CRUISING THE CHESAPEAKE

CRUISING
THE
CHESAPEAKE:
A
GUNKHOLER'S
GUIDE

William H. Shellenberger

 INTERNATIONAL MARINE
Camden, Maine

This book is dedicated
to my wife and two daughters,
without whose encouragement and
patience this book would never
have been completed.

Published by International Marine®

10 9 8 7 6 5

Copyright © 1990 International Marine, a division
of McGraw-Hill, Inc.
Revised October 1993.

Library of Congress Cataloging-in-Publication Data

Shellenberger, William H.
    Cruising the Chesapeake : a gunkholer's guide / William H.
Shellenberger.
      p.   cm.
    Includes bibliographical references (p.) and index.
    ISBN 0-07-055286-X (formerly 0-87742-254-0)
    1. Boats and boating—Chesapeake Bay (Md. and Va.)—Guide-books.
    2. Yachts and yachting—Chesapeake Bay (Md. and Va.)—Guide-books.
    3. Chesapeake Bay (Md. and Va.)—Description and travel—Guide
-books. I. Title.
GV776.C47S53   1990
797.1'09755'18—dc20   90–39047
                                                              CIP

Questions regarding the content of
this book should be addressed to:

International Marine Publishing
P.O. Box 220
Camden, ME 04843

Typeset by ProtoType Graphics, Nashville, TN
Printed by Fairfield Graphics, Fairfield, PA
Maps by Alex Wallach
Edited by J. R. Babb, Heidi V. N. Brugger, Sara E. Rubinow,
and Roger C. Taylor
DESIGN BY LURELLE CHEVERIE

Contents

Acknowledgments

No one writes a book of this type without a great deal of help from many others, and this one is no different. I would like to express my appreciation to many of those people without whose help and/or forbearance this book would not have been possible.

First and foremost, thanks to my immediate family and cruising companions, my wife, Judy, and my two daughters, Juliet and Lauren, who helped with the research of material contained in this book and put up with me while I was writing it.

Much credit goes to my brother-in-law, William MacKay. He was responsible not only for encouraging my completion of the book and a considerable amount of help in pursuing the necessary efforts to get it published, but he also went out of his way to provide me with a substantial amount of reference material which was used in it. Thanks also to another brother-in-law, Dexter Pease, who provided both encouragement and reference materials.

Special thanks go to Wayne and Sherrill Bower, Stew and Diana Kauffman, Bill and Ann Milne, and Don and Lynne Wood; all of whom provided the benefit of their experience in reviewing cruising regions of the book for accuracy, completeness and clarity. In the same vein, I would like to thank my mother, Virginia, who used her English and reading teacher background in proofreading the draft text and pointing out several areas that needed deciphering.

For provision of much of the information on land-based sights and many of the photographs used throughout the book, particular thanks go to: Gary Holloway, Samuel Britten and Jim Pottie, Aberdeen Proving Grounds; Jane White, Baltimore Office of Promotion & Tourism; Herman Schieke, Annapolis Chamber of Commerce; Paula Johnston, Calvert Marine Museum; Peter McClintock, Virginia Natural Resources Commission; Lee Ann Sink, Virginia Peninsula Tourism & Conference Bureau; Deborah Padgett, Jamestown Festival Park; Elaine Justice, College of William and Mary University Relations; and James Resolute, City of Portsmouth Department of Economic Development.

Many thanks also go to a considerable number of people who sent me much information without even including their names. For that reason, thanks to: the Kent County Chamber of Commerce; the Dorchester County Chamber of Commerce; the Somerset County Chamber of Commerce; the Crisfield Area Chamber of Commerce; the Isle of Wight/Smithfield Chamber of

Commerce; the Norfolk Chamber of Commerce; the Maryland Department of Natural Resources; the National Park Service; the Maryland Forest, Park & Wildlife Service; the Williamsburg Area Convention & Visitor's Center; the Chesapeake Bay Foundation; the Virginia Division of Tourism; the Eastern Shore of Virginia Tourism Commission; the Chesapeake Bay Estuary Program of the U.S. Fish & Wildlife Service.

My sincere appreciation goes also to the many friends and acquaintances, especially those in the Arundel Yacht Club and others too numerous to name individually, who have provided not only information but invaluable encouragement in my undertaking and pursuing this effort to its completion.

WILLIAM H. SHELLENBERGER

ACKNOWLEDGMENTS

ix

Preface

The captain takes the seadogs
ashore for their constitutional.

This book is the culmination of a more than 20-year love affair with the Chesapeake Bay. The "we" that recurs often in these pages is not editorial. "We" have always sailed the Bay as a family from the time of our first boat, a 14-foot runabout, through three others, to our present 31-foot Westerly twin-keeled sloop. The crew presently comprises, besides myself, my wife, Judy; our two daughters, Juliet and Lauren; and our Scottish and West Highland white terriers, MacTavish and Misty. The last two crewmembers may explain my preoccupation with beaches and convenient places to land.

With more than 3,000 miles of shoreline, the Chesapeake Bay offers one of the best cruising areas in the world. The harbors, creeks, rivers, bays, and bights offer plentiful opportunities for relaxed cruising, with surroundings ranging from cosmopolitan to provincial to pristine; yet nowhere in the Bay are you more than a short distance from a safe, protected harbor. Whether you choose a slip at a busy marina in the middle of a city like Baltimore, or a quiet gunkhole where your only neighbors are wildlife on the shore or surface-feeding fish, you will find what you seek in the Chesapeake.

This book addresses the entire Chesapeake Bay, from the Chesapeake and Delaware Canal in the north all the way to Cape Henry and the Atlantic Ocean in the south. No one can expect to visit every inch in the Bay and its tributaries in his lifetime; it is precisely this that makes the Bay so fascinating. We've gleaned information from literally hundreds of sources. Although as much as possible has been personally verified, things change with time and so not all information can be up-to-the-minute. We welcome comments, corrections, or suggestions for future editions.

Although it is *our* primary interest, this book is not limited to a treatise on gunkholes and gunkholing. Those of you unfamiliar with the terms *gunkhole* and *gunkholer* needn't bother to look for them in a dictionary; these words are common only in the lexicon of the inveterate cruiser. A *gunkhole* generally refers to a small, quiet, out-of-the-way body of water seldom frequented by the boating fraternity because it is difficult to find or enter. This natural exclusivity is the gunkhole's primary appeal. And to our minds, it's part of what places gunkholes among the best anchorages.

A *gunkholer* is a breed of cruiser, power or sail, who finds his way into gunkholes of all sizes and descriptions, both for the satisfaction of doing so and in search of the serenity he craves.

Anytime two or more Chesapeake cruising types

get together, the conversation swings inevitably to anchorages, especially if at least one of them has recently visited a new place, and has acquired new "local knowledge." We have all had such conversations, and they seem to follow a standard script: Everyone wants to know what the "expert" has learned. I have distilled a list of the six topics that dominate these gams:

1. *Location:* Where is the area relative to better known harbors and reference points?

2. *Recommended Approach:* What landmarks and ranges can be used for entering an anchorage? Are there shoals to beware of? Which side of the channel should be favored in which portion of the approach?

3. *Recommended Anchorages:* How enthusiastically is this harbor recommended, and why? Where are the best anchorages? Is the anchorage snug or is it open for a fetch of a mile or more in any direction? What is the range of water depth inside, and the controlling depth in the entrance? Is it peaceful or disturbed by traffic, congestion, or water skiers? Is there a time of year to avoid it? Why? When is it likely to be crowded?

4. *Description of Surrounding Area:* What is there to see? Is there a beach? Are there islands or other places to explore? Can you go ashore or is it private property? Is swimming possible? Why or why not?

5. *Facilities:* Are restaurants, marinas, or stores readily accessible? Where are they and what are they like?

6. *Special Interest Items:* Are there any historic landmarks, museums, wildlife activity, or anything else worth noting?

Remember that negative information is just as valuable as positive—sometimes more so. For example, what areas should be avoided, why, and when? And while we're on the subject of negative information, although the point of this book is not the ecology of the Bay but the enjoyment of its waters, we have watched the Bay change over time—for many years for the worse—but recently for the better.

The rockfish, once so plentiful, are scarce and protected. The bountiful bluefish are the catch of today. The famous Chesapeake Bay oysters have been decimated by a bacterial disease that has denuded once heavily populated beds, and threatens to wipe out the oystering industry. The Bay will be a far poorer place economically and aesthetically if the working skipjacks and tongers are lost.

But there is light on the horizon! Early in our cruising days, we observed the once-plentiful osprey become an endangered species. In the late 1960s, the construction of a radio tower on Bodkin Point, at the mouth of the Patapsco River, was halted permanently and a new tower erected when an osprey built a nest on the unfinished tower. Now, with a ban on the DDT that nearly wiped them out, the osprey has made such a comeback that it is rare to find a daymark or other navigational beacon in the Bay without an osprey nest on it. That unfinished radio tower still stands on Bodkin Point as a monument to this dramatic turnaround.

The seaweed and grass in the Bay were once so common that they interfered with anyone trying to swim ashore from a boat or wade off the shore in water more than knee deep. Over the years, this plant life disappeared from the waters—a visible indicator, along with algae blooms, of the progressive deterioration of the Bay's health. Recently, the weed is starting to come back due to increasing use of pollution controls. In 1986 and 1987, the algae blooms in the northern Bay, while present, decreased markedly.

Several organizations have been formed and are working actively to save and restore the Bay. In 1983, the Governors of Maryland, Pennsylvania, and Virginia joined with the Mayor of Washington, D.C. and the Administrator of the Environmental Protection Agency to establish a joint program to clean and protect the Chesapeake estuary.

Signs of progress are evidence of the active concern of the people who work and play in the Bay. If the programs are to work in the long run, the public must continue to be concerned and vigilant about the problems facing the Chesapeake Bay. It took more than 10,000 years for the rising sea to create the Chesapeake Bay as we know it and it will take time to correct the damage done in the last 300 years of use and neglect. The Chesapeake Bay and its bounty will endure only so long as we who live, work, and play in its environs remain constantly alert and active in its preservation and protection.

WILLIAM H. SHELLENBERGER

How

to

Use

This

Book

General Information

There is a lot of general information about the Chesapeake in the Introduction, including sections on references, weather, hazards to navigation, and restricted areas. We suggest you read this information first.

Regions

The basic concept in developing the structure for this guide was to divide the Bay into seven regions so that all points within each region are within a single, easy, one-day cruise for a typical sailboat (at an assumed speed of 5 knots). Powerboats, of course, are not constrained by time in quite the same way, but the same range generally applies to them due to fuel consumption and the need to refuel. This guideline breaks down in the cases of some of the longer rivers, such as the 90-mile-long Potomac, but even then there are plenty of intermediate anchorages. Partly by design and partly by coincidence, the cruising characteristics of each region described at the beginning of each chapter tend to be relatively homogenous.

Anchorages are grouped in geographical order, trending from the head of the Bay (at Cabin John Creek) to its mouth. Within each region, first the eastern and then the western shores of the Bay are covered. Most people cruise the Bay predominantly on one side or the other, regardless of region, since the trip across the Bay is generally a longish one compared with harbor hopping on the same side.

The north-south trend of coverage is frequently interrupted, however, by the same complicated geography that makes the Bay a gunkholer's paradise. One glance at a chart of the Choptank River—to pick one of many examples—will show the futility of any attempt to impose a rigid north-to-south consistency on anchorage groupings. Instead, when a tributary of the Bay is large enough to contain several or perhaps even dozens of anchorages, we begin at its mouth and proceed upstream.

This book is designed for those who are cruising the Bay, not those who are passing through on the way to somewhere else. For this reason the detailed descrip-

Regions of the Chesapeake Bay

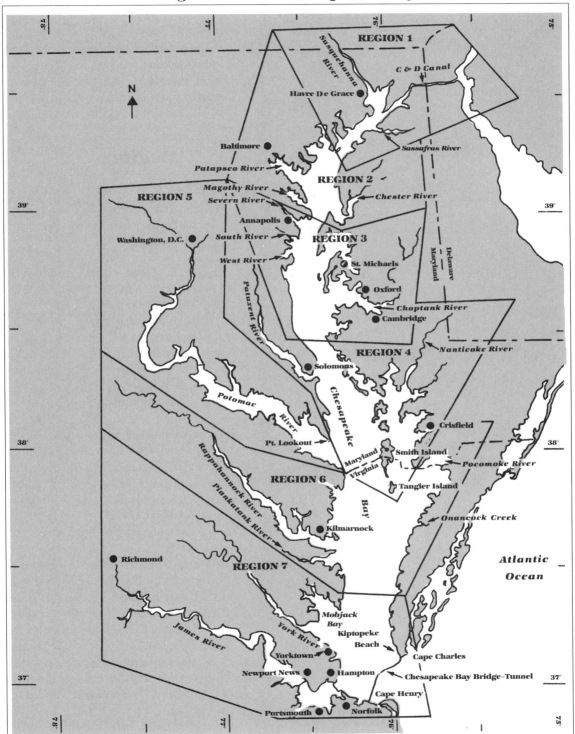

REGION 1

Susquehanna River

C & D Canal

N

Havre De Grace

Sassafras River

Baltimore

Patapsco River

REGION 2

Magothy River

Severn River

Chester River

REGION 5

Annapolis

Delaware
Maryland

REGION 3

Washington, D.C.

South River

St. Michaels

West River

Oxford

Patuxent River

Choptank River

Cambridge

REGION 4

Nanticoke River

Solomons

Chesapeake

Potomac

River

Crisfield

Pt. Lookout

Maryland
Virginia

Smith Island

Pocomoke River

REGION 6

Tangier Island

Bay

Rappahannock River

Onancock Creek

Piankatank River

Kilmarnock

Richmond

REGION 7

Atlantic
Ocean

James River

York River

Mobjack
Bay

Kiptopeke
Beach

Yorktown

Cape Charles

Newport News

Hampton

Chesapeake Bay Bridge-Tunnel

Cape Henry

Portsmouth

Norfolk

SCALE 1"=28 MILES

tion of the C&D Canal, for example, appears in Region 1, not under approaches. I am a hard-core gunkholer, and this book is organized in the spirit of gunkholing.

To show how this works in practice, let's take a closer look at the Choptank River, which is introduced in Region 3 with the typeface used for a body of water containing two to two-dozen anchorages, as follows:

CHOPTANK RIVER

Charts: 12263, 12266, **12268,** 12270

Beginning at the mouth of the river, we look first at Knapps Narrows, which connects the river mouth with the Bay proper north of Tilghman Island. Since Knapps Narrows offers an anchorage as well as a shortcut to the Bay, it's introduced with the typeface used for individual anchorages, as follows:

KNAPPS NARROWS

Charts: 12263, **12266,** 12268, 12270

Next upriver we encounter Harris Creek, which is not an anchorage but rather a complicated tributary containing many anchorages. It is introduced as follows:

CHOPTANK RIVER/ HARRIS CREEK

Charts: 12263, **12266,** 12270

and under it come such anchorages as Dun Cove, Waterhole Cove, and Briary Cove.

And so it goes, clockwise around the basin of the

lower Choptank (with a long excursion up the Tred Avon!) before we venture up into the upper Choptank toward the town of Choptank.

Ratings and facility listings (see below) are given only with individual anchorages (not with the larger bodies of water containing more than one anchorage), and with one exception in the Choptank, individual anchorages are introduced in the typeface above for Knapps Narrows. The exception is Irish Creek, which is neither an anchorage in Broad Creek, which it follows, nor large enough to contain several discrete anchorages. The hierarchical classification breaks down here a bit (indeed, no rigid structure could embrace the Chesapeake without exceptions), and author and publisher beg your forgiveness, but the Choptank is as complicated as it gets. If you can follow us here you can follow us anywhere in the Bay.

Anchorages

Anchorages are listed in geographical order from the head of the Bay to its mouth, starting at Cabin John Creek. To find a specific spot, check the index or use the running heads printed on the upper corner of each right-hand page. These will lead you to the immediate geographical vicinity and in many cases to the anchorage itself.

Ratings

Anchorages suitable for use as an overnight stay, either anchored or renting a slip at a marina, are rated in accordance with three categories: beauty/interest, protection from weather, and availability of facilities for the cruiser. (Due to the rapid changes in the availability of dockside sewage pumpout facilities, pumpouts are not necessarily found at anchorages listed as having all facilities. See Appendix C.) It is worth pointing out that these ratings are from the perspective of the transient cruiser, not the permanent resident.

Beauty/Interest

 Both beautiful and interesting. Not to be missed.

 Very attractive or interesting. Definitely worth a visit.

 Attractive or interesting.

 Nothing special, but OK.

 Not very attractive.

Protection

 Hurricane hole. May be uncomfortably hot in the summer months.

 Well protected from all directions.

 Well protected from wave, open to wind from one or more directions.

 Exposed for a mile or more in at least one direction. Use in settled conditions or as a day stop only.

 No protection.

Facilities

 Fuel (gas/diesel)

 Fuel (gas only)

 Fuel (diesel only)

 Water

 Ice

Repairs

 Moorings and/or slips

 Groceries within walking distance

 Laundromat

 Boat supplies or hardware available

 Shower

 Restaurant nearby

Sketch Maps

Sketch maps are included where appropriate to help you navigate a tricky channel or passage, identify anchorage and moorings areas, or locate shoreside services.

Caveat Yachtsman

In preparing this book every effort has been made to provide information which is accurate and up-to-date, but it is impossible to guarantee complete accuracy, and there is no substitute for experience and prudent seamanship. This guide should be used as a supplement to official U.S. government charts and other publications. The authors and publisher disclaim any liability for loss or damage to persons or property which may occur as a result of the use or interpretation of any information in this book.

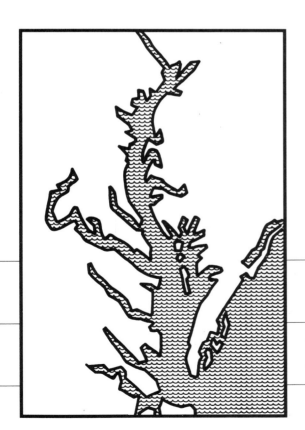

Introduction

A

Bit

About

the

Chesapeake

". . . a faire bay encompassed but for the mouth with fruitful and delightsome land."

CAPTAIN JOHN SMITH

The Chesapeake Bay is the largest inland tidal body of water on the Atlantic seacoast of the United States. It ranges 170 nautical miles long from its northern point (headwaters) at the Chesapeake and Delaware Canal to its southern opening between Cape Charles and Cape Henry. Its width ranges from about $3\frac{1}{2}$ miles in the northern portion to around 23 miles in the south. Not counting the myriad tributary rivers and creeks, 48 rivers flow into the Bay. As a result of this flow of fresh water, the character of the Bay changes as you proceed north from its mouth—from salty, near-ocean conditions, through brackish, to fresh water in the extreme northern Bay and well upstream on some of the longer rivers.

Formed about 10,000 years ago when the melting glacial ice caused a corresponding rise in the ocean level, the Chesapeake Bay is actually the drowned valley of the Susquehanna River. To be more precise, the Bay is an estuary. A bay is defined as a body of water partially enclosed by land but with a wide opening to the sea (or other parent body of water). An estuary, literally boiling tide, has both tidal flow from the ocean and a large influx of fresh water from rivers, producing a whole series of ecosystems. The action of the tides and river currents produces a diversity of chemical and physical characteristics, which permit the growth of a vast and varied collection of both animal and plant life. As a result, an estuary is the most productive habitat in nature.

Forty-eight rivers with more than 100 tributaries flow into the Chesapeake. The Susquehanna River, which originates about 400 miles to the north in the middle of New York state, is known as the mother of the Bay because she, alone, provides half of all the fresh water flowing into the Chesapeake—typically 60,000 to 80,000 gallons per second. Even with this steady flow, were the Bay suddenly emptied of all its water, it would take a year to refill it!

Naturally, the water in the Bay is saltier to the south than it is to the north, but, because salt water is heavier than fresh, the Bay's water is also saltier at the bottom than at the top. This creates an interesting phenomenon. The salty water coming in from the ocean has a net movement up the Bay on the bottom while the fresh water from the rivers has a net movement down the Bay on the top.

The combination of tidal and fresh-water currents produces a stronger and longer ebb than flood current in the Bay; the ebb current runs a good half-hour longer than the flood current in most of the Bay.

Another factor affecting salinity and, to some extent, currents is the amount of rainfall. With heavy rain, more freshwater flows into the Bay than during a dry season, with the resulting cyclic change in salinity. This change in salinity sets up a non-tidal circulation. When Bay salinity is high, saltier water is forced along the bottom up the Bay and into the tributaries and bottom water is flushed from the tributaries back into the Bay. This movement reverses when the Bay salinity is low. Normally, the Chesapeake is saltier in the late summer and fall than in the winter and spring.

Estuary Cycles

Estuaries are born, live, and die with the ebb and flow of ice ages. As glacial ice melts and the sea rises, estuaries are born. As the land rises and the water basin fills with sediment, estuaries die.

It took about 10,000 years for the Chesapeake Bay as we know it today to be formed. From 15,000 to 5,000 years ago, the sea level rose more than three feet each century, encroaching farther and farther up the continental shelf and into the wide valley of the Susquehanna River. Ten thousand years ago, there was no Bay as such. The sea had just reached the level of what is the present mouth of the Chesapeake. Five thousand years ago, the head of the Bay was near present day Annapolis. Then, 3,000 years ago, the Bay stopped growing. What was once a river valley wending its way to the sea was now a great estuary. Its shape was much like its present one. The water was clear and deep and the Bay's shores and tributaries were covered with dense vegetation.

With the cessation of the Bay's growth, the sedimentation process began. Never again would the Chesapeake be as deep and clear as it was 3,000 years ago. Sediment from the rivers began to fill up the headwaters and the deltas of each tributary, an inevitable process in the life of any estuary. In 10,000 to 20,000 years, the Bay would cease to exist in the natural course of things.

Sedimentation is an estuary's natural "weapon" against the inroads of the rising sea. From a human perspective, it is a slow process. But as long as the rivers that feed the Bay continue to flow, land will be eroded and sediment will be deposited at the margins of the Bay and its tributaries. The resulting broad flats of silt eventually are colonized by grasses and become marshes. The buildup of silt continues until the marsh becomes part of the new shoreline.

Many factors influence the speed of the sedimentation process—weather, currents, composition of the land that is affected, tides, winds, and human activity. Within the last 350 years, human activity has greatly accelerated this process. Colonists stripped the soil of its protective vegetation, clearing thousands of acres with little thought regarding soil erosion. The sediment carried to the Bay since colonial times is estimated to be four to eight times pre-colonial levels. Recent construction has increased even this accelerated pace to hundreds of times sedimentation's "natural" levels. The result is that sedimentation has significantly altered the Bay's coastline, causing colonial seaports, such as Joppatown and Port Tobacco, Maryland, to become landlocked. And the clear Bay waters of the 1600s have become the brown waters of today; visibility is now measured in inches instead of tens of feet.

Respect
for the
Environment

Pressure on the Bay environment increases constantly. Twelve to fourteen million people now live within what could be called "Chesapeake Bay Country," with more and more arriving every year.

Toxic chemicals have been dumped into the Bay waters by industries; improperly treated sewage from overloaded processing plants and leaky septic systems still ends up in the water. Even runoff from farm fields hundreds of miles from the Bay itself ends up in its waters.

A little bit of fertilizer is good; it provides nutrients for microscopic plant life upon which the entire food chain depends. Too much of a good thing, however, can be disastrous. Alga blooms alternate with massive die-offs. This, in turn, sends the dissolved oxygen in the water down to levels too low to support marine life and so more death results. Carried to an extreme, this could turn the beautiful Chesapeake into a foul-smelling, liquid desert.

Advocacy Groups.

Fortunately, there is hope for a better future. Several organizations have been formed and are working actively to save and restore the Bay. Most notable of these is the Chesapeake Bay Foundation (CBF), the original "Save the Bay" organization founded in 1966. The goal of the CBF is to promote and contribute to the orderly management of the Chesapeake with a special emphasis on maintaining a level of water quality that is capable of supporting the Bay's diverse aquatic species. CBF has programs that include in-the-field instruction in estuarine ecology; scientific investigation and legal representation for conservation and management of estuarine resources; preservation and management of significant Bay land; and research in and demonstration of low chemical input agricultural practices. Not only does the CBF serve

as an advocate for the Bay and ensure that its best interests are represented in the public forum, but it actively preserves and manages some 4,000 acres of Bay area land, holding it in its natural state and using it for educational purposes.

There are three offices for the Chesapeake Bay Foundation: 162 Prince George Street, Annapolis, MD 21401, phone (410)268-8816; Suite 815, Heritage Building, 1001 East Main Street, Richmond, VA 23219, phone (804)780-1392; 214 State Street, Harrisburg, PA 17101, phone (717)234-5550.

The government has also been doing its part. In 1983, the governors of Virginia, Maryland, and Pennsylvania; the administrator of the Federal Environmental Protection Agency; the mayor of Washington, D.C.; and the chairman of the tri-state legislative Chesapeake Bay Commission met to establish a joint program to clean and protect the Chesapeake. Four years later they met again and signed the 1987 Chesapeake Bay Agreement, which was revitalized in a subsequent meeting on

Estuaries support a diversity of wildlife. Here black ducks and mallards mingle with pintails and whistling swans. LUTHER C. GOLDMAN/SPORT FISHERIES & WILDLIFE

January 5, 1989, to endorse cooperative efforts "to eliminate all toxic discharges into the Bay, protect tidal and nontidal wetlands, remove blockages to migratory fish passages, increase public access, and formulate water quality and habitat guidelines for living resources."

Estuary waters support a diversity of life—plants, fish, birds, waterfowl, and marine and non-marine mammals. The nation's prime steward in this type of broad-based protection is the U.S. Fish and Wildlife Service (FWS). The FWS has a Chesapeake Bay Estuary Program, which is committed to reversing damage already done to the Bay, arresting further degradation, and restoring the Bay as nearly as time, technology, and resources allow, to its former productivity. In addition to its work in habitat and wetlands protection, research, technical assistance, and species conservation and protection, the FWS manages the National Wildlife Refuges and National Fish Hatcheries in the Bay area (and across the nation). The FWS produces a variety of publications—including the Chesapeake Species of Special Emphasis Series—that help educate the public regarding the living resource that is the Chesapeake Bay and what role each person can play in its restoration. Write to the service at U.S. Fish and Wildlife Service, 1825 Virginia Avenue, Annapolis, MD 21401, phone (410)269-5448.

A great deal of progress has been made. Never before have we had three state governors determined to clean up the estuary, a cadre of world-renowned environmental scientists working to unlock the Bay's many mysteries, and a well-organized and capable network of environmental advocacy organizations and citizens dedicated to the preservation and reclamation of the Chesapeake. Many programs have been implemented and many more are to come.

Although progress is evident, the work is far from done. If the programs are to work for the long run, we who live, work, and play in the Bay environment will have to do our part. The health and bounty of the Chesapeake Bay relies on our vigilance and activity for its protection—not only in public advocacy and pressure, but in our personal actions and habits.

Boaters' Responsibility. Boatowners have a special responsibility to the Bay. The Chesapeake Bay Foundation says it this way: "While the effect of a single boat on the Bay may seem insignificant, multiply it by the nearly 400,000 boats that use the Bay and such effects become both significant and increasingly apparent." Common sense and prudence can go a long way toward combining the joy of boating on the Bay with the need to safeguard the quality of the Bay environment for the future.

From the CBF Homeowner Series of booklets, "Your Boat and the Bay" addresses specific ways that individual boaters can join the movement to save the Bay. What follows are some of the ways to minimize the impact of your boat; write to the CBF for your own copy of this booklet, which has more good advice on the subject.

- If you have a Type I or II Marine Sanitation Device (MSD), always flush your system in open water that is at least 20 feet deep. This aids the rapid dispersal of waste materials and reduces damage to the shellfish beds, which are in shallow waters.

- If you have a Type III MSD, check the location of pumpout facilities on your route or near your destination and use them. (See Appendix C for a list of dockside sewage pumpout facilities.)

- Use onshore bath house facilities whenever you are docked. This minimizes the need to discharge your system.

- All anti-fouling paints release toxins into the water. Avoid using tin-based paints, such as tributylin or TBT, since these are the most toxic of the anti-fouling paints that have government approval. Fish absorb TBT through their gills and the chemical also accumulates in sediment where it affects clams and oysters.

- Use a non-phosphate detergent and a scrub brush when you clean teak, hullsides, and deck while in the water. Specialty cleaners usually have high levels of a variety of toxic substances.

- Be careful with engine oil. Wipe up all spills, no matter how minor, when changing or adding oil. Consider using a bilge "pillow" (oil-absorbing sponge) so that bilge water pumped into the Bay is oil-free.

- Dispose of old antifreeze onshore and, if possible, use a propylene glycol-based antifreeze; these are less toxic than ethylene glycol-based varieties.

- Avoid topping off your fuel tank. This often causes fuel to be spilled from overflow vents, creating miniature toxic slicks.

- Watch your wake. Boat wakes contribute to shoreline erosion, especially in those smaller creeks and coves that gunkholers love. Wakes also stir up sediment, which reduces the amount of essential light that reaches submerged aquatic vegetation—the start of many food chains in the estuary.

Cruising the Bay

The Chesapeake Bay Bridges, near Annapolis, serve as a dividing line in the Bay in more than a topographic sense. As you pass the bridges, the very character of the Bay undergoes subtle changes. The water begins to be noticeably less and less salty as you proceed farther north, as we have mentioned. The wave action changes, becoming more choppy, with lower wave heights and far fewer of the long rollers often encountered well south in the widest part of the Bay. The harbors become fewer and more crowded. Some, such as Worton Creek, are so full of moorings that there is hardly room enough to swing a cat, let alone a boat at anchor.

As may be said of anyplace, there are some drawbacks to cruising in the Chesapeake—chief among them the hot, humid weather and summer calms in July and August. No one should cruise the Chesapeake without power and, in the summer, the knowledgeable will have a good awning to provide shade and screening for protection from insects. Spring and fall are the ideal cruising times. Then, the air and water are usually pleasant and comfortable, the flying insects are seldom in evidence, and the sea nettles either have not yet appeared or have gone.

Those who like to swim tend to cruise toward the southern part of the Bay in the early part of the year then, as summer progresses and the sea nettles move up the Bay, cruise toward the northern end of the Bay. Even in the worst years for the nettles, the Susquehanna and Sassafras Rivers provide nettle-free swimming, as do the upper reaches of many of the longer rivers.

But it is all the Chesapeake Bay, one of the best cruising grounds in the country. From the southern near-ocean conditions to the northern fresh-water conditions, the Bay has countless harbors and anchorages high on the "must visit" list of the serious cruiser.

Helpful Publications

All those who cruise the Chesapeake need several publications, some for navigation and some to add to the enjoyment of the cruise. Here are some I consider to be the most useful:

NOAA Charts. A complete list of the navigation charts available from the National Oceanic and Atmospheric Administration (NOAA) is presented in the Nautical Chart Catalog 1, available from most marine stores or from the Distribution Service (C4), National Ocean Survey, Riverdale, MD 20840, at no charge. There are in excess of 35 charts which cover the Chesapeake Bay and tributaries, not counting those for the Atlantic Seaboard of the Delmarva peninsula. If you normally only cruise one area of the Bay, your best bet may be to buy the two or three full-sized NOAA charts that cover your area of interest. This list includes better alternatives if you tend to cruise a large portion of the Bay or beyond.

Better Boating Association (BBA) Chart Kit. The BBA publishes a series of chart kits that are authorized reproductions of the NOAA charts. These are far less expensive than a full set of government charts and they are easier to store and handle. The 17-by-22-inch charts are spiralbound for easy use; the kit contains the Loran C plots as well as the latitude and longitude markings. The kit you want covers both the Chesapeake and Delaware Bays (Region 4) as well as the Atlantic Coast of the Delmarva peninsula; it is probably the best choice if you plan to cruise a large portion of the Bay. A vinyl cover is available to protect the chart kit from weather while leaving the chart of interest visible. Kits are available from most marine stores and mail-order houses, or can be ordered directly from the Better Boating Association. Price is approximately $85.

Guide for Cruising Maryland Waters. A marine atlas, published by the Maryland Department of Natural Resources, this covers the tidal waters of Maryland, including the Potomac River. Adequate for cruising the Bay itself, it lacks the detail (e.g., water depth soundings) needed for gunkholing up into the tributaries. The 10-by-14-inch book provides charts with more than 200 courses, with magnetic compass directions and distances, which have been laid between buoys to most of the boating centers. In addition, the book contains the NOAA tidal current charts for the Upper Chesapeake Bay, a great aid for planning a cruise to take advantage of or avoid bucking the currents. These guides are available in most regional marine stores or directly from the Department of Natural Resources, Tawes State Office Building, Annapolis, MD 21402. Price is around $20.

Guide of Tidewater Virginia.
This is a marine atlas published by Williams and Heintz Map Corporation, Washington, D.C. It covers the tidal waters of Virginia in a manner similar to the *Guide for Cruising Maryland Waters*.

Chesapeake Bay Chart Book, MD-VA.
A collection of waterproof reproductions of NOAA charts, this book (approximately 11 by 16 inches) covers the tidal waters of both Maryland and Virginia. It is published by ADC, "The Map People," Alexandria, VA. Very useful book for those who want a more compact set of charts that address the waters of both states around the Chesapeake Bay. While weak as a guide for gunkholing, it does address the entire navigable length of the James River, a shortfall in many other chart kits.

The book came on the market in 1988 and is available from most area marine stores and mail order houses. Priced at around $30, it is a good buy.

Waterway Guide Chartbook—Chesapeake & Delaware Bays.
This collection of fold-out charts in a kit (approximately 11 by 16 inches) is comparable to the BBA kit in quality. It is published by Communications Channels, Inc., 6255 Barfield Road, Atlanta, GA 30328. This kit, or variations of it, has been around for some time. Priced at close to $55, it still beats buying the full set of NOAA Charts. It is available in most area marine stores and mail order houses.

The Boating Almanac, Volume 4.
One of the most useful and compact reference sources for cruising the Chesapeake Bay and tributaries, this 5½-by-9-inch book is published annually by Boating Almanac Company, Inc., Severna Park, MD 21146.

Published in four volumes covering the eastern seaboard of the United States from Maine through Virginia, it contains just about everything that you need to know for either extended cruising or short-range trips. Volume 4 covers the Chesapeake Bay, Delaware, Maryland, D.C., and Virginia. It contains information on marina facilities and location, launch ramp locations, area charts (not for navigation except in a pinch), NOAA Nautical Chart Catalog, tide and current tables, sun and moon rise and set tables, and much more. It even has the clearances for each of the Chesapeake Bay Bridge's spans, something I have seen nowhere else! In short, this is probably one of the best references to keep on hand, well worth a nominal yearly investment ($10.50).

Coast Guard Local Notice to Mariners.
The U.S. Coast Guard publishes this on a weekly basis to notify all mariners, be they on large ships or cockleshells, about anything affecting safe navigation on the waters covered by each district. For the Chesapeake Bay area, this publication may be obtained free of charge simply by writing to: Commander, Fifth Coast Guard District, Aids to Navigation Branch, Federal Building, 431 Crawford Street, Portsmouth, VA 23704–5004.

The Fifth Coast Guard District includes the coastal and inland waters of New Jersey, Maryland, Delaware, Virginia, and North Carolina. "The Notice" has special notices, including such things as closures of locks on the ICW, channel closures, etc; discrepancies in aids to navigation, missing markers, extinguished lights, etc; changes to charts and chart corrections; dredging operations; information on the condition and operability of bridges across navigable waterways; notice of regattas with date, time, and place; proposed projects which will or may affect mariners; and more.

If you plan to cruise or use a boat in any part of the Bay waters, get on this publication's mailing list.

The following books are just a few of the ones that can add to your general enjoyment of a Chesapeake cruise; more are listed in the bibliography in the back of the book.

Fodor's '89 Chesapeake.
Fodor's practical guides are updated yearly. This book offers a smattering of historical background and lots of useful information on hotels and motels, restaurants and eateries, and things to do. It is a basic tourist's guidebook,

available at most bookstores at a cost of about $9. Cruisers intending to spend a lot of time in the southernmost regions of the Bay and the James River area will want to get *Fodor's Virginia* too.

This Was Chesapeake Bay. This is a collection of information, which includes excerpts from ship logs, historical photographs, and the personal recollections of author Robert H. Burgess. The book covers a wide range of subjects from the Bay in the Miocene period to colonial settlements, from steamboating to naval warfare, from softshell clamming to dredging for oysters. Each chapter stands alone, so that you can read it start-and-stop fashion without hurting the overall feel of the book. Burgess also wrote *Chesapeake Circle*, which uses the same anecdotal format. Both books are published by Cornell Maritime Press of Cambridge, Maryland.

Chesapeake Bay: A Pictorial Maritime History. This book, also published by Cornell Maritime Press, is a compilation of pictures of events, objects, and vessels on and around the Bay. Written by M.V. Brewington, the collection is held together with a brief text that takes the reader from the time of the European settlements to the present.

Chesapeake. This novel by James A. Michener tells an entertaining story of the Bay and its wildlife. It is also the author's tribute to the Bay's watermen, whom he sees as the quiet heroes who live and work in the beautiful yet unforgiving waters of the Chesapeake.

Navigating the Bay

Winds and Waves

The Chesapeake Bay is considered "semi-protected waters." Although most of the tributaries are well sheltered, when the wind pipes up from the right (or wrong, depending on your viewpoint) direction the Bay can get rough enough to command your full attention. Due to the relative shallowness of the water over most of the Bay, waves tend to peak in sharp points, spaced rather closely together (trochoidal), instead of the big, wide-spaced rollers common in the ocean. As a result, the waves don't have to get very high before you have your hands full—particularly if you happen to be heading into them.

One of the nicest features of cruising the Chesapeake—if you are not in a hurry to get to a particular spot—is the fact that there are so many good harbors on both shores that you rarely need to fight your way into a strong wind in order to reach shelter. If the wind begins to "dust up," there usually is an alternate harbor where you can take refuge until the blow dies down.

The prevailing winds seem to alternate, blowing up and then down the Bay, with northerly winds predominating in the late fall and southerly breezes more frequent in the late spring and summer. Spring and fall winds usually have higher average velocities than those of summer. Flat calms or light breezes are more the norm in July and August, especially at night and in the morning. At this time of year the sailor's most useful sail is the "Iron Topsail."

Conditions in the southern Bay differ from those in the north in that the harbors are farther apart, particularly between the Choptank and Potomac Rivers. The water is generally deeper and, below the Patuxent River, the waves are generally, but not always, more like the round swells of the ocean, although they are still closer together than in the deep ocean waters. The main difference is that they don't have the sharp peaks of the trochoidal wave; this makes them easier to handle even though they may be bigger than the waves up-Bay. More than once we have been surfing down the Bay under working jib alone, watching the rollers chasing us. This is an exhilarating experience, but I wouldn't care to be going in the other direction! Fortunately, wind direction in the Chesapeake is such that, if you can afford to lay over a day when the winds are adverse, they are likely to change direction, force, or both.

A satellite view of the Bay. NASA LANDSAT

Bottom Conditions and Shoaling.

There are very few rocks in the Chesapeake—save near the mouth of the Susquehanna River and the famous White Rocks in the mouth of Rock Creek on the Patapsco River. While the seas can be steep enough to be a challenge, there is no big surf crashing on the shore to destroy a grounded boat. Running aground in the Chesapeake is very much a "so-what" affair. In fact, if you don't run aground here a few times a year, you just aren't adventurous enough!

Running aground in the Chesapeake is so commonplace that the Bay may seem little more than a series of shoals connected by channels, but nothing could be further from the truth. A glance at the charts shows plenty of shoals and a considerable number of small creeks, but also a far greater number of navigable rivers, creeks, and harbors that boats carrying a draft of 6 feet or more can follow nearly to the headwaters. For boats with 5 feet of draft or less, the number of available harbors increases dramatically. The next large jump comes at water depths of around 3 feet, accommodating shallow drafts such as on medium-sized to smaller powerboats.

Even so, Chesapeake Bay cruisers are more likely to run aground than those who cruise other waters. Since going aground here usually damages one's dignity and rarely one's boat (the exception being the planing inboard powerboat, where the prop is the lowest part of the hull), I suspect that Bay cruisers tend to be more careless. Even when care is exercised, it is easy to hit one of the many unmarked shoals when exploring small creeks and coves. And many dredged channels and harbors are constantly filling in and being dredged again, so that charts are rarely up-to-date regarding the latest controlling depths.

The judicious use of a depthsounder—or better yet a sounding pole—will permit you to poke into many a fascinating small creek which could never be attempted in other areas. The lack of rocks and the two-foot tidal range make safe adventuring far more possible here than anywhere else. Since the bottom is usually soft mud or hard sand, you need only a little effort to release your boat. (Marine insurers say that the Chesapeake is

one of the least expensive places to keep a boat because of the forgiving soft bottom.)

The small range of tide also can be a liability if you do go aground. A falling tide won't leave you very dry, but you might have to wait some time before the tide rises enough to get you off when you are really hard aground. Take heart; unless you have an "aptitude" for it, you will rarely get stuck so hard that you can't get off in just a few minutes, often by using powerboat swells.

Temperature. The summers on the Chesapeake tend to be hot and humid, especially in August. As pointed out earlier, the best times for cruising are spring and fall, from early April to mid-June and from mid-September to mid-November. As a general rule, the weather tends to be mild, but fall cruising, in particular, requires that you be prepared for a wide range of temperatures. While it can be on the chilly side in April and November, it varies considerably. We have been sailing in sub-freezing temperatures in mid-October and in shirtsleeves in November.

The accompanying climatological table may provide a better "feel" for the ranges to be expected. This table is based on records for Baltimore, but it is representative of the entire Bay. The table includes both the normal maximum and minimum ranges of temperature and the extremes recorded for the area.

Storms. To call a Chesapeake Bay line squall "just a thunderstorm" is akin to calling a tornado "a bit of wind." While technically a thunderstorm, the line squall tends to be far more impressive when you are out

---

TABLE 1. Climatological Table for Baltimore (Degrees Fahrenheit)

	NORMAL			EXTREME	
	DAILY MAX.	DAILY MIN.	MONTHLY	RECORD HIGH	RECORD LOW
April	65.8	42.6	54.2	94	20
May	75.9	52.8	64.4	98	32
June	83.5	61.4	72.5	100	42
July	87.2	66.4	76.8	102	52
Aug.	85.0	65.0	75.0	102	48
Sep.	78.6	57.6	68.1	99	35
Oct.	68.4	45.6	57.0	92	18
Nov.	56.5	34.4	45.5	83	13

on the water; its potential for damage is enormous. You have to experience the violence of one of these storms to put it in proper perspective.

The storms usually approach from the west or northwest. They can jump on you unbelievably quickly if you ignore the warning signs. The wind can go from almost nothing to 70 to 90 m.p.h. in seconds, whipping the waves into a froth and dumping buckets of water on your head. Lightning cracks and crashes; visibility drops to mere feet. Waves don't usually cause too much trouble; the wind blows their tops right off.

Don't let this or other accounts alarm you unduly. These storms don't sneak up on you. They give visible warning signs hours beforehand. Large black or gray cumulus clouds gather to the west and northwest, and often you see lightning or hear thunder. Sometimes the storms are preceded by a copper-colored haze. If you keep your eyes open, you will have plenty of time to prepare for a line squall. If a squall is en route and you don't have enough time to reach shelter, prepare to anchor or use your engine to hold your position until it is over. **(Sailors should drop all sails.)** Don't try to make any progress through the storm; lack of visibility makes this too risky. The storms rarely last more than 15 minutes or so; they just seem to last longer when you are in one.

While squalls can occur at other times, they are most common from mid-June to mid-September, generally during hot, humid weather. They rarely come before 4:00 p.m. and are most common just before sundown. While a single storm generally covers a relatively narrow path, they often come in clusters. Once we were caught out as one passed to our right and another passed to our left without affecting us. However, we were so busy watching these two that a third caught us unawares, hitting us squarely. We had a rather busy few minutes as a result!

You can never be sure what a squall will amount to before it hits. It may look really fierce and amount to little more than a rainstorm or it can blow hard enough to knock over a large port cargo crane, as happened in Baltimore in 1980. When you see signs of a squall, get your sails down and well secured and prepare to anchor, run before it, or hold position under engine. Get into a good shelter early, making sure you are well protected to the west and northwest. Assume that the storm will be bad and play it safe.

Once a squall has passed, the wind generally drops to near zero for 15 to 20 minutes—often longer—leaving you sitting in a flat calm wishing for breeze.

Predicting Weather in the Chesapeake

Starting on this topic gave me some pause. Who among us has not made the weatherman the butt of numerous jokes? He who attempts to predict the weather, be he a modern-day meterologist with access to satellite pictures and computer reports or a layman making his guess based on the current signs around him (no, no—not the entrails of a rooster!), is likely to be a subject of ridicule, rarely reverence. In fact, our family has a standing joke that has become a "classic" for reasons better not discussed: "Think it'll rain today?" "Naw! The wind's in the wrong direction." This is normally delivered in a pouring rain, or in the total absence of any measurable wind at all and heavy, black, cloud cover, or both.

With that preface, I'll make the rash statements that there are three ways of obtaining information on what weather lies in the immediate future (12 hours to two days). The first two are relatively conventional: listen to the weather reports on TV/radio or tune into the VHF-FM WE-1 or WE-2 NOAA weather radio stations for broadcasts by professional (and often wrong) meteorologists. The third is to do it yourself using a decent barometer and tracking the wind direction.

No joke! If you learn how to use the barometer and learn the historical weather patterns associated with barometric pressure trends and wind direction, you actually stand a better chance of accurately predicting the weather *in your location* than if you simply listen to broadcast weather predictions which, of necessity, cover a far larger geographical area than the one in which you are interested.

First, a short word about instrumentation. With a barometer, you generally get what you pay for! Forget the cheap barometers that cost well under $20—they make a nice wall decoration. For the accuracy and reliability necessary in a useful barometer, you have to pay at least $70. If you are really serious, look into the purchase of a barograph; this device records the changing pressure on a piece of graph paper with the use of a clockwork mechanism. Be forewarned that a barograph costs several hundred dollars. Whichever instrument you choose, you probably will have to calibrate it to a sea-level reading with the adjustment screw in the back. The simplest procedure is to listen to a *recent* weather report and correct the instrument to the reported pressure, assuming that a rapid rate of change is not in process. Repeat this calibration several times until you are confident that your instrument gives reasonably accurate readings.

You also need a wind direction indicator. For the purpose of weather prediction, you can rely on a compass and a wet finger, or spend several hundred dollars on wind speed and direction indicating instruments. (Here's how the less elaborate system works: Wet your finger and hold it up in the wind. The coldest side indicates the

TABLE 2. Predicting Bay Weather

BAROMETER	WIND DIRECTION	PROBABLE WEATHER
29.8 or less Falling rapidly	N to E	Gale Warning! Heavy Rain imminent!
29.8 or less Falling rapidly	E to S	Storm Warning! Clearing in 24 hrs.
30.0 or less Falling rapidly	NE to SE	High Wind & Rain. Clearing in 36 hrs.
30.0 or less Falling slowly	NE to SE	Rain, continuing up to 2 days.
30.0 or less Rising slowly	S to SW	Clearing in hours, fair for days.
30.1 & above Falling rapidly	NE to E	Rain in 12–24 hrs, increasing wind.
30.1 & above Falling slowly	NE to E	With light wind, rain in a few days.
30.1 to 30.2 Falling rapidly	NE to S	Increasing wind & rain in 12 hrs.
30.1 to 30.2 Falling slowly	NE to SE	Rain in 12–18 hrs, wind steady.
30.1 to 30.2 Falling slowly	SE to S	Rain in 24 hrs, wind steady.
30.1 to 30.2 Rising rapidly	SW to NW	Fair w/ rain in 2 days or less.
30.1 to 30.2 Steady	SW to NW	Fair, no change for 1–2 days.
Above 30.2 Steady	SW to NW	Cont'd fair, no change in sight.
Above 30.2 falling slowly	SW to NW	Fair for 2 days, temp rising slowly.

direction from which the wind is blowing. Now look at your compass to see what that direction is. The nearest 45 degrees normally is close enough.)

For starters, forget the words *rain, change,* and *fair* usually found on the face of a barometer. In themselves, they are meaningless save as reminders of the probable significance of a trend or direction and rate of change in the barometer reading. Since the trend is usually more important than the current pressure reading, a single reading is useless for prediction purposes. You need a series of readings, taken about once an hour for a minimum of three hours and preferably for six hours, to establish the barometric pressure trend.

Due to the influence of the sun and, to a lesser degree, the moon, there are cyclic daily variations in the pressure readings that need to be corrected for accuracy. In the latitude of the Chesapeake Bay, there is a peak-to-peak variation of about 0.04 inches of mercury (the units of pressure used) twice a day. Using Eastern Daylight (Saving) Time as your reference, correct your reading by subtracting 0.01 inch for every hour past 5:00 a.m. until 9:00 a.m. For every hour past 11:00 a.m. until 3:00 p.m., add 0.01 inch. Then subtract 0.01 inch for every hour past 5:00 p.m. until 9:00 p.m. and (if you're a nightowl) add 0.01 inch for every hour past 11:00 p.m. until 3:00 a.m. the next morning.

Having completed that exacting exercise, if you are less diligent, you can forget the fine corrections as long as you will accept a gray area in the definition of a "slow" change. A "slow" change is defined as a change, in either direction, of from 0.02 inch to 0.10 inch over a six-hour period. A "fast" change is defined as a change greater than 0.10 inch over a six-hour period.

Once you have established your set of readings for the current wind direction, and current pressure trend and current value, corrected for sea level, you are ready to attempt to "predict" the weather *in your immediate vicinity* for the next 12 to 24 hours by applying these readings to the climatological table. May you have better success than your "local" weatherman!

Tides and Currents.

The range of tide in the Chesapeake is not great. In the northern Bay it runs from 1 to $1\frac{1}{2}$ feet, while in the southern Bay, well below the mouth of the Potomac River, it may run as high as $2\frac{1}{2}$ feet.

The direction, strength, and duration of the wind has a far greater effect on water level, causing drops of 3 feet or more below the normal range or adding a couple of feet to the normal high. Strong northerlies tend to "dry out" the Bay while southerlies tend to "fill it up." To produce extreme effects, the wind has to blow from the same direction for a few days.

Except for a few marginal creeks, dredged channels, and harbors, you can ignore the tide for the most part unless you expect a strong northerly wind.

Tidal currents, although relatively mild in most of the Bay, are another matter. The maximum currents range between 1 knot and $1\frac{1}{2}$ knots, with the higher velocities on the ebb. The wind can increase these currents by roughly half a knot, particularly a north wind on an ebb current.

It is sometimes possible to minimize the effect of a foul current by hugging the shore. However, this works only if the shoreline is concave in your vicinity, such as the region between Cove Point and the Patuxent River on the Western shore. As a rule, you are better off simply scheduling your course to take advantage of aiding currents and avoiding, as much as possible, the foul currents. A set of current tables for the year is a must and, for cruising in the north, from Elk River to the Patuxent River, a set of *Tidal Current Charts, Upper Chesapeake Bay,* published by the National Oceanic and Atmospheric Administration (NOAA) is invaluable. Currents in the southern Bay are not charted at present but they follow the general guidelines I have given here.

In a few areas the Bay's currents can be substantial. The current directly under the bay bridges sometimes reaches 2 knots and can exceed that speed at the Chesapeake Bay Bridge-Tunnel in the mouth of the Bay. In the Kent Narrows, the "shortcut" between the Chester River and the eastern Bay, the current reaches an impressive speed; here we have encountered a current well in excess of 3 knots directly in the chute under the drawbridge. Fortunately, this is only a short distance. Once clear of the bridge, the current falls off rapidly.

The Chesapeake & Delaware Canal is probably the only other area where tidal currents may present a significant problem. The peak current through the 16-mile-long canal is between 2 and $2\frac{1}{2}$ knots, with currents reaching and exceeding 3 knots not uncommon. Some of the locals claim that currents of 6 knots are possible. Stating the obvious: If you plan to transit the canal, pick your time carefully.

Approaches

It may seem a little strange that a body of water as large as the Chesapeake Bay is considered to be a part of the Intracoastal Waterway, but it is. The ICW stretches from New York to Florida along the Eastern Seaboard of the United States. Admittedly, the stretch of the ICW through New Jersey is, for all practical purposes, nonexistent for any boat much larger than a runabout due to the number of bridges and shoal depth (frequent controlling depths may be 2 feet or even less). Cruising boats heading south must make the Atlantic passage from Sandy Hook, at the mouth of the Hudson River, to Cape May, with a few possible inlets in between in which they may seek shelter or rest.

The true inside route to Florida from the north really starts at Cape May, N.J. From there, the southbound cruiser has the choice of the outside route down the Atlantic Coast of the Delmarva Peninsula to the mouth of the Chesapeake and the harbors in the Norfolk area or the inside route up Delaware Bay, through the Chesapeake & Delaware Canal, and down the Chesapeake Bay to Norfolk. At Norfolk, there is again a choice; the outside route around Cape Hatteras or one of the two inside routes of the ICW, which start from the Elizabeth River at Norfolk and rejoin in Albemarle Sound, North Carolina, by Roanoake Island.

For those "snowbirds" headed back north in the spring, the reverse is, of course, true.

Northern Approaches

To be strictly correct, there is only one "northern" approach to the Chesapeake Bay, the inside route up the Delaware Bay, through the C&D Canal, and into the Elk River at the extreme northern end of the Bay. From there, the entire expanse of the Chesapeake with its hundreds of harbors and points of interest lies before you. The outside route really bypasses the entire Chesapeake and, even if you enter the mouth of the Bay, you will miss most of the better cruising grounds.

The Delmarva Peninsula Outside Route. The main advantage of the approximately 115-mile–long outside route between Cape May and Norfolk is that it is less than half as long as the inside trek up the Delaware Bay, through the C&D Canal, and down the Chesapeake Bay. For most cruisers, that constitutes about the last good thing that may be said about it. If your boat is not sturdy enough in design and properly equipped for an offshore ocean passage, don't even think about taking the outside route. While it is not normally a difficult overnight run for a capable boat, especially in the summer, a storm can come up fairly quickly—pick your weather carefully! If a storm is on the way and you are not absolutely sure of being able to enter a sheltering inlet well before it arrives, head offshore or don't start.

The last good, all-weather harbor between Cape May and Norfolk is behind the artificial breakwater inside Cape Henlopen on the south side of the mouth of Delaware Bay. While there are four or five navigable inlets along the Delmarva coast, you cannot depend upon being able to enter even the best of them under deteriorating conditions, especially against opposing ocean waves and an outgoing tidal current. All have shifting shoals and, at any given time, the channel may not be where the buoys indicate that it is located. In fact, negotiating narrow oceanside inlets anywhere is something of an art in itself and books have been written on the subject.

For better or worse, the following constitute the prime points of interest for a cruiser taking the outside route from Cape May to the Norfolk area.

BREAKWATER HARBOR: Tucked just inside Cape Henlopen, about 15 miles south of Cape May Harbor and protected by a pair of long breakwaters is the appropriately named Breakwater Harbor. Enter the harbor on either side of the 2-mile-long outer breakwater, the west end of which is a good 2 miles offshore. The east end is still about a mile offshore.

There is no need to hold the channel on the west side; there is at least 9 feet of water for a mile to either side of it. In fact, it may be better to stay out of the channel if the Cape May-Lewes Ferry (terminal located in the southwest corner of the harbor), is operating.

The east channel also has plenty of room, but stay well off the Cape Henlopen shore; it shoals a long way out. (Notice the ½-mile length of the first pier in the southeast corner of the harbor.)

The best protection is inside the inner breakwater, near the ferry terminal. There is a "tourist" store and a small restaurant inside the ferry terminal building, but, if you are looking for fuel, water, or other marine supplies, enter Roosevelt Inlet to the Lewes & Rehoboth

Canal (west of Breakwater Harbor) and proceed 1½ miles to Lewes. The canal's controlling depth is a well-maintained 8 feet. The public dock and the Inn at Canal Square are just before the drawbridge (which opens on demand).

INDIAN RIVER INLET: Twelve miles south of the tip of Cape Henlopen is the first inlet on the Delmarva peninsula. Indian River Inlet provides a passage through the strip of beach separating Rehobeth and Indian River Bays from the ocean. Unfortunately, the 35-foot vertical clearance of the fixed bridge over the inlet bars entrance to virtually all cruising sailboats. Although accessible to them, it is rarely used by cruising powerboats either, partly because of the shifting channel inside the inlet and the shallow waters of both bays.

Local powerboats and fishing boats are the primary users of this inlet. Use by these boats is evidently heavy enough to make it worthwhile to maintain a buoyage system, including lights on the jetties at the entrance and a radio beacon (R Bn-308) on the north shore, just inside the inlet. There is also a Coast Guard station located nearby.

An assortment of marinas located on the Indian River provide virtually all the marine services that you may need. There are also two marinas at the north end of Rehobeth Bay which offer most marine services except diesel fuel.

OCEAN CITY INLET: Thirteen miles south of Indian River Inlet is Ocean City Inlet, the only one of the navigable inlets that might be given serious consideration by cruising boats. Except in the case of moderate to heavy onshore winds, this inlet is relatively easy to negotiate.

Under other than benign conditions, obtain recent local knowledge or bypass the inlet entirely (unless you are feeling lucky). A tidal current well upward of 3 knots at peak can be encountered if you hit it at the wrong time. Check the tide tables for an approximation of the probable slack water times to make your entrance. Do not attempt to negotiate the inlet, especially in a sailboat, under conditions of an outgoing current and onshore winds of much over 15 knots. At best, you won't like it. At worst, you may founder or hit an obstruction, both of which will definitely ruin your day.

The entrance is clearly marked with high stone jetties and buoys to seaward. Some sort of obstruction, marked by a white/orange buoy, is located a bit to the southeast of the inlet. Do not depend on the seaward buoys to properly mark the channel as storms can readily change the channel's actual location and depth.

There is a Coast Guard station at the west end of the entrance, on the north side. A VHF-FM radio call to them to obtain information on the channel location and controlling depth prior to negotiating this inlet is a good idea.

Once inside, the Ocean City Channel leads northward to an assortment of marinas and charter boat facilities where you can obtain virtually any marine services or supplies that you might need. The channel leads, eventually, to Isle of Wight Bay. Beyond that are Assawoman Bay and the St. Martin River. Be sure to follow the channel carefully unless you plan to get out and walk!

A channel to the south of the inlet may permit anchoring in the more pristine region of the north end of Sinepuxent Bay, a little past the Commercial Fish Harbor on the mainland side. The channel continues behind Assateague Island all the way to Chincoteague Bay, but it is reputed to be shallow and subject to frequent shifting—it may not be where the buoys indicate. Although the controlling depth is reputed to be about 4 feet, if you can't get out and push your boat or you object to grounding, better forget it.

CHINCOTEAGUE INLET: A little over 34 miles south of Ocean City Inlet is the winding and changeable inlet to Chincoteague Channel. While the entrance channel is buoyed, it is quite undependable and is not recommended for use by anyone not well acquainted with recent "local knowledge" of the channel and its approaches.

If you do manage to negotiate the entrance, the channel winds through marshes and plentiful shoals inside of Chincoteague Island, past a swing bridge, to Chincoteague Bay.

Chincoteague Island is the setting for the famous children's book, *Misty of Chincoteague,* but I find little else to recommend it, especially in light of the iffy inlet and channel.

WACHAPREAGUE INLET: Approximately 20 miles south southwest of Chincoteague Inlet is the highly dubious Wachapreague Inlet. While the entrance is marked with a lighted bell buoy and assorted unlit buoys, it should be attempted only by boats with less than a 4-foot draft and under benign conditions.

This one is better left to the local fishermen. If conditions are rough, it is too dangerous to attempt, especially for a stranger. Under calm conditions, why bother? If you try it anyway, be sure to check the tide tables for the approximate time of slack water to avoid strong currents.

WACHAPREAGUE TO CAPE CHARLES: There are several other inlets on the 40 miles of Virginia coastline between Wachapreague Inlet and the entrance to the Chesapeake Bay. All have channels and shoals that shift frequently, making them virtually unusable to cruisers. For the same reasons, cruisers are well advised to steer a course well off the entire coastline in this region; a minimum of 3 miles seems prudent. It takes only a glance at the chart to confirm this blanket comment.

One possible exception is worth mentioning. If they have the skill and nerve to negotiate the fairly treacherous Sand Island Inlet into Cobb Bay, power cruisers with less than 3-foot drafts can take an inland waterway route through Sand Shoal Channel and Mockhorn Channel to Magothy Bay and then through Cape Charles Channel into the Chesapeake. (See "Region 7, Cape Charles Channel.") However, this trek is only for the truly adventurous. If occasional grounding bothers you, forget it.

On approaching the mouth of the Chesapeake, beware of Nautilus Shoal, which extends from 2 to 4 miles southeast of Fishermans Island just south of Cape Charles. In calm weather, some rudimentary navigation and prudence can permit you to save considerable distance by passing between Nautilus Shoal and Fishermans Island. However, if there is any sea making up or any uncertainty in your exact location, a wiser course is to remain well offshore until you can pick up nun "2" southeast of Nautilus Shoal or one of the shipping channel buoys before changing course to enter the Bay. (See "The Chesapeake Bay Entrance," for more information on actually entering the mouth of the Chesapeake.)

The Delaware Bay/C&D Canal Inside Route. Few people cruise the Delaware Bay for pleasure. It is normally something to endure in order to reach the Chesapeake Bay or, conversely, Cape May in preparation for the Atlantic passage north. A

rare few may head up the Delaware River to Philadelphia or beyond.

However, this passage of less than 50 miles is a vital link in the much-to-be-enjoyed inside route of the ICW, through the cruising grounds of the Chesapeake Bay, to the southern links with the routes south to escape the winter (or the path north for the summer).

The mean range of tide in Delaware Bay is between 5 and 5½ feet. The currents resulting from this, together with the shallowness of the bay and the flow of the Delaware River, can combine to make some fairly uncomfortable conditions on the Bay, especially when the current and winds oppose each other and you are headed into a strong wind. Currents can range from a low peak of about 1.3 knots to more than 2 knots at times, and crosscurrents and eddies can combine to throw the unwary well off course.

On the other hand, if your timing is good you can take advantage of the current to give you a boost either up or down the Delaware Bay. If your vessel can make 6 knots or more, you can ride the current most, if not all, of the way from Cape May to the C&D Canal or vice versa. Slower vessels should start before the beginning of the flood when departing Cape May or the ebb when departing from the C&D Canal to maximize the boost and minimize the adverse current, especially in the upper reaches.

It is preferable, but by no means essential, to transit Delaware Bay during daylight. You can save considerable distance by heading directly between the Cape May Canal and Mish Maull Shoal Light, a course of 322 degrees from the canal. This is a distance of about 17 miles, during which you pass no intermediate markers or reference points to give you a warm feeling of being on course until you intersect the shipping channel. The red occluding 4-second light of the 59-foot–high Mish Maull Shoal Light serves as a good target as soon as you are able to locate it. Once you find the shipping channel, navigation the rest of the way to the C&D Canal is easy: simply run the outside edge of the channel from buoy to buoy. There is plenty of room to parallel the channel outside of the buoys. This neatly keeps you on-course and well away from any shoals or ledges, with one possible exception. If you are running at night, beware of Cross Ledge Shoal to the east of your course, especially the ruins of the abandoned lighthouse at the south end of Cross Ledge.

The presence of large ships heading up or down the channel is a far greater danger than any possibility of

grounding. Stay out of the shipping channel itself as a matter of course, especially if a ship is anywhere in sight. Even if a ship does see you on its radar (not necessarily a high probability), it will have little choice for any kind of course change nor will it be able to stop should you become disabled within the channel (or simply get careless). Although there is a lot of shipping activity on the Delaware, wakes from even large ships are seldom a problem as they tend to keep their speed down on this passage.

On occasion, there is fog, especially in the fall and in the area of Brandywine Shoal and below. Normally, it burns off by noon but it has not infrequently lasted for a day or more. If you do travel in fog on Delaware Bay, do so only with the instrumentation that will permit you to keep close to your planned course and stay out of the shipping channel.

Between Cape May and the C&D Canal, harbors are few and far between. In fact, there really is only one, the Cohansey River, which bears much consideration. The one other possibility, the Maurice River, is too far out of the way—except to take shelter from a northwest blow that comes up after you are well under way toward the C&D Canal. Both of these rivers are on the New Jersey shore. Other than Breakwater Harbor inside Cape Henlopen or the C&D Canal itself, there are no harbors on the Delaware shore worth mentioning.

CAPE MAY HARBOR AND CANAL: In addition to being the best of all of the inlets along the New Jersey coast, Cape May Harbor serves as an excellent stopover point for the cruiser to await appropriate weather for the offshore run north or south or a favorable tide state before jumping off on the inside leg up Delaware Bay to the C&D Canal. The harbor may be entered or exited either through the inlet on the Atlantic side or, for those vessels requiring less than 55 feet vertical clearance, through the Cape May Canal to Delaware Bay. For those rare few whose timing is superb, it can even serve as a shortcut, saving several miles over the trip around the end of Cape May to head up Delaware Bay.

Like most ocean inlets, it may be impossible to enter under certain conditions, notably a heavy surf and especially with an opposing current and wave situation. In fact, some boats heading for Cape May Harbor are forced to bypass the inlet, circle around the end of Cape May, and enter the harbor through the Cape May Canal from the Delaware Bay side.

There is at least 20 feet of water on the approach to the entrance between the lighted jetties on the Atlantic inlet, although the preferred approach is to round the flashing 4-second bell buoy, red "2CM", about one-half mile northwest of the jetties. From red "2CM" it is a straight shot into and through the inlet.

Immediately after you clear the inlet, a section of the New Jersey Inland Waterway extends to starboard. The buoyed channel leading to Cape May Harbor is to port. The 1½-mile–long harbor is oriented on a north-south axis with a width of approximately one-quarter mile. In spite of its size, anchorage space is scarce, mainly because of shoaling outside of the channel. There are plenty of marinas around the harbor with all of the facilities you are likely to need or want. There is at least 7 feet of water throughout the channel down the middle of the harbor, opening out somewhat at the southern end.

The southeast corner of Cape May Harbor is the primary Mecca for transient cruising boats. Once you are a few hundred yards south of the "Tank" shown on the chart beyond the Coast Guard station on the east side of the harbor, simply pull out of the channel and find a spot to drop the hook. This may not be easy as you will have plenty of company a large percentage of the time. There is little anchorage room elsewhere. Beware of old pilings in the water toward the vicinity of the tank.

Marine facilities most visited by transients are located in Schellenger Creek to the south. Unless you have a large-scale chart, you may not find Schellenger Creek marked on it. It's the little creek that runs directly from the extreme end of the harbor, east of the entrance to the Cape May Canal. The Lobster House Restaurant is located on the old fish dock at the creek entrance. Temporary dockage is available to patrons of the restaurant.

As stated earlier, anchorage space in Cape May Harbor is fairly scarce. If you prefer to anchor out, as opposed to taking a slip at one of the marinas, and you don't need or aren't interested in the facilities or bustle of the town, try heading up the New Jersey Intracoastal Waterway to Sunset Lake, a little less than 3 miles past its junction with Cape May Inlet. Here you will find a good sized, well-protected anchorage with water depths of between 7 and 29 feet.

From the southern end of Cape May Harbor, the Cape May Canal runs for a distance of about 4 miles south to Delaware Bay. Traffic entering the canal from Cape May Harbor is supposed to be controlled by red and green lights. However, several friends have reported passing through without ever seeing these lights.

Tidal current through the canal can be substantial, frequently exceeding a normal peak of about 2½ knots. However, since you normally would time your passage through the canal for shortly prior to the flood current in the Delaware Bay, you will rarely encounter much of this current. The same is typically true for arrivals at the canal, although this is more problematical.

The speed limit in the canal is 6 knots (posted as 6½ statute miles per hour). This can sometimes be a nuisance to boats trying to clear the canal before the start of the flood tide in Delaware Bay, but you had better heed it.

The range of tide is typically 4 feet with a controlling depth in the canal of at least 6 feet MLW. Sailboats with drafts approaching 6 feet should contact the Corps of Engineers for the latest controlling depth in the canal. The Coast Guard station at Cape May Harbor also should have that information. Additional potential problems (at least for larger sailboats) are two fixed highway bridges with vertical clearances of 55 feet MHW and a swing railroad bridge that has a mere 4-foot clearance when closed. No one of our acquaintance has ever seen the railroad bridge in its closed position. Presumably, it is no longer in operation. In any event, it presents no problem.

Just inside the mouth of the canal at Delaware Bay is the northern terminus of the Cape May-Lewes Ferry. If you see the ferry coming or notice significant activity aboard the ferry as it prepares to depart its dock, give it plenty of room.

The canal exits through two lighted jetties into Delaware Bay. From there, a course of 322 degrees takes you to Mish Maull Shoal Light, saving some distance over the route around Brandywine Shoal Light.

THE MAURICE RIVER: The entrance channel to the Maurice River is located a good 7 miles off any normal route you may plan to take between the C&D Canal and Cape May. The approach takes you over Egg Island Flats in water depths between 7 and 12 feet. With a strong wind from anywhere in the southwest quadrant, it will be rough!

Look for the flashing green "3" marker paired with a red "2" nun at the entrance to the 2½ mile long channel into the river. Take a course from green "3" to the green "5" marker, then swing to port to head for the west side of the mouth of the river. Don't be misled by the green "11" marker on the east side, there is a long shoal which extends from East Point nearly into the river's mouth. There is reputed to be as much as 7 feet of water in the channel but, if your draft comes anywhere near that, we suggest that you stay out.

The town of Bivalve, a little way upriver, is the most convenient stopping place. Be sure to follow the channel on the way to Bivalve; there are plenty of stakes in the river, many of them broken off and just underwater. As the name indicates, this is an oystering port, probably the busiest on the Delaware. Don't look for typical pleasure boat facilities, there aren't any. However, you may be able to find dock space on either shore where you can tie up. Anchoring space is debatable, at best. Groceries and boat supplies are available nearby, but remember that this is a working waterman's harbor; yacht supplies are likely to be unavailable.

Port Norris, farther upstream, is reputed to have similar facilities.

THE COHANSEY RIVER: About 30 miles above Cape May or less than 20 miles below the C&D Canal and about 2 miles northeast of the shipping channel near Ship John Shoal is the Cohansey River, perhaps the only reasonable harbor on the passage between the two end points.

There are two entrances to the Cohansey: the unmarked passage through Cohansey Cove to the south of Cohansey light or through the dredged canal just to the northwest of the light. (Note: I am not certain that this light is still in operation, but it is there.) Of the two, the latter is a better choice; it is nearly 20 feet deep and the approach is marked by range lights. Again, the lights may no longer be operational. The only problem is that you may have a little trouble finding the entrance. The land is all low-lying and marshy, making it difficult to see the entrance until you are almost upon it. The easiest way to find it is to take a bearing from Ship John Shoal Light or another channel marker and follow that course, frequently checking your back bearing until you are within visual range. Err on the side of the Cohansey Light so you will know which way to turn if you have to search for the entrance.

Once through the canal, the best anchorage is in the bend just southeast of the canal. The shoreline is marshy and it will be fairly quiet and peaceful, nearly all of the traffic through the canal will be from or to the upstream reaches. Beware of a set of old pilings along the southwest shore here; some of them may be below the water.

If you need fuel or supplies, Greenwich Pier is 2 to 3 miles upriver from the canal. There are two marinas in this vicinity, both on the west (or is it north?) side of the river, where you can obtain most marine facilities you may require.

The village of Greenwich Pier is only a short walk, about half a mile, from the river. If you have the time and any interest at all in American history, be sure to visit it. There are several colonial homes here, all identified by plaques near their doors. They are occupied, so don't expect to walk in.

THE C&D CANAL APPROACH: Actually, little instruction is needed for anyone to find the entrance to the C&D Canal. The readily visible entrance will appear to port about 6 miles after you pass the obvious towers of the Salem Nuclear Power Plant on the Jersey shore to starboard. Simply honor the markers to port to avoid the extensive shoal on the Delaware side and you will enter the canal easily. If you approach at night, the floodlights lining the canal will make it unmistakable.

For more information on the canal itself, see "Region 1, Chesapeake & Delaware Canal."

Southern Approaches. There are three approaches to the Chesapeake Bay from the south: the outside route around Cape Hatteras, and the two ICW routes, both of which terminate in the Elizabeth River near Norfolk. Which route you choose is a function of the time available for the transit, the capabilities and outfitting of your boat, and the skill and interests of your crew. The ICW routes are far safer and less demanding, but are rather time-consuming and tedious, with a large number of bridges and their opening schedules with which to contend.

THE CAPE HATTERAS OUTSIDE ROUTE: Those with a capable boat and a time crunch to make the trip between the Chesapeake and points south normally opt for the ocean passage well offshore around Cape Hatteras. Since you can keep going 24 hours a day offshore and normally only travel the ICW during daylight, the outside route obviously takes only a fraction of the time of an ICW trip. Of course, the strain on the crew and the hazards of a storm are also significantly greater offshore. Details for such a passage are well beyond the scope of this book. What we will address is the approach to and entrance of the Chesapeake Bay.

There are few hazards in the approach to the Chesapeake Bay entrance from the south. Ordinary prudence would dictate a passage well to seaward of Cape Hatteras and you would normally be on a course to the entrance which would keep you away from trouble with the few outlying shoals near its mouth.

Fourteen miles east of the tip of Cape Henry, Chesapeake Light, a white superstructure with a blue base, rising 117 feet above the water on four piles, is the primary reference point for entrance into the Bay from the south to east approaches. The light also sports a radio beacon (R Bn 290) for those equipped with an RDF unit. There is no chance of mistaking it for something else, the name *Chesapeake* is emblazoned in white on all sides of the structure.

From Chesapeake Light, a course of approximately 290 degrees (plot your own course more precisely) will take you to the Bay entrance. It won't take long before you run across the string(s) of buoys marking the shipping channels. Follow them if you wish, but stay out of the channel especially if there is a ship in sight. (See "The Chesapeake Bay Entrance," later in this section for more information on the entrance itself.) If you are headed for the James River area, follow the Thimble Shoal Channel. For the York River or Mobjack Bay, Chesapeake Channel is the shortest course. For all other points north on the Bay, use the North Channel unless there is heavy wave action, in which case stay farther away from the breakers on Nautilus Shoal south of Cape Charles. (See "Region 7: Wolf Trap Light to Cape Henry," for details on harbors in the vicinity.)

THE CHESAPEAKE BAY ENTRANCE:
The mouth of the Chesapeake Bay, between Cape Henry on the south and Fishermans Island off Cape Charles on the north, is 10 miles wide. The Chesapeake Bay Bridge and Tunnel, which spans the mouth of the Bay from Lynnhaven Roads 5 miles inside Cape Henry on the south to Cape Henry on the north, divides the entrance into three channels. Thimble Shoal Channel passes between trestles "A" and "B" on the south; Chesapeake Channel in the middle passes between tres-

tles "B" and "C," and the North Channel passes under a fixed bridge with a vertical clearance of 75 feet less than a mile southeast of Fishermans Island. Which channel you choose depends mostly upon where you are coming from and where you are going.

In trestles "A" and "B" there are additional openings for small craft, each composed of a group of three spans with a vertical clearance of 21 feet and a horizontal clearance of 70 feet. Fixed green lights mark the centerline of each span and fixed red lights mark the outermost bridge support piling on each side of the openings. If you can transit these openings, you can avoid any possible confrontation with the substantial amount of large ship traffic through the two main channels, Chesapeake and Thimble Shoal. Sailboats and power cruisers of any substantial size should not attempt these openings.

THE ICW TO THE ELIZABETH RIVER ROUTES: As those who are headed up the ICW toward the Chesapeake from the south pass Roanoke Island at the top of Pamlico Sound and enter Albemarle Sound, they are faced with a choice of two different routes of the ICW, both of which terminate in the Elizabeth River south of Norfolk. The first proceeds into Currituck Sound and all the way through it to the top of the west fork in its northernmost end, where it becomes the Albemarle-Chesapeake Canal. The second requires a passage across the shallow and frequently "lumpy" Albemarle Sound and up the Pasquotank River where it connects with the Dismal Swamp Canal at the town of South Mills, North Carolina.

The first route is somewhat shorter, wider, and deeper than the second through the Great Dismal Swamp, but the latter is usually more interesting. Those planning to take the Dismal Swamp Canal should check with the Coast Guard to ascertain the controlling depth in the canal and, if the weather has been dry, whether or not it is even open to traffic.

Both routes join with the Southern Branch of the Elizabeth River within a relatively short distance of one another. From there on, you are cruising Chesapeake Bay country. (See "Region 7: Elizabeth River," for more information.)

Hazards

to

Navigation

Running aground on one of the numerous shoals, which I discussed in the previous section, is not the only thing to watch out for in the Bay. The cruiser needs to be aware of other hazards, many unique to the Chesapeake.

Crab Pots

Crabbing is one of the major industries on the Bay. Blue crabs abound in these waters, as is obvious by the unbelievable number of crab trap floats scattered throughout the Bay. In some areas, trap floats are so thick that it is difficult to navigate a boat through without hitting several. Floats range from those made commercially to bleach bottles and almost anything that floats well.

The floats themselves are no problem to boats; they are usually soft, smooth, and easily pushed aside by the bow wave. The problem is the line which fastens the float to the heavy wire crab trap on the bottom. This line can become trapped in the propeller or around the rudderpost of a boat, lifting the trap off the bottom and producing a fantastic amount of drag. There have been instances of the line being wound up around the propeller until the heavy trap slams against the hull, sometimes puncturing it. The line also can work into the propeller shaft housing, scoring the shaft and destroying the bearing.

Keep a careful watch and steer clear of trap floats. Freeing a trap line with a boathook or similar device from on deck or in a dinghy alongside is a rare bit of luck. Usually you have to dive over the side and try to work it loose. Make every effort to free the line *without cutting it*. What is a nuisance to you is the waterman's livelihood. When you cut a line, he loses that trap and any income it might have produced.

Even cruisers with the best intentions accidently foul a pot from time to time. If you should hit a trap line while under power, immediately take the engine out of gear to reduce the chance of wrapping the line around the prop, cross your fingers, and watch for the float to reappear in your wake. If it doesn't, you have no choice but to do whatever is necessary to free it before proceeding.

We once picked up a trap in mid-Bay while under sail in more than 25 knots of wind. There was nothing we could do but drag it to where we could anchor in the partial shelter of a point of land before diving over the side and cutting it free. With the heavy drag, we couldn't control the boat well enough to negotiate any harbor entrances. It was an experience we would rather not repeat. The author hopes you won't repeat it, too! (See "Crabbing: Traps and Trotlines," later in this section for more information on crab traps.)

Fish Traps

These fishing devices consist of a long line of stakes, some stretching 200 yards or more, which are used to string nets and channel fish into them. The ends of these lines are supposed to be marked with both day and night signals. In practice, they rarely seem to be lit or, if they are, the light is dim. The day markers are generally a small bush or branch of a tree, lashed to the stake at either end of the line. These are easily visible and can be used to navigate around the line of stakes. In some areas, fish traps are so thick that they present a real maze through which you must thread your way. Navigation can be difficult in the daytime. At night or in one of the rare fogs, it is nearly impossible. The boundaries of fish trap areas are plainly marked on the NOAA charts; in conditions of poor visibility, lay a course around these areas, if possible. There are fairways in many of the river channels and harbor entrances, but some of them will require careful navigation if the area is heavily populated with traps.

The areas most heavily populated with fish traps are south of the Potomac River mouth, with a real maze off Mobjack Bay. However, fish traps can be found throughout the main body of the Bay. Along the western shore, both working fish traps and abandoned stakes may be found miles offshore. If you are neglecting your navigation, they can show up all of a sudden; a dense thicket of them may prove a real test of skill to negotiate.

Restricted Areas

A quick study of the charts reveals areas where access is restricted, without revealing just what the restrictions are. Except for the area near Aberdeen Proving

Grounds in the northern Bay and the Navy bombing ranges near Tilghman Island in the southern Bay, these restricted areas don't seriously interfere with cruising. There are a couple of other restricted areas in certain parts of the Potomac River, but they are rarely in use anymore.

These ranges are patrolled by the Coast Guard or other range-associated craft. You will be warned if you happen to stray into an active target practice area.

Duck Blinds

These blinds are usually in shallow water, which you ought to avoid in any case. (They can warn of shoals in relatively unmarked areas.) However, duck blinds can be mistaken for navigational aids or beacons from a distance, so they do present a small hazard. Other than that, they are just part of the scenery.

Shipping

The skippers, pilots, and crew of the large ships that negotiate the Bay would undoubtedly take exception to being labeled a "hazard to navigation." To them, the plethora of small boats scattered throughout the Bay are the real navigational hazard. In a sense, they are right. Large ships negotiating the Bay are restricted to narrow shipping channels and are infinitely less maneuverable than the small boats that buzz around them like flies. They have nowhere else to go to avoid a small craft in one of those channels and they take more than a mile to stop even in an emergency. The prudent small boat operator must stay alert and keep well out of the way of these ships. In fact, Rule 9 (the Narrow Channel Rule) clearly states that no vessel, sail or power, shall cross a narrow channel or fairway if such crossing impedes the passage of a vessel that can safely navigate only in that channel or fairway.

This conduct holds true in encounters with smaller commercial vessels, especially tugs with tows. Many times a tug will tow a barge some distance behind it on a cable that could slice apart a small boat. Never attempt to pass between a tug and tow; you won't make it. If sailing at night, be especially careful as it is hard to distinguish a barge being towed behind a tug just by looking.

Fishing Boats and
Right of Way

The Rules of the Road are essential to the safe operation of all kinds of boats, from sailboards to giant ships. They use "common sense" to establish conventions of right-of-way between vessels on potential collision courses; these conventions determine actions that will be taken to prevent such a collision. These "rights" are established upon the basis of each vessel's relative ability to maneuver. The less maneuverable vessel usually (but not always) has right-of-way over the more maneuverable one. If both parties involved in a "meeting" situation know, understand, and abide by the Rules of the Road, there is rarely any problem. It is when the rules are ignored or misunderstood that life on the water quickly gets difficult.

One of the most heated misconceptions concerns the rights of vessels engaged in fishing, especially private powerboats who are trolling.

The rules state that "fishing vessels" have the right-of-way over powerboats and sailboats. However, this only applies to vessels using nets, lines, trawls, or other gear that severely restricts the maneuverability of the vessel in responding to the presence of another vessel on an intercept course. In addition, "fishing vessels" are supposed to display the proper dayshapes during the day and lights at night. If all of these conditions are not satisfied, the vessel is not legally "fishing" for right-of-way purposes! In practice, Chesapeake Bay commercial fishing vessels 20 or more meters in length rarely, if ever, display the "proper dayshape" while they are working; Operators of these vessels obviously feel that their identification is so obvious during the day that the dayshapes are redundant. Here tradition takes precedence over the rules. Most boats display sufficient prudence around these fishing vessels to prevent any problems.

Do trolling boats have the right-of-way over sailboats and other powerboats because they are engaged in fishing? Absolutely not! According to the Inland and International Rules of the Road, both of which specifically exclude trolling from the definition of fishing vessels, boats trolling a line or lines while under way have no special rights over other vessels—other than the Rules of the Road for the relative vessels themselves. This misunderstanding rears its ugly head again and again, fanning the flames of antagonism between powerboaters and sailboaters. There really is no need for it. Understanding and adherence to the Rules of the Road, plus common courtesy, would easily avoid any problems and the resultant antagonism. Personally, we go well out of our way, even under sail hard on the wind, to stay clear of any boats that are obviously involved in fishing of any type, including trollers. Wouldn't it be nice if these actions were reciprocated?

Last, but by no means least, there is the General Prudential Rule. In short, this means that no matter who is supposed to have the right-of-way, the skipper of a boat is required to take whatever action is necessary to avoid a collision. How's that for common sense?

General

Hazards

Sea Nettles

The sea nettle or medusa jellyfish *(Chrysaora quin-querirrha)* is probably the single biggest nuisance in the Chesapeake Bay, at least for those who like to swim or cool off in the water.

The nettles usually start to appear in June, showing up in the lower Bay first and working their way north as the season progresses. Both the density of the nettle population and the rate and maximum distance that they travel up the Bay is determined largely by the amount of rainfall in the spring and early summer. The more rain, the fewer the nettles and the slower their spread. This is probably due to both the decrease in salinity of the Bay waters and the rate of non-tidal flow of water out of the Bay. Those who like to swim tend to cruise toward the southern part of the Bay in the early part of the year. Then as the nettles move up the Bay, swimmers cruise toward the head of the Bay as the summer progresses. Even in the worst years for nettles, the Susquehanna and Sassafras Rivers provide nettle-free swimming, as do the upper reaches of many of the longer rivers.

The nettle appears to be little more than a translucent, bell-shaped, dome of jelly with tentacles underneath that can be as long as four feet. These tentacles are covered with stinging cells that are used to paralyze fish so that they can be eaten. When touched, each cell fires a microscopic "dart" filled with venom. The venom is a complex protein that causes a burning sensation on human skin. The usual result is a thin red line or welt which lasts from about 15 to 30 minutes in most cases. An unfortunate few may be hypersensitive to the venom and experience shortness of breath and severe pains which may last for days. There are innumerable "remedies" for relief from these stings (see the sidebar, "Chesapeake Bay Jellyfish," page 101) most of which seem to have their greatest effect in the mind of the believer. Personally, we have found removing any remaining cells and applying straight ammonia liberally to the affected area to be most effective in stopping the stinging. Do not apply alcohol, as this will cause any unfired cells to discharge immediately.

Don't look for the elimination of these Bay devils. Sea nettles have no known natural enemies save a certain variety of sea slug, called a nudibranch, which feeds on the nettles during their polyp stages. Nets have occasionally been used at some beaches, but the results have not been very satisfactory. Coating your body with oils or petroleum jelly is effective for a short time, but I would rather chance getting stung. The best solution for those who like to swim is to head for the far northern portion of the Bay or well up some of the longer rivers where the nettles rarely penetrate.

Insects and

Defense Tactics

Entomologists classify insects into thousands upon thousands of categories and subcategories. Those of us outside of that profession tend to use much looser terminology, the politest of which is probably *bugs*. Those who cruise the Chesapeake Bay are likely to become concerned only with the flying, biting insects. For the purposes of this book, I will divide these beasties into three categories, based on the defense tactics required, and refer to them in terms which will probably make an entomologist scream: flies, mosquitoes, and biting gnats or no-see-ums.

The main line of defense against all three is a set of close-meshed, well-fitted screens on all ports, hatches, or other openings into the cabin of a boat. If you can keep them out of the cabin, you have a haven of refuge where you can relax and at least sleep in peace. This refuge can be extended by screening in the cockpit of a cruiser or sailboat.

Making this screening sounds more difficult than it is, unless you are a neatness nut. For a cabin cruiser, it is easy. Simply make a set of screens that you can put up in place of the canvas cockpit cover. Leave plenty of material to hang loose around the snaps to aid in sealing little gaps and openings (see Figure 1).

Screening in a sailboat is a little more difficult. The

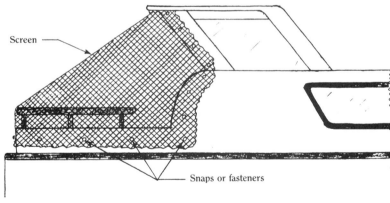

FIGURE 1.
Screening the cockpit of a cabin cruiser.

Screen

Snaps or fasteners

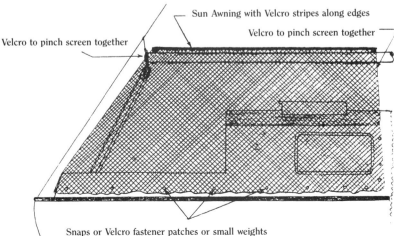

Sun Awning with Velcro stripes along edges

Velcro to pinch screen together

Velcro to pinch screen together

FIGURE 2.
Screening the cockpit of a sailboat.

Snaps or Velcro fastener patches or small weights

easiest way is to combine screening with a sun awning. Velcro strips fastened to the top edge of the awning will permit ready attachment of the screen and still preserve the flexibility needed for adjustment of the awning and movement around and outside of the cockpit. You will need to devise a means of fastening the bottom of the screen. If enough material is left at the bottom to allow several folds to drape, this can be done with judicious placement of weights and tying off to stanchions or other fittings. Closure of the screens around stays, lines, or the boom can also easily be done with Velcro. Just be sure to leave enough screen material beyond the Velcro strip to fill in the inevitable gaps (see Figure 2). This screen permits you to sit out in the cockpit well after twilight in certain "buggy" anchorages, without immersing yourself in repellent or being eaten alive.

From here on, the defense tactics vary depending on which insect is "bugging" you. Please notice that I am ignoring the wide assortment of flying insects which are pesky but do not bite. The methods used to deter their nastier cousins usually handle these offenders too.

Flies. This category covers all of the larger biting flies that show up at almost any time, anywhere, even miles offshore—horseflies, deerflies, green flies, etc., down to ordinary houseflies. All are easily kept out of the cabin by screens but can be a problem for the crew when you are under way. Very few are deterred by insect repellents—not even by the fly dopes usually found in stores that cater to campers and fishermen. Fear of their bite can be more devastating than the bite itself, since even the ominous buzz of the encircling fly can render its intended victim senseless.

On the Bay, we usually don't bother with fly dope. The most effective device I have found for keeping all sorts of flies under control, both at anchor and under way, is the time-honored fly swatter—likely one of man's first attempts at insect repellent. (Have you ever noticed how flies seem to disappear at the first appearance of a fly swatter?) The Bay's flies tend to be at their worst after a day or so of rain. The rest of the time they are comparatively sparse; a keen eye and an accurate fly swatter can prevent them from being much of a nuisance. Of course, from time to time you will have to dispose of all the little carcasses littering the deck.

Mosquitoes. Even though there are hundreds of different types of mosquitoes, all we care about is that they bite and the bites itch! After that we only care to avoid an encounter with any mosquito, regardless of which type it is. Different types of mosquitoes are active at different times of day, 24 hours a day. Although they seem to have no time constraint—when viewed as a group—they do have limits. Mosquitoes do not venture more than one-half mile offshore, except in freak cases, and are rarely a problem even at anchor if a good breeze is blowing. These bloodsuckers are at their worst a few hours after sundown.

Mosquitoes are easily kept out of a cabin by screens, but there is always the "Lone Ranger" that sneaks into the boat prior to dark, before you have fastened the screens. Once in, it finds a dark recess and lies in wait until you fasten the screens and relax your vigilance. Then it begins its ghastly maddening whine as it seeks you out.

What attracts mosquitoes? Researchers are still trying to pin that down, but so far they have determined that these insects are heat and humidity seekers—they are more attracted to people with higher skin temperatures and higher moisture transpiration rates. This means that if you have a sunburn or are simply hot and sweaty from exertion, you are a mosquito meal waiting to happen. Studies have also shown that mosquitoes perk up in a stream of carbon dioxide, which means the same exertion that makes you hot and sweaty could cause you to exhale too much and too frequently to allow these beasties to pass you by. Lastly, human skin has varying degrees of attractive chemicals; so far only lactic acid has been pinpointed as a possible lure. It seems that we are their natural prey. I have been unable to find any scientific research to buttress this claim, but personal research has shown that mosquitoes like dark, especially blue, clothing. Try to avoid wearing blue denim when you plan to do some hard work.

Repellent lotions and sprays are quite effective against these minuscule monsters, but different makes of repellent seem to have varying degrees of effectiveness for each individual, probably something that harkens back to skin chemistry. A trial-and-error process will help you find the one that works best for you. Many cruisers swear by Skin-So-Soft bath oil, an Avon product, but Letterman Army Institute of Research in San Francisco tested it and found that while it had some repellency, it was 30 times less effective than standard repellents on the market. There are also the traditional botanical repellent oils, pennyroyal and citronella. These seem to work only when the bugs aren't bad and they have to be reapplied often to keep up the repellency. Some families use them on children because they are not as toxic as the most effective repellent to date, DEET, or *N,N*-diethyl-*meta*-toluamide. Any repellent with DEET is a good start to stopping mosquitoes and no-see-ums (more on them soon). DEET is an irritant and a solvent for plastics (don't push up your sunglasses right after you apply your repellent) so you will need to try several varieties of repellent to discover which one has the right percentage of DEET—enough to repel insects but not so much that you develop a rash.

The latest round of research at the USDA's Insects Affecting Man and Animals Research Laboratory in Gainesville, Florida, has uncovered a new type of insect combatant. Permethrin is technically a contact toxicant, not a repellent, but it still gets rid of the bugs. This chemical doesn't work when applied to your skin but it is deadly to insects when it is sprayed on clothing. Any mosquito, or other insect, that lands on treated clothes dies after a few seconds. Used in combination with a DEET-based repellent, permethrin packs quite a one-two punch. Bugs will stay away from exposed skin and die when they land on treated clothes. Right now, permethrin is licensed for sale in 29 states as an aerosol spray, Permanone Tick Repellent. It was developed as protection from the tick-carried Lyme disease and Rocky Mountain spotted fever. It is too early to tell what impact such a toxicant might have on the food chain and whether it will be licensed for sale in the remaining states. It sounds like it would be terrific when used on screening around the cabin, but I will wait until all of the results are in.

Biting Gnats and No-see-ums.

Gnats are a more insidious insect, primarily because of their minute size. The Chesapeake is home to a host of biting gnats, the worst of which is the nearly invisible monster called a no-see-um. Gnats are active during daylight hours and until well after dark, with a peak of activity in the late afternoon and evening. In most cases they do not venture more than 100 yards offshore, but if you are anchored within their range and are unprepared, they can drive you to tears.

As with mosquitoes, gnats are less bothersome when a stiff breeze is blowing. Unlike mosquitoes, screens alone will not deter them from entering your cabin—they can squeeze right through the mesh! Your best line of defense is to anchor out of range and use repellents ("6–12" is my repellent of choice for gnats). Whatever your brand, it must cover every inch of exposed skin because they will simply concentrate on the untreated areas. Be sure to cover the small of your back, if your shirt rides up when you bend over. Gnats will home in on even an occasional exposure of untreated skin—and the bites can itch for a long time after the event. Although you have to be zealous in your application of repellent, be careful about applying it to your face; if it gets in your eyes it will burn severely, whatever brand it is.

I don't want to paint too black a picture. The only times we have serious problems with gnats is when we go ashore in some of the more remote areas. We have been in only one anchorage where we were bothered while we were aboard; that was in a small gunkhole off the Tred Avon River during an evening calm in late May.

In summary, if you take my advice and prepare for summer "air raids" with screening, effective repellents, and a trusty fly swatter, you should be able to go or anchor almost anywhere and feed only the occasional bug that penetrates your defenses. You may have to put up with a little good-natured ribbing about your paranoia concerning flying insects, but notice who is and isn't scratching an itch the following morning. Last evening's paranoia will be the morning's common sense.

An Abbreviated Chesapeake Romance

The First Inhabitants

Although the nearest glacial ice sheets were 200 miles north of Maryland, the area of what is now the Chesapeake Bay was "open" but much cooler than it is today. As the climate warmed and the ice melted, creating the Bay (see pages 2–3), the early inhabitants had to adapt their lifestyle to meet the changing conditions. The region's grasslands became forests; where once the natives hunted mammoth, mastodon, and other large game, they now relied on rabbits and deer as well as roots, nuts, and berries. The flooding of the Susquehanna River Valley created a holding tank for a readily available marine diet of fish, oysters, and clams.

By 1,000 B.C. the native population began to settle. The pattern of wandering after game and gathering vegetation on the way shifted to more efficient hunting with the creation of the bow and arrow (about 500 A.D.) and the cultivation of crops of corn, beans, and squash (about 800 A.D.). As farming increased, permanent settlements or villages were established. The villages were collections of rectangular bark houses encircled by a post stockade, usually with one entrance/exit that could be closed to hostile intruders. The postmold patterns have shown up at several village excavations such as the one at the Biggs Ford Village site in Frederick County, Maryland. This time of settlement, known as the Woodland Period, lasted until the arrival of Old World explorers and settlers in the 1600s.

Indians of the Chesapeake

At the time of European Contact, there were two distinct families or confederations of tribes in the vicinity of the Chesapeake. Most belonged to a large family of tribes known as Algonquins. The other tribe, one branch of the very large Iroquois Nation, the Susquehannocks (Sus-que-han'-nocks), lived along the Susquehanna River, predominantly in the vicinity of what is now the Pennsylvania-Maryland border. The warlike Susquehannocks claimed the hunting grounds as far south as the Patuxent River on the western shore and to the Choptank River on the Eastern Shore. They strengthened that

"Powhatan held this state and fashion
when Captain Smith was delivered to him
a prisoner, 1607." LIBRARY OF CONGRESS

claim with sporadic raids on the Algonquin tribes to the south. The more peaceful Algonquins were distributed around the shores of the Bay and its tributaries from the Patuxent River to Cape Henry and on most of the Eastern Shore.

The Algonquins of the Chesapeake were roughly divided geographically into three major tribes, each consisting of a number of smaller tribes. Those living south of the Potomac River were known as Powhatans. The tribes known collectively as Piscataways were distributed south of the Patuxent River, in the region between the Potomac River and the Chesapeake Bay. The remaining family, the Nanticokes dwelt on the Eastern Shore, predominantly south of the Choptank River.

It was the Powhatans that the Jamestown settlers encountered when they established their colony on the shore of the James River in 1609. The Indians gave them a friendly reception and, in spite of a substantial number of bloody incidents, relations remained peaceful. Without that peace, the colony could not have survived. By the third year of its establishment, the number of colonists had dwindled due to disease and starvation. An Indian attack could have easily wiped them out. The reason for this continued peace is not fully understood even today, but undoubtedly rested mainly with the chief of the tribe, Wahunsonacock (called King Powhatan by the colonists). Wahunsonacock had developed a grudging respect for the doughty Captain John Smith, who headed the colony during its establishment, and probably believed that he could gain an advantage over other tribes through trade goods obtained from the colonists. (Surely everyone has heard the story of how Pocahontas, the chief's daughter, saved Captain Smith's life and later married a colonist, John Rolfe.)

The Jamestown colony not only survived, but prospered. More and more colonists arrived and settled on more and more Indian land, resulting in not infrequent bloodshed between the colonists and the Indians. Even so, the shaky peace lasted until 1622, four years after the death of Chief Wahunsonacock and the assumption of the chieftainship by his brother Opechancanough.

The shaky peace crumbled when the colonists hanged an Indian for the *suspected* murder of a white trader. Opechancanough assembled a war party and on March 22, 1622, the Powhatan warriors attacked, killing 347 colonists—men, women, and children. The war was on!

For 10 years battles and skirmishes continued, with considerable losses on both sides, until a peace treaty was agreed upon in 1632.

This peace, as shaky as the previous one, lasted for 12 years. The colonists kept arriving, swelling their number to nearly 8,000. Then, in April of 1644, warriors under Opechancanough attacked again, killing nearly 500 colonists. The colonists retaliated and fighting continued for another two years, until Opechancanough was killed and another shaky peace treaty made.

The Powhatans were not the only natives to feel the pressure of European colonization. Col-

Typical Susquehannock attire at the time
of the Jamestown settlement; from Captain
John Smith's map. LIBRARY OF CONGRESS

onists had arrived in Maryland in 1634 and established their colony at St. Marys City. This time, the Piscataway tribes were the ones involved. Later, as both colonies continued to grow and expanded to the Eastern Shore, the Nanticokes and, finally, the Susquehannocks began to feel the pressure.

There was a ready and lucrative market in Europe for the tobacco grown in the colonies. Colonists continued to arrive in boatload after boatload. More and more land was needed, and taken from the Indians. In early encounters, the Indians generally reacted with curiosity, generosity, and the offer of friendship. Friendly contact exposed the Indians to European germs; many natives were decimated by disease. Repeated betrayal, trickery, and treaty violations on the part of the whites worked to create a pattern of periods of fighting followed by shaky peace between the colonists and the Indians.

Under this pressure and repeated raids by the Susquehannocks, most of the Piscataway tribes left Maryland, moving well into the wilds of Virginia, as did the Powhatans. The Nanticokes of the Eastern Shore first were established in a reservation near the junction of Chicone Creek and the Nanticoke River, but that didn't solve any of the problems and they eventually left for areas well to the north, vanishing into history. The Susquehannocks later went on the warpath against the colonists, only to be badly defeated by combined forces from the Virginia and Maryland colonies and driven back to Pennsylvania.

By the latter part of the 18th century, few Indians were left in the Chesapeake Bay area and their numbers continued to dwindle over the next hundred years. Today, a few descendants of the Nanticoke and Piscataway tribes remain on the Eastern Shore and in Southern Maryland.

The Indians may be gone but they left behind their names to label many of the rivers, creeks, and a few other places where they once dwelt. These names and a scant few traces in the shell mounds on beaches and occasional arrowheads found on the sites of old encampments are reminders that the Bay cradled people and cultures before written history.

The Colonial

Era Begins

The English, under Captain John Smith, were not the first Europeans to settle on the shores of the Chesapeake. They were, however, the first to survive and remain there.

In 1526, not far from the site of Jamestown on the James River, the Spanish attempted to establish a settlement called San Miguel de Gualdape. Between (mostly internal) fighting and rampant disease, it was soon abandoned. Repeated settlement efforts in the 1570s all failed. During this period Spaniards circumnavigated the Bay under Vincente Gonzales, but the expedition produced no charts and was soon forgotten.

The Chesapeake Bay was rediscovered in 1585— this time by an Englishman, Sir Ralph Lane from the Roanoke Island Colony in North Carolina, established by Sir Walter Raleigh. Even so, it took more than 30 years before the English capitalized on this find.

Then in May of 1607, three little ships sailed into the Chesapeake, landed briefly just inside Cape Henry (where a cross now stands to commemorate the event— the Cape Henry Memorial), and then sailed 32 miles up the James River to found the settlement of Jamestown. More ships were to follow, but the *Susan Constant, Godspeed,* and *Discovery* were the first, preceding the *Mayflower* by more than a decade. (Replicas of these three ships are at the Jamestown Festival Park, just above the site of the original settlement on the James River.)

The following year, Captain John Smith set out with a small party to explore the Bay. They spent two months gunkholing an estimated 3,000 miles of the Chesapeake, in search of the elusive Northwest Passage to the Indies. Of course they didn't find it, but they did produce the first reasonably accurate map of the Bay and its rivers, sending it to England for publication.

Despite the knowledge gained through exploration and the bounty of the Bay and its tidewaters, Jamestown almost ended in disaster. The first summer had been hard; the 105 colonists were unprepared for Virginia heat and bad food caused a lot of sickness. Even Smith became ill, but fortunately recovered. The settlers had many unfriendly encounters with Indians. Ironically it was the capture of Smith by the Powhatans that saved the weakened colonists. While he was held by the Indi-

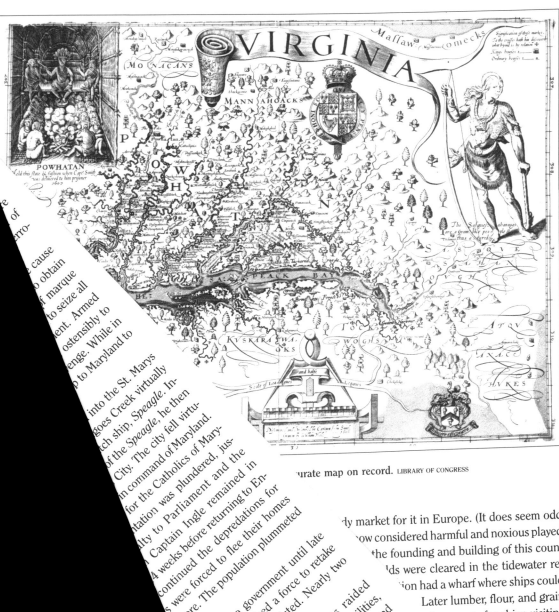

...urate map on record. LIBRARY OF CONGRESS

...ly market for it in Europe. (It does seem odd
...ow considered harmful and noxious played
...the founding and building of this coun-
...lds were cleared in the tidewater re-
...ion had a wharf where ships could
...Later lumber, flour, and grain
...ime cargo for ships visiting
...ams provided waterways
...arket and safe harbors
...aught fish and shellfish to

...terways also provided easy access
...raiders for more than two centuries
...ding of Jamestown—notably the British
...e American Revolution and the War of 1812 as
...s a wide assortment of pirates and privateers. In
...ct, it was the failure of the British to control the lower
Chesapeake, due to the intervention of the French fleet

...e of
...rro-
...e cause
...o obtain
...f marque
...to seize all
...ent. Armed
...ostensibly to
...nge. While in
...p to Maryland to
...into the St. Marys
...goes Creek virtually
...ch ship, *Speagle*. In-
...of the *Speagle*, he then
...n command of Maryland.
...City. The city fell virtu-
...for the Catholics of Mary-
...tation was plundered, jus-
...lty to Parliament remained in
...Captain Ingle and the
...4 weeks before returning to En-
...continued the depredations for
...s were forced to flee their homes
...ewhere. The population plummeted
...ttlers.
...s left without a government until late
... governor Calvert raised a force to retake
...d did so totally unresisted. Nearly two
...chy finally came to an end.
...662 to 1666 Dutch privateers raided
...t the Bay area. Before the end of hostilities,
...vateers had captured 13 or more ships and
...6 others, including the British guardships, *HMS*
...*eth*, assigned to protect the Chesapeake.
...1684 Virginia's new governor, Francis Howard, is-

off the Virginia Capes, that forced Lord Cornwallis to surrender at Yorktown, effectively ending the Revolutionary War in the colonists' favor.

Pirates

Piracy came to the Chesapeake with the colonists. Shortly before the arrival of Lord Delaware in June of 1610, a party of about 30 desperate colonists from Jamestown stole the *Swallow*, the larger of the colony's two remaining ships, in order to go a-pirating. Although the ship's ultimate fate is unknown, its theft marked the beginning of a 200-year plague of pirates, pickaroons, privateers, and assorted raiders in and around the Bay waters.

In 1634, the *Ark* and *Dove* arrived in the Chesapeake with the settlers who would establish the new colony of Maryland at St. Marys City, under Lord Baltimore's charter. The Maryland and Virginia royal charters conflicted, which set the scene for the strife that was to follow.

William Claiborne and his company had established a trading station in 1631 at Kent Island, three-quarters of the way up the Bay, under the Virginia charter. Claiborne insisted on sole trading rights with all Indian tribes in the Bay. In the spring of 1635, a small Maryland pinnace attempted to trade with the Indians and was captured by Claiborne's men near what is now Garrett Island in the Susquehanna River. This act, dubbed piracy by the Marylanders, sparked a series of ship seizures and battles between the contending parties. The matter was resolved only when the forces of Maryland's Governor Calvert captured Kent Island. The Maryland Assembly charged Claiborne with murder and piracy and returned him to England. When Claiborne lost his petition to the Lords Commissioners of Plantations the Governor of Virginia withdrew his support. Kent Island and several other islands in the northern Bay now formally belonged to Maryland. The charter conflict was resolved.

The next stage of piracy was more due to the English civil war between the Royalists (or Cavaliers) who supported King Charles and the Roundheads of Parliament, who supported Oliver Cromwell.

King Charles had just sent orders to Maryland to seize any Parliament ships and their goods when Cap-

tain Richard Ingle, who had plied the Virginia trade for more than a decade, put his pinnace, *Reformation*, in to St. Marys City in January of 1644. As soon as he arrived he was arrested, and accused of supporting Parliament and uttering treasonous words against the king. He shortly managed an incredible escape, reclaimed his ship, and sailed off.

Angered at his arrest and the subsequent warrant for what he felt were unjust charges of treason, Ingle attacked, captured, and looted several vessels anchored in St. Georges Creek at the mouth of the St. Marys River. Charges of piracy, mutiny, and "trespass" were upheld by the court. With the return to England of Ingles and the *Reformation*, the matter was, quite erroneously, considered closed.

Captain Ingle was now fully committed to the cause of Parliament. In October 1644, he managed to obtain for the *Reformation* one of the first letters of marque issued by the Lord High Admiral of England against ships, and their goods, hostile to Parliament. Armed with that, he again set sail for Maryland, ostensibly to deliver a cargo, but evidently bent on revenge. Near Virginia, he prepared his crew to "go up into Maryland plunder the Papists."

In February of 1645, Ingle sailed up the St. Marys River, took the small fort at St. Inigoes Creek, unopposed, and captured the Dutch ship *Speagle*. Installing his mate as commander of the *Speagle*, Ingle attacked the capitol, St. Marys City, taking it virtually without a fight; Ingles was in control.

A reign of terror ensued throughout southern Maryland. Plantation after plantation was looted and burned, justified by supposed loyalties to the King, or Cavaliers, or Roundheads. Although Ingle himself remained in Maryland waters only long enough to return to England, his followers plundered the colony for some time. Colonists were forced to abandon homes and seek refuge elsewhere. The population dropped from 400 to 100 settlers.

Maryland was without effective government until 1646, when Governor Calvert returned to reclaim the colony and restore order after more than a year of years of anarchy.

From 1645 to 1646, and sporadically throughout the colonial period, pirates plagued these provincial waters. Plantations were burned
Eliza

sued a proclamation prohibiting all trade with pirates and privateers by the local inhabitants. Not only did settlers continue the forbidden commerce, but many of them tried their own hand at pirating. In fact, local pirates were instrumental in establishing the College of William and Mary.

In the summer of 1688, Captain Simon Rowe, commander of the Chesapeake guardship, *Dumbarton*, stopped a small shallop manned by four men for a routine check. An investigation produced three large sea chests full of gold, silver, and other valuables. The four buccaneers—Peter Cloise (a black slave), Edward Davis, Lionel Delawater, and John Hinson—were instantly arrested on suspicion of piracy. Thus began several years of charges, countercharges, petitions, and trials, which culminated in an interesting deal, the result of a petition that the accused submitted to King Charles. The king's final decree on the matter in 1693 resulted in the release of the prisoners with most of their treasure, provided that a fourth part of it be used to establish a "Free School or College in Virginia." The College of William and Mary's first endowment was obtained from pirate booty!

Peace in Sight

In early 1700, the destruction of the pirate vessel *La Paix* (Peace) by Captain William Passenger, commander of the warship *HMS Shorham*, marked the start of a 15-year period of relatively untroubled waters, save for the occasional harassment by privateers during the War of Spanish Succession. At the close of that war, privateers of all nationalities were suddenly unemployed and so turned to piracy. Fortunately for the Chesapeake, the treasure ships of the West Indies and South America were far more lucrative targets for pirates than the Bay area's tobacco trade.

This was the time that spawned the most fearsome pirate in history, Captain Edmund Teach, better known as Blackbeard. While it is doubtful that Blackbeard actually conducted operations in the Bay itself, his legend is of such stature that he is often included in apocryphal stories of the Chesapeake Bay.

The period of relative peace lasted until the spring of 1741. The War of Austrian Succession had broken out in Europe in 1740 and its effects were soon felt in the

New World. Spanish and then French privateers began to harass the Virginia coast: This lasted until 1748, when hostilities ceased in Europe. The tidewater then remained relatively free from attack.

Patriots and
Picaroons

The American Revolution swept the Maryland and Virginia tidewater into a conflict more destructive than the early charter incidents. For almost eight years, settlers dwelling along the shores of the Bay, including its myriad rivers, creeks, islands, and marshes, were subjected to repeated raids by land and sea. Neither patriot nor Tory was spared in the high passions of that conflict, for here, in the Chesapeake tidewater area, the war was fought on two planes: one was a fairly conventional conflict between opposing armies and navies; the other was an especially nasty guerilla war, initially conducted by Tories against the patriot populace and the merchant marine in the Bay, but which frequently degenerated into acts of revenge and even piracy against both sides.

The Baltimore Clippers

Baltimore Clippers were built for speed in an era when speed on the high seas was synonymous with survival. They won the respect of the maritime nations of the world and helped establish the reputation of the port of Baltimore. In fact, in the 1790s Baltimore was the undisputed leader of the shipbuilding industry on the Chesapeake Bay.

During and immediately following the American War of Independence, the United States had little navy to speak of. As a result, the small American merchant marine had no protection on the high seas and quickly became the prey of pirates and foreign naval ships. Speed became the best survival insurance that an American vessel could have. Chesapeake Bay shipbuilders were the first to respond to this need and created one of the fastest vessels afloat in its day.

During the War of 1812, President James Madison attempted to overcome the lack of a navy by issuing Letters of Marque and Reprisal which allowed private ship owners to arm their vessels and seize the commercial cargo of vessels of hostile nations. Such a vessel was known as a privateer. Baltimore Clippers were ideally suited to operate as privateers, and American privateers captured or sank some 1700 British merchant vessels during the war. This activity was a major factor in the British decision to attack the City of Baltimore in 1814. The ensuing American victory at Ft. McHenry was described by Francis Scott Key in the words that became our National Anthem, "The Star-Spangled Banner."

In the years following the War of 1812, the very characteristic that made the Baltimore Clipper fast, the slim hull design, contributed to the ultimate demise of these sleek vessels. The limited space for cargo made the boats unprofitable for their owners. As a result, the Baltimore Clipper gave way to enlarged variations of the original clipper, which eventually led to the development of the large cargo-carrying Yankee Clippers of the 1850s.

One of the notorious Tory sea raiders, or picaroons, was Joseph Wheland, whose raids on the Eastern Shore infused local Tory strongholds with the urge to rise up and create some disorder on their own.

Wheland and crew were captured off Holland Straits in late July of 1776 by a detachment of 30 patriots. He remained in jail for five years before finally managing to secure his release. Once free, he returned to raiding with such a vengeance that his excesses were deplored by Tories and patriots alike. Following Wheland's capture, few picaroons were active on the Chesapeake until the spring of 1779—thanks to the efforts of the Virginia and Maryland State Navies.

In the summer of 1780, however, picaroons and pi-rates seemed to be everywhere in the Lower Bay. More than 25 vessels were active in outright piracy, raiding and robbing at will. By August, shipping had come to a standstill. The raiders soon took to attacking the homes and businesses of citizens along the shores of St. Marys County. By September, local picaroons and New York raiders were in control of the middle Bay region and began to focus their attacks on the Eastern Shore. Matters got worse in October of 1780 when a British fleet under General Alexander Leslie arrived to attack Richmond and Petersburg, an event which galvanized even lukewarm picaroons into action.

One year later these greedy opportunists were plundering fellow Tories as well as patriots, having degenerated into base piracy. Leaders of both sides of the Revolutionary conflict were disgusted with the picaroon/pirates and other privateers in the Bay. Lord Cornwallis, commander of the British troops at Portsmouth, Virginia, complained to his commander-in-chief that this activity was hardening the resolve of the patriots and even driving some Tories from the Crown. The French Navy soon took control of the Bay, resulting not only in the surrender of Cornwallis at Yorktown on October 19, 1781 but also in a much-longed-for respite from lawless plunder.

This respite was brief; diehard picaroons from the Eastern Shore, assorted privateers from New York, and Royal Navy deserters continued attacks on ships and shore for another 18 months. The combined efforts of the French Navy and armed barges from both Virginia and Maryland proved insufficient to capture or destroy enough of the raiders to quiet the Bay. Peace returned only when news of the formal cessation of hostilities between England and the American colonies reached Annapolis on March 29, 1783; the war was over.

The days of the Whelands, Teaches, and Ingles were gone. The fact that these were the last of the Chesapeake Bay pirates was particularly fortunate because the Bay was about to become a major site in the conflict that became known as The War of 1812. You will find references to this event scattered throughout this book in the various areas where some of the action took place.

Captain John Smith's map of the Chesapeake Bay, the earliest accurate map on record. LIBRARY OF CONGRESS

ans, Smith befriended Pocahontas, the chief's daughter. She not only intervened to save his life, but, after his release, brought substantial gifts of food to the colonists every four or five days. Pocahontas alerted Smith to a planned attack by the Powhatans, foiling her father's plans.

Smith was severely injured in an accident and returned to England in October of 1609. With his departure, the colonists lost any goodwill on the part of the Indians. During that winter many starved to death and the 32 weakened survivors prepared to abandon the settlement in the spring. The timely arrival of Baron De La Warr, known as Lord Delaware, in June of 1610 brought the supplies and new colonists necessary to save Jamestown. The colony eventually prospered, establishing the English in the Chesapeake Bay.

The Bay and its multitude of rivers turned into a watery road to riches, thanks to the cultivation of tobacco and a ready market for it in Europe. (It does seem odd that a plant now considered harmful and noxious played a major role in the founding and building of this country.) Plantation fields were cleared in the tidewater region and each plantation had a wharf where ships could come in to load tobacco. Later lumber, flour, and grain replaced tobacco as the prime cargo for ships visiting the Upper Bay. Small tidal streams provided waterways for small boats taking crops to market and safe harbors abounded for watermen who caught fish and shellfish to sell in local markets.

The Bay and its waterways also provided easy access for invaders and raiders for more than two centuries after the founding of Jamestown—notably the British during the American Revolution and the War of 1812 as well as a wide assortment of pirates and privateers. In fact, it was the failure of the British to control the lower Chesapeake, due to the intervention of the French fleet off the Virginia Capes, that forced Lord Cornwallis to surrender at Yorktown, effectively ending the Revolutionary War in the colonists' favor.

Pirates

Piracy came to the Chesapeake with the colonists. Shortly before the arrival of Lord Delaware in June of 1610, a party of about 30 desperate colonists from Jamestown stole the *Swallow*, the larger of the colony's two remaining ships, in order to go a-pirating. Although the ship's ultimate fate is unknown, its theft marked the beginning of a 200-year plague of pirates, pickaroons, privateers, and assorted raiders in and around the Bay waters.

In 1634, the *Ark* and *Dove* arrived in the Chesapeake with the settlers who would establish the new colony of Maryland at St. Marys City, under Lord Baltimore's charter. The Maryland and Virginia royal charters conflicted, which set the scene for the strife that was to follow.

William Claiborne and his company had established a trading station in 1631 at Kent Island, three-quarters of the way up the Bay, under the Virginia charter. Claiborne insisted on sole trading rights with all Indian tribes in the Bay. In the spring of 1635, a small Maryland pinnace attempted to trade with the Indians and was captured by Claiborne's men near what is now Garrett Island in the Susquehanna River. This act, dubbed piracy by the Marylanders, sparked a series of ship seizures and battles between the contending parties. The matter was resolved only when the forces of Maryland's Governor Calvert captured Kent Island. The Maryland Assembly charged Claiborne with murder and piracy and returned him to England. When Claiborne lost his petition to the Lords Commissioners of Plantations the Governor of Virginia withdrew his support. Kent Island and several other islands in the northern Bay now formally belonged to Maryland. The charter conflict was resolved.

The next stage of piracy was more due to the English civil war between the Royalists (or Cavaliers) who supported King Charles and the Roundheads of Parliament, who supported Oliver Cromwell.

King Charles had just sent orders to Maryland to seize any Parliament ships and their goods when Captain Richard Ingle, who had plied the Virginia trade for more than a decade, put his pinnace, *Reformation*, in to St. Marys City in January of 1644. As soon as he arrived he was arrested, and accused of supporting Parliament and uttering treasonous words against the king. He shortly managed an incredible escape, reclaimed his ship, and sailed off.

Angered at his arrest and the subsequent warrant for what he felt were unjust charges of treason, Ingle attacked, captured, and looted several vessels anchored in St. Georges Creek at the mouth of the St. Marys River. Charges of piracy, mutiny, and "trespass" were upheld by the court. With the return to England of Ingles and the *Reformation*, the matter was, quite erroneously, considered closed.

Captain Ingle was now fully committed to the cause of Parliament. In October 1644, he managed to obtain for the *Reformation* one of the first letters of marque issued by the Lord High Admiral of England to seize all ships, and their goods, hostile to Parliament. Armed with that, he again set sail for Maryland, ostensibly to deliver a cargo, but evidently bent on revenge. While in Virginia, he prepared his crew to "go up to Maryland to plunder the Papists."

In February of 1645, Ingle sailed into the St. Marys River, took the small fort at St. Inigoes Creek virtually unopposed, and captured the Dutch ship, *Speagle*. Installing his mate as commander of the *Speagle*, he then attacked the capitol, St. Marys City. The city fell virtually without a fight; Ingles was in command of Maryland.

A reign of terror ensued for the Catholics of Maryland. Plantation after plantation was plundered, justified by supposed loyalty to Parliament and the Roundheads. Although Captain Ingle remained in Maryland waters only 14 weeks before returning to England, his followers continued the depredations for some time. Colonists were forced to flee their homes and seek refuge elsewhere. The population plummeted from 400 to 100 settlers.

Maryland was left without a government until late 1646, when Governor Calvert raised a force to retake the colony and did so totally unresisted. Nearly two years of anarchy finally came to an end.

From 1662 to 1666 Dutch privateers raided throughout the Bay area. Before the end of hostilities, these privateers had captured 13 or more ships and burned 6 others, including the British guardships, *HMS Elizabeth*, assigned to protect the Chesapeake.

In 1684 Virginia's new governor, Francis Howard, issued a proclamation prohibiting all trade with pirates and privateers by the local inhabitants. Not only did settlers continue the forbidden commerce, but many of them tried their own hand at pirating. In fact, local pirates were instrumental in establishing the College of William and Mary.

In the summer of 1688, Captain Simon Rowe, commander of the Chesapeake guardship, *Dumbarton*, stopped a small shallop manned by four men for a routine check. An investigation produced three large sea chests full of gold, silver, and other valuables. The four buccaneers—Peter Cloise (a black slave), Edward Davis, Lionel Delawater, and John Hinson—were instantly arrested on suspicion of piracy. Thus began several years of charges, countercharges, petitions, and trials, which culminated in an interesting deal, the result of a petition that the accused submitted to King Charles. The king's final decree on the matter in 1693 resulted in the release of the prisoners with most of their treasure, provided that a fourth part of it be used to establish a "Free School or College in Virginia." The College of William and Mary's first endowment was obtained from pirate booty!

Peace in Sight

In early 1700, the destruction of the pirate vessel *La Paix* (Peace) by Captain William Passenger, commander of the warship *HMS Shorham*, marked the start of a 15-year period of relatively untroubled waters, save for the occasional harassment by privateers during the War of Spanish Succession. At the close of that war, privateers of all nationalities were suddenly unemployed and so turned to piracy. Fortunately for the Chesapeake, the treasure ships of the West Indies and South America were far more lucrative targets for pirates than the Bay area's tobacco trade.

This was the time that spawned the most fearsome pirate in history, Captain Edmund Teach, better known as Blackbeard. While it is doubtful that Blackbeard actually conducted operations in the Bay itself, his legend is of such stature that he is often included in apocryphal stories of the Chesapeake Bay.

The period of relative peace lasted until the spring of 1741. The War of Austrian Succession had broken out in Europe in 1740 and its effects were soon felt in the

New World. Spanish and then French privateers began to harass the Virginia coast: This lasted until 1748, when hostilities ceased in Europe. The tidewater then remained relatively free from attack.

Patriots and Picaroons

The American Revolution swept the Maryland and Virginia tidewater into a conflict more destructive than the early charter incidents. For almost eight years, settlers dwelling along the shores of the Bay, including its myriad rivers, creeks, islands, and marshes, were subjected to repeated raids by land and sea. Neither patriot nor Tory was spared in the high passions of that conflict, for here, in the Chesapeake tidewater area, the war was fought on two planes: one was a fairly conventional conflict between opposing armies and navies; the other was an especially nasty guerilla war, initially conducted by Tories against the patriot populace and the merchant marine in the Bay, but which frequently degenerated into acts of revenge and even piracy against both sides.

The Baltimore Clippers

Baltimore Clippers were built for speed in an era when speed on the high seas was synonymous with survival. They won the respect of the maritime nations of the world and helped establish the reputation of the port of Baltimore. In fact, in the 1790s Baltimore was the undisputed leader of the shipbuilding industry on the Chesapeake Bay.

During and immediately following the American War of Independence, the United States had little navy to speak of. As a result, the small American merchant marine had no protection on the high seas and quickly became the prey of pirates and foreign naval ships. Speed became the best survival insurance that an American vessel could have. Chesapeake Bay shipbuilders were the first to respond to this need and created one of the fastest vessels afloat in its day.

During the War of 1812, President James Madison attempted to overcome the lack of a navy by issuing Letters of Marque and Reprisal which allowed private ship owners to arm their vessels and seize the commercial cargo of vessels of hostile nations. Such a vessel was known as a privateer. Baltimore Clippers were ideally suited to operate as privateers, and American privateers captured or sank some 1700 British merchant vessels during the war. This activity was a major factor in the British decision to attack the City of Baltimore in 1814. The ensuing American victory at Ft. McHenry was described by Francis Scott Key in the words that became our National Anthem, "The Star-Spangled Banner."

In the years following the War of 1812, the very characteristic that made the Baltimore Clipper fast, the slim hull design, contributed to the ultimate demise of these sleek vessels. The limited space for cargo made the boats unprofitable for their owners. As a result, the Baltimore Clipper gave way to enlarged variations of the original clipper, which eventually led to the development of the large cargo-carrying Yankee Clippers of the 1850s.

One of the notorious Tory sea raiders, or picaroons, was Joseph Wheland, whose raids on the Eastern Shore infused local Tory strongholds with the urge to rise up and create some disorder on their own.

Wheland and crew were captured off Holland Straits in late July of 1776 by a detachment of 30 patriots. He remained in jail for five years before finally managing to secure his release. Once free, he returned to raiding with such a vengeance that his excesses were deplored by Tories and patriots alike. Following Wheland's capture, few picaroons were active on the Chesapeake until the spring of 1779—thanks to the efforts of the Virginia and Maryland State Navies.

In the summer of 1780, however, picaroons and pirates seemed to be everywhere in the Lower Bay. More than 25 vessels were active in outright piracy, raiding and robbing at will. By August, shipping had come to a standstill. The raiders soon took to attacking the homes and businesses of citizens along the shores of St. Marys County. By September, local picaroons and New York raiders were in control of the middle Bay region and began to focus their attacks on the Eastern Shore. Matters got worse in October of 1780 when a British fleet under General Alexander Leslie arrived to attack Richmond and Petersburg, an event which galvanized even lukewarm picaroons into action.

One year later these greedy opportunists were plundering fellow Tories as well as patriots, having degenerated into base piracy. Leaders of both sides of the Revolutionary conflict were disgusted with the picaroon/pirates and other privateers in the Bay. Lord Cornwallis, commander of the British troops at Portsmouth, Virginia, complained to his commander-in-chief that this activity was hardening the resolve of the patriots and even driving some Tories from the Crown. The French Navy soon took control of the Bay, resulting not only in the surrender of Cornwallis at Yorktown on October 19, 1781 but also in a much-longed-for respite from lawless plunder.

This respite was brief; diehard picaroons from the Eastern Shore, assorted privateers from New York, and Royal Navy deserters continued attacks on ships and shore for another 18 months. The combined efforts of the French Navy and armed barges from both Virginia and Maryland proved insufficient to capture or destroy enough of the raiders to quiet the Bay. Peace returned only when news of the formal cessation of hostilities between England and the American colonies reached Annapolis on March 29, 1783; the war was over.

The days of the Whelands, Teaches, and Ingles were gone. The fact that these were the last of the Chesapeake Bay pirates was particularly fortunate because the Bay was about to become a major site in the conflict that became known as The War of 1812. You will find references to this event scattered throughout this book in the various areas where some of the action took place.

Shellfishing

Oystering

Oysters have been harvested on the Chesapeake Bay for several thousand years. Archeologists have discovered evidence of Indian shell mounds dating to 5,500 B.C. in various sites around the Bay. Even so, no one can look at an oyster-on-the-half-shell without wondering about the courage, or foolhardiness, of the person who, millenia ago, ate the first one! The first colonists were aware of the oyster and some left written notes which contained references to the huge quantity and individual size of these shellfish. One writer, comparing the Chesapeake oyster to those he knew in England, claimed the New World oysters were often four times the size of those he had known.

In spite of that, the colonists did not consider oysters prime sources of food and would only eat them in any quantity when little else was available. Commercial harvesting of oysters did not exist until the early 1800s, and even that was a result of New Englanders traveling to the Chesapeake for oysters because their own oyster beds were exhausted.

Maryland has had more people making their living from the oyster than any other state. The industry not only boomed, it ran out of control. Reaching a peak in 1885 with a harvest of about 15 million bushels, the competition was so fierce that it started "the oyster wars." This was not a friendly commercial rivalry; as one wag said, "If all the bullets fired in the oyster wars were

The Chesapeake Bay Oyster

The famous Chesapeake Bay Oyster *(Crassostrea virginica)* is not really a species limited to the Chesapeake Bay. This gastronomical delight is widely distributed around the eastern coast of North America, from the Gulf of St. Lawrence to the Gulf of Mexico. Although there is much rivalry over the supposed superiority of oysters from a particular region, presumably because of special flavor imparted to the creature from the waters in which it grows, they are all the same animal.

In the more southerly waters of the United States, oysters may be found in clusters right up to the tide line. In the Chesapeake, however, they cannot tolerate the freezing temperatures found in extremely shallow waters. Therefore, they are found in waters 8 to 25 feet deep. These oyster beds, or bars, are located throughout the Chesapeake. Oysters seem to thrive best in the mid-Bay region; there the waters are salty enough to suit the oysters but too brackish for many of their predators.

One predator, which has received quite a bit of publicity lately, is MSX. In 1957, this mysterious disease virtually wiped out the oyster population in the Delaware Bay. The term MSX stands for *multinucleate sphere unknown;* research revealed MSX to be a one-celled protozoan. Even after MSX made its way down the coast and entered the bay in 1959, it was originally confined to Virginia waters since it can survive only in relatively salty water. Periodically, lack of adequate rainfall has increased the salinity of the middle Bay, permitting MSX to reach as far up the Bay as the Choptank River. Harmless to humans, MSX is debilitating to the oyster and renders it unappetizing.

In spite of the severe damage caused by MSX, oysters are unlikely to be wiped out. Those resistant to the disease will survive and, hopefully, their offspring will also be resistant to it, allowing the oyster population in affected areas to eventually recover. Research is under way to develop artificial propagation procedures to "seed" strains of resistant oysters on affected beds to speed the spread of the resistance through the natural oyster population in the area.

While oysters can survive on a wide variety of hard bottoms, the soft silty bottom found in much of the Bay would smother them. For that reason, the beds tend to be clustered in select areas where there are suitable hard anchorages for the oysters. These beds are charted and well known (by name, even) to the commercial oystermen and the Natural Resources Police who regulate them. The state creates many bars by dumping old oyster shells in clusters to form new bars. These old shells are obtained from two sources: "fresh" shell is obtained from Bay area oyster-shucking houses; "fossil" shell by dredging old, non-producing beds. A frequent sight in the Bay is a barge or barges loaded with heaps of shells being moved to a new location

where the shells are blasted over the side by powerful streams of water from turret-mounted hoses.

The oyster is sequentially hermaphroditic. That is, when it first becomes sexually mature at about one year, it is usually a male. After its first spawning season, it becomes a female and remains so for the rest of its life, which can be as much as 10 to 12 years barring "harvesting" or predation.

In the Chesapeake, the oysters usually begin to spawn in early June, or when the water temperature first reaches about 68 degrees F, reaching a peak at a temperature of around 72 degrees F, and virtually halting when the water temperature reaches the mid 80s. When ready to spawn, the sex organs of both male and female are so swollen that they completely overshadow all of its other organs. The female spawns by opening and closing its valves (the two halves of its shell) in a bellows-like motion every few minutes to dispel a cloud of eggs. The male is not quite so obvious. He merely opens his valves a small amount and allows the sperm to trickle out and be swept away by the water.

In a single spawning season, a female oyster produces on the order of 500 million eggs. The male releases over 3 trillion sperm into the water over the same period. Even with these astronomical numbers, fertilization is only by chance encounter between the free-floating eggs and sperm. Of the eggs that are fertilized, only a dozen or so will successfully grow to maturity and reproduce. The rest are lost to predators or fail to find a suitable surface on which to grow and mature.

About four hours after fertilization of the egg, the egg begins to transform into a larval stage, called a trochophore. Over the next 24 hours, the larvae develop rapidly. By the end of this period, the young oyster becomes a veliger—a stage which resembles a tiny clam. It now has a complete digestive system, two valves, a foot (the only time in its life that it has one), a padlike organ with cilia for swimming (called a velum), and two light-sensitive spots that serve as primitive eyes.

The veligers actively swim about, dispersed throughout the depth of the water, feeding on other planktonic organisms and being fed upon themselves by predators of all types.

The oyster remains in the veliger stage for about 15 days until it reaches a size about as big as one of the periods on this page. The oyster now sinks to the bottom to find the place where it will spend the rest of its life. This act is called spatting, although the young oyster is not properly called a "spat" until it has attached itself to the object (called a "clutch") that will become its home.

The veliger will spat on any hard substance, although it seems to prefer to attach itself to other oysters or their empty shells. If they are unable to find a suitable clutch, they end up enveloped by the mud of the bottom and suffocate.

Shortly after attaching to the clutch, the spat reabsorbs its foot and velum and its eye spots disappear. It will never move again.

During the first day after adhering to its clutch, the spat produces enough shell to afford it some degree of protection. Under favorable conditions of food supply and temperature, the spat will grow to about the size of a dime in approximately three months, normally reaching sexual maturity in a year.

When an oyster is getting ready to spawn, most of the food it takes in is directed toward the production of eggs or sperm. It is fat and firm, with its impressively swollen gonad. After spawning, it becomes a deflated shadow of its former self. This is the main reason for the rule-of-thumb that oysters are not to be eaten in R-less months; these months correspond to spawning season. With our current rapid, refrigerated transportation, there is no health reason for this anymore; oysters just aren't particularly appetizing during these months.

Actually, even though September is a month containing an "R", the oysters still have not yet really recovered from their ordeal and are better when harvesting waits until October. Many claim that the oysters are not really back to their best condition before November.

---

recovered, they would satisfy the market for fishing sinkers for near a century!" (For more on the oyster wars, see the sidebar in Region 4, page 243.)

Most present-day oystering in Virginia is done on privately leased bars regulated by the state. This ap-

proach worked well until the combination of MSX (a one-celled protozoan that attacks and debilitates oysters) and overfishing nearly destroyed the oystering industry in the southern bay; it still hasn't fully recovered.

Oystering in Maryland is a public fishery—it works on the principle that the bottoms of the Bay are public. Anyone can oyster in the Maryland Bay waters at his or her own financial risk and does not have to work for someone who holds a lease on a particular oyster bed. The beds are maintained and policed by the state for use by any licensed waterman. This, in turn, has resulted in a fiercely independent breed of waterman. It is a hard life and certainly not one to make a waterman rich, but he is his own man and runs his own life as he sees fit, subject only to regulation by weather and state laws. Only? The law sets regulations on when he can fish, where he can fish, and the minimum size of anything he catches that he can keep. Still, they are a rugged breed, perhaps one of the last of the traditional American rugged individualists, possibly an endangered species.

With the exception of the relatively recent addition of diving for oysters with underwater breathing gear, there are really only two ways that oysters are harvested on the bay: through the use of an assortment of tongs, or dredging. Currently, tongers and divers are allowed to oyster from September 15 to March 30; dredgers are restricted to the slightly narrower range of November 1 to March 15 each year. In addition, oystering is permitted only Monday through Saturday from sunrise to sunset. Any oyster smaller than three inches must be returned to the bed for continued growth, only the larger ones may be kept and sold. These regulations are rigidly enforced by Maryland's Natural Resources Police.

As a result of gear restrictions imposed by the state, the tongs and dredges used today are little different from those used more than a century ago. The improvements have been mostly in the use of power winches to replace manual effort in all except hand tonging.

Tongs. Other than in details of the design of the metal "basket," hand tongs haven't changed since the first known use of tongs in 1701. In its simplest form, tongs resemble a pair of garden rakes hinged together with a basket of sorts attached to the back of the head of each "rake." The handles will vary from about 12 to as much as 30 feet in length, depending upon the depth of the water to be worked.

Hand tonging remains the most common
form of oystering in the Bay. DE GAST

Taking oysters by tonging demands considerable physical strength and a remarkably good sense of balance. It obviously is confined to relatively shallow water. Oysters are so scarce and this method so inefficient that the tonger rarely reaches the 25-bushel daily limit. Even so, hand tonging remains the Bay's most common form of oystering and there are sound economic reasons as well as other advantages to this seemingly perverse and old-fashioned preference.

Unlike either power tonging or dredging, the initial equipment investment is small; repairs are few and inexpensive when needed. The lightweight, small equipment permits the tonger to use skiffs and other small boats and to work near home in creeks or rivers where dredgers and power tongers are prohibited from operating. This, in turn, reduces fuel expenses.

Oyster tonging is not a business for any but the strong, hardy, and fiercely independent. Tongers must stand by the boat's gunwale, lower the tongs to the bottom, pull the handles apart, then bring the handles back together to rake up oysters into the basket part of the tongs. (How tongers can tell if they have any oysters in the tongs or just debris I don't know, but many claim that they can "feel" oysters on the bottom through the handles of the tongs.) When the tonger thinks that he has a good haul or "jag," he raises the tongs, hand over hand, until he can swing the head aboard over a culling board to dump his catch. The assembly, complete with catch, can weigh as much as 70 pounds! This process is repeated until a good haul is sitting on the culling board; then the singlehanded tonger turns to cull the catch. If there is a helper to cull, the tonger never stops tonging until regulations force him to or the boat is in danger of sinking, whichever comes first.

In 1887, a Patuxent River blacksmith, Charles L. Marsh, devised a set of tongs that operated remotely by lines attached to a winch. He promptly patented the mechanism, which became known as "patent tongs."

With this system, watermen could reach oysters in never-before accessible water depths, and they could work faster and with far less physical effort than with hand tongs. The first patent tongs operated by a hand winch, frequently mounted on a mast with a boom that swung out to drop the patent tongs over the side or back

In deeper Bay waters oystermen use patent and hydraulic tongs. DE GAST

to drop the catch inboard. These winches were power driven as soon as appropriate engines became available.

In 1958, another Calvert County waterman, William Barrett, and a local blacksmith, T. Rayner Wilson, modified the patent tong with a hydraulically driven mechanism. This new design could be run by one person and operated twice as fast as the earlier version.

The hydraulic tongs were so efficient that they supplanted the earlier version, virtually driving those oystermen who did not invest in it out of business, and caused a change in the law. As a result of a court case in 1971, current hydraulic tong use is limited to the Bay proper and a few other areas (such as the mouth of the Patuxent River) where the water is too deep to be worked by shaft tongs.

Dredging. There were many different types of sailing craft designed for use on the Chesapeake Bay, ranging from the early dugout canoes to the skipjack, which was the last of the commercial sailing craft to be developed. There is no single design for the skipjack. They started as fairly small craft in the 1890s, based on the V-bottom crabbing skiff commonly used to run trot lines in shoal waters of the Bay. Called bateaux, and in some locales dead-rise, they all had the wide beam, low freeboard, shallow draft, and V-bottom so suitable to oyster dredging, or "drudging," as the watermen say.

Maryland has the only remaining sail-powered oyster-dredging fleet in North America. This skipjack is at berth in Wenoa, Deal Island.

The jib headed and "Leg O'Mutton" mainsail sloop rig with a clipper bow makes the skipjack readily recognizable from a distance.

The early skipjacks stayed close to home and sold their catch either locally or to "buy" boats from the cities. Within 10 years, the skipjack had become large enough to carry its catch to whatever Bay destination the captain wished.

Maryland has the only remaining sail-powered oyster-dredging fleet in North America. The main reason for its continued existence is based on the law, passed in 1865, restricting oyster dredging to sail-powered boats. Amended in 1967 to permit the use of gasoline-powered "push boats" on Monday and Tuesday of each week, this law is still in effect and enforced. There are now only 15 to 20 working skipjacks left on the Chesapeake, a drastic drop from the hundreds that plied its waters after the turn of the century.

The rough and tumble tactics used by dredger captains back then are long gone and good riddance to them; today's captain is a businessman as well as skipper. He must find oysters, keep a good crew through-out the season, and make enough money to stay in operation—which of these is the hardest to accomplish is debatable. One thing is certain: the success or failure of an oyster-dredging operation rests squarely on the captain and his abilities.

The best chance to see one of these graceful, fascinating boats is to go to Chesapeake Appreciation Day on the first Saturday before November 15, where skipjack races are held off Sandy Point, near the Bay Bridges. This race is possible because the boats are in the area anyway for the start of the Bay's oystering season, traditionally begun near Annapolis. Most cruisers rarely see a skipjack in operation, let alone dredging for oysters. These boats work when most cruising boats have given up for the season. Skipjacks dredge all winter, limited only by storms and ice.

A dredge, which is dragged over an oyster bar, is by far the most efficient oyster-harvesting method ever used on the Bay—too efficient, some say. The dredge has a roughly triangular metal frame with a toothed raking bar along its lower leading edge, which loosens oysters as the device is dragged along the bottom. The

Oyster dredge and winch on the deck of a skipjack
at the Calvert Marine Museum, Solomons.

bar's width cannot exceed 44 inches. Some larger ones can be found, but these were built to be operated only over leased beds by local oyster companies and, therefore were not subject to state regulation. Most boats carry three or four pairs of dredges aboard, each pair with a different design of raking bar to be used for different types of bottoms. To the rear of the dredge frame is the collecting basket or "dredge bag," usually made with a bottom half of iron links or chains joined with S hooks and the remainder of mesh cording. The dredge bag collects the oysters plus assorted other debris broken free by the raking bar.

In operation, the dredge is lowered over the side of the boat and its line let out until the captain judges the lead of the line is right for the depth of the oyster bar. Two dredges usually operate at the same time, one on each side of the boat. The dredges are towed until the captain judges that the dredge bags are full or no more oysters can be gathered at that site. Then, each dredge in turn is brought to the surface and raised aboard with a winder (a winch designed for this purpose) and its contents are dumped on the deck.

The crew lowers the dredges over the side again and dredging continues while they cull the catch to select legal size oysters, those at least 3 inches long. As oysters are culled, the "keepers" are tossed into four piles, two piles forward and two aft. This keeps the boat in trim and leaves a clear working space in the middle. Then the crew dumps everything else back overboard.

This process is repeated all day long. The boat makes pass after pass, each parallel to the previous one, until the bar is exhausted or (with luck) the harvest limit is reached. Then the watermen either offload their catch onto a buy boat or return to port to offload and return home. Those who traveled far to reach their working area may elect to stay overnight in a sheltered creek or river near their dredging grounds. The next day, they repeat the process.

Diving. In recent years, several of the younger watermen have tried using underwater breathing apparatus for oyster harvesting. At first, the traditionalist watermen felt that this approach was "unfair"; that divers would take all of the "good" oysters from the beds. Cooler heads soon prevailed, helped by government regulations to restrict where the divers could operate and the realization that the murky Bay waters forced a diver to rely on "feel" rather than easy visual selection.

Oyster divers cannot work the same beds used by tongers, with a few minor exceptions. They must dive on beds in the main Bay or some of the larger river mouth areas, all of which are clearly and carefully defined on maps produced by the Department of Natural Resources; these areas are policed diligently. The restrictions, combined with the frigid winter waters (which make diving a cold operation even with the protection of a wet suit), make it highly unlikely that divers will dominate the oystering industry.

A few divers use Scuba gear, but most operate with an air pump in the boat which provides air through a long hose attached to a full face mask. This allows the diver to stay down longer and eliminates the need to recharge and carry bulky air tanks on board. In addition divers have a ready guide to the boat above.

A diver's boat is manned by at least two oystermen. One dives and gathers oysters into a basket; the other tends the air pump, controls the boat, and hauls the basket of oysters aboard when signaled by the diver. Presumably, the initial culling is done by the diver on the bottom and finished by his partner tending the topside operation.

The Inland Navigation Rules Act of 1980 requires a vessel engaged in diving operations to display the international code flag Alpha, a blue and white swallow-tailed flag. Rarely does anyone other than a commercial salvage diver display this flag. Instead, most fly the traditional "Diver Down" flag, a rectangular red flag with a white diagonal stripe. If you see either of these flags, you are required to keep well clear.

Like tongers, divers operate from small, relatively open boats, generally the same skiffs used for crabbing, oyster tonging, or clam dredging. There is no real need for any cabin accommodations, other than for some protection from the weather. And divers, like the tongers, go home every evening.

Clamming

There are two kinds of clams of commercial interest found in the Chesapeake Bay: the hard clam and the soft-shelled clam, better known as manninose. Both are harvested and sold commercially, but few people not involved in the business have a clear understanding of how they are taken or with what kind of equipment, even though these clammers, especially those harvesting the soft-shelled clams, present some of the Bay's more unusual sights.

Hard Clams. The hard clam has a thick, heart-shaped shell. This is the clam the American Indians called quahog and used for wampum. Quahogs are categorized by size: the young, small ones are littlenecks and cherrystones; the large ones are called chowders. The first two are eaten raw on the half-shell. Larger quahogs are tougher and are usually cooked as their name suggests. The littleneck name refers to two small siphons that can be seen just below the cut muscle on freshly shucked clams. Their shortness means that hard clams cannot burrow deeply. The hard clams *(Mercenaria mercenaria)* require relatively high salinity (at least 15 parts salt per thousand parts water), which restricts their growth to the lower Bay waters. The heaviest concentrations are found from the lower James River to the lower York River on the western side of Virginia's portion of the Bay and on the lower portion of Virginia's Eastern Shore. Strangely enough, cherrystone clams aren't limited to the vicinity of Cherrystone Inlet on the Eastern Shore, but these succulent clams are traditionally bountiful at that location.

Harvesting of hard clams is done one of two ways. On the lower Eastern Shore, the tidal flats are so extensive that even the small range of tide exposes enough of the flats to permit gathering clams by the traditional method of wading the flats with bucket and clam rake to rake through the mud, picking up the clams exposed by the process. The method is effective, but messy.

The other technique uses tongs, much like oyster tongs but with a finer mesh on the basket. These are used from a boat anchored over a clam bed. Since clams normally live between the tide line and about 20 feet of water, this method is also quite effective.

Manninose (Soft-Shelled) Clams. The soft-shelled clam has a thin, easily broken shell. It is elongated, not as round as the hard clam. The siphons of the soft-shelled clam are long and retractable, but they cannot be completely withdrawn into the shell. These long siphons enable the clam to burrow much deeper than its hard clam cousin. The manninose, which stems from the Indian name, are best prepared steamed, fried, or in chowders. The manninose *(Mya arenaria)* are found throughout the Bay, except near the headwaters where the water is close to being fresh. They live in all types of bottoms (except soft mud) and in shallow waters (0 to 20 feet deep). They burrow into the hard mud, using a long "snout" to take in water from which they filter out their food. Unlike oysters, clams can move, mostly vertically in the mud, which allows them to survive in silting conditions that would smother oysters.

Most of the clams harvested in the Chesapeake Bay area are not eaten locally. The majority are shipped out of the area save those bought by watermen who use them for eel bait. For some reason, an appreciation for the taste of these clams has never taken hold in the region.

Clamming is a relatively young industry in the Chesapeake. Its development is the result of a shortage of New England clams, which occurred in the 1950s, caused by overfishing and disease; and a clam dredge, which was invented in 1950 by Fletcher Hanks of Oxford, Maryland and put into commercial use in 1952. With the high demand from New England and the existence of efficient dredging equipment, clamming in the Chesapeake moved into high gear. Hanks' clam dredge accounts for the entire commercial harvest in Maryland; its use is prohibited in Virginia's waters.

The clamming boom was short-lived, however. Catches started falling off and the state imposed a maximum catch limit of 40 bushels a day for a boat and restricted the maximum working depth of the dredges to 15 feet. Combined with the effects of Hurricane Agnes in June of 1972, which devastated the crop, this nearly killed the industry. It still survives, but the harvest has yet to reach pre-Agnes levels.

For obvious reasons, the Department of Natural Resources designates clamming areas that are distinctly separate from oyster beds and the laws against clam dredging in unauthorized areas are strictly enforced.

In operation, the clam dredger's conveyor is

Try Your Hand at Shellfishing

While I encourage you to try clamming and oystering, get to know the rules covering these activities so your experiences are legal.

CLAMMING. Neither Virginia nor Maryland require a fee or a license if you are clamming for personal consumption. If you are interested in small-scale clamming for market, you will need a gear license, the fees for which vary according to the type of equipment you use. In Virginia, for example, hand tongs or hand rake fees run $15 per year for residents. Nonresidents must pay a $350 annual fee in addition to the gear licensing fee. Clamming for personal consumption must be done with a hand rake in Maryland; using any other equipment puts you in the commercial clamming category. This applies to divers as well as surface clammers.

Clamming in both states is restricted to "Clean Areas," which are marked by signs. If you have any doubts about an area you want to clam, call the Virginia Marine Resources Law Enforcement Division at (804) 247-2200; this office will help you contact the Marine Patrol officer operating nearest you (there are 80 officers patroling the Virginia waters of the Bay). In Maryland contact the Department of Natural Resources at (410)974-3216.

Maryland restricts your clamming take to one bushel a day; Virginia has no size or quantity limits.

OYSTERING. In Maryland the restrictions for clamming apply to oystering for personal consumption/recreation. You are limited to one bushel a day and must stick to the Clean Areas, which are marked by signs. There are no fees.

The Virginia Public Oyster Grounds are open only from October to March, limiting the appeal of this "sport" for cruisers. In addition, the laws governing oystering in Virginia waters are incredibly complex. You will need to read the Virginia Code Book and familiarize yourself with additional regulations and orders. For those who must know, contact Lyle Varnell, Statistic Program Director for Fisheries, Virginia Marine Resources, Law Enforcement Division, P.O. 756, 2401 West Avenue, Newport News, VA 23607; (804) 247-2200.

A hydraulic clam dredge in operation. JOAN B. MACHINCHICK

mounted on the starboard side of the boat and rigged to hinge at the rear so that the front end, with its hydraulic jets, can be lowered to the bottom. Then the conveyor belt and water pump are started. The boat moves slowly forward while the high-pressure jets, just forward of the lower end of the conveyor belt, blast clams loose from the mud. The clams are forced back onto the chain-mesh conveyor belt where they are carried up to the side of the boat. As the clams and other debris pass by him, the waterman picks out the "keepers" (legal clams must be at least two inches long) and allows everything else to continue on to drop off the end of the belt, back into the water behind the boat.

The original systems needed three engines: one to operate the boat, one to drive the belt, and one to drive the high-pressure water pump. Today, most boats are diesel powered and the main boat engine is used to drive everything on the rig except the water pump. A second engine is used solely for the pump.

Most clamming operations take place in the spring, after the oystering season and before the crabs really start to run. Frequently the waterman uses the same boat for tonging oysters in the winter, then mounts the dredge for clamming in the spring, and finally removes the rig to crab throughout the summer and fall until he can resume tonging for oysters again, completing the circle.

Crabbing

The Beginning. Although crabs have been caught and eaten long before recorded history, commercial crabbing as a significant industry really didn't start in the Bay until the late 1870s. The first recorded shipment of soft-shell crabs was from Crisfield to Philadelphia sometime in 1873 (give or take a year). Suddenly, the crabbing industry leapt into being, reaching a peak take in 1920 of 50 million pounds. The current take from the Chesapeake Bay ranges from 25 million to 40 million pounds annually. Since it takes about one and three-quarters "typical sized" crabs to make one pound, the sheer number of crabs caught and sold each year boggles the mind. And this doesn't include the take by amateurs.

Well, then, what about the blue crab and crabbing?

No one should cruise the Bay without knowing something about the creature itself, the industry based on it, and how anyone on or near the Bay can take advantage of this bounty.

The Blue Crab.

The blue crab (*Callinectes sapidus*, which means savory, beautiful swimmer) is widely distributed along the east coast of the United States down into the Gulf of Mexico. While obviously not unique to the Chesapeake Bay, it is extraordinarily abundant there. It is so abundant that, in the Bay region, it is simply referred to as "the crab" and everyone knows exactly what animal is meant.

The crab is an aggressive creature found throughout the Bay—from the salty, ocean-like waters of the mouth of the Bay to the almost-fresh waters of the head of the Bay. It feeds on virtually anything that it can catch, including recently deceased fish, plant materials, oysters, and the soft-shell stage of its own kind. While predominantly a bottom-feeder, the crab is an excellent and very active swimmer. The paddle-like set of its fifth pair of legs, called swimmerets, allow it to move far more swiftly through the water than would be expected from its relatively awkward appearance.

The front pair of its five sets of legs are armed with claws that can really catch your attention if you handle the crab carelessly. (The only safe place to grab a crab is in back of the carapace.) The middle three pairs of legs are used for walking, the traditional sideways scuttle with which the crab on land moves with surprising speed.

The first set of legs are what give the blue crab its name. A good part of the claws really are blue. The rest of the crab is a dull green. It is only when it is cooked (steamed or boiled, depending on your preference) that it turns the bright orange-red, the way most people see them just before devouring them in gustatorial delight.

Until they reach the adult stage, the immature crabs are preyed upon by virtually every other marine creature. The adult blue crab has only one serious predator—man. From the casual, amateur crabber with his baited line and net to the commercial crabber with his trotline or dozens of traps, it seems that every man is out to "get" the blue crab. There are times when the crab traps in the Bay are so thick that you would swear there was no space between them for any crabs to pass. Even with catches that number well into the millions of crabs every year, the crab population seems undiminished. Harvests steadily increased from the 1930s to the

1970s. Then the crab catch went through a 10-year decline. Since 1980, catches are on the rise again. One Smith Island crabber was known to claim that if it weren't for the crabbers catching so many, those crabs would multiply so much they might just take over the world.

While most people today are at least aware of the appearance of the hard crab (even if they have never eaten one), few would recognize the soft crab, a hard crab which has just shed its shell. Before reaching full size, a crab sheds its shell, or moults, 18 to 20 times, increasing its size by one-quarter to one-third each time. Only the last couple of moults produce what we call the soft-shell crab. Until then, the crab is too small to be gastronomically interesting.

The moulting process itself has several stages. In the first stage, when the crab is called a peeler, a hard crab has a fully formed soft shell under the hard shell and is ready to start the moulting process. In the next stage, during which the crab is called a buster, the crab cracks its old shell just before shedding it. These first two stages are what commercial crabbers carefully look for when they catch crabs. Peelers and busters are sorted out and placed in special holding pens, called "peeler pounds," to be harvested as soft crabs when they shed their shells.

As soon as the old shell is shed, the creature is called a soft crab, or soft shell. At this stage, the crab is totally defenseless and virtually immobilized. This period, before the shell starts to harden, lasts about nine hours, unless arrested by man. During the first two hours, the crab rapidly absorbs water to increase its size to the maximum for its next stage. It is during this period that the softshell crab is harvested and packed in ice to prevent further development (and bring the maximum price).

For 9 to 12 hours after shedding, the crab is called a paper shell. During this period, the shell is beginning to harden and is papery to leathery in texture, thus its name. At this stage, it still has commercial soft-shell crab value, although not as much as the true soft crab stage.

For the next 12 hours, before the shell becomes truly hard, the crab is a buckram. During this stage, the shell is stiff and brittle. A crab in this stage is simply left alone by the waterman until it hardens and can be added to a hard crab catch.

In order to sound like a true crab expert, you need to know a few more names for the crab. Young females are referred to as sally crabs. The adult female crab is a sook. The previous set of names also apply at different stages of a sook's life; so she can be a paper shell, for instance. A female carrying eggs is equally referred to as a busted sook, a sponge crab, or (less often) a berry crab. The adult male is called a jimmy or a channeler.

Each summer, the sook is either already in or migrates to the saltier waters of the lower Bay where the fertilized eggs, which she is carrying as a result of her mating the previous summer, will hatch. She extrudes between 1 and 2 million eggs; these form a large mass, or sponge, which attaches to her abdomen. They develop as she migrates to the saltier waters of the lower Bay, turning darker in color as they develop, from the orange or yellow of newly deposited eggs to the dark brown of those almost ready to hatch. This is the reason that the sponges of sooks caught in the mid or upper regions of the Bay are noticeably lighter in color than those caught in the lower, saltier part of the Bay. Most of the sooks will produce a second sponge of eggs in the same summer and a few will even produce a third.

After the last set of eggs hatch, the sook usually dies. A rare few may survive for another season, but they will be barren, neither mating again nor producing any more eggs.

When the eggs hatch, they bear no resemblance to anything we might recognize as a crab. The larvae, or zoea as they are called, are microscopic in size; they join the surface plankton to feed and be fed upon. The zoea moults several times, making noticeable changes in shape each time.

With the last moult as a zoea, the larva metamorphoses drastically into a new form called a megalops. This stage is the first one that is large enough to be seen without significant magnification. For the first time, the creature has claws. It resembles a cross between a crab and a lobster. It can swim, although somewhat erratically, but is still at the mercy of any significant currents, frequently being washed out to sea. The incursion of the so-called "water fleas," which cause bathers at the beaches near the mouth of the Bay some degree of skin irritation and itching, is actually the megalops. Those claws may be tiny, but they can already be felt.

Normally, the megalops stage only lasts for about 12 days but, under unfavorable conditions, it can prolong this stage for as long as three months or until it can find its way back to less salty water to continue on to the next stage.

With its next moult, the surviving megalops again goes through a metamorphosis. Although less than one sixteenth of an inch in size, the "BB"-sized animal is now recognizable as a blue crab. Save for reproductive organs, it is now complete and can perform all of the activities of the crab as we know it. It is now secure from most of its enemies and can concentrate on feeding and growing as it begins its long journey up the Bay or several of the larger rivers towards the brackish water that it prefers.

By late fall, the crabs are as big as two inches across, having moulted every 10 to 15 days or as many as eight times. Now the water is beginning to really get cold and the little crabs move to deep water and bury themselves in the mud to wait out the winter.

By the late summer of their second year, the crabs have reached their adult size of 4 to 6 inches and undergo one more change, that of attaining sexual maturity. Only in the female is there any external sign of this change; the abdominal apron changes from a "V" shape to a nearly circular one. It is during this moult— and only during this moult—that the female can be fertilized by the male.

The process starts with an elaborate courtship ritual. The male approaches a receptive female well before her actual moult starts and begins his courtship dance, a series of postures and movements. If the female is really ready, she will back towards him, waving her claws in and out. The male will grab her and try to put her in the proper cradle-carry position, with her underneath him and surrounded by his walking legs as if in a cage. She soon settles down and allows herself to be carried.

The cradle carry lasts from two days to as long as a week before the female moults. This is the stage of the "doubler" which may frequently be seen as the male paddles along near the surface with the female contentedly riding in her cradle. This process has two great biological advantages: it provides protection for the female during her vulnerable and difficult last moult, and it insures that a suitable male is present during the very brief time that the female is capable of accepting him.

When the female's moult begins, the male stands over her, enclosing her in the cage of his walking legs. On completion of the moult, a process of several hours, the male helps the female, now a soft shell, to turn on her back in a face-to-face position under him. When ready, the female opens her abdomen, now nearly circular in shape, to expose her two genital pores into which the male inserts his two genital organs. She then extends her abdomen over the male's back, a position they maintain for five to twelve hours.

The male continues to cradle carry the female for another two days while her shell hardens and her muscles recover. Upon release, the sook, for that is what she now is, starts her migration back down to the salty waters of the lower Bay to wait out the winter buried in the mud. The sperm is not utilized until the following spring, when the life cycle starts all over again with the fertilized eggs of the sook. The male remains behind where he may moult a few more times and mate again with a female the next summer.

Now that we have gone through its terminology and life cycle, let's move on to the business of catching, cooking, and (of most interest to us) eating the Chesapeake Bay blue crab.

Of course, before they can be cooked and eaten, they first have to be caught. There are four basic ways hard crabs are caught: Amateurs (chickenneckers) generally catch hard crabs with hand lines and dip net or scoop them with a hand net from the bow of a moving boat; the professionals use either crab pots or trotlines. Softshell crabs are different. Amateurs tend to skim the softshell crabs from the shallows, flats, or pilings where they seek shelter during this vulnerable phase. Professionals keep peelers or buckrams in pens until they shed their shell as described above.

Only those hard crabs which measure at least five inches from point to point on their carapace may be legally kept. All others must be returned to the water. In addition, in Maryland waters, all females carrying eggs (the sponge sook), regardless of size, must be released.

In Virginia, there is a substantial winter crabbing industry dredging for hibernating crabs, using dredges not unlike those used for oyster dredging. In fact, about 60 percent of all of the crabs provided on the eastern seaboard of the United States during the winter and early spring months come from winter crab dredging in Virginia. Since most of the crabs in the southern Bay are sooks with eggs, this seems at odds with sensible conservation measures.

The Workboat. There is probably no such thing as a "standard" workboat design for crabbing. However, while details and deckplans may vary, the workboats used by commercial watermen all have several common features, all based on practicality and utility. Everything said here about crabbing boats holds true for oyster tonging and clam dredging craft since the same boat is generally used in each of these seasonal activities to keep the waterman employed throughout the year.

First and, perhaps, foremost, the boats have to be stable and have low freeboard. These boats are taken out in all kinds of weather and the waterman, frequently

A waterman works his trotline in the Wye River. JOAN B. MACHINCHICK

alone, has to lean over the side to snag a float and haul up his trap. Just think about doing that in a boat that rolls with every ripple!

Virtually every workboat we have seen has a set of controls located amidship, on the starboard side. There are a few "lefties," but these are rare. Steering is traditionally by a large wooden lever, although a few have more conventional helmsman stations. Everything is set up to allow a single waterman to perfectly control his boat without ever having to leave his station where he works his pots, even if he has a crew to help out.

Of course, the boat has to be big enough to securely carry enough bushel baskets to hold the crabs the waterman expects (or hopes) to catch and still allow room for him to work and sort the catch as it comes in. This usually means a boat of 30 to 40 feet LOA. Smaller boats are used, but they quickly become self-limiting.

Once these basic requirements are met, details begin to vary. Some boats have a small cabin forward to protect the operator when he is not actively working the set of pots. Some are comparatively open to weather, with only a small windshield for protection from spray. Some have a structure over the deck to provide shade and to carry some of the large collection of traps when initially setting the string or picking it up to move it elsewhere; some have nothing. The design of each and every one evolved over time to meet the needs of these hardy watermen.

Traps and Trotlines. The most prevalent sights on the Chesapeake Bay, at least from late spring until well into the fall, are literally acres of floating, tethered objects—bleach bottles, cork floats, small buoys—of every shape and color. These are the most visible sign of the magnitude of the crabbing industry's mainstay, the crab pot.

Usually rectangular, about 2 feet by 2 feet by 3 feet, and made of heavy-gauge chicken wire and reinforcing rods with a weighted bottom to help keep the trap upright, the crab trap, or pot, is a very simple device, but quite an effective one. One side (sometimes both sides, and sometimes all four) has a circular hole with a truncated cone of the same wire leading into the pot. Bait—usually salt eel because of its durability, but sometimes fishheads—is secured near the middle of the trap. (There isn't a real waterman alive who will admit to using chicken necks.) A float of the crabber's choosing and marked with his designated color code is attached to the top of the trap by a stout line approximately 20

Navigational Hazard or Livelihood at Risk?

Skippers please take note: The floats at each end of the trotline are usually relatively large (a foot or more in diameter) and colored a bright red or orange. This isn't for the waterman's benefit—he knows exactly where his line is. It is to help warn other boats, especially pleasure craft, where the end of his line lays to allow them to steer clear of the trotline and not to interfere with his efforts to work it. It certainly seems reasonable for passing boats to pass far enough behind him to avoid both the boat and the trotline. One jostle of the trotline and all the crabs on it may drop off, at least for that pass. Surely we all can afford to give the working waterman this simple courtesy.

Trotlines and crab pots are navigational hazards, but they also represent the waterman's livelihood. Watermen already have to adjust their work time to accommodate pressures from pleasure boaters; weekend hours get shorter every year as the number of cruisers increases. They also must compete for water space: Marina development reduces workable water bottom because of the poor water quality around marinas. And few marinas rent to watermen because their boats are noisy and messy. The slip shortage forces watermen to travel farther and farther to reach workable shellfish beds. The waterman can ill afford the time and money ($22 apiece) to replace traps that cruisers destroy through carelessness.

feet long. Pots are usually placed in 10 to 20 feet of water, the most common place to find hard crabs during the main season.

A hungry crab attracted by the bait searches around the pot until it finds the opening and enters the trap through the cone. Once inside, it will attempt to get away, not the same way it came in but by swimming up through one of the two holes into the area known as the "church," from which it rarely escapes. Apparently, it is baffled by the shape and placement of the smaller aperture of the cone. There the hapless crab remains, along with as many of its relatives as manage to make the same bad decision, until the crabber returns, hauls up the pot, and retrieves all the legal-size crabs in it. Undersize crabs, less than 5 inches across the back, are thrown back, the trap is rebaited and set back into the water to await its victim(s).

Maryland law states that no crab pots are to be set in tributaries of the Bay. In Virginia, it is unlawful to place crab pots within navigable channels that are marked with aids approved by any agency of the government. This essentially has the same result.

Since there are plenty of crabs in the rivers and creeks off the Bay, a different, albeit less productive, means of commercial crabbing has developed—trotlining. In reality, this is simply an adaption of the old English fishing practice called "longlining" made suitable for catching crabs instead of fish. Bait, predominantly salt eel pieces, is tied every few feet to several hundred feet of heavy cord or line, with weights attached to each end. The line is then carefully flaked into tubs of brine to preserve the bait and ready the trotline for use.

The boats used for trotlining range in size from a rowboat to 30- and 40-footers. No matter the size of the boat, all have one thing in common—a roller mechanism mounted outboard of the starboard gunwale.

To deploy his trotline, the waterman selects a likely area in one of the rivers or creeks off the main Bay. A buoy with enough line to reach the bottom is attached to the weight at each end of the trotline. Then, one buoy and its corresponding weighted end of the trotline are dropped into the water and the waterman proceeds in a straight line, paying out the trotline as he goes, until the other end with its float passes over the side. The trotline is now deployed. Some watermen, usually those with the bigger boats and a helper, will deploy two or more trotlines to increase their catch. The next step is to catch the crabs attracted to the bait.

Catching crabs on a trotline is simple in principle. Putting it into practice effectively takes a fair amount of skill, learned only by experience.

To work the deployed trotline, the crabber lifts one end of the line (remember that buoy?), places it over the roller mounted outboard of his gunwale, and proceeds slowly along the line toward the float at its other end. As the line passes over the roller, it gently lifts the bait—hopefully with a crab stubbornly attached—from the bottom and brings it to the surface, where the crabber waits with a metal mesh dip net.

As soon as the crab can be seen, the waterman deftly scoops it up with his net, swings all "keepers" aboard and into a temporary basket, then turns back to the water to watch for the next crab on the line to appear. The whole process takes bare seconds for the experienced professional. If the crabber is alone, he stops periodically to cull the crabs, keeping the legal ones and sorting them into bushel baskets to be sold later on. All others are returned to the water.

If he feels the crabs aren't "running" well in the area he has chosen, he may pick up and redeploy his line elsewhere, sometimes many times in a day.

Chickenneckers. *Chickenneckers* is the not-exactly-complimentary monniker watermen use to refer to the assortment of amateur crabbers using individually baited lines to catch crabs. Somehow this name does not seem inappropriate since chicken necks are, or at least were, the traditional crab bait used by amateurs. Today, whether the amateur is using chicken necks, salt eel, or filet mignon for crab bait, in the Bay he (or she) is and forevermore a chickennecker.

Reduced to its simplest elements (and ignoring the semiprofessional crabber who sets a string of pots or runs a trotline), amateur crabbers normally use either of two basic methods to catch crabs for their own use: hand line and dip net, or hand trap. How you prepare any crabs you catch is a matter of personal choice. There are as many recipes as there are people who cook them. I have included some regional favorites in "Chesapeake Bay Recipes," page 194.

HANDLINE AND DIP NET: This is the original, basic method used by chickenneckers to catch crabs from time immemorial. With a dip net, some cord, a few weights, and bait, you are fully equipped to catch crabs (some assembly required). Of course, something to hold any crabs that you may catch is a rather good idea, too; allowing angry, aggressive blue crabs to run around your feet can be somewhat disconcerting. A basket, a bucket, or an empty ice chest (some ice isn't a bad idea either if available) will do just fine. Water in the holding container is a bad idea as the crabs will soon deplete the oxygen in the water and suffocate. Crabs can last a day or more out of the water, provided they are protected from the sun. Uncooked, dead crabs spoil with amazing speed and should never be cooked and eaten.

So how do you go about catching crabs with this ex-

Lauren Shellenberger chickennecking with some friends.

otic equipment? First, the required assembly: (1) Cut to lengths of about 20 feet as many pieces of cord as you think you will be able to tend or have room to place with minimum danger of tangling together. (2) Tie a weight to one end of each 20-foot cord. It need not be very heavy, just enough to keep the bait on the bottom. A couple of large metal washers, a nut, or anything comparable will do just fine. It is important that the weight be less than one ounce to allow you to "feel" the crab on the line. (3) Make a small slip knot in the cord right next to the weight, slide a piece of bait into the loop, and pull it tight. Handline assembly is now complete and you are ready to go.

Now, where do you go? That's easy—nearly anywhere in the saline waters of the Bay where the water is between 6 and 20 feet deep and you can find a place to both stand and tie the free (unbaited) end of your handline. Of course, your spot also needs to be close enough to the water to allow you to reach 1 to 2 feet below the surface with your dip net. This tends to rule out bridges, but docks and most boats are ideal. Before you set up, make sure that you have permission to be crabbing there if you don't own the place!

Boats give you more freedom concerning where you crab, but there are a few practical restrictions, most of which are related to unwanted motion of the boat. Once a crab grabs the bait, you need to draw it to the surface gently. Any sudden tugs and the crab will probably drop off. This obviously means that, aside from the discomfort to the crew, you don't want to try crabbing by handline in an area subject to frequent waves or wakes. By the same token, if your boat tends to "sail" at anchor (swinging widely back and forth), you should either find a more protected spot or put down a second anchor to steady you. Aside from the danger of tangling the crabline in your propeller or twisting the lines together, you would be moving the bait around, which would reduce the probability of catching anything.

Once you have a stable platform, tie the free end of each line to something and drop the baited end into the water. Each line should be long enough to reach the bottom with a little slack. Separate the lines enough so they won't interfere with each other. Then wait and watch the lines.

Any lines that start to move off away from the others probably are being dragged by a crab. Gently try lifting each line in turn. If a crab is on the bait, you will feel it tugging through the line. Slowly and gently start pulling up the line, preferably with someone else standing by with the dip net. If you are alone, you will have to bring up the line hand over hand with your third hand holding the net! As the bait nears the surface, lower the net be-

Try Your Hand at Crabbing

In 1993, Virginia enacted legislation requiring recreational crabbers to obtain a license from Marine Commission agents for $5. Maryland has proposed similar legislation that will be addressed by its legislature in early 1994. Virginia now sets a limit of two pots or traps per person; Maryland allows up to five traps per person. Both states limit the quantity of your catch to one bushel per day per person (but no more than two bushels per boat) and both limit the size of each crab to 5 inches spine to spine (or tip to tip; the spine is the tip of the spike). All waters in both states are open to crabbing from April 1 to December 31.

There is one difference in crabbing regulations for the two states. Maryland prohibits the taking of sponge crabs—female crabs with egg masses. Virginia holds that any crab, including a berried female or sponge crab, is fair game as long as it meets the size requirements. While you can keep a sponge crab, it is better for the future of crabbing to toss it back. As an added incentive, the quality of sponge crab meat is not as high as that of other stages.

low the surface a couple of feet away from where the line breaks the surface. When you can see the crab, swing the net underneath it and raise it smoothly and swiftly up under the crab, bait and all. There is a knack to doing this, learned only through practice. Many a crab will escape during the learning process—and thereafter, for that matter.

Once you have your crab, check to see if it is legal (5 inches across the back). If not, throw it back. (You probably will see it again before long.) If it is legal, dump it

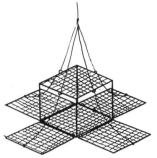

FIGURE 3. A crab hand trap.

top of the trap, are attached in such a way that, when the trap is resting on the bottom and the line to the trap is slack, all four sides hinge out and lay flat, leaving it wide

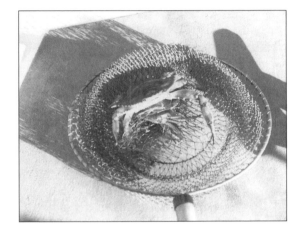

Once the crab is in the dip net, the trick is to get it out.

from your net into your holding container. (Note: A metal mesh net is easier to empty than a twine net. The points, legs, and claws of the crab tend to get stuck in the twine mesh and you may have to risk fingers to extract it.)

To pick up a live crab bare-handed, grab it just behind the carapace. It is easy to do, but watermen wear gloves and just let the crab bite, then they remove it. We take the chicken's way out and use a pair of tongs, which you'll need anyway if you choose to cook the crabs on board.

HAND TRAP: Catching crabs with this method is something like combining a hand line with a dip net. The typical trap consists of a metal mesh cube, usually about a foot in each dimension. (Yes, I know that some are pyramid-shaped, but the cube is most common and easier to make and store.) Most of them fold flat for storage. When assembled, there is a fixed mesh panel on the top and bottom. Four lines, joined a little above the

Dismantling a Crab

Now that you have your crabs and they are ready to eat (never mind whether you caught and cooked them yourself or bought them in that condition), what do you do? This bright-colored critter sitting in front of you is armor plated and bristling with sharp points. How do you get past these defenses and obtain that succulent crab meat?

There are an assortment of variations on a crab-dismantling theme, and I will probably provoke the ire of various "experts" by outlining this one, but this is my method.

First, make sure that you are armed with the traditional crab mallet, a six-inch–long hammer with a wooden head about one inch in diameter by two to three inches long. This is not to subdue the aggressive crab—boiling or steaming them accomplished that. Use the hammer to crack the claws and front legs so you can get at the meat. A collection of newspapers spread out to absorb the juices and debris from the process is also a good idea unless you plan to hose down the area (and yourself) afterward.

Break off the claws at the joint with the carapace. Set them aside to crack open at your leisure. That's the easy part.

Then break off and discard the rest of the legs. Turn the body over, abdomen up, and use a thumb or knife point to pry up and lift off the apron flap. Discard the flap.

With thumb or knife point, lift off the top shell and discard it. This will expose the tube-like gills (dead man's fingers) and the soft yellow "mustard". Tear or scrape off the grey gills and the yellow "mustard", exposing the semi-transparent membrane covering the edible crab meat. Hold the crab on each side and break it apart at the centerline.

The meat under the membrane cover in each half of the crab can be exposed by removing the cover with a knife or by slicing halfway through the center of each half. Either approach exposes the large chunks of meat, which can then be removed fairly easily with fingers or knifepoint.

Crack open the claws with the mallet and you are ready to feast on the succulent crab-meat. Handle it according to your desires or individual preference, but enjoy! (For crabmeat recipes, see the sidebar in Region 3, "Chesapeake Bay Recipes.")

open. Bait is suspended from the top of the trap to lure a crab inside.

The idea is that a crab will be occupied trying to pull the bait loose or attempting to eat it in place; when the crabber periodically pulls up each trap to check it, the sides of the trap will slam shut with the crab inside. It does get a little tricky if a big, fiesty crab is inside when you try to empty the trap. Consider trying to keep all four sides together with one hand, holding up the trap with the other hand, and opening only the side you want the crab to fall from while balancing the whole assembly over your crab container!

Other than that, the main disadvantage of this technique is that the only way to tell if a crab is in the trap is to haul it up and look. It also requires a little more investment in equipment and space to store it. On the other hand, you don't need a dip net and you can use this method from a bridge. For whatever reason, we have yet to catch a single crab with the two-hand traps we carry aboard, although we have had great success with the hand lines and dip net with both methods in use at the same time. You explain that one, I can't!

Fishing

Fish, Fishermen

and the Bay

In the early days of this country, the numbers of fish were such that the early colonists, once they learned how from the Indians, were able to catch remarkable quantities of fish from the bountiful waters of the Bay even with their comparatively primitive methods, usually haul seines. In fact, salted herring, which could be preserved for months, remained a staple for settlers and residents in the tidewater region well into the 20th century. Although the quantities of fish have been greatly reduced in recent years for a variety of reasons, the Bay can still be called nothing less than bountiful.

Today, there is an enormous range of fishing activities on the Bay, probably unsurpassed anywhere else in the world. There are more than two hundred species of fish living in the Chesapeake Bay and its tributaries.

Sport fishing, with fly or hook and line, is done in every conceivable manner, from the hoary bamboo pole and worm bait dangled off a dock or bank, to rowboats in the rivers and creeks, to gold-plated powerboats rigged with an impressive array of trolling gear. There are even "surf-casters" who fish off the Bay beaches, although I am sure that they operate somewhat differently than surf-casters on ocean beaches, if only due to the lack of any real surf in most parts of the Bay. The forms of fishing most obvious to the cruiser are the charter "head boats," drifting with the wind or current, loaded with crowds of fishermen standing shoulder-to-shoulder along the sides of the boat, and the private powerboats moving around in loops dragging trolling lines behind them. The latter are often a source of conflict with sailboats, and some cruising powerboats, over the right of way. (See "Fishing Boats and Right of Way" under "Hazards to Navigation" in this section.)

Chesapeake Sport Fish and Fishing

While there are more than 200 species of fish living in the tidal waters of the Chesapeake Bay, only a relative few of these species are sought after by sport fishermen. These include bluefish, flounder (fluke), white and yellow perch, spot, wahoo, dolphin, albacore, catfish, sea trout (grey trout, weakfish), hickory and American shad, kingfish, shark, black drum, red drum (channel bass), striped bass, mackerel, speckled trout (spotted sea trout), and cobia.

Once striped bass (rockfish) and American shad were popular targets of sport and commercial fishermen alike. Then, during the '70s and '80s the population decline of these fish caused enough concern for them to be placed on the endangered species list in Maryland and all harvesting halted. In 1989, the population had increased to healthier levels, thanks to the reversal of degraded water quality in the Bay and stocking with hatchery production. A restricted rockfish season is now in place in both Virginia and Maryland, with stringent limits on both the maximum and minimum size and number of fish that each individual hook and line fisherman may keep.

Not all species are found throughout the Bay, nor do some of them remain in any particular region of the Bay at all times. Beyond some very rough geographical areas (see the table), I make no guarantees regarding where they may be found. All species are known to be in

TABLE 3. Where They Are Biting

FISH	AREA OF BAY (Upper to Lower)	WHEN
STRIPED BASS	• Choptank River	• May to December
	• Susquehanna River (to dam) and Flats	• End of May to mid-October
	• Lower Patuxent River	• May to October
	• Potomac River (to D.C.; best from Rt. 301 to mouth)	• May to October
	• Magothy River (mouth)	• Spring and fall
	• Severn and South Rivers (mouths)	• Occasional runs in spring and fall
SHAD (both Hickory and American)	• Susquehanna River	• Early April to July (Hickory); mid-May to late June (Am.)
	• Potomac River (especially Port Tobacco River area)	• May to June
	• Pocomoke River (mouth)	• May to June
SEA TROUT	• Lower Patuxent River (guides at Benedict and Solomons)	• May to October
	• Tangier Sound, mouths of Nanticoke, Wicomico, and Manokin Rivers	• Mid-July through fall
BLUEFISH	• Lower Patuxent River	• May to October
	• Pocomoke River	• Occasionally
COBIA	• Potomac River, especially Smith Creek area (guides near Wayne)	• August to late October

STRIPED BASS (ROCKFISH)

FLOUNDER (FLUKE)

COBIA (BONITA)

SEA TROUT (GREY TROUT, WEAKFISH)

BLUEFISH

SPECKLED TROUT (SPOTTED SEA TROUT)

BLACK DRUM

RED DRUM (CHANNEL BASS)

FIGURE 4. Edible Fish of the Chesapeake Bay.
VA MARINE RESOURCES COMMISSION

the following areas of the Upper Bay: the Bay Bridges area, Turkey Point, Spesutie Island, Battery Point, Pooler Island, Worton Point, Tea Kettle Shoals, Eastern Neck Island, Hickory Thicket, and Love Point. In the Middle Bay, fishermen frequent Dolly's Lumps, Brick House Bar, Bloody Point, Dastern Bay, Poplar Island, Holland Point and Tilghman Island with success. Lower Bay known hot spots include Sharps Island, Winter Goose, James Island, Round Ragged Point, Little Choptank River (mouth), Taylors Island and Cove Point. If you really want to find fish, you should go out with a guide or an experienced Bay fisherman, either private or charter. At the least, talk to bait-and-tackle shop owners. There is an annual periodical, *Fishing in Maryland* (Virginia used to have a similar publication but no longer does), found in most Bay area tackle shops and many marine stores. It covers the types of sport fish to be found in different areas of the Bay at different times of the year, but you do need some Bay fishing experience—some of the vaunted "local knowledge" so valuable anywhere—to be able to effectively utilize this information. Most of the newspapers in the Bay area run a column on fishing during the main season.

Bluefish (a fairly recent denizen of the Chesapeake in significant numbers) are migratory, traveling over great distances to a variety of locations, and their schools are sizable. The striped bass (rockfish) also follow a migratory pattern, although they never school in anything like the sheer number common with bluefish.

Perch are usually found in many of the tributaries off the main Bay, especially in the north. Most fishermen bottom-fish for them right at the mouths of these tributaries and sometimes out in the Bay itself.

Flounder, spot, sea trout (weakfish), and catfish are found in both Maryland and Virginia waters, while red drum (channel bass), black drum, and cobia are generally only found in the waters of the southern Bay, where the salt content of the water is higher.

Both Maryland and Virginia have instituted laws requiring sport fishermen in the tidal waters of the Chesapeake Bay or its tributaries to obtain fishing licenses. Those fishing the tidal Potomac can obtain a Potomac River Fisheries license for the Potomac and its tributaries or either a Maryland or Virginia saltwater license. A boatowner can obtain either a personal license or a boat license that covers him and any guests on board. The two states and the Potomac River

Fisheries Commission have reciprocal agreements and each honors all licenses. Costs are: Maryland individual license, $5; boat license, $25; Virginia and Potomac River Fisheries individual license, $7.50 (Virginia also has a 10-day permit for $5); boat license for boats under 27 feet, $30, for boats 27 feet and over, $60. Each state has different regulations and they are subject to change. For the most recent information, contact: Maryland Department of Natural Resources, Tawes State Office Building, Annapolis, MD 21401, (410)974-3216; and/or Virginia Marine Resources Commission, 2600 Washington Ave., P.O. Box 796, Newport News, VA 23607, (804)247-2248 or 247-2200.

Sport fishing is a subject about which volumes have already been written and is an area beyond my personal ken anyway. Suffice it to say that there are multitudes of charter "head boats" available for those fishermen who are interested in that sort of fishing, and even more private powerboats bottom fishing or trolling in all areas of the Bay.

While the type of fish caught varies with the seasons and the movements of the various species of fish, commercial fishing today is a year-round activity. Commercial fishing in the Bay is roughly divided into two basic categories by the type of equipment used. Fish traps are used to catch eels and, to a lesser degree, catfish. Everything else is caught through the employment of different types of nets. Although there are other types, there are three kinds of nets in predominant commercial use: purse seines, gill nets, and pound nets. These three types of net are the only ones the cruiser is likely to notice, even if he or she doesn't know what they are.

Eeling

Did you ever wonder at the source for all those eels used in the multitudes of crab pots and trotlines? It turns out that eeling is a substantial industry on the Bay, carried out right under our noses, so to speak. In the spring, at least, many of the floats that we see, especially those in the tributaries of the Bay, are not attached to crab pots, as most of us probably assume, but to eel pots, a different device altogether.

In spite of its snake-like appearance, the eel *(Anguilla rostrata)* is a true fish. Close examination will show that they have scales, fins, and gills that we are used to seeing on other species of fish. But they are unlike other species in behavior as well as appearance.

Through various articles and TV programs, most of us are aware of the habits of anadromous species, such as the salmon, which live most of their lives in the ocean waters but return well up freshwater creeks and streams to spawn where they were originally hatched. The eels do something similar, but with a backward twist. Eels spend most of their lives in the brackish waters of the Bay and its tributaries, leaving those waters to head out into the blue Atlantic, especially the Sargasso Sea, to spawn.

When the young hatch, they begin a truly amazing journey from the far reaches of the Atlantic between Bermuda and the West Indies to the waters of the Bay and its tributaries, a trip which can take up to two years. Considering that the tiny young, or elvers, are only two to three inches long by the time they reach the Bay, such a journey is remarkable. They continue on their way back to the rivers, streams, and ponds from which their parents came. The fact that they can find their way back to a place only their parents have seen, not the elvers themselves, is a feat even more remarkable than the return of the salmon to their birthplace!

While eels are considered a delicacy in many other parts of the world, most Americans don't eat them, probably because of their appearance. They are harvested in the Bay solely for export (predominantly to Belgium and the Netherlands, where they are prized as gourmet fare) and for use as bait, mostly for crabs.

Eels destined for exportation are kept alive, first in special boxes in the waterman's boat, then in large tanks with circulating water on shore. They can remain alive for a week or more in the large tank until an eel-exporting company collects them and ships them to their final destination. The rest of the catch is salted down to be sold (or used by the eeler himself) for crab bait.

Most commercial eeling takes place in the spring, as soon as the water temperature rises enough to awaken the eels from their winter hibernation in the river-bottom mud. In the summer and fall, eeling activity falls off rapidly as the watermen switch their efforts to crabbing, but it does continue sporadically into the late fall.

The first commercial eel pots were based on designs used by the Indians and made from white-oak splints woven, just like a basket, around a cylindrical mold. Although the materials have changed over the years, the pot's basic design has varied, with a few exceptions, only slightly. Today, most eel pots are made from a galvanized wire mesh. The pots are typically about two feet long with a diameter of seven to nine inches. Internal funnels, which allow the eel to enter easily but rarely to escape, are made of a variety of modern materials, such as wire, solid metal, and synthetic netting. Some watermen use cube-shaped pots that look like crab pots, except they are usually smaller and made from a much finer mesh.

The eel pots are baited with crushed soft-shell clams, horseshoe crabs, or a mixture of the two; nearly any *fresh* bait can be used. (There is a pattern evident here. Soft-shell clams not used for people food are used for eel bait. The eels caught with the clams, not exported for food, are used for crab bait. The crabs caught with the eels are *all* eaten by people.)

The eeler sets his eel pots on the bottom, preferably with the open end facing downstream, attached to a buoyed line long enough to reach the surface with a little slack. Eels, attracted to the bait, swim into the pot through the funnel or funnels and there they remain, unable to find their way back out.

The pots are hauled just like crab pots. The buoy line is hooked and the pot hauled to the surface. Lifting it on board, the eeler opens the end, dumps the eels into his "live tank," rebaits the pot, resets it, then moves on to the next buoy in line and repeats the process. This continues until his tank is full or darkness falls, whichever comes first. Then he heads home to transfer his catch to the large "live tank" on shore or starts salting those eels intended for bait.

There are other methods of catching eels, such as spearing and using unbaited "fyke" nets, or baited-and-hooked long lines (like the trotlines used for crabbing, but with the whole line buoyed with small floats), but none is used commercially.

The Menhadden Fleet

(Purse Seining)

Purse seining is a method used by the menhaden fleet based near the town of Reedville, Virginia, on Cockrell Creek, off the Great Wicomico River. At present, only one company, Zapata Haynie, still engages in the business of catching and processing fish for products used for animal feed, fertilizer, and making paint and cosmetics. The boney, oily, and unappetizing menhaden are almost exclusively the fish used for this purpose. They are likely the fish Indians taught settlers to plant with their corn seed, since the Indian name, *munnawhatteaug*, means "that which manures."

The menhaden (*Brevoortia tyrannus*), a species of herring, is a sea-going fish which frequently visits tidal estuaries like the Chesapeake Bay. While they spawn at sea, the juveniles and, with fair frequency, the adults will move into brackish or even fresh water of estuaries to find food and to escape from voracious bluefish.

While the adult menhaden will be only about a foot long and weigh only about a pound, by sheer numbers they are the most common fish in the sea. Scientists estimate that there is a greater poundage of menhaden swimming the seas than any other species! They cluster together in vast schools which literally cover acres and, unlike most other species, do not scatter when attacked by other fish or stressed. Instead, they cluster closer together and remain near the surface, a fact which makes them especially easy to net.

The menhaden itself is not sought by sport fishermen but, as the schools are followed by predatory fish, such as bluefish, which are of considerable interest to these fishermen, menhaden schools are watched for and quickly recognized by them. This sighting is made easier because the menhaden are so oily that a school actually leaves a slick on the water surface as they pass.

Menhaden, or pogies, are also the fish that often sicken and die in great numbers in the Bay in summer months. The cause of their death is not well understood, but this "fish kill," as it is commonly called, apparently has little or nothing to do with pollution or any other clearly identifiable manmade problem, in spite of media hype to the contrary.

You won't see any purse seining operations in Maryland waters of the Bay, they are prohibited there. However, you can hardly fail to see at least a few of the seiners in Virginia waters. They also operate in the Atlantic Ocean off the Carolina capes and as far north as Maine. Once dependent on sightings of menhaden schools from towers mounted on the fishing seiners, the menhaden fleet now uses light planes as spotters. When a spotter locates a large school of fish, the seiners head for the location as fast as they can. On arrival, they launch smaller boats which carry the end of the purse net out from the boat, around the school of fish, and back to the boat. Then the net is closed at the bottom and drawn in, or pursed, until the fish are compacted together close to the seiner.

The closely packed menhaden are then taken on board with a giant suction pump, which is something like an oversized vacuum cleaner. The size of the catch is measured by how long it takes to pump the fish aboard.

When the operation is complete and the holds of the seiner are full, the ship returns to port to off-load its catch at the processing plant, where the fish are cooked and the oil pressed out.

The oil is used in making paints and soaps. Another little item produced from this fish oil is nitroglycerine, as well as other more stable explosives. A large portion of the munitions consumed in World Wars I and II were derived from the humble pogie. The fish meal remaining after the oil is removed is dried and used in cattle feed and for fertilizer.

Pound Nets

As you cruise the Bay, some of the more puzzling sights to the uninitiated are the lines of stakes with a cluster of similar sticks at one end, seemingly at peculiar locations. Those who give them a casual glance and attempt to pass between any of these stakes may be in for an unsettling time of it. These stakes represent the supports for a pound net, a method used by generations of watermen and local farmers to catch fish. There is a net strung between these stakes. While it can foul your propeller or other underwater parts of a boat, resulting in a great deal of trouble for you, your course can cause a lot more trouble for the pound netter since these nets are his livelihood.

The nets are supposed to be marked on each end of the string with a white light placed at least six feet above high water and strong enough to be visible for a mile. (Unfortunately, the lights we have encountered have tended to be rather dim or extinguished.) There is usually a bush or basket placed on the same poles to make them readily visible in the daytime. However, should you enter an area peppered with nets, you may find yourself in a maze that can drive you into a state of gibbering. For this reason those regions marked on the chart as fish trap areas are best avoided by a wide margin.

The principle of the pound net is fairly simple; the

A pound net on the Bay. The actual pound is in the background. The stakes in the foreground mark and support the leader net. JOAN B. MACHINCHICK

implementation and use takes a bit of skill and not a little effort. They range in size from relatively small nets placed close inshore to extensive rigs (we have seen some that look to be a hundred yards long) placed a good distance offshore.

Normally, the nets are placed perpendicular to the shoreline, or at least to the flow of the tidal current, with the trap portion, or pound, located on the side of the net towards deeper water. Typically, they are placed in water depths of from 10 to 20 feet. As schools of fish swim along the shore or some other path which "channels" them, they encounter the leader, the portion of the net strung across their path. Their natural instinct leads them to turn toward deeper water, where another set of nets is strung to direct them into the main pound net where they are trapped in a smaller net, or pocket.

The net may be left in position for months at a time, but it gets checked daily at each slack current. This net with its catch is normally too heavy to be hauled aboard the fisherman's boat, so it is raised toward the surface by working around the pound, lifting each side until the fish are gathered together near the surface. Then the fish are scooped out of the water with large dip nets and dumped into a holding receptacle, which varies with the size of the boat. After the fish have been removed, the net is reset and the cycle resumes.

Pound nets are rare in the northern Bay these days and are becoming less common in the southern Bay as diminishing catches and increasing government restrictions combine to make their operation less and less profitable. They are being replaced with the less expensive and more easily maintained gill nets or are being abandoned altogether. (The stakes from an abandoned pound net are supposed to be removed, but frequently are not.)

Gill Nets

A gill net is very much what its name implies, a net with a mesh designed to trap a fish by its gills. The mesh will allow the head and gills to pass through but is too small for the rest of the fish's body. When the fish attempts to back out, its gills (actually its gill covers) become caught in the net and the fish is held securely until the fisherman collects it.

In the past, gill nets were much less prevalent than either pound nets or haul seines. (A haul seine is the simplest and most ancient form of seining. The seine has two wings and a bunt, or bag. One end is held on shore while the net is laid from a boat. The other end is then landed, surrounding a semicircle of water and the two ends are hauled up on the beaches.) Today, haul seines are virtually nonexistent and pound nets are in decline. Gill net use is on the rise because they are less expensive to buy and maintain than other nets, small enough to be worked by one person, and more selective (a function of net gauge), making compliance with government regulations easier.

The Department of Natural Resources regulates both the gillnetting season and the mesh size of the net to protect specific declining species of fish (such as the recent ban on harvesting rockfish). As of November 1, 1984, the mesh size was restricted to a range of 4 to 6 inches. This size prevents larger fish, such as rockfish preparing to spawn, from being "gilled" and permits smaller fish to swim through the net.

Gill nets are usually deployed in a straight line across the anticipated path of schooling fish, normally in water depths of 6 to 10 feet, supported by stakes driven into the bottom. These are the lines of stakes that you see stretching for as much as a hundred yards. They are marked at each end with a light and there is usually a bush attached to the top of the stake at each end of the line to make the setup, especially the ends of it, more visible by day.

The net is fastened to the stakes and may or may not also have intermediate floats attached to the top of the net. Weights secured to the lower edge of the net keep it on the bottom. It is important in both making and setting the net that it hang straight in the water so that the fish cannot easily see it. Most nets today are made of twisted nylon netting (and increasingly of nearly invisible monofilament), which is not only cheaper than cotton or linen netting used in the past but is more durable and harder for the fish to see.

As in the case of pound nets described earlier, *under no circumstances should you attempt to pass between these stakes*. You will not only foul the net, getting assorted parts of your boat entangled in it, but you will also damage the net, for which you will be financially responsible (an average gill net runs about $200 per 300-foot length).

Gill nets are sometimes deployed in two other configurations: as anchor or drift nets. Neither is especially apparent to the casual cruiser, but it is a good idea to be aware of them, especially in the mouths of the larger southern Bay rivers and near the shore and shoals. Occasionally they show up in the northern Bay. Once one sprang "overnight" in the mouth of the Patapsco River where one had never been before. We were sailing at night and nearly came a cropper on it! Fortunately, we saw it at the last moment and veered off in time.

Anchored gill nets are usually set in water deeper than 10 feet and have buoyed anchors at each end securing the net in place on the bottom. As in the case of the staked gill net, weights keep the lower edge of the net on the bottom while floats suspend the upper edge to hold the net vertically in the water. The top edge of the net is an indeterminate distance below the surface, hopefully deep enough so that boats passing over it can clear its top.

Drift gill nets are buoyed at the top so that the top edge of the net is at or near the surface while weights keep the bottom down so that the net is vertical. These nets usually have a large float at one end and the other end attached to a boat. A rare few may be left to drift with the tide, but that seems a really risky operation for the fisherman as well as a hazard to other boats. In any event, should you see a commercial fishing boat, especially in the southern Bay, moving in an apparently inexplicable manner, watch out for a drift net behind it!

REGION 1

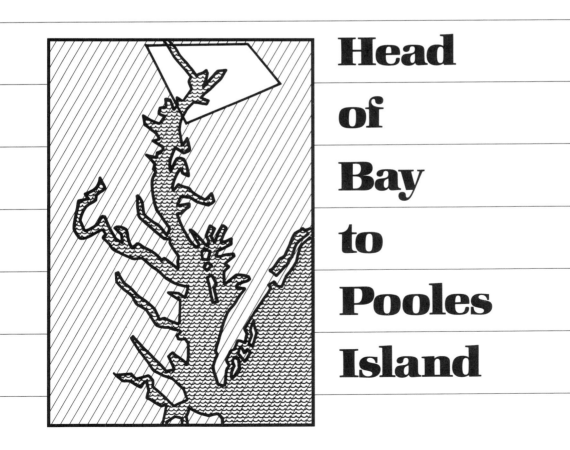

Head
of
Bay
to
Pooles
Island

Head of the Bay to Pooles Island

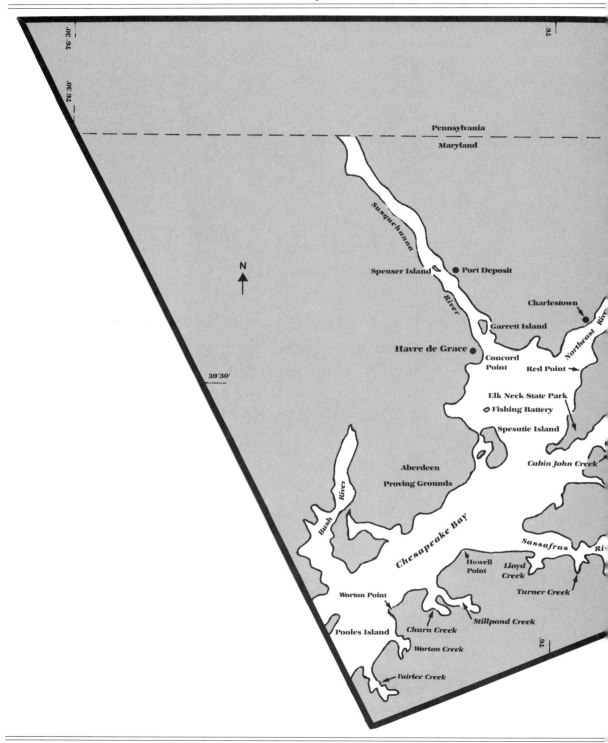

N

Pennsylvania

Maryland

Susquehanna

River

Spenser Island • Port Deposit

Charlestown

Garrett Island

Northeast River

Havre de Grace •

Concord Point

Red Point →

39°30'

Elk Neck State Park

Fishing Battery

Spesutie Island

Cabin John Creek

Aberdeen Proving Grounds

Bush River

Chesapeake Bay

Sassafras River

Howell Point

Lloyd Creek

Turner Creek

Worton Point

Stillpond Creek

Pooles Island

Churn Creek

Worton Creek

Fairlee Creek

76°30'

76°30'

76°

76°

SCALE 1"=**5.7** MILES

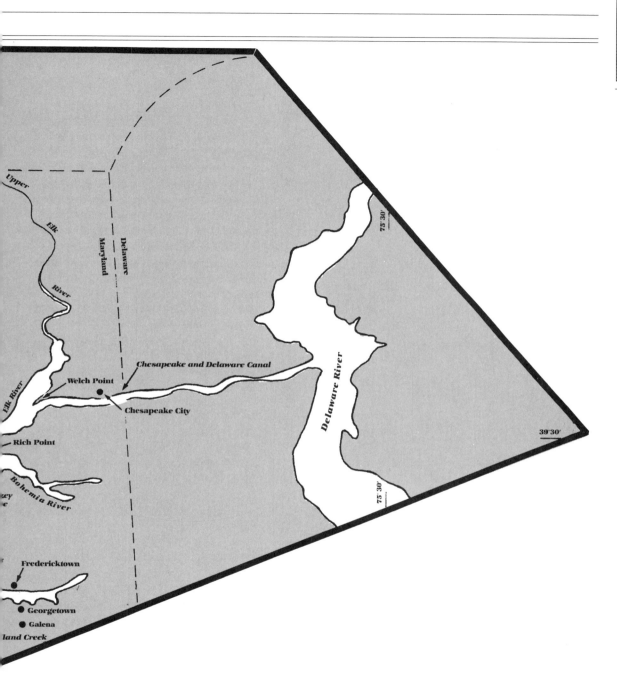

Upper

Elk

River

Maryland

Delaware

75°30'

Elk River

Chesapeake and Delaware Canal

Welch Point

Chesapeake City

Delaware River

39°30'

Rich Point

75°30'

Bohemia River

Fredericktown

Georgetown

Galena

land Creek

The extreme northern part of the Chesapeake Bay is more closely akin to a large freshwater river than a tidal estuary. The water in the Upper Bay is only lightly brackish and, as you proceed up most of the tributaries, it becomes fresh. Crabs and oysters are relatively rare and sea nettles seldom, if ever, penetrate. The area is scenic and thinly settled, at least in comparison to areas near Baltimore farther south.

Like the tines of a pitchfork, the head of the Bay is split into four forks by the Susquehanna, Northeast, Elk, and Sassafras Rivers. The Bohemia River and the Chesapeake & Delaware Canal form additional forks off the Elk River. All offer secure and interesting harbors to the visiting yachtsman, with all the facilities needed for resupply or repairs. Farther to the south, Pooles Island and Worton and Fairlee Creeks form a transition area where the water changes from the nearly fresh water of the head of the Bay to the more brackish waters of the main part of the northern Bay.

Most of the western shore, between the Susquehanna River and Pooles Island, is a Restricted Area be-longing to Aberdeen Proving Grounds. Landing there is strictly prohibited at all times; this includes swimming or any person touching the bottom, shore, or a pier within the Restricted Area. The entire Restricted Area is closed Monday through Friday from 7:00 a.m. to 5:00 p.m., except on national holidays. Additional closed times are announced over broadcast and VHF-FM radios. When actual firing is in progress on the range, patrol boats warn the unwary out of the area. When the area is open, boats may navigate through it, fishing or crabbing is allowed, and water-skiing is permitted up to within 200 meters (approximately 220 yards) of the shore. For specific information, call (410)278-2250, VHF-FM Radio Channel 16, or CB Channel 12. A detailed map is also available from APG Public Affairs, Aberdeen Proving Grounds, MD 21005.

As a direct result of the above, the approximately 15 miles of western shore associated with the proving grounds, except for the U.S. Army Ordnance Museum on the main part of the post, will not be discussed in any detail here.

Eastern
Shore

THE ELK RIVER

Charts: 12273, **12274**

Many consider Turkey Point at the mouth of the Elk River to be the true "top of the Bay." Near here, the Elk, Sassafras, Susquehanna, and Northeast Rivers all join forces with the Bay. The Elk River itself offers little of direct interest to the cruiser except for a few potential day stops along Elk Neck State Park. In colonial times there was a major port at the headwaters, which was burned out by the British forces during the War of 1812. Now it is silted in and pretty much forgotten, save for a mark on the charts showing Old Frenchtown Wharf. The Elk River connects the C&D canal and the Bohemia River with the rest of the Bay. However, there are still quite a few harbors and points of interest worth mentioning here.

CABIN JOHN CREEK

No facilities

Charts: 12273, **12274**

Approaches. Less than 2 miles up the Elk River from Turkey Point, Cabin John Creek lies on the east shore. Although a little shallow (5 feet Mean Low Water), this creek is a popular anchorage with shallow-draft vessels for swimming and a convenient "duck-in" shelter for some occasions. Unfortunately, you cannot proceed very far into the creek and it is exposed to the northwest, the most common direction for a "blow." Not unexpectedly, there are no moorings or marine facilities. A good beach on the south side of the creek lends itself to swimming, wading, and beachcombing.

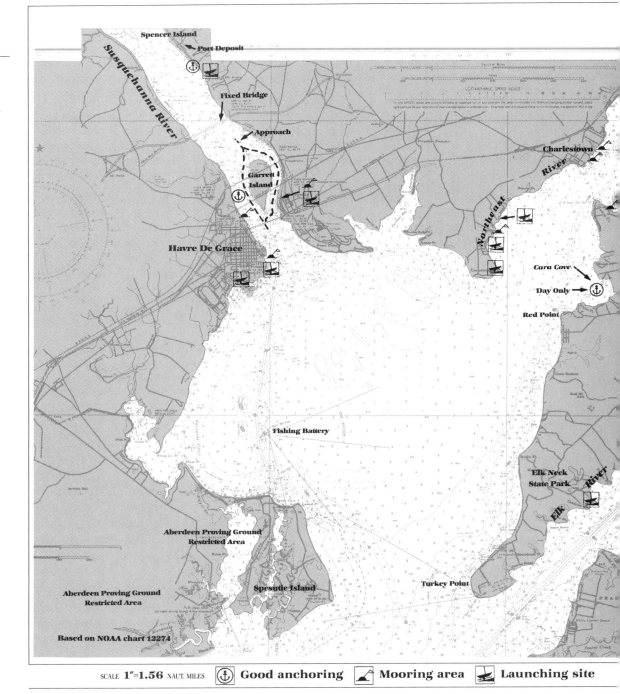

Spencer Island

Port Deposit

Susquehanna River

Fixed Bridge

Approach

Garrett Island

Havre De Grace

Charlestown

River

Northeast

Cara Cove

Day Only

Red Point

Fishing Battery

Elk Neck State Park

Elk River

Aberdeen Proving Ground Restricted Area

Aberdeen Proving Ground Restricted Area

Spesutie Island

Turkey Point

Based on NOAA chart 12274

SCALE 1"=1.56 NAUT. MILES ⚓ **Good anchoring** ⚓ **Mooring area** **Launching site**

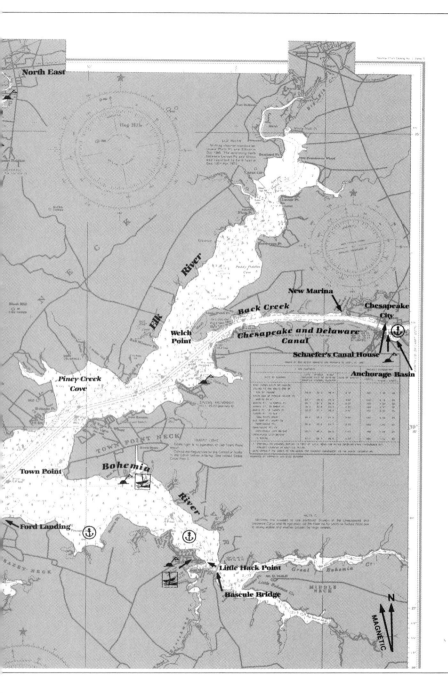

ELK NECK STATE PARK

☆2 |1| •

No facilities

Charts: 12273, 12274

Approaches. To port as you proceed up the Elk River, most of the land is a part of Elk Neck State Park. Consisting of more than 1,700 acres, the topography of this park is quite varied. It ranges from sandy beaches to marshlands to woodlands that are more than 100 feet above sea level. It is a wildlife sanctuary.

Anchorages. While anchoring off any of several beaches is possible, there is little or no protection from either the elements or the wakes from boat and ship traffic. There are boat launching and rental facilities in Rogues Harbor about 1½ miles above Turkey Point and directly across the Elk River from a large housing development with look-alike white houses stacked cheek-to-jowl. The launching facility is designed for small powerboats or daysailers. Other trailerables with a draft well under 3 feet also can make use of the facility. Trailers and cars can be parked at a separate area just up the hill.

You can anchor off this cove, but lack of protection from weather and ship wakes makes it less than a desirable anchorage. For just putting a small boat in for the day or even windsurfing, it is a good spot.

BOHEMIA RIVER

☆3 |2|

Charts: 12273, 12274

Approaches. Slightly more than 3 miles up the Elk River from Turkey Point lies the mouth of the Bohemia River. Nearly a mile wide with 7- to 10-foot depths, no buoyage is necessary, but give Town Point a wide berth if you are approaching from the north. The Bohemia frequently serves as a stopover point for boats planning to transit the C&D Canal, 4 miles to the north.

Anchorages. The first, and probably best, anchorage within the river is Veasey Cove, 1 mile to starboard from the river's entrance. Although exposed to the northwest, it is otherwise well protected. In calm weather or with southerly winds, many local boaters prefer to anchor closer to the river mouth, by the bluffs which extend from Ford Landing to Veasey Cove, in order to make use of the gradually sloping beach and a nice sandy bottom. The only problem may be an occasional wash from shipping traffic in the Elk River. If the weather is threatening, you would be better off moving farther upstream. Although a good number of boats will be found anchored in Veasey Cove on summer weekends, the number dwindles rapidly in the evening as the "locals" up anchor and go home.

Dockages/Provisions. If you are looking for marine facilities or prefer to tie up at a marina overnight, there are plenty of facilities upstream. There are three marinas on the north shore, just inside Rich Point. At least one of these, Two Rivers Yacht Basin, has a dockside sewage pumpout facility. There are five more marinas on the south shore farther upstream, just before the bridge. One of these, Long Point Marina, also has a dockside sewage pumpout facility. Among these marinas, you should be able to find just about any facilities you want or need.

Although there are several homes on the river, most are hidden by trees. This presents cruisers with an unspoiled, wooded shoreline, which greatly adds to this river's appeal.

The bridge over the river is now fixed, in spite of what charts may say, with a vertical clearance of less than 10 feet. This, of course, bars passage to all sailboats and larger powerboats. It is probably not worth the trouble to go above the bridge as the channel above is narrow, winding, sometimes shoaling, and virtually unmarked. This is really runabout country and, in warmer weather, there is usually a collection of these shallow-draft boats zipping around, with or without a skier in tow. Hard-core gunkholers may want to give it a try anyway.

If you wish to explore the river above the bridge, we recommend that you do so by dinghy or rent a rowboat from Austins Boat Yard on Little Hack Point near the bridge. As long as you stay in the channel, you will find 7- to 10-foot depths for 1½ to 2 miles beyond the bridge in both Little and Great Bohemia Creeks. Don't expect to find a good spot to anchor where you won't be in danger of bumping a shoal should the wind change direction.

UPPER ELK

RIVER

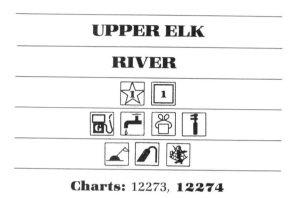

Charts: 12273, **12274**

Anchorages. Above the Bohemia, there is little to recommend on the Elk River. Piney Creek Cove on the west shore, opposite Old Town Point Wharf, is a possible anchorage for those with drafts less than four feet. Personally, I wouldn't recommend it because of its lack of protection from weather and ship wakes.

Dockages. This leaves Harbor North Marina as the only place to stay overnight before entering the C&D Canal. It is about one-half mile up a dredged channel northeast of Courthouse Point. This marina, which claims to hold 10 slips available for transients, monitors VHF-FM Channel 16, and I suggest contacting them in advance by radio or phone at (410)885-5656 if you intend to use their facilities.

Above the entrance to the canal, the Elk River shoals and should be left to boats with less than a 3-foot draft. There are at least four fair-sized marinas in the area between Henderson, Locust, and Plum Points, all of which cater to powerboats. If you have the draft to allow it, a short cruise up this region of the Elk promises to be a scenic trip to take at least once. Repeated trips are best left to the resident boats.

THE CHESAPEAKE

AND DELAWARE CANAL

Charts: 12274, **12277**

History. Originally opened on July 4, 1829, the canal has been modified three times to improve and expand its capability. Originally a 22-foot-wide barge canal, the C&D was purchased by the U.S. Government in 1919 and converted to a sea-level waterway with a width of 46 feet and depth of 12 feet. In 1938, it was again improved, widening it to more than 200 feet with a depth of more than 25 feet. Finally, it was widened to more than 400 feet with a depth in excess of 40 feet to accommodate modern ships. As a sea-level link between the northern Chesapeake Bay and Delaware Bay, the canal is heavily used by commercial shipping and a vital part of the Intracoastal Waterway.

At least on the Maryland portion of charts, the C&D Canal seems to have two names—Chesapeake & Delaware Canal and Back Creek. The reason for this is simple: Back Creek was transformed into the C&D Canal.

Approaches. Although it appears tranquil on the surface, the canal demands constant attention. In addition to commercial traffic—freighters and tugs with barges (and their wakes)—cruisers need to watch the water for frequent debris, washed in from the Delaware. Most of all, pay attention to the current. Official publications list the peak current at between 2 and 2.6 knots. However, currents frequently are well in excess of 2 to 3 knots. According to some of the locals, it can reach close to 6 knots at times! It is extremely important to pick your transit times so that the current is either slack or aiding your progress. In addition, if you are attempting to dock or pass structures, such as the bridge at Chesapeake City, beware of dangerous eddies. It is always safer to err on the side of caution.

The canal is under the supervision of the District Engineer, Army Corps of Engineers, Philadelphia, which enforces certain restrictions for canal transit. This control of the canal extends from Welch Point on

Pay attention to the current in the Chesapeake & Delaware Canal, especially because of dangerous eddies near structures such as the Route 213 bridge at Chesapeake City.

the Maryland side to Reedy Point on the Delaware side. Between these points, water-skiing and transiting under sail are prohibited. All small pleasure craft in the canal must relinquish the right-of-way to deeper draft vessels having limited maneuvering room. (A prudent procedure in any case.) Other than that, all vessels proceeding with the current have the right-of-way over vessels heading in the other direction. Smart cruisers stay out of the center of the canal, just in case. A large ship probably will not be able to stop for or maneuver around an incapacitated small craft in mid-channel.

Located at Old Town Point Wharf on Town Point Neck, just north of the Bohemia River, and at Reedy Point, Delaware, are red and green traffic control lights. Red indicates that the canal is closed to traffic, green that it is open. TV cameras located at these two points monitor traffic through the canal. In the case of emergency, the dispatcher at Chesapeake City also monitors Channel 16 on VHF-FM radio. Although no clearance is required for pleasure craft, it is a good idea to check

in with the dispatcher prior to transit.

The channel is well marked with buoys and lights throughout its length. Be advised that the *colors of the buoyage system reverse at the Chesapeake City bridge*. As you enter from the Elk River on the Maryland side, the red lights and even-numbered markers are on the south side of the canal. Past the bridge, they reverse so that between the bridge and Delaware Bay the red lights and even-numbered markers are on the north side. At night, the canal is lighted with mercury vapor lights, positioned roughly 140 feet back from the edge of the channel and 250 feet apart on both banks.

Anchorages/Dockages/Provisions.

Within the 16-mile length of the canal, there is really only one place where you can stop, Chesapeake City. Anywhere else would be downright risky, not to mention foolhardy! Here you will find an anchorage, possibly a slip or two, fuel, some marine supplies, and restaurants. Chesapeake City is where ships transfer be-

Anchorage at Chesapeake City in the C&D Canal on the canal's south side.

tween Delaware and Chesapeake pilots. A small pilot boat will come alongside the moving ship and the pilots will climb up or down a ladder along the ship's side. If you happen to be having dinner at Schaefer's Canal House at this time, you will hear the maitre d' announce the name of the ship, its tonnage, cargo, and ports of call.

On the north side of the canal you can tie up at Schaefer's Canal House for a meal or to spend the night. Be sure to provide adequate bumpers to protect your vessel and beware of the current as you approach the dock. There is no charge if you tie up for dinner. If you remain overnight, there is a charge (around $.60 per foot) which includes electricity. Fuel, ice, marine supplies, some groceries, and other necessities are also available. Privacy at the dock is minimal as diners tend to stroll up and down the dock inspecting all the boats as if they were on display.

Many pleasure craft that spend the night in the canal prefer to anchor in the anchorage basin on the south side of the canal (South Chesapeake City) where there is between 4 and 10 feet of water. There is (or at least was) a mud shoal in the center of the entrance. Keep well to starboard on entering to avoid it. With a deep-draft vessel, enter at high or at least half tide, if possible. There is a marina with haul-out facilities as well as a restaurant in the basin. The preferred anchorage is in the eastern half of the basin. On the west side of

the basin, small vessels can tie up for 24 hours free of charge at the Government Wharf. Permission to tie up here for longer must be obtained in advance from the dispatcher in Chesapeake City.

Things to Do. South Chesapeake City is the location of the C&D Canal Museum, housed in the gray stone pumphouse built before 1829 for one of the old canal locks. The museum is open Monday through Saturday and major nonreligious holidays between 8:00 a.m. and 4:15 p.m.; Sundays and Easter through Thanksgiving, between 10:00 a.m. and 5:30 p.m. Most of the exhibits are in the old boiler room where the steam power to operate the old pumping engine was once generated. The museum's slide show covers the 150-year history of the canal; there are dioramas, ship models, and assorted exhibits, and a moving model which shows how the old locks worked. If you stop at Chesapeake City, make a point to visit the C&D Canal Museum.

THE SASSAFRAS RIVER

Charts: 12273, **12274**

When Captain John Smith first explored this river in 1607, he named it the Tockwogh, in reference to the edible plant we call sassafras, which was used by the Indians living along the banks to make bread and for a variety of other purposes. Shortly after the arrival of the Calverts in 1634, the name Tockwogh yielded to Sassafras as the river's official name. The name remains, and it is still one of the loveliest rivers on the Bay.

Wildlife abounds along the shores; in the early morning, you may see deer coming down to the water to drink (yes, it is fresh). In some places, the banks bordering the river rise gently to meet wheatfields, barely visible beyond the camouflage of lush trees. Elsewhere, the banks soar to 80 feet above the river. High on these bluffs or nestled below are several beautiful old mansions, which can sometimes be glimpsed behind the deep foliage. The Sassafras has an immense estuary. A couple of miles upstream, it narrows, becoming much like a succession of small landlocked lakes, which provide endless variety and opportunity to explore.

The approach is one of the easiest on the Bay. There is deep water all the way to the Route 213 bridge and the channel is well marked. You can run aground, but if you just follow the buoys you probably won't. Anchorages abound.

Sassafras River and Stillpond Creek

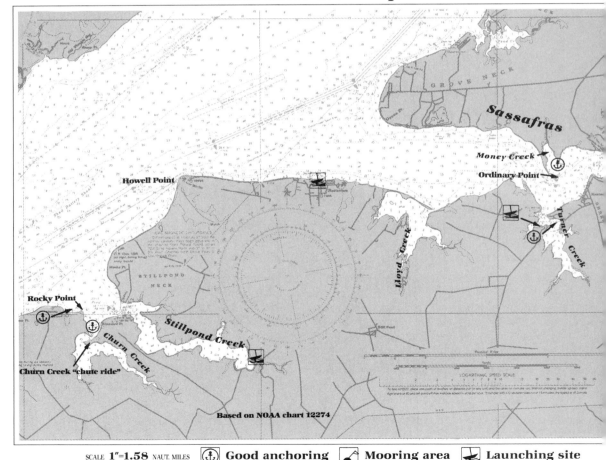

Based on NOAA chart 12274

SCALE 1"=1.58 NAUT. MILES ⚓ **Good anchoring** ◿ **Mooring area** ⛵ **Launching site**

LLOYD CREEK

No facilities

Charts: 12273, **12274**

Lloyd Creek is definitely not an anchorage in any sense of the word. Fifteen years ago it was possible, just barely, for a boat with less than a 4-foot draft to get into the mouth of this creek. Even then there was no place to go and little room to consider anchoring. Since then shoaling has done its work to the point that no one, save a few shallow-draft runabouts, even thinks about it.

TURNER CREEK

No facilities

Charts: 12273, **12274**

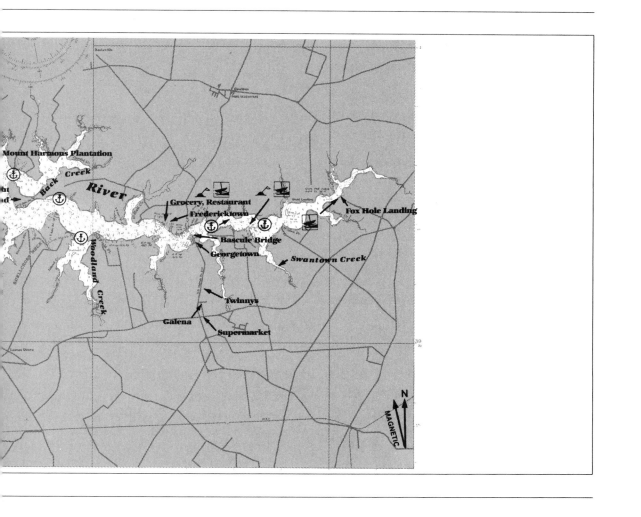

Approaches. The first possible anchorage as you proceed upstream is in Turner Creek, which has at least 6 feet of water in a narrow channel that continues about halfway to the head of the creek and is well protected from weather in all directions. Homes line its banks, making it less pastoral than other creeks along this river. Turner Creek also is decidedly more difficult to negotiate: The entrance channel is narrow and winding, presenting a bit of a challenge even though it is well marked. Feel your way in cautiously!

Anchorages. About one-half mile in from can 1, at the end of the creek entrance channel, is the Turner Creek Public Landing, on the point off the southwest side of the creek, directly ahead. There is a fair amount of room to anchor once you have cleared the entrance channel, although the creek shoals quickly a little past the point with the public landing. There are a few private moorings in here but no marine facilities of any kind. Just inland from the public landing is the Kent Museum, open between 10:00 a.m. and 4:00 p.m. on the first and third Saturday of each month. Near the museum is the huge colonial mansion known as "Knock's Folly."

There may be prettier anchorages on the Sassafras, but this one is by far the best protected from wind and wakes until you reach Georgetown.

ORDINARY POINT

No facilities

Charts: 12273, **12274**

Approaches/Anchorages. The next anchorage is a good one, on the north side of the Sassafras, just east of Ordinary Point. Stay well out from the mouth of Money Creek since the water shoals rapidly as you head north from the tip of Ordinary Point. This area has one of the nicest sandy beaches on the river. Unfortunately, it is open to passing traffic, which is heavy with power cruisers (that make large wakes) on most summer weekends. A frequently used tactic to reduce the effects of the wakes is to drop your main anchor off the bow and

carry out a stern anchor to hold the bow pointed toward the channel.

Ordinary Point, itself, was given the name because it had a colonial tavern, called an "ordinary," which served travelers using the ferry that was also located here. Today, there are no signs of either the "ordinary" or the ferry docks. There is a pair of stone steps on the point, but no one knows if they ever had anything to do with the tavern.

BACK CREEK

No facilities

Charts: 12273, **12274**

Approaches. About 1½ miles upstream from Ordinary Point is Back Creek, which has a narrow entrance channel. Favor the north side of the creek for the first one-half mile in from the entrance, holding about 200 yards off the north shore. After clearing the northern tip of Knight Island, head southeast across the creek until you are close to the southeast shore. This is the shallowest portion of the entire creek and should not be attempted if you carry more than a 4-foot draft. From this point, continue upstream along this shore; the water will stay between 5 and 15 feet deep.

Anchorages. This part of the creek is well protected on all sides and is usually very peaceful, unless some water-skiers take it into their heads that they own the place. Stay out of McGill and Dowdel Creeks near the head of Back Creek; both have less than 2 feet of water. A good anchorage would be across from McGill Creek in the 11-foot spot.

WOODLAND CREEK

No facilities

Charts: 12273, **12274**

Anchorages. Another popular anchorage is in the mouth of Woodland Creek, about 3 miles above Ordinary Point and 2 miles from the excellent marinas and restaurants in Georgetown. This is a fairly well-protected anchorage with several small sandy beaches and all of Daffodil Island to explore.

Approaches. Boats drawing more than 4 feet should proceed with caution, because the depths drop to 4 feet or less as you approach Daffodil Island. Only runabouts or dinghys should proceed beyond Daffodil Island because it becomes extremely shallow. In fact, it may be easier to wade. The bottom is hard sand.

GEORGETOWN/
FREDERICKTOWN

All facilities

Fredericktown is on the north shore of the Sassafras, just short of the Route 213 bridge. Georgetown is on the other (south) side of the bridge. For convenience, in all further references I'll simply call it "Georgetown." An assortment of fine marinas and all the facilities that you are likely to need or want are in Georgetown.

Anchorages/Moorings. Anchoring space is scarce among all the moorings, but you can either rent a slip or mooring for the night or move a short distance downstream to anchor.

Georgetown on the Sassafras River, with the Kitty Knight House on the hill in the background.

Where to Eat. Georgetown has at least two excellent restaurants: the Kitty Knight House, on a hill overlooking the Georgetown Yacht Basin, and The Granary, on the other side of the river next to the Georgetown Yacht Club. (The Granary burned in 1985 and has now been completely rebuilt.)`

History. The Kitty Knight House, by the way, has an interesting history. During the War of 1812, legend says, it was the only house in Georgetown not burned by the British. Two days after they burned Havre de Grace, a contingent of British marines and sailors in several small boats made their way up the river, accompanied by the notorious Admiral Cockburn. Ignoring the British warning not to resist, the local militia opened fire. The poorly trained militia couldn't stand up to the British regulars and was forced to retreat. In retaliation to being fired upon, the British promptly began to set fire to all of the houses in Georgetown and Fredericktown. The strong-willed and salty-tongued Catherine (Kitty) Knight, then in her late thirties, wasn't about to tolerate such an indignity and beat the fire out with her broom. Admiral Cockburn was so impressed with Kitty's courage that he called off his men, saving the house. The Kitty Knight House still stands on the hill looking down the length of the Sassafras River just as it did more than 175 years ago.

Provisions. The five marinas in Georgetown provide just about every service a yachtsman could desire, including complete hull, rigging, and engine repair. If you can't find what you need at one of the marinas or shops here, one of them can probably get it for you. The Georgetown Yacht Basin has a dockside sewage pumpout facility. Georgetown Yacht Basin also has a sail loft and rigging shop. Skipjack Cove Marina has sailboats of various sizes for charter. All of the marinas have heads, showers, and marine supplies. There are also at least two laundromats.

Things to Do. From Georgetown Yacht Basin, it is about a mile walk south on Route 213 into the town of Galena. Formerly called Downs Cross Roads, it was renamed for the variety of silver discovered in 1813 and mined near the town. (The mine was closed during the War of 1812 to prevent the British from using it.) Here you will find several interesting old shops, including a tiny but well-stocked pharmacy and a supermarket.

About two-thirds of the way into Galena, you pass Twinny's Place, an unimposing little restaurant reminiscent of a turn-of-the-century diner. There are only about nine tables and five stools at the counter in the dining room. The menu is posted in several locations on the walls, you have to look for them. Why stop? That's easy; it is a friendly little place with down-home atmosphere and great food. I don't know where they get their ice cream, but we have never tasted better. (Of course, a walk along a road in the heat of a Maryland summer greatly enhances the flavor of anything cold.) An apocryphal sign over the kitchen area reads: "This is not Burger King. You can't have it your way." Not true! Don't miss a visit to Twinny's.

UPPER SASSAFRAS

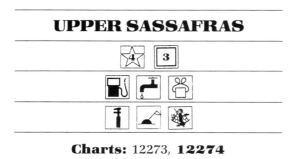

Charts: 12273, **12274**

Approaches. It is possible to navigate beyond the Route 213 drawbridge (12-foot vertical clearance, closed) at Georgetown, although not many take the trouble to do so. The bridge will open between sunrise and sunset Monday through Friday and at any hour on Saturday and Sunday between May 30 and September 30. At other times, advance notice to the Coast Guard is required. We are told that it will soon be manned 24 hours a day year-round, but have not confirmed any change to the previous schedule.

The river is navigable for another 2 miles above the bridge, where it passes by high, wooded banks with an occasional herd of cows on the north shore. It is certainly far less traveled and more secluded than the lower part of the river. To us, that is an attraction in itself. An additional advantage is the lack of frequent wakes from large power cruisers from the marinas below the bridge.

Dockages/Provisions. There is a marina on the south side, just before Swantown Creek, which

takes pains to blend into the wooded surroundings. Gregg Neck Boatyard offers gasoline and diesel fuel, as well as slips for transients. It also has a dockside sewage pumpout facility. The docking fee is "negotiable." (If the owners take a liking to you, you might overnight for nothing!) It is a small, family-run yard, reminiscent of the Bay marinas of two or more decades ago, and the owners obviously like their work.

Anchorages. Probably the best anchorage above the bridge is in the mouth of Swantown Creek in 5 to 9 feet of water. Don't proceed into the mouth of the creek beyond about level with the mooring area of the marina as it shoals quickly.

If you want to get away from the hustle and bustle and wakes of powerboat traffic, try this area!

STILLPOND

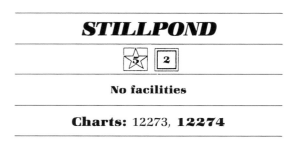

No facilities

Charts: 12273, **12274**

During the summer months, Stillpond is one of the more popular anchorages in the northern Bay. Rumor has it that the name is a corruption of the Elizabethan English name Steel's Pone, meaning Steel's favorite. Another version has it that the name originally was Steel's Pond.

Located roughly midway between Howell Point at the mouth of the Sassafras River and Worton Point, this area is far enough north that sea nettles are rarely, if ever, a problem and far enough south to be readily accessible from the more populated areas near the Bay Bridges.

Approaches/Anchorages. This anchorage is well protected from all points of the compass except the northwest. When there is a blow from this direction, knowledgeable cruisers get out in a hurry, push as close as possible to the western side of the anchorage, or work their way into Stillpond Creek. If you have a choice in this situation, pass into Stillpond Creek. The entrance is well marked and, if you don't have a draft over 5 feet, you shouldn't have any trouble (barring the possibility of recent shoaling at the entrance.) Entering at the change of tide is not for the timid as there is a substantial current. Once past the bar, you have 5 to 9 feet of water for well over a mile from the entrance. To port just inside the entrance is a U.S. Coast Guard Station, established in 1969. This station is the search and rescue operation center for the entire Upper Chesapeake. Visitors are welcome any time.

The first bend in the river past the Coast Guard station may present some problem to boats with more than a 3-foot draft; the channel is very difficult to find, tending to restrict access to the deeper water farther upstream past this bar to very shoal-draft vessels. However, if you hug the shore to starboard just past the bend (almost close enough to touch some of the tree branches), a 5-foot-draft vessel can get through at even very low tide. You will need to feel out the channel cautiously the first time. (To find it the first time, I got out and walked!) For this reason and the lack of reasonable anchorage room by the Coast Guard station, larger vessels should be careful if the weather looks threatening.

I don't recommend trying to enter Churn Creek in anything larger than a dinghy or a small outboard. Although the water is deeper than the 2 feet indicated on a chart, there is no marked channel and very little room to maneuver. If you do manage to get inside, there are depths of between 3 and 10 feet for about a mile. (There are a couple of small sailboats permanently moored in here, so it is possible.) More important, when the tide is turning, there is a very strong current, possibly as much as 5 knots at the peak, through the entrance. You neither want to buck this flow nor be driven ahead of it in anything big and heavy.

Things to Do. On the other hand, it is this very current that makes the mouth of Churn Creek one of the more fascinating aspects of visiting Stillpond in the summer months. On a falling tide, if you take a cushion, raft, or dinghy and launch yourself from the sand spit into the current, you will experience an exhilarating ride through and beyond that chute. If you watch the swirls in the water, you can take advantage of the eddys on the eastern side to bring you almost back to the starting point where you can take that ride over and over again with relatively little effort on your part. Go to the left and the current will carry you over the 1- to 2-foot deep shoal most of the way to where boats anchor. Unfortunately, the incoming current isn't nearly as exciting.

In the main part of Stillpond, tranquillity is the norm, except with a strong northwest wind. Along the western and southern shores are several nice, sandy beaches. There is a long, wide shoal, extending well out from the south and southwest shore, which prevents anchoring closer than a couple of hundred yards. This shoal makes for a long walk—that's right, walk—ashore if you choose to stop here. There are other, equally attractive, beaches along the western shore and you can anchor much closer to them.

Rocky Point, on the western shore, gets its name honestly. There is a large outcropping of sandstone here. The waves have washed out small caverns under these rocks, which thrum and gurgle as the water washes into them. Children find them fascinating! Off these rocks, the water is about 2 feet deep for a distance of about 50 yards. The only drawback is that the bottom is covered in round stones 6 to 10 inches in size which make walking in the water a little difficult—they roll under your feet.

Proceed past the point toward the Bay and you come to perhaps one of the prettiest sandy beaches in the Bay. The beach slopes gently into the water and continues to deepen gradually. You can anchor to within less than 50 yards of the beach. It is a nice spot to be during the heat of a midsummer day, but I don't recommend overnight anchoring here. Holding seems to be good, but you are exposed to the entire sweep of the Bay to the north and west. Should the wind decide to blow during the night, you could get uncomfortable fast.

On summer weekends, Stillpond tends to be a bit crowded for our taste. Boats line the entire length of the shore and fill the southern portion on the Churn Creek side. Swimming, fishing, crabbing, and other typical Bay activities are in process all the time then. If you shun crowds and plan to visit Stillpond in summer, do so on a weekday.

WORTON AND FAIRLEE CREEKS

Charts: 12273, **12278**

Worton and Fairlee are good intermediate stopovers for gunkholing and relaxed cruising between the extreme northern Bay and the Bay Bridges region. Although not well suited for a large number of transient boats, either one is a pleasant one-day stopover for the solitary cruiser.

WORTON CREEK

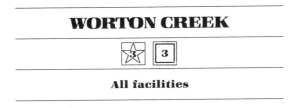

All facilities

Charts: 12273, **12278**

Worton Creek is due east of the northern tip of Pooles Island. It is completely sheltered beyond the narrow entrance channel, providing a snug haven to wait out inclement weather. Space to anchor is scarce, except for a small area to the west of the junction of Worton and Mill Creeks which recently has been cleared of moorings. However, moorings are usually available for the transient yacht (at least those drawing less than 4 feet). The shoreside facilities are readily available, but you will need a dinghy since there is no launch service.

Approaches. When approaching the entrance to Worton Creek, stay far enough to the north side of the estuary to permit approaching the red nun "2" buoy from the northwest, thereby avoiding the shoal off Handy's Point. Swing wide around nun "2" and head due south so that you don't come too close to green can "3" until *after* it comes abeam, then turn to port and pass close to it. After passing can "3" and can "5" just beyond it, head toward the center of the opening between Green Point Wharf and the sand spit opposite. While there is a shoal to the north of this sand spit, you can pass very close to the eastern side of the spit as the depth there drops sharply to about 8 feet within 6 feet of the shore.

Moorings. From here to Worton Creek Marina at Buck Neck Landing, you have only to follow the channel between the rows of moored boats on either side. There is at least 6 feet of water all the way to the gas dock, where you can lay alongside long enough to arrange for a mooring at the office, refuel, or pick up ice or sundry supplies. If you carry much more than a 5-foot draft, do not approach any of the other piers as you will stand an excellent chance of grounding at low water.

Chessie—
The Bay's Own Sea Monster

Shades of Loch Ness and things that go bump in the night! Can it be that the bountiful waters of the Chesapeake harbor a real, live, sea monster?

Since the late 1970s, when a few scattered sightings of "something" very unusual in the waters near the mouth of the Potomac River were reported, the answer appears to be a definite "maybe."

In that period, there were more than a dozen sightings by different people at different times, all of whom provided a remarkably similar description of a large, snake-like creature swimming through the water with a vertical, undulating motion. This was enough for the *Richmond News-Leader* to dub the creature "Chessie". (Obviously, implying its family resemblance to Scotland's Loch Ness monster, "Nessie.")

There was quite a bit of speculation on what, if anything, all of these people had actually seen. The press had a field day!

Then, in the spring of 1982, a resident of the northern tip of Kent Island had the presence of mind to grab his video camera and make a tape showing a long, snake-like object swimming past, a bare 100 yards offshore! Here was grist for the TV mill and the media made the most of it.

A team of scientists from the Smithsonian Institution was the first to study the tape in an attempt to identify what the "object" might be. After an exhaustive study, the team announced simply that the object appeared to be a "dark, elongated, animate object . . . which undulates in a vertical plane." That was it; nothing more was ventured. The implication was that the "object" was a large, swimming snake (ignoring the detail that most snakes swim with a *horizontal* undulating motion), but the team stopped short of any identification, claiming that "there wasn't enough evidence on the tape for a positive identification."

Johns Hopkins University got into the act by enlarging and computer-enhancing the video picture(s). The end result was still unsatisfying. The only conclusion: "The videotape is not a fake." The Hopkins analyst wouldn't even declare whether the "object" was a long, thin animal or something like a "large turtle leaving a long wake behind it."

The only consistent conclusion resulting from the tape was that there definitely was "something" there and it could not be identified as anything previously known to the Bay.

Sightings continued and a group called the "Enigma Project," a collection of scientists who study unexplained phenomena, became interested and made a study of a decade of sightings in the Bay—including more than 50 eyewitness accounts. The results were interesting, to say the least, and added a bit more to the puzzle. The sightings, which predominate in the Upper Bay, appeared to indicate that the "creature" only appears between the months of April and September and that it follows the migratory pattern of bluefish up and down the Bay, leading to the hypothesis that it feeds on the bluefish.

It seems that there really is "something" out there, but there is an enormous amount of confusion as to just what that "something" actually may be.

Theories abound. Some say that it may be a giant anaconda somehow transported from South America on a banana boat and escaped into the Bay. Some think it may be some form of prehistoric whale, while others vote for an oversized eel or possibly even a large, lost manatee. Others, after deep reflection, wonder if it isn't something that no one else has seen before, at least within recorded history.

Scattered reports of sightings continue to come in at apparently random intervals. Whatever she, he, or they may be, we don't know. Nevertheless, "Chessie" has joined the ranks of such other fascinating and unexplained phenomena as the long-sought Loch Ness monster. There's a lot of water out there in the Bay, and much more beyond its mouth in the ocean. Who can say what creatures man has yet to find in its depths?

For now, Chessie remains the substance of legend!

Things to Do. Once on your mooring or (if you are lucky and a little more adventurous) at anchor, you have several options for recreation. With the possible exception of late August, the swimming and beachcombing are excellent along the northeast end of Handy's Point, especially off the sandy spit you passed on the way in. You can dive off this spit into deep water, but watch out for passing boats. Unfortunately, in late August the bottom often purges, making the water look dirty and uninviting. We have been told that there is an old Indian mound on the northern portion of Handy's Point, near the small pond; we have never searched for it.

Provisions/Facilities. There are two marinas just inside the entrance, Green Point Marina and The Wharf at Handy's Point. Both welcome transients and offer both fuel, ice, and small marine stores. The Wharf also has a laundromat and a dockside sewage pumpout facility.

At the head of the creek, Worton Creek Marina, in addition to the usual marine engine and hull repair facilities, has a limited hardware and grocery selection, ice, soft drinks, beer, and a laundromat. They also have a dockside sewage pumpout system. A shower and head facility is located halfway up the slope of the hill overlooking the marina.

At the top of the hill above the marina is the Harbor House Restaurant, where we have often had superior meals at reasonable prices in a quiet, relaxing atmosphere. The building gives diners a pleasant view of the anchorage from most tables.

Anchorages. If you don't care for the congestion in Worton Creek, can't get a mooring or slip, are unable to find room to anchor in adequate depth, or simply are more adventurous, Tims Creek could be your alternative. This is a gunkholer's delight. The entrance is tricky, and quite difficult to find and negotiate. Tims Creek branches to the northeast three-quarters of the way through the entrance channel to Worton Creek. However, the entrance channel is extremely narrow and very close to the east shore. It is unmarked and definitely not for the timid! Don't try it on a low tide or if your draft approaches 5 feet, unless you are fond of dredging new channels. In fact, if you draw 6 feet or more, you would be wise to pass up both Tims and Worton Creeks altogether.

If you do manage to make it into Tims Creek, the

only anchorage is in the bight made by the sandbar extending to the southeast from the sandy spit at the mouth of the creek. You can anchor in good holding ground with at least 5 feet of water at low tide, well sheltered from the weather, in comparative isolation, off a good, sandy, swimming beach. You still will be within easy dinghy range of all of the Worton Creek facilities. Don't try to proceed much farther upstream; it gets progressively shallower.

FAIRLEE CREEK

All facilities

Charts: 12273, **12278**

Approaches. The entrance to Fairlee Creek lies directly to the east of the southern tip of Pooles Island, less than 2 miles from the well-marked shipping channel. While it's an easy approach to the first of the creek entrance markers, the red "2" lighted buoy, the entrance itself is "interesting": You must follow the markers carefully, even though a couple of them may be hard to believe.

From red "2," steer a course of 182 degrees to take you between the next pair of red and green buoys. Red "4" is practically on the beach, but the entire approach was dredged to a depth of eight feet in the fall of 1992, widening the channel to about 75 feet. As you pass red "4," a line of green cans guides you in. You can pass close enough to the beach to almost shake hands with someone ashore. If you need reassurance, use the private marker labeled "7A" on the shore directly ahead as an aiming point. Turn sharply around the end of the sandspit to starboard to enter the creek. Be careful! When the tide is running, and in the summer season, this can be tricky. Do *not* try this under sail.

Once through the narrow inlet, you can relax; the water runs about 7 feet deep. Past the huge collection of piers and slips belonging to Great Oak Landing to port, the water depth decreases to 5 feet (near the center of the creek) for most of the distance to the headwaters, shoaling rapidly towards the sides.

Things to Do. Great Oak Landing was a private club until 1976, when it was opened to the public. In 1980, it changed hands and additional slips were added, a process that has continued over the past several years. This resort has every facility and amenity—its airport, however, has been closed. Dockage is free for guests while they are at the restaurant. There is launch service for anchored or moored boats (sound your horn twice).

Great Oak Landing, as big as it is, occupies only one cove on the creek. Across the creek from Great Oak Landing, the sand spit that you cleared on the way in provides an excellent sheltered harbor and beach for swimming. There is a 7-foot water depth to within a few feet of the shore and you often will find sizeable boats with their bows on the sand and their sterns in deep water. Unfortunately, the entire sand spit is heavily posted with No Trespassing signs, due to past problems with fires and littering. People still go ashore, to be periodically chased off by the sheriff. During the peak boating season, this area tends to be crowded, so if you have a draft of less than five feet, you may want to head farther upstream.

Anchorages. Upstream, you can anchor almost anywhere without worrying about traffic and, once away from the creek entrance, in relative seclusion. There are several other sandy beaches along the shores—none as nice as the one at the entrance—but the shoals stretch for a long way off the beaches.

This is a lovely location any time of year. However, due to the shallowness of the water, in the very hot weather of July and August the water may be uncomfortably warm. As a result your cabin could be hotter at night than you would expect, even when the air temperature drops to a comfortable level.

Western

Shore

THE NORTHEAST RIVER

Charts: 12273, **12274**

As you approach Turkey Point on the way into the Northeast River, give it a good berth and start looking for red "2", a little over 2½ miles ahead. Once you reach red "2", stay close to the buoys. To port lie the Susquehanna Flats—an area notorious for craft running aground.

The scenery here is magnificent. The 100-foot high, wooded bluffs of Elk Neck State Park rise to starboard above sandy beaches. Although Elk Neck to starboard and the Susquehanna Flats to port cause most people to believe that the river begins at Turkey Point, officially you are still in the Chesapeake Bay!

The Northeast River begins at red "6" off Red Point. The only reason for folks to deliberately enter the Northeast River with the intent to remain overnight is if they plan to visit one of the clusters of marinas here; this river offers no good, secure anchorages to entice the cruiser. Elk Neck, however, has several nice beaches that warrant a daystop, and the high wooded bluffs provide some beautiful scenery. Elk Neck used to be inhabited by a tribe of the Iroquois Nation, the Susquehannocks, so many people search the beaches here for Indian artifacts. Literally thousands of items have already been found.

CARA COVE

No facilities

Charts: 12273, **12274**

About 5 miles above Turkey Point, Cara Cove opens to starboard, providing a partially sheltered anchorage for boats with less than a 4-foot draft. Totally exposed to the southwest through northwest, it does offer some possibilities. A pretty spot, with a beach under the high wooded cliffs, it should serve as only a daystop if there is any possibility of bad weather.

HANCE POINT CREEK

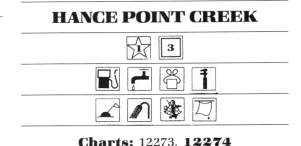

Charts: 12273, **12274**

Just past Hance Point, roughly 7 miles above Turkey Point, Hance Point Creek opens up to display a pair of extensive marinas and the Hance Point Yacht Club.

Dockages/Provisions. Right inside the point is Sheltered Cove Yacht Basin. The fuel dock is immediately ahead as you pass through the protecting bulkhead at the entrance. Here you will find a laundromat and the Jackson Marine Store, which is about a hundred yards inland from the docks.

The next marina down, Bay Boat Works, is equally extensive. Judging from the size of a couple of sailboats there, the marina must have at least 5 feet of water in the entrance and at the piers.

Both marinas cater primarily to powerboats and both offer slips to transients. There is no anchorage here. To spend the night, you'll have to take a slip.

CHARLESTOWN

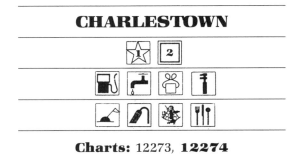

Charts: 12273, **12274**

History. Across the Northeast River from Hance Point is Charlestown. This town began about the same time as Baltimore, in 1742, and the two were rivals for shipping interests until the Revolutionary War. Balti-

more had the edge in both facilities and location, and Charlestown went into a decline. In 1780 the county seat was moved from Charlestown to Elkton; then the hurricane of 1786 provided the coup de grace when it cut a channel that made Havre de Grace the more easily accessible port. Today Charlestown is a small country town with a cluster of marinas.

Dockages/Provisions. The first and largest of the marinas, Charlestown Marina, has a long causeway on its south side; this blocks waves from the wide open direction to the main Bay, a nicety that also protects the other two marinas to the north of it. An outer steel bulkhead protects the rest of the piers from the easterly direction. Gas, diesel, and marine supplies are available here and at the Avalon Yacht Basin (no diesel) just to the north. A short walk into town enables you to try out the Market Street Cafe, which was once a general store and is now a restaurant with a display of antiques.

Charlestown has no anchorage. To spend the night you'll have to take a slip at one of the three marinas.

NORTH EAST

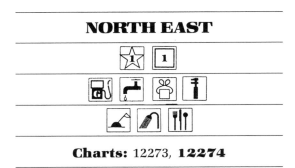

Charts: 12273, **12274**

Located at the head of the Northeast River, the town of North East was founded in 1658. One of the oldest buildings still remaining is the St. Mary Anne's Episcopal Church, established in 1706 as North Elk Parish. The present building was built in 1742. The rest of the town offers plenty of stores for shopping, but it is a fair walk from the waterfront.

Anchorages/Dockages. Tucked away in the northeast corner of the Northeast River, east of where the river necks down to a relatively small stream, is an anchorage basin. Although relatively shallow, there is plenty of water for any boat with a draft of 4 feet or less. In the east corner is the Anchor Marina catering to powerboats. To the immediate west of the marina is the Harbor House restaurant, which sports multiple piers that seem designed to accommodate many small- to medium-size powerboats. Those wanting to dine at the restaurant may tie up free of charge.

Things to Do.   To the west of the restaurant is a large public park with pavilions, a playground, ball fields, and a picnic area. Here you will also find the Upper Bay Museum, which is dedicated to preserving the heritage of the commercial and recreational hunter, and houses an extensive collection of hunting, boating, and fishing artifacts native to the Upper Chesapeake. The museum is sponsored by the Cecil-Harford Hunters Association, dedicated to the propagation and conservation of waterfowl and upland game, and the improvement of their environment. The museum is open 9:00 a.m. to 4:00 p.m. on Sundays between Memorial Day and Labor Day.

Migrating Waterfowl: Ducks, Geese, and Swans

One of the more fascinating sights on the Bay occurs every fall when hundreds of thousands—or is it more properly millions—of Canada geese, snow geese, tundra swans, and assorted species of ducks arrive in the Chesapeake, either on their way farther south or to spend the winter. They literally blanket the water in some creeks and bays, or crowd wing-to-wing in fields to glean grain missed in harvesting. It is a sight that many cruisers go out of their way to observe. And the noise these birds create "talking" to each other is nothing short of phenomenal!

Migration of waterfowl—and other birds—remains somewhat of a mystery and much of what we do know about it is stranger than fiction. It seems that this drive is triggered by the amount of light, or the length of the day, in the birds' habitat. Light levels cause a reaction in the birds' glandular systems that makes them grow restless. But that is not the whole story. Some waterfowl apparently know the route they will travel instinctively. Others, such as geese, have this knowledge "impressed" upon them, or taught, by their elders. And migrating waterfowl

Mallards.
PETER CARBONI/U.S. FISH & WILDLIFE SERVICE

Mallard with young.
HANS STUART/U.S. FISH & WILDLIFE SERVICE

Black ducks (foreground) and mallards.
F. S. TODD/U.S. FISH & WILDLIFE SERVICE

Canvasbacks (female on left).
REX G. SCHMIDT/SPORT FISHERIES & WILDLIFE

Canvasback hen on her nest.
JEROME STOUDT/SPORT FISHERIES & WILDLIFE

Canada geese.
REX G. SCHMIDT/SPORT FISHERIES & WILDLIFE

Whistling swan.
DAN YOUNG/U.S. FISH & WILDLIFE SERVICE

have something in common with all mariners—the ways they navigate. Night-flying fowl use celestial navigation; others orient themselves by the earth's magnetic poles; day-flyers follow a series of recognizable landmarks.

Most of the waterfowl using the Bay summer (and reproduce) near the Arctic Circle in Canada, with some in Alaska and others in Greenland. Some, such as the canvasback duck, summer in the North American prairie. When the weather starts to cool and the day grows shorter, heralding winter and its harsh conditions, these birds gather in flocks—often extended families—of various sizes to migrate south to more benign conditions. This migration follows well-established routes, which combine to form the continent's four major flyways: the Atlantic, the Mississippi, the Central, and the Pacific. The Atlantic Flyway is the one that channels waterfowl to the Chesapeake.

On a map of North America, the Atlantic Flyway resembles an irregularly shaped funnel. At the top, it goes from Alaska and the Northwest Territories to the western shores of Greenland, tightening to a narrow band on the Atlantic Coast somewhere between New Jersey and Virginia. (This tightening accounts for the spectacular quality of this migration in the Bay. Of the estimated 100,000 whistling swans on the North American continent, half winter in the Chesapeake Bay/Currituck Sound area!) From there it hugs the coastline down to the Caribbean and South America.

Species of ducks frequenting the Atlantic Flyway include: American black duck, mallard, American widgeon, northern pintail, green-winged teal, blue-winged teal, northern shoveler, and gadwall. (Canvasbacks and redheads follow this route; their species are just not as plentiful in number.) Each species reaches its peak migration at a slightly different time in the fall. For instance, whistling (tundra) swans and canvasback ducks seem to consistently arrive in the Bay at about the same time.

Historically Bay waterfowl were present in large numbers during the winter and they were hunted vigorously. Market gunners killed thousands of ducks, geese, and swans, and sold them to commercial markets in Baltimore, Philadelphia, and New York. Market gunning was an honorable and respected profession back then, meeting the needs of a hungry nation. And these hunters were incredibly efficient. Huge guns, often multibarreled, killed dozens of waterfowl with a single shot. Many market gunners became outlaw gunners when this commercially approved slaughter was banned after the Migratory Bird Treaty Act (1916), which established hunting seasons and bag limits. The legal bans and changing national appetites gradually reduced the number of birds killed.

The 1916 treaty between the U.S. and Canada—along with successive agreements with Mexico in 1936, Japan in 1972, and the Soviet Union in 1976—focused attention on the harvest of migratory gamebirds through regulatory controls, habitat preservation, and research. These treaties certainly saved many species of birds from extinction and have allowed some waterfowl to rebuild their numbers. In fact, recovery of the Bay waterfowl populations in the last 50 years has been remarkable.

Even so, many species continue to decline in number. Seven years ago more than 600,000 Canada geese wintered in Maryland. Recent winter counts estimate that between 312,000 and 377,000 Canada geese use the area—the lowest count in 20 years. In the period of time between 1954 and 1985, the canvasback population has plummeted from 400,000 to 50,000. Black duck counts dropped to 41,000 from 220,000 during the same period.

Habitat disruption is one of the big reasons for this decline. Water pollution from municipal waste, industrial discharge, and agricultural and residential runoff has killed aquatic plants and insects on which the birds feed. Some birds suffer from the long-term effects of DDT or other pesticides on their ability to reproduce. Then, too, development of the shores and wetlands to meet human desires for marinas, homes, and recreation spots has reduced the amount of available habitat. For wary breeds, such as the black duck, the mere increase of human presence can cause birds to abandon use of an area.

It will take continued commitment from residents, vacationers, industry, and government agencies to reverse the damage already done and to—as much as is possible—restore the Bay estuary to its previous viability and variety. This area is so rich that it is difficult for those who have not witnessed its decline to appreciate the

damage that has been done. It supports swans, geese and ducks—even in the summer—and the mass migration in the fall impress all who see it. Every fall the Chesapeake is alive with the flapping and calling of different flocks of waterfowl by the thousands—a sight we never tire of watching and at which we marvel annually.

IDENTIFICATION TIPS. You probably will enjoy this seasonal spectacular even more if you can identify some of the birds you spot. Canada geese are very straightforward: They have a black head and a prominent white patch on their cheeks; their body is brown with a white undertail. Snow geese are white with black wingtips; their feet and bill are pink.

There are two kinds of swans that use the Bay—whistling or tundra swans and mute swans. Mute swans are white and have a large orange bill with a black knob at its base close to the eyes. Mutes hold their necks in an S-curve and fan their wing feathers when they display. They are very romantic in appearance. Whistling swans are pure white with black bills and hold their neck straight, so they are easy to distinguish from mute swans.

Ducks are much more difficult to tell apart. Even avid waterfowl watchers have to bone up before the migration begins. Mallards are probably the most plentiful species in the Bay. They belong to a group of ducks called dabblers or puddle ducks, which means that they stick their head underwater and put their rump in the air when feeding in shallow waters. Dabblers can take off vertically, needing no running start. Male mallards have iridescent green heads and necks and a deep reddish brown breast that is separated from the neck by a distinct white band. Their body is gray and their bill is bright yellow. When they fly, their wings have a purple sheen. Females, which are otherwise a drab mottled brown, also display this flash of purple when on the wing.

Northern pintails are also abundant and the males are easily distinguished by their long pointed tail, which is as long as their neck. They have a chocolate brown head, framed on either side by streaks of white that follow down to the white chest. Their back and sides are gray. Female pintails are less recognizable, being a mottled brown and having a less prominent tail.

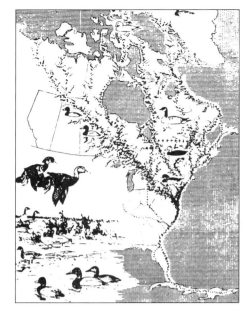

Waterfowl flyways
of North America.

Black ducks are hard to identify. Both males and females are dark, mottled brown. They are dabblers, like the mallards, but unlike mallards are wary of humans.

The King of the Chesapeake Bay waterfowl is the canvasback duck. This bird was once prime fare for market hunters. Its diet of starchy roots made it a popular gourmet item; King Edward, King George, and Queen Victoria all had standing orders for canvasback. Declining water quality killed off many of the plants that fatted the "cans," so it began to eat small clams. This change in diet made the canvasback less palatable. Canvasbacks are large, white-bodied birds with reddish brown heads and a black breast and tail. The female has a brown head and breast as well as a darker body than the male. Their bills are long, black and wedge-shaped and their heads are elongated, especially in flight. Canvasbacks are diving ducks—they need that running start to take off.

Each year, on a weekend in mid-July, the town of North East holds a Water Festival in the anchorage basin off the park. There are lots of water events including a Bay-craft boat parade, various boating skills contests, a water-ski show, and the hilarious bathtub race. If you are interested, information on the schedule for the year can be obtained from the Administrative/Park Office, 300 Cherry Street, North East, MD 21901.

THE SUSQUEHANNA RIVER

Charts: 12273, 12274

The Susquehanna River alone is responsible for about half of the entire supply of fresh water to the Bay. Stay here for a couple of days and you will leave with the cleanest bottom that your boat has had since it was launched freshly painted! The fresh water kills off all the marine organisms—including slime—that have been growing on your hull in spite of the antifouling paint. If only for this reason, I feel that it is worth the trip here. The most interesting portion of the Susquehanna River, the region from Havre de Grace to Port Deposit, lies to the northwest of the Susquehanna Flats.

The takeoff for cruising the Susquehanna is the red-green "A" midchannel buoy between Spesutie Island and Turkey Point. (Note: Many of the main Bay buoys are being renumbered, and this may be one of them. However, it is the only one there.) The channel from here is well marked and considerably more forgiving than it may appear from a glance at the chart. However, do not stray far from the channel as a few additional feet can shift you from 10 feet of water to hard aground rather suddenly.

From red-green "A", a course of 343 degrees magnetic takes you past can "1" to nun "2", a distance of 2 miles. From nun "2", the channel veers a few degrees to port. You should be able to see can "3", which is less than a mile away. As you leave can "3" to port, you will see a cluster of red and green buoys about one-half mile ahead. It is a little difficult to tell which one is what until you get closer, but be sure that you head between nun "6" and can "5" before swinging to starboard to pass between nun "8" and can "7". From here on, follow the buoys. Don't be misled by Fishing Battery Light, a white lighthouse located on one of a cluster of little islands in this area. If you head directly for the lighthouse, you will run aground.

The islands to the west of the channel are the result

of past channel dredging. Held in place by brush, they offer very nice sandy beaches for swimming, sunbathing, or camping. In calm weather during the summer, many small boats cluster around these islands. The swimming is great and you are never bothered by sea nettles. Watch the depth carefully as you approach, these islands are surrounded by extensive, shallow shoals. Anchor within 100 yards or less of the channel if you have a draft over 1 foot. Do not spend the night here—it is totally exposed and can get nasty in a storm.

HAVRE DE GRACE

All facilities

Charts: 12273, **12274**

History. The town of Havre de Grace owes its name to General Lafayette. As the story goes, he came to America in 1782 to visit General Washington. During that time, he traveled from Washington's home at Mount Vernon to attend a meeting of the Continental Congress in Philadelphia. His route took him through a town, then known as Lower Susquehanna Ferry. As he was admiring the beauty of the place, he was informed that a countryman of his, on first sight of the place, was heard to exclaim, "C'est Le Havre de Grace!" General Lafayette is reputed then to have replied, "It is, indeed, much like Le Havre. In this new free country, it may fittingly be called Le Havre de Grace." Three years later, Lower Susquehanna Ferry was officially given the name Havre de Grace, Harbor of Mercy.

As you approach Havre de Grace, you see the white Concord Point Lighthouse with its black top. This lighthouse, built in 1827, was in continuous operation for more than 150 years. No longer in service, the light is still a useful landmark. It has now been restored and is open for visitors from 1:00 to 5:00 p.m. on Sundays, May through October. A small floating dock in front of the lighthouse makes it easy to anchor off and visit the site by dinghy.

During the War of 1812, the British, under Rear Admiral Cockburn, attacked the town of Havre de Grace. The few militia in town fled and the British burned the town to the ground, unimpeded except by one man.

Concord Point Lighthouse and monument, Havre de Grace.

Close by the Concord Point Lighthouse, there is a cannon-surmounted monument to John O'Neil bearing a bronze plate inscribed with the following, which says it all better than I:

"This Cannon of the War of 1812 marks the site of the battery on Concord Point where John O'Neil served the guns single-handed during the British attack upon Havre de Grace, May 3, 1813, until disabled and captured. He was relieved from the British Frigate *Maidstone* through the intercession of his young daughter, Matilda, to whom Admiral Cockburn gave his gold-mounted snuff box in token of her heroism. As a tribute to the gallant conduct of her Father, the citizens of Philadelphia presented a handsome sword."

Things to Do. Past the lighthouse, follow the redbrick walk to stairs, which lead to the Havre de Grace Decoy Musuem. The museum, which opened in November 1986, is dedicated to the art of decoy-making and contains four primary points of interest: the decoy exhibit of master carvers, the "Life-Like Display of R. Madison Mitchell" (master carver), a panorama, and a display of various types of gunning boxes. Admission is free.

Between the lighthouse and the Decoy Museum is the Havre de Grace Maritime Museum, intended to

The swing railroad bridge at Havre de Grace.
Garrett Island is in the background.

showcase the area's nautical heritage and the local
interest in wooden boats.

Dockages/Provisions.   Although they are
a little difficult to count, Havre de Grace contains no
less than six marinas, all well within walking distance
of the center of town. Everyone we have met there has
been unfailingly polite, courteous, and as helpful as
possible. There are facilities here to satisfy virtually any
cruising need you might have, including a dockside sewage pumpout facility at Havre de Grace Marina. A short
walk into town brings you to shops, restaurants, and
grocery stores. Although excellent transient slips are
available, we have always preferred to proceed upstream
to anchor for the night.

GARRETT ISLAND

REGION

⊠3 2

Charts: 12273, **12274**

Approaches.   As you proceed upstream, the
first obstacle that you encounter is a railroad bridge. It

has a closed vertical clearance of 52 feet at mean high
water. If you are in a sailboat, be sure that you know your
maximum mast height, including any radio antennas.
Actually, only the biggest boats, those in excess of 35
feet LOA, will have any trouble. Even these can pass if
they really want to do so, but they must notify Conrail
Railroad Company in Philadelphia 24 hours in advance. The phone is (215)596-2876, however you may
have some difficulty getting someone to answer; let it
ring.

Once past the first bridge, pay careful attention to
your chart and, particularly, to the navigation aids on
the river. Look sharp; there are big rocks here, not the
usual sand or mud of the Chesapeake Bay.

The easiest route upstream is to pass to the west of
Garrett Island where there is deep water all the way. If
you should choose the east route past the island, swing
hard to starboard as soon as you pass through the first
bridge. Then parallel the bridge, maintaining a distance
of between 25 to 50 yards from the bridge until you are
well past the tip of Garrett Island. This takes you clear of
the shoal extending toward the bridge from the island,
keeping you in at least 9 feet of water. Regardless of
which side of the island you pass, the remaining bridges
present no problem. The lowest of them has an 86-foot
clearance.

Anchorages.   Along the western route past the
island, the first good anchorage is to port, anywhere
along the western shore just past the Route 40 bridge
(the second bridge). Pull in until you get a sounding of
between 10 and 15 feet and drop the hook. The holding
is excellent and the densely wooded banks under the
high hills in the background make for a well-protected,
secluded anchorage, except in a blow from the northwest. Even then, the bridges upstream provide a surprising amount of protection. There are rarely many, if
any, other boats here even in midsummer. (The trains
crossing the two railroad bridges do make a bit of a
racket but we seldom hear them much once we go below
deck for the night.) Stay close to Garrett Island as you
proceed upstream but don't try to anchor near it on the
western side: The water is too deep (30 feet or more) to
anchor comfortably; you will be in the mainstream of
any traffic, which can include barges from Port Deposit;
and there are rocks all along the shore which make
landing there difficult. Be sure to leave can "21" to port
after you pass the third bridge. From here, the deep water runs along the east side of the river.

Dockages/Moorings. If you choose the eastern route past the island, you can anchor to the east of it. The shore on this side of the island is appealing, with several small sandy beaches frequented by campers. Other than campers, the island is uninhabited (although my wife has been regaling our offspring with tales of the "madman who lives in the woods of Garrett Island," a story whose source I have never been able to determine!). For those used to anchoring in most tributaries of the Chesapeake, prepare for some problems. The water is between 50 and 60 feet deep. At least three marinas in Perryville, on the east bank of the river opposite Garrett Island, and Havre de Grace Marina on the west bank, offer slips or moorings to take care of that little problem, if necessary.

GARRETT ISLAND TO
PORT DEPOSIT

⭐2 1

No facilities

Charts: 12273, **12274**

Anchorages. From the north end of Garrett Island, it is just over 2 miles to Port Deposit. Above the I-95 bridge, anchorages are in short supply. If you intend to remain overnight, retreat below two or three of the bridges to anchor or take a slip, unless the weather is expected to remain mild. (Who believes the weatherman?)

Approaches. Above Garrett Island, remain in the north half of the river to avoid the long shoal extending from can "21" all the way upstream in the southern half. As you reach the I-95 bridge, stay clear of the northern three spans to proceed beyond it. On the upstream side, about 100 yards past the bridge, there is at least one piling—and probably more—just at or below the surface, ready to snag the unwary.

Once you are clear of the bridge, there is 25 to 30 feet of water in the north half of the river until you reach Port Deposit.

A condominium complex and marina (Tome's Landing) are being built in Port Deposit—plans for transient

facilities are unclear. In the summer, trailers line the shore below town. At one time, gas for smaller powerboats was available at the floating dock of a little restaurant there.

In the summer of 1988, we were anchored a little south of Port Deposit when my youngest awoke us in the wee hours of the morning to "Come, look! You have to see this!" With a bit of grumbling, we arose. Sure enough, there was something to see—the little restaurant to the west of the line of trailers was on fire. And a spectacular fire it was! The flames were leaping well over 100 feet into the sky. The propane tanks for the stoves must have been feeding the flames. Fire engines arrived but all they could do was keep the fire from spreading. When morning arrived, the little restaurant was ash. I don't know if it was, or will be, rebuilt.

Above Port Deposit, the river begins to shoal quickly and cruising boats should not proceed much beyond the downstream tip of Spencer Island, a short distance past the Port Deposit construction yards. Look upstream and the reason is obvious. These are big rocks, not the forgiving mud bottoms of the main Bay. Clearly visible beyond the jumble of rocks is the huge Conowingo Dam and its hydroelectric plant. Beyond the dam is a lake 1 mile wide and 14 miles long, but you cannot get to it from here by boat.

ABERDEEN PROVING
GROUNDS

Charts: 12273, **12274**

Aberdeen Proving Grounds is not a cruising area. In fact, it is surrounded by a restricted water area that is closed to navigation from 7:30 a.m. to 5:00 p.m. daily except Saturday, Sunday, and national holidays. During periods of active firing, the area is patrolled by boats from APG's "navy" to prevent anyone straying into the area at an "inopportune moment." APG is included here because it is an area that we find a "point of high interest," well worth paying a visit if the opportunity presents itself.

Unfortunately, there is no harbor or public docking facility to permit boaters to visit Aberdeen Proving Grounds directly by water. In addition, the entire shoreline is restricted; no one is permitted to land on the

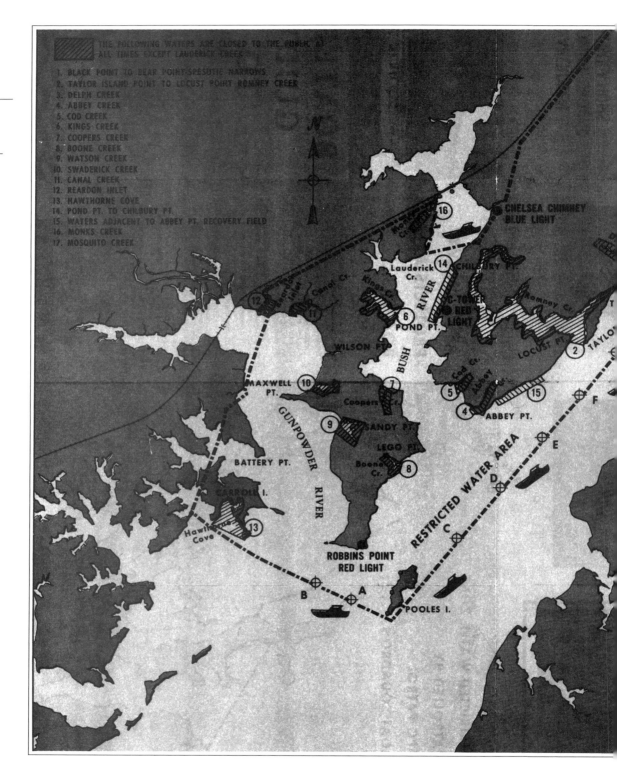

THE FOLLOWING WATERS ARE CLOSED TO THE PUBLIC AT
ALL TIMES EXCEPT LAUDERICK CREEK

1. BLACK POINT TO BEAR POINT-SPESUTIE NARROWS
2. TAYLOR ISLAND POINT TO LOCUST POINT ROMNEY CREEK
3. DELPH CREEK
4. ABBEY CREEK
5. COD CREEK
6. KINGS CREEK
7. COOPERS CREEK
8. BOONE CREEK
9. WATSON CREEK
10. SWADERICK CREEK
11. CANAL CREEK
12. REARDON INLET
13. HAWTHORNE COVE
14. POND PT. TO CHILBURY PT.
15. WATERS ADJACENT TO ABBEY PT. RECOVERY FIELD
16. MONKS CREEK
17. MOSQUITO CREEK

Aberdeen Restricted Area.

shore or even to approach within 200 meters at any time. The reason is obvious if you stop to think about it. The waters, shorelines, and islands within the installation are used in weapons and ammunition testing and research. Hitting a "dud" shell or some other form of ordnance could set it off and really ruin your day!

However, APG's fascinating U.S. Army Ordnance Museum and many outside collections of historical and modern weaponry make it worth docking in Havre de Grace and finding some form of transportation (taxi, rental car, friendly local, etc.) to get there.

The proving grounds conducts one open house each year, usually on Armed Forces Day, the third Saturday in May. The highlight of the day is a firepower demonstration with some of the heavier and more impressive weapons systems. We still remember one demonstration of a post-Civil War Gatling gun and a modern 20mm Vulcan cannon, which were set up to fire the exact same number of rounds, 500 shots. The vintage weapon took nearly two minutes to complete firing. The

IMPORTANT NOTICE TO BOATERS

The adjoining map illustrates the waters, shorelines, and islands within Aberdeen Proving Ground's restricted water zone. Normally, these restricted waters are closed from 7:30 to 5 p.m. daily except on Saturday, Sunday, and national holidays.

However, the shaded areas on the map which are listed above are closed to the public at all times.

Opening of the restricted water zone is granted for navigational and fishing purposes only.

Navigation includes anchoring a boat within the restricted waters or using the restricted waters for water skiing provided that no boat or person touches any land (either dry land or underwater land) within the Proving Ground reservation and that no water skier comes closer than 200 meters to any shoreline.

Persons outside of any vessel for any purpose, including, but not limited to, swimming except for purposes of water skiing as outlined above, scuba diving, or any other purpose is considered in violation of navigation. Violators are subject to prosecution under 18 U.S.C., section 1382, and other applicable statutes.

Landing of boats or personnel on the shorelines or islands within the restricted zone is prohibited at all times.

Entrance into the restricted waters for navigational purposes during periods of firings can be made only by securing a clearance from either the installation's B-Tower Control by telephoning 278-2250/3971, personal or radio contact on ship-shore FM channel 16 and citizen band channel 12 with range control (call letters AAAA) or B-Tower AAAA-1, Carton Point AAAA-2, and Meeks Point AAAA-3. Loud speakers and flashing red or blue lights as warning signals are installed on all patrol boats.

ABERDEEN RESTRICTED AREA BUOY-
Can Buoy, yellow with letters.
Maintained June 5 to October 1.

U.S. Army Ordnance Museum at Aberdeen Proving Grounds has an outstanding collection of weaponry. It is worth docking at Havre de Grace and finding transportation in order to go see it.

Vulcan exhausted its ammunition in seconds! During open house, the visitor can see more than 50 displays and exhibits, which detail the mission of nearly every agency at APG. The day's events conclude with the traditional retreat ceremony at 5:00 p.m., with the sounding of taps and lowering of the flag to signify the end of the day. All events are free and large groups can be accommodated.

The U.S. Army Ordnance Museum on APG is open to the public year-round. Its collection policy is to maintain significant items in the evolution of the various types of ordnance equipment, both U.S. and foreign, resulting in the most complete collection of weapons in the world. In addition to providing instruction to army personnel, they accommodate more than 200,000 visitors each year. Photographing exhibits is permitted. The museum hours are Tuesday through Friday from noon to 4:45 p.m.; Saturday and Sunday from 10:00 a.m. to 5:00 p.m.; closed Mondays, Christmas, and Thanksgiving.

BUSH RIVER AND POOLES ISLAND

Charts: 12273, **12274**

This whole area has been kept relatively isolated because of the joint barriers of the proving grounds and a low bridge on the Bush River. It will probably stay that way for the foreseeable future.

BUSH RIVER

Charts: 12273, **12274**

Nearly two-thirds of the Bush River, from its mouth to just below the railroad bridge close to the headwaters,

lies within the Restricted Area of Aberdeen Proving Grounds. There are no anchorages below the bridge and the water shoals to 3 to 6 feet in the region above the bridge. The bridge itself has a vertical clearance of 12 feet for a width of 35 feet and definitely does *not* open on demand. Those who need to have the bridge opened in order to pass through and have a strong desire to do so must make arrangements through the Bush River Yacht Club, Long Bar Road, Abington, MD 21009.

Approaches. While official restrictions prohibit passage through the Restricted Area 7:00 a.m. to 5:00 p.m. Monday through Friday, unofficially locals claim that, in practice, passage up or down the river is allowed except when firing is in progress. At those times, an Aberdeen Proving Grounds Patrol Boat is stationed near Chilbury Point at the upper part of the restricted area of the river and another one in the main Bay near the river mouth to stop traffic. The story goes on to state that these delays are usually only on the order of a half hour. Of course, if you have any doubts, official restrictions have "the right of way."

In any event, if you do choose to make the 7-mile passage up the river and proceed past the railroad bridge, the Bush River opens out, looking more like a landlocked lake than a tributary of the Chesapeake Bay. The water has the bay's typical rich color of milk chocolate rather than the clearer waters of a lake.

Anchorages/Dockages. There are some sailboats here, but this is really powerboat country. Past the bridge, there is a host of marinas, primarily on the shores of Otter Point Creek, with two more on opposite shores of the upper Bush River itself. Otter Point Creek carries a depth of 3 feet for a distance of just under 1 mile from its entrance. In the Bush River, where it proceeds toward Church Creek, 3- to 5-foot depths are found as far as Church Point. You can anchor in either of these two branches if your draft permits you to get there at all. The considerable runabout and small powerboat traffic in the region creates an uncomfortable chop for an anchored boat throughout most of the daylight hours. Of course, if you happen to be in one of those small powerboats, this is an ideal location. The waters are protected and there are plenty of launching ramps and facilities catering to powerboat activity.

POOLES ISLAND

No facilities

Charts: 12273, 12278

This mile-long, wooded island holds down the southeast corner of the Aberdeen Proving Grounds Restricted Area. The attractive island, with its sandy beaches, may tempt you to explore, but it is all U.S. Government property—landing on the island is strictly prohibited. If there is any doubt in your mind, simply read any of the several signs posted around the island which state: "U.S. ARMY PROPERTY, NO TRESPASSING, (DANGER) UNEXPLODED SHELLS, KEEP OFF".

The island was first named Powells Island by Captain John Smith, after one of his companions, during his exploration of the Chesapeake in 1608. By the time the map of his voyage was published in 1612, the name had become "Powels Isles." By the time of the publication of the famous Augustine Herman "Map of Maryland" in 1659, it had somehow become "Pooles Island." Barring any further slips of the pen, it will remain Pooles Island.

During the American Revolution, the island was 255 acres in size and was owned by John Bordley, a patriot. He not only donated all of the livestock from the island to the Continental Army, but raised crops on the island and donated them to the army for the duration of the war.

Pooles Island was one of many Chesapeake islands occupied by the British during the War of 1812. The British not only plundered everything on the island, but set up a gun battery to cut off trade in the Upper Bay. How effective this battery really was remains unknown due to lack of records.

Still standing but no longer operational is a lighthouse on the northwest corner of the island. Built in 1855 it was in continuous operation until 1939. Like the rest of the island, the lighthouse is off-limits.

From 1873 until the island was taken over by Aberdeen Proving Grounds in 1917, there was a peach orchard on the island which reputedly produced peaches of superior flavor. Virtually all of the "Pooles Island Peaches" were sold in nearby Baltimore.

Today, the island is quiet—uninhabited except for the wildlife. There is a herd of deer, which may occasionally be glimpsed from passing boats, and a sizable great blue heron rookery there. Bald eagles are occasionally seen in the area and may be nesting on the island.

The island is now about 190 acres in size, indicating a loss of only about 65 acres in the last 200 years, pretty good by Bay standards. In comparison, the much larger Sharps Island in mid-Bay has completely disappeared in the same time. This particular Bay landmark should be around for some time to come.

The Bald Eagle

The national emblem of the United States, the Bald Eagle (*Haliaeetus leucocephalus*, which means white-headed sea eagle), is truly a magnificent creature. A large bird, it weighs from 7 to 14 pounds, measures $2\frac{1}{2}$ to $3\frac{1}{2}$ feet long, and has a wingspan of 6 to 8 feet, impressive talons and beak, and a fierce, stately appearance. (The female birds are larger than males.) The white head and tail, which appear when the adult is 4 or 5 years old, make it one of the most easily identified raptors.

A mature bald eagle.
KARL KENYON/U.S. FISH & WILDLIFE SERVICE

Although this bird's armed with formidable talons and beak, it subsists primarily on fish, although it is not above eating ducks, geese, small mammals, rodents, snakes, and turtles. Even stranger, while it is quite capable of catching live, healthy prey, it seems to prefer to feed on dead or dying fish, a habit which lost it Benjamin Franklin's support for national symbol. Unlike the osprey, which will dive from a considerable height, plunging into the water to capture a fish, the eagle will fly along just above the surface of the water, reaching with a taloned leg to grab an unwary fish swimming close to the surface. This is not as effective as the osprey's dive-bombing technique. Perhaps this is why the eagle often plays robber baron, stealing the legitimate prey from other birds, especially osprey. Being larger and faster, the eagle will harass an osprey with repeated passes until the terrified opponent drops its fish. Then the eagle dives to reclaim its prize, usually before it hits the water.

Nesting eagles are becoming more common again in the Chesapeake region. An eagle's nest, or aerie, is usually a massive structure, growing 6 to 8 feet in width and as deep as 10 feet. The aerie is an untidy collection of sizable sticks and branches which are jammed into place to form a platform. This platform is then lined with assorted materials such as broom sedge, pine needles and other soft material. At least one theory holds that the whole mass is really held together by layer after layer of guano!

In the lower and middle Bay area, bald eagles prefer a large old loblolly pine for a nest site. These trees provide an excellent supporting structure for the nest and grow close to the marshes and open water which the eagle hunts. In the upper Bay region, eagles build nests in hardwood trees, mainly because loblolly pines there don't grow large enough.

Eagles mate for life and a pair will return to the same nest again and again, adding to it each year. Most eagle pairs maintain two or more nests in an area, alternating the one in actual use each year. Apparently, they guard even the unused nests, driving off other birds that attempt to use the site.

Bald eagles are found throughout the Bay, but they can by no means be considered common. In fact, they are still on the endangered Chesapeake Bay species list. A recent estimate (1987) by the Chesapeake Bay Estuary Program of the U.S. Fish and Wildlife Service counted 167 nests on the Bay. Some of the reasons for their relative scarcity are their intolerance of the human population increase and the decreasing habitat. A pair of eagles requires at least a square mile of territory, a factor which limits

their number in even prime habitat. The greatest limiting factor, however, was the post-WWII pesticide problem, which put the Bay eagles, as well as osprey and peregrine falcons, on the endangered species list. Chesapeake Bay eagles had some of the highest recorded DDE levels (DDE is a by-product of DDT) in their tissues and eggs in the United States. In 1972, when DDT was banned in the States, there were fewer than 90 pairs of breeding eagles in the Bay area. Historical records indicate that more than 1,000 pairs of eagles nested here in the early 1900s.

Bald eagle chick.
CRAIG KOPPIE/U.S. FISH & WILDLIFE SERVICE

The bald eagle has responded to actions taken to prevent its extinction: the ban on DDT, rigorous enforcement to prevent illegal shooting, and habitat protection. Chesapeake Bay now has one of the highest concentrations of bald eagles in the lower 48 states, and the U.S. Fish and Wildlife Service estimates that the Bay supports roughly 20 percent of the breeding eagles on the East Coast.

While the highest density of bald eagle winter population is in the Blackwater Wildlife Refuge, they can be found throughout the Bay if you look. Populations shift seasonally. Bald eagles also winter in the areas of the Pocomoke, the Rappahannock (Virginia) and Mason Neck

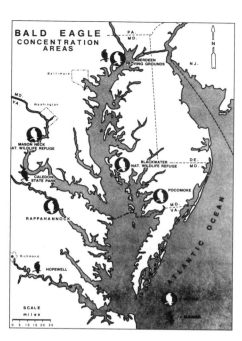

BALD EAGLE
CONCENTRATION
AREAS

Bald eagle
concentration areas.

National Wildlife Refuge. In the summer, they congregate in Hopewell, and Caledon State Park (both in Virginia). But you will have the best chance of sighting a bald eagle near the Aberdeen Proving Grounds, where this raptor spends time in both summer and winter.

In 1989 there were six pairs of eagles nesting in the impact area of APG in the northern Bay. These eagles and their nests are possibly the best protected eagles in the world. First, no humans (or at least extremely few) are going to be intruding into the nesting areas due to the possibility of setting off a dud bomb or shell there. (Remember, that is the main reason for the existence of the Aberdeen Restricted Area!) Second, the APG has established an Endangered Species Project, which is primarily focused on the eagles. In addition to studying them, the APG has established a circle of 100 meters radius around each of the nests where "nothing takes place"—that is, there is no firing in or near the protected area and none of the APG personnel go near the nests for any reason. Third, there is an abudant food supply for the eagles. According to Jim Pottie, APG project team leader, there was a count of between 100 to 200 eagles in the APG area in the summer of 1989, most of them considered transient, but such a high count is encouraging nevertheless.

The eagle is definitely making a comeback in the Chesapeake Bay area! Seeing one of these great birds on the wing is always an impressive sight. One that, with luck and some care, we will be able to continue to see well into the distant future.

REGION 2

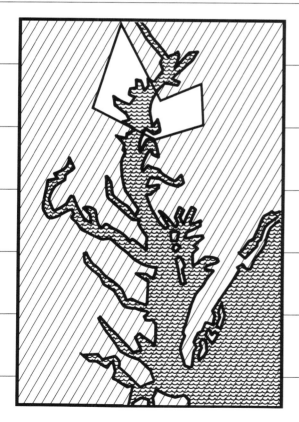

Pooles
Island
to
Bay
Bridges

Pooles Island to Bay Bridges

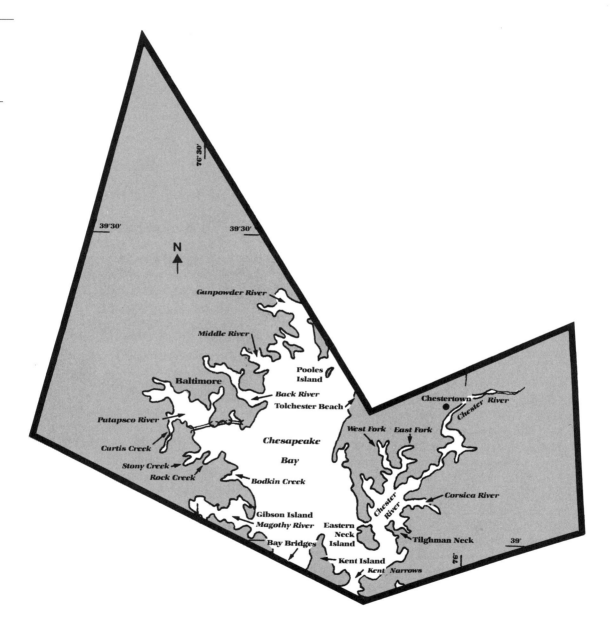

Pooles Island, near Fairlee Creek, and the Chesapeake Bay Bridges serve as dividing lines in the Bay in more than a topographical sense. As you pass each of these points, the very character of the Bay begins to undergo subtle changes. As you proceed north from below the bridges, the water begins to be less and less salty; the wave action changes, becoming more choppy, with lower wave heights and far fewer of the long rollers often encountered below the bridges. Even the shoreline changes, although that may be more in the mind's eye than in actuality. The harbors become fewer, more crowded, and, some say, not as attractive as those farther south. The change as you head north past Pooles Island is not quite as evident. The main difference is that the water rapidly loses salinity, becoming more fresh. The sea nettles rarely penetrate north of this island, making it an excellent area for swimming throughout the summer.

Regardless of changes, it is all Chesapeake Bay country—one of the best cruising grounds in the U.S.A. Many harbors and anchorages here belong on the "must visit" list of the serious cruiser.

Chesapeake Bay Jellyfish

There are three basic types of jellyfish found in the Chesapeake Bay: the infamous sea nettle, the winter jellyfish, and comb jellies. The first two have long tentacles covered with stinging cells, which make them rather unpopular with people who like to go into the water. The last type consists of a considerable number of different kinds, all harmless to anything but plankton.

THE SEA NETTLE The sea nettle (scientific name *Chrysaora quinquecirrha*) is the best known of all of the Chesapeake Bay jellyfish, perhaps better known than any other form of marine life, and for good reason. The adults, or medusae, invade the middle and lower Bay in such numbers during the summer months that you can't enter the water without getting stung unless you wear full protective clothing over your skin.

Jellyfish are capable of limited propulsion by the repeated contraction and expansion of the bell of the medusa. However, they are mostly

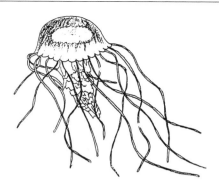

FIGURE 5. **The medusa stage of the sea nettle.**

carried by tidal and other currents. This has the peculiar effect of causing them to be extremely concentrated in some areas and relatively scarce in others, even at the peak of their population. The areas of concentration change, usually in a matter of hours.

Sea nettles are saltwater creatures. They cannot survive in fresh or low-salinity water. As a result, they are rarely seen north of Pooles Island and Fairlee Creek; their density as far south as the Little Choptank River fluctuates based on spring rainfall—more rain means fewer nettles.

The sea nettle develops through several stages. The fertilized egg is carried inside the adult female medusa until it develops into the planula larva. The planulae are released into the water and sink to the bottom where they attach to hard structures on the bottom such as oyster shells. Soon the planulae bulges and become a polyp, which looks a lot like a sea anemone. When the water temperatures warm in the spring the polyp develops into a medusa through a process called strobilization. During this period, the top of the polyp develops what looks like a stack of saucers. Each saucer is released to become an Ephyra, which is a tiny medusa. The medusa is the only stage we are likely to see; all of the others are tiny and don't bother us anyway. The medusa stage of the nettle varies in size from the small, approximately 1-inch diameter, immature medusa bell with tiny tentacles to the full-grown adult with a large bell (up to 6 inches in diameter) and innumerable tentacles, which can attain a length of several feet! Needless to say, at this stage they can make us painfully aware of their presence.

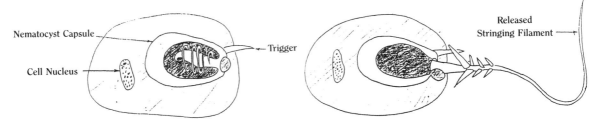

Nematocyst Capsule

Cell Nucleus

Trigger

Released Stringing Filament

FIGURE 6. Sea nettle stinging cell.

After the medusae spawn in the late summer, they die. That's why, no matter how dense the population during the summer, they are all gone by October and the cycle starts over again. (The jellyfish you may see after that time are the winter jellyfish, a different species.)

The medusa is an opportunistic carnivore, feeding on any prey that swims into its stinging tentacles. Sometimes you can see small fish or shrimp inside the nettle, where it is being digested.

There are literally hundreds of nematocysts on each of the myrid tentacles of the sea nettle. Each stinging cell, or nematocyst, contains a coiled thread covered with an alkaloid type of venom. There is a small hairlike projection on the surface of the cell that acts as a trigger. When anything touches this trigger, the cell fires, releasing the microscopic needle, which can easily penetrate thin skinned parts of the human body. Interestingly enough, the needles cannot penetrate the thick skin on the palms, a phenomenon which has allowed many a mischievous child to pick a nettle up by the bell and hurl it at an unfortunate companion.

A minor brush with them can cause inflammation and a stinging sensation where they touched, usually disappearing in 15 to 30 minutes. Normally, these can be treated by first removing any remaining tentacles, scraping or rubbing the affected area with sand, then applying calamine, witch hazel, ammonia, or vinegar. Do *not* apply alcohol as this will trigger any unfired nematocysts.

Severe, multiple stings can be dangerous to a person especially sensitive to the venom. Emergency treatment in this case is the same as for bee stings in an allergic person. Should the victim begin to wheeze or feel faint, apply ice packs and seek prompt professional medical care.

WINTER JELLYFISH The winter jellyfish *(Cyanea capillata)* adult stage occurs only during the winter and early spring months (late November to early June). As a result, it is not nearly as well known as the sea nettle, although sometimes it can be as plentiful. Winter jellyfish cannot reproduce in low-salinity waters and are rarely seen in great quantity very much farther north than the Little Choptank River, although we have seen them in the Chester River at times.

In the spring, the adults are sometimes mistaken for sea nettles that have somehow "wintered over," surviving due to a mild winter. They can easily be distinguished from the colorless sea nettle as they are a brownish orange and their tentacles are not nearly as long, even though the bells are similar in size. Their sting is comparatively weak.

COMB JELLIES There are two species of comb jellyfish found in the Bay; the pink comb jelly *(Beroe ovata)* and the sea walnut *(Mnemiopsis leidyi).* While the comb jellies are far more numerous than the sea nettles in the Bay, we rarely notice them as they are virtually invisible in the water and don't bother us. They are also quite small, seldom growing much over four inches long. We are most likely to notice them in two ways: when they are most plentiful in the

SEA WALNUT

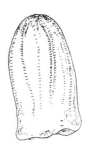

PINK COMB JELLY

FIGURE 7. Comb jellies.

summer months it may feel like you are swimming in gelatin as you brush against groups of them; and at night, especially in late July and August, disturbing the water will cause them to luminesce with a soft green light—sometimes the bow wave and wake of a boat traveling at night will be aglow with them.

They are present year-round, but their population begins to rise sharply in the spring, reaching a peak in the late summer. They feed exclusively on plankton and have no stinging cells. The sea walnut is found almost throughout the Bay, as far north as the vicinity of Pooles Island where the salinity is so low that even the sea nettle is rare. The pink comb jelly is not as tolerant of low salinity and is rarely found much above the bay bridges.

Comb jellies are rather fragile and easily break apart if handled out of the water. Our offspring frequently capture them in a bucket in the evening then disturb the water to watch them glow. There is a luminescent band inside their bodies which appears to be a glowing green wire. They are fascinating little creatures, with a grace and beauty that transcends their apparent simplicity.

Eastern

Shore

TOLCHESTER
BEACH,
SWAN
CREEK,
AND
ROCK
HALL

104

TOLCHESTER BEACH, SWAN CREEK, AND ROCK HALL

Charts: **12272,** 12273, 12278

Until you reach Rock Hall and the Chester River region, this section of the Eastern Shore has few offerings. While Tolchester serves as a harbor of refuge, only Swan Creek has any anchorage.

TOLCHESTER

All facilities

Charts: **12272,** 12273, 12278

About midway between Fairlee Creek and Swan Point is Tolchester Marina, in an artificial harbor just south of Tolchester Beach. This is the only harbor of refuge on that 10-mile stretch on the Eastern Shore. Here you will find all the facilities that you are likely to need, including a laundromat, which is a real find on any extended cruise.

Approach/Dockage. To enter, simply head between the jetty pilings until you are within the dredged basin inside. Pull up to the fuel dock to get information or directions on where you can stay. You have to take a slip at the marina to stay here; this is not an anchorage. Only two transient slips are available and they are assigned on a first-come-first served basis. No reservations are taken.

Eastern Shore with Chester River

TOLCHESTER
BEACH,
SWAN
CREEK,
AND
ROCK
HALL

105

MAGNETIC

N

KENT IS

Chestertown

Chester River

Centreville Landing

Corsica River

East Fork

Lookout Tower

Holton Point

Shoaling

Reed Creek

Sailor R&R Facility

N "2"

West Fork

Langford Creek

Chester River

Tilghman Neck

C "3"

See Detail Map

C "11"

Piney Point

Hall Point

Tolchester Beach

Eastern Neck Island

Rock Hall

Huntingfield Point

Swan Point

Rock Hall Harbor

"4" Fl.R 4 sec

Supplies

Chester River

Fl. 6 sec

Chesapeake Bay

Love Point

Rock Hall Harbor

R "12"

SOUNDINGS IN FEET

Based on NOAA chart 12272

SCALE **1"=2.62** NAUT. MILES

Good anchoring   Mooring area   Launching site

SWAN CREEK

Charts: 12272, 12273, 12278

Approaches. Swan Creek is approximately 6 miles north-northeast of the northern tip of Kent Island. The approach to the creek is interrupted by Swan Point Bar, which extends about 2½ miles south-southeast from Swan Point. Although the bar is not really much of a barrier for shoal-draft boats, use caution when crossing it if you have a draft approaching 4 feet. Those with drafts exceeding 4 feet should round can "3" marking the southern limit of Swan Point Bar, even though it is a little longer. If you are approaching Swan Creek from the south or from the mouth of the Chester River, the bar is no problem because you will be running parallel to it.

Once you're inside Swan Point Bar, the approach is easy. Pick up Huntingfield Point Light "4," a single piling that is hard to see until you are within a mile of it. Come to within 100 yards of this light before turning to head due magnetic north, past can "5," to nun "6" at the mouth of Swan Creek. From there, simply stay near the center of the creek until you reach the prime anchorage opposite "The Haven," a bay-like appendage extending southeast of the main creek. Hold close to the red "8" daymark in the one-foot spot at the mouth of "The Haven" to avoid the unmarked shoal on the north shore of the creek, opposite the daymark.

Don't be intimidated by the moorings belonging to Swan Creek Marina that extend out into the channel. Hold close to them. Stay out of The Haven unless you are in a shallow-draft boat or are headed for the marina there. Outside of its dredged channel, The Haven is very shallow, effectively negating it as an anchorage.

Anchorages. Up to a mile past the red "8" daymark, most of the north-south portion of the creek is suitable anchorage. Almost any type of anchor holds well in the soft mud bottom. While this portion of the creek is completely protected from wave action, the surrounding land is so low that it offers little protection from the wind. On a hot summer night, when any breeze is welcome, this is a prime anchorage. The water depth ranges from 7 feet to almost nothing, depending on how close to shore you drop the hook. It remains reasonably deep to within about 50 yards of the western shore, but the eastern side shoals farther out. Water-skiiers have not been a problem, but the anchorage is often crowded, especially on summer weekends.

Things to Do. At other than high water, there are some sandy beaches on the eastern shore, backed by dense stands of trees. Except for scattered farms and the town of Gratitude, the area is relatively uninhabited. The swimming is generally good even late into the jellyfish season, although you should inspect the water for these beasties in late July and August. Mosquitoes can be a bit of a problem on breezeless summer nights, so be prepared with netting and repellents.

Dockages/Moorings. For those who prefer to tie up, the two marinas at the mouth of the creek often have transient slips available; one of them, Swan Creek Marina, also has moorings available.

Gratitude Marina is located on the Bay side of Gratitude, right in the mouth of Swan Creek, to starboard on entering. Although exposed to the Bay, its slips are completely protected by large wooden breakwaters surrounding its piers, creating a small artificial harbor.

Swan Creek Marina is located in a little cove just around the point, called Deep Landing. This marina now comprises two yards, one on each arm of the cove. In the past few years, its growth has been phenomenal. Its character has also changed. Years ago, it was full of powerboats, with a few sailboats on moorings. Now, it has mostly sailboats, with a sprinkling of powerboats.

Located well back in The Haven is the Y-W Yacht Basin. There you will find more than 100 open slips, a dockside sewage pumpout station, and facilities for complete engine and hull repairs. There are a number of good-sized sailboats here to support the claim that the depths in the channel and the marina hold at about 6 feet mean low water.

TAVERN CREEK

Charts: 12272, 12273, 12278

Tavern Creek, just west of the mouth of Swan Creek, is inaccessible due to shoaling to about 1 foot across all the approaches. If there is any way into this 4-foot deep creek, I don't know it. By the same token, I don't consider it cruising territory even for a gunkholer.

ROCK HALL

All facilities

Charts: 12272, 12273, 12278

Approaches. About a mile south of the entrance to Swan Creek, you can easily see the entrance jetties to Rock Hall Harbor. To approach Rock Hall, follow the same instructions needed to enter Swan Creek until you reach the flashing red "4" off Huntingfield Point. From here, swing to starboard to can "1" near the dredged approach to the jetty entrance. Once you pass between the green "3" and red "4" lights, head directly for the jetty entrance. From here, simply follow the markers. You can either follow them north around the perimeter of the harbor or take the passage straight across. (The northern course is a little easier to follow.) In either case, you will be in about 9 feet of water all the way to "Sailing Emporium," the large marina in the southeastern corner of the harbor. You must retrace your course to get back out as the channel does not complete the circle along the southern shore.

Dockages/Provisions. In recent years, Rock Hall's look has changed radically. Once a shallow harbor exclusively used by watermen and their power-boats, the entire harbor area has been enhanced to make it more attractive to yachtsmen, while keeping the commercial watermen who have fished there for generations. Now marinas, marine stores, restaurants, and grocery stores as well as a sprinkling of arts and crafts shops have sprung up along Rock Hall's Main Street. There is even a museum in a wing of the town's municipal building. Be sure to stop at Durding's Store at the intersection of Sharp and Main Streets for a step back into the 1930's, including a fantastic soda fountain.

History. An early ferry—reputedly used by George Washington on eight separate occasions—once crossed the Bay here, but no trace of the landing now remains. It was here that Colonel Trench Tilghman began his ride to carry the word of the surrender Cornwallis at Yorktown to the Continental Congress in Philadelphia.

Things to Do. Speaking of the American Revolution, the annual, old-fashioned Fourth of July celebration in Rock Hall has become something of a major event in the area. The Rock Hall Volunteer Fire Company holds a fish fry that draws quite a crowd. The menu includes such delicacies as fried eels, baked beans, oven-baked fresh bread, and a large assortment of other tasty fare. A boat-docking contest between watermen at the public docks on Bayside Avenue is followed by a seafood bash, which includes traditional fried clams, crab cakes, and all the fixings. On the Fourth itself there is a parade, complete with theme floats and other entries. Other events include a whistling contest, a sack race, a turtle race, a tug of war, Bluegrass music, and the traditional flea market and craft tables. It is crowded, so if you go by boat, go into Swan Creek and walk over to Rock Hall from there.

LOWER CHESTER RIVER

Charts: 12263, 12270, **12272,**

12273, 12278

Looking something like a J-shaped umbrella handle, the broad sweep of the lower part of the Chester River starts from Love Point Light at the northern tip of Kent Island and hooks around Eastern Neck Island to swing to the north for a distance of about 5 miles. Then it turns to the northeast, splintering into a spray of interesting creeks with an assortment of excellent, well-protected anchorages. While the main Chester River winds its way from here into the heart of the Eastern Shore for another 15 to 20 miles, the cruiser need look no farther for some of the best anchorages on the river.

Eastern Neck Island is a 2,285-acre wildlife refuge,

ROCK
HALL

LOWER
CHESTER
RIVER

107

established in 1962 by the U.S. Fish and Wildlife Service. It also happens to be the site of many Woodland Indian artifact discoveries dating back 2,700 years. There are no harbors on the island usable by cruising boats. However, the Ingleside Recreation Area on the northwest side is frequently used by those who like to wade the Bay "flats" in search of soft crabs. The area also has crabbing and car-top boat launching facilities, wildlife trails, a boardwalk, and bayside observation deck. (For more information on the refuge, contact Eastern Neck National Wildlife Refuge, Route 2, Box 225, Rock Hall, MD 21661.)

As you enter the Chester River from the Chesapeake Bay, follow a compass course of 162 degrees from Love Point Light until you pick up can "3". (You need not honor can "3," there is plenty of water all around it.) From can "3," come to a course of 150 degrees until you reach can "7" if you plan to head upriver. If you are heading south through the narrows, assume a course of 155 degrees to the red/green quick-flashing buoy at the entrance to the Kent Narrows Channel. The compass courses are helpful as the buoys cannot be seen until you are within a mile or less from them. For the upriver course, head 130 degrees from can "7" to the flashing 4-second can "9." Stay at least three-quarters mile off Eastern Neck Island at all times as the shoal extends a surprising distance offshore and it has some nasty lumps in it. (We once "located" a log there by tacking in a little too close one dark night.)

If you enter the Chester River from Kent Narrows, can "9" is easily visible as you clear the last daymarks on the way out of the Kent Narrows Channel.

A course of 55 degrees from can "9" takes you past can "11" to the lighted red "12" between Hail Point and Tilghman Creek. (Note: This is not the Tilghman Creek off the Miles River; this one is not navigable.) Both can "11" and the red "12" buoys are difficult to see, even with binoculars, until you are less than a mile from them.

Can "11" is directly off Hail Point where, in colonial days, ships were hailed and inspected before going farther upriver. Whatever the original reason, the purpose of this hailing and inspection appears to have been forgotten today.

For all practical purposes, once you have cleared can "11" off Hail Point, you can head due north, ignoring nun "14" but staying well off Piney Point to starboard, until you pick up either can "1" off the mouth of Grays Inn Creek or the green-red "LC" buoy about a

mile southwest of Nichols Point off the entrance to Langford Creek. The green-red "LC" buoy marks the outer point of the shoal extending from Nichols Point where Langford Creek splits off from the main Chester River.

From here you can either continue on upriver or head into the Corsica River to starboard. Any shoals in the main river are well marked and navigation presents no problem until you reach the Route 213 bridge at Chestertown.

KENT HAVEN

Charts: 12263, 12270, **12272,** 12273

Kent Haven is actually an artificial harbor, located on Kent Island about 3½ miles upriver from Love Point Light. This represents the first place on the Chester River where you can find refuge or supplies. The next closest is Kent Narrows, the channel to which is approximately 3 miles farther upriver.

Dockages/Provisions. This harbor opened several years ago under the name Castle Marina. It was a dredged yacht basin, whose entrance silted in fairly rapidly. Since then, it has changed hands and been renamed Kent Haven Yacht Harbour. The entrance channel has been dredged. The present ownership plans to maintain a minimum of 5 feet in the channel at low tide. Kent Haven Yacht Harbour is a condominium marina, but transients are welcome. A swimming pool and restroom/shower facilities are close to the harbor and a restaurant and bar (The Yachtsman's Inn) is located in an old mansion, a short walk from the water. To stay here, you'll have to take a slip; there is no anchorage.

Approaches. The easiest approach to this harbor is to run to the flashing red "6" buoy located in the Chester River, southwest of Eastern Neck Island. From red "6" a course of 240 degrees takes you directly to the marina entrance, a distance of about 2 miles. You can, of course, chart a more direct course, but this approach is easy and neatly avoids all of the shoals; it makes the entrance unmistakable. (An alternative course is 185 degrees from Love Point Light.) The entrance channel is marked by a flashing pair of lights, green "1" and red "2." From them, follow the double row of privately maintained markers into the yacht basin. The fuel dock is directly ahead.

KENT NARROWS

All facilities

Charts: 12263, 12270, **12272,** 12273

For those traveling to the Miles River area from the north or to the Chester River from the south, Kent Narrows provides a shortcut saving several miles over the route around Kent Island. However, it is not a passage for the timid and sailboats above the dinghy class should not attempt it without auxiliary power. Although well marked, the channel on the Chester River side is narrow and has a couple of doglegs to be negotiated. In a couple of places the shoals frequently bow out into the channel to snag the unwary. In addition, there is a substantial current to contend with during changes of the tide. This current is strongest directly under the Route 50 drawbridge where it has been known to exceed 2 knots.

In spite of these difficulties, the passage through the narrows is used extensively and well worth the bit of extra effort involved. With a little foresight and planning, nearly all of the complications can be minimized or eliminated through proper selection of your transit time.

A number of documents can assist you in planning for the easiest passage through Kent Narrows. The most important are a large-scale chart of the Chester River with an inset showing Kent Narrows in detail (such as NOAA chart 12272, Chester River—Kent Island Narrows & Rock Hall Harbor), a current copy of the tide and current tables for this area (Fort McHenry and Sandy Point respectively), and a set of the Tidal Current Charts for the Upper Chesapeake Bay. Plan your arrival time at Kent Narrows for high tide and slack water or at least with a favorable, instead of opposing, current.

The Kent Narrows drawbridge (Route 50) is known to have a current of 2 knots and sometimes more during changes of tide.

Kent Island Narrows

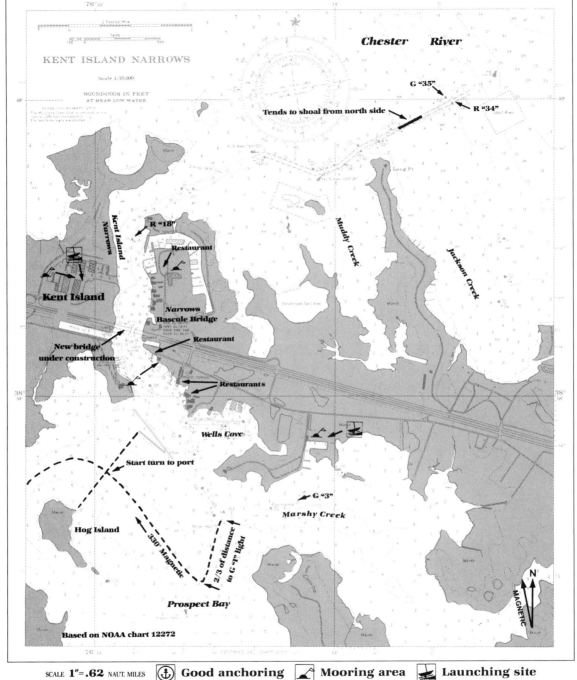

KENT ISLAND NARROWS

Scale 1:10,000

SOUNDINGS IN FEET
AT MEAN LOW WATER

Chester   River

G "35"

R "34"

Tends to shoal from north side

R "18"

Restaurant

Muddy Creek

Jackson Creek

Long Pt

Kent Island Narrows

Kent Island

Narrows
Bascule Bridge

Restaurant

New bridge
under construction

Restaurants

Wells Cove

Start turn to port

Hog Island

330 Magnetic

*2/3 of distance
to G "I" light*

G "3"

Marshy Creek

N

MAGNETIC

Prospect Bay

Based on NOAA chart 12272

SCALE **1″= .62** NAUT. MILES   **Good anchoring**   **Mooring area**   **Launching site**

The buoyage system is referenced to the Chester River. That is, if you are entering the Chester River via Kent Narrows (i.e., heading north), keep all *red* markers to starboard (right) and all *green* markers to port.

Approaches.

When approaching Kent Narrows from the mouth of the Chester River, the simplest course is to take a heading of 165 degrees from Love Point Light to bring you to the red "6" buoy in the Chester River. As you reach this buoy, the Kent Narrows bridge will be visible to starboard. *Do not head toward the bridge.* Instead, come to a course of 142 degrees to head toward the red-green buoy at the entrance to the Kent Narrows Channel. The new Route 50 bridge can be seen from over 5 miles away and completely masks the old drawbridge from view. The channel daymarks will become visible before the red-green buoy but you should maintain this course until quite close to the buoy to avoid the shoal to starboard.

From the red-green buoy, head directly between the red "34" and green "35" daybeacons to enter the channel. The channel tends to shoal on the northwestern side between daybeacons "35" and "33," so favor the southeastern side of the channel in this area, unless oncoming traffic precludes this option. Controlling depth of the channel is marked on the charts as 6 feet at mean low water. If it has been dredged recently, it may be closer to 9 feet. However, an abnormally low tide or a strong northerly wind can shave this to less than 4 feet, which is why the transit should be made close to high tide. Once clear of this area, simply follow the markers through the two doglegs into the narrows proper. Favor the southeast side of the channel between markers "23" and "21" as the channel can bow in that direction by 20 to 30 feet due to shoaling.

After you clear the red "18" daymark in the narrows proper, the only remaining obstruction is the old drawbridge. The new Route 50 bridge has a vertical clearance of 60 feet at MHW and presents no problem. The old drawbridge is still operational for local traffic and when closed has a vertical clearance of only 18 feet. Unfortunately, it still does not open on demand for boat traffic but opens every hour, on the hour, for any boats waiting to pass through. Hopefully, they will

adopt an open-on-demand policy in the near future.

According to the Rules-of-the-Road, the vessels with the current behind them are supposed to have the right-of-way in proceeding through a restricted passage such as this bridge. In actual fact, those vessels holding into the current waiting for the bridge to open often manage to pass through first as they do not have to turn around before heading for the opening. The General Prudential Rule-of-the-Road takes precedence here so there is rarely a significant problem (short of assorted ruffled feathers) resulting from the situation.

Plans for a new Route 50 bridge over the Kent Narrows have been approved, and construction started in the spring of 1990. The new bridge will have a vertical clearance of 65 feet above mean high water for a horizontal width of 182 feet. The existing bridge will remain for local traffic as Maryland Route 18. While it has not yet been specifically stated, we can expect the drawbridge to resume opening-on-demand as soon as the new bridge becomes operational.

Once you are past the obstacle of the bridge, the rest is easy: simply honor the rest of the markers until you clear the narrows. Swing a little wide of the green "3" daybeacon to insure clearing the tip of the shoal, which extends to the south from the cinderblock breakwater to starboard and head directly toward the green "1" lighted spar at the north end of Prospect Bay. Leaving this green "1" to starboard and following a course of 180 degrees takes you to the green "1" buoy east of Parson Island, where Prospect Bay opens into Eastern Bay and the mouth of the Miles River.

Dockages/Provisions.

Although many people use Kent Narrows as a convenient shortcut, with possibly a fuel stop, it offers a considerable number of attractions. In addition to the half dozen or so marinas, with the usual assortment of fuel, supplies, hardware, and repair capability, there are also several restaurants, all but one on the south side of the bridge. With a little planning, the interval between bridge openings can be put to good use.

Anchorages.

Often overlooked in the hurry to pass through the narrows is an excellent anchorage, hidden behind Hog Island near the southern end of the Kent Narrows Channel. Kirwan Creek provides a sheltered anchorage with good holding ground in 8 to 9 feet of water, about a mile away from the marinas and restaurants in Kent Narrows proper.

To enter this anchorage from the narrows, you first must clear the green "3" daybeacon and proceed approximately two-thirds of the way to the green "1" lighted spar before turning to a course of 330 degrees and entering the approach to Kirwan Creek. This course keeps you roughly midway between Hog Island to port and the cinderblock breakwater to starboard, neatly avoiding both sets of shoals. Once you have reached a line between the northern tip of Hog Island and the center of the breakwater, start swinging to port and remain in the center of the creek until you have reached your selected anchorage anywhere to the west or southwest of Hog Island or farther upstream. There is adequate depth here to anchor within less than 100 yards from either shore. Goodhands Creek, opening due west of Hog Island, offers a good alternate anchorage.

The area is pleasant and quiet with a few small sandy beaches where you can land to beachcomb, wade, or swim (unless the sea nettles take over the water). It is completely protected from wave action and provides a reasonable amount of shelter from the wind without eliminating the cooling breezes needed in hot weather. In warmer weather, be sure to come equipped with a good set of screens and insect repellent for the evening hours, which is when the sizable mosquito population becomes active.

QUEENSTOWN CREEK

☆4 3

🛒

Charts: 12263, 12270, **12272**, 12273

History. About 2½ miles past the entrance to Kent Narrows Channel is the approach to Queenstown Creek. Although never more than a small village, Queenstown was a small colonial port, which was used as an outlet for cargoes of grain, hemp, and tobacco and as a receiving point for manufactured goods from Europe. During the War of 1812, the British considered Queenstown important enough to warrant a joint attack by their land and sea forces.

Today Queenstown Creek is shoaled in so that only a narrow channel remains, making for a precarious entrance to the pretty, well-protected harbor inside. The entrance channel was dredged to a depth of at least 10 feet in 1985, making entrance much easier but, like most of the Bay, it has a tendency to shoal with the winter storms. If you have a draft approaching 6 feet, pay particular attention to the entering instructions and do not enter on a falling tide.

Approaches. All approaches to the creek entrance should be made by leaving nun "2" close to starboard and heading directly toward the lighted green "3" spar, the first of the actual channel markers. Leave green "3" close to port and head directly toward the red "2" light well inside the entrance, leaving green "5" about 10 to 20 feet to port. The simplest way to ensure remaining in the channel is to maintain your heading so that the red "2" lines up with the left edge of the white house on the shore behind it. Do not line up with the right edge of the house or you may bump. If you keep your speed down on negotiating the entrance, you should pass without difficulty. Running aground here is pretty much a "so what" situation since the bottom is soft and forgiving.

Anchorages. Hold this course until you are 30 to 50 yards from red "2" before swinging to port to head for the anchorage area. Assume a course that will take you to a point approximately 30 to 50 yards off the pier to starboard. A duck blind or its remains are adjacent to the pier on the side closer to the creek entrance. As soon as you come even with the pier, change course to port again to head for the center of the creek to avoid the shoal to starboard just past the pier. From here on, you can anchor just about anywhere. There is a minimum depth of 7 feet nearly from shore to shore. Boats with deeper drafts should not proceed very far into Salthouse Cove (to starboard) as the water does start to get thin there.

The upper part of Queenstown Creek beyond Salthouse Cove carries at least 6 feet of water until a short distance past Ditchers Cove, where the creek makes a 45-degree bend to the north. There is an overhead power cable in this part of the creek with an authorized vertical clearance of 66 feet. Somehow, this clearance appears to be a lot less when you are watching your mast approach it! You are better off anchoring short of the cable, although you can find seclusion just around the bend if you have the nerve to go that far.

If you choose to enter Queenstown Harbor, continue around red "2" to starboard as you clear the entrance channel. Once in the harbor you will see a number of workboats tied to stakes in the water. You can lay alongside the town dock for a maximum of two hours but finding space is a bit iffy during summer weekends. Alternatively, you can anchor just short of the workboat mooring stakes and take a dinghy ashore if you can find room.

Provisions. From the town dock, it is a short walk into town, where you will find a post office and a small convenience store. If you need some groceries or supplies, take Del Rhode Ave. (to the right of the Post Office) about ⅓ mile to Bob's Mini Mart at Route 301. Bob's has a nice selection of groceries and an excellent deli.

GRAYS INN
CREEK

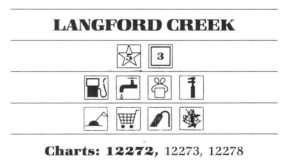

Charts: 12272, 12273, 12278

Approaches. The entrance to Grays Inn Creek, on the northwest side of the river, is about 12 miles up the Chester River from Love Point Light or about 2 miles past nun "14." Don't let the unmarked shoals at the creek entrance disturb you; they are no problem if you follow the entrance instructions.

Head due north from can "11" near Hail Point until you pick up Langford Creek can "1," just south of Grays Inn Point. Start your approach from can "1." Set a course of 320 degrees to head directly toward or slightly to the north of the end of the pier on the southwest shore, just inside the creek mouth.

Anchorages. Once you have entered the mouth of the creek, past a line between Grays Inn Point and Little Gum Point, you are in the clear. Simply remain more or less in the middle of the creek until you reach your chosen anchorage.

Not too many cruising boats enter Grays Inn Creek, possibly due to fear of the entrance shoals. Those that do usually anchor in the mouth of one of the convenient little bights or coves between Browns Point and the entrance to the creek. The character of the creek changes at Browns Point. Until this point, the land is low-lying and covered in marsh grass with muddy shores. At Browns Point, there is a screen of trees above a nice sandy beach with deep water very close to shore. From this point, the creek rapidly narrows and several houses appear.

Holding ground anywhere in the creek is good and the traffic, if any, is usually extremely light. The swimming is excellent through most of the summer and sea nettles are rare.

Provisions. Ice is available at Steamboat Landing on the north shore of Herringtown Creek, which branches off to the northeast opposite Browns Point. Gas is available both at Steamboat Landing and at Hills Marine Railway next to the landing. No other supplies are available. (No, I don't know where Grays Inn was or even if it still exists.)

LANGFORD CREEK

Charts: 12272, 12273, 12278

The mouth of Langford Creek is located about 12 miles up the Chester River from Love Point Light, just east of the mouth of Grays Inn Creek. At Cacaway Island, 2 miles upstream from its mouth, Langford Creek splits into the East Fork, the West Fork, and Davis Creek. For cruising, the East Fork with its rolling farmlands and relatively sparse settlement is far more attractive than the West Fork. The land in the area is predominantly farmland with a scattering of residences, which are sizable estates, on the western fork.

Anchorages. Langford Creek abounds with excellent anchorages. All are well protected and most have at least some kind of sandy beach for beachcombing or swimming. While most of the land is low-lying, heavy growths of trees all along the creek provide good shelter from the wind. Throughout the creek swimming is good at all times that the weather and water are warm enough to be comfortable. Sea nettles are rarely a problem, even in late August, unless it is a particularly bad year for nettles. (In 1987, for example, the nettles were present in quantity all the way to the headwaters.)

History. Like many other areas around the Bay, this region has its reminders of times and events that helped shape this country. One of the numerous skirmishes of the War of 1812 was fought at the head of Langford Creek. Men from the British ship, *H.M.S. Menelaus*, engaged in the harassment of the Eastern Shore, were met and repulsed by men of the area in a place called Caulk's Field (inland and between the two forks) near the old St. Paul's Church. A landmark in its own right, the 277-year-old St. Paul's Church was constructed in 1713 on the site of the original wooden channel, which dated from 1699.

Approaches. To enter Langford Creek, head due north from can "11" off Hail Point until you pick up either can "1" off Grays Inn Point or the green-red "LC" buoy off Nichols Point. From either of these, you can see both can "3" and can "5" which mark the left side of the entrance to Langford Creek. Head directly for can "5," but be sure not to stray to the west of an imaginary line drawn between can "3" and can "5" or you may run afoul of the 1-foot shoal off Deep Cove to port. Incidently, *Deep Cove* is a real misnomer as it has a maximum depth of only 3 feet and a depth of only 1 foot at the entrance.

If you are navigating upstream, Orchard Point provides a necessary reference. From Langford Creek can "5," set a course to take you slightly to the left of the watchtower located on Orchard Point (labeled "Lookout Tower" on the chart), but beware of the fishing stakes often placed to the right of your course. This course takes you to can "7", which is almost impossible to see until you are within one-half mile of it. Do not try to pass west of this can; it appears to be closer to the

eastern side of the creek than you would expect, but it is there because of a long shoal that makes out from Drum Point. After rounding can "7," swing to port and remain at least 200 yards off the eastern shore of the creek until you cross an imaginary line between nun "2" at the mouth of Davis Creek to port and the watchtower to starboard. At this point, Langford Creek divides into Davis Creek, the West Fork, and the East Fork. Here you have to decide which branch you want to enter.

LONG COVE

Charts: 12272, 12273, 12278

As you proceed upstream from can "5," the marinas in Long Cove offer the first facilities. Long Cove buoys can "1" and can "3" mark the 8-foot–deep channel into the cove. Since the water close to the marinas is a bit on the thin side (the approach depth is 6 feet, but you can't depend on more than 3 feet MLW), other than shoal-draft boats should try elsewhere.

There is no good anchorage here.

LAWYERS COVE

No facilities

Charts: 12272, 12273, 12278

The Rock Hall Yacht Club is located in Lawyers Cove, just above Long Cove, but there is even less water than at Long Cove and I can't recommend trying it without some up-to-the-minute local knowledge.

DAVIS CREEK

Charts: 12272, 12273, 12278

Davis Creek, to port, offers a good, easily accessible anchorage. Although somewhat more built up than other areas on Langford Creek, it is pleasant and peaceful enough once you have gone a little past the marina at its mouth.

Anchorages. The best anchorage is right in the first bend of the creek where it turns to the right. This is a quiet, pretty little area where you can anchor in complete security and good holding in about 7 feet of water.

Provisions/Facilities. If you are looking for marina facilities or resupply of essentials, the best facilities within 10 miles are right here at Lankford Bay Marina. It has gas, diesel, ice (block and cube), water, and a small store with a limited amount of marine supplies and even some food. There is no restaurant in the area. You may have a little trouble finding the fuel dock as it is hidden past the last of the boat slips as you proceed toward shore. Just turn sharply to port after passing the last slip and you enter a short channel running parallel to the shore, leading to the fuel dock. Hold to within about 50 yards of the marina docks as you approach the fuel dock—it is somewhat chancy for deeper draft boats, although there is 8 feet alongside the dock.

The Davis Creek Yacht Club, which holds a series of fall races through the first week of November, also operates out of this marina.

While Davis Creek is a pleasant enough anchorage, more attractive anchorages are close at hand in the two forks of Langford Creek.

WEST FORK

No facilities

Charts: 12272, 12273, 12278

Approaches. If you proceed up the West Fork of Langford Creek, favor its west side but watch out for the unmarked, 0-foot shoal which extends a good 100 yards or more off Island Point and the 2-foot shoal off Eagle Point, both to port as you head upstream. (We have personally "surveyed" the shoal off Island Point, under full sail, and can attest to its presence!)

Anchorages. There are numerous little coves on the western shore of this branch into which you can nestle for the night. Unfortunately, none seems to offer a place to land and the beaches, if any, leave a bit to be desired. Perhaps the best of these is Bungay Creek, with a close second just inside the entrance to Shipyard Creek, well upstream. These are small, tight, secure little anchorages, but anywhere on the West Fork is well protected from both wind and wave.

The entire West Fork is significantly more populated than the East Fork, which is why I feel that the East Fork is a far better choice.

EAST FORK

No facilities

Charts: 12272, 12273, 12278

Anchorages. As you enter the East Fork of Langford Creek, Cacaway Island, perhaps the best anchorage on Langford Creek, lies to port. Unfortunately, in 1989 "No Trespassing" signs went up on the island. No one seems to know what precipitated this. Even so, if you are wading or on the beach, it is doubtful if anyone will come to chase you off as long as you aren't harming anything. (Note: The island divides the east and west forks of Langford Creek.) A dense stand of tall trees on the island provides excellent shelter from the critical northwest. The height of the mainland and trees on it provide good protection from all other directions while still leaving the anchorage open to cooling breezes. At the extreme northern end of the island, a sand spit reaches out into the creek, offering a pleasant, sandy beach where you may go ashore to bask in the sun, swim, or build sandcastles. To the west of this spit, along the entire eastern shore of the island, there is deep water almost up to shore. In fact, near the end of the spit, the depth drops to 8 feet at less than that distance from shore! On the other side of the spit, however, the water is no more than thigh deep all the way across to the mainland.

In the evenings, you often may see raccoons or opossums (which means white animal in some Algonquin language of Virginia) come down to the water to drink or search for clams. Except for the animals, the privately owned island is uninhabited and not very exciting to explore.

A short distance upstream from Cacaway Island, there is a nice anchorage in the mouth of Wann Cove. Stay at least 100 yards offshore to avoid grounding. There is a small beach around the perimeter of the cove and, due south of where you should be anchored, the sandy hook of Hawbush Point offers a beach where it curves around the mouth of Kings Creek. Stay out of Kings Creek in anything larger than a dinghy or small runabout as there isn't much water.

To the northwest of Wann Cove is an unnamed cove with 9 feet of water nearly up to the southern shore of the entrance, where a small bank rises sharply. If you draw 4 feet or less, you can anchor inside the cove, but it is probably smarter to anchor right in the mouth.

About 1 1/2 miles above Cacaway Island is Phillip Creek, which provides a reasonable alternative anchorage when Cacaway is crowded—as it often is on a holiday weekend during the main boating season. Although a little tricky, you should enter trouble-free if you favor the northern shore and do not proceed much beyond 300 yards east of the large house on the north shore. The holding ground is good and the sand bar at the entrance provides a sandy beach, at least at low tide. There is another bar farther in, closer to where you probably will anchor, but it is all mud.

Across from and a little to the north of Phillip Creek is the Lovely Cove anchorage, which we did not find as inviting as several of the others, although some people

like it. It is too "public" for our tastes and has no place to land. Other than that, Lovely Cove is a pretty little place to drop the hook. You can anchor to the inside of the narrow point on the south side of the cove entrance, but watch the depth as it shoals rapidly.

Just beyond Lovely Cove, in a bend of the river protected by a small bar, is a better anchorage, close to a nice sandy beach. From this point on, you can anchor almost anywhere out of the mainstream of traffic and feel protected from the weather, if not from the occasional power cruiser leaving a large wake.

Don't try to enter either of the two little creeks between Lovely Cove and Island Point; they don't have much water past their mouths.

The East Fork of Langford Creek is navigable as far upstream as Flat Point. Past Flat Point, the water depth drops to 4 feet or less and there are submerged piles off the next upstream point. If you so desire, you can explore the creek for about another mile by dinghy before completely running out of water in the marshy headwaters.

REED CREEK

No facilities

Charts: 12272, 12273, 12278

Almost due south of Nichols Point, which marks the eastern side of the mouth of Langford Creek, is the entrance to Reed Creek, an anchorage often avoided by many because of the reputedly "tricky" entrance. However, with a little care this creek can be entered easily.

Approaches. As you round Piney Point on Tilghman Neck while heading upstream in the Chester River, hold to within one-quarter mile of the shore of Tilghman Neck. This will guide you directly to can "1" that marks the entrance to Reed Creek. The "tricky" part is that you cannot head directly from green can "1" to red nun "2," which is clearly visible in the entrance, because of the unmarked shoal that bows out into the channel from the small point on the eastern side of the entrance. Therefore, from can "1" set a course that would take you about 50 yards to the right of nun "2."

Hold this course until you have passed the point on the east shore, then swing to port onto a new course that leaves nun "2" close to starboard (but no closer than 10 yards). Once past nun "2," you are in. Simply remain near the middle of the creek favoring the west shore until you reach your selected anchorage. The water depths at the entrance are between 7 and 10 feet and a 7-foot depth is carried for over a mile upstream, with a few deeper areas.

Do not attempt to enter Grove Creek, to port as you pass nun "2," unless you have a draft under 3 feet. While there is deep water inside, a bar at the mouth restricts access to very shoal-draft vessels—a shame as it is a pretty little creek. (Gunkholers take note: Here is a challenge.)

Anchorages. As you pass nun "2," swing to starboard and head due west. To starboard is the long sandbar, which protects the creek. A sandy beach stretches all along the bar and you can land here to stretch your legs. In the middle of the bar is a classic mudhole which provides a playground for those of that particular bent. The first of three excellent anchorages is right here, just before the creek makes a sharp bend to the south.

A small bay halfway up the creek provides another popular anchorage. However, the shore is lined with homes and offers no landing place.

Just past this bay, where the creek narrows again, is the third popular anchorage. For about one-quarter mile farther up from this point, the creek is lined with farm fields and trees. The banks are muddy, but below them are a few small, isolated beaches at low tide where a dog can be "watered." There is no good place to land where you can stretch your legs.

Anywhere you drop the hook in this creek is a good choice. All locations are quiet, serene, and well protected from all directions. There are no marine facilities of any kind on this creek. The closest fuel and supplies are on Langford Creek, 3 to 4 miles away.

CORSICA RIVER

No facilities

Charts: 12272, 12273

Approaches. A little more than 12 miles up the Chester River from Love Point Light is the Corsica River entrance. A course of 113 degrees (magnetic) from red nun "16," off Nichols Point in the Chester River, takes you directly to nun "2" in the narrowest part of the approach to the Corsica. An alternative approach is to take your departure from the red/green "N" buoy marking the center of the approach to the Corsica and head directly toward nun "2." Favor the north shore as you pass nun "2" to avoid the 2-foot shoal to starboard. This shoal extends to, but not yet past nun "2." After you clear nun "2," the rest of the river is nearly 10 feet deep from a short distance off each shore, save for a 4-foot shoal extending a good 300 yards to the north about midway between Middle Quarter and Tilghman Coves.

In the mouth of the river, between Town Point and Holten Point, Pioneer Point Manor has been leased by the Russian Embassy for use as an R&R resort. I do not recommend landing on this point to explore.

We were sailing past Town Point a few years ago when we noticed a pompous man strutting down the beach accompanied by another man, quite evidently a bodyguard. Much to our surprise, they suddenly stopped, the first man peeled off *all* of his clothes, turned, and strutted into the water. In a few moments, it became obvious that he was ordering his companion to join him, which, with some obvious reluctance, he did. We soon sailed out of sight and never saw the conclusion of the episode. Even now, we never pass the mouth of the Corsica without training glasses on Town Point to see if any more Russians were engaging in that particular form of R&R.

Anchorages. Once within the entrance, it is feasible to anchor almost anywhere. However, the three best locations are probably in the bight between Town Point and Middle Quarter Cove, in the bight between Wash Point and Rocky Point, or in the mouth of Emory

Creek. All of these have good holding ground and are reasonably well protected from the usual storm directions. None is likely to be bothered by traffic or water-skiers and each has some kind of beach on which you can land without bothering any of the locals. These three areas offer plenty of room for both solitary cruisers and a sizable collection of assorted boats. The shores abound with wildlife and there are usually clams for the picking.

Above Emory Creek, numerous bends or bights in the river offer excellent anchorages. Simply pick a spot which minimizes the fetch along the river and you will find a good anchorage.

The last usable anchorage on the Corsica is in the vicinity of Jacobs Nose, a mile upstream from Emory Creek. Just pull to one side to get out of the main traffic pattern and anchor upstream of nun "6."

Although the river is navigable all the way to Centreville Landing at the headwaters, it is probably not worth going much farther upstream than Jacobs Nose as the river narrows and soon begins to shoal, except for a narrow channel.

There are no facilities readily accessible from the river except for the possible trip upstream to Centreville Landing and a 1-mile walk into Centreville. Centreville is home to the oldest surviving courthouse in Maryland (1792) and a museum. There is also a supermarket.

COMEGYS BIGHT

No facilities

Charts: 12272, 12273

Anchorages. About 2 miles upstream in the Chester River from the Corsica River entrance is Comegys Bight. This bay-like appendage to the river provides a fairly well-protected anchorage, except from the south to southwest where it is open to a several-mile–long stretch of the Chester. For this reason and the lack of any particular attraction, we have never remained there. There are far better anchorages nearby, such as in the Corsica River.

UPPER CHESTER RIVER TO CHESTERTOWN

Charts: 12272, 12273

Once you pass Comegys Bight, the river narrows and begins to resemble many of its tributaries. There are no proper anchorages, although you could anchor anywhere out of the mainstream of traffic in perfect security. There are several small creeks which look interesting, but stay out of them; all are shallow.

ISLAND CREEK

Charts: 12272, 12273

On a practical basis, the first place on this stretch of the river where a cruiser might consider stopping is Kennersley Pointe Marina on Island Creek, off Southeast Creek, about 7 miles above the mouth of the Corsica River. Until recently Island Creek was inaccessible to most boats and there was no reason to try it anyway. Now there is a pleasant little marina and a channel has been dredged to a depth of 8 feet for a width of 50 feet.

Approaches. Five private markers make the approach relatively easy, provided you pay attention. As you approach Southeast Creek, continue past most of its mouth to round nun "2," which is close inshore to Deep Point on the far side of the creek mouth. Give nun "2" a wide berth and favor the shore side until you clear the marker. Then hold close to the five private markers, leaving them to starboard and the small island to port. The marina will be directly ahead of you. There is not much room to anchor. Don't plan on it.

Dockages/Provisions. This is one of the increasingly rare family-run marinas on the Bay and it is quickly recognized as such by the relationship of the Navis family with the boaters there. Nine of the 50 slips normally are kept open for transients and can accommodate rather large boats. Reservations are recommended. In addition to marine services, with the exception of diesel fuel, the Navis family provides free transportation to church or Chestertown (11 miles away by road) in a 15-passenger van. This marina has a pool, a welcome item if the nettles are in (and they do sometimes come this far up the Chester). Both block and crushed ice are available.

ROLPH'S WHARF

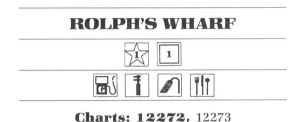

Charts: 12272, 12273

Approaches. The next potential stopping place is Rolph's Wharf Inn and Marina, about 1 mile beyond the mouth of Southeast Creek. Start looking for the marina to starboard within one-half mile after passing Southeast Creek.

Provisions. Only gasoline is available here, no diesel, and ice is a little scarce. During the summer, there is a pleasant little restaurant.

Dockages. Transients are welcome but, unless you prefer to rent a slip, it is not a good place to remain overnight. Aside from the fetch along the river, the slips are totally exposed to wakes from powerboat traffic on the river.

CHESTERTOWN

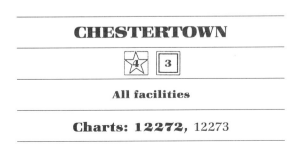

All facilities

Charts: 12272, 12273

Once past Rolph's Wharf, the next stop is Chestertown, on the west side of the river just before the Route 213 bridge. At Chestertown you will find a full set of marine facilities, although repairs are limited. If you can't find everything you need here, you aren't asking the right people!

Anchorages. Anchoring in the river near the Route 213 bridge can get "interesting" due to the 180-degree change in the current flow with the change of tide. A plow is the best anchor to use; a Danforth tends to break out as the current reverses. We were anchored here one Fourth of July to watch the fireworks and, although we had three other boats rafted to us, thanks to our 35-pound plow and all-chain rode we were one of the relatively few boats, in a rather large crowd, that did not drag when the current did its switch.

The Route 213 drawbridge has a vertical clearance of 12 feet at mean high tide. If you need to have the bridge raised, it will open on demand between 6:00 a.m. and 6:00 p.m. from April 1 to September 30. At all other times, you must give six hours notice. Instructions are posted on the bridge near the drawspan.

Although the river has at least 7 feet of water all the way to Crumpton, about 7 miles past Chestertown, and about 5 feet for a mile past Crumpton, the trip is probably not worth the effort. It is a pretty river with no special points of interest to see and no appealing anchorages.

History. Chestertown was established as the county seat in 1698 and was an important and busy port in colonial times. Washington College, founded in 1782, is also located here. While Annapolis has more surviving beautiful 18th century homes, Chestertown has a whole street of them, all together. Several homes on Water Street were built by shipping merchants during the 18th and 19th centuries.

Chestertown has a favorite historical tale, which any of the residents will be happy to recount in detail. It seems that the citizens of Chestertown held their own version of a "tea party" on May 23, 1774, when they boarded a ship just arrived from England, the brigantine *Geddes*, and dumped her cargo of tea into the water to protest the 1774 tea tax imposed by England on the colonies.

Each year, the town celebrates the anniversary of its "tea party" with parades and other activities on Memorial Day weekend. Festivities start on Friday evening with a cocktail party at the Wilmer Park Pavilion overlooking the Chester River. On Saturday, a parade begins at 10:30 a.m., with horsedrawn carriages, a fife and drum corps, and more. Around the area colonial craftsmen display their wares and talents—blacksmith, potters, broom makers, weavers, woodworkers, and others. There is also food a-plenty, featuring local and Eastern Shore delicacies, and music in the air. At 2:00 p.m., a crowd of shouting citizens, dressed in colonial garb, will race to the waterfront, row out to the "British ship" in the harbor, and, with some brawling, throw crates of "tea" overboard. The official closing of the event is 6:00 p.m.

Western

Shore

GUNPOWDER RIVER

Charts: 12272, 12273, **12274**

The entire region of the Gunpowder River, from Oliver Point to the Bay, lies within the Restricted Area belonging to Aberdeen Proving Grounds. The entire area is normally closed from Monday through Friday, 7:00 a.m. to 5:00 p.m., except on national holidays. The area is also closed at other times, which are announced over VHF-FM radio; patrol boats direct personnel out of the danger area during periods of active artillery range firing.

When the area is open, boats may navigate through it, fishing or crabbing is allowed, and water-skiing more than 200 meters offshore is permitted. At no time is swimming allowed nor may any person or boat touch the bottom, the shore, or a pier within the Restricted Area. (This regulation is undoubtably due to the probable presence of dud shells and explosives lying on the bottom.)

While there are launching ramps and small boat facilities above the fixed bridge (vertical clearance 12 feet), much more accessible launching and other facilities may be found elsewhere. There are no anchorages worthy of the name on this river.

For the above reasons, any detailed description of this area is omitted here. We recommend that all transient cruising boats avoid it.

SALTPETER AND

DUNDEE CREEKS

No facilities

Charts: 12272, 12273, **12274**

Saltpeter and Dundee Creeks share a common entrance, which is completely within the Aberdeen Restricted Area. Even without that problem, both creeks are fairly shallow, limiting access to boats of less than a 4-foot draft. Even shallow-draft vessels risk grounding

Western Shore, Seneca Creek to Patapsco River

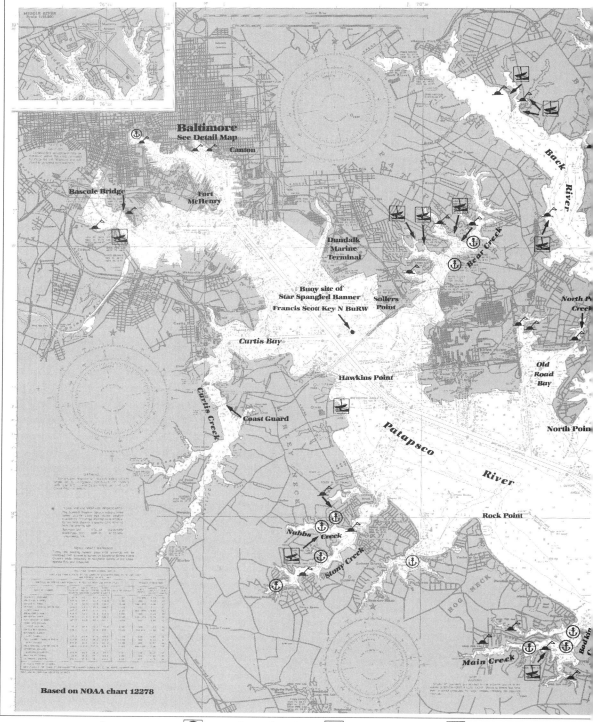

Baltimore
See Detail Map
Canton

Bascule Bridge

Fort
McHenry

Dundalk
Marine
Terminal

Back River

Bear Creek

Buoy site of
Star Spangled Banner
Francis Scott Key N BuRW

Sollers
Point

North P.
Creek

Curtis Bay

Hawkins Point

Old
Road
Bay

Curtis Creek

Coast Guard

Patapsco

River

North Poin

Nabbs Creek

Rock Point

Stony Creek

Main Creek

HOG NECK

Based on NOAA chart 12278

SCALE **1″=1.72** NAUT. MILES   ⚓ **Good anchoring**   **Mooring area**   **Launching site**

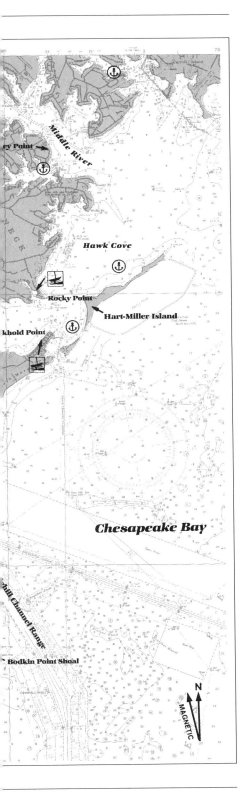

Middle River

cy Point →

Hawk Cove

Rocky Point

Hart-Miller Island

khold Point

Chesapeake Bay

ill Channel Range

Bodkin Point Shoal

N

MAGNETIC

---

on the unmarked shoals. This is normally runabout country only, and that by virtue of a launching ramp on the east side of Dundee Creek.

There are better anchorages nearby; skip this one.

SENECA
CREEK,
MIDDLE
RIVER,
AND
BACK
RIVER

123

SENECA CREEK, MIDDLE RIVER, AND BACK RIVER

Charts: 12273, 12278

This is a busy, built-up area of the Bay. You'll find plenty of provisions and places to eat, but little in the way of peace and quiet.

SENECA CREEK

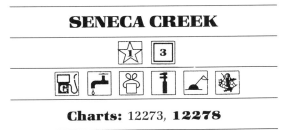

Charts: 12273, 12278

Approaches. Seneca Creek is located just above the mouth of Middle River and the entire eastern shore of this creek is within the Restricted Area described above.

Anchorages. A possible anchorage in 5 to 8 feet of water is just past the point where the creek turns to the west. Although there are three marinas on this creek, the creek is shallow, except for a narrow channel, and heavily built up, offering little to interest the transient cruiser. This is predominantly powerboat country—and even those belong to residents.

Hawthorn Cove, right at the mouth of Seneca Creek, looks much more appealing but lies entirely within the Restricted Area, as well as being totally open to the south.

More interesting creeks and far better anchorages exist nearby. Skip this one too.

SENECA
CREEK,
MIDDLE
RIVER,
AND
BACK
RIVER

124

MIDDLE RIVER

All facilities

Charts: 12273, **12278**

Approaches. This river is probably the most civilized tributary on the Bay. A cursory exploration reveals every inch of shoreline to be privately owned and built up. Although there are a number of navigable creeks splintering off of Middle River as you proceed upstream and numerous marinas all over the area, if you are looking for quiet and solitude in unspoiled surroundings, look elsewhere. There are marina facilities and restaurants on virtually all the little creeks off the main part of the river. Pay attention to your chart as there are a number of shoals, not all of which are well marked. In particular, stay well off Booby Point on the south side of the mouth of the river; an unmarked shoal there extends for a good third of a mile to the east from this point. (Is it possible that the frequency of inattentive mariners "surveying" this shoal is the source of the name of the point?)

If you are not looking for marina facilities, this river holds little of interest. Sue Creek, on the southwest shore near the mouth of the river, may be the exception. It is the location of the hospitable Baltimore Yacht Club, which has an attractive clubhouse situated on the top of the hill on Sue Island, at the mouth of the creek.

There are two unmarked shoals which you have to negotiate in order to enter Sue Creek. One extends to the east from Sue Island and the other to the southeast from Turkey Point on the other side of the creek entrance. The easiest way to find the entrance for the first time is to take your departure from the red "4" buoy just off Bowley Point (marked as Bowley Bar on some charts). From red "4," head directly for the green "1" flasher on a 14-foot–high piling at the entrance and you will neatly avoid both shoals. Hold close to the "1" marker and the docks to port as you enter the creek— there is a shoal on the starboard side that extends roughly to the middle of the entrance.

Dockages/Provisions. Don't go farther than the yacht club docks if you draw close to 6 feet as the water starts to get thin. Slips are usually available for

visiting yachtsmen from other recognized yacht clubs. Other than gas, diesel fuel, and a restaurant, there are no supplies available here or elsewhere on Sue Creek.

If you draw less than 5 feet, you can proceed well up the main branch of the creek, as far as the Red Eye Yacht Club, which is on the south side of the creek, nearly to the headwaters, near the last fork in the creek. The Red Eye claims to have transient slips available.

Anchorages. If you choose to anchor, the best location is probably under the lee of the high bank on the south shore, opposite Sue Island. The bottom is soft mud with good holding and the immediate vicinity is relatively unpopulated.

BACK RIVER

All facilities

Charts: 12273, **12278**

History. The mouth of Back River is guarded on the Bay side by Hart-Miller Island. Older charts show these islands as separate, but the gap between them no longer exists. In the early 1980s, Hart and Miller Islands were selected as the site where the spoil from the dredging of Baltimore Harbor would be dumped. For some time, this decision stirred up quite a controversy. As it turned out, the dumping created no problem and may have actually enhanced the islands. On the Bay side, a long bulkhead has been constructed to retain the spoil. This wall extends from the south end of Hart Island and curves around to the northern tip of Miller Island where it terminates.

Things to Do. Hawk Cove, on the Back River side of the islands, provides the primary point of interest to the boating population. The bulkheading company has deposited a huge amount of sand, which not only filled in the gap, but created a nice beach area, open to the boating public. The main part of the islands is marked "No Trespassing."

While the beach is a nice attraction during the warm summer months, don't plan to stay aboard your boat for any length of time while anchored in that region.

Back River entertains considerable powerboat traffic, which causes an unpleasant chop during most of the day. In addition there is a long fetch to the north and northwest; a wind from that direction can make this an uncomfortable anchorage. We don't recommend remaining overnight here unless you are sure that the wind will be out of the south or southeast (the prevailing direction during the summer).

Approaches. The primary approach to Back River is the same as for Middle River. Although there are plenty of navigation markers, all you have to do to enter Back River is to guide on Hart-Miller Island, staying off at least 100 yards. Once you reach the southwest corner of Hawk Cove, simply honor any markers you see. There is a dredged channel which passes between the mainland and the tiny island just south of Hart Island, providing a shortcut to Hawk Cove or the upper part of Back River from the main Bay. The entrance is easy to find from the Bay as a 105-foot high tower, which is the rear Craighill Channel Range Light, marks the east side of the channel entrance and can be seen from miles away. However, this channel is narrow, and shoaling to 2-feet has been reported, so it is best left to shoal-draft powerboats.

Provisions. There are numerous unmarked shoals in Back River, the shoreline is heavily populated, and there are no interesting creeks or tributaries to explore. The river has a number of marinas, if you are in need of supplies or repair, but little else to recommend it.

PATAPSCO RIVER

Charts: 12273, 12278, **12281**

The Patapsco River points like a finger into the heart of Baltimore, one of the world's largest ports. Located about 150 miles from Cape Henry and about 50 miles from the Chesapeake & Delaware Canal, the Port of Baltimore is even busier today than it was in the heyday of the clipper ships.

Just a few years ago, yachts cruising the Bay did not go beyond Rock Creek, near the mouth of the Patapsco, without some specific reason. But the times are changing—and changing rapidly. The harbor is cleaner and Baltimore has completely renovated the Inner Harbor area and is continuing the process toward Fells Point and other parts of the city.

The Patapsco has three distinctly different portions. Two—the outer portion from the Francis Scott Key Bridge to the Chesapeake Bay, and the Inner Harbor of Baltimore—offer harbors of interest to cruising boats. Between them, the remaining portion, consisting of the part of the river from the Key bridge to Ft. McHenry (with the possible exception of some of the upper portions of Curtis Creek), is lined with the shipping port facilities and shipyards which, while of direct interest only to commercial shipping, can be fascinating to observe as you cruise past. This is where boats gather to watch the fireworks from Fort McHenry on the Fourth of July.

The outer portion of the Patapsco River constitutes the real cruising ground of this river. This area is roughly bounded to the northwest by the Francis Scott Key Bridge, to the northeast by North Point, and to the southwest and south by Rock Point and Bodkin Creek.

Until the spring of 1989, Sevenfoot Knoll Lighthouse served as a convenient aiming point for an approach from the south or east. The squat, 42-foot high, red-painted, screwpile-type structure has been moved to Baltimore's Inner Harbor where it is part of the permanent maritime displays. Functioning in its stead is a much less obvious platform light. The easiest approach is to plot a course to take you a good mile to the north of Bodkin Point. Bodkin Point Shoal extends more than 3/4 mile to the east of the tip of Bodkin Point.

If you are approaching from the north, the front Craighill Channel Range light, a 39-foot–high cylindrical white concrete lighthouse, serves as your guide. You can leave this light to either side but be careful of the 4-foot shoal 1 mile to the east southeast of it.

Beware of the unmarked shoals which extend from North Point on the north side of the Patapsco River entrance and from Rock Point on the south side. Once clear of these shoals, you can choose to enter Old Road Bay, continue on up the Patapsco toward Baltimore, or approach either Rock Creek or Stony Creek.

Ahead of you, clearly visible from miles away, is the Francis Scott Key Bridge, spanning the Patapsco River between Hawkins and Sollers Points. With a vertical clearance of 195 feet, this bridge presents no obstacle to boating traffic (although a ship did manage to hit one of the bridge supports a few years ago).

Seeing Fort McHenry from the water is more thrilling after you have toured it on foot. These are the inner ramparts.

To the north of the shipping channel, just before the Francis Scott Key Bridge, is the abandoned Fort Carroll. Started in 1848 as a part of the defense structure for Baltimore, this was supposed to be a four-story, 40-foot–high fortress that would hold as many as 350 cannons. Robert E. Lee, then a lieutenant, was in charge of the construction. After three years of effort and the expenditure of more than $1 million (a much more impressive amount of money in those days), Congress refused to provide more funds and construction ceased. In 1854, a small lighthouse was erected on the unfinished fort. Today, Fort Carroll remains unfinished, unmanned, and inhospitable to visitors who would like to land. No Trespassing signs are posted, but visitors can tour around the structure by boat.

Past the Francis Scott Key Bridge, you can see Fort McHenry in the distance. A red, white, and blue buoy in the water past the bridge marks the spot where the ship upon which Francis Scott Key wrote "The Star Spangled Banner" was anchored during the bombardment of the fort in 1814. Seeing Fort McHenry from the water is still a bit of a thrill, especially if you have first toured the fort by land. Unfortunately, docking is neither permitted nor practical at the fort. In calm conditions, you might try anchoring southwest of the fort near the dis-

continued spoil area and land by dinghy. However, watch the depth carefully and be prepared to haul your dinghy out of the water over the riprap (big rocks) protecting the shoreline. Be very careful not to anchor in the pipeline area extending south across Middle Branch from the southern tip of the point on which the fort is located.

At Fort McHenry, the river forks. The right (north) fork leads to Baltimore's fascinating Inner Harbor. The left fork offers little, except a couple of marinas.

The variety of creeks branching off the Patapsco River provides a range of cruising grounds—some well worth the visit, others probably not worth the trip.

BODKIN CREEK

Charts: 12273, 12278, **12281**

Right at the mouth of the Patapsco River, on the southern shore, is Bodkin Creek. While neither as scenic nor as secluded as many of the rivers and creeks on the Eastern Shore, Bodkin Creek holds several attractions for those who enjoy being in and around the water as well as on it. There are no restaurants or supply facilities available within reasonable access of the water, although ice is available at Ventnor Marina on Ventnor Point (marked as Graveyard Point on most charts, but no one calls it that) just a little way up Main Creek. Haulouts and repairs are available at Ventnor Marina, Carback's Marina well up Main Creek, and Bodkin's Boat Yard on Back Creek. Germershausan's and Pinehurst Boat Yards on Locust Cove also offer repairs, predominantly for powerboats.

Approaches. Although narrow, the entrance to the creek is well marked and, with a little prudence, is not difficult to negotiate. If this is your first time entering this creek, enter slowly, under power. The entrance should be approached well north of Bodkin Point Shoal, marked by green spars "3" and "5." Use a current chart, as not only has the shoal shifted but the buoyage system and spar locations were changed in 1976 and another green daymark added in 1986. Leave the green "7" dolphin near the entrance close to port and head directly between the red "10" and green "9" daymarks. These daymarks are located at both the narrowest (about 50 feet wide) and shallowest part of the channel. If your draft is much over 5 feet, enter only at high water. A bar across the entrance just inside the "9" and "10" daymarks allows creek access only to vessels with a 6-foot draft or less. Head from the daymarks to leave the green "11" dolphin on Cedar Point (opposite Old Landon Point) close to port. Once beyond this marker, the creek maintains a fairly constant 8- to 10-foot depth all the way to the headwaters. Don't try to cut inside the red "12" daymark off Spit Point (between Main Creek and Back Creek); you won't make it.

Anchorages. There are two excellent anchorages off sandy beaches on the main creek. The first, and most heavily used, is just inside Cedar Point off Bodkin Neck where you can anchor in 8 to 10 feet of water to within 50 yards or less from the shore. Beware of submerged logs in the extreme northeast corner of the anchorage. Almost all of the visible portion of Bodkin Neck is undeveloped and its sandy stretches are open to exploring, beachcombing, or just lying on the sand

basking in the sun. There is no telling how much longer this situation will last, however. Efforts are under way to build condominiums and a marina here, although the builders have encountered considerable resistance. The beach slopes gently into the water with the depth dropping more and more sharply as you move northwest along the beach until, close to the channel, it drops suddenly to an 8-foot depth less than 10 feet offshore. Normally, sea nettles are no problem; if they invade, simply move upstream.

The second anchorage is about a mile upstream on the southern side of Main Creek between Jubb Cove and Goose Cove. Although smaller than the first anchorage and without much of a beach, we prefer this spot over the other—water-skiers are much less of a nuisance; it is quieter, less frequented by other boats; and we rarely ever see a sea nettle. The short beach used to end in a 15-foot cliff. Until the mid 80s, the top of the cliff was uninhabited and thickly wooded. Now the whole area is rapidly being developed and the top of the cliff is thick with houses. There is no longer a place to land here.

To the south of Spit Point is a third attractive anchorage, in the little cove to the north of Old Bee Point. While it is well protected from weather, as is the entire creek, there is no place to land and you are still exposed to powerboat and water-skier wakes.

The other two branches of Bodkin Creek, Back Creek and Wharf and Locust Creeks, are both packed solid with homes; they have little to see and no place to land.

OLD ROAD BAY

Charts: 12273, 12278, **12281**

Approaches. Old Road Bay is located on the north side of the entrance to the Patapsco River, just past North Point. While there is a relatively narrow, well-marked channel leading from the main part of the Patapsco into Old Road Bay, this channel is intended for deep-draft ships. Cruising boats can ignore it for all practical purposes. In fact, if you hold a course to leave the red "2" daymark west of North Point well to starboard, you can enter with no problem.

Dockages. The west fork, Jones Creek, has about four marinas on it but should be left strictly to shoal-draft vessels. The surroundings are heavily industrial.

Provisions. The east fork, North Point Creek, has several marinas and a narrow channel that carries at least 7 feet up to the headwaters. This branch is not as industrial but, other than to put in for fuel (gas only) or some supplies, you should look elsewhere for an overnight stay.

ROCK CREEK

All facilities

Charts: 12273, 12278, **12281**

Approaches. Past Rock Point on the south side of the Patapsco River, approximately 4 miles upriver from Sevenfoot Knoll Light, Rock Creek is an excellent refuge in rough weather and probably the most convenient stopover enroute to and from Baltimore's Inner Harbor. Stay well off Rock Point as there is a shoal extending for more than one-half mile to the north.

The mouth of the creek is easily identified by the White Rocks, a large rock formation located about one-half mile northwest of Rock Point. A friend of ours claims that the seagulls maintain the whiteness of these wonders of the Bay, the only known rocks of this size in the entire Chesapeake. With 12 feet or more of water all the way to most of the marinas, the wide, well-marked channel extends straight into the creek, due southwest of the White Rocks.

Dockages/Provisions. All six marinas here offer fuel and ice. Most have repair facilities and a marine railway or travelift. White Rocks Marina and the Cross Current Inn each have a bar and a restaurant. For those with a membership in a recognized yacht club, bar and restaurant service is also available at the Maryland Yacht Club, immediately to port as you clear the

green "3" light off Fairview Point.

Transient slips are usually available at the marina, and there are well-protected anchorages in the mouth of Tar Cove and Wall Cove. No anchoring is permitted upstream of Water Oak Point due to a state water purification system. Bubbles welling to the surface and a series of warning buoys mark the no anchoring area. Marinas and residences take up the shore, leaving no place to land. However, the wooded banks help create a mood of privacy.

STONY CREEK

Charts: 12273, 12278, **12281**

Approaches. On the south side of the Patapsco River, about a mile to the west of the White Rocks, is the entrance to Stony Creek. Be sure to start your entrance from nun "2," about one-half mile northeast of the reddish brown rocks that guard the entrance to the creek. From nun "2," a heading of 240 degrees takes you to the red "4" lighted marker on a piling. (This flashing 4-second red "4" is nearly on shore and hard to make out on the chart.) Maintain this course until you have passed the reddish-brown rocks to port and are quite close to red "4." (You may have the feeling that you are going to hit the shore.) When the lighted flashing 4-second green "5" is abeam, swing to port to pass midway between green "5" and red "6." The channel is narrow here, so be sure to stay in the middle. As soon as you pass red "6," swing to starboard toward nun "8." Once past nun "8," you are in and the creek opens up with deep water from shore to shore. From here on, you have about 15 feet of water.

The next obstacle you encounter is the drawbridge (vertical clearance 18 feet MHW), about one-half mile from the entrance. This bridge is manned 24 hours a day and opens on demand except for two hours (7:00 to 9:00 a.m.) in the morning and two hours (4:00 to 6:00 p.m.) in the evening, during weekday rush hours. Blow one long and one short blast on your horn to request that the bridge be raised. For emergency passage, you can call the bridge tender on Channel 13, VHF-FM.

Anchorages. Anchor anywhere past nun "8." Although the area is well settled, the creek is quiet, peaceful, and fully protected from the weather. A 6mph speed limit, instituted in 1990, makes the entire creek beyond the bridge a no-wake zone. Water-skiers can use the area from the Patapsco River creek entrance to the bridge. Nabbs Creek, well up Stony Creek, and Back Cove off Nabbs Creek also offer protected, quiet anchorages. All have depths over 10 feet.

Provisions. Gas (no diesel) is available at Greenland Beach Yacht Basin, to starboard just past the bridge and at Greenhaven Marina on the south side, well up Stony Creek.

normal vertical clearances of 25 and 8 feet MHW respectively.

Passing a fifth bridge (a drawbridge with a vertical clearance of 12 feet MHW closed) will take you to the Bear Creek headwaters, which carry 8 to 9 feet of water almost to the end. However, the shore is built up and we see no good reason to go there—not even to anchor for the night.

There is one relatively secluded area where you can anchor, to starboard just after you negotiate the fourth bridge. The shore is wooded and a sandy beach stretches for about 100 yards. During our last visit, there was a wreck of a 30-foot powerboat well up on the beach. It will probably stay there until it disintegrates. We used to recommend Lynch Cove, to port after the fourth bridge, as an anchorage, but now the shore is completely built up. Anchor Bay East Marina to port in the mouth of Lynch Cove and Lynch Cove Marina near the headwaters both have gasoline.

BEAR CREEK

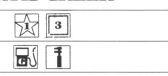

Charts: 12273, 12278, **12281**

Approaches. The entrance to Bear Creek is on the north side of the Patapsco River, just before the Francis Scott Key Bridge. In spite of the number of marinas and boatyards on the creek, several of which hope to attract transients as well as residents, there is little here to entice the transient cruiser. The area is simply too commercial and built up. In addition, the water is usually discolored by pollution from the local industries; never swim here.

Anchorages. The only anchorages which could even be considered are after you negotiate four bridges. The first bridge (actually an extension of the Key Bridge) is a fixed bridge with 53 feet of clearance MHW. The second bridge, once a drawbridge, has been discontinued and its span has been removed. The third and fourth are a drawbridge and a swing bridge, with

CURTIS CREEK

Charts: 12273, 12278, **12281**

Approaches. On the south side of the Patapsco River, about 1½ miles past the Francis Scott Key Bridge, is the entrance to Curtis Bay and Curtis Creek. One of the largest U.S. Coast Guard bases on the East Coast is located just past Stedds Point near the entrance to this creek. This is a shipbuilding and buoy maintenance facility, which is capable of constructing both steel and fiberglass Coast Guard vessels. The base is normally closed to the public; group tours can be arranged for the weekends. The base is open to the public on Armed Forces Day, when they give demonstrations of Coast Guard activities.

Facilities. Hull repairs are available at Smith & Sons Shipyard on the east side of the creek before you reach the Coast Guard station. Gas (no diesel) is available at the Launching Pad Marina in Marley Creek, near the headwaters of Curtis Creek.

Anchorages. The first half of Curtis Creek is heavily commercial; the water is dirty and the area could hardly be called scenic. However, if you pursue your course upstream past the industrial area, the upper reaches of the creek offer a couple of nice anchorages in Marley Creek or Furnace Creek. Swimming is definitely not recommended as the water quality is questionable. The region does offer an alternative to anchoring in Baltimore harbor or traveling several more miles to another creek.

BALTIMORE

All facilities

Charts: 12273, 12278, **12281**

Approaches. As you approach Fort McHenry, the Patapsco River forks. Although there are a couple of small marinas located in the Middle Branch to port past the swing bridge, most of the left fork is highly industrialized and of little interest. The right fork leads to the Inner Harbor of Baltimore, a trip worth taking.

On the Fourth of July each year, a huge fleet of boats descends on the Inner Harbor area and its outer reaches to watch the extensive fireworks display put on by the city. Somehow, the idea of watching fireworks in the vicinity of Fort McHenry, the birthplace of our national anthem, on Independence Day provides an extra thrill found in few other places in the country.

Anchoring anywhere in the region between the Francis Scott Key Bridge and Fort McHenry is not normally recommended because of the shipping traffic. Each year, more than 4,000 ships (about 11 per day) enter Baltimore Harbor. There are hundreds of business organizations in the area associated with the shipping industry in one manner or another. Except for companies that provide a direct service to the private boating population, most people are only vaguely aware of the surging and varied activities associated with each ship entering the harbor. All most of us see are the piers, factories, and ships as we cruise by, especially the huge Dundalk Marine Terminal to starboard past the bridge. Enough cargo passes through these terminals to make Baltimore the third largest seaport in the U.S., just behind New York City and Norfolk.

Baltimore's Inner Harbor with the prominent World Trade Center as seen from the south side of the harbor.

Leave Fort McHenry to port and proceed up the north (right) fork, labeled Northwest Harbor on the chart. Just past the fort, the Canton Marine Terminal lies to starboard. This is the largest privately owned marine terminal on the East Coast and one of the oldest, founded in 1829. The name stems from the estate of John O'Donnel, a captain in the East India merchant service and a colonel in the Maryland Militia, who settled in Baltimore in 1780. He named his waterfront estate after Canton, his favorite Chinese port. Nearly 50 years later, his son formed the Canton Company, which eventually became today's terminal.

Things to Do. As you proceed upstream, a cluster of marinas at Fells Point will be to starboard. Baltimore's original shipbuilding and maritime center, the Fells Point area is alive with the port's commercial activities and the market there is well worth a visit. Cobblestone streets lead to an assortment of shops, pubs, restaurants and the Fells Point Fishmarket. Over 350 of the original residences in this area still remain, many of them restored to their former elegance under Baltimore's downtown renewal project. All but one are still private residences. The "one" has been converted into an inn, right on the waterfront at the end of Broadway. Brown's Wharf, a set of renovated brick warehouses, houses a collection of specialty shops.

There is some public dockage just past the tip of Fells Point itself, at the end of Ann Street, to the east of the large red brick Recreation Building on (what else) the Recreation Pier. If you are lucky or plan far enough ahead, you can tie up for a few hours to visit Fells Point or, possibly, remain overnight. Call ahead to the Fells Point harbormaster's office (396-4507) between 8:30 a.m. and 4:30 p.m. Monday through Friday, especially if you have any desire to spend the night there. If you just show up and take your chances, be sure to check in with the dockmaster promptly. The harbormaster's office is in the city hall, at Holiday and Fayette streets, a couple of miles away. As of this writing, there is no charge for tying up, but others may be scheduled for the dockspace. If one of those happens to be a cruise ship, such as the *Port Welcome*, you won't want to argue with her. If you decide to put in on the spur of the moment, especially on a weekend, give it a try. However, for the reasons just cited, it is a better idea to plan ahead and contact the office beforehand.

As you pass Fells Point and the huge landmark sign of the Domino Sugar Company (reputed to be the largest neon sign in the world), you are entering Baltimore's Inner Harbor. Space does not permit anything close to a full description of the Inner Harbor. There are so many activities and things to see and do that it would take a full book to describe them all. Revitalization of the downtown Baltimore area began in 1959 and the Inner Harbor, in particular, now bears no resemblance to its previous, less than attractive appearance.

To starboard is the huge, tent-like structure of the Pier 6 Concert Pavilion, a summertime concert hall with programs ranging from jazz to performances of the Baltimore Symphony Orchestra.

Pier 5 contains the Clarion Hotel, Harrison's Restaurant and the Lady Maryland Foundation.

Pier 4 is the Baltimore Maritime Museum, with its collection of ships and the old Sevenfoot Knoll Lighthouse that used to stand off Bodkin Point in the mouth of the Patapsco River. This is also the location of the "Six Flags Power Plant." Once it supplied electric power to the city's streetcars. For a while, it held four nightclubs called P. T. Flagg's. Now it stands empty.

Pier 3 holds the fabulous National Aquarium, which contains more than 5,000 specimens of marine creatures in natural environments, as well as the largest coral reef exhibit in the continental U.S. It even has a large room in which a tropical rainforest is recreated. The submarine USS *Torsk* and the Lightship *Chesapeake* are tied to the west side of the aquarium pier. (Note: The ships' locations are subject to change.) There is space for private boats to tie up along the east side of the pier and a little space near the submarine on the west side.

Just past the aquarium, the 30-story, pentagonal tower of the World Trade Center dominates the skyline. The top floor of the building, ostentatiously called the "Top of the World," is open to the public (Monday through Saturday, 10:00 a.m. to 5:00 p.m.; Sunday, 12:00 to 5:00 p.m.) and sponsors various art exhibits, including oil paintings and marine photography. The five-sided panoramic view of Baltimore and the Patapsco River from the top of this building is spectacular. There is an admission fee.

Next is the U.S. Frigate *Constellation*. (Visiting hours: May 15 through October 15, 10:00 a.m. to 5:45 p.m.; October 16 through May 14, Monday through Saturday 10:00 a.m. to 3:45 p.m., Sunday 10:00 a.m. to 4:45 p.m.) This is a working restoration of the first of six frigates designed and built for the fledgling U.S. Navy. She is, arguably, the oldest American warship

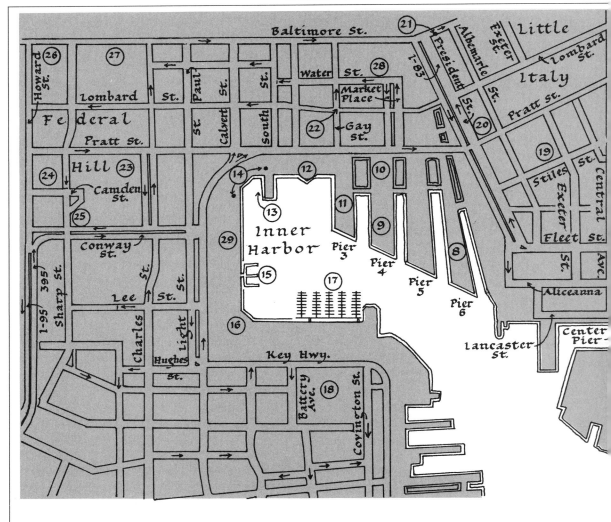

KEY

FELLS PT.
1. Licorice Factory Marina
2. The Anchorage Marina
3. Bay View Marina
4. Thomas Point Marina
5. Recreation Pier
6. Public Dockage
7. Fells Pt. Fishmarket

SCALE 1"=663 FEET

BALTIMORE INNER HARBOR / FEDERAL HILL

⑧ Pier 6 Concert Pavilion
⑨ Baltimore Maritime Museum
⑩ Six Flags Power Plant (Closed)
⑪ National Aquarium
⑫ World Trade Center
⑬ U.S. Frigate CONSTELLATION
⑭ Harborplace
⑮ City Piers
⑯ Maryland Science Center
⑰ Inner Harbor Marina

⑱ Federal Hill Park
⑲ Little Italy
⑳ Star Spangled Banner House
㉑ Shot Tower
㉒ "Corned Beef Row"
㉓ Convention Center
㉔ Festival Hall
㉕ Old Otterbein United Methodist Church
㉖ Baltimore Arena
㉗ Morris Mechanic Theatre
㉘ ㉙ Information

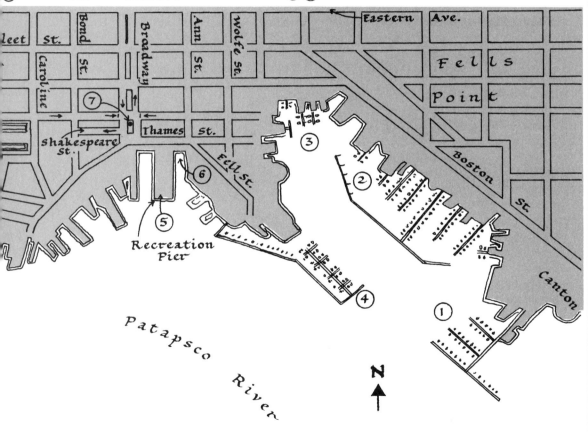

Note: Arrows indicate flow of traffic on one-way streets.

continuously afloat and in commission since 1797, which is when she was launched from Fells Point. Visitors can examine this ship both above and below deck, pondering on the days of "wooden ships and iron men."

In the northwest corner of the Inner Harbor is Harborplace. Each of the two buildings is not really one place, but many. The two-story glass and metal pavilions contain: markets for produce, fish, meat, and dairy foods; a trading hall featuring other food items; an indoor park where a variety of international foods is served over-the-counter; a bazaar for crafts and gift items; and (at last count) 12 traditional and contemporary cafes and restaurants. The two buildings are of similar construction on the outside, but inside they are quite different. The one to the left (from the water) is almost completely food oriented, the one to the right is retail oriented.

If you can find space, you can tie up along the seawall, right off the west pavilion of Harborplace. To the south of Harborplace are the public piers where you can get a slip, if you are lucky. There are no reservations, it's first come, first served. See the harbormaster as soon as you get in; the office is just south of the Harborplace food pavilion. There is a fee both for berthing in slips and for tying to the seawall. This fee has been increasing each year. Both choices are very public. People will be wandering by above you at all hours of the day or night. You can anchor out in the harbor (depth greater than 30 feet), but that too has a fee, and a paddleboat flotilla runs around the harbor constantly, reducing that option's appeal.

In the southwest corner of the Inner Harbor is the Maryland Science Center. The hours are Tuesday through Thursday, 10:00 a.m. to 5:00 p.m.; Friday through Saturday, 10:00 a.m. to 10:00 p.m.; Sunday, 12:00 to 6:00 p.m.; closed Monday. The unusually shaped building houses a variety of technical exhibits and displays, as well as a planetarium. The center encourages visitors to see, touch, and use many of its exhibits of the Chesapeake Bay, Baltimore, and general science. Be sure to pay it a visit.

When she is in port, the *Pride of Baltimore II*, a replica of a Baltimore clipper, is berthed in front of the science center. (See the accompanying sidebar for the tale of the loss of the *Pride of Baltimore I*, and the construction of the *Pride II*.)

Dockages/Provisions/Facilities.

On the south shore of the Inner Harbor, directly oppo-

The Prides of Baltimore

In the latter part of the 18th century, American shipbuilders recognized and responded to the need for fast and maneuverable ships as a means of countering the British command of the high seas, especially during the Revolutionary War. Chesapeake Bay shipbuilders were the first to respond to this need, creating the Baltimore Clipper. These small, swift, and sleek vessels were some of the fastest ships of their day. In addition to running blockades, many of them were armed during the War of 1812 and contributed to the capture or sinking of roughly 1,700 British merchant ships. In fact, it was their success which led the British to attack Baltimore in 1814, to destroy the shipyards where the clippers were constructed.

Even after commercial needs outgrew the capacity of these relatively small ships, they remained a model for later ship designs which ultimately led to the design and construction of the giant "Yankee Clippers" which helped to make America a world maritime power. The yacht, *America*, which won the prize (later to be called the America's Cup) in a regatta held at the British World's Fair of 1851, was also based on the design of the Baltimore Clippers.

Her name was the affectionate title given to another Baltimore Clipper, the *Chasseur*, which operated out of Baltimore during the War of 1812. The *Chasseur* and her captain, Thomas Boyle, are considered the apotheosis of privateering. They became world renowned for harassing shipping along the English seacoast and singlehandedly blockading the coast of England. Upon their return home the *Niles Register* described *Chasseur* as "the most beautiful vessel that ever floated on the ocean; those who have not seen our schooner have but little idea of her appearance. As you look at her, you may easily figure yourself the idea that she is about to rise out of the water and fly in the air, seeming so light to sit upon it." Crowds in the city hailed her as the "Pride of Baltimore."

In 1977, a replica of one of the Baltimore Clippers, the *Pride of Baltimore*, was launched and set sail from the Inner Harbor of Baltimore to serve as a goodwill ambassador for the state of Maryland and, of course, the United States. For nine years, she sailed the world, visiting more than 125 ports and accepting visits aboard from more than a million people from all walks of life.

Then, on 14 May 1986, disaster struck. With almost no warning, a violent Atlantic storm struck the *Pride,* knocking her down. Her movable ballast (true to the original design) shifted and she was unable to recover. The storm passed almost as quickly as it had come but the *Pride,* along with her captain and three of her crew, was gone.

In the days that followed, the crowd at the Inner Harbor never seemed so subdued as they passed what had been the berth of the *Pride,* now empty save for a solitary wreath with a card that read, "For the *Pride of Baltimore* and her gallant crew," signed, "The Arundel Yacht Club." There is a special sadness that we feel at the loss of a ship, especially one as unique as the *Pride.*

As tragic as the loss of the original *Pride* may have been, it served as a catalyst to begin the construction of a new clipper ship, the *Pride of Baltimore II.* The tradition would continue.

A nonprofit corporation was formed in October of 1986, donations were solicited, and a new ship, *Pride II,* was designed and constructed. The official launching ceremony took place on April 30, 1988 in Baltimore's Inner Harbor, accompanied by a huge crowd, a substantial fleet of private boats, and much celebration. Baltimore, Maryland, and the United States again

had a majestic goodwill ambassador to the world.

The *Pride of Baltimore II* is owned by the State of Maryland as represented by the Department of Transportation acting by and through the Maryland Port Administration. She is operated by Pride of Baltimore, Inc., a private, non-profit organization made up of business leaders. (Donations are still needed to support and maintain the *Pride II.* Tax deductible contributions can be sent to: Pride of Baltimore, Inc., 100 Light Street, Baltimore, MD 21202.)

site the National Aquarium, is the Inner Harbor Marina, probably the best place for a cruiser to tie up while visiting Baltimore. There are more than 150 slips arranged along floating piers with water and electricity at each. Showers and restrooms are close ashore; gas and diesel fuel is available, as is a fair-sized marine store. There is even a small convenience store nearby. Transients are welcome, but prior arrangement for a slip is a must. This marina is so popular that slips are booked well in advance. Here you can leave your boat in perfect security. The docks are closed off by a fence and the area is patrolled constantly. Only those with boats there, and their guests, are allowed on the dock. The marina also has an agent for both dinner and theater reservations, as well as the ability to provide information on Baltimore events and activities.

More Things to Do. Behind the marina is a field where, nearly every summer weekend, the city holds one of its ethnic festivals, each representing one or more of the diverse Baltimore neighborhoods. Numerous public holiday activities are held here too.

Dominating this field is the rectangular-shaped knoll of Federal Hill. Once used as a lookout point for ships approaching the harbor, it is now a public park and still provides a magnificent view of the harbor and its approaches.

You can easily discover more of Baltimore by walking a few blocks in nearly any direction from the Inner Harbor.

To the east, just beyond Pier 6, is the well-known neighborhood of "Little Italy" with its collection of excellent Italian restaurants.

Just north of Little Italy is the "Star-Spangled Ban-

The maiden voyage of the
Pride of Baltimore II. GREG PEASE

ner House," once the home of Mary Pickersgill, the woman who made the huge flag that flew over Fort McHenry during the British bombardment and inspired Francis Scott Key to pen his poem, "The Star-Spangled Banner." The house is now a museum, which, in its garden, features a map of the U.S.A. with each state constructed from its native stone. It's open Monday through Saturday, 10:00 a.m. to 3:30 p.m.

Within another block is Carroll Mansion, home of the longest-lived singer of the Declaration of Independence, Charles Carroll.

Another block to the north, easily visible from quite a distance, is the 234-foot high, redbrick Shot Tower. Built in 1828, the tower was used to produce shot of various sizes for guns from shotguns to cannon. Molten lead was poured through a sieve, with appropriate sized holes, at the top of the tower. As they fell, the droplets formed round balls which were quenched into that shape in vats of cold water at the bottom of the tower. While the tower is no longer in actual use, a sound and light show recreates the process for visitors. It is open Tuesday through Saturday, 10:00 a.m. to 4:00 p.m.; Sunday, 12:00 to 4:00 p.m. There is no admission fee.

A little to the west of the tower are two blocks of East Lombard Street, known as "Corned Beef Row," home of the best kosher delicatessens in the city.

Just north of the Inner Harbor, within a couple of blocks, are the Convention Center and the Civic Center, where circuses, sporting events, exhibits, and assorted other activities are held.

About six blocks north, near the junction of Eutaw and Lexington Streets, is the Lexington Market, two square blocks of assorted foods, both raw and prepared. Just short of the market is the Old Europe, a German deli with some of the best sausage you'll find anywhere, as well as enough other German items to make you feel as if you have walked into old Germany!

A few more blocks to the west, at 203 Amity Street, is the home of Edgar Allen Poe. In fact, Poe is buried in Westminster Churchyard nearby, on Fayette and Green Streets.

Beyond easy walking distance of the harbor are many more points of interest, all accessible by bus, subway, or taxi as well. There are museums, the Baltimore Zoo, seven theater/concert halls (not counting university and assorted amateur performance centers), baseball (Orioles), soccer (the Blast), ice hockey (Skipjacks), and Pimlico Race Track, where the Preakness (the mid-

dle leg in the Triple Crown) is run on the third Saturday in May.

There are probably more than 25 restaurants in easy walking distance from the Inner Harbor, as well as theaters, stores, and many other points of interest. More projects for the area are on the drawing board now and even more are promised in the future. Baltimore has revitalized and changed its character for the better.

(For more information than you can ever hope to use, contact the Baltimore Office of Promotion and Tourism, 110 West Baltimore Street, Baltimore, MD 21202; (301)837-4636.)

MAGOTHY RIVER

Charts: 12273, 12278

The mouth of the Magothy River is located at the southern tip of Gibson Island. If you are in doubt, look for the 52-foot–high white column of Baltimore Light positioned a little over 1½ miles to the east of the entrance. Although traffic tends to be heavy through this relatively narrow entrance, it is well marked and nearly everyone seems to have sense enough to keep to their right as they pass through it. The bar extending to the

Baltimore Light, a cassion-style
lighthouse, is about 1½ miles to the east
of the entrance to the Magothy River.

Magothy River

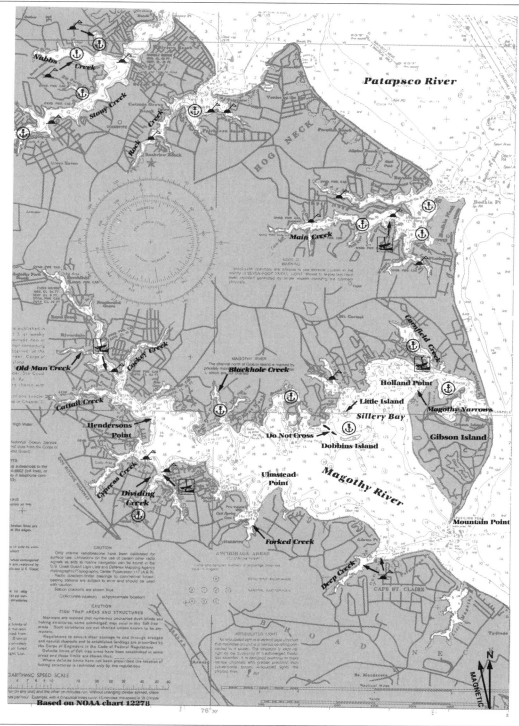

Patapsco River

Nabbs Creek

Stony Creek

Rock Creek

HOG NECK

Main Creek

Old Man Creek

Cockey Creek

Blackhole Creek

MAGOTHY RIVER

Cornfield Creek

Holland Point

Little Island

Sillery Bay

Magothy Narrows

Gibson Island

Cattail Creek

Hendersons Point

Do Not Cross

Dobbins Island

Cypress Creek

Dividing Creek

Ulmstead Point

Magothy River

Mountain Point

Forked Creek

Deep Creek

CAPE ST. CLAIRE

B R O A D N E C K

Based on NOAA chart 12278

76° 30′

SCALE **1″=1.24** NAUT. MILES   ⚓ **Good anchoring**   **Mooring area**   **Launching site**

south from Gibson Island does not extend all the way to the markers and it drops off sharply from the point where it is no longer clearly visible under the water.

Once you are clear of the entrance, the river opens out, providing a broad sweep where sailboat races with fairly large boats are frequently held. From here, you can choose from among a considerable number of creeks or coves in which to anchor and explore.

DEEP CREEK

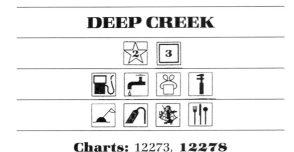

Charts: 12273, 12278

Approaches. On the south shore of the Magothy River, Deep Creek is the first creek to port as you enter the river. There is no good, attractive anchorage here and we do not recommend spending the night, except in a slip.

Provisions. The two marinas located here are the only source for gasoline for some distance. Fairwinds Marina is on the south shore, just before the lighted "3" marker, and Deep Creek Marina (formerly Capt. Clydes Marina) is on the opposite shore a little farther into the creek. Deep Creek Marina also has a small package store and a restaurant and bar, but space to tie up alongside is rather limited and boats with drafts of 5 feet or more should not try it. The restaurant features seafood and friendly, efficient service. Both bar and restaurant are well patronized by locals, always a good sign. Incidentally, there is good lighting at the fuel dock so that approaching after dark is easy.

Deep Creek occasionally serves as a temporary port for some of the skipjacks during their winter dredging for oysters. There is some debate as to whether this is because the marina and restaurant stay open throughout the winter or vice versa.

GIBSON ISLAND

Charts: 12273, 12278

Gibson Island is the large island to starboard as you enter the Magothy. This island is unique to the Bay in that it is a totally private island, connected to the mainland by a narrow causeway blocked by a guardhouse on the mainland side. Only members of the Gibson Island Club and their guests are permitted on the island.

Moorings. Members of recognized yacht clubs who arrive by boat at the Gibson Island Yacht Yard on the north side of the island, adjacent to the causeway, will be welcomed. However, the club has only a few guest moorings and arrangements for their use should be made in advance with the commodore or a member of the squadron. During the main boating season, there is a club launch, which provides water taxi service to the club boathouse. The clubhouse is on the Bay side of the island, about a half-mile walk from the boathouse.

Approaches. As you clear the end of the sandspit off the southern tip of the island, swing to starboard and head for the gap between Dobbins Island and Gibson Island. Stay at least 300 yards off Gibson Island to avoid all shoals. Continue paralleling the shore into Magothy Narrows (west of Holland Point). Be sure to leave the lighted green "3" to port and the lighted red "4" to starboard. There is 10 feet of water all the way into the yacht basin.

Anchorages/Provisions. Directly opposite Holland Point is Cornfield Creek, on the mainland. Fuel (gas and diesel) is available here at Weder's Marina. Don't look for any other supplies in the immediate area—there aren't any. You can anchor here in full security, but the next anchorage is a bit more attractive.

As you pass Holland Point, Eagle Cove opens to starboard. You won't find the name on any chart that we know of, but that is what locals call this cove. Favor the Purdy Point side as you enter and anchor closer to Purdy Point than Holland Point to avoid the shoal in the west side of the cove. This is a well-protected an-chorage which appears to be uninhabited. A small sandy beach is backed by a marsh and woods. None of the houses on Gibson Island are visible from here.

Dockages. If you proceed past Eagle Cove, as soon as you pass Purdy Point, the Gibson Island Yacht Yard Basin described earlier opens up to starboard. Here is a completely landlocked harbor where you are able to watch ships and small boats passing on the Bay while completely protected by the causeway to the is-land. Space is limited here.

DOBBINS ISLAND

No facilities

Charts: 12273, **12278**

Approaches. To the west of the center of Gib-son Island, approximately 2 miles from the mouth of the Magothy River, lies Dobbins Island, usually called Dutch Ship Island by the locals. The narrow, one-quarter–mile long, wooded island has sheer cliffs rising in excess of 20 feet above the water; it is clearly visible as you finish negotiating the entrance channel to the Ma-gothy River from Chesapeake Bay.

Be sure to honor the green "1" lighted marker at the edge of the shoal extending from the eastern end of Dobbins Island. After rounding this marker, give the shoal a reasonably wide berth and head for the sandy beach extending from the western tip of the island.

Anchorages. This will take you directly to the prime anchorage north of the island. The preferred area to drop the hook is close off the northwest corner of the island where a sandy spit extends into a narrow finger of a shoal stretching to the mainland. At low tide, more than one-third of this shoal is above water and it is possible to wade from the island to the mainland with-out getting into water deeper than your hips. Do not at-tempt to enter the anchorage from the west.

The island is virtually unapproachable from the south due to a skirt of very shallow (1 foot or less) shoals leading to sheer, red clay cliffs rising from a minuscule

beach. The northern side of the island has deep water (8 to 12 feet) ranging from 20 yards offshore in the cen-tral northern portion to as close as 10 feet offshore in the extreme northwestern portion of the island. The an-chorage itself is protected from weather on all sides ex-cept the northeast, where it is open to Sillery Bay for a maximum reach of about 1½ miles. Although the chart indicates a soft bottom, oyster shells littering the sticky clay bottom in the western part of the anchorage make it difficult to properly set a lightweight anchor, such as a Danforth. Once the anchor is set, holding appears to be good and there is plenty of room for several dozen boats to swing.

One-half mile due north of Dobbins Island is Little Island on which there is a solitary house nestled deep in the trees. Under no circumstances anchor to the west of Little Island as the utility cables for the island run across the bottom to the mainland here. Circumnaviga-tion of Little Island is quite easy but please note that the island is very firmly *private*.

Things to Do. Dobbins Island, although pri-vately owned, is uninhabited and the owners appar-ently do not object to people from boats landing on the island. Every day during the summer, especially on weekends, numerous people take advantage of this gen-erosity. However, there are signs requesting that you take all trash with you, a warning which, if ignored, could cause the island to be closed to the public.

In the northwest corner, the island has a very nice, sandy beach, which stretches from the narrow finger of a shoal, mentioned earlier, to a steep slope leading to the pleasantly wooded upper crest of the island. The view from the crest is a panorama of the lower Magothy River with a vista extending to the Chesapeake Bay Bridges 7 miles away. Tall trees cover the entire island while the undergrowth, ranging from light to dense, is crisscrossed with trails providing shaded avenues for ex-ploring.

During the peak boating season, this anchorage usually contains a considerable number of boats and, on weekends in particular, is very popular with water-skiers. By all means avoid this anchorage over the Fourth of July weekend, which is a mob scene. Prior to Memorial Day and after Labor Day, the island and the anchorage are relatively deserted.

The closest facility for gas, ice, and soft drinks in the vicinity of Dobbins Island is Grays Creek Marine Rail-way, which is just inside the right fork of Grays Creek.

GRAYS CREEK

Charts: 12273, **12278**

Approaches. The entrance to Grays Creek is one of the rare exceptions where it is much deeper and easier to negotiate than you would expect from all the indications on nautical charts. Although it is quite narrow, the entrance channel is well marked and used regularly by boats with drafts of 5 feet. The entrance itself is hard to see until you are almost on top of it. To find it, simply head for the eastern side of Little Island. Before you get very close to the island, you will be able to see the red "2" daymark, followed by the rest of the entrance channel daymarks. None of the markers are lighted, so do not try this at night—at least on the first try.

Once you are past the entrance, the creek opens up into two forks. Do not continue up the right fork past the marina as it shoals fairly quickly.

Anchorages/Provisions. The best anchorages are in the left fork, which has 9 feet of water and protection from the weather in all directions. The second cove to port is probably the best place to anchor, in 7 feet of water. Don't expect to find a convenient place to land except at the small marina on the right fork. The shoreline is completely built up and all private property.

BROAD CREEK

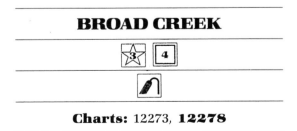

Charts: 12273, **12278**

Approaches. Located on the north shore of the Magothy River, Broad Creek is easily accessible and offers a couple of well-protected anchorages. A course

of 310 degrees from the entrance to the Magothy River from the Chesapeake takes you directly to the pair of red and green daymarks at the entrance to Broad Creek. Favor the starboard side until you are at least 200 yards past the green "3" daymark to avoid the edge of the shoal that stretches from Rook Point to well south southeast of the marker. Although there is 13 to 14 feet of water nearly shore to shore, continue to favor the east shore in order to avoid the 2-foot shoal that reaches halfway across the creek from the west shore midway between Broad Point and the head of the creek. Don't get too close to the east shore until you are well past the little cove to starboard as there are 3-foot shoals projecting out into the creek on either side of the entrance to the cove. (The cove is shallow so don't try it in anything but a dinghy or runabout.)

Broad Creek makes an abrupt, right-angle turn to the east just past the 2-foot shoal to port. As you reach this turn, you see a tiny island ahead of you. A shoal extends to the southwest and around to the mainland from the island, so leave it well to port. You can hug the starboard shore closely with no problems.

Anchorages. The best anchorage is in 9 to 10 feet of water in the fully protected hook of the creek past the little island. The shoreline is unsettled except for the small North Shore Marina on the north side of this hook of the creek. Tall trees come almost to the edge of the high bank on the south shore, making a snug little anchorage, and the island has an attractive beach where you can land. Wading can be a little sticky; the bottom is soft mud just a short distance off the sandy beach.

Going aground here is easy, but the bottom is so soft that it is only a minor inconvenience—and with a little care avoidable. This is probably the most secluded, best protected, private anchorage on the Magothy River.

FORKED CREEK

AND COOL SPRING

COVE

No facilities

Charts: 12273, **12278**

Anchorages. On the south shore of the Magothy River, just past Ulmstead Point, Forked Creek offers a pleasant, well-protected anchorage.

Approaches. A long sandbar nearly closes off the entrance to Forked Creek but you can squeeze past it easily by holding close to the red "4" daymark opposite the end of the bar. There is at least 5 feet in the channel until you pass the end of the bar. Then the depth increases to 10 to 13 feet nearly to the head of the creek. The surrounding land is high and wooded, except where the large houses of Ulmstead Estates stand. The docks belonging to Belvedere Yacht Club, part of the Ulmstead development, are on the east side of the creek, just inside the entrance bar. There are no facilities or supplies available here.

Do not attempt to enter Cool Spring Cove. A 1-foot bar at the entrance keeps you from the depths of 10–13 feet indicated inside the cove.

BLACKHOLE CREEK

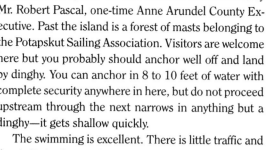

No facilities

Charts: 12273, **12278**

Approaches. On the north shore, about 3½ miles from the entrance to the Magothy from the Bay, is Blackhole Creek. This secluded, well-protected little harbor is the home of the Potapskut Sailing Association.

Many experienced cruisers manage to run aground coming in, but if you honor the red "10" light in the middle of the Magothy River before turning to the north you easily avoid the first hazard, which is the long thin shoal extending south from Chest Neck Point on the east side of the entrance to Blackhole Creek. From red "10," head directly toward the red and green entrance markers to the creek and you enter nicely.

Anchorages. The first anchorage is in the bight to port, immediately after you pass the green "1" light at the entrance to the creek. Directly ahead after

you enter is the green "3" marker on an island owned by Mr. Robert Pascal, one-time Anne Arundel County Executive. Past the island is a forest of masts belonging to the Potapskut Sailing Association. Visitors are welcome here but you probably should anchor well off and land by dinghy. You can anchor in 8 to 10 feet of water with complete security anywhere in here, but do not proceed upstream through the next narrows in anything but a dinghy—it gets shallow quickly.

The swimming is excellent. There is little traffic and that is limited to a 6-knot speed. Blackhole Creek is a wildlife sanctuary. You may find pike and perch here—and perhaps some soft crabs in the shallows.

No facilities or supplies are available here.

MILL CREEK

Charts: 12273, **12278**

Located on the south shore of the Magothy River, this creek provides an excellent, sheltered anchorage. Dividing Creek and Mill Creek share the same entrance approach, with Dividing Creek forking to the west and Mill Creek to the east. If you are short of groceries, there is a small beach on the west side of the approach (Crystal Beach side) where you can land and walk a short way to a good store. Don't plan on staying here: it is too exposed both to weather and the wakes from boats passing by in the Magothy.

Approaches. While no navigation aids are shown on a chart, there are private markers to assist you in entering Mill Creek. There is a red barrel where the two creeks separate, which should be left to starboard. From here, swing to port and thread your way between the shoals off the southern shore and the sandspit off Stony Point. Head for a second red barrel just past the sandspit. Pass between the barrel and a stake (if it is still there) and you are in. From here on there is 7 to 12 feet of water nearly shore to shore up to the head of the creek. About halfway up the navigable part of the creek is an overhead cable with a clearance of 48 feet.

Anchorages/Provisions. Anchor any-where in here; the high wooded bank protects you from weather and wakes. All of the homes in this residential area are well back from the water, giving the illusion of seclusion.

To port, just inside the sandspit at the entrance, is Ferry Point Yacht Basin, which offers gas (no diesel), ice, limited hardware, and a snack bar. They also offer retail seafood. There is 10 feet of water alongside the gas dock; one or two transient slips might be available.

The best anchorage is past the next bend in the creek where it opens out a bit. Choose either the small cove to starboard or immediately past this cove near the head of the creek. The high banks provide plenty of shelter but, conversely, tend to minimize the cooling breeze so essential in midsummer.

DIVIDING CREEK

Charts: 12273, **12278**

Most of what has been said about the surroundings in Mill Creek applies to Dividing Creek. There are more houses and they are more visible. Still this is a pretty anchorage with complete protection from weather and wakes.

Approaches. After you pass the first red barrel (left to starboard) just before the junction of Mill and Dividing Creeks, swing to starboard to enter the creek. Favor the starboard shore until you have passed the first point to port at the entrance to the creek.

Anchorages. The best anchorage is to port just after you clear this point. The high banks and tree-lined shore make for an attractive spot.

If you proceed upstream, favor the west shore as you pass the next point to port. There is a shoal off this point not clearly indicated on the chart. Past this point, the creek forks. Stay out of the starboard (west) fork as it shoals quickly. You can continue about half the remaining distance up the south fork in 7 to 8 feet of water before it, too, begins to shoal. There is a small boatyard

where the creek forks but no supplies or facilities for the cruiser.

CYPRESS CREEK

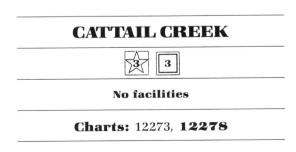

Charts: 12273, **12278**

Approaches/Anchorages. Still on the south side of the Magothy River, Cypress Creek offers sheltered anchorages in both forks of the creek. Simply honor the two green daymarks, "1" and "3," and you can enter the creek with ease. Stay in the middle and you will find 8 to 9 feet of water to at least halfway up either fork.

Provisions. Just before you enter the creek, Magothy Marina to port offers gas and diesel fuel, as well as premix for outboards. You can get ice, but little else in the way of supplies. To port, inside the creek just before the fork, is Cypress Marine, Inc., which stocks some hardware and has a laundromat (no fuel, though). Struble's Marina on the west fork of the creek does not offer much for the transient cruiser.

Cypress Creek is protected from weather and the holding is good. The area has a high population density and the shore is lined with private homes, except for the marinas in each fork. Many outboard enthusiasts come here, perhaps because no speed limit is posted.

CATTAIL CREEK

No facilities

Charts: 12273, **12278**

Approaches. Before you reach the entrance to this creek, the Magothy River begins to narrow and there is at least one shoal waiting to trap the unwary. As you pass Hendersons Point with its green "13" light, look carefully for the red "14" light and be sure to honor it. Red "14" is located at the end of a 0- to 2-foot shoal, which extends nearly two-thirds of the way across the river from the north shore. It is even harder to find when you are returning from upriver, so make note of the landmarks after passing it to insure honoring it on the way back.

Cattail Creek opens to port about a quarter mile past red "14." There is a green "15" daymark at the end of the shoal off Focal Point (Falcon Point on older charts) on the north side of the entrance. Favor the south side of the entrance, staying off green "15" as the shoal extends well to the southwest of the marker. There are two privately maintained lighted markers at the end of two piers to port on the south side of the entrance.

Anchorages. As you pass these markers, hold to the middle of the creek to avoid the half-foot shoal extending from the west side of the little cove to port. From here on, just stay in the middle and pick your anchorage.

While this is another populous area, the shores are high and wooded and the houses blend into the scenery. The high banks provide protection from weather and traffic is light. There are no facilities here and no place to land, but this is a pretty anchorage, well worth the visit.

COCKEY CREEK

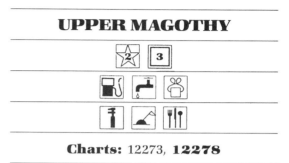

No facilities

Charts: 12273, **12278**

Approaches. About a quarter mile past the green "15" daymark at the mouth of Cattail Creek, Cockey Creek forks to the right off the Magothy River. Entrance to the creek is easy. There are no projecting shoals and 7 to 12 feet of water is carried at least three-quarters of the way up the creek. The largest boats need to beware of the overhead power cable at the mouth of the creek, although the clearance of 63 feet MHW is more than adequate for most.

Anchorages. This is a creek of strange contrast. The eastern bank is high and wooded, with unobtrusive houses nestled in the trees. By comparison the western bank is overbuilt, with houses looming over the edge of the high bank. This means that there is no privacy for anyone anchored below. If that bothers you, as it does us, go elsewhere. Otherwise this anchorage is quite attractive and well protected.

UPPER MAGOTHY

Charts: 12273, **12278**

Past Cockey Creek, the Magothy River becomes more a small creek than the wide river it is downstream. There are no projecting shoals to cause you problems until you reach the head of navigation a quarter of a mile short of the bridge over the river. The built-up shores leave no place to land except at the two marinas and the Riverdale Inn Restaurant.

Provisions. Cyr's Marina, on the west shore of the Magothy just past Cockey Creek, offers gas, ice, and complete engine and hull repairs.

Old Man Creek, which forks to the left just past the wide spot on the Magothy, is more attractive than the main river in this area. However, the shoreline is completely built up and it is all private property. The Beall Boat Shop is located here but offers nothing for the transient cruiser.

Where to Eat. Cruisers may want to investigate the Riverdale Inn Restaurant on the west shore of the Magothy, a few hundred yards past the entrance to Old Man Creek. The Riverdale has some of the best food on the Bay at reasonable prices and at least a dozen slips for rather large boats to tie up while dining there. The service is good and the people are friendly.

The entrance to the Sandy Point State Park launch basin from the Bay.

SANDY POINT

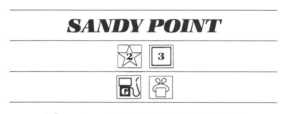

Charts: 12270, 12273, **12278**

Sandy Point State Park is located on Sandy Point, just to the north of the western end of the Chesapeake Bay Bridges. It features a fine sandy beach and a dredged channel and basin where you can enter and anchor in complete security if you want to make use of the beach or park facilities.

While not really intended for use by larger, deep-draft boats, the basin provides launch ramp facilities and a refuge for small craft. To find the entrance head for the northwest corner where the Bay Bridges meet the mainland. Parallel the bridges, and the marked entrance with its long breakwater opens ahead of you. Simply follow the markers into the basin in Mezick Ponds. Anchoring overnight is not permitted. (In the case of a blow, I have little doubt that this restriction would be waived.)

The controlling depth in the entrance and the basin is in excess of 7 feet, so most cruising boats can use it, but the only good reason to is as a refuge from a storm. This facility with its dozen or so launching ramps is intended to be used solely as a small boat launching facility. This and the availability of gasoline are the attractions for cruisers.

Sandy Point State Park is the site of the annual

Sandy Point Lighthouse and the Bay Bridges.

Skipjack races off Sandy Point. MARYLAND TOURISM

Chesapeake Appreciation Days celebration, usually held the first weekend in November (subject to a week variation in either direction). This event runs from 9:00 a.m. to 5:00 p.m., Saturday and Sunday, featuring Maryland seafood, exhibits on Bay life, air shows, and live entertainment. In short, something for everyone. There is an admission fee to the festivities.

The Annual Skipjack Races are usually held at the same time, in the main Bay, some distance off the point. This is a competition to determine the fastest boat in the nation's only remaining sailing oyster fleet. Weather permitting, there is often a large fleet of spectator boats anchored between Sandy Point and Sandy Point Lighthouse, a half-mile offshore, to get a better view of the races. If you want to watch the races from shore, better bring a good pair of binoculars or a strong telescope.

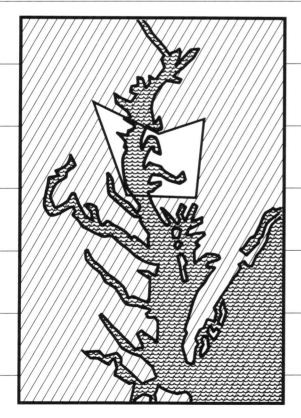

Bay Bridges to Little Choptank River

Bay Bridges to Little Choptank River

BAY
BRIDGE
TO
LITTLE
CHOPTANK
RIVER

148

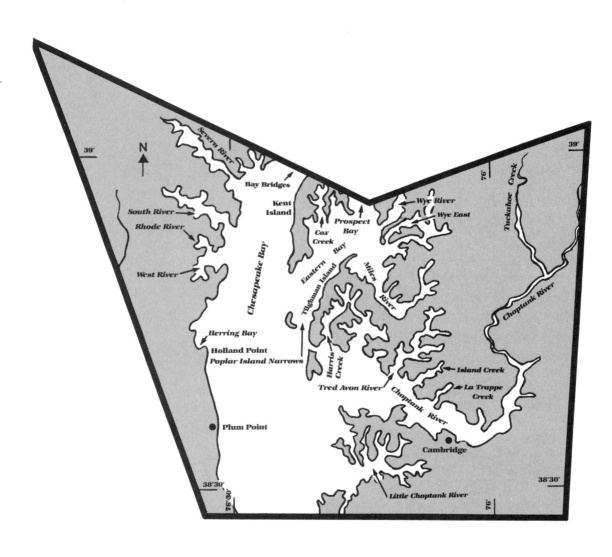

SCALE **1″=9.8** MILES

As you pass under the Bay Bridges, avoid the center span, which is used by large ships transiting the Bay. There is no need to use the center span; all of the other spans have plenty of clearance (see Table 4: Bay Bridge Clearance Heights).

Flukey wind shifts often trouble those sailing under the bridges, so give yourself plenty of room to maneuver in case you are suddenly headed by the wind and have to bear off.

Past the bridges, a fleet of ships usually is anchored off the mouth of the Severn River. With few exceptions, these ships are bulk carriers waiting to enter Baltimore Harbor to take on or off-load cargo. Most carry grain or coal and are waiting their turn at Baltimore's port facility. The grain carriers must be inspected by the U.S. Department of Agriculture. Those that are not clean or are infested with insects or rats, must be fumigated, which causes additional time at anchor.

Past the Bay Bridges, the Bay water suddenly increases in salinity. As a result, you see different marine life, more ocean-dwelling creatures appearing as you move farther south. Horseshoe crabs and cow-nosed rays are the most obvious. You will find the shells of the crabs on shore and, during the summer months, will see plenty of rays cruising just under the surface or making short rushes along the surface with a lot of noise and spray. The rays also have a habit of swimming slowly just under the surface with one or both tips of their "wings" just above the water, looking for all the world like the fins of a couple of sharks. (Sharks are so rare that I doubt you will see one, and if you do, don't worry; there has never been a recorded account of a shark attack in the Chesapeake Bay.)

One of the most striking features of this part of the Bay is the cluster of islands which encloses a small, shallow bay known as Poplar Harbor. These low islands, visible from more than 5 miles away, are all that is left of what was a 1000-acre island in colonial times. Now they serve as a convenient reference for those trying to find the entrance to Knapps Narrows from the Chesapeake Bay.

BAY
BRIDGE
TO
LITTLE
CHOPTANK
RIVER

149

TABLE 4. Bay Bridge Clearance Heights

The pilings are numbered from Sandy Point, on the Western Shore, to Kent Island and the clearances are listed in feet between Mean High Water and the lowest point of the structure in the center of the span. Some of the spans have a lower portion called a "knee," not listed here.

SOUTH BRIDGE		NORTH BRIDGE	
PIER NO.	CLEARANCE	PIER NO.	CLEARANCE
WESTERN SHORE			
6–7	31		
7–8	33		
8–9	23		
9–10	28		
10–11	34		
11–12	19		
12–13	27		
13–14	34		
14–15	42	21–22	42
15–16	43	22–23	43
16–17	52	23–24	52
17–18	61	24–25	61
18–19	70	25–26	70
19–20	79	26–27	79
20–21	88	27–28	88
21–22	98	28–29	98
22–23	115	29–30	115
23–24	**	30–31	125
24–25	168	31–32	168
*25–26	186	*32–33	186
26–27	168	33–34	168
27–28	**	34–35	127
28–29	119	35–36	119
29–30	98	36–37	108
30–31	88	37–38	99
31–32	**	38–39	88
32–33	78	39–40	78
33–34	67	40–41	67
34–35	58	41–42	58
35–36	47	42–43	47
36–37	77	43–44	53–60
37–38	63	44–45	63
38–39	52	45–46	37
39–40	38	46–47	38
40–41	34	47–48	34
41–42	40	48–49	30
EASTERN SHORE			

*Main Span— Shipping Channel   **Information not available, presumed same as north bridge.

COURTESY OF CHESAPEAKE BAY YACHT RACING ASSOCIATION'S "THE TRAVELER"

Eastern

Shore

KENT ISLAND/

BAYSIDE

Charts: 12263, **12270,** 12273, 12282

As you proceed south from the Bay Bridges, the only harbors on the 9-mile stretch of Kent Island to Bloody Point, at the southern tip of Kent Island, are four marinas in artificial harbors. Some of these can accommodate relatively deep-draft vessels; others are better left to those with shoal drafts.

PIER ONE

MARINA

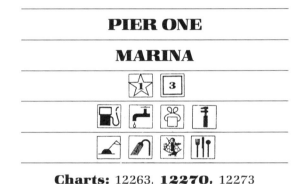

Charts: 12263, **12270,** 12273

Approaches/Dockages. The first of these harbors is Pier One Marina, just south of the Bay Bridges. The entrance channel is 6 to 8 feet deep and nearly one-half mile long, dredged through the shoal off Kent Island. It is well marked with ranges and leads into a protected inner basin capable of handling very large boats. The marina maintains both a restaurant and motel, and claims to have 8 feet of water beside the long fuel dock.

Provisions. A boat drawing at least 4 feet can negotiate the entrance channel. This is primarily powerboat country. There is no anchorage, although boats can tie up along the fuel dock, away from the pumps, long enough to visit the excellent restaurant there (Hemmingway's). For an overnight stay, you need a slip at the marina, assuming one is available.

Kent Island and Eastern Bay (with Rich Neck)

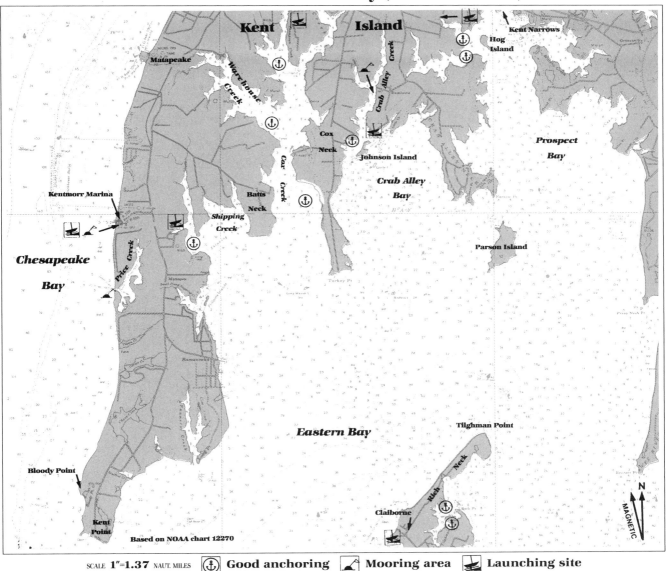

Kent Island

Matapeake

Kent Narrows

Hog Island

Ware house Creek

Prospect Bay

Cox Neck

Johnson Island

Crab Alley Creek

Crab Alley Bay

Cox Creek

Kentmorr Marina

Batts Neck

Shipping Creek

Chesapeake Bay

Price Creek

Parson Island

Eastern Bay

Tilghman Point

Bloody Point

Rich Neck

Claiborne

Kent Point

Based on NOAA chart 12270

N

MAGNETIC

SCALE 1″=1.37 NAUT. MILES   Good anchoring   Mooring area   Launching site

MATAPEAKE HARBOR

OF REFUGE

☆1 2

No facilities

Charts: 12263, **12270**

Approaches. Matapeake Harbor of Refuge is located about 2 miles below the bridges. Established on the site of the old ferry landing, the harbor has made effective use of the bulkheads and breakwaters left from the ferry. Be careful when you enter Matapeake—the entrance channel has shoaled in recent years and vessels with more than a 5-foot draft shouldn't try it.

This harbor is intended for use in emergencies only; visiting boats are not encouraged to remain overnight, except in a genuine emergency, such as a severe storm. There is a picnic area and a public launching ramp for small boats, mostly used by fishermen, inside the bulkheaded area. A few slips next to the Maryland Marine Fisheries Repair Base dock may be used on occasion. There is also some room to anchor, but not much.

KENTMORR MARINA

☆1 3

Charts: 12263, **12270**

Approaches. Kentmorr Marina is located roughly midway between the Bay Bridges and Bloody Point. The easiest way to locate the entrance from the Bay is to take your departure from the south white/orange "S" measured mile marker positioned just under a mile offshore. A course of 120 degrees from this marker takes you directly to the harbor entrance.

This harbor is totally manmade and the entrance is subject to frequent shoaling. As a result, we cannot rec-

ommend it for any boats with more than a 4-foot draft; powerboats or other shoal-draft boats should have no trouble. In fact, a fleet of more than 20 charter fishing boats is based here, which indicates the focus of activities.

Provisions/Facilities. The marina is quite large, with all the facilities you may want or need, except a laundromat. If you ask nicely, the management can probably help you out there also. There is a restaurant, cocktail lounge, and a snack bar to assuage hunger or thirst. They also have a swimming pool.

Dockages. There is no anchorage here. If you plan to stay overnight, you must reserve a slip, preferably in advance.

QUEEN ANNE MARINA

☆1 3

Charts: 12263, **12270**

Approaches. This marina is a little over 1 mile below Kentmorr Marina, near the entrance to Price Creek. Price Creek is actually a shallow salt pond, which has been dredged near the marina, originally to a depth of 5 feet MLW. The dredged channel has a tendency to shoal, so vessels with a draft of 4-feet or more should not try to enter without recent local knowledge, especially if the sea is running. The marina monitors CB Channel #2, but not VHF-FM, a good clue that they cater primarily to powerboats.

Dockages/Facilities. Shoreside facilities are available at the marina and it is a center for fishing boat charters. However, while transient slips are offered, they are reputed to be in short supply.

Don't plan on anchoring out. There isn't any room with adequate depth in the pond.

EASTERN BAY

Charts: 12263, **12270**

As you reach the southern tip of Kent Island, the slightly tilted Bloody Point Bar Light, a 54-foot-high redbrick cylinder, is the primary reference for entry into Eastern Bay when approaching from the north. You can pass to either side of this lighthouse (but it's best to stay west of it) and head straight for the green "1" bell buoy directly south of Kent Point. While you can cut inside of the "1" bell buoy, it is better to honor it as you will need this as a reference to be sure of clearing the shoal that extends to the southeast from Kent Point. From green bell buoy "1," set a course of 72 degrees to the red "2A" buoy off Claiborne, on Tilghman Island; hold this course for at least a mile beyond the green "1" to clear the shoal. Once past the shoal, you can bear off to the north if you are heading for one of the creeks on the southeast side of Kent Island or come left a little to head around Tilghman Point into the Miles River or proceed around Parson Island and on up to Kent Narrows.

If you are approaching Eastern Bay from Poplar Island Narrows to the south, simply hold at least one-half mile offshore until you reach the red "2A" buoy off Claiborne. Take your departure from there to any of your destinations on or beyond Eastern Bay.

SHIPPING CREEK

No facilities

Charts: 12263, **12270**

Approaches. A course of 5 degrees from the red "2A" off Claiborne takes you to the flashing red "2" marker at the mouth of Cox Creek. The green "1" daymark, which indicates the southern side of the entrance to Shipping Creek, will be clearly visible to the west. Give green "1" about 100 yards clearance as you round it because the shoal extends about that that far northwest of the marker. If you bump, alter course a little farther north and you should quickly find 12 feet of water. Another shoal (off Batts Neck) on the right side of the channel prevents you from heading directly into the mouth of Shipping Creek. Try heading midway between the largest of the houses on shore and the south side of the creek entrance until you are about halfway between the shore and the green "1" daymark. Then head north northwest until you can see the opening of the entrance into Shipping Creek to port. Don't make the mistake of heading toward the right fork. There isn't much water there. Once into Shipping Creek proper, simply keep to the middle.

Anchorages. You can anchor anywhere up to the first cove to port in at least 6 feet of water. The anchorage is well-protected, with farmland on the western shore and a scattering of nice-looking homes to the east and farther up the creek.

Don't proceed past this cove as the creek quickly shoals. (Although you may see several workboats and perhaps a sailboat or two upstream, don't try it without current local knowledge.)

If there is a strong easterly wind, pass up this creek— the anchorage will be lumpy.

Bloody Point Light is the primary reference for entry into the Eastern Bay from the north.

COX AND WAREHOUSE CREEKS

No facilities

Charts: 12263, **12270**

These two creeks share a common entrance and really should be considered as two forks of the same creek. Both are attractive, but we prefer to anchor in Warehouse Creek.

Approaches. As you pass the flashing red "2" at the entrance to Cox Creek, continue on course for about 100 yards before swinging slightly to starboard to head for the next marker. This will ensure that you clear the shoal off Turkey Point. (If you are in doubt, hold a course about midway between Cox Neck and Batts Neck shores, favoring the west side.) You may choose to anchor here or proceed upstream past the red "4" to where Warehouse Creek splits to the northwest from Cox Creek. Be sure to stay in the middle of the creek and proceed slowly, preferably with a depthsounder running, as the edges of the creek shoal a bit abruptly.

Anchorages. This is a pleasant location with a few large homes on the south shore of Warehouse Creek and a wooded marsh on the north shore. You can anchor anywhere in here, completely protected from weather and waves. Plan to use a relatively short anchor rode because of the shoals and shallows on both sides. To the north northwest, you can clearly see the Bay Bridges but you will be in nearly complete solitude. Good screening is essential in the warmer weather since the nearby marshes provide excellent mosquito habitat.

CRAB ALLEY CREEK

Charts: 12263, **12270**

Approaches. The entrance to Crab Alley Creek is on the west side of Crab Alley Bay, but you cannot head directly for it from anywhere outside of this little bay as there are several unmarked shoals.

When approaching from the south through Eastern Bay, take your departure from red "2A" off Claiborne. From "2A," a course of 35 degrees, on a line midway between Bodkin Island and Parson Island, takes you past the shoals off each island. Bodkin Island is easily recognized from a long way off by the single pine tree which grows on it—looking like the classic palm tree usually depicted on cartoons of a desert island. Once Bodkin Island is abeam to port, head due north (010° magnetic) to leave the green can "1" ahead of you to port.

When approaching from the Miles River, a course of 341 degrees from red "4," north of Tilghman Point, takes you directly to the Crab Alley Bay can "1." From Kent Narrows, simply stay at least three-fourths mile off Parson Island (hold the distance you have off the island as you round green "1") at all times until you can assume a course of about 340 degrees to can "1."

From Crab Alley Bay can "1," swing a little to port and pass between the red "4" daymark and the green "3" buoy to enter Crab Alley Creek. Once past red "4," swing to starboard to leave the red/green daymark close to starboard and pass up the left fork of the channel. The right fork leads up a narrow channel, reportedly shoaled past its red "2" daymark.

Provisions. There are a few tiny marinas and boatyards at the end of the right fork, but they have little in the way of supplies and there is no fuel available. The Bay Boat Shop, located well up the main creek, is another tiny marina which offers repairs and marine supplies, mostly oriented to powerboats.

Anchorages. Hold close to Johnson Island, forming the east side of the creek, as you pass its southern tip to avoid the shoal to port. You will find the best anchorage in the mouth of the small cove to port, opposite the middle of this island. If you proceed farther upstream, simply remain in the middle and you can continue to at least the point where the creek forks before it begins to shoal. If you anchor up here, keep a relatively short rode because of the shoals to either side of the narrow creek.

The entire creek is well protected from weather and waves—but not from the wake from the occasional workboat. As in most of the creeks on Kent Island, come prepared with good screens and mosquito repellent in the warm weather.

CLAIBORNE

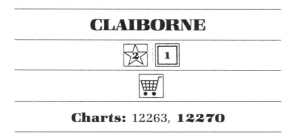

Charts: 12263, **12270**

Prior to the completion of the first of the Bay Bridges in the early 1950s, there was a ferry dock at Claiborne Landing used by the ferries from Romancoke on Kent Island and by Bay steamers. When this service was discontinued, the landing became a public dock and launching ramp, mostly used by local small craft.

Provisions. This is not a good harbor for cruising boats. Until 1992, there was an interesting country store and post office in Claiborne, a short walk from the public dock. The owners of the store and post office have won a battle against the U.S. Postal Service to keep the post office open, but the country store is no longer in business, and has been replaced by a public telephone and soda machine. Martha Hamylin still runs the post office and would love to have any cruisers come and chat.

TILGHMAN CREEK

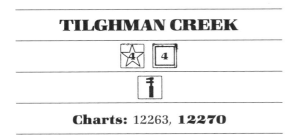

Charts: 12263, **12270**

A well-protected and attractive anchorage, Tilghman Creek is reached easily from anywhere in this part of the Bay. It makes a convenient stopping place for those bound across the main Bay from the Eastern Shore or to the Miles River/Kent Narrows area from the Bay.

Approaches. Except for the final stages of the approach to the entrance, navigation is easy. Swing wide around Tilghman Point and continue south or south southwest until you are due east of the green "1" light at the mouth of Tilghman Creek and you will have no trouble with the pair of finger shoals extending south and south southwest from Rich Neck below Tilghman Point. From here, a compass course of 270 degrees brings you safely to the green "1" light on a spar at the mouth of the creek. Leave the "1" marker at least 50 yards to the south of your course until it is abeam to port. Then swing to a course that brings the green "3" daymark close to port (to within 30 feet) to avoid the entrance shoal to starboard. Once you pass the red "4" daymark (don't cut number 4 too close), you are in. The creek opens out and the water is deep enough to allow you to maneuver easily. (We don't recommend entering under sail.)

Anchorages. Leave the first cove to port alone. It is shallow except for a narrow segment along the north shore. The best anchorage is in the first cove to starboard in 11 feet of water, off a long sandy beach. There is plenty of room for several boats.

In the event that this cove is too full, the mouth of the second cove to port makes a nice alternative. Don't go much past the two piers as the water in the cove gets a bit thin farther in.

Farther up, where the creek forks, is another nice place to anchor, although it is not a good place to land. You can take a dinghy over to the tiny boatyard, Locust Hill Boatworks, at the end of the left fork to land and walk into Claiborne. From the boatyard, walk to the end of the road and turn right. About a quarter of a mile down this road, you come to Claiborne's general store and post office.

Although the boatyard offers inboard engine and hull repairs, no marine facilities are available to cruisers on this creek; come prepared.

GREENWOOD
CREEK

THE
WYE
RIVER

156

UNNAMED COVE

[No rating] 3

No facilities

Just over one-half mile southeast of the entrance to Tilghman Creek is a cove, unnamed on any chart I checked, which presents a little bit of a puzzle. According to the latest and largest scale chart I have been able to find, the entrance is barred with an extensive, 2-foot shoal. From the outside of this cove, I see no obvious evidence that it has been dredged recently. We have seen one good-sized sailboat in there; so there must be a way in. Unfortunately, we never have had nor taken the time to look more closely.

It appears to be a nice anchorage, in 9 to 10 feet of water, if you can figure out how to get there. I leave this one as a challenge for other incurable gunkholers.

PORTER CREEK

No facilities

Charts: 12263, **12270**

Approaches. About 1½ miles below Tilghman Creek, just short of Hambleton Point, is the entrance to Porter Creek. This one, too, is unmarked on the chart in terms of navigation aids or any indication of a deep entrance channel. However, a privately marked, dredged entrance channel leads to a pleasant little anchorage in 7 feet of water, surrounded by a few fancy houses on expansive plots of land. (I don't know the entrance depth, but have seen some fair-sized sailboats inside and assume that it must be 4 feet or more.)

Anchorages. There is no place to land but, if that isn't a requirement, this is a nice spot. To enter, simply follow the markers in. Then swing to port and continue upstream until the water just starts to shoal.

Porter Creek is relatively open to the north through northwest and could get uncomfortable in a strong

northerly. There are far better anchorages nearby. Except to say you have been there, pass it by.

GREENWOOD CREEK

Charts: 12263, **12270**

Greenwood Creek is located on the Eastern Shore of Eastern Bay, just east of Piney Neck Point. We have seen several good-sized sailboats negotiating the entrance to this creek, but it is totally unmarked so you would have to feel your way in. We have been told that there is an elusive 5-foot channel. By now, we doubt that it is more than 4 feet. In any event, we haven't tried it.

If you draw less than 4 feet, you should be able to make it past the entrance bar and find a scenic, well-protected creek, 8 feet deep all the way to the headwaters. This creek has no facilities of any kind.

THE WYE RIVER

Charts: 12263, **12270**

While most of the rivers and creeks on the Eastern Shore are appealing, the Wye River is special. The river splits into two main forks, the Wye East and the Wye West Rivers, which enfold Wye Island. (Actually the proper name for the west fork is the Wye River. I chose to call it the Wye West River to avoid confusion.) Wye Narrows connects the East and West Wye Rivers north of Wye Island, completing the ring of water to make it an island. The small, fixed bridge (vertical clearance 10 feet) that connects Wye Island to the mainland prevents circumnavigation of the island, which otherwise would be easy since there is deep water all the way around.

Wye Island itself is sparsely settled. A one-time wild-life refuge, there are only one or two houses on the island now. We have been told that there are future plans to develop Wye Island.

On other shores of the Wye, you will find manor houses, estates, and many lesser but large homes. The water is sometimes discolored from sediment but unpolluted and clean. There is rarely any sign of the refuse or trash you often will find washed ashore in some other

Wye River Region

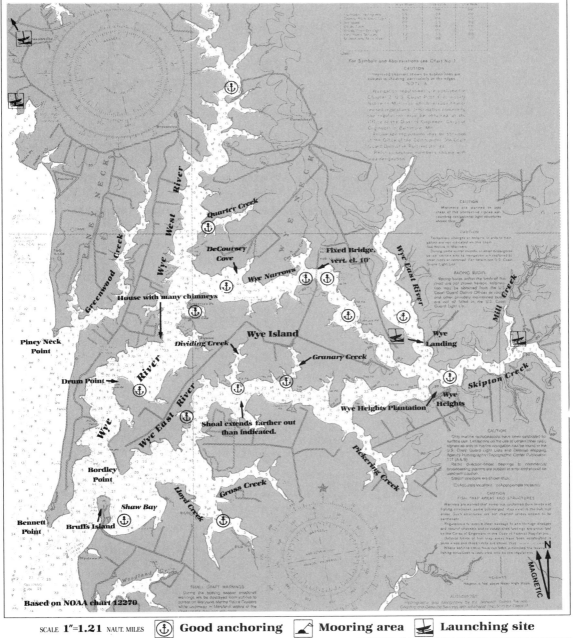

SCALE **1″=1.21** NAUT. MILES   ⚓ **Good anchoring**   **Mooring area**   **Launching site**

rivers on the Bay. No matter which part of the Wye you cruise, snug anchorages abound in the numerous creeks or coves on the river.

If you are approaching the mouth of the Wye from the north through Eastern Bay, plot a course to take you between the green can "3" buoy at the end of the shoal off Bennett Point and the red nun "2" buoy at the north end of a shoal off the mouth of the Wye—all that is left of an island. You can pass into the mouth of the Wye on either side of can "3" but, if you pass inside of it, hold to within less than 50 yards of the can or you may run aground on the long shoal off Bennett Point. An intriguing, private lighthouse on the tip of Bennett Point makes identification of this point easy from a substantial distance away.

If you approach from the south, out of the Miles River, simply guide on the east shore, holding about one-half mile off of it. This equates to a course of 18 degrees from nun "12" at the mouth of the Miles River to red "4" in the mouth of the Wye River and neatly avoids the shoals to port and starboard.

Once past can "3," head into the Wye favoring the eastern side of the river until you are well past the lighted red "4" marker on a piling just inside the mouth of the river. As you approach Bruffs Island, you must decide whether to cruise the Wye East or Wye West River. Regardless of which you choose, good anchorages abound; we can list only a few of those we consider the best.

WYE EAST RIVER

Charts: 12263, **12270**

As you round Bruffs Island to enter the Wye East River, hold at least 50 yards off the shore of the island to avoid its shoal, but watch out for the shoal extending south from Bordley Point on the other side. It juts out farther than indicated on the chart. You must beware of a few other unmarked shoals on this branch of the Wye. Except for these, stay near the middle of the river and you will have no problems. (Note: All marks in the Wye are state maintained and may not appear on NOAA charts.)

Leave the red "2" daymark, past Shaw Bay, fairly close to starboard and assume a course to leave the green "3" daymark ahead at least 25 yards to port. (Green "3" blends into the shore behind it so it may be a little hard to see until you pass red "2.") When you pass green "3," continue on the same course until you reach the middle of the Wye East segment that runs north-south. The shoal off the point to port extends well to the east of green "3."

The next shoal to guard against may not be apparent from the chart. This one extends well to the south from the east side of the entrance to Dividing Creek. However, if you stay at least 100 yards off that point until it is past your beam and you are 50 to 75 yards from the south bank of the Wye East before you turn to port to head upstream, you clear the shoal easily.

The last unmarked shoal is opposite the Wye Heights Boathouse, just before the entrance to Skipton Creek. Give the point to port a wide berth. This shoal is hard and harbors a submerged piling.

SHAW BAY

 3

No facilities

Charts: 12263, **12270**

Anchorages. Shaw Bay is the first good anchorage on the way up the river. Here you can anchor anywhere in good holding, but most choose to anchor well into the southwest corner of the bay. Do not attempt to land anywhere on Bruffs Island; it is private property and closed to the public. The shore opposite Bruffs Island is sandy and extends almost the entire length of the east side of Shaw Bay. You can land here to walk and beachcomb to your heart's content. We usually find horseshoe crab shells, as well as indications of some marine life more common to the ocean.

Shaw Bay is a beautiful anchorage. On summer weekends, it is usually crowded, but it can hold many boats comfortably. For more seclusion, continue upstream.

LLOYD CREEK

No facilities

Charts: 12263, **12270**

While this creek is not quite as snug as others farther upriver, it is comfortable and well protected except from the northwest. If you happen to like Canada geese it is a fantastic anchorage in the fall. Then literally thousands of geese land to feed in the fields on all sides of this creek. They are noisy, which may keep light sleepers awake at night.

Approaches. A select group of cruisers manage to keep running aground here; we have never been able to understand why. Stay near the middle of the creek, favoring the west side of the center line, as you enter and you should avoid the 2-foot shoal that extends to the west from the east shore of Lloyd Creek, south of Gross Creek, *nearly* to the center of the creek.

Anchorages. The best anchorage is well into the creek, in the area where the creek hooks sharply to the southwest. Most charts indicate a tiny island at this bend in the creek, but it is just a duck blind. Don't expect to land; there is no good place for it.

GROSS CREEK

No facilities

Charts: 12263, **12270**

Approaches. Gross Creek extends to the east, just past the entrance to Lloyd Creek, but a bar at its entrance restricts access to vessels with less than 4-foot drafts. (That was the depth when we last visited; it may be less now.)

Anchorages. If you can get past the bar, you will find a 6- to 8-foot depth inside all the way up to the fork in the creek, so you can anchor where you will. Don't enter either fork, since the water is less than 3 feet in spite of what the chart says.

WYE ISLAND COVE

No facilities

Charts: 12263, **12270**

Anchorages. This cove is unnamed on the chart so we dubbed it this for want of something better to call it. Located on the west shore, about midway up the north-south part of the Wye East River about one-half mile past the green "3" daymark, this snug anchorage can accommodate about a half dozen boats. The cove is lined with trees, which break the wind nicely but not the cooling breezes in the hot summer months. Behind the trees are the fields of Wye Island, providing a very secluded anchorage.

Approaches. The entrance is easy; simply continue up the Wye East River until the entrance to this cove is abeam, then turn and head straight in. Don't proceed more than three-quarters of the way to the head of the cove unless you draw less than 4 feet. Up to there, the water is 7 to 10 feet over a mud bottom. A small beach here, near the entrance, is a mixture of sand and mud. While minimal, it does allow you to land and stretch your legs a little.

This is a superb anchorage in the late fall when the winds howl and the geese fly.

DIVIDING CREEK

No facilities

Charts: 12263, **12270**

This creek is narrow and relatively deep, with high banks (for the Chesapeake) covered with tall trees, forming a screen of woods between the water and the fields of Wye Island. Here a great blue heron stalks the shallows and osprey circle overhead, as do numerous other birds. Raccoon and muskrat can often be seen along the shores, especially in the early morning or late afternoon. You are in the minority if you miss sighting a variety of wildlife here.

Approaches. The entrance is easy if you pay proper respect to the shoals extending out into the Wye from either side of the entrance. Keep to the middle of the Wye River until the entrance to Dividing Creek is

Osprey

The osprey, or fish hawk *(Pandion haliaetus)*, is a large, impressive bird, with a wing span reaching five to six feet. White underneath, it has a striking brown, black, and white pattern under its wings and tail and on its upper side. A black streak extends back from each eye and it has the classic fiercely curved beak of a raptor.

The osprey inhabit the Bay from early April until the fall, nesting from late April through July and sometimes even later. Then they go south for the winter, returning each spring.

As recently as the 1960s, osprey were relatively rare in the Bay area. Pesticides washing into the Bay were absorbed into the food chain, concentrating more and more heavily in creatures higher up in the chain. DDT, especially, reached a high concentration in fish, the sole diet of the osprey. The result was a thinning of the shell of the bird's eggs; the weight of the brooding parents crushed the fragile eggs. The young that did hatch often were deformed. The osprey became an endangered species.

With the banning of DDT and other pesticides, the osprey is once again a common sight on the Bay. It seems as if every daymark and lighted spar in the Bay sports an osprey's untidy nest.

An osprey cruises the Eastern Shore.
LUTHER C. GOLDMAN/SPORT FISHERIES & WILDLIFE

The adult osprey return to the same nest year after year, adding to it each time. Some nests reach massive proportions, frequently obscuring the marker unless they are removed by man. These raptors seem to prefer nesting on these man-made havens out in the water, using the tops of dead trees only if all markers are already "taken."

They fish tirelessly all day, cruising 50 to 100 feet above the water looking for fish near the surface. On spying its prey, an osprey folds its wings and plummets into the water, often disappearing below the surface to sink its talons into the fish. With its prey secure, the bird appears to fly right out of the water with considerable splashing, then fly to its nest to feed itself or its offspring.

Ospreys fiercely defend their nests, the two parents taking turns fishing and guarding, screaming a loud "kee, kee, kee" at any and all who come too close, even (or perhaps especially) boats. Frequently, one or both of the adults will fly off the nest to make passes (mock attacks) at the trespassers.

Aside from crows, which snatch or eat eggs in an unprotected nest, humans are the osprey's only real enemies. However, osprey are sometimes "mugged" by bald eagles. If an eagle is in the area when an osprey makes a catch, the eagle may attack as the osprey is making its way back to its nest. Taking advantage of its superior size, strength, and speed, the eagle dives at the osprey, talons outstretched, to scare the osprey into dropping its fish. Rarely actually making contact, the eagle keeps up the harassment until the fish is dropped. When the fish is dropped, the eagle will shear off and dive after the fish, usually catching it in midair. Then the osprey, seeming resigned to its role, goes off to make another catch.

An osprey on the wing is an impressive sight, but this raptor can be confused with eagles, turkey vultures, and even gulls when observed at a distance. The osprey holds its wings in a crooked or low M position; an eagle holds its wings in an almost flat position, while a turkey vulture holds its in a flattened U position. Both turkey vultures and eagles have dark undersides; the osprey's undersides are white. Gulls, like raptors, enjoy riding thermal updrafts near ridges. Their white undersides can confuse osprey-watchers, however, gulls have relatively larger heads and proportionately longer wings. Now that you have the wherewithal to identify osprey in flight, work on becoming sharp enough to identify the fish it has caught and carries!

abeam, then turn and head directly into the middle of the entrance. Favor the port side of the creek until you clear the point to starboard.

Anchorages. From here on, you can anchor anywhere in complete security. Dividing Creek is well-sheltered from both weather and the wakes of passing boats.

The depth is 7 to 9 feet almost to the head of the creek. It begins to shoal within about 100 yards of the end of the creek, so be careful if you venture that far. This creek is such an attractive anchorage that on weekends it draws many boats. One early October, we counted 99 boats at anchor, probably due to the fact that it was blowing pretty hard and this creek provides the best protection in the area. During the week, you often can have this spot to yourself.

QUARTER COVE

No facilities

Charts: 12263, **12270**

Approaches. Almost directly opposite the entrance to Dividing Creek, this "cove" looks as much like a creek as many so named—at least in this area. The approach to the entrance is wide open and 7 to 9 feet of water is carried all the way to the head of the cove. From the point where the cove narrows simply stay in the middle and you will remain in deep water.

Anchorages. This anchorage is pleasant enough, but not secluded; there are several homes on the shore. You can land on the sandy beach on the east side of the mouth of the cove to walk, swim, or beachcomb. However, there are better anchorages nearby.

GRANARY CREEK

No facilities

Charts: 12263, **12270**

This creek is very similar to Dividing Creek. In fact everything said about Dividing Creek applies to Granary Creek. However, one house on the west bank, about halfway down the creek, breaks the bucolic splendor.

Approaches. The entrance is simplicity itself: Just pay attention to your chart and head directly into the mouth of the creek. Favor the west side of the entrance to avoid the short shoal that projects a little off the east side of the entrance. There are no other shoals to worry about. Seven to 8 feet of water is carried all the way to the headwaters.

Anchorages. You couldn't ask for more protection in an anchorage. This creek doesn't seem to attract quite as many boats as Dividing Creek, perhaps because it is a little farther up the Wye East River. Anchor anywhere once you are in.

PICKERING CREEK

No facilities

Approaches. Pickering is a relatively long and narrow creek, with a number of unmarked shoals waiting to snag the unwary. Although the water depth ranges between 8 and 10 feet to the head of the creek, the shores are well built-up with homes, making this creek less attractive to us than several others in this region.

Anchorages. The banks are high and lined with trees, providing good protection from weather. If you sound your way in carefully, you will find a secure anchorage, but you may not find anywhere to land.

SKIPTON CREEK

No facilities

We feel that this creek is special, if only because the anchorage is within sight of the gardens belonging to Wye Heights Plantation, an old colonial estate. The house itself can be seen as you approach the mouth of the creek. The imposing brick structure, with its four large white columns, overlooks the junction of Wye Narrows, Skipton Creek, and the Wye East River. A herd of coal-black sheep wanders the grounds between the house and the river, presumably keeping the grass trimmed. Farther back from the water is a compound with a herd of reindeer! Twice while anchored here we have been invited by the owner to land and stroll through his classic English gardens.

Approaches. The Skipton Creek entrance is easy, provided that you avoid the shoal off the point opposite the Wye Heights boathouse in the Wye East River and give the point on the right side of the mouth of the creek a wide berth.

Anchorages/Provisions. The best anchorage is just after you enter the creek, in 7 feet of water. Boats with drafts of 4 feet or more shouldn't try to proceed any farther than a little beyond the next point—the creek starts to shoal from there on. Cube ice is available at Wye Landing on the upper Wye East River, just past the entrance to Skipton Creek.

This creek ranks among one of the prettier anchorages on the Wye and the sea nettles don't usually show up here. There is a healthy snapping turtle population; we always have been inspected carefully by one or more of these critters shortly after anchoring.

Of Turtles and Terrapins

One of the largest and most frequently seen of the tidewater creatures, the common snapping turtle *(Chelydra serpentina)* inhabits nearly all of the creeks and rivers in the Bay, from brackish to fresh waters. They can grow to be as much as 18 inches across and weigh up to 90 pounds. Most weigh in at around 30 pounds—still a lot of turtle! Mortality due to predation is high among the juveniles, but the adult snapper fears only humans and, if not caught and killed, may live to be 50 years old.

Snapping turtle.
FRANK DUFRESNE/SPORT FISHERIES & WILDLIFE

Snappers are indiscriminate scavengers, tackling anything that might be edible. They will devour anything they can catch—carrion, small shellfish, fish, live ducklings, other turtles, and even the young of their own species.

On several occasions we have anchored in a quiet cove and within minutes watched as the resident snapper swam out to and around our boat several times, giving us the once over. We have often wondered if he were curious or simply determining our edibility.

In fact, people are the predators in this relationship. The snapping turtle is caught commercially with traps, handlines, and dip nets and sold as food. (The State of Maryland prohibits catching snappers from state waters by the use of a hook and line, trotline, bow and arrow, spear, gig or gig iron, or any other device capable of piercing any part of the turtle.) Frequently hibernating snappers are harvested in the winter from the muddy creek bottoms by probing for them with a pointed stick. The captured turtles are sent to Baltimore, Philadelphia, New York, and other markets. Snapper reportedly makes a good soup, though I cannot attest to it personally.

Snappers live, eat, and mate in the water, the latter activity being very noticeable. Adult snappers are rather noisy about their mating—and the related fighting—hissing and thrashing in the upstream waters, creating more racket than seems possible for their size. As dramatic as the mating ritual may be, it works for the snappers; they have been around for millennia with little likelihood of becoming extinct in the near future.

About the only time a snapping turtle willingly leaves the water is when the gravid female crawls out to lay her clutch of eggs in a nest dug above the high water mark. She lays about 40 leathery shelled, nearly white eggs—each a little less than two inches in diameter. She then covers the eggs and goes on her way. Those eggs not found and eaten by raccoons, skunks, or man hatch in about 80 days.

The hatchlings emerge as fully formed miniature versions of adult snappers and scramble for the water. Those not picked off by birds, other predators, or other snappers will feed and mature, eventually mating and continuing the cycle.

A less pervasive but better known Bay turtle is the diamond-back terrapin *(Malaclemys terrapin terrapin)*. This turtle was once so plentiful that, in 1797, Maryland enacted a law prohibiting feeding it to slaves more than twice a week. This legislation was designed to protect the slaves from a monotonous diet, not the turtle from being eaten. By the late 18th century, however, the diamond-back was considered such a delicacy that it was hunted almost to extinction. Today legal restrictions and a greatly reduced

market are helping this turtle make a comeback. A few gourmets still consider the diamond-back tablefare; some "table turtles" are raised commercially in ponds and pens—one such operation is near Crisfield; others are caught in the wild. (Legal size for terrapins in the State of Maryland is six inches along the bottom of the shell.)

Diamond-backs are found in brackish creeks and marshes, although they can survive in fresh water. They feed underwater on mollusks and crustaceans but aren't so picky that they won't eat all sorts of other fare, including insects and an occasional fish.

Diamond-back turtle.
NELL BALDACCHINO/U.S. FISH & WILDLIFE SERVICE

Timid by nature, diamond-back terrapins frequently are found sunning themselves on logs, but they will flee quickly into the water's protection at the slightest disturbance.

The diamond-back reaches a maximum length of nine inches. At its more typical size of eight inches, a female weighs a little more than a pound. The males tend to be smaller, reaching a length of five to six inches. Coloring varies from individual to individual, except for the throat and mouth area, which is usually off-white with black markings. The shell is sculpted in the distinctive pattern that gives the diamond-back its name.

Like the snapper, the diamond-back hibernates through the winter, emerging in the spring to mate and reproduce. A female terrapin matures at four to five years of age, which is when she lays her first clutch of eggs. She will continue to lay until she is about 40 years old.

The female leaves the water when she is

ready to lay, moving up into a marsh where she excavates a nest. There she will deposit anywhere from 6 to 24 nearly spherical, one-inch-diameter eggs. She then covers the clutch with debris, somewhat indifferently, and leaves the eggs to fend for themselves. Those eggs not eaten by predators will hatch in just less than three months. The eggs are preyed upon by raccoons, skunks, muskrats, and other animals. (While there are no regulations regarding snapper eggs, Maryland prohibits the possession, destruction, or disturbance of diamond-back terrapin eggs.) The young turtles are the favored prey of crows and herons until they are big enough that their size protects them. Even so, the real limit to the diamond-back population is shrinking habitat and human predation.

EASTERN WYE NARROWS

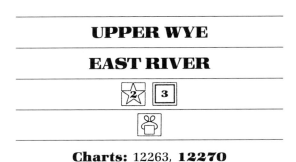

No facilities

Charts: 12263, **12270**

The eastern half of Wye Narrows branches off the Wye East River directly opposite the mouth of Skipton Creek. Although Wye Narrows runs between the Wye East and Wye West Rivers, the bridge that connects the north end of Wye Island with the mainland divides Wye Narrows into halves, both geographically and in terms of the character of the surroundings.

Approaches/Anchorages. Pay careful attention to your chart and stay in the middle of the waterway until you reach the first of two wide spots, southeast of the bridge. This is the best anchorage in this half of the narrows. There is 7 feet of water nearly up to the shore, except for a shoal that projects to the east from a point in the northwest corner of this miniature bay. The holding is good, but the land is low-lying and the banks are muddy, rising directly from the water—no beach.

If you continue toward the bridge, favor the east shore to avoid the shoal, mentioned earlier, which projects into the middle of the channel. The next anchorage is just short of the bridge, in 8 to 12 feet of water. Anchor near the bridge on the north side of the waterway, but don't get too close to the northeast corner of this "wide spot" to avoid the shoals there. There is almost no traffic over the bridge, so you need not worry about noise from that source.

As noted, the bridge is fixed, with only about a 10-foot vertical clearance. For all practical purposes and most cruising vessels, this is the head of navigation on the eastern half of Wye Narrows.

UPPER WYE EAST RIVER

Charts: 12263, **12270**

Approaches/Provisions. Just above the junction of the Wye East River and Wye Narrows is Wye Landing, on the east side of the river. This is a public launching ramp for trailered boats, so it tends to be rather busy on summer weekends. Wye Landing is also the sole place on the Wye where you can replenish your ice supply. Both blocks and cubes are available, as is bait for fishing and crabbing. No other supplies are available. While it may be possible to tie up briefly alongside the pier upstream of the launching ramp, deeper draft boats should anchor and land by dinghy. This spot is popular with runabouts, making it too active an anchorage for us.

Although the Wye East River is navigable by shoal-draft vessels for up to 2 more miles, most cruising boats have to call it quits less than a mile past Wye Landing. The first point on the starboard side is about as far as the river carries 5 feet of water. From there on, the river begins to shoal and depths of 2 and 3 feet occur with regularity.

History. The nearby village of Wye Mills is home to the Wye Oak, the oldest white oak in Maryland, reputed to be more than 400 years old. The Wye Oak is also the largest of its kind in Maryland—with a height of over 95 feet and a horizontal spread of about 165 feet, it is one of the largest in the United States.

WYE "WEST" RIVER

Charts: 12263, **12270**

The Wye West River doesn't have as many attractive anchorages as the eastern branch, but has plenty of well-protected coves, creeks, and bights to keep this branch high on the cruiser's "must visit" list.

Navigation here is straightforward. The few projecting shoals are well marked for the most part. Those that do not have markers are obvious on the chart and easily avoided.

DRUM POINT

No facilities

Charts: 12263, **12270**

Anchorages. The first good anchorage on the Wye West River is just off the south shore, in a bight due east of Drum Point. This bight is about one-half mile wide and has plenty of room for a lot of boats. The shore is sandy and, especially on Drum Point itself, provides an excellent beach for swimming, wading, or simply sunbathing.

The area is fairly open to winds from the north and northeast and a blow from that direction can make this a lumpy anchorage. The bottom is soft and the holding not very good, even with a plow anchor. We were once in the middle of a small raft that was caught by a blow with winds of 20 to 30 knots. The anchor boat had a 35-pound CQR plow anchor down with a 9:1 scope out; it plowed a furrow in the bottom for about 100 yards before we managed to break up the raft.

Probably the most popular anchorage on the Wye West River, Drum Point is a crowded anchorage for the whole boating season. For more seclusion, continue on.

BIGWOOD COVE

No facilities

Charts: 12263, **12270**

The first cove to starboard, about a mile past Drum Point, is Bigwood Cove. There is a large house with a surprising number of chimneys on the point opposite this cove. Once we were so engrossed in trying to count them that we managed to run aground off the point. That took a certain amount of talent since the shoal doesn't project out all that far.

Approaches/Anchorages. Entering the cove is relatively easy. Simply continue up the Wye River until the entrance to the cove is abeam, then turn and head directly for the center of the entrance. Within less than 100 yards, the cove forms a crude T. Stay out of the south fork, it is too shallow. The best anchorage is just inside the north fork.

Bigwood Cove provides a nice, secluded anchorage in 6 to 8 feet of water for one or two single boats. The shore is uninhabited and privacy is virtually insured. However, the shoreline is marshy and the cove is open for a reach of about a mile to the southeast. The cove is worth poking into, but an extended stay may not be a good idea.

GRAPEVINE COVE

No facilities

Charts: 12263, **12270**

Anchorages. Grapevine Cove opens to starboard just a few hundred yards past the big house on the point opposite Bigwood Cove. If you like privacy, try this cove, a secluded, well-protected little anchorage in 6 to 7 feet of water for half a dozen boats to anchor. There are rarely any boats and, once you are well into the cove, you are out of sight from most of the main river. The shoreline is undeveloped and the banks rise rather steeply from the water. The only beach is revealed at low tide, and is muddy. Holding is good, but the cove is so well protected that you probably could use a brick for an anchor and never know the difference. Conversely, it is a little too snug to be comfortable in the sticky, hot summer weather.

Approaches. While there is 9 feet of water in the entrance channel, you have to feel your way in due to the shoals on either side. Approach the entrance on a southeast course to avoid the shoal on the south side of the entrance.

UNNAMED COVES, WEST SHORE

No facilities

Anchorages. On the west side of the Wye West River, directly opposite Grapevine Cove, is an unnamed cove with two horns. Either of these "horns" provides a secure albeit unsecluded anchorage and is easier to enter than Grapevine Cove. However, the shoreline is all private property and you cannot land without the owners' permission.

WESTERN WYE NARROWS

No facilities

Charts: 12263, **12270**

Just past Grapevine Cove, the western part of Wye Narrows opens up to starboard. The entrance is broad and deep (10 to 14 feet) and navigation is straightforward.

You can anchor anywhere fairly close to the southern shore, where a series of sandy beaches stretches all the way from the entrance to the bridge.

Approaches/Anchorages. DeCoursey Cove is the first cove to port, about one-half mile from the entrance to the narrows. This cove provides a secure anchorage in 6 to 7 feet of water, but feel your way in because the shoals on either side of the entrance extend a long way across. Head directly north from the middle of the narrows, toward the lone house on shore, and you will clear the shoals easily. Don't look for the tiny island shown in the mouth of the cove on some charts; it no longer breaks the surface of the water. In midsummer, you may want to anchor well out from shore to avoid the clouds of no-see-ums that inhabit the north shore.

As you pass DeCoursey Cove, beware of the shoal projecting into the narrows from the east side of the cove entrance and the one projecting to the north directly opposite the point on the east side of DeCoursey Cove entrance.

The next cove to port is Covington Cove, a sheltered anchorage with 5 to 6 feet of water. The entrance is easy—there is 7 feet of water almost from shore to shore in the mouth of this cove. Don't travel up either horn of this cove as the water gets a bit thin for deeper draft boats. In hot, sticky summer weather you should avoid this cove. It is too protected to permit any breeze, which means no relief from heat or no-see-ums.

At this point, you have reached the fixed bridge (10 feet MHW vertical clearance) mentioned in the Eastern Wye Narrows section, and must stop.

QUARTER CREEK

No facilities

Charts: 12263, **12270**

Approaches. Continuing up the Wye "West" River, to starboard, just past the mouth of the Wye Narrows, is Quarter Creek. The entrance is straightforward and the creek carries 6 to 8 feet of water to its headwaters.

Anchorages. You can anchor anywhere here in good holding. The relatively high banks and the surrounding tall trees provide full protection from the weather and the curved entrance cuts off wakes from the Wye River.

No houses are visible from the creek so this anchorage is quiet and secluded. The first point to starboard after you enter has a small, sandy beach where you can land to swim or wade at other than extreme high tide. Most boats do not venture this far up the Wye West River, making this anchorage more private than you might expect, considering its attractiveness.

UPPER WYE
WEST RIVER

☆3   3

No facilities

Charts: 12263, **12270**

Past Quarter Creek, the Wye River narrows. Here numerous coves and creeks provide tight, secure anchorages. Be sure to check your chart before entering any of them and carefully feel your way in. Most shoal quickly past the entrance.

Anchorages. Actually, you can probably anchor anywhere on this part of the Wye River. Just pick a nice-looking spot and drop the hook. The whole river, from Quarter Creek north, is a gunkholer's delight.

MILES RIVER

Charts: 12263, **12270**

If you are approaching from Eastern Bay, a course of 161 degrees from the red "4" buoy off Tilghman Point takes you directly to the nun "12" buoy off Deep Water Point, where the Miles River begins to constrict. This course also neatly skirts a shoal, all that is left of an island, off the mouth of the Wye River.

If you are approaching from Kent Narrows, you may pass to either side of this shoal without lengthening your course. From the green "1" can off Parson Island, a course of 182 degrees takes you west of the shoal, to the red "10" buoy. Then a course change to 160 degrees takes you to the nun "12" buoy off Deep Water Point. Alternatively, a course of 174 degrees from the Parson Island green "1" takes you to can "1," which marks the eastern edge of the "late island" shoal. Beware of altering course too far to the east, because there is a shoal extending well to the southwest from Bennett Point at the mouth of the Wye River. From can "1," a course of 186 degrees takes you to the Deep Water Point nun "12." The compass courses are helpful because the buoys are almost impossible to see from more than a mile away.

Nun "12" serves as a reference for all of these approaches, but this red nun is difficult to see until you are about one-half mile from it. From nun "12," you can navigate virtually unaided the rest of the way up the river.

At Deep Water Point, the buoy numbering system changes from the Eastern Bay system to the Miles River system. One-half mile south of nun "12" is the green "1" lighted (Fl 4 sec.) spar, southeast of Deep Water Point; this marks the tip of the shoal extending west from Fairview Point. You must honor this marker and nun "2" beyond it. You can ignore nun "4" for all practical purposes, if you remain at least 300 yards off the western shore when heading into St. Michaels. The region between nuns "2" and "4" in the mouth of Long Haul Creek is often the scene of round-the-buoy regattas on summer weekends. Steer clear of here if a race is in progress.

At nun "4," St. Michaels is to starboard and the mouth of Leeds Creek is to port. Directly ahead, the rest of the Miles River continues for several more miles.

About 2½ miles past nun "4," the river makes a right-angle turn to the northeast, around the end of Long Point. As soon as you clear Long Point, the mouth of Hunting Creek opens up to port. The river continues to be navigable for another 5 miles, with more anchorages beyond the drawbridge, 3 miles ahead.

LONG HAUL CREEK

⭐2 □3

🚰 ⛴

Charts: 12263, 12270

Approaches. Long Haul Creek, to starboard as you pass nun "2," is the home of the Miles River Yacht Club. The entrance to this creek is not difficult, even without the club buoys put out during the yachting season. After rounding nun "2," simply line up the range lights on the club dock, on the southwest shore of the creek, and follow the range all the way to the dock.

Dockages/Anchorages. If you choose to stop in this creek, you can often obtain a slip at the club. Failing that, you can anchor out in either the south or north fork of the creek. Should you choose the former, stay near the south shore to avoid the shoal waters along the opposite side. For the north fork, simply stay near the middle until you pass the little point to port. You can anchor just past this point, fully protected from weather and wakes, in about 8 feet of water.

Provisions/Facilities. Water and electricity are available at the yacht club dock. For fuel or supplies, head for St. Michaels about a mile away.

ST. MICHAELS

⭐5 □3

All facilities

Charts: 12263, 12270

For most of its 300-year history, St. Michaels has been a workingman's community. Like many of the towns on the Chesapeake Bay, it has become a tourist attraction in the last decade or so.

The town is small for its reputation. St. Michaels is famous for its yacht harbor, maritime museum, crab and seafood restaurants, and old houses dating back 200 or

more years. In St. Michaels harbor, expensive yachts can be found docked hull-to-hull with the workboats of clammers, oyster tongers, and trotline crabbers. Boutiques and gift shops—even an art gallery—are interspersed with hardware stores, laundromats, and a foundry.

History. According to the Chesapeake Bay Maritime Museum, the earliest recorded reference to St. Michaels was made in 1631 by a Captain Claiborne of Kent Island who traded at a town on "Shipping Creek." The town, unnamed at first, grew up around a log church built in 1670 by Edward Elliot. The church was rebuilt on the same site three times, resulting in the present handsome, 100-year-old building made from massive stones quarried near Havre de Grace.

In 1680, the town was named St. Michaels, after the archangel. Later, it became a shipbuilding center. By the time of the American Revolution, there were about 25 boatyards, which built everything from punts to schooners. During the War of 1812, St. Michaels shipyards produced privateers and gunboats that harassed British shipping.

The British finally became so incensed that several Men-of-War were ordered up the Chesapeake to shell St. Michaels and destroy her shipyards. On the evening of August 10, 1813, the fleet arrived off St. Michaels and proceeded to shell the village. Anticipating the attack, the townsmen, under the leadership of Brigadier General Perry Benson, hung lanterns high in the trees around the town and darkened all the houses and outbuildings. The British gunners, thinking that the town was on a hill, overshot it with every round except one. That one cannonball crashed through the roof of a house owned by William Marchant, a shipwright, and bounced downstairs past Mrs. Marchant, who was carrying her daughter down those same stairs at that very moment. The house has since been known as "the cannonball house."

Most of the shipyards are gone, and the main industry is now seafood—both the catching and the serving of it. The 1,500 residents of St. Michaels still carry on their day-to-day business much as they always have, and their lovely, placid town holds a strong attraction for cruising people.

Approaches. As you pass nun "2" in the Miles River, stay at least 300 yards off the western shore and head for flashing red "2" and green can "3" at the entrance to St. Michaels harbor. (You can pretty much ignore the nun "4" buoy in the Miles River.) As you pass between red "2" and can "3," you will be heading directly toward the Chesapeake Bay Maritime Museum on Navy Point. There is no mistaking Navy Point. Perched on the end of the point is the six-sided, cottage-type lighthouse which was moved to the museum from Hooper's Straight in 1966 to save it from demolition. First lighted in 1879, it is one of only three lighthouses of this type left in the Bay region. To starboard is a little creek where you can anchor in relative peace and quiet, or you can head for the marinas and restaurants in the main harbor to port.

Where to Eat. During the main boating season, several of the restaurants maintain free water taxis for those on boats or at the maritime museum who want to dine there.

As you enter the main harbor, you can't miss The Crab Claw Restaurant. It is one of the four restaurants directly accessible from the water and has several slips on its west side where you can tie up a boat as long as 40 feet while dining there. From the dining room on the second floor, you have an excellent view of the harbor, and you can often watch oyster boats unloading their catch at the main dock directly below. As the name suggests, the emphasis at The Crab Claw is on crab and crab dishes, although other fare is offered. We have yet to be served a meal that has been less than excellent, and the prices are reasonable.

In the southwest corner of the harbor, diagonally across from the lighthouse, is Longfellow's Restaurant,

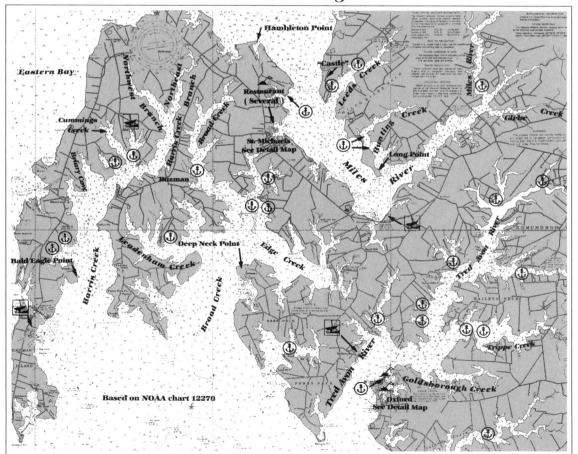

St. Michaels Region

Based on NOAA chart 12270

SCALE **1″ = 2.12** NAUT. MILES   Good anchoring   Mooring area   Launching site

St. Michaels

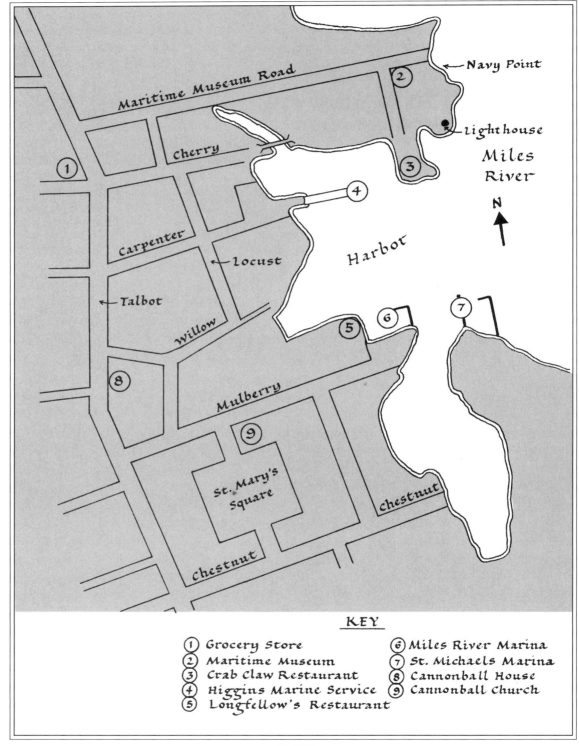

Maritime Museum Road

Cherry

Carpenter

Locust

Talbot

Willow

Mulberry

St. Mary's Square

Chestnut

Chestnut

Harbor

Navy Point

Lighthouse

Miles River

N

KEY

① Grocery Store
② Maritime Museum
③ Crab Claw Restaurant
④ Higgins Marine Service
⑤ Longfellow's Restaurant
⑥ Miles River Marina
⑦ St. Michaels Marina
⑧ Cannonball House
⑨ Cannonball Church

SCALE 1″= 300 FEET

certainly the fanciest of the four restaurants on the main harbor. If you go by water, you need a dinghy, because the landing dock is inadequate for anything larger. Longfellow's has a wide selection of delicious meals offered in an elegant, air-conditioned room overlooking the harbor. The service is excellent; the prices are fairly high, but Longfellow's accepts major credit cards.

If you are on a tight budget, try the Quarterdeck Restaurant, next to Longfellow's. It is associated with the Miles River Marina, where you can either tie up during dinner or rent a slip for the night. The Quarterdeck is more representative of Eastern Shore waterfront restaurants.

In the cove on the other side of Navy Point is The Inn at Perry Cabin. Previously a nightclub, it is now a fancy bed & breakfast and restaurant (coat and tie required).

Dockages/Things to Do. With the exception of The Crab Claw, Navy Point is occupied entirely by the Chesapeake Bay Maritime Museum. Some of the buildings are new but others date back to the mid-1800s. Slips are available to museum "Boating Members" on a first come basis, and they tend to fill up early on summer weekends. There is both a dockage and an admission fee, but members may visit the museum as often as they like at no additional charge. No electricity is available at the docks, but water and trash disposal are.

The main part of the museum is on the outer half of Navy Point. The buildings house a waterfowling exhibit, a waterman's exhibit, and a display of small boats indigenous to the Chesapeake. Outside are more exhibits, such as the fog bell tower and the original 1,000-pound bell from Point Lookout, a boat workshop, the Hooper's Straight Lighthouse, and the floating exhibits. Newly recovered boats are restored and the existing fleet maintained with the museum's own marine railway and boat shop. When a relic of the sailing past is discovered on one of the salt marshes of the Bay, it is often brought to the museum for restoration. As a result, the fleet is growing every year.

Anchorages. Transient slips are usually available at the harbor marinas but, if a slip is not available or you choose to anchor out, you will find the anchorage in the harbor to be quite small, and crowded on holidays and weekends during the cruising season. The holding is also far from the best here. Alternative anchorages are available across the Miles River in Leeds

MILES
RIVER

171

Old Hoopers Straight Lighthouse was moved in 1966 from the Strait to Navy Point at the St. Michaels Maritime Museum. This view is looking west from the entrance to St. Michaels Harbor.

Creek or, as previously mentioned, in either branch of Long Haul Creek beyond the Miles River Yacht Club.

LEEDS CREEK

⬚★3 ⬚3

No facilities

Charts: 12263, **12270**

Leeds Creek is located directly across the Miles River from St. Michaels. For decades, this creek has provided a convenient, easily entered, alternative to remaining overnight in St. Michaels harbor. Recently, the shoals at the mouth of the creek have been encroaching on the entrance channel, making the proper channel more difficult to find and follow.

Approaches. If you are approaching from the north, give the green can "1" buoy off Fairview Point a wide berth until it is abeam. The shoal extends well to the north and west of the buoy. Once the buoy is abeam, turn to port and, leaving can "1" about 50 yards to port, assume a course tangent to the first point on the south side of the creek until you are a little more than 200 yards past can "1." Then swing to port to assume a course to take you about three-quarters of the way to the north side of the creek mouth. Proceed slowly and sound your way in because the shoal has been growing each year. Once the tip of Fairview Point is abeam, you are in. Favor the north side of the creek as you proceed upstream so that you avoid the two protruding shoals extending from the south side of the creek.

Anchorages. The first anchorage is in the cove to port after you enter. A fascinating "castle" stands at the head of the cove. The story is that it was built by a member of the Winchester family who was afraid of being assassinated. As a result, he constructed his home like a fortification, complete with secret rooms and "hidey holes." We can't vouch for the truth of this story, but the building is an impressive sight and the cove is a nice anchorage in its own right.

The next good anchorage is in either of the twin coves to port, just under a mile from the creek mouth. The first cove is more secluded—no buildings or tall trees line the banks. Favor the west side of the cove to avoid the shoal to the northeast. The second cove has deep water shore to shore, but a couple of houses there reduce privacy. For some reason, the first little cove is a favorite haunt of horseshoe crabs. We find several complete shells from these interesting creatures, ranging in size from a couple of inches to more than a foot across, every time we come here.

From here on, the creek is protected by a small dogleg, allowing you to anchor anywhere in full protection from the weather. All but shallow-draft powerboats should stay out of the inviting-looking cove to starboard past the dogleg. There is a bar at the mouth and the water is only about 4 feet deep once you are inside.

You can proceed upstream almost to the fixed bridge, just short of the towns of Copperville and Tunis Mills. The bridge's 6-foot vertical clearance bars passage to all but small runabouts or dinghies—besides, the water starts to shoal here. Beware of submerged pilings off the point to starboard a couple of hundred yards short of the bridge.

HUNTING CREEK

No facilities

Charts: 12263, **12270**

Approaches. About 2½ miles past St. Michaels, after the Miles River makes a sudden hook to the northeast, the entrance to Hunting Creek will be to port. Even though there is about 10 feet of water very close to the southern tip of Long Point, stay well off since there are also some submerged pilings.

To enter the creek, just stay in the middle, avoid the points and honor the red and green daymarks. The creek is navigable for a good 2 miles from its mouth.

Anchorages. Anywhere you anchor in here is fully protected from wind and wave; passing traffic is limited to an occasional workboat.

There are no facilities on this creek; most of the banks appear unspoiled and houses are sparse, although this condition is unlikely to last much longer. For now, it is a beautiful, serene creek.

This creek holds at least one very vivid memory for us. One October, we anchored here in temperatures over 80 degrees. The following morning, we awoke to a blizzard with 2 inches of snow already on the deck! Looking ashore to the island, we saw a small herd of deer peering back at us through the blowing snow. I still wonder which of us was the more perplexed. (Needless to say, we stayed put until it cleared.)

UPPER MILES RIVER

No facilities

Charts: 12263, 12266, **12270**

From Hunting Creek, the Miles River is navigable for another 5 miles. The banks are lined with beautiful homes and the river itself is peaceful. The drawbridge 3 miles above Hunting Creek opens on demand, sunrise to sunset. Otherwise 6 hours notice is required.

Anchorages. It is feasible to anchor anywhere along the sides of the river in full security, having only to contend with the wakes from local powerboats.

Past the bridge, the river splits into three forks. The first fork, Glebe Creek, shoals fairly rapidly about one-half mile past its mouth, however the entrance offers a nice anchorage. The next fork, Goldsborough Creek, is navigable for about a mile, also offering well-protected anchorages. The third fork, the main Miles River, continues for about 2 miles, although here it is narrow and looks more like a small creek than the wide river you have been negotiating up to this point. It, too, provides secure anchorages anywhere along its length.

POPLAR ISLAND
AND NARROWS

Charts: 12263, 12266, **12270**

At the northern entrance to Poplar Narrows, which runs between the islands and the mainland, is red nun

"8," a reminder that the buoyage system in the narrows is still referenced to Eastern Bay. When entering Poplar Narrows from the north, you must treat the navigation markers as if you are leaving Eastern Bay. The red markers are left to port and the green markers to starboard until you reach the lighted green "1" marker south of Poplar Island. Navigation here means threading your way through numerous crab pots. Even though regulations state that from Memorial Day to Labor Day no crab pots are to be placed in a 50-foot channel through Poplar Island Narrows, usually you have to avoid many pots.

There is a shoal that extends nearly a mile to the northeast of Valient Point on Jefferson Island, one of the islands in the Poplar Island group. Allow plenty of room to clear it as you enter Poplar Island Narrows. If you are not a good judge of distance, hold close to nun "8" and then come to a course of 192 degrees until you pick up can "5," east of Coaches Island (the southernmost of the island cluster). From there, follow the markers until you reach the lighted green "1" marker at the southernmost part of Poplar Island Narrows. Give the last two markers a wide berth because of the shoal southeast of Coaches Island. Boats drawing 6 feet or more probably should not attempt the passage through the narrows because of shoaling in this area. (A good friend of ours has a boat with a 6-foot draft. We once led him through the narrows, warning him that he may bump a couple of times, and he did—exactly twice.)

POPLAR HARBOR

No facilities

Charts: 12263, 12266, **12270**

Approaches. Although you occasionally find sizable sailboats anchored in Poplar Harbor, the approach is restricted to shoal-draft vessels. If you carry a draft of 5 feet or more, don't try it unless grounding doesn't bother you. If you do try it, take your departure from the red "6" marker west of Ferry Cove in Poplar Narrows on a course of 267 degrees toward the northern tip of Bare Island (the first one northwest of Coaches Island).

Anchorages. Once inside Poplar Harbor, you can anchor in 5 to 6 feet of water, fairly well protected from wave action. Here you can watch the traffic on the Bay go by. Anchoring here is recommended only in fair weather as gusty winds can make it a bit "lumpy." Don't enter at all if the wind is strong out of the north. Northerlies have a tendency to blow the water out of the Bay; you may find yourself stranded.

CHOPTANK RIVER

Charts: 12263, 12266, **12268,** 12270

The Choptank River is the largest river on the Eastern Shore. Although it is navigable for most boats as far as Denton, 45 miles upriver from the mouth, and as far as Greensboro for shoal-draft boats, there is little reason for any but the confirmed gunkholer to proceed much beyond the town of Choptank, 8 miles above the bridge at Cambridge (vertical clearance 50 feet). The river is deep, well marked, and protected enough for you to anchor nearly anywhere along the banks of the river, but it winds among low-lying, buggy marshes beyond Choptank and the best cruising grounds are below this point.

At one time, a substantial island was located in the mouth of the Choptank river, south of Tilghman Island. In 1675, the island was nearly 900 acres in size and belonged to a doctor, Peter Sharp, for whom it was named. By 1847, the wind, waves, and storms of the Chesapeake had eroded to island to half its size, about 473 acres. From then on, the erosion accelerated, reducing

Sharps Island Lighthouse, looking west. The island has long since been reduced to a shoal outside the mouth of the Choptank River. Ice floes have forced the lighthouse askew, but it is still in service.

the island to a mere 94 acres in 1900 and finally to nothing but a shoal in 1963. A series of lighthouses were built on the island, all but the last becoming undermined by the waters or ice and being destroyed. The present lighthouse was originally built in 1882 on a 5-acre circular plot of land, which disappeared along with the rest of the island. The lighthouse now stands in 10 feet of water. The brown painted circular lighthouse was tilted by ice in 1973 and even further by more ice in 1976. It has assumed a rakish angle, making it easily identifiable from a distance, marking the north end of the shoal that was once Sharps Island.

KNAPPS NARROWS

Charts: 12263, **12266,** 12268, 12270

At the mouth of the Choptank River is a peninsula pointing south toward the now-submerged Sharps Island. The southern half of this peninsula is actually an island by virtue of a narrow channel from the Bay to the Choptank River, which separates Tilghman Island from the mainland. This channel, Knapps Narrows, saves 5 miles in the passage from the northern Bay into the Choptank River. The channel is heavily used by both local watermen and pleasure boaters who cruise the Choptank River and its tributaries.

Knapps Narrows is not merely a convenient passage for casual yachtsmen. For more than 400 years it has been the home of a sizable fleet of the traditional workboats of the Bay watermen. From late spring through early fall, pleasure craft mingle with the workboats. During the winter months, the yachts disappear, leaving the water to the workboats.

Approaches. As you pass the southern end of Poplar Island, you can see the lighted green "1" marker at the entrance to Knapps Narrows. If you have trouble picking it out from the shoreline, a course of 155 degrees from Poplar Island "1" will take you directly to it.

There is usually shoaling on the Bay side of Knapps

Narrows, particularly if winter gales have been severe. After it was dredged in 1980, another red marker was added. (It is re-dredged periodically.) The new marker has eased the approach. The controlling depth is typically 6 to 7 feet, if you stay in the center of the channel. Even so, check with someone who has been through recently if you are making your first passage for the season. It has a bad habit of shoaling in the vicinity of the red "4" light on the Bay side.

Be sure to hold close to the red "4" light as you approach it, then swing sharply to starboard and head directly for the middle of the entrance to the narrows. In this way you easily avoid the encroaching shoal northeast of red "4" and allow yourself to enter the narrows proper. From here, favor the south side of the channel until you reach the drawbridge. You can hold to within 10 feet of the south shore in this section, but don't try it on the north side unless you like plowing through mud.

At the bridge, the buoyage system reverses. In other words, when you enter from the Bay side, all green markers are left to port. Immediately on passing the bridge, you must leave all green markers to starboard.

Although we do not recommend passing through the narrows at night, the bridge opens on demand 24 hours a day. Each time we have made the passage, the bridge operator has been alert and very responsive. Everyone we met there on both commercial and private craft has been courteous, and this bridge is devoid of the "me first" attitude often encountered in Kent Narrows. Sometimes the current through the narrows is fairly strong, but it has never caused us any problems.

Once you clear the bridge, you are in deep water throughout the passage until you reach the flashing red "6" marker at the start of the channel into the Choptank River from the narrows proper.

Leave red "6" close to port and hold a course parallel to a line drawn between the green markers to starboard but no closer than 50 feet to them. The markers are not directly on the edge of the channel, but offset about that distance to the south of it. Don't get too far to the north either, as the channel is not more than 100 feet wide. Hold this course until you have passed the lighted green "3," the last channel marker. If you are proceeding north into Harris Creek, hold this course for at least another 400 yards before heading toward the mouth of the creek. This ensures that you clear the shoal to the north. For any other destination on the Choptank, you can come to your new course as soon as you reach green "3."

Dockages/Provisions. Although definitely a waterman's harbor, Knapps Narrows is also frequented by pleasure craft and has facilities designed for them. There are three large marinas, that cater to yachts and smaller pleasure boats. Four other boatyards cater primarily to the local watermen and their craft. There are at least two restaurants right on the waterfront near the bridge. One of these, the Bay Hundred, is located at Knapps Narrows Marina, adjacent to and northwest of the drawbridge. Temporary dockage while eating at Bay Hundred is available at the marina, although depth at the fuel dock can be "iffy." Directly across the channel is the Bridge Restaurant. The "Bridge" changed hands recently and we are unaware of any changes the new management has made. One thing we know hasn't changed; you can still see watermen offloading their catch at the pier. A warning: Do not fill your fresh water tanks from the hoses so conveniently placed on the outside of the Bridge Restaurant. Those hoses are used to wash down the oyster and clam unloading area on the pier with *seawater* pumped from the narrows.

Although not obvious to the casual observer, the Tilghman County Dock is in the artificial cove adjacent to the Bridge Restaurant. There is some confusion as to exactly which part of the pier belongs to the restaurant (which charges a fee to tie up overnight) and where the County Dock portion begins (which does not charge a fee). The rule of thumb that we use is the County Dock starts with the portion of the pier immediately south of the corner of the restaurant building and continues clockwise all the way around the cove.

The narrows is an excellent place to refuel, restock supplies, or to sit down to a meal at a good restaurant, but it is not a good place to spend a quiet night. The waterway is always busy and, even if you can find a place to tie up for the night, you are sure to be awakened in the wee hours of the morning as the watermen get underway.

On the Choptank River side of Tilghman Island, about a stone's throw south of Knapps Narrows, is a small basin populated by workboats and a few skipjacks. Harrison's Chesapeake House (hotel and restaurant) is located here. If you have a draft that permits entrance (the channel was just under 6 feet MLW in 1988) and are looking for a super meal, try it! You can tie up off the end of any of the three piers just inside the entrance channel long enough for a meal (which, incidently, we guarantee will be outstanding). We do not recommend anchoring overnight, although the channel and basin are dredged to a mean depth of 6 feet. A strong east wind makes mooring at Harrison's piers uncomfortable at best.

CHOPTANK RIVER/ HARRIS CREEK

Charts: 12263, **12266,** 12270

Once you are clear of Knapps Narrows, the approach to Harris Creek is easy. Simply honor the markers as you proceed up the creek. You have to contend with only one unmarked shoal, which extends to the southwest from Indian Point on the east side of the creek, just past Dun Cove. If you hold to within a couple of hundred yards of green "7" off Seaths Point, you avoid it easily.

This creek has many anchorages. The most popular one, in Dun Cove, provides excellent protection from weather and is the closest harbor for convenient passage to or from Knapps Narrows. If you are looking for more seclusion, pick one of the creeks or coves farther up Harris Creek.

DUN COVE

No facilities

Charts: 12263, **12266,** 12270

Two miles to the north of the eastern end of Knapps Narrows, Dun Cove is an appealing spot to spend the night. Both arms of this cove are excellent anchorages.

Approaches. After passing the green "5" marker in Harris Creek, due east of Bald Eagle Point, head directly for the red "6" marker east of Dun Cove before turning to head directly into the middle of the entrance to the cove. Shoals project from both the north and south sides of the entrance, so keep to the middle at all times.

Anchorages. Anchoring in the south arm of the cove is perfectly satisfactory, but the north arm of the cove is more popular because it is better sheltered. In either case, the bottom is mud and clay, which serve as good holding ground, and the surrounding trees break the wind. It is surprising how suddenly a howling wind and foul weather moderate as soon as you turn into the protection of either arm of Dun Cove.

Except for the farmhouse at the extreme end of the north arm of the cove, the surroundings are woods on one side and fields on the other. There are sandy beaches where you can land to stretch your legs, although the land off the beach is posted with "No Trespassing" signs. It is not surprising that this anchorage is a favorite spot for cruisers. As a corollary, the cove is often crowded on weekends during the boating season.

WATERHOLE COVE

No facilities

Charts: 12263, **12266,** 12270

The next anchorage above Dun Cove is Waterhole Cove. There are several homes on the shore, but the impression is of a relatively unspoiled shoreline. The holding is generally good and there are some small sandy beaches to the west and one off Smith Point to the north.

Anchorages. While you can tuck well into the west side of the mouth of the cove to gain the protection of Smith Point from the north to northeast, most cruisers elect to anchor farther out to catch the cooling breezes in the warm weather. This anchorage's main disadvantage is being wide open to the east and southeast. Normally, this is no problem, but one night we did have to break up a raft at 2:00 a.m. when the wind shifted and started to blow hard from that direction.

BRIARY COVE

No facilities

Charts: 12263, **12270**

Briary Cove is almost a clone of Waterhole Cove. The same description fits it except that there is less room to anchor because of the shoaling along each shore and there is an unmarked 4-foot shoal extending two-thirds of the way across the entrance from the point on the northeast side of the mouth. Since there are better anchorages nearby, we recommend passing up this one.

UNNAMED COVE

No facilities

Charts: 12263, **12270**

Between Briary Cove and Cummings Creek is an attractive little cove that is not named on any of our charts. It is a pretty little spot but relatively open to the southeast unless you draw less than 5 feet and can get around the point into the left fork. The bottom is soft mud. You may drag a bit if the wind pipes up, but you probably won't drag very far as your anchor will soon bury itself deep into firmer mud.

Our general impression of this cove is one of pristine surroundings. Try it. You probably will find yourself in your own private anchorage!

CUMMINGS CREEK

Charts: 12263, **12270**

Approaches. If you feel your way through the narrow entrance channel into Cummings Creek, you are likely to have a private little anchorage all to yourself. Leave the quick-flashing marker close to starboard and stay in the middle to enter.

Anchorages. The depth of Cummings Creek is 6 to 7 feet inside the left (west) fork, but you can anchor in 7 to 8 feet of water in the left fork or right in the mouth of the right fork, well protected from weather in all directions except the southeast. Don't proceed past the mouth of the right fork; it shoals quickly. The couple of small boatyards in here offer nothing for the transient. The concrete launching ramp indicates some runabout traffic, which may make you decide to anchor elsewhere. Even so it is worth a look around.

UPPER HARRIS

CREEK

No facilities

Charts: 12263, **12270**

The creek is navigable for more than a mile above Cummings Creek and you can anchor in numerous places along the way, all the way up into the Northeast Branch. Don't try to enter the Northwest Branch; there is a 2-foot bar across its mouth.

CHOPTANK RIVER/
BROAD CREEK

Charts: 12263, 12266, **12270**

Perhaps one of the most underrated cruising grounds in the vicinity of the Choptank River is the Broad Creek area. In discussions concerning cruising the Choptank River, you seldom hear Broad Creek or its several tributaries mentioned. The reason is not clear, but the omission may have to do with the lack of fuel and supplies on Broad Creek or its tributaries. The nearest point for fuel and supplies is in Oxford on the Tred Avon River, about 7 miles from the green "1" light at the mouth of Broad Creek. I find the lack of facilities odd since the region abounds in attractive scenery and excellent anchorages—both in the main creek and its offshoots.

Broad Creek winds its way north for about 6 miles from its mouth on the Choptank River to its headwaters. From the flashing green "1" light at the mouth of Broad Creek, a course of 10 degrees takes you directly to the lighted red "4" marker off Deep Neck Point. Do not stray very far to the east of this course or you may run afoul of the wide shoal off Deep Neck near the course midpoint.

As you approach the red "4", do not let yourself become confused by the readily visible group of red and green daymarks beyond it. Simply ignore all the daymarks until you clear red "4," then change course to head either into Leadenham Creek to the west or to a northeast course to head farther up Broad Creek proper. Be sure to leave the red "6" daymark to starboard. At red "6" you can either swing to port to head up Broad Creek or swing right toward red "8" to enter Edge Creek or San Domingo Creek. In either direction, attractive anchorages beckon and worrisome shoals are well marked.

BALLS CREEK

No facilities

Charts: 12263, **12266,** 12270

The first creek to port as you proceed up Broad Creek, Balls Creek is the home of a fleet of watermen. Although well-marked, the entrance, with its three doglegs, is nerve-racking the first time through and the creek itself offers little. The low banks are muddy and the bottom is stoney toward the sides of the creek, making anchoring a little uncertain. We recommend passing it up.

LEADENHAM CREEK

No facilities

Charts: 12263, **12266,** 12270

Approaches. As you approach the red "4" light off Deep Neck Point, you can begin to swing to port as soon as you can see the pair of red and green daymarks marking the entrance to Leadenham Creek. Although there are no more markers after these two, that presents no problem. Just stay near the middle of the creek. If you plan to continue up Leadenham Creek, swing to port immediately after passing the green "1" daymark, otherwise you may find yourself heading up Grace Creek.

Anchorages. The best anchorage on the Leadenham is in the unnamed cove that opens to starboard about one-half mile past green "1." This pretty cove, with 10 feet of water and good holding, is well protected from all directions except the south. Even from the south, the maximum fetch is little more than one-half mile. We once weathered a pretty good blow here in complete comfort. There are only a couple of houses in the northwest corner of the cove and, although all of the land is private property, there are lots of sandy beaches along the eastern side—backed by a screen of trees in front of a farm field—where you can land to stretch your legs a little.

The next opening to starboard is Caulk Cove, where you can anchor securely in 8 feet of water. This is an attractive anchorage, but the muddy banks offer nowhere to land. The same can be said about the remaining portion of Leadenham Creek. Don't travel much beyond the point where the creek bends sharply to the northwest; from there on it begins to shoal.

GRACE CREEK

Charts: 12263, **12266**, 12270

Approaches. As you pass the red "2" daymark at the entrance to Leadenham Creek, swing to starboard and you easily enter Grace Creek. There is no tricky channel and it is well marked where needed.

Anchorages. The first and best anchorage is in the little cove to port less than 400 yards past red "2." This is out of the way of any traffic and the holding is good, in soft mud. To the west there is a beach, which appears to be sandy, backed by a screen of trees in front of a field.

As you continue up Grace Creek toward Bozman, you find a series of watermen's docks and the P. T. Hambleton Marine Railway. On a good day, you may be able to purchase some seafood. No fuel is available.

UPPER BROAD

CREEK

No facilities

Charts: 12263, 12266, **12270**

Approaches. If you swing to port on reaching red "6" at the junction of Broad and Edge Creeks, you can continue into the upper reaches of Broad Creek for 3 miles. Simply stay to the middle of the creek. The few projecting shoals are well marked and the many bights offer a number of spots where you can pull in and anchor.

Anchorages. Most of the shoreline is lined with private homes, with the exception of Hambleton Island to starboard, until you get well up into the headwaters.

From the part of the creek that runs north-south up to the head of navigation, you have a number of attractive spots in which to anchor in relative seclusion. All are well protected and have the mud bottom that offers good holding. Once while exploring this part of the creek, we were overtaken by a line squall. We simply dropped the hook right where we were and rode it out in comfort and security.

EDGE CREEK

No facilities

Charts: 12263, 12266, **12270**

As you reach red "8" to the north of Cedar Point, you are entering the mouth of Edge Creek. Unless you have a definite reason for doing so and some local knowledge, do not try any of the tributaries off Edge Creek, except San Domingo Creek. They are full of shoals and in most the water is uncomfortably thin. We recommend proceeding no farther than Drum Point, just past the mouth of San Domingo Creek, if you are in a sailboat.

There is an overhead power cable across Edge Creek with a vertical clearance of only 26 feet. This is normally not a problem since it is nearly at the headwaters and the water is too shoal for any sailboats, but powerboats with tall antennas should be careful.

SAN DOMINGO CREEK

No facilities

Charts: 12263, 12266, **12270**

Approaches. As you clear red "8" in Edge Creek, come to a southeast course to the green "9" marker. Give this marker a wide berth as you turn to enter San Domingo Creek. The shoal from the south end of Hambleton Island gradually is extending to the southeast and, during our last trip, had progressed well past the marker. Keep a good 100 yards off the marker and you will enter San Domingo Creek with no trouble.

Once into the creek, stay in the middle. There are only two projecting shoals, both well-marked by daymarks green "11" and red "12". If you have a draft of 4 feet or less, you can proceed to within one-half mile of St. Michaels in the headwaters of the creek. There is a public dock where watermen tie up at the extreme end of the east fork of the very northern end of the creek. If you have a draft of more than 2 feet, your only approach is in a dinghy. From here it is about a half-mile walk into the town of St. Michaels, entering by the "back door."

Anchorages.   There are several excellent anchorages on San Domingo Creek. If you have no need to go ashore to stretch your legs or explore, proceed past Hopkins Point and you can anchor almost anywhere with full protection from wind and wave. Some of the better anchorages are in the fork of the creek to starboard, immediately past the red "14" daymark.

Alternatively, you might choose the mouth of the branch to port, about 600 yards past red "14." Beyond that, you are into the headwaters of the creek where the water starts to shoal.

In all cases, the bottom is mud over a clay base, which makes for very good holding ground.

If you are looking for relative solitude and a place to land and explore, Hambleton Island offers at least two secure anchorages and several small sandy beaches. The charted depths are deceptive. There is actually more water and the deep water is closer to shore than indicated by the NOAA charts—at least this was true in places we tried.

Hambleton Island is actually two islands, although they have only the one name. From the evidence of the shoal between them, it is obvious that these two islands were connected in the not too distant past. Having explored this connecting shoal by dinghy and finding what looked to be about one foot of water between the two parts of the island, we were floored when we observed a medium-size workboat blithely cross over it and proceed on into Broad Creek. The attitude of the local watermen toward shoals and their ability to avoid or ignore them never ceases to amaze us!

There are two good potential anchorages off Hambleton Island, both attractive to cruising boats of any size. The first is off the southern portion of the island, in a little bight immediately to the southwest of the

green "11" daymark (middle of the lower island). Do not try to anchor immediately to the northwest of green "11" or even get close to it; there are submerged pilings and a shoal there. The island has a nice beach right near this anchorage and a somewhat larger one on the north side right around the point.

The second anchorage is anywhere to the east of the northern portion of the island; you can anchor to within 50 yards of the beach in 9 to 11 feet of water over a soft mud and clay bottom. Don't go into the inviting cove to the north of the island; there is only one foot of water between the island and the mainland.

Once you pass the initial barrier of high banks and brush above the beach, you can try exploring the islands. It is easier to land at high tide either by beaching a dinghy or tying to one of the fallen trees and using the tree as a bridge onto the island proper. At low tide, a dinghy grounds 20 to 50 yards from the beach and you have to wade through the mud and sea nettles in order to land. It is also harder to reach any of the fallen trees. At high tide, most of these problems go away.

Once you are on the island, walking is fairly easy and the poison ivy, although present, is not profuse enough to deter exploration.

The southern portion of the island is about six-tenths of a mile long; the shoal between the two parts is about two-tenths, and the northern portion of the island is about two-tenths, for a distance of just over a mile from the southern tip of the south portion to the northern tip of the north portion of Hambleton Island. Either portion has ample room for you to exercise your legs.

Wherever you choose to anchor on San Domingo Creek, you should have peace and quiet. In spite of the numerous piers and sizable boats in this area, everyone is extremely courteous to and considerate of anchored visiting boats—and the water traffic is very light.

CHOPTANK RIVER/ IRISH CREEK

No facilities

Charts: 12263, **12266**

Tred Avon River Region (Irish Creek to Island Creek)

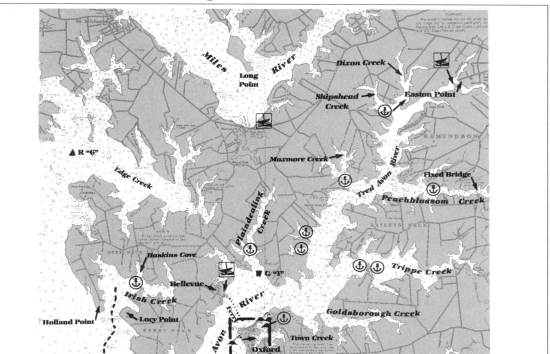

SCALE **1"=1.65** NAUT. MILES ⚓ **Good anchoring** ⚓ **Mooring area** ⚓ **Launching site**

Approaches. Entering this creek is tricky—contrary to its straightforward appearance on the chart. Although sailboats as large as 35 feet regularly negotiate Irish Creek, the channel is a true test of piloting skills and a challenge to every dyed-in-the-wool gunkholer.

The first part of the entrance *is* straightforward. Pick up the green "1" can and head to leave the red "2" nun close to starboard. After rounding red "2", head to leave the green "3" daymark less than 50 yards to port. Now comes the test. You cannot take a straight course from green "3" to red "4." A shoal protrudes from the southwest shore at Lucy Point, so you must take a gentle arc to port until halfway between the markers then

follow the same curve back to red "4." Proceed slowly and use a lead line or pole on either side of the boat to warn you when you are getting too far to one side or other of the channel. If the duckblind off Holland Point is still there, you can use it as if it were another green marker to guide you.

Anchorages. Once past red "4," you are in. Be sure to honor the red "6" daymark off Edwards Point before swinging to starboard. Anchor anywhere in this quiet, well-protected harbor with few other boats, save those belonging to people who live there. Perhaps the most attractive anchorage is in 9 feet of water right in the mouth of Haskins Cove.

The creek carries 6 to 10 feet of water throughout, except in the extreme eastern portion where it bends sharply to the north. Don't enter very far into the attractive little cove between Lucy and Edwards Points as it shoals quickly.

CHOPTANK
RIVER/
TRED
AVON
RIVER

182

CHOPTANK RIVER/ TRED AVON RIVER

Charts: 12263, 12266

About 7½ miles from the mouth of the Choptank River is a large, 35-foot high, lighted spider (Choptank River Light), which marks the mouth of the Tred Avon River. From this point, the river wanders to the north and east with a variety of creeks and coves offering anchorages ranging from secluded to commercial. Many of the shoals upriver used to be unmarked, presenting a minor navigational hazard. Now, there are enough strategically placed markers to keep you off the mud, if you are prudent.

While the Choptank River Light serves as an excellent reference, visible for several miles, it need not be honored when approaching the Tred Avon. Definitely leave the lighted green "1" marker off Benoni Point to port. From Benoni Point, a course of 18 degrees takes you to the lighted red "2" spar west of Oxford, a distance of just over 2 miles. From there, with a few exceptions in the tributaries, piloting upriver as far as the head of navigation at Easton Point is a matter of honoring the markers.

Anchorages abound along the 6 miles of river between Oxford and Easton Point. You can drop the hook in varying degrees of sylvan surroundings and still be no farther than a few miles from resupply points for ice and other amenities. If you are looking for restaurants or need supplies or repairs, Oxford is the place to go. If you seek seclusion, head upriver.

OXFORD

All facilities

Charts: 12263, 12266

Where to Eat/Things to Do. As you clear Bachelor Point, civilization appears to starboard

Tred Avon Ferry, which runs between Oxford and Bellevue, Maryland, is the oldest free-running ferry route in the United States.

Oxford

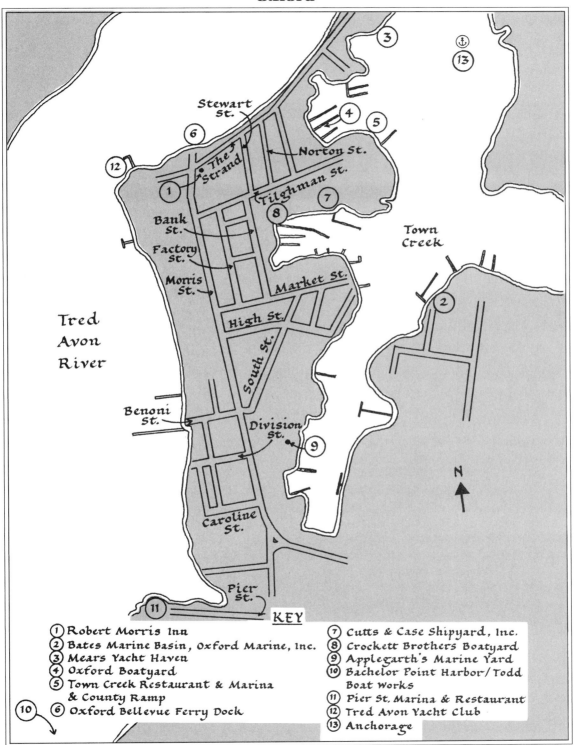

Stewart St.

The Strand

Norton St.

Tilghman St.

Town Creek

Bank St.

Factory St.

Morris St.

Market St.

High St.

South St.

Tred Avon River

Benoni St.

Division St.

N

Caroline St.

Pier St.

CHOPTANK
RIVER/
TRED
AVON
RIVER

183

KEY

1. Robert Morris Inn
2. Bates Marine Basin, Oxford Marine, Inc.
3. Mears Yacht Haven
4. Oxford Boatyard
5. Town Creek Restaurant & Marina & County Ramp
6. Oxford Bellevue Ferry Dock
7. Cutts & Case Shipyard, Inc.
8. Crockett Brothers Boatyard
9. Applegarth's Marine Yard
10. Bachelor Point Harbor/Todd Boat Works
11. Pier St. Marina & Restaurant
12. Tred Avon Yacht Club
13. Anchorage

SCALE 1" = 730 FEET

CHOPTANK
RIVER/
TRED
AVON
RIVER

184

in the form of the Pier Street Marina and Restaurant in Oxford. There is deep water and dock space available for those visiting the restaurant. Use caution when laying alongside the dock in the face of a strong breeze from the southwest quadrant as the area is unprotected from that direction. If you want to spend the night, transient slips are available. The restaurant has reasonable prices and high value for your money, but fancy it isn't.

Almost immediately after rounding the red "2" marker off the Tred Avon Yacht Club, you come to a wharf commonly called the Oxford "town dock," although its name is the Oxford-Bellevue Ferry Dock. This is one of the terminals for the Tred Avon Ferry, the oldest free-running ferry route in the United States, established in 1760. One story holds that the first ferry route here was established in 1683. Whatever the actual date, this is the best known car ferry on the Eastern Shore. Except for the period from Christmas to March 1, the ferry operates seven days a week. Although the hours vary for summer and winter, basically it operates from a little after sunup to sundown. Tolls are (in 1988) $3.75 per car and driver plus $.25 for each additional passenger; bicycles and trailers, $1.50; motorcycles, $2.00.

The 300 feet of dockage space along the wharf is available to transients at no charge, but it is too exposed to wakes and weather for a lengthy tie-up. You would do better to anchor off the long, sandy, town beach (called The Strand), and take a dinghy in to shore. The Strand extends from the ferry dock eastward about halfway to the Town Creek entrance. In the warmer weather, beware of children swimming and diving near the town dock as you pull in.

Within about 100 yards straight inland from the dock is the Robert Morris Inn, an excellent restaurant but a bit on the expensive side. Most major credit cards are accepted. On Friday and Saturday nights, dinner is first come, first served—no reservations. The structure of the inn incorporates the original home, built in 1710, of Robert Morris, Sr., one of the financiers of the American Revolution.

Provisions. Much more appealing for either a temporary stop or overnight stay in Oxford is Town Creek, the mouth of which is less than one-half mile beyond the Oxford town dock. The first marker is a lighted red "2" spar, not to be confused with the lighted red "2" to the west of Oxford which was mentioned earlier. The Town Creek Channel is well marked with pairs of red

and green daymarks all the way to the end of the creek. The first facility to come into view is Mears Yacht Haven to starboard, perhaps the most convenient place for resupply of ice and fuel. It is very busy during in-season weekends and you may have to hold off and wait your turn to approach the fuel dock.

Just beyond Oxford Boatyard, following Mears, is the Town Creek Restaurant and Oxford Carry-Out Food Service, two restaurants in one building, with almost 200 feet of free dockage for customers. The reasonably priced meals are excellent and, except for holiday weekends, you might get permission to leave your boat tied up at their pier long enough for a tour of the town. Everything in town is within easy walking distance of wherever you may land around the town.

Dockages. Farther up Town Creek are four more marinas or boatyards from which you may choose, each with varying degrees of capability and facilities. Worthy of note and just across the street from Applegarth's Marine Yard is Pope's Tavern, one of Oxford's more "interesting" restaurants. Here you may take yourself back to the turn of the century, complete with ceiling fans, wooden floors, and a selection of penny candy. The room is not large, but the sandwiches and crab cakes are good as is a cold glass of beer on a hot summer's day.

Anchorages. If you so desire, you can anchor out in Town Creek away from wave action, if not always protected from the wind. However, the grassy clay bottom makes it difficult to set a lightweight anchor, such as a Danforth, and the surrounding land features cause the wind to come in puffs from flukey directions. Town Creek has a fair amount of boat traffic at times. For these reasons, one of the other anchorages off the Tred Avon may be a better choice for anchoring overnight.

PLAINDEALING

CREEK

☆3 2

No facilities

Charts: 12263, **12266**

Approaches. Due north of the mouth of Town Creek is Plaindealing Creek, its entrance shoal clearly marked by a green "1" daymark.

Anchorages. Less than one-half mile past the daymark you can drop your anchor in a little cove to port in good holding ground, sheltered from both wind and wave, except from the southeast.

There is deep water for about another one-half mile, but this cove is the best anchorage. It is possible to land on a narrow strip of sandy beach on the point of land to the north of the cove. The surroundings are quiet and pleasant with a few houses and plenty of trees. We prefer other places on Tred Avon for longer stays.

UNNAMED CREEK SOUTHWEST OF PLAINDEALING

No facilities

Charts: 12263, **12266**

Anchorages. This unnamed creek is not a bad anchorage unless it breezes up from the southeast. Six feet is carried up to the point where it bends to the west. Then it shoals rapidly to 3 feet or less as you proceed upstream. The soft bottom provides good holding under most conditions.

There is no place to land as the shoreline is all privately owned, with the possible exception of the marshy point on the west side of its mouth. There is at least 5 feet of water in the little fork to the west inside this marshy point where you can find full protection from wave, if not wind, in the event of a southeast blow.

This creek provides a quieter alternative to Town Creek while still within about a mile of the town of Oxford. You can take a dinghy around the point and southwest to the western (Bellevue side) termination of the Oxford-Bellevue ferry. Leave your dink inside (north) of the quay leading to the ferry dock and ride the ferry (toll) to Oxford to avoid taking a small dinghy across the

busy Tred Avon. It saves about a mile of rowing distance and the ferry is fun to ride.

GOLDSBOROUGH CREEK

No facilities

Charts: 12263, **12266**

Heading east from Oxford on the Tred Avon, you pass Goldsborough Creek to starboard. Although I am sure that it has its good points, it is too civilized for our tastes.

Anchorages. There is a good anchorage in 8 feet of water just past the small point on the north shore, but you won't find a place to land.

TRIPPE CREEK

No facilities

Charts: 12263, **12266**

Approaches. While the entrance to Trippe Creek is straightforward, there are a couple of shoals lying in wait for the unwary. The first one, which extends off the east shore, can be avoided easily by holding close to the green "1" daymark at the mouth of Trippe Creek. After clearing this daymark, steer north northeast until approximately due east of the point north of green "1" at the creek entrance. From there, simply stay in the middle of the creek until you clear Deepwater Point. This brings you clear of the shoal west of the point.

Anchorages. While you can anchor almost anywhere once you are fully within Trippe Creek, there are three "best" locations. Our favorite is in the mouth of the unnamed cove to the southeast of Deepwater Point, close to a tiny strip of sandy beach on the outside of the point of land by the cove. If the wind is from the northern quarter, many people seem to like Snug Harbor on the north bank. We prefer the second unnamed cove to the eastern end of the north bank because Snug Harbor's banks are lined with private homes. Wherever you anchor, holding is good and the water is clean, with 7 to 15 foot depths.

CHOPTANK
RIVER/
TRED
AVON
RIVER

186

UNNAMED COVES

No facilities

Charts: 12263, **12266**

Anchorages. A little above the mouth of Trippe Creek, to the west of the red "10" lighted spar, two unnamed coves provide secure, secluded anchorages in 7 feet of water, with tree-lined banks that screen farm fields. The lower cove was promptly dubbed "Turtle Cove" by the younger members of our crew after we watched about two dozen turtles swimming into the entrance one morning. Both coves have sandy beaches, excellent for swimming, wading, or beachcombing. This land is private, so stay below the high water mark. In 1990 this area was marked for housing development. There goes another secluded cove.

These coves also share a problem common to many of the low-lying areas along the eastern shore, biting gnats or no-see-ums, and, unfortunately, the coves are not large enough to permit anchoring far enough off shore to be out of their range. These anchorages are untenable during the late spring and summer months, unless you come prepared with adequate screening and appropriate repellents and insecticides.

MAXMORE CREEK

No facilities

Charts: 12263, **12266**

Approaches. The mouth of Maxmore Creek, just north of Long Point, provides the next anchorage along the Tred Avon. There is 8 feet of water almost up to shore on Long Point. Most of the rest of the creek is navigable if you have a 5-foot draft or less.

Anchorages. Inside Long Point is the best place to anchor. The voracious no-see-ums frequent this cove too; come prepared for them.

PEACHBLOSSOM

CREEK

No facilities

Charts: 12263, **12266**

Approaches. Peachblossom Creek to starboard is well worth a visit even if you never get your anchor wet. The banks rise steeply and are lined with large houses—perhaps estates—which are nestled in the trees. All of the land appears to be privately owned and developed. The creek is wide and carries at least 6 feet of water (with no protruding shoals) to within one-half mile of the Route 333 bridge.

Anchorages. You can anchor almost anywhere in the creek proper, but stay out of Le Gates Cove; once past the entrance, it gets rather shallow.

SHIPSHEAD AND

DIXON CREEKS

No facilities

Charts: 12263, **12266**

Approaches. The last proper anchorage off Tred Avon River is in Dixon Creek which appears to port. Shipshead and Dixon Creeks share an entrance and both are navigable, but Dixon Creek is a better choice. Stay well off the point of land to starboard as you enter the creek since the shoal projects somewhat farther out than is apparent from the chart.

Anchorages. You can travel almost to Bloomfield if you have less than a 5-foot draft, but the best anchorage is along the western bank of the Dixon Creek, just before the point where the creek splits.

There are low-lying fields on either side of the creek but no beaches, except for one or two small and muddy ones at low water. It is possible to land briefly, if necessary, but this is all privately owned farmland. Although the gnats are here, they are not as bad as in the other anchorages on the western side of the river. Be prepared for them if you do anchor.

EASTON

POINT

Charts: 12263, **12266**

Dockages/Provisions. Just more than a mile above the mouth of Dixon Creek is Easton Point. Here you can get marine supplies and gas (no diesel) at Easton Point Marine, which has a head and showers that are yours to use for the asking—something to remember if the weather is sticky or you have been out for several days. The people running the store are courteous and pleasant, characteristics common to most people we have met on the Eastern Shore.

Things to Do/Where to Eat. The city of Easton, Talbot County county seat, is 1½ miles away from Easton Point. With a population of over 8,000, Easton offers a wide range of stores, movie theaters, and restaurants. The Tidewater Inn, a 120-room colonial hostelry, has a good reputation, especially for local seafood dishes. Each November it is the site of the an-

nual Waterfowl Festival, which attracts literally thousands of people. Easton is close enough to walk to or you can call a taxi from Easton Point Marine.

CHOPTANK RIVER, ISLAND CREEK TO CAMBRIDGE

Charts: 12263, **12266**

This section covers both shores of the Choptank River from Island Creek and Castle Haven Point upriver to Cambridge.

ISLAND CREEK

No facilities

Charts: 12263, **12266**

The entrance to Island Creek, due east of the Choptank River Light, has been progressively shoaling in. Although the chart indicates 5 feet in the channel, if you have a draft approaching that, you should verify the actual controlling depth in the channel before trying it.

Approaches. Once you are in, you will find plenty of water depth (9–20 feet) throughout the creek. There are, however, two places where you need to watch your depth carefully. Both are near the creek's headwaters, off the last two points on the northern shore where it forks. The second of these shoals projects more than halfway across the mouth of the northern fork at the end of the creek.

Anchorages. Any anchorage out of the mainstream of traffic is in good holding and fully protected from weather. This Eastern Shore creek is one of the few with a completely developed shoreline, which means there is no place to land. If landing is not a cri-

CHOPTANK
RIVER,
ISLAND
CREEK
TO
CAMBRIDGE

187

teron and you have a draft that allows you to get into Island Creek, it is an attractive anchorage.

The closest facilities are in Oxford.

CHOPTANK
RIVER,
ISLAND
CREEK
TO
CAMBRIDGE

188

CASTLE HAVEN

No facilities

Charts: 12263, **12266**

Approaches. About 2 miles southeast of the Choptank River Light, on your way up the Choptank River, you can see a sizable cove to starboard. Do not, under any circumstances, head directly for it. There is a long finger of a shoal, barely submerged, which extends from the tip of Castle Haven Point to the red nun "2" buoy past the mouth of this cove. Swing wide round this buoy and head for the south side of the cove entrance until you are a good 300 yards past nun "2." Then swing a little to starboard, to head for the end of the point on the northern side of the entrance, until you are just past the center of the entrance.

Now you can head directly into the cove, keeping in the middle, until the first constriction, where two small points on opposite sides stretch toward each other. Proceed beyond here with caution; it starts to shoal rather quickly.

Anchorages. The land is low-lying and marshy, except for the site of a lone house on the northern shore. Castle Haven offers good protection from all but the east, where it is wide open to a fetch of more than 2 miles. This gunkhole is interesting to poke into—once.

LECOMPTE BAY

AND CREEK

No facilities

Charts: 12263, **12266**

Mouth of the Choptank River

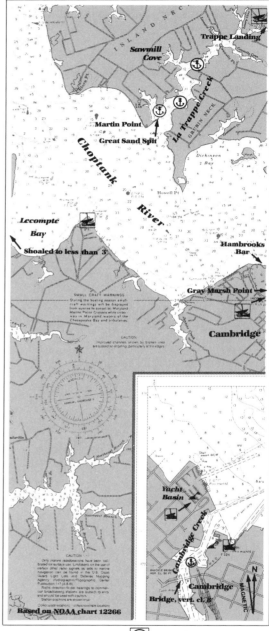

SCALE 1"=**1.45** NAUT. MILES   **Good anchoring**

 Mooring area **Launching site**

Approaches. Just below Castle Haven is the wide mouth of Lecompte Bay. This bay has 7 to 10 feet of water throughout but is wide open to the entire northeast quadrant. A nice place to visit but not a snug harbor.

The chart indicates a well-marked channel into Lecompte Creek. This channel has had a lot of shoaling so don't expect to get through it with anything over a 3-foot draft.

Anchorages. A nice little anchorage sits just inside the entrance, once you make it in, but the shores are marshy and the area is a bit on the "buggy" side. Look elsewhere!

CHOPTANK
RIVER,
ISLAND
CREEK
TO
CAMBRIDGE

189

LA TRAPPE CREEK

Charts: 12263, **12266**

Approaches. La Trappe Creek is located on the northeast shore of the Choptank River, directly opposite Lecompte Bay. The entrance is marked with a large, black beacon (perhaps replaced with a green one by now) which resembles a miniature lighthouse. Swing wide around the point on the west side of the creek mouth before approaching the beacon. Stay 20 to 40 yards off the beacon and head so that the red "2" (also a miniature lighthouse) beyond it is a little to starboard; the water is 10 feet deep all the way into the creek.

Anchorages. To port just inside the creek is one of the finest anchorages in this part of the Bay. Give a wide berth to the end of the sand spit as you swing around it and you can anchor behind Martin Point in 7 to 8 feet of water. There is deep water to within a few feet of the sand spit, but don't get too far to the west side of the cove; it starts to get shallow. Martin Point is posted "No Trespassing," but you may land at the end of the sand spit to swim, wade, or beachcomb. The rest of the point, with a nice sandy beach, is closed to the public as a result of the thoughtless boaters who left piles of litter here in the past.

The next attractive anchorage, with 10 feet of water and good holding, is in the bight just past the first point to starboard on your way upstream. The high, wooded shores provide plenty of protection from wave and weather. The shoreline is uninhabited and you can land on a small sandy beach.

There is a pretty little anchorage, with 6 feet of water,

in the mouth of Sawmill Cove, about one mile upstream from the mouth of the creek. There are a couple of houses here, but they don't detract from the scenery.

The creek is navigable (6 to 7 feet of water) to Trappe Landing, the home of Dickerson Boat Builders.

The La Trappe is one of the most beautiful creeks on the Chesapeake Bay. On the way upstream, it narrows and the trees lean over the water, giving something of an "other world" sensation to those familiar with the rest of the Bay. The water is a deep shade of chocolate, which makes you feel more like you are driving down a road than cruising a waterway. Don't let this "other worldliness" keep you from catching a look at the many large mansions or estates along the way. Don't attempt to travel beyond Trappe Landing or you will promptly run out of water.

CAMBRIDGE

All facilities

Charts: 12263, **12266**

Approaches. Cambridge is located about 7 miles southeast of the Choptank River Light, just short of the Route 50 bridge over the river. As you pass Hambrooks Bar and Gray Marsh Point, just northwest of Cambridge, be sure to honor all the red markers to avoid the 2-foot shoal that extends way out into the river. From can "23" off Hambrooks Bar, head for a point on the bridge about one-third of the way across from the Cambridge side, a course of 148 degrees. This takes you directly to the green and red pair of markers where the deep, dredged channel into Cambridge Creek harbor begins. You can either follow the markers into Cambridge harbor or use the outer markers as a take-off point to enter the Municipal Yacht Basin, also the site of the Cambridge Yacht Club.

If you choose the yacht basin, look for the wooden bulkhead just to the right (about 350 yards) of the entrance to Cambridge Creek. A pair of red and green lighted markers on this bulkhead indicates the entrance into the basin. Head directly to these markers from the outer green "1" at the beginning of the Cambridge channel. This course takes you through the channel to the basin entrance with ease. Don't enter the basin if you draw more than 5 feet.

Dockages/Provisions. The clubhouse of the Cambridge Yacht Club, a gift from Francis Du Pont in 1938, is immediately to the right as you enter the basin. The club honors membership cards from other yacht clubs and maintains a few guest slips. The water depth is a little iffy, more amenable to powerboats than sail. Fuel, water, and showers are available here.

The Municipal Yacht Basin is to port upon entering the bulkhead area. The basin has a few slips for transients up to 60 feet, but the same caveat on water depth as for the yacht club applies here. A restroom, shower, and laundromat are in the same building that houses the dockmaster, located to the far right of the basin on the shoreside. The dockmaster is on duty most of the year with extended hours in the summer months.

To enter Cambridge Creek, simply follow the markers into the turning basin at the mouth of the creek, 10 feet of water all the way. Once in the turning basin, swing to starboard into the narrow channel leading to Cambridge Creek proper. The Yacht Maintenance Company comes up quickly on your left. Primarily a repair facility, it also has numerous slips, some of which may be available to transients.

Ahead to starboard is the 600-foot-long service dock of the Phillips Oil Company Marina, an automobile service station with pumps near the water to serve boats. Tie up alongside and walk into town. Starboard of Phillips is Clayton's Restaurant, with plenty of free dockage in 6 feet of water.

Anchorages. Anchor out in the basin, but stay out of the middle to avoid the boat traffic, mostly watermen but occasionally some rather large vessels.

Past the bridge, there is some room to anchor but it is a little narrow and in the company of numerous condominium slips. With the exception of 12:00 noon to 1:00 p.m. every day, the bridge opens on demand to the standard call of one long and one short blast on a horn or a call on VHF-FM Channel 13. We prefer to anchor in the turning basin before the bridge.

Where to Eat/Things to Do. The town has several restaurants, laundromats, convenience stores, grocery stores—in short all the shopping you could wish for in a small city. Although founded about 300 years ago, Cambridge has few of the original, colo-

nial buildings due to a series of fires over the years. On the bright side, the cutesy tourist trap shops and fast food places common to several other waterfront towns are also missing here. If you hunger for fast food, take the 1- to 2-mile walk to Route 50, "fast-food paradise." The Rouse Company has put together a redevelopment plan for Cambridge Creek, which will soon cause some significant changes to the area. Already, a mini-mall has opened and a couple of townhouse complexes have sprung up. A large hotel and a marina complex are on the boards.

Cambridge offers plenty to see and do, but we don't recommend spending the night there, except perhaps in a slip at the municipal basin. We like to leave in time to get back into La Trappe Creek, 4 miles away, to anchor for the night.

UPPER CHOPTANK RIVER

⭐2 | 3

⛽ | 🚰 | 🚿 | 🎣 | ⚓ | 🍴

Chart: 12268

The Route 50 drawbridge has been replaced with a fixed bridge that has a maximum vertical clearance in the main channel of 50 feet. The center portion of the old drawbridge has been removed and the remaining portions jutting out from either shore have been converted into fishing piers.

Approaches. Do not run upriver for the first time after dark: The river is well marked, but an unmarked shoal extends to the north from Whitehall Creek to starboard just past where the river bends to the northeast. There is also a narrow section just west of Goose Creek, marked by buoy cans "33" and "35" and the lighted red "34" marker. None of the little creeks are navigable until you reach the Warwick River.

Dockages/Anchorages. The Warwick River has a narrow dredged channel up to Dorchester Oil Company at Secretary where you could probably get permission to dock, but why bother? Anchor in the

Choptank for the night, or land by dinghy. Secretary was named in honor of Lord Dewall who owned the land while serving as Secretary of the Province of Maryland in the mid-1600s. The oldest church in the United States in continuous use, Old Trinity Church, built in 1675, is located here.

The next creek up offers a small marina and restaurant by "Suicide Bridge." (If you know how the bridge got its name, I would like to hear the story.) The creek shoals to 3 feet, accessible only to shoal-draft vessels.

The next reasonable place to anchor is near the town of Choptank. Do not enter the old steamboat basin, which has less than 2 feet. Anchor out on the edge of the channel. You could also try the Choptank-Towne Yacht Basin that offers gasoline and some transient slips.

Although there is deep water all the way, unless you are a real diehard, don't bother proceeding beyond Choptank. There are no other creeks or coves to pull into until Tuckahoe Creek, which is more than 40 miles up the Choptank River past winding, marshy banks. If you make it as far as Tuckahoe Creek and brave its winding marshy channel, you qualify as an expert gunkholer.

LITTLE CHOPTANK RIVER

Charts: 12263, 12264, **12266**

On the eastern shore, just south of the mouth of the Choptank River, lies the Little Choptank River with several first-class harbors beckoning the cruiser. It is a trip of 5 or 6 miles from the green "1" lighted spar—positioned nearly a mile to the southwest of Hills Point in the mouth of the river—to the nearest good shelter. The land in this region is low-lying, nothing over 20 feet above sea level, but the trees on the shore provide adequate wind breaks and the nooks and crannies provide good shelter from the waves. The lack of easily identified landmarks means you have to pay careful attention to your position because there are a number of unmarked shoals. As in most of the Bay, the bottom here is forgiving and the only damage likely to result from a grounding is to your dignity.

Whether you are approaching the Little Choptank from the north or south, James Island serves as a conve-

nient reference. It is characteristically low, but the trees on it are visible from a good distance away. Approach no closer to the island from the west to the northeast than three-fourths mile in order to avoid the shoal around it. Since the green "1" marker between James Island and Hills Point is difficult to see from a distance, simply guide around James Island and head directly for the lighted green "3" beacon to the southwest of Ragged Island as soon as you can see the beacon. From green "3," you should be able to see the lighted green "5" beacon to the southeast. Leave both markers well to port and you will travel in 20 to 50 feet of water until you are about 200 yards past beacon "5." From there on, typical depths are between 9 and 20 feet, with some deeper spots. Green "5" is your departure point for approaching the assortment of creeks off the Little Choptank where you will find the best anchorages.

SLAUGHTER CREEK

Charts: 12263, **12264**, 12266

Approaches. A course of 190 degrees from green "5" in the Little Choptank takes you to the first channel marker into Slaughter Creek, although you should be able to see the marker from green "5." Subject to continual shoaling, the channel has been dredged recently so there should be at least four feet of water through it. Make sure that you stay in the channel through the bar. A storm may have caused additional shoaling, so go slowly. Leave the lighted red "2" beacon about 20 feet to starboard on the way in, then bow a little to port and swing in a smooth arc back to the red "4" beacon as the shoal encroaches from the west. Then swing right to head between the red "6" and the green "7" markers.

Once into the creek proper, stay in the middle where you have a minimum of 7 feet of water all the way to the Coast Guard station and Taylor Island Marina, just before the fixed bridge. The only reasonable way to explore past the bridge is by dinghy. Bring plenty of repellent as the marshy shores are well populated by mosquitoes. There is no place to land except at the marina; the banks are all muddy and there is no such thing as a beach.

Dockages/Provisions. Taylor Island Marina is a small place, but they offer slips, gas, diesel, ice and a few other supplies. There is also a small snack bar. Believe it or not, the Coast Guard station here is a

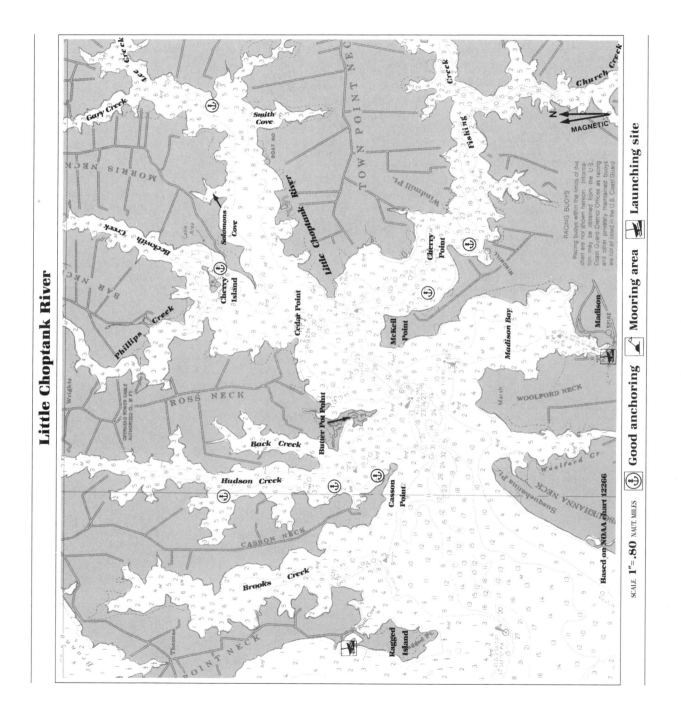

Little Choptank River

RACING BUOYS

Racing buoys within the limits of this chart are not shown hereon. Information may be obtained from the U.S. Coast Guard District Offices as racing and other privately maintained buoys are not as listed in the U.S. Coast Guard.

MAGNETIC

Based on NOAA chart 12266

SCALE 1"=.80 NAUT. MILES

⚓ Good anchoring   ⛵ Mooring area   ⛴ Launching site

houseboat at the marina! At the other side of the bridge, about one-half mile by road, is a general store. It also can be reached by dinghy or boats with less than a 3-foot draft.

Unless you specifically want to visit the marina, there are better anchorages off the Little Choptank. Pass this one by.

BROOKS CREEK

No facilities

Charts: 12263, 12264, **12266**

Approaches. The entrance to Brooks Creek is to the north of the green "5" beacon in the Little Choptank River. Swing wide around green "5" and head directly for the pair of daymarks designating the narrow entrance to the creek. With careful piloting you can get about another mile into the creek through the relatively narrow channel. The creek has shoaled badly since the charts were updated—this is now shoal-draft country. If you are in a sailboat of any size, don't try it; you will have to turn around and go back out. Our last time in we surveyed the channel the hard way.

Even so, many fairly large sailboats often anchor in the center of Brooks Creek as far as several hundred yards up past the two points at its mouth. This is exposed to the entire south quadrant and, while we don't find it particularly appealing, some do.

Anchorages. The first cove to port is a snug, tree-lined, attractive anchorage, only for those with a draft less than 3 feet.

The rest of the creeks off the Little Choptank all offer better anchorages, so we skip Brooks Creek.

HUDSON CREEK

No facilities

Charts: 12263, 12264, **12266**

Approaches. To enter Hudson Creek, assume a course of 76 degrees from the Choptank River green "5" beacon and start looking for the green "7" daymark, about 1½ miles ahead. From here on, pay careful attention to your navigation: It is easy to become confused if your attention lapses. Daymark "7" is the turning mark for the entrance to Hudson Creek. As you pass the marker, maintain your course for at least another 300 yards before swinging slowly to port to a course of about 15 degrees. Do not head directly for the green "1" daymark in Hudson Creek from green "7" since a shoal bows to the east of a line between these two marks. (For the same reason, do not proceed east of a line between Hudson Creek green "1" and Little Choptank green "9," off Butter Pot Point. There's another shoal there.) Hold close to green "1" as you pass it and head directly toward the red "2" daymark.

Leave red "2" close to starboard as you swing around it. Less than one-half mile past red "2", you pass the green "3" daymark, which should be left close to port. From here you are on your own; there are no more markers, but neither are there any more projecting shoals. Stay in the middle and proceed slowly (as you should in any case) and you will have no problems.

As you move upstream, there are widely scattered homes to starboard, with well-kept lawns on large plots of land. To port, the land is undeveloped and marshy. All of the land is close to the same level as the water, which must make the residents rather nervous during the spring tides.

As you cruise toward the headwaters, the area has a noticeably, yet undefinably different feel. Perhaps *peaceful* best describes it. In any event, it is worth the trip up the creek at least once, if only to see the sights and return immediately. Several inviting coves beckon from the western shore, but if you draw more than 4 feet you are better off viewing them from a distance.

Anchorages. The creek is navigable for 3 miles from its mouth up to the point where it forks near the head of navigation, less than one-half mile from the town of Hudson. However, the best anchorage is near the mouth, just inside Casson Point. Here you can pull well out of the channel and anchor in 7 feet of water within 100 yards of an inviting sandy beach. This anchorage is well protected from any wave action and, thanks to the trees, reasonably sheltered from the wind, save from a north or south direction. There is very little traffic on this creek and few houses in sight. Holding is good and most cruising boats that visit Hudson Creek anchor here or in the mouth of the next cove to port upstream.

Now for the fly in the ointment: That inviting beach just mentioned is posted "Private No Trespassing." A little investigation, however, reveals a similar beach on the inside of the tip of Casson Point, past the clump of trees, devoid of legal deterrent. No one seemed to object to our landing there.

Back Creek, to the northeast of red "2," offers an anchorage in about 6 feet of water, provided you can get past the 3-foot bar at the entrance to the creek.

Immediately to port past the green "3" daymark, a beguiling cove presents itself to port. Proceed on a course up Hudson Creek until you are well past the cen-

Classic Bay Recipes

The following recipes are a sampling of a wide variety of dishes concocted from the bounty of the Chesapeake Bay and its environs. All of those presented have been prepared aboard our boat during one or more of our cruises, generally from items that we have caught ourselves or bought on the shores of the Bay.

CRABFEAST Perhaps nothing is more traditional to the cusine of the Chesapeake than a crabfeast, whether on shore with a large number of participants or aboard a boat where the "guests of honor," the Chesapeake's blue crabs, have been freshly caught from that same boat. Some may argue that the specific type and quantity of ingredients or the cooking technique used is not strictly "correct," but this one is a simple way of preparing and serving crabs whether on a boat with its limited cooking capability or ashore. It works for us!

Ingredients

1. One large pot with tight fitting lid. (The bigger the better.)

2. Enough water to fill the pot two-thirds full. (An alternate approach is to use only about three cups of water or beer and steam the crabs. Note that steaming requires a pot with a very tight-fitting lid.)

3. Four to five crabs per person. (Do not use any crabs that even *appear* to be dead and under no circumstances should live crabs and cooked ones be allowed to come in contact with each other. To avoid bacterial contamination, cooked crabs should not be stored in the same container that held live ones.)

4. One-fourth cup of Old Bay Seafood Seasoning.

5. One-half cup of salt (or use seawater).

6. Plenty of old newspaper to cover table (or be prepared to wash down the boat if you eat the crabs aboard).

7. Mallets and nut crackers.

Directions

Bring the water to a hard boil; add the Old Bay Seasoning and stir.

Add as many crabs as the pot will hold and cook for approximately 20 minutes. They should be a deep, bright, red color when cooked. (Have the lid of the pot handy as you drop the crabs in—this aggressive meal sometimes tries to exit the pot.)

Cover a table with paper. Pile the cooked crabs in the center. Select your crab(s) and enjoy. (Note: They seem to taste best when accompanied by ice-cold beer.)

CRAB IMPERIAL A' LA DRAUSSEN

This recipe assumes the availability of an oven, although it is possible to cook this crab imperial with a dutch oven or equivalent on the top of a stove.

Ingredients

1. One pound of crab meat.

2. Three-fourths cup mayonnaise.

3. One egg.

4. One tablespoon chopped sweet pickle.

5. One teaspoon Old Bay Seafood Seasoning.

6. Four large scallop shells.

7. Paprika.

Directions

Mix the first five ingredients.

Divide mixture into the scallop shells. Sprinkle with paprika.

Bake at 350 degrees (F) for 30 minutes.

Serves four.

MARYLAND CRABCAKES   This is a simple recipe, but it is unlike the crabcakes you will find in virtually any restaurant due to the minimal amount of filler (bread crumbs) and the maximum amount of crabmeat. Expensive if you haven't caught the crabs yourself, yes, but the taste is very hard to beat!

Ingredients

1. One pound of crab meat (pick out any shell and cartilage).
2. One egg.
3. One-half cup mayonnaise.
4. One teaspoon dry mustard.
5. One teaspoon Old Bay Seafood Seasoning.
6. Bread crumbs.
7. Butter or margarine for frying.

Directions

Mix the first five ingredients together in a bowl. Add only enough bread crumbs to keep the mixture from breaking apart.

Divide and shape into 6 patties.

Melt butter or margarine in a frying pan. Add the crabcake patties and cook until brown on both sides (about 5 minutes per side).

Serve either with crackers and pickle slices or on a bun with tartar sauce and pickle slices.

Serves three to six, depending on appetites.

OYSTER FRITTERS   It is a close tie between eating the Bay's oysters right out of the shell or with the following recipe.

Ingredients

1. One pint oysters (the fresher, the better).

2. Three-fourths cup flour.
3. One and one-half cups pancake mix. (You can substitute any biscuit mix.)
4. One teaspoon baking powder.
5. One egg.
6. One-half teaspoon each salt and pepper.
7. Three-fourths cup milk. (You may need a little more.)

Directions

Mix items 2 through 7, adding more milk if needed to make a smooth batter.

Add oysters to the batter and stir.

Drop by the tablespoon into a pan containing hot grease.

Cook until the batter is firm and browned on the outside.

Serves four.

MARYLAND BEATEN BISCUITS   These biscuits are a beloved reminder of Maryland's past—but they are an acquired taste. They are best eaten with a stew or hearty soup.

Ingredients

1. Seven to eight cups flour.
2. One cup of lard.
3. One-half teaspoon salt.

Directions

Blend the ingredients adding water by the tablespoon until a stiff dough results.

Place dough on a wooden surface and beat with an axe handle for 10 to 15 minutes! (Some cooks reputedly used large stumps in the kitchen yard.)

Form dough into small biscuits.

Prick top with a fork and bake at 450 degrees (F) for 15 to 20 minutes.

Yields about six dozen.

ter of the mouth to the cove before attempting to enter. Favor the north shore as you approach and anchor just within the point on the southern shore in 5 to 6 feet of water. It looks as if you could pull very close to the southern shore just inside this point and still be in 5 feet of water.

Farther upstream, there is a larger cove about three-fourths mile beyond green "3." Not deeper, except right at the entrance, it is less snug than the first cove. The chart shows 5 feet of water in the middle of the cove but 2-foot shoals line the perimeter.

Another half mile beyond the second cove is a pair of small coves open for exploration if you draw less than 5 feet. In both coves you can pull in close to shore and anchor in about 5 feet of water. These coves abut a marsh, which offers some solitude, and the songs of the wild at night. At least this used to describe the area, which has been subdivided for development.

On the eastern side of the creek, about midway between the second cove and the pair of coves just mentioned, is an inviting cove. Decline its invitation; there is a 1-foot bar at the entrance.

From here to the head of navigation there are no more suitable anchorages. Shallow-draft boats can travel up the left fork of the creek almost as far as the town of Hudson, but for most cruising boats the fork in the creek should be considered the head of navigation.

MADISON BAY

Charts: 12263, 12264, **12266**

Approaches. The entrance to Madison Bay is marked by a lighted red beacon, located southeast of Hudson Creek. Hold close to this marker on a course from the Little Choptank green "9" until you are 100 yards past it. Once inside, the channel opens up into a wide bay with 7 feet of water in the middle third.

Anchorages. While it is quite feasible to anchor in most of Madison Bay, it is exposed to the north-west and the screen of shoaling around the perimeter doesn't permit approaching much closer than 400 yards off the shore. It is quiet and there is little boat traffic through the area, but we much prefer other anchorages on the Little Choptank.

Provisions. The only reasonable place for resupply in the Little Choptank for boats with drafts of more than 4 feet is at Madison Landing, tucked away in the southernmost corner of Madison Bay. A few years ago, Madison Bay was a real chore to navigate. Today, it has a well-marked, dredged channel. At Madison Landing you can get gasoline and diesel fuel, soft drinks, beer, some limited groceries—even a pretty good meal (so we have been told). The approach to Madison Landing is well marked and you can carry 6 feet all the way to the fuel dock.

Dockages. Most of the slips at the marina are for workboats, which means a noisy, early morning departure. As a result we don't spend the night here.

FISHING CREEK

No facilities

Charts: 12263, 12264, **12266**

Approaches. The entrance to Fishing Creek is past McKeil Point, which separates Fishing Creek and Madison Bay. You must hold a course fairly close to the Little Choptank green "9" and "11" markers in order to avoid the unmarked shoal that extends well to the west of the tip of McKeil Point. From green "11" swing to starboard and head directly toward the red "2" daymark in the entrance to Fishing Creek. Leave this mark close to starboard as you swing around it to head for the green "3" daymark in the creek.

Anchorages. Once past green "3," you can anchor anywhere along Cherry Point, off a very nice, sandy beach. Since this is exposed to the northwest, anchor here only if the weather promises to remain fair.

Squeezing past the end of Cherry Point to obtain access to the rest of the creek can be a little tricky. A draft of more than 5 feet may deny you the better anchorages on Fishing. From green "3", head directly toward red "4" until you are within 50 yards of it. Then swing to port to pass within 50 feet of it. As red "4" comes abeam, start to swing gently to starboard to keep it abeam until you are pointing straight into the middle of the rest of the creek. Hold this course until you are past the tip of Cherry Point. From here on the creek opens out and all you need do is to remain somewhere near the middle to go nearly to the headwaters. (No, the chart doesn't lie; there are shoals in Fishing Creek, but passage is nowhere near as scary as it may appear.) The best anchorage on the creek is in the bight to the south, immediately after clearing Cherry Point. You can anchor in 9 feet of water off a sandy beach, well protected from weather.

Things to Do. If you like crabs, pull into the mouth of the little cove near the house on the shore, but feel your way carefully. This is one of the best places to crab. We once pulled up 25 crabs in 30 minutes, using six baited lines along the sides of the boat! We would have done even better, but "Dad" had some trouble extracting crabs from the twine dip net we used.

Additional Anchorages. Upstream is more populated, although the mouths of the unnamed little creeks branching off the main creek offer several places to anchor. There are a couple of snug little anchorages in Church Creek, about a mile beyond Cherry Point. These are in the first two coves to port after entering Church Creek. Past the second cove, the creek shoals to about 4 feet or less, effectively limiting further exploration to shoal-draft boats or a dinghy.

By all means, put Fishing Creek on your must-try list.

PHILLIPS CREEK

No facilities

Charts: 12263, 12264, **12266**

Approaches. Phillips Creek splits off the Little Choptank to the north just past the last navigation marker, the flashing green "13" off Cedar Point. Watch out for the long bar off the tip of Morris Neck on the east side of the creek entrance. If you head from green "13" to the end of the point directly to the north, where Phillips Creek swings to the northwest away from Beckwith Creek, you can clear all the shoals.

Anchorages. Anchor anywhere in the little bay west of Cherry Island with 6–7 feet of water. There is only one house in the vicinity, making this one of the area's more private anchorages. Usually there are few, if any, boats anchored here.

If you sound your way carefully, you can feel your way through the unmarked channel around the point of land west of Cherry Island for almost another half mile up Phillips Creek. Proceeding beyond Cherry Island into the main part of Phillips Creek is a good test of a gunkholer.

BECKWITH CREEK

No facilities

Charts: 12263, 12264, **12266**

Approaches. On the east side of the little bay on Phillip Creek is Cherry Island with its large square tower. You can enter the mouth of Beckwith Creek by heading north through Phillip Creek until the tower is nearly abeam then turn and head east until it is again abeam on the port side.

Anchorages. Once past the tower, you can anchor to the southeast of Cherry Island in 8 feet of water.

It is possible to feel your way about another half mile upstream, but only confirmed gunkholers should try it. Be ready to survey a few shoals on the way.

LITTLE CHOPTANK

HEADWATERS

 ⬚3

No facilities

Charts: 12263, 12264, **12266**

Anchorages. The Little Choptank is navigable for about 2 miles past the mouth of Phillips Creek. There are alluring anchorages in the mouths of Solomons Cove (4 feet of water), Smith Cove (5 feet), and the unnamed cove beyond Smith Cove (5 feet near the north side of the mouth). In this part of the Little Choptank you can anchor anywhere that appeals to you. The river has 5 feet of water all the way up to the last fork where it splits into Gary and Lee Creeks, which shoal rapidly beyond both entrances.

Western
Shore

This side of the Bay is much more populated than the eastern side. There is little of the shoreline that has not been developed into residences or businesses. However, you still can find excellent anchorages, which give the illusion of, if not actual, seclusion. Many are attractive even though the shore is lined with homes.

WHITEHALL BAY

Charts: 12263, 12270, **12282,** 12283

Whitehall Bay is a popular good weather anchorage and the three creeks branching off it offer secure, attractive anchorages plus assorted marine facilities. It is only a short run to Annapolis from here, making the area a popular anchorage for those wanting to visit Annapolis but not wanting to contend with its crowded, busy harbor for the night.

WHITEHALL BAY
ANCHORAGE

No facilities

Charts: 12263, **12282,** 12283

Approaches. Because North Shoal extends a surprising distance to the west and south of Hackett Point, it is easier to approach the 4-second flashing, red "2" spar marking the entrance to Whitehall Bay from the south than the north. A course that stays midway between Hackett Point and Greenbury Point brings you directly to the red "2" marker with no problems. You can't miss Greenbury Point. It's the one sprouting all the large antennae.

When approaching from the north, stay at least one-half mile offshore from Hackett Point. Underestimate that distance and you may be grounded.

Leave the red "2" marker close to starboard on entering Whitehall Bay. Hold your course, which should be due north, until you are about 300 yards past the marker, then head for your chosen anchorage.

Anchorages. The best anchorage in Whitehall Bay itself is in the northeast corner, off the long sandy beach. This beach is private property, which means that you are not likely to get permission to land there. The anchorage is protected from all but the south. Normally, this presents little problem as most southerlies are mild. However, in a strong blow from the south or southwest, the long fetch quickly makes this anchorage uncomfortable. Should this happen, the prudent course of action is to move into one of the nearby creeks off Whitehall Bay: Mill Creek, Whitehall Creek, or Meredith Creek. All three offer full protection from all directions and, except for Meredith Creek, are not difficult to enter.

MILL CREEK

Charts: 12263, **12282**, 12283

Mill Creek lies tucked away in the western corner of Whitehall Bay. Its narrow entrance and high banks are well camouflaged by the scenic shoreline. It offers complete protection from wind and weather in any of the several possible anchorages, as well as a couple of "hurricane holes." On the down side there is no convenient landing place on the creek other than at the Riverside Inn. Private property or terrain makes landing elsewhere impossible.

Approaches. After entering Whitehall Bay and proceeding about 200 yards past the red "2" spar, swing northwest on a course of 310 degrees to head directly toward the first of the daybeacons marking the entrance to Mill Creek. As you pass between the first red and green markers, stay in the center of the umbrella-handle–shaped entrance channel; the edges rise very quickly. While there is a slight amount of shoaling between nuns "2" and "4," the charts claims a 6-foot controlling depth for the channel. The charts are correct,

but you may want recent local testimony to confirm them.

Anchorages. The first, and perhaps the best, anchorage on the creek lies just inside Possum Point as you clear the entrance channel. The high banks of the creek provide wind break from all directions except the southeast. To the southeast, Possum Point, which is a large sandbar, provides complete shelter from wave action while permitting a cooling breeze to sweep the anchorage. The sandy beach of Possum Point provides a very attractive-looking place to stretch your legs, but don't land there. The impressive antennas on the shore belong to a Navy communications facility. In the past a few trespassers shot at insulators on the towers and, as a result, the Navy keeps a close watch on anyone approaching the area.

Immediately to starboard at the entrance to Mill Creek is Burley Creek. The surrounding high banks and trees make it a very snug hurricane hole. It also provides a very comfortable anchorage on chilly spring or fall evenings. Conversely, Burley Creek is not the place to spend a hot, muggy night. There are a number of large, attractive homes on this creek but no place to land and room for only a couple of boats to anchor.

Martins Cove lies to port about one-half mile past Possum Point. More a small creek than a cove, it is very similar to Burley Creek. The homes lining the banks, although far less ostentatious than those on Burley Creek, appear to be well kept. Martins Cove offers a nice, snug anchorage for two or three boats that need to ride out some very unpleasant weather, but avoid it in hot weather because breezes there are rare.

Where to Eat. For an excellent, inexpensive meal, continue upstream on Mill Creek to the Riverside Inn. This bar/restaurant sits on top of a 30-foot high bank to port just beyond Martins Cove. It is easily identified by its sign and its large pier with a pair of fuel pumps and tray-like tanks of water, holding scores of crabs. An open-air patio with tables overlooks the creek. Most diners use the main building only in bad weather. Don't expect a lot of frills—just good food and drink.

Additional Anchorage. You can continue up the creek almost to the headwaters, while passing large, expensive homes to starboard and much smaller, perhaps more interesting ones to port. Be sure to leave the point above the Riverside Inn well to port to avoid the unmarked shoal that extends more than halfway across the creek. A distance of about two-thirds of the way across the creek from the point to port will keep you out of trouble. The end of the shoal is now marked with a small green buoy, but it is easy to miss and looks like it is too far to that side of the creek to be correct. Believe it!

Once clear of the point, you can anchor in the north corner of this loop of the creek. If you do, try to stay well out of the channel; a number of watermen leave at sunrise or earlier and will have to pass you.

Just past what we call "Sneaky Point" are a couple of small marinas to port on the southeastern shore, but neither has fuel or facilities for transient yachts.

Past the marinas, the house lots become more spacious, the creek rapidly narrows, begins to shoal, and is quiet (except when there is a shoot at the nearby gun club). If you can see the bridge over the headwaters of the creek, turn around and get out.

WHITEHALL CREEK

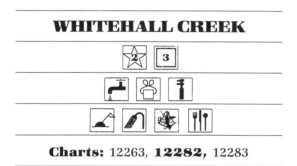

Charts: 12263, **12282**, 12283

Whitehall Creek has a number of things in its favor to attract the cruiser—an easy entrance, a number of well-protected and attractive anchorages, and marine facilities for transients. It also offers a few places to land and stretch your legs.

Approaches. After passing Whitehall Bay red "2," continue another 200 yards before swinging to a northeast course to pick up the red "4" daymark at the entrance to Whitehall Creek. From red "4," simply honor the next two markers and you will enter the creek, easily clearing the sheltering bar at its mouth. As soon as you round red "6," you are in well-sheltered waters and can anchor in full security nearly anywhere that strikes your fancy.

The first cove to port, just before the green "7" day-

mark, contains Scott's Marine Services. This tiny marina with limited facilities specializes in fiberglass repairs. One or two boats could anchor in here for shelter from storms but there are much better anchorages farther up the creek.

As you proceed up Whitehall Creek, be sure to find and honor the green "7" daymark. This marker warns of the last extensive shoal of any significance, which lies in wait for the unwary.

Anchorages. The next branch of the creek, to port, is called Ridout Creek. This creek is perhaps the finest anchorage on Whitehall Creek. It is navigable for nearly a mile from its entrance, progressively narrowing down to allow you to select your desired degree of "snugness." There are still a few places to land, mostly on the south side of the creek, but you have to look for them. It is usually not crowded, except for the occasional rendezvous weekend at one of the larger yacht clubs there.

Just past the mouth of Ridout Creek, a small cove opens to starboard offering a secluded anchorage with 8 feet of water for more than half its length. It is worth looking into to see if it suits your fancy.

Provisions/Facilities. Farther up the main branch of the creek, the Whitehall Yacht Yard may be found to starboard. Here you can anchor anywhere in 8 to 10 feet of water, unless you wait for the snuggest anchorages, which lie around the next bend in the creek past the marina.

MEREDITH CREEK

No facilities

Charts: 12263, **12282**, 12283

Approaches. If you look on a chart, this creek appears to be impossible to enter because of a 1-foot shoal barring the entrance. This is not quite true. You can get into the creek, but don't try it without either recent local knowledge or having someone precede you in a dinghy, sounding for the channel every foot of the way. Sailors should not even attempt this in windy conditions. However, if you do manage to negotiate the entrance, you will find a lovely spot, secluded, and serene, in which to drop the hook.

Any cruiser who succeeds in entering this creek automatically becomes a member of the unofficial "Meredith Creek Gunkholers Association," and thereby must swear to keep secret the information on how to negotiate the entrance. Am I kidding? See for yourself, but be prepared to pull yourself off a shoal!

SEVERN RIVER

Charts: 12263, 12273, **12282,** 12283

The Severn River offers a plethora of harbors, anchorages, and sights-to-see, ranging from the cosmopolitan to the provincial and wild. A beautiful river in its own right, alluring side creeks and coves beckon the boater. The major attractions are close to its mouth—harbors for easy stop-over on the way up or down the Bay; all the marine facilities, supplies, and attractions that you can imagine; and Annapolis, state capitol, home of the U.S. Naval Academy, and much, much more. Farther up the Severn is an assortment of quieter anchorages, many of which are worth a visit in their own right.

Approaches. If you remain on the Severn River itself, you must continue upstream beyond at least the first of the two bridges over the river; anchoring below that bridge is prohibited. In spite of appearances, the bridges present little obstacle. A new fixed bridge with a vertical clearance of 65 feet replaced the old Route 450 drawbridge in the summer of 1994. The drawbridge has been removed but the remains of the old bridge could possibly stay and serve as fishing piers.

There used to be a second bridge, an old, unused, permanently open, swing bridge, which once served a railroad line. The entire bridge has been removed so there is no obstacle to water traffic.

The last bridge (Route 50) presents no difficulty in terms of its vertical clearance (80 feet). You can ignore the orange rectangles painted on two of the supporting columns for one span. They no longer have any meaning.

After clearing the Route 50 bridge, you can enjoy the peace of many quiet anchorages, as well as the excitement and bustle of Annapolis just minutes away. The Severn River anchorages are as follows.

Anchorages. You can anchor in 15 feet of water on the north shore, in a bight about midway between the two bridges, but there are old pilings there, some of which may be just below the surface. I recommend foregoing that spot in favor of the mouth of Weems Creek, to the southwest, just short of the last bridge. If that fails to suit your fancy, you can choose from the many excellent anchorages farther up the river—all obvious from a glance at the chart and easy to find.

LAKE OGLETON

No facilities

Charts: 12263, **12282,** 12283

Approaches. On the southern side of the mouth of the Severn River, about a mile in from Tolly Point, is the entrance to Lake Ogleton. The outside marker for the 8- to 10-foot-deep dredged entrance channel is difficult to discern until you are within a mile of it. Some charts appear to show the green 4-second flashing "1" marker on the wrong side of the channel. Don't worry about it; just leave green "1" to port on entering as you normally would. Line up the first two green markers as you approach the channel to avoid the shoals on either side of the entrance, which extend well to seaward from the first marker.

Anchorages. Once past the first marker, simply honor the red and green markers beyond it until you pass the last green marker. Beyond the last mark, on the southern shore you face Oak Point, which divides Lake Ogleton roughly into two parts. You can anchor in comfort on either side if you don't push too far to the extreme east or west where it starts to shoal.

Don't expect to be able to land. All of the waterfront is private property. The anchorage is fully protected from weather in all directions and the holding, although mud, is normally adequate. This is an excellent anchorage for those who wish to be close to Annapolis without spending the night in Annapolis Harbor, or who want to get a jump on a trip farther up or down the Bay the next day. We have entered this anchorage late at night many a time for just that reason.

BACK CREEK

 1   3

All facilities

Charts: 12263, **12282,** 12283

Severn River Region

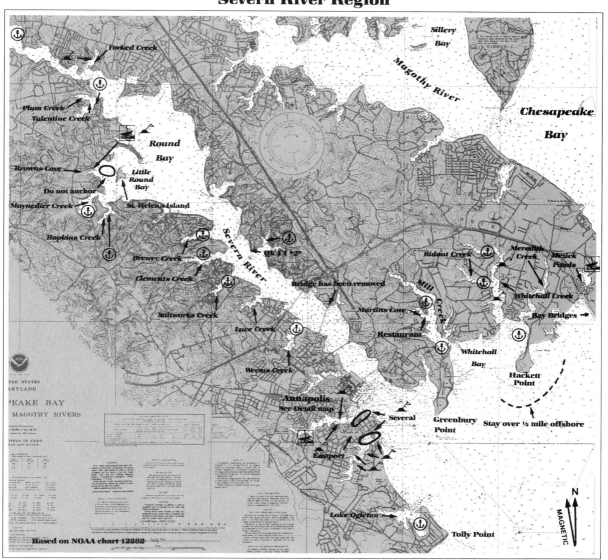

SCALE **1"=1.55** NAUT. MILES   Good anchoring   Mooring area   Launching site

Dockages/Anchorages. Back Creek may be the first option that comes to mind as an alternative to anchoring in Annapolis Harbor. Unfortunately, it, too, suffers from congestion and heavy traffic. The entrance is fairly wide but tricky when visibility is poor or restricted, and anchorage room is limited. Unless you plan to tie up at one of the marinas here, we advise you to move upstream on the Severn River or back around Greenbury Point to one of the anchorages off Whitehall Bay.

SPA CREEK

(ANNAPOLIS)

All facilities

Charts: 12263, **12282,** 12283

Here is where you will find Annapolis. The sound of its name conjures visions of fleets of pleasure craft gliding through the harbor and beyond in a kaleidoscope of motion.

Approaches. Entering the harbor is easy. On the way into the Severn, simply honor the 40-foot–high "spider" light (red) and the nun "10" beyond it. From nun "10," head to leave the green, flashing 6-second light off Horn Point well to port. Once clear of Horn Point shoal, you can turn and head directly into the harbor, where there are no shoals.

Dockages/Provisions. For all practical purposes, Spa Creek is synonomous with Annapolis. The mouth of Spa Creek is Annapolis Harbor. Both sides of the creek are lined with hundreds of boats in marinas, boatyards, and private piers around the creek. If you arrive reasonably early in the day you should be able to find a transient slip at one of the marinas in the area. However, if your heart is set on tying up in Annapolis, make advance reservations.

Between Back Creek and Spa Creek, which bracket the Eastport section of Annapolis, there are close to 30 marinas, not counting yacht clubs, sailing associations, and temporary tie-ups. This count includes only the

ones in the immediate Annapolis Harbor area. There are even more marinas located farther up the Severn River, across the mouth of the Severn in Mill and White-hall Creeks, and in the South River, just a short run around Tolley and Thomas Points. The majority of these marinas welcome transients. Supplies and fuel are readily available throughout the area.

The Spa Creek bridge does not necessarily open on demand, especially during landlubbers' rush hour (7:30 to 9:00 a.m. and 4:30 to 6:00 p.m.). This makes anchoring upstream impractical; passing under the bridge two times is a nuisance. Upstream there is little room to anchor and transient dockage is limited. Spend the night at Lake Ogleton, across the mouth of the Severn to Whitehall Bay, or farther upstream on the Severn.

Slips and bulkhead space are also available on the Annapolis City Dock on a first-come, first-served basis. Normal procedure is to pull into a vacant space not roped off or tie to a bulkhead before paying dockage. The city has also placed forty moorings in the harbor area, leaving no room to anchor. The mooring fee is $15/day from Memorial Day through Labor Day. From April to May and September to October, moorings are

Each October Annapolis is the site of a two-week boat show—one week for sailboats (shown) and one for powerboats. ANNAPOLIS CHAMBER OF COMMERCE

available for a month at a rate equivalent to 2 weeks. However, you can still anchor farther up Spa Creek for free.

On the weekends during the boating season, especially holiday weekends, casual transients should stay clear of the congested harbor—perhaps even the mouth of the Severn River. If you plan to visit the harbor area, try to do so during the week or wait until off-season. Even then, you will have plenty of boats to keep you company, but you will also have more room to maneuver.

Annapolis is expensive. Supplies usually fetch full price; the restaurants are not cheap; dockage fees and repair costs can be significantly higher than in outlying areas.

In 1988 and again in 1989, the mayor of Annapolis, Dennis Callahan, opened the city dock to free use by workboats from late fall through April 1. He also initiated an effort to reopen the old McNasby's Oyster House in Eastport with the idea of joining with the Maryland Waterman's Association to turn the building into a seafood buying and packing co-op. These are the first of several steps taken to avoid driving all of the watermen out of Annapolis—the result of converting waterfront buildings and warehouses into offices and condominiums, as well as raising docking fees.

Things to Do.

Every visitor must tour Annapolis itself. There is a lot to see: more than a hundred 18th century houses, the oldest state house in the country, the home of William Paca (a signer of the Declaration of Independence), St. John's College (founded in 1696), the United States Naval Academy, restaurants, shops and more. There are marinas, marine supply stores, yacht sales agencies, sailmakers, repair facilities, and dockage; if it has to do with boats, it probably can be found in Annapolis.

During a two-week period in October of each year, in-the-water boat shows are held at the City Dock, one week for sailboats and one week for powerboats. These shows get bigger and better every year. The shows are so popular that visitors have to park at the naval academy football stadium and take special buses from there to the show site. Incidently, don't try to visit the show by water, at least not in Spa Creek.

Sightseeing here is best done on foot, especially in the summer when the streets are clogged with traffic and parking space is almost nonexistent.

Regardless of where you land, the starting point for any cruiser's tour of Annapolis has to be at the City Dock. The harbormaster's office and visitor information center here can provide you with far more information than this book can include. Surrounding the City Dock are a variety of restaurants, several "watering holes," the seafood market, assorted stores of all types, and Fawcetts Yacht Chandlers, right on the waters of the dock area.

A short walk north along Randall Street takes you to the United States Naval Academy. You can enter there at Gate 1, or turn left on King George Street and enter at Gate 3, a couple of hundred yards up the street. Gate 1 takes you to Ricketts Hall, the Visitor Center, where you can arrange for a guided tour of the academy seven days a week throughout the year. Gate 3 brings you directly to Preble Hall, where the museum is located, or, with a quick right turn, to the Navy Chapel, where the body of John Paul Jones, the "Father of the U.S. Navy," lies preserved in an alcohol-filled crypt. Wander the grounds and be sure to catch the Brigade Noon Formation if you can.

The naval academy started as the Naval School in 1845, founded by the Secretary of the Navy, George Bancroft, and situated on 10 acres of old Fort Severn. Five years later, it became the United States Naval Academy. Today, the naval academy is designated a National Historic Site. It is frequently called Annapolis, much to the chagrin of some Annapolis residents.

The historic areas of the city are centered on Maryland Avenue and State Circle, where the original town was laid out by Governor Francis Nicholson in 1696. As you leave Gate 3 of the academy and proceed south along Maryland Avenue, you come upon the fabulous Georgian mansions of the Chase-Lloyd House and the Hammond-Harwood House, which face each other just south of King George Street. Both were built in the 1760s and both are open to visitors.

A short jaunt down Prince George Street takes you to the not-to-be-missed William Paca House and Garden. Built by Paca, another signer of the Declaration of Independence, before he became Governor of Maryland in 1782, the building was scheduled to be demolished in 1965. The Historic Annapolis organization not only prevented its demolition, but went on to restore the house and its once-magnificent garden. The latter took the help of archaeologists in unearthing most of the garden from beneath a parking lot and the deteriorated Carvel Hall Hotel building.

The focal point of Annapolis is the State House, lo-

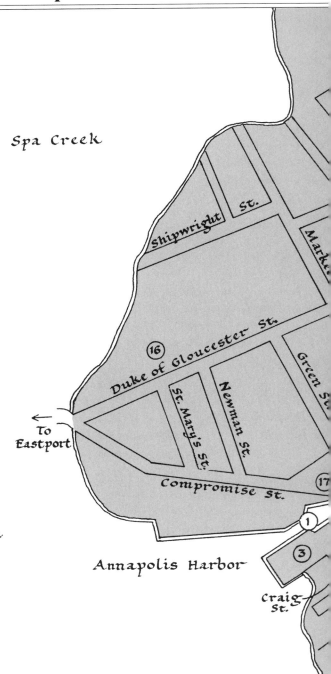

Spa Creek

Annapolis Harbor

KEY

① City Dock
② Maryland State House
③ Visitor Information Center-
   City Dock, Harbormaster
④ Visitor Center, U.S.
   Naval Academy
⑤ U.S. Naval Academy
⑥ Navy Chapel & Crypt
   of John Paul Jones
⑦ Naval Academy Museum
⑧ William Paca House
   & Garden
⑨ Hammond - Harwood House
⑩ Chase-Lloyd House
⑪ Governor Calvert House Inn
⑫ Government House
⑬ St. Anne's Church
⑭ Banneker - Douglass Museum
⑮ Anne Arundel Co. Courthouse
⑯ St. Mary's Church
⑰ Market House

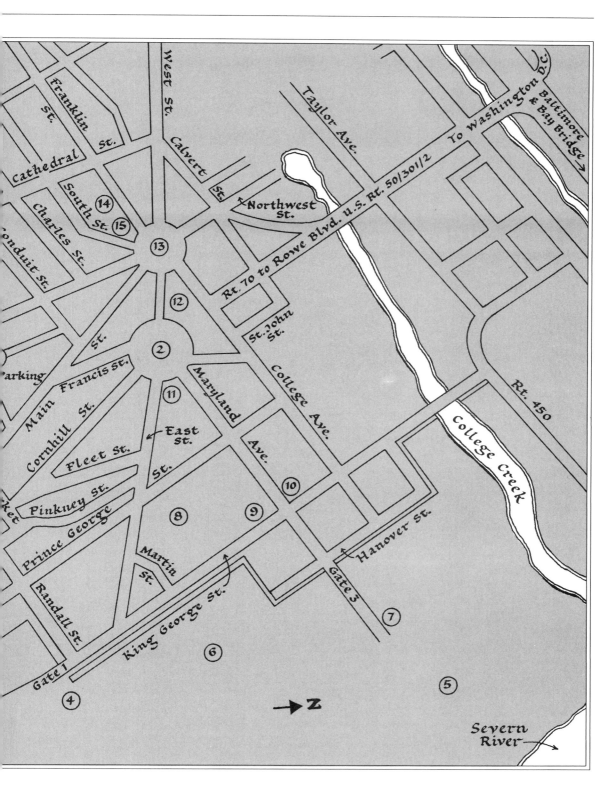

Franklin St.

West St.

Taylor Ave.

To Washington D.C.

Baltimore & Bay Bridge →

Cathedral

Calvert St.

Charles St.

South St.

Conduit St.

(14)

(15)

(13)

↑ Northwest St.

Rt. 70 to Rowe Blvd. U.S. Rt. 50/301/2

(12)

St. John St.

Rt. 450

(2)

Parking

Main

Francis St.

(11)

Maryland Ave.

College Ave.

College Creek

St.

Cornhill St.

East St.

Fleet St.

St.

(10)

Pinkney St.

(8)

(9)

Prince George

Martin St.

Hanover St.

↑ Gate 3

Randall St.

King George St.

(7)

(6)

Gate 1

(5)

(4)

→ Z

Severn River →

The State House (lower left) is the focal point of Annapolis.
This aerial view is looking southeast. ANNAPOLIS CHAMBER OF COMMERCE

cated on the highest point of land in the area and ringed by State Circle. Built between 1772 and 1779, this is the oldest state capitol still in continuous legislative use, and a National Historic Landmark. It is also the only state house to have served as the nation's capitol, which it did from November 1783 to August 1784. Tours of the State House are available year-round at no charge, at 11:00 a.m., 2:00 p.m., and 4:00 p.m., except for Thanksgiving, Christmas, and New Year's Day. The tour includes a slide show.

Nearby is the Governor Calvert House, now an inn for dignitaries, and the Government House, residence of the Governor of Maryland.

A little farther on is Church Circle, dominated by St. Anne's Church and the Anne Arundel County Court-house. A hundred yards down Franklin Street is the Banneker-Douglass Museum, featuring the history of Afro-American life and culture in Maryland.

A walk down Duke of Gloucester Street toward the Spa Creek bridge takes you past St. Mary's Church and the Charles Carroll Mansion, which was home of yet an-

other signer of the Declaration of Independence (not open to the public).

Cross over the bridge and you are in the Eastport section of the city, with more marine supply stores, marinas, restaurants, and "watering holes" than I am able to describe. Call the Annapolis Information Center at (410)268-TOUR or the dockmaster at (410)263-7973 for more information. Discover the rest for yourself!

WEEMS

CREEK

No facilities

Charts: 12263, **12282,** 12283

Although Weems Creek is navigable for more than a mile from its mouth, the bridges over it limit normal cruising boats to the area just inside the mouth. The shore is all private property, leaving no place to land without express invitation.

Approaches. When approaching the mouth of the creek, be sure to steer clear of the shoal on the north side of the entrance, marked by the red/green buoy. Leave the buoy well to starboard on entering and head for the center of the creek mouth.

Anchorages. You can anchor anywhere inside the creek mouth up to the first bridge. The entire area is well protected with good holding in about 10 feet of water. Don't bother trying to pass the pair of bridges over the creek. The first bridge is a swing bridge with a 5-foot vertical clearance when closed. Trying to get it to open is more of a problem than it is worth. Past the swing bridge is a fixed bridge with a 28-foot vertical clearance, so only powerboats have access to the upper part of the creek.

COOL SPRING CREEK

No facilities

Charts: 12263, **12282**

Approaches. To starboard, just past the Route 50 bridge, Cool Spring Creek lies almost hidden amid the high banks of the northeast shore of the Severn River. Provided that it hasn't shoaled in, the entrance is easy, but hard to see unless you know where to look. Beware of the shoal protruding to the south from the north side of the entrance. Sound your way in carefully.

Anchorages. Once in, you are in a snug, well-protected anchorage for just a few boats. In warmer weather, it is so snug that there are no cooling breezes. Here too, the shore is all private property and there is no place to land. Unless you want to try it just to see if you can negotiate the entrance, try elsewhere.

LUCE CREEK

No facilities

Charts: 12263, **12282**

At first glance, Luce Creek looks to be an attractive anchorage. A second look at the chart shows a 4-foot bar at the entrance with the expectation that it will shoal in over time. Although it is well protected, we suggest that only shoal-draft vessels or cruisers with recent local knowledge attempt the entrance.

The community marina here has no transient facilities. The shoreline is private property, so there is no place to land. Head for the more attractive anchorages farther upstream.

SALTWORKS CREEK

No facilities

Charts: 12263, **12282**

An intriguing, well-protected, easily entered creek, Saltworks Creek bears your investigation. Steep banks provide more than adequate shelter from weather.

Approaches/Anchorages. Once you are clear of the shoal extending eastward from the north side of the creek entrance, you have 8 to 10 feet of water all the way to the overhead power cable (vertical clearance 46 feet) at the headwaters. This is an attractive anchorage but shares the same problem with most in this region; the private shoreline offers no place to land.

CHASE CREEK

No facilities

Charts: 12263, **12282**

Approaches. Almost directly across the Severn River from Saltworks Creek, Chase Creek has a quick-flashing red "2" buoy marking the shoal on the upstream side of the entrance. This not only provides warning of the shoal but also makes the entrance easy to find in almost all conditions. As you pass the small spits, which guard both sides of the entrance, the creek opens out into a Y-shape. Other than the one by the red "2" buoy at the entrance, there are no shoals.

Moorings/Anchorages. Moored or anchored boats, predominantly sail, fill the left branch. The right branch has fewer boats and is a little less developed. The high banks provide plenty of protection and, even though the shore is all private property, you have the illusion of partial seclusion. A sandy spit of land here is a possible landing, at least at low tide.

CLEMENTS CREEK

No facilities

Charts: 12263, **12282**

Although a little wider, Clements Creek is nearly a clone of Saltworks Creek. It has the same high banks, good protection, and private shoreline. There is no place to land.

Moorings/Anchorages. This is an attractive anchorage so you will find plenty of other boats anchored or moored here. No supplies or marine facilities are available.

BREWER CREEK

No facilities

Charts: 12263, **12282**

Approaches. Just upstream from Clements Creek, Brewer Creek provides a snug, secure anchorage. Simply stay in the middle on entering and you will find 10 to 15 feet of water almost to the end of the creek.

Anchorages. The best anchorages are from half way to three-quarters of the way up. Not too long ago this anchorage was surrounded by high wooded banks; now it is solidly residential and the shoreline is all private property.

There are no facilities, no supplies, and there is nowhere to land.

ROUND BAY

Charts: 12273, **12282**

Round Bay provides no secure anchorages but deserves mention because of its unique character. Located about 5 miles up the Severn River, Round Bay opens out to provide an excellent, protected area for sailing small boats. If it weren't for the brackish water, you might believe that you were in a large landlocked lake.

On the west side of Round Bay is St. Helena Island, a private island located right in the middle of Little Round Bay. In mild weather, you can anchor inside Long Point to the north of the island. Be sure to stay clear of the cable area to the west of St. Helena Island. You can anchor anywhere else in Little Round Bay in reasonable protection but the shore is all private and there is no place to land, except at Smith's Marina just inside the mouth of Browns Cove. Gas but not diesel is available at the marina. The approach is risky for boats with drafts of more than 4 feet.

MAYNEDIER CREEK

No facilities

Charts: 12273, **12282**

Approaches. Maynedier Creek and Hopkins Creek share a common entrance to the southwest of St. Helena Island. Although both of these creeks are unmarked, there is only one shoal of which you need beware on your approach. This shoal extends to the northwest from the little point on the mainland due south of St. Helena Island. If you hold close to the red "2" marker off St. Helena Island, even this shoal presents no problem.

Anchorages. Once you've entered the creek proper, it opens out into a bowl shape. The steep banks provide good protection from weather all around except to the southwest where you can look right up a small valley. Anchor anywhere on the east half of this circular "bay," which has 8 to 10 feet of water; the western half is shoal.

HOPKINS CREEK

No facilities

Charts: 12273, **12282**

Approaches. As you enter the mouth of Hopkins Creek, hold close to the sandspit to port to avoid the shoal off the shore to starboard. This is one of those sandspits from which you can dive into about 10 feet of water.

Anchorages. Once past the sandspit, you can anchor anywhere in the creek in 8 to 11 feet of water. The steep banks all around make Hopkins Creek one of the snuggest "hurricane holes" you are likely to find anywhere on the Bay. The same snugness cuts off

breezes so Hopkins is not a comfortable hot-weather anchorage.

UPPER SEVERN RIVER

Charts: 12273, **12282**

Anchorages. Once past Round Bay, the river narrows and you can find numerous anchorages in Valentine, Plum, or Forked Creeks, or simply in a bight of the Severn River itself. While it may be possible to squeeze into Yantz Creek, I don't recommend trying it unless you are in a small boat with a shallow draft that you can get out of and push.

The river remains deep as far as Indian Landing, where the Anne Arundel County Department of Education has a dock and recreational facilities, which may be used by cruising people if prior arrangements are made. Beyond Indian Landing, the river shoals rapidly so don't go past this point.

FISHING CREEK

No facilities

Charts: 12263, **12270**

Approaches. This little-known creek lies between the Severn and South Rivers, tucked away just north of the tip of Thomas Point. The entrance must be approached from the northeast because of the shoal extending to the east from the tip of Thomas Point. Stay to the northeast of a line between Thomas Point Lighthouse and the point on the north side of the creek mouth until you can leave the flashing red "2" marker close to starboard. From there on, simply honor the markers until you reach the basin near the Coast Guard Station.

South River to West River

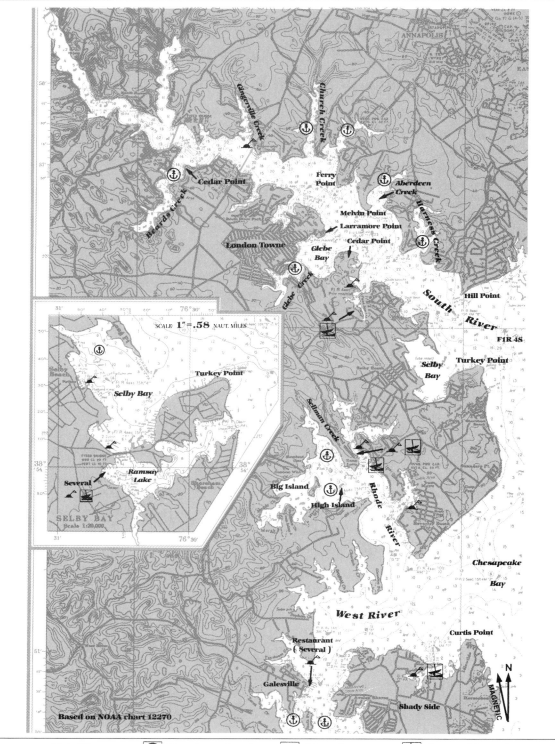

SCALE **1″=1.16** NAUT. MILES   Good anchoring   Mooring area   Launching site

Anchorages. There is 5-6 feet of water at MLW through most of the basin. However, be sure to anchor away from the Coast Guard Station and well out of the path to the exit markers. The coasties may be called to depart at all hours of the day and night and they tend to do so "flat out." Their wakes can be impressive.

There is nothing in particular here to attract the cruiser except as a convenient stopover point for the night on a passage up or down the Bay to save some distance. There are better anchorages nearby. I'd recommend passing this one by.

SOUTH RIVER

Charts: 12263, 12270

Prior to the American Revolution, South River was used by the shipping trade. In fact, Londontowne, about 2 miles upstream from the river's mouth, rivaled Annapolis. It was one of three Anne Arundel County sites addressed in a 1683 General Assembly act designed to promote trade. The water was not deep enough at Londontowne to serve the traffic a state capital would generate, and Annapolis quickly eclipsed it. The Publik House is now the only surviving structure from the original town.

Numerous marinas and boatyards are scattered throughout the South River, as well as many restaurants accessible from the water. Although commercial traffic is light, South River carries a substantial amount of traffic, much of it from Selby Bay. Even so, South River is not nearly as busy as the Severn or Middle Rivers, in spite of comparable population densities.

Navigation here is easy. Although you have to contend with several shoals during your approach, they are well marked, so you have only to use a bit of prudence to stay out of trouble. The approach to the mouth of South River is simplicity itself. Thomas Point Lighthouse serves as a highly visible, and picturesque, reference point, which aids in the recognition of and approach to the entrance to South River. The red nun "2" can be ignored with impunity—it is located in 13 feet of water—but honor all remaining markers on the river.

Two bridges cross the river. The first one is the Route 2 bridge at Edgewater. This bridge was rebuilt re-

cently with a center arch that, at 53 feet, is high enough for all but the very tallest sailboats to clear. The second bridge, at Riva, is a fixed bridge with a 50-foot vertical clearance; it will stop some sailboats. In 1987, this bridge replaced an unreliable and almost always broken drawbridge.

SELBY BAY

Charts: 12263, 12270

Tucked away just inside the mouth of the South River lies a small body of water that gives cruisers a choice. In Selby Bay the visiting yacht can enter the busy, bustling world of heavily populated marinas with all their attendant facilities, or anchor out in relative seclusion. The latter option offers the best of both worlds: You can anchor close to an undeveloped shoreline full of small wildlife, yet never be more than minutes away from the facilities you might need.

Approaches. As you enter the mouth of the South River, a course of 321 degrees takes you to the green "5" daymark off Turkey Point. Hold your course for at least 200 yards past the green "5" daymark before swinging to port to head directly for the red "2" lighted mark at the entrance to Selby Bay. This will insure that you clear the shoal off Turkey Point, as well as the submerged pilings reported there.

Anchorages. As you approach the red "2" marker, you must quickly decide which Selby Bay you wish to enjoy. For marina facilities, continue on; to anchor out, let red "2" slide past, then turn to starboard to a northwest course which leaves the red "4" marker well to port. There are two finger-like shoals, parallel to this new course, which extend from the shore to these two red markers; you now pass between them.

Once inside the shelter of Long Point, you can anchor just about anywhere. The relatively low surrounding land allows a cooling breeze, but you are well protected from wave action and the holding ground is good. Stay out of the inviting little cove to starboard on Long Point. It has only 2 feet of water.

Long Point is an uninhabited, marshy peninsula with some sandy beaches where you can land to beachcomb or, if the jellyfish have not yet come in, swim. The remains of a wrecked boat still should be visible on the shore. In the evening, the crickets and treefrogs sing you to sleep, while on the opposite shore the lights of the houses and marinas announce the presence of considerable human activity. Very little human noise carries the distance to this anchorage. What little sound does carry is drowned out by nature's serenade.

The amount of boating activity in this area makes it necessary to display a good anchor light. In addition, I highly recommend the use of good screens in the summer—mosquitoes like this marshy shoreline.

Dockages/Facilities. If you opt for the world of marina facilities, you have a choice of two courses from the red "2" marker at the bay entrance. One larger marina, Selby Bay Yacht Basin, is located in the northwest corner, but most of the facilities are clustered in the southern corner of Selby Bay.

To reach the marina cluster, head south southwest from red "2" off Long Point. Keep the green "1" daymark to port and the lighted red "4" to starboard and you will have no problem reaching your destination. A casual glance at the chart will disturb you; the southern corner of the bay shows 1, 2, and 3 feet of water, but don't be alarmed. A more careful examination reveals a reasonably deep channel that runs near the southern shore most of the way around the bight where the marinas are.

As you approach Holiday Point Marina, watch out for runabouts and small power cruisers exiting Ramsay Lake through the fixed bridge to port.

Do not attempt to anchor anywhere in the bight where these marinas are located. You either will run aground or block traffic.

Somewhat more accessible and less congested is Selby Bay Yacht Basin, located due west of the red "2" marker off Long Point. Head west from red "2," so that you leave the red "4" marker close to starboard. As you clear red "4," head directly toward the green "5" marker on the corner of the large building ahead of you. That building is the part of the marina containing the fuel dock and a platform from which you can view all of Selby Bay. Children, especially, seem to enjoy climbing

to the top of this observation platform and looking around.

Associated with Selby Bay is Ramsay Lake, a nearby landlocked tidal pond. The only real access to the lake is through the stone abutments of the bridge connecting Turkey Point to the mainland. During changes of the tide, there is a substantial current through these abutments. Despite the current, the water is quite shallow, marked as 2 feet on the chart. The bridge itself has a vertical clearance of only 10 feet, which, together with the shallow water, restricts access to the lake to relatively small powerboats. Even so, traffic is substantial, especially on weekends.

DUVALL CREEK

No facilities

Charts: 12263, **12270**

The markers in the mouth of Duvall Creek are privately maintained, and the channel is narrow. Though charts show a 2-foot shoal across the mouth, the channel depth holds at a minimum of 5½ feet MLW, making it accessible to most sailboats, unless there is a strong northerly, which can blow the water out.

Approach the first two markers, "1" and "3," on a line roughly midway between the two mid-river markers "6" (off Turkey Point to the south) and "8" (off Hill Point to the north). Head directly for the green "1" daymark, turning to starboard at a distance of 15-20 feet to leave it, a small green buoy, and the green "3" daymark all fairly close to port. Maintain this course until you are past the end of the sandspit to port. Anchor anywhere.

HARNESS CREEK

No facilities

Charts: 12263, **12270**

Approaches. Harness Creek is the first good foul-weather anchorage on the South River. The entrance is unmarked but not difficult. After you pass the red "8" marker off Hill Point, maintain your course until the opening into Harness Creek is at about a 45-degree angle off your starboard bow. Then turn and head directly for the entrance. As you enter, favor the east side where you have a minimum of 11 feet of water all the way in.

Anchorages. Once in the creek, you can anchor anywhere, secure from foul weather from any direction. The sandy point to starboard on entering offers a nice beach to stretch your legs or "water a dog." If you follow the east shore around carefully, you come to the gap in the marsh that allows entrance to the famous Harness Creek "hurricane hole." You can negotiate this gap with a good bit of water *under* you but not much *around* you until you are through it. Once in this hurricane hole, a couple of boats can weather any blow, completely protected by the high banks and dense woods. This very protection makes it the last place to anchor in during hot, sticky weather.

Although we never have had any problem, we have heard several reports of boats having trouble getting their anchors to set properly and hold in the upper part of the creek. Since this is quite a popular anchorage during the main boating season, we recommend that you get in early, set your anchor carefully, and check it even more carefully before turning in.

If this anchorage is too crowded for your taste, simply head for one of the other creeks up the river.

BREWER CREEK

Charts: 12263, **12270**

Just across South River from Harness Creek, Brewer Creek offers anchorage in pretty, wooded, high-banked surroundings. The creek is open to the north for some distance, unless you have a shoal draft, which enables you to pass the 2-foot bar into the inner cove.

If the weather is expected to remain fair, give Brewer Creek a try. Otherwise, head for another anchorage.

ABERDEEN CREEK

No facilities

Charts: 12263, **12270**

Approaches. The next creek on the way upriver is Aberdeen Creek. For some reason, many cruisers fail to pay attention to the shoal that extends to the east from Melvin Point to port when entering this creek. Even though the creek is unmarked, there is no good reason to run aground. If you keep in the eastern third of the creek's entrance, you have 15 to 17 feet of water all the way in. Once you have passed the mouth, the creek opens out and all you need do is to keep a prudent distance off the shore.

To starboard on entering is a group of buildings belonging to a children's camp. Melvin Point to port is wooded, curling down and to the east where it ends in a marsh. The shoal mentioned above extends from this point.

The shoreline around the creek is wooded but relatively low, permitting a welcome breeze on hot summer nights. The creek is open to the south southeast unless you proceed nearly to the headwaters. This is not the usual direction for a significant blow, however, so the openness is not a problem.

An attractive anchorage and a favorite rendezvous spot for boating clubs, this spot is rarely crowded.

GLEBE CREEK

Charts: 12263, **12270**

ALMSHOUSE CREEK

No facilities

Charts: 12263, **12270**

Approaches. Directly across the South River from Aberdeen Creek, a green "11" flashing marker indicates the tip of the shoal off Cedar Point on the east side of the entrance. Do not cut inside this marker! Not only is there a shoal, but also a collection of old pilings—indicated on the charts—some of which are still visible above water. Favor the south side of the entrance to avoid the shoal, which extends to the east from Larramore Point and has its own collection of pilings. Stay with the south shore as you continue through Glebe Bay; there is a 2-foot shoal right in the middle of the bay. There is a piling in the water about where you would expect the 2-foot shoal. Although it really doesn't mark the shoal, give it a wide berth and you will avoid the shoal and pass through Glebe Bay with no problems.

Glebe Bay is attractive, but it is too exposed to provide a comfortable anchorage. Continue on and pass into Glebe Creek. By skirting the southeast shore of Glebe Bay about 150 to 200 yards offshore you easily reach the low-lying point of land that protects the entrance to Glebe Creek.

Anchorages. From here on, there is deep water (11 feet) from a short distance offshore all the way across the creek. You can anchor anywhere in here, well protected from wave and weather. Be careful how you set your hook! The bottom is covered with leaves, which make it difficult for a Danforth to dig in; test your anchor accordingly.

This anchorage is lined with modest homes. It is attractive but can be a bit noisy, at least during daylight hours.

History. The next creek upstream, to port, is Almshouse Creek, named for the Almshouse, which was once the Cortelyou mansion in London Towne and is now known as the London Towne Publik House. As mentioned earlier, London Towne was a leading port before Annapolis became Maryland's capital.

From 1694 until the 1790s, a public ferry served to connect London Towne with Annapolis. As one of the provisions of the ferry's license, the ferry operator had to maintain specific service standards, which included providing meals and lodging to those waiting to cross on the ferry. As a result, the license holder, William Brown, constructed the Publik House in the mid 1760s. For a while, the building served as the governor's residence. In 1828 it was purchased by the county for use as a poorhouse, a role it served until 1965.

Things to Do. In 1970, the London Towne Publik House and Gardens was designated a National Historic Landmark, restored to its colonial appearance, and now operates as a historic site museum. It is open to the public 10:00 a.m. to 4:00 p.m., Tuesday through Saturday, and 12:00 to 4:00 p.m. on Sunday. It is closed on Mondays, Easter Sunday, Thanksgiving, Christmas, and the months of January and February. Boats may tie up at the public pier here at no charge during the regular hours of the Publik House.

Approaches. Entrance to Almshouse Creek is easy: Keep clear of the green "15" marker at the west side of the entrance and you have 11 to 14 feet of water all the way in. The area is built-up and has become entirely too "public" for our tastes. Since no fuel or facilities are available, we recommend visiting the Publik House but anchoring elsewhere.

CRAB CREEK

No facilities

Charts: 12263, **12270**

Approaches. Although completely unmarked, the approach to Crab Creek is relatively easy. After you pass red "14" off Ferry Point, maintain about the same distance offshore and swing around Ferry Point to the entrance to Crab Creek. Favor the starboard side of the entrance, leaving a piling there well to port.

A small cove to port right after you enter makes anchoring possible for one or two boats. However, there are better anchorages farther up, past the sandy hook on the east side of the creek. A glance at the chart may cause you to pause, but the narrow channel carries plenty of water (12 feet). Hug the sandy spit at a distance of 75 to 100 feet off the beach and you can pass into the upper part of the creek with relative ease.

Anchorages. Although you can anchor anywhere in here, the better anchorages are past the second point to starboard, in 10 to 12 feet of water. Most boats can proceed almost all the way to the headwaters, although the creek shoals to 5 feet in the last one-quarter mile.

The high banks inside provide plenty of shelter from the weather and the only waves you get are from other boats. There are no marina facilities and the houses are well screened by trees and shrubbery, so all are relatively secluded. By all means try this anchorage.

CHURCH CREEK

No facilities

Charts: 12263, **12270**

Church and Crab Creeks share more than a common approach—they also share all the positive aspects, making Church Creek another recommended anchorage.

Approaches. Approach as if you were going to enter Crab Creek, but just before you would enter it, swing to port to head directly for the entrance to Church Creek, which then is clearly visible. This course neatly avoids the 2-foot shoal to port.

Anchorages. Pass the first point to starboard before anchoring to provide yourself with full protection from wave and weather. Although you can anchor anywhere in here, the best anchorage is in the north fork of the little cove to port after you enter. The same description used for Crab Creek surroundings also applies here.

WAREHOUSE CREEK

Charts: 12263, **12270**

On the southern shore, just before the Route 2 bridge at Edgewater, is Warehouse Creek. Like most of the creeks on the southern side of South River, the shores are developed and therefore less attractive as anchorages go.

Warehouse Creek Boatyard is located here, but it has neither fuel nor other facilities for transient boats other than inboard engine repairs, if needed.

UPPER SOUTH RIVER

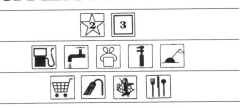

Charts: 12263, **12270**

Anchorages. Past the Route 2 bridge are several other creeks or anchorages worth exploring. Gingerville Creek, to starboard immediately past the bridge, provides a couple of coves and bights below high banks where you can anchor in security. Just past Gingerville Creek is a small, interesting cove to starboard. Beards Creek, to port, just before the Riva Road bridge offers some anchorages near its mouth. Past South River Boat and Engine Works is a cable area that covers most of the navigable portion of the creek, which precludes anchoring there.

The vertical clearance of 53 feet for the fixed Route 2 bridge will allow most boats to proceed another mile upstream to the fixed Riva Road bridge (vertical clearance 25 feet), which will stop all sailboats. Powerboats can continue past the bridge into Broad Creek and the headwaters of the South River itself.

RHODE RIVER

Charts: 12263, **12270**

Approximately 4 miles southwest of the Thomas Point Lighthouse lies the Rhode River with its three distinctive little islands. The area is much more reminiscent of many of the Eastern Shore anchorages than those on the more congested and built-up western shore of Maryland. Once you are well into the river, the shoreline is relatively sparsely settled and has high wooded banks.

RHODE RIVER

ANCHORAGES

Charts: 12263, **12270**

Approaches. The approach to the mouth of the West River, from which the Rhode River branches off, is easiest from the north. A compass course of 240 degrees from Thomas Point Lighthouse brings you past the green "1" buoy to the red "2" light in the mouth of the West River, just about a mile north of Curtis Point.

The approach from the south is a little more com-

plex due to a long, wide 3- to 4-foot shoal that extends for about 1½ miles northeast of Curtis Point. While shoal-draft boats can pass over the outer third of this shoal, it is more prudent to hold close to the green "73" bell buoy of the Chesapeake Bay main shipping channel. (Note: The Coast Guard is in the process of changing these buoy numbers. To prevent confusion, this buoy is the one about 2½ miles east northeast of the tip of Curtis Point.) Then follow a course of 292 degrees to the green "1" buoy at the approach to the West River. Then a course of 240 degrees takes you to the West River red "2" marker.

A course of 284 degrees from red "2" takes you directly to the red "2" lighted beacon at the entrance to the Rhode River, which is difficult to see until you get fairly close. Be sure to honor the Rhode River red "2" unless you are very fond of kedging off shoals.

Provisions. There are several small tributaries on the Rhode River—places to restock supplies and fuel or to explore—but we do not recommend anchoring in any for an extended period because the anchorage near the three islands is far superior in every respect. Bear Neck and Cadle Creeks are the closest places for resupplying fuel and provisions. One caution: While the chart shows 5 to 7 feet of water in Cadle Creek, there is a 4-foot (or less) bar at its mouth, which restricts entrance to shoal-draft vessels. For groceries or a restaurant, head for Galesville on the West River, a little over 3 miles away. Muddy Creek to the southwest of Big Island is just that, muddy and shallow. Sellman Creek to the north of Flat Island is a nice anchorage to use if the Big Island one is too crowded.

Anchorages. The first reasonably good anchorage on the river is in the large bend, Canning House Bay, to the west of the mouth of Cadle Creek, where you can anchor fairly close to shore by some attractive sandy beaches. The holding is good and the area is sheltered from wave action and somewhat from the wind, but it is exposed to wakes from the plentiful passing traffic. For that reason, most people continue upstream to anchor among the three islands.

After clearing the red "6" daymark, give the green "7" light, where the Rhode River bends sharply to the west, a wide berth as you approach it. This course avoids the shoal between the green "7" light and the mainland to the south of the light. As you clear the marker, you have a clear view to port of the anchorage among the islands. Our recommended approach is to pass to the south of High Island so that you avoid the shoals extending north from High Island and south from Flat Island. These shoals don't present any real problem, but we see no reason to flirt with even possible trouble.

Holding in the area is excellent; the heavy mud bottom provides good security with any type of anchor. The best place to drop the hook is to the east of Big Island, unless there is a strong easterly wind. In that event, simply run around the north side of Big Island and anchor in its lee. There is about 7 feet of water to within roughly 50 yards from the shore. Do not try to pass to the south of Big Island as the water shoals to 2 feet or less between the island and the mainland.

As the names would lead you to believe, High Island is relatively high in relation to its size while Flat Island is so low that it appears in danger of submerging at any time. Flat Island is all that remains of a small peninsula, which used to extend from the mainland. High Island is also disappearing—its high banks crumbling into the water. You can land on and explore both Flat and High Islands, but be careful of the poison ivy that flourishes on High Island. Big Island, the last of the trio, is big only when compared to the other two. It is approximately 500 yards long by 100 yards wide, its high banks covered with heavy underbrush and pine trees. It is posted with "Private, No Trespassing" signs. Evidently this is enforced; no one tries to land there, even though it is uninhabited.

To the north of High Island, on the mainland, is Camp Letts, which is a well-cared-for, pleasant place to stretch your legs if you land well to the west of the main camp, inside Sellman Creek.

The Rhode River is a popular anchorage, especially with power cruisers, and the area between Big and High Islands is usually peppered with anchor lights after sundown during the height of boating season (Memorial Day to Labor Day).

WEST RIVER

Charts: 12263, 12270

The approach to the mouth of West River is the same as described for the approach to the Rhode River up to the West River red "2," north of Curtis Point.

Although there are several marinas in Parrish Creek, just inside Curtis Point, normally the only boats to traverse the narrow dredged channel belong to those who have slips there.

WEST RIVER
AREA ANCHORAGES

Charts: 12263, 12270

Approaches. From red "2," a course of 260 degrees takes you to the flashing 4-second red "4" spar, leaving the green "3" can to port. The creeks along the north shore of the river are all too shallow to be of interest. Once you reach red "4," you need to pay careful attention to your navigation as the channel narrows and bends, with shoals extending from both shores.

A course of 200 degrees from red "4" takes you to the green "5" daymark opposite the mouth of Cox Creek. If you draw less than 5 feet, you can enter Cox Creek, which provides a pleasant, well-protected anchorage. Favor the south side of the creek on the way in. The best anchorage is just opposite the mouth of Tenthouse Creek in about 5 feet of water.

As you clear green "5," find and leave the flashing 4-second red "6" marker off Councillors Point (on the south side of the mouth of Cox Creek) well to starboard. For some reason, this marker is easy to miss and, if you fail to honor it, you will find yourself trying to plow another channel.

Dockages/Provisions. Once you are clear of red "6," the channel opens out again and you can head directly for your selected destination. All the marina facilities you may need are in Galesville, as well as a couple of restaurants and a small grocery store.

Anchorages. Anchor in the basin where Smith Creek bends to the west or pass to the east of Chalk Point and anchor in South Creek. Unless you draw well under 5 feet, don't proceed up South Creek much past the Chesapeake Yacht Club to port in Shady Side.

All the shore is privately owned. If you must go ashore for any reason, you have to land at one of the marinas. The West River offers marina facilities and well-protected anchorage, but no seclusion.

HERRING BAY

Charts: 12263, **12270**

Rockhold Creek represents the last harbor for a distance of more than 30 miles along the western shore, except for a handful of man-made basins. Even so, it is only for those who draw less than 4 feet. There is little room to anchor, so if you stay you probably will have to tie up at a marina.

Long Bar extends southward from Parker Creek to beyond Fairhaven. Boats with drafts of less than 4 feet can cut across the southern half of the bar, but proceed carefully—the bottom is hard oyster shell.

ROCKHOLD CREEK

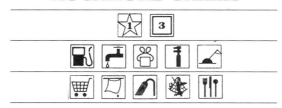

Approaches. Pay close attention as you travel up the dredged entrance channel. Although well marked, you can easily drift out of the channel between the marks and find yourself on the flats. At one time, only very shallow-draft boats could approach the two marinas in the mouth of Tracy Creek, preferably inboard-outboard or outboard boats. The considerable number of large sailboats there now indicates an improved channel depth. No boats can proceed past the fixed bridge over Tracy Creek; the bridge is low and the creek promptly shoals to next to nothing.

Dockages. Most of the marinas are clustered along the shores of Rockhold Creek below the fixed bridge (vertical clearance 14 feet), with a few on the

eastern shore above the bridge where the water depth drops to 3 feet MLW. On the west side of Rockhold Creek, just before the bridge, is the Happy Harbor Restaurant. This is a "just plain folks" place which hasn't changed much in 20 years. You can still get a great meal there at a reasonable price. There is room for one or two shoal-draft boats to tie up at the dock for dinner. (Remember, this is powerboat country.)

Provisions. Supplies and fittings are available in a number of places, and the town of Deale itself, about a mile above the fixed bridge, has an excellent hardware store that caters to the marine trade.

This is not an anchorage. To spend the night, you must take a slip at one of the marinas or go elsewhere.

HERRINGTON HARBOR

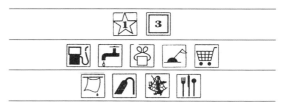

Charts: 12263, **12266**, 12270

Once called Rose Haven, Herrington Harbor has had a somewhat spotty history. Founded in 1947 by Joseph Rose, the Rose Haven Yacht Club was intended to be the focus of the Rose Haven community. The club fell into disrepair and both the entrance and a large part of the basin silted in. In 1978, it was sold and the new owners dredged and enlarged the entrance and basin and refurbished the shoreside facilities. They also opened the facilities to the public, with the intent to cater to cruising groups.

Approaches. The entrance to Herrington Harbor is in the southern part of Herring Bay, just to the west of Holland Point. If you are approaching from the north, remain a good 1½ miles offshore until you can pick up the quick-flashing green "1" marker at the entrance to Herrington Harbor channel. Leave the green "1" marker to port and follow the daymarks into the basin. The channel has a controlling depth of 5 feet for a width of 60 feet. Boats with close to a 5-foot draft should proceed cautiously as the entrance is forever in danger of shoaling. Most of the resident boats are large powerboats, but as many as a quarter of the boats are good-sized sailboats. The latter indicates some serious effort to keep the entrance channel open to a reasonable depth, so perhaps it is now deeper than the previous 5 feet.

The fuel dock is the third pier to port on entering. Tie up here for directions to where you can stay if you want to visit the restaurant (clearly defined by the "lighthouse"). If you are looking for a slip for the night, make advance reservations during the boating season. Don't plan to anchor out; there is absolutely no room for it.

Dockages/Facilities/Provisions.

Although open to the public, Herrington Harbor has all the trappings of a yacht club, complete with pool, tennis courts, a restaurant and lounge, and a motel. It also has a laundry. The facilities are open to slip holders and guests, but the harbor does advertise slips for transients.

Herrington Harbor offers high-class shoreside accommodations and lots to do. Try it, unless you "want to be alone."

CHESAPEAKE BEACH

(FISHING CREEK)

Charts: 12263, **12266**

About 2 miles south of Holland Point is the entrance to Fishing Creek, better known as Chesapeake Beach. Unless it has been dredged recently, we recommend that boats with drafts of more than 3 feet stay out. As with many such places on the Bay, the problem is not the water depth in the basin but the shoaling in of the entrance channel. The controlling depth of the entrance was 6 feet in 1983; I don't know what it is now.

CHESAPEAKE BEACH

All facilities

Charts: 12263, **12266**

Approaches. Stay at least a mile offshore until you are able to pick out the green "1" entrance marker outside the breakwaters with a pair of red and green markers at the end of each jetty. Approach roughly perpendicular to the shoreline. Favor the north side of the approach to avoid the ruins of an old pier on the south side.

Anchorages/Dockages. Once inside, there is some room (not much) to anchor in about 7 feet of water or you can get a slip at Kellam's Marina. You may tie up alongside the Rod & Reel Dock at no charge if you plan to eat at the restaurant; some dockage for transients is available. The Rod & Reel and Kellam's both sell fuel and groceries are available nearby.

A sizable fleet of charter fishing boats is located here. The harbor is not pretty but does offer good shelter from wind and wave, if you get in the channel entrance before the storm hits. Don't try the entrance in a storm!

There is a low (10-foot clearance) fixed bridge so only powerboats can continue farther. The covered and open slips past the bridge belong to the marina and two restaurants.

BREEZY POINT

HARBOR

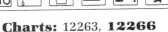

Charts: 12263, **12266**

Just north of Plum Point is Breezy Point Harbor, an artificial basin dredged into a marsh. There is plenty of water in the basin, but the entrance frequently shoals, presenting transients with an iffy situation. This is a shame; inside is a rather nice marina with a restaurant, snack bar, and some limited marine supplies. Our advice is to stay out unless you are a powerboat with no fixed propeller and rudder, unless you know that the entrance was dredged recently; you can contact the marina at (410)257-2561 to check on the controlling depth at present.

REGION 4

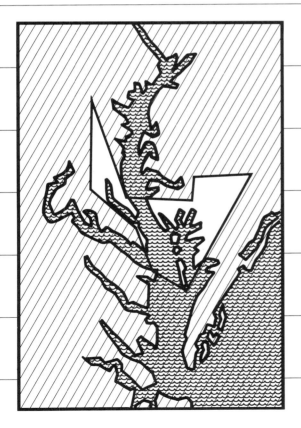

Little
Choptank
to
Potomac
River

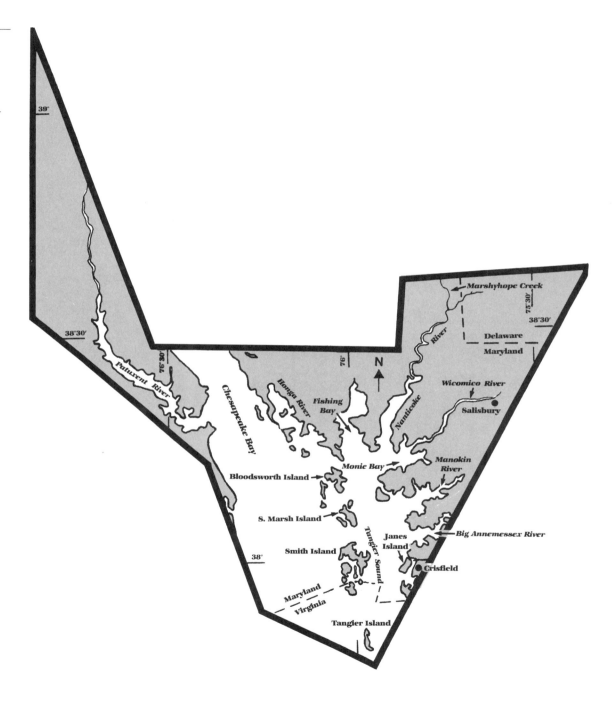

39°

38°30'

76°30'

Patuxent River

Chesapeake Bay

Honga River

Fishing Bay

76°

N

Nanticoke River

Marshyhope Creek

75°30'

38°30'

Delaware
Maryland

Wicomico River

Salisbury

Monie Bay

Manokin River

Bloodsworth Island

S. Marsh Island

Tangier Sound

Janes Island

Big Annemessex River

Smith Island

38°

Crisfield

Maryland
Virginia

Tangier Island

From the Little Choptank to the Potomac River, the character of the Bay changes again. On the eastern shore, the harbors disappear and there is a long (for the Bay) stretch of low-lying marshy islands with no receptive harbors until you reach Hooper Strait. Even then, attractive harbors on the eastern shore are rare until you reach Smith Island.

The western shore, similarly short of harbors until you reach the Patuxent River, has a totally different character. Here you find the high, fossil-laden Calvert Cliffs, which stretch from just south of Herring Bay to Cove Point. After a short interruption, they resume to sweep on into the mouth of the Patuxent River. High on these cliffs, about 4 miles north of Cove Point is Calvert Nuclear Power Plant. In fair weather, you can go ashore (by dinghy) and tour the plant, which has an interesting display of fossils from the Calvert Cliffs.

Just north of Cove Point is the Cove Point Natural Gas facility, a huge imposing structure with a pier that looks like it was designed for giants. Most charts warn you to stay a minimum of 200 yards away from this facility, but we prefer a minimum distance of at least one-half mile. Don't miss the Cove Point Lighthouse. It is a classic lighthouse, complete with lightkeeper's house.

South of the Patuxent River, you pass some peculiar-looking structures about 2 miles offshore, midway between Cedar Point and Point No Point. Stay well away from them; they are targets for a U.S. Navy bombing range.

If you are headed for the Potomac River, you can cut well inside Point No Point Lighthouse to save some distance. The light is really intended for large ship traffic.

HONGA RIVER

Charts: **12230,** 12261, 12263, 12264

The Honga River opens to the north off Hooper Strait, at the south end of Hooper Island. The river has a deep, wide channel for most of its length but no anchorages. The Honga is worth the trip if you are interested in the three relatively unspoiled fishing villages along its shores. These workboat harbors have narrow, dredged channels and small basins where gasoline and some supplies are available.

A passage, called Fishing Creek, offers a shortcut into the Honga River at the northern end of Hooper Island. Unless it has been dredged recently, it is only suitable for the shallow-draft workboats skippered by local watermen. The controlling depth was less than 4 feet in 1986 and keeps shoaling. Don't try it in anything but a light-displacement, shallow-draft boat.

FOX CREEK

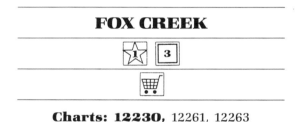

Charts: **12230,** 12261, 12263

Approaches/Provisions. Hearns Cove is off Fox Creek on the eastern shore, around Crab Point and up a narrow, dredged channel with a reported controlling depth of 5½ feet. Swing wide around the red "2" marker off Crab Point and head straight to the first of the channel markers into Hearns Cove. Supplies are within a short walk of the basin in the small village of Wingate. The quarters here are tight and there is no place to anchor. You may have trouble even finding a place to tie up among the workboats.

Anchorages. Just past the green daymark off Pauls Point, Fox Creek makes a right-angle bend to the northwest. Six feet of water is carried in a nearly straight line to within 400 yards of the shore of Asquith Island, forming the west side of the creek. This region presents a possible anchorage in a nearly unpopulated region. It is open for more than 2 miles to the southeast and the low land provides limited protection from the wind. This may well be the closest thing to a good anchorage (with more than two feet of water) that you find on the Honga River.

MUDDY HOOK COVE

Charts: 12230, 12261, 12263

Dockages/Provisions. Almost due west of the entrance to Fox Creek, on the western side of the Honga, is Muddy Hook Cove, a small basin up a narrow channel with a reported controlling depth of 6 feet. There is a 200-foot–long dock at Rippons Harbor where you can tie up. Fuel is available. There is a crab house nearby in the town of Hooperville and you can get fresh seafood in season. The harbor is exposed to the east and space at the dock is scarce. There is no anchorage and, unless you can manage to rent a slip, remaining overnight here is not a good idea (except if you are already in a hard blow).

BACK CREEK

Charts: 12230, 12261, 12263, 12264

Anchorages/Approaches. Six miles up the Honga River from Muddy Hook Cove, also on the western shore, is Back Creek. This is the snuggest of the three potential harbors on the Honga River, thanks to a dogleg in the narrow, dredged channel. The channel controlling depth is somewhat uncertain so, unless you are in a shallow-draft boat, check the depth with one of the locals before trying it. Even then, proceed slowly and with caution.

Provisions. Fuel is available at Rippons & Tolley, right by the dogleg, and you can get some supplies in the nearby town of Fishing Creek.

FISHING BAY

Charts: 12230, 12231, 12261, 12263

At the eastern end of Hooper Strait, the broad expanse of Fishing Bay opens to the north. This is a wide, shallow bay surrounded by low, marshy shores. Why this body of water is called a bay and not a river or creek is beyond me; it looks more like a river than the nearby Honga. There are no good anchorages or cruiser-oriented harbors.

A number of small streams wind their way through the marshes into Fishing Bay—only four of them identifiable by channel markers leading into them. The first one, on the western side, is Tedious Creek. About 2 miles north of that creek, still on the western shore, is Goose Creek. Just over a mile above Goose Creek, on the eastern shore, is McReady's Creek. Two miles past McReady's Creek, on the western shore, is the last available harbor on Fishing Bay, Farm Creek. These are all workboat harbors and, except for Goose Creek, you can't get into them unless you have a draft of 3 feet or less. Goose Creek is reputed to have a controlling depth of 5½ feet. All have some gasoline available and, except for Goose Creek, have some supplies relatively nearby, but you'll have to ask to find them.

After you pass the entrance marker to McReady's Creek, there are unmarked shoals on both sides of Fishing Bay. Proceed with caution to the entrance to Farm Creek. Above Farm Creek, the bay rapidly shoals to depths of 2 to 5 feet. Cruisers with a draft of 3 feet or less can continue on to explore the rest of Fishing Bay but the water depth is iffy all the way. This is an area reserved for small, shallow-draft boats.

NANTICOKE RIVER

Charts: 12230, **12261,** 12263

Most cruising boats can navigate the Nanticoke River all the way to Seaford, Delaware, a distance of more than 35 miles from its mouth. The channel is well marked; the shoreline is low and marshy. You can anchor anywhere out of the main part of the river once you pass upstream of Chapter Point. The bends in the river provide adequate protection from weather, but you need good screens for protection from the flying bloodthirsty insects. Below Chapter Point, there are three possible harbors, for relatively shallow-draft boats only.

NANTICOKE

No facilities

Charts: 12230, **12261**

The town of Nanticoke offers a dredged cove on the eastern side of the river, just past Roaring Point. A pair of jetties provide protection to the small harbor. The controlling depth is reputed to be 5½ feet, with deeper water in the turning basin. This is a county boat landing intended for small boats. It is not made to cater to larger cruising boats.

Provisions. Although supplies should be available in Nanticoke, you may have trouble finding room to tie up at the dock. The County Boat Landing has some slips but their availability is problematic.

BIVALVE

Charts: 12230, **12261**

The town of Bivalve offers a short entrance channel and a well-protected basin, but the controlling depth is about 4 feet. To get there you have to negotiate the somewhat tricky eastern channel on the Nanticoke River between Ragged Point and the Wetipquin Creek.

Dockages/Provisions. Fuel and ice are available on weekends in "season" at the Cedar Hill Boat Ramp & Park. Cedar Hill has 150 slips and welcomes transients. To stay overnight, you must take one of the slips; this is no anchorage.

WETIPQUIN CREEK

No facilities

Charts: 12230, **12261**

Approaches. The entrance to Wetipquin Creek is unmarked and difficult to follow and the controlling depth is reputed to be 4 feet. If you line up with a clump of trees on the western shore and head toward the right side of the wharf ahead, you should be able to follow the channel into the creek. Proceed carefully, preferably using a lead line or pole to feel out the channel. You should find 4 feet if you manage to stay in the channel. Unless you can squeeze well into the creek, this area is exposed to the northwest. Most shoal-draft boats should be able to get far enough in to find good shelter.

Anchorages. Try anchoring farther up the Nanticoke, past Chapter Point. You will feel much more secure. The Wetipquin is a little too tight for comfort.

REWASTICO CREEK

No facilities

Chart: **12261**

Approaches. This creek is an anchorage for shoal-draft boats that can manage to get over the 3-foot bar at its mouth. If you can get in, you can explore this little creek for more than a mile. For those with shoal draft and nerve, proceed for 3 miles upstream as far as Jenkins Landing. After you pass the mouth of

Manumsco Creek, anyone tired of boating can get out and walk!

Anchorages. Just past the second bend in the creek is a possible anchorage. Here I can almost guarantee that you will find yourself all alone in a pleasant little creek that meanders through a tidal marsh. Don't expect to land—it's all mud.

THE INLET

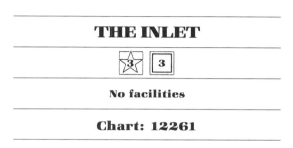

No facilities

Chart: 12261

Things to Do. About one-half mile past the mouth of Rewastico Creek is a barely visible entrance, labeled "The Inlet" on the chart. The Inlet offers gunkholers a unique experience: the opportunity to explore a tidal marsh uncorrupted by civilization. Any cruising boat worthy of the name can travel this narrow but deep body of water that winds its way through a couple of miles of marsh. Here you can observe wildlife and plants in their wetland habitat—something usually possible only for small boats whose drafts are measured in inches rather than feet.

Approaches. About a mile into the passage, there is a fork to the left, which you can follow for nearly one-half mile before it shoals at another split. The right fork leads on for another mile where it connects with two other waterways through the marsh. The left branch is Rags Thorofare, which, if you could get past the 1-foot shoal about one-third of a mile into it, would lead you back to the Nanticoke River just above Marshall Point. The right branch is Bridge Thorofare, which leads into Rewastico Creek at its second bend—only if you can clear the 2-foot shoal that is two-thirds of a mile past the junction of the three "thorofares." These little passageways have between 6 and 21 feet of water depth until you reach the two shoaling spots mentioned.

While I don't recommend trying to anchor in here, if you are looking for a good introduction to the "art" of gunkholing, I can't think of a better place to start.

VIENNA

Chart: 12261

History. The town of Vienna is one of the oldest settlements in Maryland, settled the late 1600s. In its history, it has had two ferry services alternating with two different bridges. The first ferry was established in the 1670s and in service until 1828, when the first bridge was built. In 1860, the bridge was declared unsafe and dismantled, and the ferry service was reestablished. It continued in operation until 1931 when the present Route 50 bridge over the Nanticoke was built.

During the American Revolution, Vienna was such an important source of supplies for the Continental Army that the British raided it at least five times. They also raided it during the War of 1812 but were repelled from a breastworks constructed from ship ballast set up along the river. The remains of this breastworks can still be seen on the south side of the town, near the Nanticoke Manor House.

Things to Do. Much of Vienna's past survives today in its architecture. The town has made a determined effort to restore many of its fine old homes, and has produced a walking tour brochure to guide visitors around the two-block historic area, right on the waterfront. There are 22 points of interest on the tour, including the Nanticoke Manor House, built in 1861; Governor Hicks House, built between 1780 and 1800; the Federal period Houston House; the colonial Tavern House; the one-room ferry house, and St. Paul's Episcopal Church, one of the earliest churches in Dorchester County. The old Customs House, at the foot of Church and Water Streets, dates back to 1768 when Vienna was proclaimed to be the customs district of the area as it was authorized by the Maryland Assembly as the original location of Baltimore (which never came to pass). The Customs House was closed in 1865 as the true Baltimore became Maryland's center of commerce.

Provisions/Anchorages. The bend in the river here provides enough shelter to permit an-

Vienna waterfront.

choring. The Route 50 bridge opens on demand, 24 hours a day. During heavy road traffic periods, you may have to wait a while for response. The Vienna Public Launching Ramp, just south of the Route 50 bridge, makes a good place to land and leave a dinghy—I wouldn't try bringing in a large boat—should you want to tour the town or buy some groceries.

MARSHYHOPE CREEK

No facilities

Chart: 12261

About 4 miles above the town of Vienna, Marshyhope Creek splits off to the west from the Nanticoke River. There are no navigation markers on this creek, but you can follow it all the way to the town of Federalsburg, a distance of more than 12 miles, in water never shallower than 5 feet. Except for the shoals at the entrance, there is plenty of water nearly from shore to shore.

Approaches. To enter the creek, take your departure from the red "38" marker in the Nanticoke River and head straight for the tip of the point on the right (north) side of the first bend of Marshyhope Creek. When about midway between this point and the one just before it on the Nanticoke River side, swing to port slightly to head for the center of the creek. You should find a minimum of 7 to 8 feet of water if you are in the right place. If the creek starts to shoal, stop and use a sounding pole or lead to determine which way to turn for deeper water. Once you are past the aforementioned point, you are in and should have no more problem with water depth, although a 5-foot spot at the end of the first U bend in the creek could catch you by surprise.

Anchorages. Here you can anchor nearly anywhere in security; other traffic is usually a rarity.

SHARPTOWN

No facilities

Chart: 12261

The swing bridge over the Nanticoke River here has a vertical clearance of 8 feet but opens on a 24-hour-a-day basis. I have not investigated this area because it hosts too much come-and-go traffic from small craft, the result of the launching ramp there.

BROAD CREEK

No facilities

Chart: 12261

Three miles beyond the bridge at Sharptown, the entrance to Broad Creek opens to starboard. The entrance is easy; simply stay in the middle. There are enough bends to protect you from waves, but the land is too low to offer wind break. This is a pretty little creek. If you are looking for an anchorage, give it a try.

This winding, well-marked creek is navigable as far as the town of Laurel, 6 miles upstream. The controlling depth is reputed to be 5 feet, but there is deeper water as far as the town of Bethel, halfway to Laurel. Here a fixed bridge with a vertical clearance of 30 feet effectively stops any cruising sailboat. Just past Laurel, a fixed bridge with a vertical clearance of 2 feet puts a halt to virtually all boat traffic.

SEAFORD

Chart: 12261

Approaches. The town of Seaford, Delaware, represents the head of navigation for the Nanticoke River, although there is water for some distance beyond it. There is a swing railroad bridge (no vertical clearance closed) followed by a drawbridge (3 feet vertical clearance). Nothing beyond these bridges has beckoned

The Woodland Ferry

This is neither a harbor nor an anchorage. This is the site of one of the four remaining ferries on the Delmarva Peninsula and the only one operated in Delaware. The other three are all in Maryland.

The first ferry was established in this location in the 1790s and continued to be operated by the Cannon family until 1843 when the operation was taken over by Sussex County. Nearly a hundred years later, in 1935, it became a state-run free ferry and continues in that role today.

It operates seven days a week, year round, from sunrise to sunset, and averages 70 crossings a day. Each crossing takes two to three minutes. The ferry can carry only three or four vehicles each trip, depending on their sizes. It has one motor, but a transmission directs the power to the proper propeller. With a propeller at each end, the ferry is always going "forward" no matter in which direction it is crossing the river.

If you are boating in this area and see the ferry start to transit, you must give way to it. This is a cable-guided ferry. That is, a steel cable is stretched from shore to shore and the ferry is hitched to it, using it as a guide to cross the river. Normally, the cable is on the bottom and is no impediment to other boating traffic. However, passing ahead of or behind the ferry while it is in transit is not a good idea as the cable is raised by the ferry as it passes and the cable is near the surface for some distance from the ferry. Whitehaven and Upper Ferry, on the Wicomico River, each have a cable ferry, too.

enough to motivate me to go to the trouble of getting either one to open.

Provisions. Walkers Marine, near Lewes Creek, 2 miles downstream from Seaford offers fuel, repairs, and some marine supplies. Select groceries are available in the town of Seaford, a short walk from the public launching ramp just below the railroad bridge.

WICOMICO RIVER

Charts: 12230, **12261**

With the possible exception of Webster Cove and Wicomico Creek, there are no good harbors on this river until you reach Salisbury, about 20 miles up river from its mouth. On the way upstream, the banks are low and marshy and the water sometimes changes to "interesting" colors. The channel is wide and well marked all the way and the controlling depth is at least 10 feet. Keep a lookout for fairly large commercial traffic and give it plenty of room. Although the many bends in the river seem to offer protection from the weather, the commercial traffic makes this an unsuitable anchorage unless you can really get well off to the side.

MONIE BAY

No facilities

Charts: 12230, 12231, 12228, **12261**

Monie Bay is wide and shallow and offers no shelter other than in two of its tributaries, Dame Quarter Creek and Monie Creek. Even those are usable only by shallow-draft boats.

Anchorages. Dame Quarter Creek has a marked channel leading into it from the south side of the entrance to Monie Bay. Its controlling depth is reputed to be 4 feet, but seems less. If you can get in at all, it has a reasonably protected anchorage just inside its mouth, well short of the launching ramp there. In anything larger than an inboard/outboard, I would not feel comfortable spending any time here.

Monie Creek is located at the extreme northeast corner of Monie Bay and there are no channel markers. The controlling depth is 3 feet, and if you can handle that, there are a couple of possible anchorages. Favor the eastern side of Monie Creek until you reach Nail Point. Then favor the left side of the creek until you round the next bend in the creek. A possible anchorage

in 7 feet of water lies just inside Nail Point in the western corner of the creek's first bend. There is a 3-foot spot just past the bend, then it deepens and you can proceed for at least another mile, anchoring at whim. The effort you take getting in will undoubtedly be rewarded by seclusion.

ELLIS BAY

No rating

Charts: 12230, 12261

The wide expanse of Ellis Bay opens up to the west just past Mollies Point. It is too shallow and exposed to be useful for anything but wading.

WEBSTER COVE

Charts: 12230, **12261**

Webster Cove is an artificial harbor located a good half-mile up a narrow dredged channel. At one time the controlling depth was 6 feet, but what it is today, I don't know. In any event, I wouldn't even think about going in there with a draft much over 3 feet unless I checked locally first.

Dockages/Provisions. The main attraction here is the Harbor Club, operated by Harvey Hastings. It has 120 feet of dock space, including the gas (no diesel) dock, for those who want to try the restaurant. There are also some slips of uncertain depth at the nearby Somerset County Dock and Ramp.

WHITEHAVEN

No rating

Charts: 12230, **12261**

History. The town of Whitehaven is a quiet Eastern Shore town with a collection of old, stately homes. It dates back to 1685 when its charter was granted by Lord Baltimore. Today, its main point of interest is the cable ferry, one of two on the Wicomico River. A ferry of one kind or another has operated here since the first one was established in 1692. Now, the ferry is a free, cable ferry much like the one at Woodland on the Nanticoke River.

Navigation Alert. The Whitehaven ferry can carry three or four vehicles, depending on their size, on each trip across the 1,000 feet of river. Be sure to stay well clear of the ferry if you approach while it is in transit to avoid the steel cable, which is brought near the surface in the vicinity of the ferry.

Since the traffic is rarely even as high as 300 cars a day in the summer, the peak season, this ferry is likely to continue in operation for the foreseeable future. The reason is simple. It's cheaper to operate and maintain the ferry than to construct a bridge, which would be needed if ferry service were discontinued.

WICOMICO

CREEK

Charts: 12230, **12261**

The cable ferry at Whitehaven. Steer clear of it to avoid the steel cable which is brought to the surface near the ferry itself. MARYLAND TOURISM

Approaches. Two miles above Whitehaven, Wicomico Creek opens to starboard. The channel into this creek is well marked, but pay close attention to the markers. Look for the red "2" daymark in what looks like the middle of the main Wicomico River. You must round this before swinging to starboard and heading for the green "3" daymark in the creek itself. From green "3," stay in the middle until you clear the next marker to port. From there on, it is deep water all the way to Walkers Marine past the big horseshoe bend in the creek.

Anchorages. Once into the horseshoe, you can anchor just about anywhere in good security. Just get over to one side so that you don't block traffic from the marina.

I am not sure just how far the creek is navigable, but it looks like it may be worth exploring.

UPPER FERRY

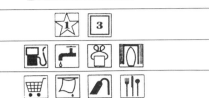 No rating

Charts: 12230, **12261**

Upper Ferry is just that; the upper of two cable ferries across the Wicomico River. Like the one at Whitehaven, this ferry is free, operated by Wicomico County since the early 1950s. Prior to that time the ferry was privately operated and a toll was levied for the 3-minute crossing. Apparently some of the road maps haven't caught up with the times as several still indicate a toll.

Navigation Alert. This ferry is smaller than the one at Whitehaven; it carries no more than two vehicles. It is powered by an outboard motor mounted alongside the pilot house. To change directions, the whole motor is turned around, a simple yet elegant solution. Differences aside, the same caveat regarding the steel cable applies: Give the ferry plenty of clearance if you approach when it is in transit.

Facilities. In the bend of the river just below the cable ferry is White Marine, which offers complete hull and engine repairs.

However, there are no transient facilities.

SALISBURY

Charts: 12230, **12261**

Provisions. Those who come all the way up the Wicomico River to the town of Salisbury will find 20 slips reserved for transients at the Port of Salisbury Marina. The marina offers most basic marina services, including a dockside sewage pumpout facility, and there are plans to make it a full-service marina. A short walk into the the town of Salisbury enables you to restock groceries and other supplies, as well as shop, eat at a restaurant, or both.

This "Winter Lakeshore: Snowy Owl with Bonaparte's Gull" by Larry Barth is one of many award-winning carvings at the Wildfowl Carving and Art Museum in Salisbury.

History/Things to Do. Salisbury, the county seat of Wicomico County, is both an industrial and shipping center. If you have just made the long trek up the river, the latter may surprise you, but it goes hand in glove with the industry there. Thanks to a pair of fires in 1860 and 1886, virtually everything in the town belongs to the 20th century, with the single exception of the Poplar Hill Mansion, built in 1795. The mansion, known for its architectural work (especially the cornices), is a short distance from the river on Elizabeth Street. It is open to the public on Sundays from 1:00 to 4:00 p.m.; a donation is requested.

The Wildfowl Carving and Art Museum is located in Holloway Hall at Salisbury State College, a moderate walk down Camden Avenue from the river. The museum has a collection of exquisite bird carvings and antique duck decoys as well as some fairly elaborate displays of prairie falcons and doves. The museum is open daily from 10:00 a.m. to 5:00 p.m. There is a small admission fee.

DEAL ISLAND

Charts: 12230, **12231**

Between the east side of Tangier Sound and the north entrance to the Manokin River is Deal Island with its two harbors of Chance (at the north end of the island) and Wenona (at the south end). In spite of a scattering of summer cottages along the waterfront, mostly near Chance, this is very much a waterman's island, with a way of life reminiscent of several decades ago.

A good half of the island is marsh and even the "high ground" is very close to water level. Just wander by a churchyard and notice the large, heavy slabs of stone atop most of the graves. The water table is really close to the surface here.

The people are friendly and helpful but there is little reason to wander far from either of the harbors on the island other than to see a slice of life on the Chesapeake. The low marshy island is a good breeding ground for mosquitoes; be prepared for them if you plan to spend the night here.

CHANCE
(UPPER THOROFARE)

Charts: 12230, **12231**

The harbor at Chance, Maryland, is on Upper Thorofare, the narrow body of water that separates Deal Island from the mainland. To be strictly correct, the town of Chance is on the mainland, north of Upper Thorofare, not on Deal Island itself. However, since nearly everyone refers to the harbor simply as "Chance," we'll be no exception.

Approaches. The entrance channel to Chance was dredged to a depth of 10 feet in 1987 and, as of 1989, there was still at least 9 feet of water at mean low tide. Entrance is easy: honor the buoys on the way in. For those approaching at night, there is now a lighted range, which you may use to keep in the entrance channel until you can rely on the harbor lights to see where you are going.

Anchorages/Dockages/Provisions.
When you enter the turning basin of the harbor, you will see that this is very much a working waterman's harbor. Even so it is attractive enough to draw rendezvous from several of the cruising clubs on the Bay during the summer. During the fall, it is likely to be crowded with workboats and you may have some trouble finding a space to anchor, let alone tie up. There are three marinas, a hardware store, and a seafood store/restaurant right on the water in the harbor.

Two of the marinas, Last Chance Marina and Scott's Cove Marina, are on the north side of the turning basin. Both have fuel, ice, water, engine and hull repairs, and some transient slips. Scott's Cove Marina has a bulkheaded basin at the end of a dredged channel. Last Chance is slightly farther into the harbor. The third Marina, Windsor's Marina, is located past the fixed bridge (10-foot vertical clearance) and offers only slips and a shell launching ramp for small powerboats.

MANOKIN
RIVER

BIG
ANNEMESSEX
RIVER

236

On the south side of the turning basin is Island Seafood, Inc., which has 200 feet of dockage for those wanting to buy seafood or take a meal at the small restaurant. The wharf next to Island Seafood is Deal Island Hardware, which offers fuel, ice, marine supplies, and some groceries. Be careful when approaching the wharf; I am not certain about the depth alongside, although I have been told that it is "adequate."

Additional groceries and some other supplies are also available south of the bridge, on the road through Deal Island to Wenona. The short walk down this road takes you to the grave of Joshua Thomas, the "Parson of the Islands." There is also a chapel dedicated to him nearby.

WENONA

(LOWER THOROFARE)

⭐ 1   3

👤   🛒

Charts: 12230, **12231**

At the south end of Deal Island is a long, narrow, dredged passage—called Lower Thorofare—between Deal and Little Deal Islands. It leads to the harbor at the little town of Wenona. This is another working waterman's harbor.

Approaches. The channel was dredged to a 10 foot depth in 1987 and a small fleet of skipjacks uses it regularly. The depth in the channel is still reasonably close to 10 feet deep, although the channel itself is narrow and poorly marked.

Anchorages/Dockages. Most of the harbor is shoal so if you do make it in, you won't be able to anchor unless your draft is a foot or less. The piers to port have around 8 feet of water alongside and up to about 80 feet out from them. This is the only place for deeper draft boats to maneuver or stay. You will probably find a couple of skipjacks and some crab skiffs tied up alongside the piers. The locals are friendly; hail someone and ask where you can either tie up or anchor.

Provisions. Visit this harbor at least once. Some groceries and ice are available nearby. One of the piers has a peeler pound for crabs. However, the greatest appeal of the Lower Thorofare is to the gunkholers among us. Those who suffer from grounding angst better pass it by.

MANOKIN RIVER

Charts: 12230, **12231**

This wide river is rather disappointing in that it has no good anchorages and it is full of outlying shoals. The only place to put in is at Goose Creek Marina located in the mouth of Goose Creek on the south side of the entrance to the Manokin River. Deep-draft boats will find this difficult to reach.

There is a well-marked channel that goes past Carmel Point, where some shelter can be found. Even so, it is too exposed for me to consider it a secure anchorage. Those who travel up the Manokin do so simply to see what the river looks like. It looks as if you could take 4- or 5-foot draft up to to St. Peters Creek.

BIG ANNEMESSEX RIVER

Charts: 12230, **12231**

Daugherty Creek, on the south side of the Big Annemessex, leads to the Daugherty Creek Canal, the back door to Crisfield. Proceed slowly into Daugherty Creek past the markers until you enter the canal. Once in the canal, there is 6½ feet for a width of 60 feet all the way to the Little Annemessex River. At the south end of the canal, the buoyage system changes. *Leave the red markers to port from here on as they are now referenced to the Little Annemessex River.*

Boats drawing less than 5 feet can make their way upriver as far as Persimmon Point. Thanks to the bend in the river, some shelter can be found here.

Manokin and Big Annemessex Rivers

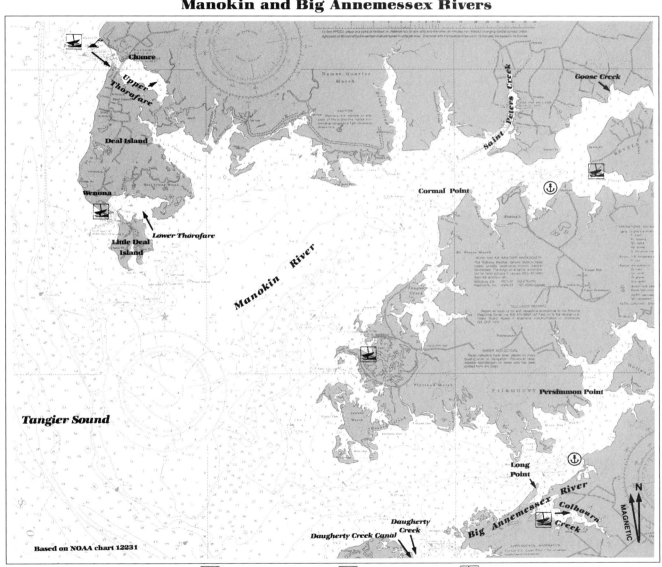

Chance

Upper Thorofare

Deal Island

Wenona

Little Deal Island

Lower Thorofare

Manokin River

Tangier Sound

Saint Peters Creek

Goose Creek

Cormal Point

Persimmon Point

Long Point

Big Annemessex River

Colbourn Creek

Daugherty Creek

Daugherty Creek Canal

N

MAGNETIC

Based on NOAA chart 12231

SCALE 1"=1.53 NAUT. MILES   ⚓ **Good anchoring**   **Mooring area**   **Launching site**

COLBOURN CREEK

No facilities

Charts: 12230, **12231**

There are no anchorages on the Big Annemessex River other than Colbourn Creek. Colbourn Creek offers a well-protected spot with 5 feet of water, if you stay in the middle and don't go beyond the first bend in the creek. Feel your way in carefully. Although there is 5 to 7 feet of water in the entrance channel, it is unmarked and curves close to Long Point.

LITTLE ANNEMESSEX RIVER

Charts: 12228, 12230, 12231

When approaching the mouth of the Little Annemessex River from any direction, head for the 37-foot–high, black, Janes Island Lighthouse, southwest of Island Point on Janes Island. If you are coming from the north, be sure to pass at least one-half mile to the west of the lighthouse, honoring the red "8" buoy. As soon as you can see the small green "1" can southeast of the lighthouse, turn to head directly toward it. You can get away with leaving it to either side, there is at least 7 feet of water for a couple of hundred yards north of it. From can "1" on, the channel is well marked and easy to follow.

The river makes a right-angle bend to the north around the southern end of Janes Island and continues past the town of Crisfield until it turns into Daugherty Creek Canal, a shortcut inside Janes Island to the mouth of the Big Annemessex River. Janes Island is all tidal marsh, except for the area at the southern end of Daugherty Creek Canal where Janes Island State Park offers campsites and slips for campers.

Harbors on the Little Annemessex River are remarkably few. In fact, it is possible to get into a total of three creeks plus the canal. The real place of interest on the river is the town of Crisfield.

Crisfield Harbor on the Little Annemessex River. CRISFIELD CHAMBER OF COMMERCE

OLD HOUSE COVE

 3

No facilities

Charts: 12228, 12230, 12231

Anchorages. The first cove to port as you enter the Little Annemessex River is Old House Cove, a fair-sized basin at the southern end of Janes Island. The entrance was dredged to a depth of 5 feet in 1979; what it is now is anyone's guess. Inside, the water depth ranges between 3 and 4 feet, at least in the middle. If you are in a shoal-draft boat, such as an outboard or inboard/outboard, give it a try.

BROAD CREEK

  1

No facilities

Charts: 12228, 12230, 12231

This is not an anchorage. In fact, it is called a creek only out of courtesy; it is really a shortcut through the marshes between the Little Annemessex River and about the middle region of Pocomoke Sound. Unfortunately, the controlling depth is only a little more than 3 feet, limiting its use to very shallow-draft boats. In actual fact, it is probably used only by local watermen and an occasional inquisitive gunkholer.

JENKINS CREEK

 3

Charts: 12228, 12230, 12231

Jenkins Creek is little more than a narrow channel leading to the Crisfield County Wharf and Launching Ramp. While some small, shallow-draft boats might find a few places to anchor, this is used as water access for fishermen. The restaurant near the ramp area is there almost by coincidence as it is not cruiser-oriented.

CRISFIELD

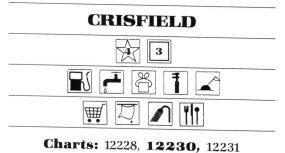

Charts: 12228, **12230,** 12231

Approaches. The only real harbor on the Little Annemessex River is Somers Cove, a good-sized basin serving the town of Crisfield. The entrance to Somers Cove is rather obscure, almost impossible to see until you are on top of it. As you approach the green "11" beacon, you will see a large brick building among a cluster of others on the east side of the river. Head for this building and look for the small sign that points the way into the deep, narrow channel between the packing plants and into Somers Cove.

Dockages. The channel soon opens up into the basin and the piers and building of Somers Cove Marina appear just off your port bow. While you can anchor out in the basin, this marina is of such high quality that we recommend (against our usual counsel) that you take a slip for your stay here. Its popularity has grown to the point that reservations are a good idea during the peak boating season. We have been told that reservations usually are not accepted during the period of the Crab Festival, 15 August to Labor Day. Then slips are available on a first-come, first-served basis.

Facilities. At the Somers Cove Marina you are greeted promptly and pleasantly, and a marina employee not only directs you to your slip but also helps you tie up. The main building houses the marina office. In an adjoining building there are very clean heads and showers, as well as a coin-operated laundry. The combi-

The Somers Cove Marina with the
U.S. Coast Guard Station in the background.

History. The town of Crisfield was established
in the mid-1600s with the name of Annemessex, the
Algonquin Indian name meaning "Bountiful Waters."
The primary industry, however, was agriculture until the
early 1800s, when fishing became the focus and the
town's name became Somers Cove. In 1860, oystering
brought the oyster fleet to Somers Cove, along with
steamships and a railroad line. The last was largely due
to the efforts of a Princess Anne area lawyer in whose
honor the town was renamed again. Legend has it that
the real reason for naming the town after Mr. Crisfield
was to sooth his "ruffled feathers" after he fell through a
rotted pier into the harbor. In any event, the fishing industry really took off and Crisfield promptly dubbed itself "The Seafood Capitol of the World." In fact, much
of the town is literally built on oyster shells. Today, the
oystering industry has dwindled from its heydey, but
crabbing still holds full sway. At the city dock, you find a
crab barrel factory, oyster dredge repair shops, and
packing plants.

nation to the lock on the doors is provided to each visitor on request.

The marina's landscaped grounds are large and
park-like with a wide walkway bordering the basin. The
piers are painted white and the 14-inch pilings are
something of an overkill for this landlocked harbor. The
complex includes a swimming pool, which is very popular in hot weather.

For half of the year, Crisfield is a quiet community,
mostly of watermen. The rest of the year, May through
October, it is one of Maryland's major crabbing centers
and fully justifies the new version of its self-adopted title, "The Crab Capitol of the World."

The entrance to Somers Cove is hard to see. As you approach green "11" beacon you will see a
large brick building among a cluster of others on the east side of the river. Head for this building and
look for the sign that points the way into the deep but narrow channel between the packing plants.

Crisfield

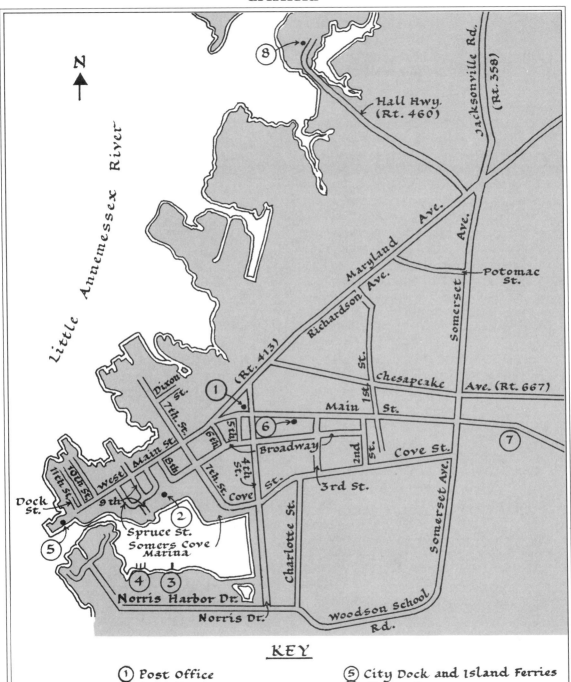

N

Little Annemessex River

⑧

Hall Hwy.
(Rt. 460)

Jacksonville Rd.
(Rt. 358)

Maryland Ave.

Richardson Ave.

Somerset Ave.

Potomac St.

(Rt. 413)

① Dixon St.

7th St.

1st St.

Chesapeake Ave. (Rt. 667)

Main St.

5th St.

6th St.

⑥ Broadway

4th St.

2nd St.

Cove St.

⑦

West Main St.

8th

7th St. Cove St.

3rd St.

10th St.

11th St.

Dock St.

9th

Charlotte St.

② Spruce St.
Somers Cove Marina

⑤

Somerset Ave.

④ ③

Norris Harbor Dr.

Norris Dr.

Woodson School Rd.

KEY

① Post Office
② J. Millard Tawes Museum
③ Coast Guard
④ Boat Ramp

⑤ City Dock and Island Ferries
⑥ City Hall
⑦ Public Library
⑧ McCready Hospital

SCALE 1" = .25 MILES

Things to Do. By all means, walk into and explore the town. The shops have a turn-of-the-century atmosphere and the people are unfailingly pleasant. Buyer beware: This book may be the only place where you receive fair warning about the 5 percent nuisance tax levied on customers who use a credit card!

The J. Millard Tawes Historical Museum provides an interesting and full look at Maryland history from pre-European times to the present, with special emphasis on Governor Tawes and other prominent Crisfield individuals and businesses. Museum hours are 10:00 a.m. to 5:00 p.m. daily from Memorial Day through September 30; 10:00 a.m. to 4:00 p.m. daily March through May and in October. The museum closes its doors to the public during the months of November, December, January, and February. Admission fees are $1.00 for an adult and 50 cents for a child. Adjacent to the museum is an information center, which is worth a look before you continue your exploration of town. The center is also a stop on the "Crisfield Crab Line," a red-and-white-striped jitney bus that travels a circuit of town shops and restaurants. There is a nominal fee (50 cents last time I checked).

On the river waterfront, there are several ferries that go to Smith Island or Tangier Island. This is a good way for you to visit these islands if you don't wish to negotiate the narrow channel into the harbor and deal with the problem of finding a place to tie up or anchor. The cost is $12 to $20 per person, depending on the cruise line you choose and its options.

Over the Labor Day weekend each year, Crisfield holds the "Hard Crab Derby" where specially groomed crabs are raced on a wet, inclined platform. Related activities (fishing tournament, beauty pageant, land and water parades, and many others) build this crab event into a real festival, attracting large crowds. It takes an intrepid crew to bring a visiting boat into this maelstrom.

SMITH ISLAND

Charts: 12228, 12230, 12231, 12261

At the turn of the century, there were several islands with significant populations. Now all but two—Smith and Tangier—have succumbed to the erosion of wind and wave.

Captain John Smith visited the island during his exploration of the Chesapeake in 1608, giving it his name. By the late 1600s, Smith Island had been settled and, much later, took an active part in the War of 1812. All of the settlers were of British origin or ancestry and even today the population of around 900 is nearly pure Anglo-Saxon, bearing names such as Evans (a name shared by about half the population), Crockett, Parks, and Tyler. Their speech is laced with a faint touch of Elizabethan English, although it is being rapidly diluted by TV and radio. This is an island populated almost entirely by watermen. Their business is crabbing in the summer and oystering in the winter.

Most of the island is low-lying marshland, with a few scattered trees. Marshland means mosquitoes, so come prepared with good screens and repellent if you plan to spend the night. For the same reason, try to visit the island in the spring or fall rather than summer, but by all means visit it.

There are three villages on the island. The largest of these, Ewell, can be reached from either the main Chesapeake Bay or from Tangier Sound through the channel called Big Thorofare. The other two, Tylerton and Rhodes Point, are accessible from Tangier Sound, up a long narrow channel (Tyler Creek), provided you can find your way over the bar that stretches from Horse Hammock Point on Smith Island all the way south to Tangier Island. There is also a channel in from the main Bay on the west side of the island, but shoaling is a frequent problem there.

BIG THOROFARE

Charts: 12228, 12230, 12231

Approaches. There are two entrances to the main Smith Island harbor at Ewell. The shortest approach is from the Bay side, where its entrance is marked by a pair of lighted beacons. The controlling depth in the first part of the channel is 7 feet, presenting no problem to most cruising boats. Immediately after passing the red "10" daymark, you must make a 90-degree turn to the south to enter the channel to Ewell.

The controlling depth of this channel is indicated as 4½ feet; however, the range of tide here is around 2 feet and, if you take advantage of the tide, most cruising boats can make it through the passage. The church steeple in Ewell serves as a good reference point once you have turned into the southbound channel.

The other approach is up a 4-mile-long channel from Tangier Sound. A course of 295 degrees from Janes Island Light takes you to the lighted green "1" beacon at the channel entrance. The controlling depth is 7 feet so most cruising boats should have no trouble. Watch out for the ferries from Crisfield; squeezing by them can be a little tight in the narrow channel.

If you are passing through Smith Island between the Bay and Tangier Sound, take note that the buoyage system reverses at Ewell.

Anchorages/Dockages. Once you reach Ewell, you can tie up along the right-hand dock on the town side. If you anchor out, the short section of channel running southeast from Ewell is a possibility. A better anchorage (but less convenient to Ewell) is the part of the channel (in from the Bay), which extends to the east of the 90-degree bend at marker "10." Here the channel is unmarked but has 7 feet of water and is a snug anchorage except in the case of a strong west wind.

Provisions. In Ewell, fuel and water are available at the docks; other supplies, and a couple of excellent restaurants, in town.

TYLER CREEK

$\star$ 3 | 3

⚓

Charts: 12228, 12230, 12231, 12261

Approaches. In order to try Tyler Channel to reach the towns of Tylerton or Rhodes Point, you need a draft of 5 feet or less so that you can cross the bar extending to the south from Horse Hammock Point. To cross the bar depart from the lighted red "6" bell buoy in the middle of Tangier Sound, right on the Maryland-Virginia State line. From red "6," a course of 270 degrees (due magnetic west) heading directly toward tiny

The Oyster Wars

What became known as the "oyster wars" started in 1870. The wars involved two sets of conflicts: one between the hand-tongers and dredgers, and one between the dredge boats from Maryland and Virginia (and later, "pirate" dredgers from New England).

When the oyster dredge was first used in the eighteenth century, it immediately caused conflict with the hand-tongers who could only work beds in relatively shallow water. Dredgers could take oysters anywhere that they didn't run aground. At first the argument was fairly mild but, by 1871, thousands of dredge boats were invading river waters supposedly reserved for hand-tonging and the argument escalated into a shooting "war" between the tongers and dredgers—a rivalry that continues to a limited extent today. These battles led to the formation of Maryland's scandal-ridden "Oyster Navy," which was eventually replaced by the Natural Resources Police we know today.

The conflict peaked on the Chester and Choptank Rivers. The oyster police force commissioned in 1868 by Maryland proved woefully inadequate to deal with the "pirate" dredgers. As dredgers grew bolder and conflicts between oyster police and dredgers grew more frequent, tongers increasingly attempted to take matters into their own hands. In 1888, a group of Chester River tongers went so far as to obtain two cannons, mount them on the shore and bombard the dredge boats. The tongers, however, were unable to hit anything with the little one-pounders. The dredgers retaliated, stealing ashore one night, overpowering the lone guard, and taking away the cannons. Some versions of the story say that the dredgers stripped the watchman and sent him out into the cold with a message of defiance to the tongers.

The pirate dredgers then made a serious mistake. Assuming a fog enshrouded ship in the Chester River to be a police steamer, they opened fire on it. The ship was the passenger steamer, *Corsica*, with many women and children on board. This attack so enraged the public that the oyster navy's flagship, the *Governor McLane*, with a 12-pound howitzer mounted on her decks, was dispatched to clear the pirates out of the Chester. After some considerable effort, she managed to force the pirates to move elsewhere.

The conflict between tongers and dredgers continued nearly to the present day, although with much less violence, up until the Maryland Marine Police were established [1964] and were able to keep a much diminished oyster fleet under their watchful eye. (In 1972, the Marine Police became the Natural Resources Police under the Department of Natural Resources, which was previously called the Department of Chesapeake Bay Affairs.)

In addition to a technological aspect, the Oyster Wars had a territorial basis. The controversy between the states of Maryland and Virginia dated back to the Compact of 1668, under which Virginia received about 15 thousand more acres than Maryland felt Virginia was entitled to.

This constant source of friction was not relieved by the 1785 renegotiation of the compact in which representatives from both states met with George Washington at Mount Vernon. The new agreement gave Maryland sovereignty over the Potomac to the high-water mark on the Virginia side but gave Virginia equal access to the river. It also allowed for reciprocal rights in the Pocomoke River on the Eastern Shore. This compact remained in force until after the Civil War (War Between the States), even though it really didn't solve the problem of oyster fishery rights. Related to that problem, the real boundary line across the Chesapeake Bay between the two states was hotly argued.

It wasn't until after federal arbitration that the Jenkins-Black Award of 1877 defined the boundary as beginning at a point on the Potomac where the line between Virginia and West Virginia strikes the river at low water; over to Smith Point; and across the bay to Watkins Point on the Pokomoke. Virginia got the larger share of the Tangier and Pocomoke Sounds oyster beds, much to the chagrin of the Marylanders. Marylanders who ran over the line to take oysters risked arrest and confiscation of their boats by the Virginia police. However, Virginia did nothing to prevent its dredge boats from crossing over to take Maryland oysters and Maryland authorities were reluctant to do any-

thing that might rekindle the boundary dispute. The Maryland oystermen promptly took matters into their own hands in December 1883 and open warfare erupted!

Virginia dredges that ventured into Maryland waters met a hail of bullets from the furious Maryland watermen. Retaliating against the Virginia poachers, Smith Island watermen began pirating oysters in Virginia waters. On one occasion, the Virginia police schooner, *Tangier,* pursued the watermen back to Smith Island, only to be met by determined resistance from Marylanders on the shore who were fortified with repeating rifles. Discretion being the greater part of valor, the *Tangier* retreated back to its home port.

By March 1894, the conflict between Maryland and Virginia and their watermen reached such a level that communications between the two states ceased altogether. The Potomac River was also a frequent scene of gunfire as the Maryland Oyster Police tried to enforce the oyster laws on Virginians. As the respective lawyers quarreled, the oyster beds were becoming exhausted, the beds were not being reseeded, and many of the remaining oysters were being smothered with silt. Hard times soon fell upon the Bay's oystering industry as a result.

This state of affairs lasted until 1959, when a popular Virginia waterman was killed by Maryland police gunfire on the Potomac River. This death caused a wide-ranging shakeup of the Maryland oyster police and focused enough public attention on the situation that the two states finally tried to settle their differences. Even so, it wasn't until President John F. Kennedy signed the Potomac River Fisheries Commission Bill into law on December 5, 1962, that the governors of the two states finally sat down at a luncheon to commemorate the end of generations of conflict.

Since that time, open warfare in the Chesapeake Bay over oysters has ceased. Oyster inspection has become a routine matter and those who directly remember the gunfire over it are few. Old oyster ports such as Crisfield, Tilghman Island, and others are now "picturesque" tourist attractions as well as the remnants of a once vast oystering industry.

Herring Island takes you across the bar. You won't be able to make out Herring Island until you are actually crossing the bar. Continue on this course for a good 300 yards after the water starts getting deeper again, then swing to starboard to a course of 350 degrees to the first of the Tyler Creek channel daymarks, red "2." Past the red "2" daymark, head towards red "4," more than a mile away, by feeling your way carefully with lead line or depth sounder. Any time the depth drops below 8 feet you are getting out of the channel. Be sure that you make corrections in the right direction as the water gets thin fast.

At Tylerton there is a line of fish houses in the water, just past the green "1" daymark at the beginning of the channel to Rhodes Point. The controlling depth of this channel is reported to be 6 feet but only for a width of 40 feet; this channel is reserved for the adventurous. At one time, boats with drafts under 3 feet could make it all the way out to the Bay through this channel. It may still be possible, but check with the locals before even considering the attempt. Shoaling in Sheep Pen Gut north of Rhodes Point is the usual problem.

TANGIER ISLAND

Charts: 12225, **12228,** 12230

About 8 miles south of the entrance from Tangier Sound to Big Thorofare on Smith Island is the entrance to Tangier Island. Until the mid-1960s, this was the only entrance to the tight little harbor on Tangier Island. Now, it is possible to pass completely through the island in a dredged, well-marked channel.

If you are approaching from the Tangier Sound side, stay well off the island until you can see the 15-foot–high green "1" marker at the beginning of the eastern entrance to the channel. This marker should be approached on a heading of between 240 and 300 degrees to ensure that you avoid the long shoal extending southward from Smith Island and the shoal extending eastward from Tangier Island.

Approaching from the Bay side is a little different, especially from a southwest quadrant. Before the island itself is clearly visible, you may be able to see what appears to be a large ship proceeding on an east-west

The main harbor at Tangier Island, looking northwest to the entrance from the Bay side. PETER McCLINTOCK/VA MARINE RESOURCES BUREAU

course much farther to the east of the normal shipping channels than you would expect. That ship is a U.S. Navy bombing and gunnery target; stay well clear of it. It is in the center of the 1-mile–diameter prohibited area marked on the chart. It is also the center of a 6-mile–diameter restricted area, which is closed to traffic when the range is in use. There are other wrecks in the vicinity, also part of this Navy bombing range, but they are not as clearly visible as this ship.

Because of this bombing range, vessels approaching from the south or southwest would be wiser to pass east of the Tangier Sound Light at the southern tip of Tangier Island and head for the eastern channel entrance. Otherwise, plot a course to take you well north of the

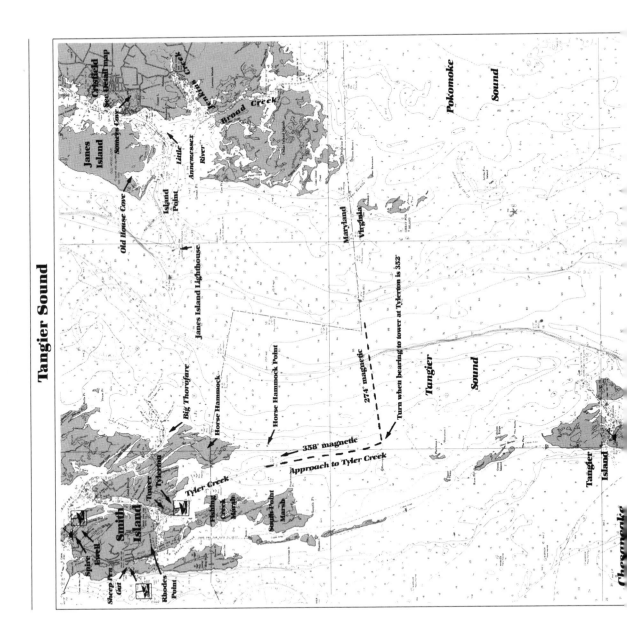

target ship before heading in to the western channel entrance.

On approaching from the Bay side, the spire of the church in the middle of the island is visible before anything else can be made out clearly. Head directly for this spire and you soon can pick out the 15-foot–high green "1" at the channel entrance. Be sure to leave this to port. While subject to shoaling, the channel controlling depth is nominally 7 feet and prudent cruisers should have no trouble.

Be sure to note that, like the channel through Smith Island, the buoyage system changes at the town of Tangier. That is, on entering from either entrance, keep the green markers to port and the red markers to starboard until you reach the town. If you continue through the channel from there, heading either to the Bay or Tangier Sound, keep the green markers to starboard and red markers to port. (A simple way to keep this straight is to look at the marker numbers. If the numbers descend, keep the red markers to port.)

Be careful of the ferry from Crisfield if it is heading your way. The channel is narrow and it can be a bit of a tight squeeze in the region near the center of the island. In fact, the Bay entrance is now considered the main entrance and, if only to avoid the ferry squeeze, is preferable if you have the choice.

Southwest of Tangier Island, the chart indicates a large danger area labeled "*San Marcos* Wreck." This was once the U.S. Navy battleship *U.S.S. Texas*, which served during the Spanish-American War. In 1911, she was renamed the *San Marcos* and towed to her current location to serve as a gunnery target. Blasted to a hulk by the battleship *New Hampshire* in 1911–1912, she again served as a gunnery target during World War II. Afterwards, the *San Marcos* was said to be responsible for at least seven shipwrecks, and in the late 1950s she was dynamited to leave a depth of about 20 feet over the highest part of her remains. While no longer really a hazard to navigation, the prudent mariner gives her location a wide berth.

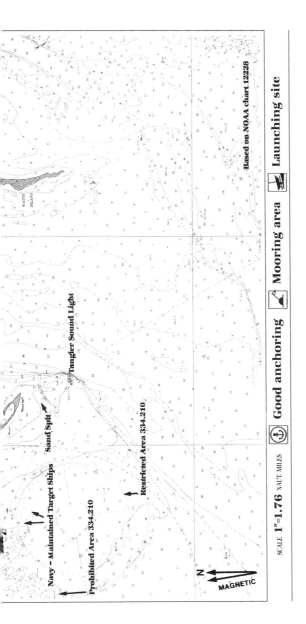

Based on NOAA chart 12228

Launching site

Mooring area

Good anchoring

SCALE 1"=1.76 NAUT. MILES

Tangier Sound Light

Sand Spit

Navy – Maintained Target Ships

Prohibited Area 334.210

Restricted Area 334.210

N
MAGNETIC

TANGIER

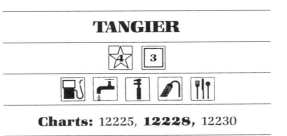

Charts: 12225, **12228**, 12230

Dockages/Moorings. There is little room to anchor among the local fishing boats which are moored to stakes in this harbor. Fuel may be available at the Tangier Oil Company docks, but you are not en-

Tangier is the only town on the island and it is a working fishing village. Settled in the late 1600s by a family from Cornwall, the island's inhabitants still have traces of Cornish in their speech.

couraged to tie up there or at the other docks used by the local fishermen. In fact, during the boating season (Memorial Day to Labor Day), visiting boats are not always welcome due to crowding of the harbor and its few facilities. Even so several piers are available for visiting boats and some signs indicate transient dockage for rent.

The town of Tangier, the only town on the island, is a working fishing village. The people, especially the children, are friendly and somewhat curious about visitors from the "outside." With TV and radio, most of the island mannerisms of speech have all but disappeared. As on Smith Island, a small assortment of surnames serve the islanders. The most common is Crockett, followed in frequency by Pruit and Parks.

Where to Eat. Go to Hilda Crockett's Chesapeake House for excellent seafood. Be sure to get there early—no later than 5:00 p.m. Meals are served daily from April 15 through October, and are "good enough to justify the ferry ride."

Bed & breakfast lodging is also available with reservations. Call ahead at (804)891-2331. The Chesapeake House is closed November 1 to April 1. Some limited groceries and supplies are available in town; be warned that all shops close on Sunday.

Anchorages. If you can't find any room in the harbor or if you would like to spend the night in solitude, boats with drafts of less than 6 feet can find their way into the snug little anchorage inside the hook at Sand Spit, at the extreme southern tip of Tangier Island. Stay a good half-mile off the island until you reach the tip of the hook, then hold close to the hook as you ease around it. You will find a well-protected anchorage surrounded by marsh with about 6 feet of water. (Remember, marsh means mosquitoes, so come prepared with screens and repellent.)

Western

Shore

The western shore of the Bay in this region is relatively inhospitable. The long line of the Calvert Cliffs continues all the way into the Patuxent River, broken only by one artificial harbor and the Patuxent River, an excellent cruising ground all by itself.

LONG

BEACH

249

Calvert Cliff State Park.
Lusby, Maryland. MARYLAND TOURISM

LONG BEACH

Charts: **12263,** 12264

Of all of the artificial harbors on the 30-mile stretch of the western shore above the Patuxent River, Flag Harbor at Long Beach is probably the most likely to be accessible.

The first guide to look for is the set of domed towers belonging to the Calvert Cliffs Nuclear Power Plant. The entrance to the marina is just over 2 miles north of these towers. If you are in approximately the right area, you should see a line of light colored houses near the water level followed by another line of houses higher up on the cliff. Just past this upper line of houses, you should see a dark opening in the shoreline: This is the entrance to the marina.

Head toward this dark opening on a course perpendicular to the shoreline. There are now two lighted markers on dolphins at the entrance, as well as a quick flashing white range light just inside the harbor to mark a spoiler jetty to starboard as you enter.

FLAG HARBOR

Charts: **12263,** 12264

Dockages. This is largely a sailboat marina, although there are some sizeable powerboats here.

There is no room to anchor, but transients are welcome. There are some transient slips for boats up to 38 feet. Individually owned slips are often available for a flat fee. There is no longer any free overnight docking, nor do you have to listen to a condominium sales pitch.

Facilities. The management is striving to keep the entrance channel open to a depth of 7 to 8 feet and seems to be successful at achieving this objective. The marina is all modern construction and its facilities include fuel, water, ice, showers, a swimming pool, and tennis courts.

PATUXENT RIVER

Charts: 12230, 12263, **12264,** 12284

Located about halfway down the relatively inhospitable western shore of the Chesapeake Bay between Herring Bay and the Potomac River, the Patuxent River offers some of the best cruising grounds on Maryland's western shore. While the river is navigable for more than 40

Flag Harbor Marina, looking toward the entrance from the Bay, has some slips for transients but no room to anchor.

Patuxent River

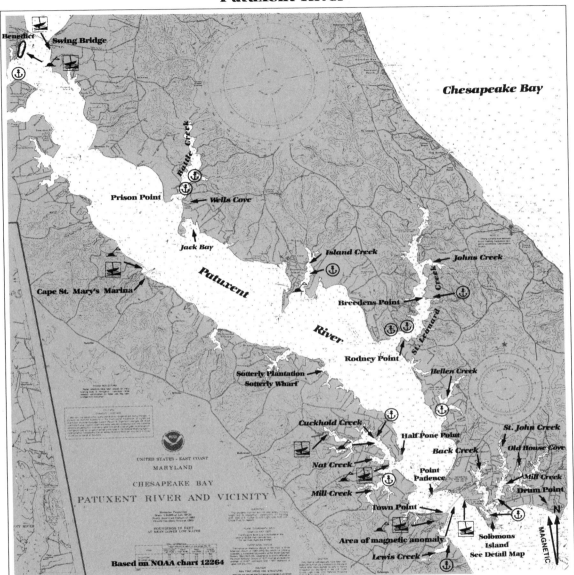

SCALE **1"=2.2** NAUT. MILES   ⚓ **Good anchoring**   ⚓ **Mooring area**   ⚓ **Launching site**

miles from its mouth, all of the good harbors are within about 18 miles of its entrance, the best ones less than 8 miles above Drum Point.

When approaching the mouth of the Patuxent River from the south, there are two shoal areas where you should be especially careful. The first of these is off Cedar Point where the chart shows an abandoned lighthouse in ruins. Actually, unless you look closely, the lighthouse appears to be in reasonably good repair. Although the bell buoy that replaced the lighthouse is almost a mile farther offshore, you can approach within 200 yards of the lighthouse in at least 10 feet of water on the offshore side. The danger lies in the possibility of the current or wind pushing you much closer than you intended to go because rocks are there.

The second shoal is off Hog Point, extending due

Cove Point Light on the Bay's western shore,
just below the natural gas facility.

north from the point. If you draw less than 6 feet, this is not a problem, but the ice in winter has a tendency to destroy the lighted "1" spar here and the temporary buoys used as replacements are hard to see. Should you cross inside of the marker with your depth sounder running, you will see the bottom come up alarmingly fast. Although there is no real danger, the relatively sudden change from 20 to 30 feet of water to 6 feet or less can be a real heart-stopper if you are not expecting it.

Once clear of the Hog Point shoal, a course of 272 degrees from number "1" takes you directly to the flashing red "6" marker that indicates the southernmost point of the sunken island in the entrance to Solomons Harbor. This course takes you a few hundred yards offshore of Drum Point Light. Mounted on a 30-foot-high tower, Drum Point Light is easily seen from a considerable distance, even against the shoreline. You either can use this tower as a reference or, within limits, ignore it completely since the water is around 40 feet deep to within a short distance of the shore.

A simpler approach to the Patuxent is from the north. After rounding Cove Point, if you stay at least 400 yards offshore, you have to try really hard to hit anything except crab pot floats, which are abundant, or a few fishing stakes. (Note: If you approach at night, stay more than a half-mile offshore as the fishing stakes are invisible then until it is too late.) Once you can see Drum Point Light, head directly toward it. Actually you want to head a bit to the south of the light, which is on the shore.

Drum Point Light in the Patuxent River near Solomons has three red sectors, northeast, south to east southeast, and west. The first two may be used as a guide to entering the Patuxent River at night. From the

Bay, locate the Drum Point Light and maintain a course to keep you in the white sector of its beam. If it suddenly turns red, you are off course either to the north or south. Which way you need to correct should be obvious. The west red sector is a guide to those exiting the Patuxent River around Solomons to avoid the shoals south and east of Solomons and on past Drum Point. (See chart for any clarification.)

About 1 mile to the northeast of Drum Point, a series of cliffs appear to starboard. Although they have neither the name nor the fame, these cliffs are essentially the same as the Calvert Cliffs. In actual fact, they are an extension of the same formation. It is possible to anchor to within 100 yards of the beach (you can get a lot closer, but we lost our nerve at that point), land, and search the cliffs for sharks teeth and Miocene fossils (15 to 30 million years old). If you have children aboard, and even if you don't, be sure to visit these cliffs at least once. The main advantage to stopping here rather than at the more publicized Calvert Cliffs is that, in the event of a storm, you are not far from shelter in Solomons Harbor.

Once past Drum Point, you have the option of putting in to Solomons for supplies, a meal at a restaurant, or whatever, or continuing on to the more sylvan harbors farther up the Patuxent. Incidentally, the Governor Johnson bridge upriver from Solomons has a 140-foot vertical clearance; you can get under it no matter how high your mast may be. If you use a compass-driven electronic autopilot, be careful in this area; there is a large magnetic anomaly in the vicinity of the bridge.

SOLOMONS

All facilities

Charts: 12230, **12264**, 12284

Near the mouth of the Patuxent River, Solomons Island beckons to many boaters cruising up or down the Bay. Unless you demand solitude, the area serves as a wonderful stopover during a cruise. It offers anchorages, marinas, restaurants, groceries, hardware, and an interesting marine museum. The harbor is well protected and the creeks fanning off from it provide anchorages

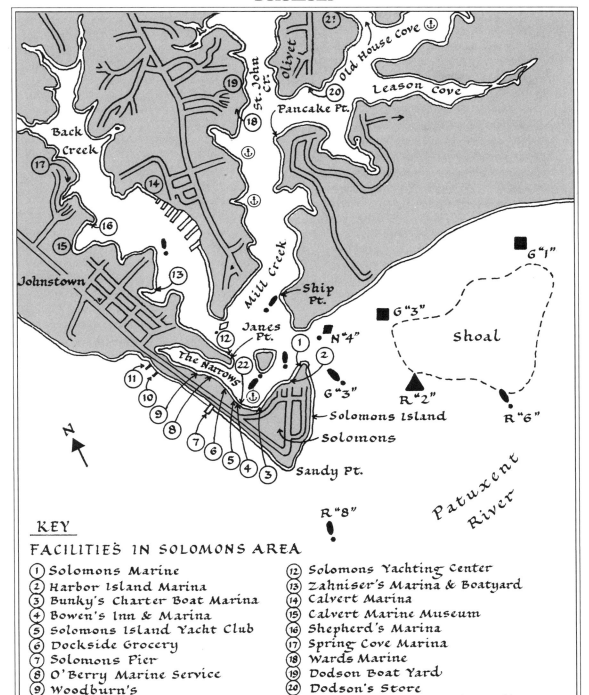

Back Creek

Johnstown

St. John Cr.

Olivet

Pancake Pt.

Old House Cove

Leason Cove

Mill Creek

Ship Pt.

Janes Pt.

The Narrows

Solomons Island

Solomons

Sandy Pt.

Shoal

G "1"

G "3"

N "4"

G "3"

R "2"

R "6"

R "8"

Patuxent River

N

KEY

FACILITIES IN SOLOMONS AREA

1. Solomons Marine
2. Harbor Island Marina
3. Bunky's Charter Boat Marina
4. Bowen's Inn & Marina
5. Solomons Island Yacht Club
6. Dockside Grocery
7. Solomons Pier
8. O'Berry Marine Service
9. Woodburn's
10. Skipper Boat Rental
11. Island Carry Out
12. Solomons Yachting Center
13. Zahniser's Marina & Boatyard
14. Calvert Marina
15. Calvert Marine Museum
16. Shepherd's Marina
17. Spring Cove Marina
18. Wards Marine
19. Dodson Boat Yard
20. Dodson's Store
21. W. Fletcher & Son Marine Railway
22. Lighthouse Inn

SCALE 1"=1,170 FEET

out of the mainstream of traffic. Few other harbors on the Bay offer as much in the way of facilities for the cruiser as Solomons Island.

Approaches.

As you clear Drum Point on the way in, you have a choice of two channels past the shoal at the harbor entrance. In daylight, either channel is acceptable, although the outside channel is preferred by most. Both are well marked. At night, use the outside channel as lighted markers "3," "4," and "6" make it by far the easier approach. None of the inner channel markers are lighted.

As you swing around the bulkhead on the northeastern end of Solomons Island, a triangular-shaped man-made island appears off your port bow. This was once the site of a natural island called Mollyleg or Moll's Leg or Molly's Leg, which was wiped out by a hurricane over 50 years ago. I am not sure why the island was rebuilt unless it was used as a repository for spoil from harbor dredging. In any event, the majority of marinas, restaurants, shops, and other facilities are in the cove to the west and south of this island.

Immediately to your left, on the southern side of the harbor entrance, are the docks belonging to the Chesapeake Marine Biology Laboratory. Here, tied up in the shadow of the huge Exxon tanks, you usually can see some of the research vessels used by the laboratory.

Dockages / Provisions / Facilities.

Just past the Exxon tanks are the docks of the excellent Harbor Island Marina. The pilings and platform of the first dock you come to have a good bit of soft creosote, of which you should be wary when laying alongside. The marina keeps space for visiting boats along its outer piers and you may wish to take advantage of this courtesy to visit the Harbor Island Inn located there.

Adjacent to the Harbor Island Marina is Bunky's Charter Boat Marina, which offers its services to Bay anglers. Just past Bunky's is a package store and a small gift shop, which also carries a good line of boating clothes.

Next is Bowen's Inn and Marina. Transients are welcome to tie up to its pier overnight (limited space and there is a charge) or to visit the dining room or bar (no charge to tie up). However, Bowen's Marina is only open from April 15 to October 1. The restaurant is also closed on Mondays.

Off season, the Solomons Island Yacht Club is an ex-

cellent place to spend the night, particularly for members of recognized yacht clubs.

Farther along, past the Solomons Island Yacht Club, is Dockside Grocery. If it's groceries you need this is the place to stop. It has a wide selection of most food supplies that you are likely to need or want and usually has a good price on beer by the case.

Where to Eat.

On the Patuxent River side, directly across the thin neck of land from Dockside Grocery, is Solomons Pier Restaurant. The restaurant is located on a long finger of a pier extending out into the Patuxent River. There is dockspace for a few boats to tie up, but the water depth is uncertain and there is no protection from waves or wakes from the river. It changed hands in 1985 and has become a "fancy" place instead of the "just plain folks" place it once was. It's also quite a bit more expensive.

Just past Dockside, between Solomons Island Neck and Langley Point, is a small body of water called the Narrows. On the northeastern shore of the Narrows is the large Langley Point Marina and the Pier I, a busy little restaurant which has docks where you may tie up while enjoying a meal there. On the western side of the Narrows is a place that offers charter fishing boats. The Narrows is far too busy a place for anchoring at any time.

Additional Dockages/Provisions.

Often overlooked by newcomers, Back Creek, extending to the north of Mollyleg Island, has several more marinas and the intriguing Calvert Marine Museum.

Zahniser's Marina and Boatyard is located in the first cove to port, less than one-half mile past the tip of Langley Point. Aside from a recently opened gift shop, Zahniser's has the only dockside sewage pumpout facility in the Solomons Island area.

Off the starboard bow is the large and hospitable Calvert Marina. Calvert has a pier set aside for transients, adjacent to their carry-out restaurant, which is open in the summer months. They also have a ships store, a swimming pool, and, that site of washday miracles, a laundry.

As you come even with the main docks of Calvert Marina, a little cove opens up to port. On the north side of this cove is Shepherd's Marina, which is reputed to maintain a few slips for transients. There is now a boat sales office where there was a restaurant a few years ago.

Things to Do. Tucked away back in the cove is the Calvert Marine Museum. Operated by the Calvert County Historical Society, the museum is open daily year-round. Although reputed to have as much as 200 feet of dockspace for visitors at the museum pier, there is really only one space, in front of the lighthouse, to lay alongside the pier. Museum boats take up most of the dock space. If you can't find a spot at the museum dock, you can either anchor out in the cove and land by dinghy or pull into a transient slip at Shepherd's Marina and walk to the museum from there—or, for that matter, from any part of Solomons. Whatever you have to do to get there, by all means visit the museum.

There is no charge for tying up at the museum dock, if you can find room. For admission, the society requests a voluntary donation to help support the museum. Inside, there are exhibits on local maritime history; estuarine natural history and paleontology. There is a shipcarving and model-making shop and underwater exhibits—by themselves worth the trip. There is also a small gift shop. Outside are a few small exhibits, a small boat shed, and the screw-pile Drum Point

Lighthouse. (The lighthouse is only open for visitors for certain hours of the day but it appears to be typical of the type. In fact, it looks to be a twin of the lighthouse at the St. Michaels Marine Museum.) The museum also offers hour-long cruises on a converted 1899 bugeye, *Wm. B. Tennison.* From September through March, visitors can see working oyster boats at Broomes Island, Chesapeake Beach, and Solomons Island. Across the street from the museum is a Visitor Information Center.

There are more marinas upstream. Spring Cove Marina has a restaurant, a general store, and bike rentals. A new Holiday Inn has been built at the headwaters, with its own marina. Just behind the Holiday Inn on Route 4 is a shopping center with a pizza parlor, post office, liquor store, convenience store, laundry, and the newly relocated Woodburn's Food Market. The marine store (1st Marine) just happens to be one of the few places that can repair and recondition propellers. (The owner tells me that he can handle only small propellers, those no larger than five feet in diameter.)

Anchorages. Don't try to anchor for the night anywhere in Back Creek. It is crowded with boats and will not make for a restful night. Instead, head up into Mill Creek, to the northeast of Mollyleg Island. The best anchorage in the area is the region along the west shore of Mill Creek between markers "3" and "5." You can pull in fairly close to shore and still anchor in about 10 feet of water. There are a couple of sandy beaches where it is possible to land. This short stretch is the only part of Mill Creek not lined with homes. That probably won't last and the Solomons area will be the poorer for it when it goes. If this portion of Mill Creek is crowded, simply move farther upstream. Anchorage here is adequate, but most of the shore is private property and you cannot expect to be able to land.

Another alternative anchorage is Old House Cove, either just inside the mouth of the cove or in the broad part of Mill Creek just past the cove. The bottom in both places is hard mud, making for good holding. Don't try to anchor in Leason Cove; the holding is reputed to be as poor as the holding in Old House Cove is good.

If you don't have to go ashore, you can anchor almost anywhere in either Mill Creek or St. John Creek and spend a peaceful night. You can follow Mill Creek upstream until you start to plow mud, or poke into any of the other branches until the water gets uncomfortably thin, with virtual impunity. In spite of the popula-

A view of the Calvert Marine Museum's waterfront and Drum Point Lighthouse. The Patuxent Small Craft Guild maintains the museum's small craft collection, including the skipjack *Marie Theresa* in the foreground. PAULA JOHNSON/CALVERT MARINE MUSEUM

tion density, the water traffic on Mill Creek is surprisingly light. You cannot anchor in the basin on the south side of the Patuxent River, across from Solomons. It is part of the Patuxent Naval Air Test Center and is not open to the general public.

LEWIS CREEK

No facilities

Charts: 12230, **12264,** 12284

Virtually unnoticed by cruisers, Lewis Creek is hidden on the western shore of the Patuxent River just south of Town Point. Nearly everyone who ventures into this area bypasses this creek in favor either of Town Creek or of continuing farther up the Patuxent. This is probably because the chart indicates that the entrance is impassable by cruising boats. This is not the case; you just have to know how to get through the entrance.

Approaches. On the south side of the entrance, there is a sandy hook with a green "1" daymark right at its tip. On the opposite side of the entrance is a large patch of marsh grass backed by a small hillside, which gives warning of shoaling on that side. The entrance is best approached on a due-west course, guiding directly at the middle of the sandy beach of the hook. Approach slowly, holding almost close enough to the beach to jump ashore and follow the beach around the point. Don't get too close to the green "1" as you can expect a little shoaling past it. Once on a course toward the big boathouse to starboard, you are in.

Anchorages. The creek has 6 to 11 feet of water throughout, right up to its end. The banks are high and wooded, providing a well-protected and secluded anchorage for boats adventurous enough to negotiate the entrance. There are only a few houses on the shore. This is a truly secluded spot.

TOWN CREEK

Charts: 12230, **12264,** 12284

Town Creek, the second navigable creek on the western shore of the Patuxent River, literally lies in the shadow of the Governor Johnson bridge, which crosses the river just a little to the northwest of Solomons. Since this bridge was built, the right fork of the creek is accessible only to vessels with a vertical height of less than 30 feet.

Approaches. The entrance to the creek is deep and easily negotiated. Simply honor the lighted red "2" marker at the mouth of the creek, leaving it close to starboard. The rest of the creek has 8 to 10 feet of water, except in the last half of the creek's left fork, where it shoals to about 4 feet.

Dockages/Provisions. There are several marinas in here, two of which serve transients. To starboard, just before the bridge is Homeport Marina, indicated by a small sign with that name. Near the water is a small, tan, masonry building, which houses the showers and the laundromat. Past the bridge, at the head of the creek's right fork, is the Town Creek Marina, which offers package goods, a restaurant, and a bar with nightly entertainment.

While not an unattractive area, the creek shoreline is residential and there are far better harbors elsewhere on the Patuxent.

MILL CREEK

Charts: 12230, **12264**

Approaches. As you pass the bridge and round Point Patience in the Patuxent River, you are soon able to see the common approach shared by Mill and Cuckhold Creeks off your port bow. A course of 344 degrees takes you from the red "8" light at the tip of Point Patience to the green "9" Patuxent River lighted marker, which also indicates the south side of the approach into Mill and Cuckhold Creeks. As you pass green "9," swing to port and follow the daymarks past Half Pone Point into the creek mouths. As you clear the last red marker off Half Pone Point, swing to port to enter Mill Creek. There is plenty of water in all branches of Mill Creek, just be sure to give all points a prudent berth.

Dockages/Provisions. Directly in front of you as you complete the approach is Clarke's Landing. The restaurant and bar here offers slips to transients using their facilities. It would be wise to ascertain the depth in any of these slips before using one.

In the end of the first cove to starboard in Mill Creek is the Placid Harbor Conference Center. While they do not really cater to the marine trade, they do offer some slips, showers, heads, and ice. Other conference center facilities are not open to the general public. Look for the dockmaster to obtain permission before using any of the slips.

The rest of the creek is pretty and wooded, although most of the shoreline in the smaller branches is lined with homes.

Anchorages/Things to Do. You can anchor nearly anywhere here with good protection. We have found the best anchorage to be in the bight to port just after entering the creek, near the cliffs. There are some nice, small sandy beaches along here where you can land to stretch your legs and, if you have a dinghy, just inside the point is a small pond in the marsh, which you can explore.

CUCKHOLD CREEK

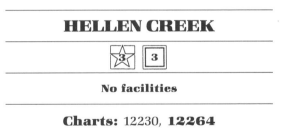

Charts: 12230, **12264**

Approaches. The same approach instructions as stated for Mill Creek apply here. After clearing Half Pone Point, swing to starboard to enter Cuckhold Creek. (Sorry, we have not been able to discover the origin of the name.) Immediately to port is Nat Creek, which has plenty of water but was too crowded to interest us.

Dockages/Provisions. About one-half mile past Nat Creek, where the Cuckhold Creek widens a bit, Blackstone Marina appears to port. The marina has a marine store, showers, and heads, as well as gas and diesel fuel. Just past Blackstone's, Weeks Marina offers ice and limited hardware, however it does not really cater to transients.

The creek is navigable almost to the headwaters of the two forks at its end. It is interesting to note that the farther upstream you go, the browner the water gets.

Anchorages. You can anchor anywhere in Cuckhold Creek, but we prefer less developed anchorages. We recommend Mill Creek or one of the other harbors on the Patuxent for overnight anchoring, but feel it is worth a quick trip up this creek to give it the once-over.

HELLEN CREEK

No facilities

Charts: 12230, **12264**

About a mile past the entrance to Mill and Cuckhold Creeks, Hellen Creek lies to starboard. This creek looks interesting, but, unless you can find the narrow 7-foot-deep privately marked channel, the bar across its entrance limits access to very shallow-draft vessels. If you can get in, there are plentiful, well-protected anchorages in 7 to 11 feet of water. Negotiating the bar is a test of nerve and skill.

ST. LEONARD CREEK

Charts: 12263, **12264**

Approaches. A little more than 3 miles past Point Patience is the entrance to St. Leonard Creek, perhaps the prettiest part of the Patuxent River. A course of 355 degrees from the red "8" at the tip of Point Patience takes you directly to the green "1" daymark in the mouth of St. Leonard Creek. The entrance is difficult to see until you are almost on top of it. About 400 yards to the west of the St. Leonard Creek green "1" daymark is the lighted red "14" Patuxent River marker. *Do not go between them;* they indicate the same shoal. Leave green "1" to port and enter the mouth of St. Leonard Creek. The creek has no more markers, but they really aren't needed.

Give Rodney Point a wide berth as you proceed up the creek. The rest of the creek is easy to navigate, as a glance at the chart shows. There is 7 to 20 feet of water nearly from shore to shore for the entire 3 miles of St. Leonard Creek. Simply stay near the middle and you won't get into trouble while you enjoy the quiet, pastoral scenery on this beautiful creek. There are few houses and, with one exception, no commercial development.

History. It was in St. Leonard Creek that the little flotilla of Commodore Barney was bottled up when they fought to turn back the British during the War of 1812. After a valiant effort, they pulled off a surprise attack which sent the British fleet reeling back to Point Patience, whereupon Commodore Barney was able to escape with his fleet relatively intact upstream on the Patuxent River to Benedict. Unfortunately, the British fleet was soon reinforced, Barney's flotilla was forced to scuttle their gunboats and the British went on to burn

The destruction of the U.S. Chesapeake Flotilla in Washington, D.C. LIBRARY OF CONGRESS

Washington, D.C. Today, there are continuing efforts to find and salvage artifacts from these scuttled gunboats.

Anchorages. The first anchorage is in Mackall Cove, the little cove to port, almost at the mouth of the creek. The high wooded banks and 12 feet of water make this one of the snuggest anchorages in the area. Conversely, there is little of the air circulation needed in hot weather. Mackall Cove is definitely a cool weather anchorage.

Just past Rodney Point is one of the creek's most popular anchorages. From Rodney Point around to the east is a beautiful white sandy beach below a wooded bank. Here you can wade, swim, beachcomb, or build sandcastles to your heart's content. Anchor inside the point in about 14 feet of water with good holding. During the boating season, you probably won't be alone, but there is plenty of room for all.

The next good anchorage is just below the cliff at Breedens Point. If you really like seclusion, make your way into Hollins Cove, just to the east. Here there is room for just a couple of boats to swing, completely protected from all directions.

Directly west of Breedens Point, on the opposite side of the creek, is an unnamed cove which lies between high wooded banks. This is a great hurricane hole to duck into in the event of a line squall. The homes on both sides preclude landing, and it is too close for hot weather anchoring.

Where to Eat. A little farther upstream, right where Johns Creek branches off St. Leonard Creek, is Vera's White Sands Restaurant and Marina. If you want a slip for the night or plan to go to the restaurant (which you definitely should visit at least once), pull up to the gas dock for a slip assignment from the dockmaster. Showers and heads are in the restaurant building on the hill above the docks, as is the swimming pool. Vera is who really makes this facility unique. Once a Hollywood starlet, Vera is a gracious lady with a taste for the exotic, who still presents a commanding appearance. There is never any question who she is when Vera makes her appearance. Once having met her, you'll never forget her.

You can proceed farther upstream, but sailboats are advised not to proceed beyond Planters Wharf Creek due to the overhead power cable (vertical clearance 38 feet).

SOTTERLY

PLANTATION

No facilities

Approaches. Almost directly across the river from the mouth of St. Leonards Creek is Sotterly on the Patuxent. The plantation overlooks a large sweep of the river. This is a working plantation, which dates back to the early 18th century.

Easily accessible from the water, Sotterly welcomes visitors. There are two docks where you can tie up to visit, although overnight dockage is neither expected nor desirable with St. Leonard Creek so close. One of these docks is a T-shaped pier that juts out into the Patuxent River. The other, perhaps a better choice, is in the little cove just north of the pier. To enter the cove, favor the southern side of the entrance, swinging close to the pier, then pull into the dock on the south side of the cove. Here your boat will be well protected from weather and wave while you are visiting the plantation.

History/Things to Do. The dockhouse has a phone which you can use to call a car to pick up your crew and take them up to the lovely Georgian mansion. Actually, it is a pleasant half-mile walk up the dirt road past the bordering raspberry bushes.

Originally, Sotterly was part of a 4,000-acre land grant made in 1650 to Thomas Cornwallis by Lord Baltimore. This tract was subdivided in 1710 and the 890 acres that became Sotterly were purchased by James Bowles, who started construction on the manor house. Bowles died in 1727 before much could be completed. Two years later, his widow married George Plater II, a prominent lawyer. It was George Plater II and his son, George Plater III, who were responsible for most of the construction of the present manor.

The manor house stands on the top of a sloping bank, now a sheep pasture, which provides a fantastic panorama down to and across the Patuxent River. Be sure to walk in the English country garden north of the house.

The staff at the plantation welcomes either small or large groups which, for a nominal fee, they conduct on a

Sotterly on the Patuxent, a working plantation, is open to visitors and easily accessible from the water.

tour of the manor. With advance notice, they will cater luncheons, teas, or receptions for groups of over 25. The plantation is operated by the Sotterly Mansion Foundation, which may be reached by phone at (301) 373-2280 or by writing to P.O. Box 67, Hollywood, MD 20636.

and Fishing Center, in the little cove to port just after you pass the narrow mouth of the creek, offers groceries. Be prepared to go in by dinghy; it gets shallow there.

The shoreline is low and marshy to starboard and at the headwaters; built up to port. There is reasonable protection in 8 to 10 feet of water once you get in.

ISLAND CREEK

Charts: 12263, **12264**

Approaches. The entrance to this creek, although marked, is tight and subject to shoaling. You have to feel your way in if you have more than a 3-foot draft because the channel meanders more than indicated by the chart and the few markers.

Provisions. There are three small marinas here where you can get some limited supplies. Len's Market

BATTLE CREEK

No facilities

Chart: 12264

Approaches. The entrance to this creek is marked with two buoys at a dogleg in the channel through the shoals in its mouth. There is also a snag indicated to starboard just prior to a 3-foot shoal opposite Prison Point. Swing well north of the red marker in the Patuxent River to the west of Jack Bay and set a course to head toward the east end of the sandspit inside the mouth of the creek past Wells Cove. As the tip of Prison Point comes abeam, swing slowly to port and feel your way in until the water depth drops to about 15 feet. From then on, remain in the middle and you should fare well. The creek has 7 to 18 feet of water for two-thirds of the way up before it starts to shoal.

Things to Do. There is good protection in here but the shore is thickly settled until you get away from the mouth of the creek. You can proceed for a distance of about 1½ miles upstream from the creek mouth before the water starts to drop below 7 feet. At the head of the creek is one of the northernmost stands of bald cypress in America—some of the trees are reputed to be 600 years old. Make the 1½ mile trip to the Battle Creek Cypress Swamp Sanctuary only at high water and in a shallow-draft boat. It is open 10:00 a.m. to 5:00 p.m., Tuesday through Saturday; 1:00 p.m. to 5:00 p.m., Sunday. Try the self-guided elevated tour.

There are no marine facilities on this creek, but the Cape St. Marys Marina, directly across the Patuxent River from the entrance to Battle Creek, has fuel, water, ice, a dockside sewage pumpout facility, engine repairs, a restaurant, and a novelty shop.

UPPER PATUXENT

RIVER

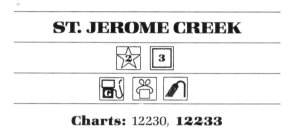

Chart: 12264

Dockages/Provisions. Above Battle Creek, no protected anchorages out of the main part of the river are passable by other than very shallow-draft boats. There is some dockage at Benedict, the principal town on the upper part of the Patuxent, just below the swing bridge. Supplies are available dockside or in stores in the town. You can anchor in the mouth of Indian Creek, just below Benedict, but watch the depth as you feel your way in.

Approaches. The swing bridge at Benedict has a closed vertical clearance of 16 feet, but it opens on

signal from 6:00 a.m. to 6:00 p.m. At any other hour, advance notice is required (phone, 535-1740).

The river is navigable for more than 10 miles above the swing bridge but narrows progressively as you proceed upstream. How far you can actually go depends on your draft and your nerve; NOAA chart 12264 has a chartlet, which goes up to Nottingham, a dozen miles beyond the bridge.

Anchorages. There are no protected harbors or tributaries off the main river, but none are necessary. Just pull to the side of the river in a comfortable-looking bend and drop the hook. This section is still a pretty river and, if you have the inclination, worth a look. Some parts are fairly well populated but others are nearly pristine. Few cruising boats take the trouble to travel this far upriver; they are missing something.

ST. JEROME CREEK

Charts: 12230, **12233**

Just south of Point No Point, about midway between the Patuxent River and the Potomac, is St. Jerome Creek, a harbor of refuge to relatively shallow-draft vessels. If you carry a draft of 4 feet or more, don't try it. Under no circumstances attempt to enter at night unless you are very familiar with this creek.

Approaches. The approach is straightforward. The course from Point No Point Light to the first marker at the entrance of St. Jerome Creek flashing 2-second green is 258 degrees for 2.3 miles. At this point you can find and honor the markers in the entrance.

Anchorages. Once past the last daymark, turn sharply to the north and anchor anywhere in the northern fork of the creek. Stay out of the shallow south fork.

Provisions/Facilities. Trossbach Marina in the southern corner of St. Jerome Creek offers gasoline, ice, and showers, but ready access is only for shallow-draft boats.

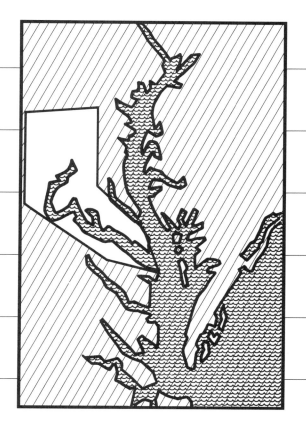

REGION 5

Potomac River

Potomac River Region Overview

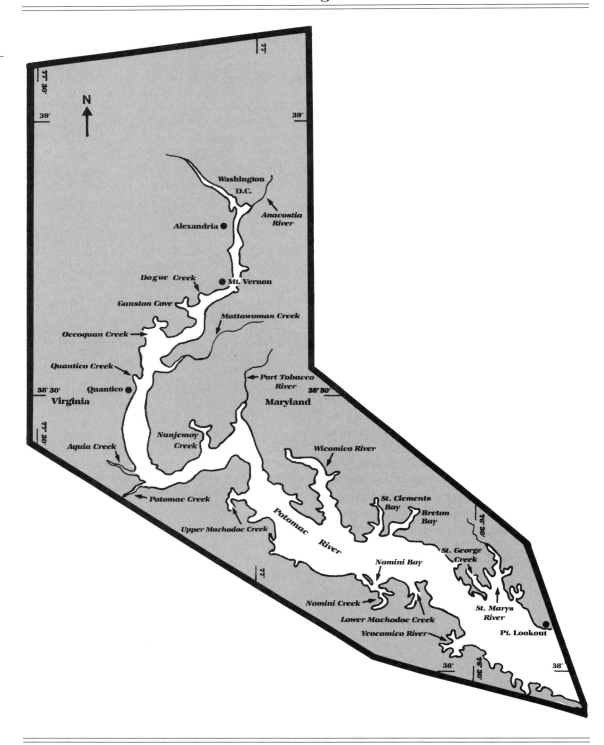

Often overlooked by those who cruise the Chesapeake Bay, the lower portion of the Potomac River offers cruising grounds that can rival those of the Bay itself. The mouth of the Potomac is 10 miles wide, comparable to the upper Bay, with low-lying land that creates an illusion of an even greater expanse. Within the 95 miles of river from Point Lookout to Washington, there are nearly 30 rivers or creeks—some are inviting, some impassable. The best cruising grounds lie within the first 30 miles of the entrance. Good harbors are scarce in the last 65 miles of the run to Washington, but they do exist.

The mean range of tide varies from about 1½ on the lower river to about 3 feet at Washington. As with the rest of the Chesapeake, tide and currents here can be greatly influenced by the wind. Winds from the north or south can make any resemblance between the tide-and-current tables and the actual conditions purely coincidental. Luckily the waters are forgiving. Like the Chesapeake, the Potomac's bottom tends to be soft mud; running aground is an inconvenience but no great hazard. The current, however, can be much more of a problem here than in the Bay. You can expect to encounter some currents on the order of 1.5 knots or more. Besides affecting your progress, such currents can throw your navigation well off when visibility is restricted.

Under conditions of opposing wind and current, the mouth of the Potomac can become extremely uncomfortable in a surprisingly short time. This area also has a reputation for squalls, so get into port early, particularly in the summer months.

Mouth

of

Potomac

to

Port

Tobacco

River

☐

LOWER POTOMAC RIVER

Charts: 12230, **12233,** 12285

Warnings notwithstanding, the lower Potomac is a vast expanse of placid waters with numerous rivers, creeks, and bays containing plentiful, well-protected harbors, and surroundings varying from secluded without supplies to public with full facilities. The upper portion of the Potomac, although somewhat lacking in harbors, more than makes up for that deficiency with more points of interest.

For sailors, the first 30 miles of the river allow plenty of room for tacking, since it is at least 4 miles wide. Unless you are a real die-hard, we don't recommend cruising the Potomac and its tributaries without power.

The real line of demarcation between the Chesapeake Bay and the Potomac River is Point Lookout on the Maryland side of the river; Smith Point on the Virginia side is not as sharply defined. Under certain conditions, a line in the water—possibly caused by the effects of wave action on bottom sediment or the mixing of main Bay and Potomac waters—extends southward from Point Lookout for as far as a couple of miles across the mouth of the Potomac. To the east of this "line" you are in the Chesapeake Bay. To the west and north of it, you are cruising the Potomac River.

Point Lookout, itself, is now a state park with all sorts of recreational facilities. On the inside of the point, in a bight labeled Cornfield Harbor (it really isn't a harbor), there is a channel leading into the public boat launching and rental facility. However, this is strictly for small powerboats; the maximum depth is 4 feet and it definitely is not an overnight anchorage area.

During the War Between the States, a Union prisoner of war camp was located at Point Lookout. Officially called Camp Hoffman, the compound covered 26 acres, surrounded by a 12-foot high fence and patrolled by guards on a catwalk on the outside. Inside, there was a ditch marking the deadline beyond which any prisoner would be shot. For the prisoners, Hoffman was hell. It frequently has been compared to the Confederate prison camp at Andersonville in the poor treatment of its prisoners.

The camp was protected by three earthwork forts

and picket boats patrolled the shores. Today, there is little left but a piece of the prison wall and one wall of one of the forts. A monument stands nearby, marking the common grave of the more than 3,000 Confederate soldiers and some civilian sympathizers who died there.

SMITH CREEK

All facilities

Charts: 12230, **12233,** 12285

The mouth of Smith Creek lies on the Maryland side of the Potomac, about 6 miles from Point Lookout. The entrance, although narrow, is well marked and easy to negotiate. This creek is often used as a harbor of refuge, and the six marinas inside offer all the facilities you are likely to need.

Approaches. You might have some trouble locating the first of the entrance markers, a lighted red "2" spar, feeling uncomfortably close to the land before you pick up "2" for certain. This feeling is illusory; your depth sounder will indicate depths in excess of 20 feet if you are even approximately on course. Hold reasonably close to the green "3" marker right in the middle of the creek as you pass it since there are some shoals to either side, especially to the southwest of the marker. Once past green "3" (you have to take a dog-leg to the west after passing "3"), there is deep water from shore to shore all the way to the headwaters of both branches of the creek. There are numerous coves or creeks here, so there is a good chance of finding one unoccupied if you seek privacy.

Dockages/Facilities. All of the marine facilities are in the east fork of the creek (Jutland Creek). If you need supplies, fuel, or prefer a slip for the night, head up this branch.

Anchorages. The west fork offers more solitude. You can anchor anywhere up to a distance of about 1 mile above the point where the creek forks. Holding is good and you will be well protected from the

weather in all directions. The first cove to starboard is surrounded by tall trees which makes it both private and gives excellent protection from a blow.

ST. MARYS RIVER

Charts: 12230, **12233,** 12285

For the main part, the St. Marys River is a pretty river surrounded by wooded hills and farmland. The few thickly settled areas are quiet and well kept. St. Marys not only offers sheltered anchorages but also many historic sites to lure the tourist in us all. Even those with no appreciation for its history will enjoy the 8-mile trip from the entrance to the head of navigation of the St. Marys River.

In 1634, two small ships filled with colonists sailed up the Potomac River, past the mouth of the St. Marys River, and landed briefly on St. Clements Island. There they erected an altar and cross, giving thanks for their safe voyage.

Leaving St. Clements Island, the colonists sailed the *Ark* and the *Dove* up the St. Marys River. Led by Leonard Calvert (brother of Lord Baltimore), they established the colony of Maryland and named the first settlement and provincial capital, St. Marys City. In 1695, the provincial capital was moved to Annapolis—a blow that caused the settlement to dwindle and almost disappear into history.

Few traces of the original settlement remain, but an 800-acre outdoor museum, including the reconstructed brick State House, the rebuilt Trinity Episcopal Church, and several other colonial buildings now occupy the original site. (For more information, see the section on St. Marys City.)

The approach to the St. Marys River is easy. From Point Lookout to the mouth of the river, steer a course to keep you at least one-half mile offshore. This enables you to clear the few shoals that could cause any difficulty. Pass well to the south of the red "2" light at the mouth of Smith Creek to avoid the long shoal off Kitts Point at the mouth of the St. Marys River.

As you enter the St. Marys, continue to keep at least one-half mile offshore, especially as you approach Fort Point where an unmarked 3-foot shoal to starboard extends about one-half mile into the river. By the time you get to this point, you should have decided whether you want to put into St. George Creek or continue up the St. Marys River.

As you clear Fort Point (which doesn't look like much of a point), you can see the large Naval Test Facility to starboard. There is also a Coast Guard facility located in St. Inigoes Creek nearby. Although you can't see much of the base, you will see some signs of activity

and cannot miss the Coast Guard aircraft taking off and landing at the airfield.

About here you have to make another decision regarding your destination. You can proceed up the St. Marys River towards St. Marys City; put into Carthagena Creek for fuel or supplies, or enter St. Inigoes Creek, which has some of the best protected anchorages on the St. Marys River.

Smith Creek to Breton Bay

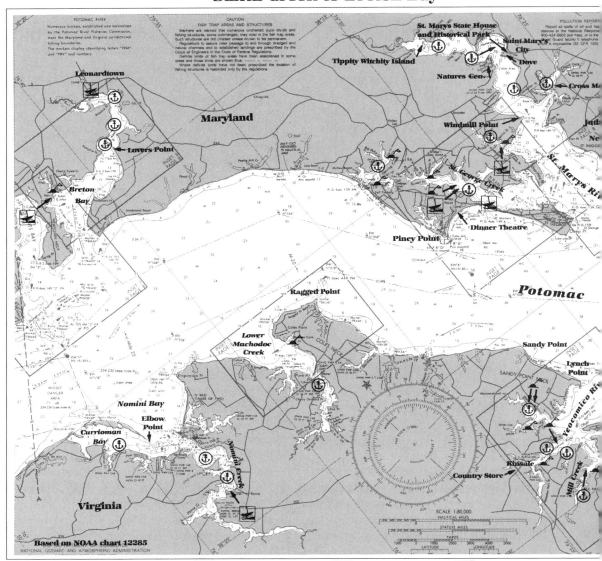

SCALE 1"=**2.65** NAUT. MILES   **Good anchoring**   **Mooring area**   **Launching site**

ST. GEORGE CREEK

Charts: 12230, **12233**, 12285

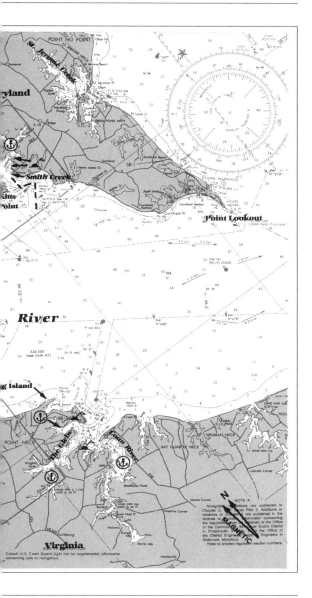

Facilities/Where to Eat. There are a couple of marinas on this creek and, on the Potomac side of the peninsula, about midway between Piney Point and Straits Point, the Oakwood Lodge and Dinner Theatre, which is within walking distance. However, unless you plan to visit the Harry Lundeberg Maritime Training School or the Oakwood, I recommend proceeding to more attractive creeks and anchorages up the St. Marys River. The island at the mouth of St. George Creek is low and marshy, with a few clumps of pines.

Anchorages. If you are planning to continue up or down the Potomac the following day, you could anchor in Price Cove. Its proximity to the Potomac makes it a good spot in which to overnight. Price Cove is near the St. George Creek entrance. It is roomy enough that you won't feel crowded if you share the spot with several other boats. Well protected from weather, the cove still gets a cooling breeze and is large enough that you can anchor offshore to avoid becoming an insect luau. Tall trees and a nice shore-side beach add to the cove's attraction. On the down side, a few boats have had trouble getting their anchors to hold in the bottom.

CARTHAGENA CREEK

Charts: 12230, **12233**, 12285

Provisions. The only place on the St. Marys River where supplies are available is Dennis Point Marina in Carthagena Creek. Just a few years ago, entering this creek was more of an adventure because it was a little short of markers. Today, the entrance is well marked and, if you honor the markers, no trouble to negotiate.

Approaches. As you approach the flashing green "1" off Edmund Point, you can see the first of two green daymarks, "1" and "3," off Graveyard Point. You may have some trouble recognizing them because they tend to blend into the background until you are within one-half mile of them. Leaving the green "3" to port, head directly toward the 15-foot red "4" flasher at the mouth of the creek. Leave the red "4" close to starboard and the green "5" daymark well to port.

Dockages/Facilities. The fuel dock of Dennis Point Marina lies straight ahead, under the large Gulf sign. In addition to the usual marina facilities (water, fuel, electricity, and slips), Dennis Point Marina has a small snack bar/cocktail lounge and a limited selection of groceries and hardware. On each of our visits, we were impressed with the friendliness and cooperation of the personnel. This marina has been run by the same family for 20 years and reflects that care, interest, and attention.

The shore of Carthagena Creek is wooded and the entire creek is quiet. You can cruise nearly to the headwaters of the creek, approximately 1 mile past the marina, in 7 feet of water. Except for the marina, there appears to be no convenient place to land and the banks look pretty muddy.

ST. INIGOES CREEK

No facilities

Charts: 12230, **12233**, 12285

Approaches. On the eastern side of the St. Marys River, almost directly opposite the entrance to Carthagena Creek, is St. Inigoes Creek. As you enter St. Inigoes, be sure to stay well off the southern shore. Some shoals protrude well out into the creek there; do not be misled by the sizable dock at the Coast Guard Station.

Anchorages. The first anchorage is in the entrance to Molls Cove, which has room for several boats to swing. (There is a shoal on the west side of the shore but it doesn't bar the entrance.) Holding is good and the anchorage is sheltered, except from the west. Cross Manor, said to be the oldest house in Maryland, is located on the eastern side of Molls Cove. The main house and several of the outbuildings were constructed in 1644, just 10 years after the founding of St. Marys

City. It is still an impressive, well-kept structure, but is not open to the public.

Perhaps the best anchorage in St. Inigoes Creek is beyond the point where Cross Manor stands. As you clear the point, the creek widens and you can drop the hook in 10 to 13 feet of water to within 50 yards of shore. On the sandy point nearby is the wreck of what appears to be a steel-hulled boat, lying completely over on its side. At low tide, less than one-quarter of it protrudes above the water. The point with this wreck is about the only place on St. Inigoes Creek where you can land. The rest of the shore is lined with private homes.

Milburn Creek and Church Cove each have an anchorage. Be warned that the names of the creeks and coves shown on the chart do not necessarily agree with the local names. For example, what the chart refers to as Molls Cove is locally known as Church Creek. This is one of the rare cases in which local knowledge, normally so valuable, can confuse you or, worse, get you into trouble.

As you leave the mouth of St. Inigoes Creek, be sure to honor the lighted "3" marker off Windmill Point. Once you are past Windmill Point, navigation is straightforward. The entire river contains deep water up to within 50 yards (sometimes less) from shore.

CHANCELLOR POINT

No facilities

Charts: 12230, **12233**, 12285

Anchorages/Things to Do. Barely 1 mile past the mouth of St. Inigoes Creek, on the east side of the St. Marys River, is a small sandy spit of considerable interest. First, it forms a pocket in the river, providing a surprisingly protected anchorage, even with a 1-mile stretch of the river open to the north. Second, a smooth sandy beach, open to the public, slopes gently into the water, making for excellent swimming and wading. Third, this is the site of the Chancellors Point Natural History Area and Nature Center. The nature center has an exhibit hall, several nature trails, a picnic area, and a full-time "curator," who is willing to explain the area's indigenous species, both living and fossilized.

The natural history area includes a recreation of an Indian longhouse and an exhibit of the Stone Age tools used to build it.

Those going ashore in midsummer should beware the no-see-ums. While they don't venture far offshore, they will drive you crazy on the beach if you are without a good repellent. This is the only place on the St. Marys River where we've had problems with these little vampires.

ST. MARYS CITY

No facilities

Charts: 12230, **12233,** 12285

The *Dove*, a Jim Richardson reconstruction of one of the ships that carried the first colonists to Maryland. JACK HEVEY/HISTORIC ST. MARY'S CITY

Approaches. No visit to the St. Marys River is complete until you have been to Historic St. Marys City. Once you clear Chancellor Point, you can see Church Point, the original site of the city. Church Point has two

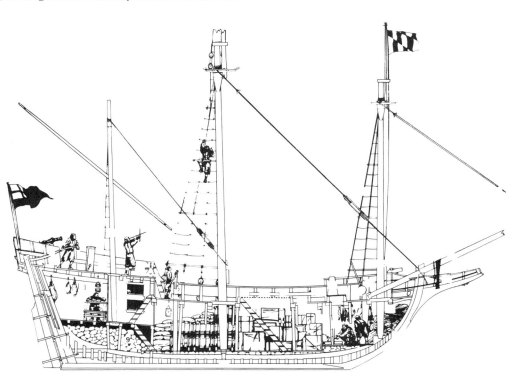

Maryland Dove.

landmarks that clearly identify it: On the top of the hill, Trinity Episcopal Church and, just to the right of the church, the reconstructed red brick State House. Next to the State House are some restored houses from the original St. Marys City, which now house a visitors' center, exhibit, and a gift shop. Historic St. Marys City includes the *Dove,* a full-sized replica of one of the two ships (the other was a supply ship called the *Ark*) that carried the first Maryland colonists. The *Dove,* usually tied to a pier directly below the State House, is open to the public for a nominal fee. Built by well-known Cambridge, Maryland boatbuilder Jim Richardson, who inspired James Michener's boatbuilding section in *Chesapeake,* she is normally staffed by at least one of the crew members, if not the master, who will be able to answer any questions about the vessel or its use, often spiced with anecdotes of some of her cruises.

Things to Do. Historic St. Marys City is a living history museum. Actors play the parts of the villagers and colonists, assuming the dress, accents, and atti-

The State House, a reconstruction of the 1676 original. The militia is mustering on the river lawn in one of the town's living history reenactments. JANET CONNOR/HISTORIC ST. MARY'S CITY

tudes of the period. Their skits never fail to entertain. The museum consists of four exhibit areas: The Brentland Farm Visitor Center with orientation exhibits, an archaeology exhibit hall, and a gift shop; the Governor's Field with the *Dove,* the Reconstructed State House of 1676, Farthing's Ordinary (a recreated 17th-century inn and modern outdoor restaurant), and several archaeological sites; the Godiah Spray Tobacco Plantation, a working farm of the 1660s period; and the Chancellor's Point Natural History Area, which is the site of the Chesapeake Indian Lifeways Center. The visitors center is open daily except Christmas, Thanksgiving, and New Year's Days. Exhibits are open Wednesday through Sunday from Memorial Day through Labor Day; weekends from the end of March to Memorial Day and from Labor Day to the end of November. Hours are 10:00 a.m. to 5:00 p.m. Admission is $5 for adults and $2 for children ages 6 to 12 years.

Anchorages. A good anchorage exists off the dock where the *Dove* is tied up, and a nice beach stretches from the base of the hill to the end of Church Point, where you can land in a dinghy. Alternatively, round Church Point and anchor in the better protected Horshoe Bend near the St. Mary's College Boating Center. Sometimes you can tie up at the pier used by the college's sailing fleet long enough to see the local sights. Other than that, there is normally no dockage available at Historic St. Marys City, making anchoring out a necessity if you want to visit the town or the *Dove.*

HEADWATERS OF THE
ST. MARYS RIVER

 ⟨3⟩ ⟨2⟩

No facilities

Charts: 12230, **12233,** 12285

Approaches. Past Historic St. Marys City, high wooded banks and farmlands line the shores. As you approach the headwaters, you will encounter the improbably named Tippity Witchity Island. Do not pass beyond; the water shoals rapidly and there is little left of the St. Mary's River. As you approach Tippity Witchity

Island, beware of the ½-foot spot to the southeast where there is supposed to be a wreck.

Anchorages. The best anchorage here is in 7 feet of water to the south southeast of the island, where you are sheltered from all but the southeast.

History. Prior to the War Between the States, this island was called Lynch Island. No one is certain, but it seems a good bet that it was named after the Lynch family who owned it. There is an interesting story behind its present name. A somewhat disreputable ex-Confederate smuggler, Captain H.W. Howgate, operated several floating bordellos in Washington. In 1879, a flood destroyed most of them, and the survivors were ordered from the city. The good captain purchased the former Lynch Island in the St. Marys River and constructed a gambling house and bar, with three bedrooms upstairs dedicated to his "girls." The place was called the "Tippling and Witchery House," which quickly corrupted to "Tippity Witchity." Business, dependent on crews from visiting ships, was sporadic, and the doors closed in 1881, a short two years later. The house itself persisted into the early 1940s before being destroyed by vandals.

A new house now occupies the island, on the site of its notorious predecessor, but it is a private home guarded by a large black dog whose mission is to protect the island from interlopers. Don't try to land.

COAN RIVER

Charts: 12230, **12233,** 12285

Seven miles from Point Lookout, or 13 miles from Smith Point, are the three branches of the Coan River on the Virginia side of the Potomac. Each offers seclusion in well-protected anchorages, and one has marina facilities.

The main entrance to the Coan is marked by the Potomac River 4-second flashing green "5" buoy located about 3 miles off-shore. If you are not already familiar with the entrance, use this marker as the starting point for your approach. From here, a course of 232 degrees takes you past the nun "2" and nun "4" buoys, which mark the starboard side of the channel into the Coan. From nun "4," take a heading that leaves the lighted

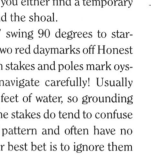
4-second flashing green "5" buoy close to port. The next marker, a red "6" lighted spar, is critical: It marks the end of the long shoal off Travis Point (Lewisetta). Winter ice has taken out this spar more than once. If it is missing move slowly until you either find a temporary buoy or feel your way around the shoal.

Once you clear red "6," swing 90 degrees to starboard and head toward the two red daymarks off Honest Point. A large number of fish stakes and poles mark oyster grounds in this area; navigate carefully! Usually these stakes are in 8 to 10 feet of water, so grounding should not be a problem. The stakes do tend to confuse you as they seem bereft of pattern and often have no fairways between them. Your best bet is to ignore them and follow the proper navigation markers. As you approach the red "8" daymark, you must choose among the three branches: the Main Branch to the south, The Glebe straight ahead, or Kingscote Creek to the north. Kingscote Creek is the only branch with marina facilities.

MAIN BRANCH

No facilities

Charts: 12230, **12233,** 12285

Approaches. The entrance to the main branch of the Coan River is a little tight and requires careful attention to the chart, particularly off Walnut Point. Do not assume a straight course between the red "10" and "12" markers; you need to swing to starboard to avoid the shoal.

Anchorages. Many boats choose to anchor just to the south of Walnut Point, but more secluded anchorages lie upstream. There is deep water, 8 to 13 feet, all the way to the headwaters. You have your pick of good places to anchor in here. The shores are predominantly wooded with few dwellings. Finding an isolated cove or bight where you can anchor all by yourself should be short work. Low tide reveals a number of sandy beaches where you can land to stretch your legs.

THE GLEBE

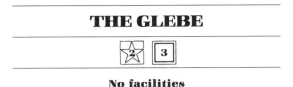

No facilities

Charts: 12230, **12233**, 12285

Approaches. The entire entrance to The Glebe appears to be blocked with oyster stakes. Don't let them bother you; they are all in deep water. As you enter, stay near the middle of the creek and pick your way through the stakes. Once past this congestion, you have clear passage, but beware of the unmarked shoals that extend from each point of land.

Anchorage. The first cove to starboard, unnamed on the chart, is called Fishermans Cove locally. You can anchor in its mouth or move around the slight bend to the west. This small anchorage is a perfect, snug place to ride out a storm. Watch out for the unmarked shoal extending to the south from the starboard side of the cove entrance.

The next cove to port has a jumble of oyster stakes at its mouth. A private marker at the edge of the shoal extends to the northwest from the point to port at the mouth of the cove. You can ignore the oyster markers and enter well into this cove if you favor its eastern side. Watch out for the unmarked shoal extending from the south of the cove; it nearly splits the cove in half.

Farther upstream are anchorages galore. You can pull into Wrights Cove or round the bend and anchor in the mouth of Glebe Creek in 7 feet of water. If your draft is less than 5 feet, squeeze through the narrow pass into the headwaters of Glebe Creek, where there is 6 to 8 feet of water. The whole area is well protected from wind and wave in all directions.

KINGSCOTE CREEK

Charts: 12230, **12233**, 12285

Provisions. The northern branch of the Coan River, Kingscote Creek, contains a popular harbor at Lewisetta. This is your one stop for fuel, ice, and some supplies. An interesting country store is located at the end of a remarkably long dock.

Approaches/Anchorages. Private markers aid your entrance into this creek, but they are not on the chart. If a strong wind from the south to southeast is due, try anchoring farther up the creek where there is more protection. The wooded banks give the impression of isolation, but the conveniences of Lewisetta are less than a mile away.

YEOCOMICO RIVER

Charts: 12230, 12233, **12285**

The Yeocomico River, 4 miles upstream from the Coan River, offers myriad anchorages and your choice of 10 marinas. The countryside is Chesapeake pretty and locals are friendly and helpful. The Yeocomico is a very popular stop for yachts. With so many anchorages I will mention only a few. Although all branches have plenty of water, watch your chart for the shoals that extend from most of the little points of land—not all of them are marked. One other note of caution: Beware of numerous fishing stakes and traps as you approach the mouth of the Yeocomico, especially by Hog Island in the mouth of Judith Sound to the east. The water is deep but if you are careless you could get tangled in the nets while picking your way through.

The flashing red "2" marker, about 1 mile to the east of Lynch Point on Sandy Point Neck, is the starting point for the entrance to the Yeocomico. The approach is easy because the entrance is broad and deep, however, the fishing and oyster stakes could confuse you. Once you clear the 4-second flashing green "3" marker off Barn Point, you must decide which of the three primary branches of the Yeocomico you want to enter. The South Yeocomico extends to the south for about 1 mile, then splinters into a spray of creeks and coves. The West Yeocomico extends straight to the west. The Shannon Branch, which extends to the north, offers the least of the three.

SOUTH YEOCOMICO

RIVER

☆4 | 3

⛽ 🚰 🍞

🚰 ⛵ 🛶

Charts: 12230, 12233, **12285**

Approaches. As you clear the green "3" marker, swing to port to head directly for the red "2" daymark at the mouth of the West Yeocomico River. On Mundy Point, just south of the red "2" daymark, are the long low buildings of the W. J. Courtney Co., a fish cannery. Pass quite close to the docks and you will avoid the long shoal that extends northwest from Tom Jones Point opposite the cannery.

Anchorages. As you pass the red "4" daymark off Walker Point, the river begins to divide. To port is Palmer Cove, an attractive anchorage with 7 to 8 feet of water. The entrance is about 400 yards wide and inside there is plenty of room for a number of boats. The bottom is soft mud, so set your hook accordingly.

To starboard is the entrance to Mill Creek, one of the river's more thickly settled branches. There are no facilities up this creek, just some tidy little homes. However, you have room to anchor if lack of a place to land doesn't bother you.

To port, opposite the red "6" daymark, is the entrance to Dungan Cove, where you can anchor in relative seclusion with 7 to 9 feet of water. The last time we visited this cove, its shores were still undeveloped.

Facilities/Provisions. If you are in need of fuel, ice, or other services, there are a couple of marinas on this branch of the Yeocomico. On the north shore, opposite Dungan Cove, is Krentz Marine Railway, which offers fuel, ice and transient slips. On the south shore, just past Dungan Cove, Olverson's Marina has fuel, ice and transient slips for powerboats.

Additional Anchorages. There are sev-

eral places to anchor in this branch beyond Dungan Cove—just pull over to the side anywhere that appeals to you. Our preference, however, would be to head back to Dungan Cove or Palmer Cove for overnight anchorage.

WEST YEOCOMICO

RIVER

☆4 | 3

⛽ 🚰 🍞 🚰 ⛵

🛒 🏕️ 🛶 🍴

Charts: 12230, 12233, **12285**

Approaches. Hold close to the red "2" daymark at the mouth of the West Yeocomico as you swing to starboard to enter the river. This ensures avoiding the shoal that stretches to the north from Mundy Point. Hold to the middle of the river until you are at least 300 yards past the "2" marker or opposite the entrance to Wilkins Creek to port.

Anchorages. Wilkins Creek is readily accessible so a number of boats choose to anchor there. It is protected and has several sandy beaches at low tide.

Dockages/Facilities/Provisions. To starboard, just inside Horn Point, is a little bight which is the home of the Yeocomico Marina and the Moorings, a little restaurant with excellent food. You can tie up at the marina for fuel, supplies, or a meal. As an alternative you can pass just a little further upstream, anchor in the next little bight, and then land by dinghy.

Kinsale, the leading town on the Yeocomico, is at the head of this branch. The marina there is newly reopened and there is a general store at the top of the hill near the landing which is worth the short hike to see. We were lucky enough to be there one June when they were holding a special country jamboree. Although we didn't land, we anchored off the town and were serenaded for hours by the sounds of bluegrass.

HERRING
CREEK

LOWER
MACHODOC
CREEK

276

SHANNON BRANCH

Charts: 12230, 12233, **12285**

Approaches. This branch of the Yeocomico is easy to enter. As you clear the green "3" marker, swing to starboard, leaving the green "5" of Shannon Branch close to port. There is deep water fairly close to both shores and you can hold close to White Point if you wish.

Dockages/Facilities. The Shannon Branch is the way to White Point Marina on White Point Creek. We were well treated here.

Sandy Point Marina is on the northeast shore, opposite the mouth of White Point Creek. It has a dockside sewage pumpout facility in addition to the conventional marina facilities.

Anchorages. There is a pretty anchorage in 9 feet of water just north of the bar between White Point Creek and Shannon Branch, but, to our minds, the Shannon Branch cannot stand up to the competition from the South and West Yeocomico Rivers.

HERRING CREEK

Charts: 12230, 12233, **12285**

Almost invisible from the Potomac, Herring Creek is about 2½ miles above Piney Point on the Maryland side of the river. Once you know that it's there, it's surprisingly easy to approach and enter. Simply run up the coast, staying a prudent distance offshore, until you can see the pair of flashing 15-foot–high navigation markers and the jetties at the narrow entrance to the creek.

HERRING CREEK

ANCHORAGE

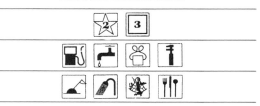

Charts: 12230, 12233, **12285**

The entrance channel seems to have stabilized at 6 feet, which permits passage to most cruising boats. Inside the creek the depth ranges from 7 to 8 feet in the middle, with outcropping shoals around the periphery.

Anchorages. Anchor where you will; it is all well protected from wind and wave. There is room for plenty of boats to swing. Be sure to put up a good anchor light since you can expect some traffic well after dark.

Dockages / Facilities / Provisions. Tall Timbers Marina is to starboard just inside the entrance. Head for it if you need fuel or supplies. The marina often has a transient slip for the night, but contact it in advance to be certain. If you are in the vicinity on Friday night, be sure to try the buffet at "The Reluctant Navigator."

Cedar Cove Marina is straight ahead, near the creek's headwaters. It offers fuel and engine/hull repairs. Make a careful approach; the depth nearby is 5 feet with only 4 feet alongside.

LOWER MACHODOC CREEK

Charts: 12230, 12233, **12285**

Lower Machodoc Creek, 11 miles above the Yeocomico, is exposed to the northwest, unless you squeeze around the narrow sand spit labeled "Narrow Beach" on the chart.

LOWER MACHODOC

CREEK ANCHORAGE

Charts: 12230, 12233, **12285**

Provisions. You can get supplies at any of the three marinas in Branson Cove, just inside the entrance. A short distance from the marinas is the Driftwood II, where you can get a great meal at a good price. Reservations are a must Saturday nights. Groceries and facilities are also available up the creek at the town of Hague.

Anchorages. If you do squeeze past Narrow Beach Point by markers "4" and "6," you come upon a well-protected anchorage with 7 to 10 feet of water. You have to feel your way through the narrow channel off the tip of the point. Hold close to the red markers, then favor the side opposite the point in order to clear the shoal extending to the south from the tip of the point. A couple of private stakes in the water mark the two shoals south of the sand spit's tip.

Past the point, you can anchor anywhere; we recommend the cove inside the sand spit. There is 7 to 14 feet of water in this part of the creek and at least 6 feet of water as far as Parham Point, which was an old sidewheeler steamer dock from 1900 until World War I.

NOMINI BAY

AND CREEK

Charts: 12230, 12233, **12285**

About 3 miles above Lower Machodoc Creek is Nomini Bay and Creek. The entrance channel to Nomini Creek is tight—attempt it only in good visibility. You must follow the markers religiously and sometimes they are hard to see.

NOMINI CREEK

Charts: 12230, 12233, **12285**

Approaches. Once you are past the entrance, the creek opens up and several attractive anchorages present themselves. Pay careful attention to the chart—you have to contend with several unmarked shoals as well as numerous oyster stakes, not to be mistaken for channel markers.

Once you pick up the green "1" lighted marker at the entrance, the channel is well marked and straight until you reach the lighted green "5" marker off Icehouse Point. From there, it bends to starboard and runs straight to the red "8" daymark, off Hickory Point. Red "8" can be hard to see. If you cannot find it from green "5," point your bow at the white house in the trees on the odd-shaped point about 1 mile ahead, where the creek bends sharply to the east. (On the chart this point resembles a crab's claw.) After you clear red "8," you have to negotiate past the oyster stakes; then you are in the clear. Give the "crab claw" point wide berth to avoid the shoal that extends to the north of it. Once past the tip of the claw hold close to the western shore to avoid the 1-foot shoal and (probably submerged) piling on the opposite shore. Beyond here, merely keep to the middle.

Anchorages/Things to Do. This is a picturesque anchorage. If you are even an occasional tourist, you should put into Mount Holly and take the short taxi ride to Stratford and Wakefield, the birthplaces of Robert E. Lee and George Washington, respectively. Dockspace for boats drawing under 4 feet is available at the Mount Holly Steamboat Inn for those visiting the restaurant. Motorlaunch service is available for boats anchored off the dock.

If you need supplies, try McGuires Wharf or put in at Nomini just past the swing bridge (vertical clearance closed, 5 feet).

Pierce Creek, beyond Mount Holly, is shallow, accessible only to boats drawing well under 4 feet.

CURRIOMAN BAY

Charts: 12230, 12233, **12285**

At the mouth of Nomini Creek is the entrance to Currioman Bay. It is reputed to be well marked—we haven't tried it—and I've been told that if you manage to pick up the correct red "2" nun (the first one to starboard, not the red "2" for Nomini Creek) and don't get confused by the markers at the Nomini Creek entrance, the entrance to Currioman Bay isn't all that difficult. Beware of the long, narrow, *submerged*, tip of Elbow Point to starboard.

The bay is too open to be comfortable if the weather turns bad. If you are looking for supplies or a secure, protected anchorage, Nomini Creek is much to be preferred. On the other hand, the protecting bar on the Potomac side of the bay offers you an isolated beach and a

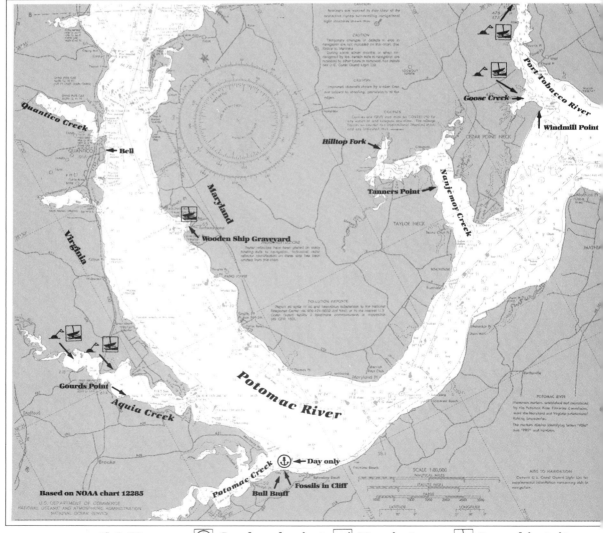

St. Clements Bay to Mattawoman Creek

SCALE **1″=2.78** NAUT. MILES   **Good anchoring**   **Mooring area**   **Launching site**

good place to stretch your legs. Try wading out on Elbow Point just to see how far it goes.

BRETON AND
ST. CLEMENTS BAYS

Charts: 12230, 12233, **12285**

On the Maryland side of the Potomac, 6 miles across the
river from Lower Machodoc Creek, Breton Bay and St.
Clements Bay share a common approach. They also
share a reputation for some of the best cruising waters
on the Potomac.

The approach is marked by a red-green nun. While
you may pass to either side of this nun, beware of Heron
Island Bar to the west, all that remains of its namesake
island. The eastern side of this shoal is indicated solely
by a privately maintained marker.

BRETON
AND
ST.
CLEMENTS
BAYS

279

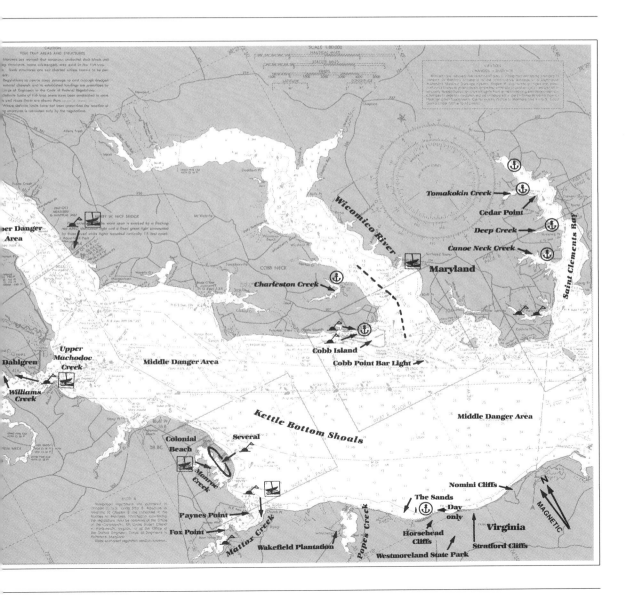

BRETON
AND
ST.
CLEMENTS
BAYS

280

BRETON BAY

Charts: 12230, 12233, **12285**

Approaches. From the red-green buoy, a course of 027 degrees takes you past the red "2" light, which marks the mouth of Breton Bay, directly to the red "4" daymark inside. Just inside the entrance, Combs Creek and Cherry Cove Creek offer yachtsmen facilities (except diesel fuel). Although the chart indicates that the entrances are unmarked, both creeks have private markers, which make the entrance fairly easy. There is about 7 feet of water inside, although the channels are reputed to be no deeper than 5 feet. If you do go into Combs Creek, watch out for the overhead power cable (vertical clearance, 50 feet) just past Combs Creek Marina.

Anchorages. The upper portion of Breton Bay offers several good anchorages along the north shore, just below Leonardtown. Watch out for the shoal off Lovers Point, marked by the flashing red "8" light, and the obstruction reported to be about 400 yards north of the marker.

Breton Bay is navigable all the way up to and a little beyond Leonardtown Wharf. Beyond this point, there simply isn't any more water, either horizontally or vertically.

ST. CLEMENTS BAY

Charts: 12285, **12286**

In 1634, the original Maryland colonists from the *Ark* and the *Dove* erected a wooden cross on the southern tip of St. Clements Island, at the mouth of St. Clements Bay, in thanks for their safe crossing of the Atlantic Ocean. Shortly after that, the colonists sailed back to the St. Marys River to found St. Maries Citty. The original cross is long gone, but a large, new stone cross was erected in 1934 in memory of that first landing. The new cross provides a landmark that unquestionably identifies the island from a long way off.

Approaches. The large cross on St. Clements not only clearly identifies the island, but serves to warn cruisers headed upriver that they are about to enter the lower limit of what is called the Middle Danger Area. This is a region that has been established to permit firing in this portion of the Potomac by the U.S. Naval Weapons Laboratory at Dahlgren, Virginia. Boats may not enter this area while firing is in progress without the permission of the Navy range boat. These boats can be identified by a square red flag during daylight hours and, at night, by a 32-point red light at the masthead. If you see one of these boats, you can ask for instructions regarding where you can and cannot go. Don't get too worried; this area is rarely used for firing.

The entrance to St. Clements Bay requires careful navigation, mostly due to Heron Island Bar. (See the approach to Breton Bay.)

Anchorages. There are several creeks with good anchorages on the western side of St. Clements Bay. All are easily accessible and have at least 6 feet of water.

The first is St. Patrick Creek. This is the one to choose if you need marina facilities. The privately marked entrance and channel are fairly narrow. There has been some shoaling so I am unsure of the present depth. There is no good place to anchor, but you can stay the night at a transient slip, usually available at Kopel's Marina or Cather Marine. Kopel's will supply a courtesy car if you need transportation to a nearby restaurant. If you prefer to swing at your own hook, find another creek.

The next creek is Canoe Neck Creek. The entrance is wide and easy, and there are a number of bights with good anchorages. Skip the first two little coves to port; both are chock-full of homes and boat docks and the second one has a 2-foot bar at its entrance. The rest of Canoe Neck Creek is more inviting. Perhaps the nicest anchorage here is in the first cove to starboard, on the north shore. An extensive shoal projects from the point on the southeast side, so keep well to port as you enter. This anchorage tenders relative seclusion and, at low tide, some beaches on the eastern side of the cove where you can land. The second cove on the north side is also secluded; there is a single house with a dock at the end of the cove. Actually you can anchor anywhere in Canoe Neck Creek in complete safety; these are my top choices.

Next is Deep Creek. Although Canoe Neck Creek has more area and bights, Deep Creek has a reputation for more scenery. This single, nearly straight creek doesn't have the usual protecting shoal at its entrance. You could probably enter blindfolded. Regardless, you can anchor anywhere inside.

The last creek, Tomakokin Creek, is the least built-up of the three. This little creek is to port as you round the "5" light off Cedar Point. You can proceed about half the creek's length before it shoals. Tomakokin is somewhat exposed to the east, but this far up St. Clements Bay, you could probably anchor anywhere with full security.

WICOMICO RIVER

Charts: 12285, **12286**

Slightly more than 4 miles past St. Clements Island is the mouth of one of the four Wicomico Rivers on the Chesapeake. This one has many outlying shoals and no navigable creeks or well-sheltered anchorages, except for Neal Sound directly north of Cobb Island at the mouth. (Note: To the southwest of Cobb Point Bar Light, the chart shows a reported obstruction. Steer clear of that area; ruins and piles lurk just below the surface.

NEAL SOUND

(COBB ISLAND)

Charts: 12285, **12286**

Approaches. With the possible exception of Mattox Creek on the Virginia side of the Potomac, Neal Sound is the last available port for a considerable distance for vessels going up the Potomac. If you are in a boat drawing 4 feet or less, you can enter from the downstream side and leave by the upstream channel, saving quite a distance. (The fixed bridge between the mainland and Cobb Island has a vertical clearance of 18 feet, which effectively prevents sailboats from using this passage.) If you draw more than 4 feet, use only the downstream side. Even then, refer to a current chart and watch out for shoaling near daymark "4." Recent reports indicate that the upper channel is now badly silted in.

The entrance to the Wicomico River is well marked and easy to follow, if you keep your wits about you. From the red-green nun southeast of the 18-foot–high flashing "1W" on Cobb Point Bar, a course of 357 degrees takes you to the red "2W" daymark. From red "2W," a course of 337 degrees takes you to flashing green "3W" at the eastern (downstream) entrance to Neal Sound.

From the flashing green "3W," head for flashing red "2" at the dredged entrance to the Cobb Island Channel. Leave red "2" and the next daymark, red "4," to starboard. Favor the port side of the sound where the water is deepest.

Dockages/Anchorages. Sailboats must berth at marinas below the fixed bridge between Cobb Island and the mainland, but powerboats can enter the marinas above the bridge. The best anchorage and shore facilities are found in the basin east (below) of the bridge.

Facilities/Where to Eat. Cobb Island Marina, the last on the left before reaching the bridge, has excellent facilities including a restaurant. There is a grocery store nearby. I recommend a walking tour of the island—it is a pleasant walk and the islanders are particularly friendly.

POPES
CREEK

MATTOX
AND
MONROE
CREEKS

282

UPPER WICOMICO RIVER

No facilities

Charts: 12285, **12286**

Approaches. If you choose to explore the rest of the Wicomico, a course of 11 degrees from "2W" at the river's mouth takes you to the flashing green "5W." From green "5W," swing to a course of 357 degrees to avoid White Point Bar to starboard and head on up the river.

Anchorages. If you draw less than 5 feet, Charleston Creek to the west of green "7W" offers the only protected anchorage on the rest of the river. While it is possible to proceed considerably farther up the Wicomico River, the numerous shoals and obstructions and lack of sheltered anchorages make doing so less appealing.

POPES CREEK

Charts: 12285, **12286**

Between Nomini Bay and Popes Creek are the high Nomini, Stratford, and Horsehead Cliffs where you can search for fossils, much like at the better known Calvert Cliffs of the Chesapeake. Back of Horsehead Cliffs is the 1,300-acre Westmoreland State Park, well worth climbing the cliffs to visit. (There is a path, which leads upward from the beachside picnic grove at the area marked The Sands on the chart.) The park has cabins, camping, hiking trails, and a boat ramp. You can swim at the beach or in the new Olympic-size swimming pool.

At Popes Creek is Washington's Birthplace National Monument (shown on the chart as northwest of Popes Creek). Wakefield is not only a national monument, it is also a working 18th-century plantation with a Georgian-style manor house (the original burned long ago), the family burial plot, and a picnic area. You may try to take a dinghy in, but even by dinghy there is no good place to land. [It's a 3-mile walk from The Sands.] Popes Creek itself is inaccessible by water, but Mattox Creek, a couple of miles upstream, offers a quiet anchorage and you can visit Wakefield from there.

MATTOX AND MONROE CREEKS

Charts: 12285, **12286**

Mattox and Monroe Creek share a common approach and both offer well-protected anchorages and many marinas from which to choose. The navigational aids serving these two creeks are somewhat difficult to see against the shoreline as you approach.

MATTOX CREEK

Charts: 12285, **12286**

Approaches. Mattox Creek is easily identified by the two large tanks on Paynes Point on the north side of its entrance. This creek offers a quiet, protected anchorage and all the marine facilities that you are likely to need during a short stay. The entrance is easy and the channel is well marked. The channel has 6 to 7 feet of water most of the way in, however boats with drafts over 5 feet should not proceed much beyond Fox Point.

Just past Fox Point is the Harbor View Marina & Resort, which is open to the public. Cruisers have a variety of services here. In addition to the mundane amenities, there is a laundromat and a dockside sewage pumpout facility. There is also a grocery store and a marine supply store.

You can either tie up at the fuel dock to arrange for a slip for the night or anchor out just about anywhere in the creek. Swimming is reputed to be good and the scenery is easy on the eye.

MONROE CREEK

All facilities

Charts: 12285, **12286**

Approaches. If you approach Monroe Creek from the flashing 4-second red "2" east of Gum Bar Point, leave red "2" well to starboard and assume a course of 230 degrees to take you down the middle of the approach to Mattox and Monroe Creeks until you are on a line between Mattox Creek green "1" and Monroe Creek red "4." Then a course of 323 degrees takes you directly to red "4" and the narrow entrance channel into the harbor. Favor the port side of the entrance to avoid the shoals that extend westward from the spit to starboard. This entrance can be subject to strong currents. Plan to pass through when the current is not running strongly. You need a considerable amount of power to buck an adverse tidal current in this area.

Dockages / Facilities / Provisions.

Colonial Beach, on the long peninsula between the creek and the Potomac, has facilities for resident and transient alike, including full-service marinas and restaurants with their own docks. This is the last diesel fuel source for deep-draft boats (more than 5 feet) until the marinas in Washington. It also serves well as a base from which to branch out and visit nearby historic sites. Monroe Creek is a logical stopping point both for breaking the long run to Washington and for resupplying your boat.

Colonial Beach came into its own as a resort around 1882 and, by 1911, was serviced regularly by the famous sidewheeler steamboats. In the 1950s a long pier extended out into the Potomac, capitalizing on the fact

that the Maryland border extended along the Virginia side of the Potomac. This was significant because gambling was legal in Maryland but not in Virginia. The pier burned down but was never rebuilt because the laws changed, negating the need for this feature. Colonial Beach is still a popular resort area, drawing people from far and wide, especially for its Potomac River Festival and outdoor art festival.

The first marina to starboard, Bay Yacht Center, claims to have about 7 feet of water at the gas dock and 4 to 6 feet elsewhere. Other facilities farther up the creek offer restaurants, motels, and other amenities for the cruiser. Be careful of the depth; it gets more iffy the farther up you go. Do not anchor out without a great deal of care. The wiser course is to take a slip for the night or go back to Mattox Creek and anchor there.

The town residents are friendly and helpful and the tree-lined streets make for pleasant walking. This is the place to get taxis for the drive to Wakefield or Lee's birthplace, Stratford Hall, which has a working grist mill, in addition to more conventional restorations.

UPPER MACHODOC CREEK

Charts: 12285, 12286

Seven miles above Mattox Creek is Upper Machodoc Creek, occupied by the U.S. Naval Weapons Laboratory at Dahlgren. Once a prohibited area, it is no longer restricted.

DAHLGREN

Charts: 12285, **12286**, 12287

Approaches. The approach to this creek should start from the flashing 4-second green "29" buoy near the middle of the Potomac River. There is an inshore approach, but I prefer the middle of the river. From green "29" simply follow the markers into the creek.

Provisions. Boats drawing less than 5 feet can get supplies at Dahlgren Marine Works near the headwaters, past the Coast Guard station to starboard.

The middle of the creek has 5 feet of water to just beyond the first bend. It shoals toward the sides and in Williams Creek.

Port Tobacco River to Washington

PORT TOBACCO RIVER

Charts: **12285,** 12288

Continuing upstream from Upper Machodoc Creek, you pass under the Route 301 bridge, which has a vertical clearance of more than 100 feet. Shortly after passing this bridge, you enter the Upper Danger Area, similar to the Middle Danger Area mentioned earlier and with the same caveats. Pay attention to the channel markers in the Potomac; there are several unmarked shoals that you are better off leaving undiscovered.

PORT TOBACCO RIVER ANCHORAGE

Charts: 12285, **12288**

Approaches. The Port Tobacco River, which is on the Maryland side where the Potomac makes a sharp bend to the west 5 miles above the bridge, is a pretty place. It is, however, too open to the north and south to be a comfortable anchorage except under optimum conditions. The holding ground is somewhat uncertain. Observe all daymarks in this river, particularly the green "1" off Windmill Point at its mouth.

Provisions. Of the three marinas on the river, only one—Goose Bay Marina in Goose Creek, to port after you clear green "1"—is readily accessible to any but very shoal-draft vessels. The other two are at the headwaters. All are better left alone by anyone with a draft of 4 feet or more.

High on a hill at Chapel Point, overlooking the river, is the nearly 200-year-old St. Ignatius Catholic Church. The view from the hilltop is worth the climb.

NANJEMOY
CREEK

POTOMAC
CREEK

AQUIA
CREEK

286

The town of Port Tobacco, now a short distance beyond the headwaters of the river, was a busy port in early colonial times. Even though it was a major tobacco shipping port in the 1700s, the origin of the town's name had little to do with tobacco. It is a corruption of the name of a local Indian village, variously reported as Potapaco or Pertafacco.

NANJEMOY CREEK

Charts: 12285, 12288

The next creek on the Maryland side, Nanjemoy Creek got its name from an Indian word for "poor fishing." The tendency of the water to get a little thin and a maze of fishing structures, especially at the entrance, greatly reduces the creek's appeal. Blossom Point Proving Grounds is on the point to the east of the creek entrance, as is a 287-acre wildlife sanctuary, operated by the Maryland Nature Conservancy. Possibly as a result, this is one of the least populated creeks off the Potomac.

As a historical note, John Wilkes Booth rowed across at Blossom Point during his flight from the capital after shooting Lincoln.

I have been told that depths in the Nanjemoy are greater than indicated by the chart. However, unless you draw well under 5 feet, navigation is going to be touchy. If you try it, hug the eastern shore on your way in until you find the locally maintained buoys near Tanners Point. These take you the rest of the way up the creek to near Hilltop Fork—if your draft is 3 feet or less. Beyond the fork, get out and walk!

Gunkholers might like to poke in here once, but they won't find any good anchorages. The Nanjemoy's an unspoiled creek and would be quite attractive if it only had a bit more water in it.

POTOMAC CREEK

Charts: 12285, 12288

Potomac Creek, 9 miles beyond Nanjemoy Creek on the Virginia side, features a tight entrance, big mosquitoes, and thin water. If you draw 4 feet or more, stay out.

For the amateur archeologist, Bull Bluff on the south side of the entrance offers the possibility of finding fossilized sharks' teeth. You can anchor quite close to shore in 6 to 7 feet of water, but the area is exposed so I don't recommend staying overnight. This is also one of many sites that claims to be where Pocohontas saved Captain John Smith from her father, Chief Powhatan.

WAUGH POINT

Facilities. Waugh Point Marina, on the south shore of the creek near green daymark "5," reportedly has at least 6 feet of water alongside the gas dock (no diesel), but I have not verified this. It does have a dockside sewage pumpout facility.

AQUIA CREEK

Charts: 12285, 12288

Three miles above Potomac Creek, still on the Virginia side of the river, is Aquia Creek.

AQUIA CREEK

ANCHORAGE

Aquia is a reasonable anchorage for boats with drafts under 5 feet, although it shoals quickly outside the narrow channel. If you draw less than 4 feet, you can proceed upstream as far as the fixed bridge (vertical clearance, 26 feet), just over 2 miles from the creek mouth.

The Misbegotten Wooden Warships

On the Maryland side of the Potomac, about 5 miles above the mouth of Aquia Creek, lies a monument to bureaucratic stupidity, the remains of more than 100 wooden hulls of would-be freighters, constructed during World War I. This area is not an anchorage nor is it a place to take anything other than a dinghy for a closer look. However, if you are on the Potomac, swing nearby and take a look.

The United States entered World War I in April of 1917, nearly three years after its start. The German submarine campaign had destroyed so much shipping that the U.S., under the newly formed United States Shipping Board, hastily developed a bold scheme to build and deploy a fleet of quickly and cheaply constructed wooden steamers. The theory was that the ships could be built with semi-skilled labor and would not tie up the shipyards engaged in steel ship construction.

The Emergency Fleet Corporation, which was established to execute the task, was unable to live up to the theory's promise. The entire effort was mismanaged and uncoordinated. There were innumerable delays and costs skyrocketed.

Original plans were for the construction of approximately 1,000 ships in 18 months! However, it took eight months to place the contracts for the first 300 vessels. Within a month after that, the program was a case study in bureaucratic entropy. The wrong timber for keels and hulls had been purchased and the proper timbers were only available from West Coast lumber contractors. Railway shipping of the needed timbers from the West Coast was soon at a near standstill because transportation priorities were improperly planned. As a result, a parallel West Coast program for wooden ships was initiated. Controversy and infighting between the two programs was rampant. The U.S. Navy refused to man the vessels, charging that the ships were not seaworthy. The resulting design changes increased the costs and the length of the delays.

When Germany surrendered in November 1918, only 134 ships had been completed. Only 76 had ever carried any cargo, and these were in the Pacific; not one had been deployed to Europe, the original purpose of the program. The ships leaked, and couldn't carry enough cargo to justify their operating expenses. Even so, by mid-1919, 174 wooden ships were in operation with more on the way.

After the war, most of the ships were mothballed in the James River, kept afloat only by constant effort. Finally some 200 were sold for scrap. These were towed from the James and up the Potomac to Alexandria where they were stripped of machinery and equipment and returned downriver for disposal. Tied together with a steel cable, they were burned to the waterline at Widewater on the Virginia side of the Potomac, then towed across the river to Mallows Bay where salvage crews removed much of the metal.

The fleet was forgotten until the 1930s when the ships were searched again to recover any remaining scrap metal. The scrap was sold to metal-hungry Japan and much of it came back to us as shells and other weaponry during World War II. The number of salvagers and, during Prohibition, bootlegging operators in Mallows Bay caused a local population explosion. Well managed, very coordinated entrepreneurs anchored five houseboats in or near the "Reservoir" part of Mallows Bay. These floating brothels were known as Potomac River Arks. At least one of these boats is still visible, aground on the south side of the mouth of the "Reservoir."

You still can see the hulks of Mallows Bay's misbegotten fleet, as well as some more recently abandoned boats and barges in the "Reservoir." Some hulls are difficult to recognize; Nature has reclaimed them, turning a war effort into life-supporting islands of bushes and trees.

Dockages/Facilities.   There are a couple of marinas near Gourds Point on the south side—Aquia Creek Marina & Boatyard (by the point) and Willow Landing Marina—and another (Aquia Harbor Marina) past the fixed bridge. I am not sure of the approach depths but they are reputed to be between 3 and 4 feet. The Aquia Harbor Marina has a ramp, 50 slips, showers, and a shoreside pool.

QUANTICO
CREEK

UPPER
POTOMAC
RIVER

288

QUANTICO CREEK

Charts: 12285, **12288**

About 8 miles above Aquia Creek is the Quantico Marine Base. The boat basin, maintained by the Marines, is just before Quantico Creek. It is indicated on the chart by the word *bell*. You must get permission to tie up or use a mooring in Quantico Marine Basin from the harbormaster. Beware of strong currents near the approaches to the basin.

Do not attempt to anchor in the mouth of Quantico Creek. Aside from the shoals, there is a noisy railroad line nearby. The main creek is unnavigable.

UPPER POTOMAC RIVER

Charts: 12285, **12288**

This portion of the river does not offer great cruising but makes up for that lack by offering plenty to do. In spite of increased development, there are still plenty of

Mattawoman Creek to Washington, D.C.

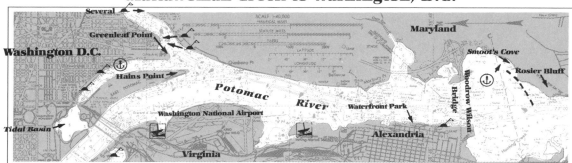

SCALE **1"=1.34** NAUT. MILES

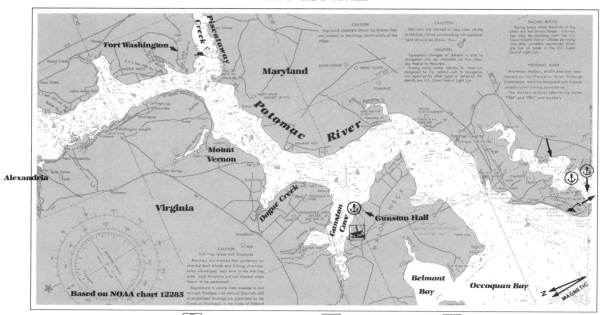

SCALE **1"=2.64** NAUT. MILES   ⚓ **Good anchoring**   **Mooring area**   **Launching site**

Based on NOAA chart 12285

anchorages in addition to the expected yacht clubs and marinas.

MATTAWOMAN CREEK

Charts: 12285, **12288**

About 4 miles above Quantico, on the Maryland side of the Potomac, is Mattawoman Creek, with its mouth flanked by the Naval Ordnance Station on the north and the Naval Ordnance Disposal Facility to the south. This is probably the first anchorage where you will encounter weekend cruisers from Washington.

Anchorages. The outer portion of the creek is convenient for anchoring, but exposed to the northwest. Better shelter lies farther up the creek. Proceed carefully to avoid grounding, especially on the 3-foot spot between the "5" light and Grinders Wharf. There is a good anchorage just west of Bullitt Neck. You can land either at Marsh Island or Thorofare Island to explore. Throughout the creek, the banks are heavily wooded and the houses are fairly well screened from view by shrubbery, giving a semblance of seclusion.

Facilities/Things to Do. Just past the first point to starboard on the way in is a small promontory, labeled Sweden Point on the chart. This is part of Smallwood State Park (often confused with Fort Smallwood State Park located in the mouth of the Patapsco River), developed by the State of Maryland. Currently there is a small pier and launching ramp, neither is large enough to handle cruising boats. In August of 1990 the park plans to open a 50-slip marina with full facilities (showers, laundromat, etc.); the marina eventually will have 200 slips. To ascertain the status of the marina, call the park at (301)743-7613. Until the marina opens, your supplies are limited to ice and gas (no diesel) if your draft permits. There is a small shop for fishing gear and sandwiches. The highlight of Smallwood State Park is the Smallwood mansion, home of General William Smallwood, who was a Revolutionary War hero and Maryland's fourth governor. The origi-

nal all-brick structure dated from 1762; the present reconstruction is open for a guided tour of the mansion, which is completely furnished with period pieces.

Technically you can continue for another mile beyond Grinders Wharf in at least 7 to 8 feet of water, but the narrow, winding channel is unmarked and probably will appeal only to the confirmed gunkholer. It is an attractive trip, through lily pads and past wooded banks, but a nerve-racking one.

OCCOQUAN RIVER

Charts: 12285, 12289

Anchorages/Approaches. On the Virginia side, the Occoquan River offers well-sheltered anchorages, all very far up a narrow channel beyond the first bridge (vertical clearance, 65 feet). The channel is reasonably well marked and supposedly maintained in excess of 10 feet since it is used by commercial barges. In fact, the portion of the channel that passes through Occoquan Bay has doubtful depths. Boats with more than a 4-foot draft are advised to proceed with extreme caution. Be sure to stay in the narrow, marked channel as the water quickly shoals to less than 2 feet out of the channel.

Swimming is good, but holding poor, and there is a current with which to contend.

Alternative Anchorage. If you carry less than a 4-foot draft, the southern quarter of Belmont Bay offers a possible alternative anchorage but you must cross a 3-foot bar to get there.

Although numerous large power and sail boats call the Occoquan home, we do not recommend it for the transient cruiser.

GUNSTON COVE

No facilities

Charts: 12285, **12289**

Approaches. Gunston Cove, bordered on the north by Fort Belvoir, offers a fairly well-protected anchorage in 6 feet of water, once you are well into it. The mouth is marked by red nun "2" near the southwest shore inside Hallowing Point. The rest of the cove is unmarked; you have to feel your way past the entrance shoals, a relatively easy matter.

Anchorages/Facilities. Once past the Gunston Hall Estate, you can anchor just about anywhere close to the southwest shore. You cannot anchor in the wide pipeline area down the middle of the cove and the Fort Belvoir Restricted Area takes up the entire northern quadrant. Pohick Bay Regional Park, well into the cove, has picnic facilities, a launching ramp, and a small dock (for very small, shallow-draft boats only).

Things to Do. Gunston Hall, the home of George Mason (author of the Virginia Declaration of Rights and Constitution and a contemporary of George Washington), is within walking distance of the boat launching area. If your draft is more than 2 feet and you want to go ashore, you have to land by dinghy. This colonial mansion, built in 1755, has been beautifully restored and preserved by the State of Virginia in concert with the Colonial Dames of America. Guided tours are conducted through the building and there is a classic boxwood garden on the side toward the river.

DOGUE CREEK

Charts: 12285, **12289**

A small military marina maintained by Fort Belvoir is located well up this narrow and shallow creek. Visiting the post itself is permitted, however, the marina is not open to the public.

Provisions/Dockages. Mount Vernon Yacht Club is on the north shore of the creek. There is a 50-foot–wide channel with 6 to 8 feet of water from the Potomac to the yacht club dock, where gas is available if you are in dire need. The yacht club welcomes transients who have an affiliation with another recognized yacht club.

The rest of Dogue Creek is quite shallow. Do not attempt it if you carry a draft of 3 feet or more; even then, be prepared to feel your way in and proceed slowly. This is not an anchorage.

MOUNT VERNON

No facilities

Charts: 12285, **12289**

About 1½ miles past Dogue Creek, on the Virginia side of the Potomac, is the famous Mount Vernon, home of George Washington. There is a dock where you can tie up temporarily if you want to visit the estate but you cannot spend the night. The narrow but well-marked channel, which you must follow to approach the dock from the main part of the Potomac, is supposed to have at least 6 feet of water (9 feet in 1984), but I suggest soliciting recent local knowledge if you are in a deep-draft vessel. The north side of the dock is reserved for visiting private boats. Visiting yachtsmen are welcomed by a security guard who collects the admission fee for visiting the grounds, if they have made the necessary arrangements in advance (703-780-2000).

Mount Vernon is open every day of the year, including Christmas. The schedule from March through October is 9:00 a.m. to 5:00 p.m. November through February it is open from 9:00 a.m. to 4:00 p.m. In addition to touring the grounds and mansion, you can talk to museum "interpreters," who can give detailed accounts of Washington's life at Mount Vernon and answer any questions. At least two hours are suggested for the tour.

PISCATAWAY CREEK

Charts: 12285, **12289**

overlook the Potomac River, with a view all the way past the Woodrow Wilson bridge to Washington, D.C.

The park and fort are open daily from 7:30 a.m. until dark. On summer Sundays, there is a parade ceremony which is worth watching; bring your camera.

SWAN CREEK

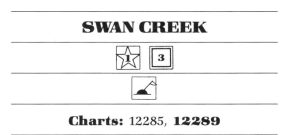

Charts: 12285, **12289**

Approaches/Dockages/Provisions.
Almost literally the "last stop" before Washington is Piscataway Creek on the Maryland side, less than 3 miles from Mount Vernon. The approach channel was recently dredged to a controlling depth of 6 feet. However, if your draft approaches that, proceed cautiously as shoals have a way of returning. The approach to Fort Washington Marina, your best bet for an overnight stay, is a bit on the thin side, even in the marked channel. In season, make prior arrangements if you intend to stay overnight. This is one of the few marinas on the upper Potomac that carries diesel fuel. It also has a dockside sewage pumpout facility.

Things to Do. Visit Fort Washington. Walk from the marina or, easier, land on Diggs Point by dinghy and walk up the hill to the fort. It is well preserved and, like the marina, operated by the National Park Service.

The original fort was too weak to withstand the British fleet, which sailed up the river to Alexandria in the spring of 1814. In September of that same year, plans were laid to construct a much stronger fort that would be able to repel a naval assault. However, the fort wasn't completed until 1824 and never received a challenge, not even during the War Between the States. Abandoned in 1872, the fort later was transferred to the care of the National Park Service.

You enter the fort via a drawbridge over a moat, which leads into a tower with a guardroom on one side and the commandant's quarters on the other. Inside the fort, the officers' and enlisted quarters (all restored) flank the parade ground. The battlements to the right

Dockages/Moorings. If it weren't for the Tantallon Yacht Club, located up a well-marked 4- to 6-foot-deep channel, Swan Creek could be totally ignored. Transients are accepted for an overnight stay, but yacht club affiliation is expected. Prior arrangements are recommended. To stay here, you must take a slip. There is no anchorage.

SMOOT'S COVE

No facilities

Charts: 12285, **12289**

Except for the Tantallon Yacht Club in Swan Creek, there are no safe anchorages or marinas beyond Piscataway Creek until you have reached the Woodrow Wilson Memorial Bridge, 5 miles upstream. This drawbridge has a vertical clearance of 50 feet and, therefore, rarely has to be raised.

Anchorages/Approaches. Smoot's Cove to starboard just below the bridge is a possible anchorage. Once you are in, there is plenty of water. The problem is getting over the entrance shoals. Use the red "90" lighted buoy just past Rosier Bluff as your turning mark. Swing to starboard to a course of 85 degrees toward the Maryland shore, feeling your way with your depth sounder until the water starts to deepen again. Then hold about the same distance offshore and follow the curve of the cove until you find a place to anchor. You must come back out the same way as this is the only route through the shoals.

ALEXANDRIA

☆3 1

Charts: 12285, **12289**

History. To port, immediately above the Woodrow Wilson bridge, is the town of Alexandria, a commercial and cultural hub off and on for more than 250 years. Old Town Alexandria was founded as a seaport in 1749; Scottish merchants were the principal city founders. Known as George Washington's hometown, this is where Washington and fellow patriots attended the theater, church, and political meetings during the formative years of the revolution. Until recently Old Town Alexandria was rather seedy, with rotten wharves and grungy warehouses. Today it has been named a National Landmark by the National Register of Historic Places. Changes are still being made to transform Old Town Alexandria into a center for shopping, dining, and the arts.

Things to Do. Just above the bridge is Waterfront Park where the schooner *Alexandria* is tied up. A classic Scandinavian cargo vessel built in Sweden in 1929, she was remodeled for passengers in the early 1970s. Her length is 92 feet on deck and 125 feet overall. *Alexandria* spreads more than 7,000 square feet of red sail and her planking is three-inch oak on eight-inch double-sawn oak frames. Formerly the *Lindo*, she was acquired in 1983 by the Alexandria Seaport Foundation, through its Compass Rose Program, in order to fulfill its mandate to preserve Alexandria's proud maritime heritage. You can board her when she is not reserved for a dockside reception, party, business luncheon or executive meeting. Her personnel can tell you all you want to know about her history and about the city of Alexandria.

Alexandria began as a Potomac River seaport. Today commerce and recreation share its shoreline. NINA TISARA/ALEXANDRIA TOURIST COUNCIL

Alexandria

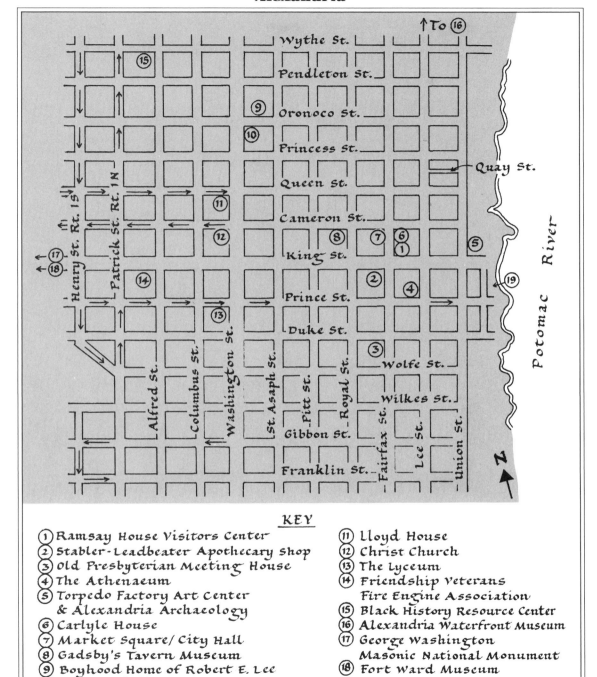

UPPER
POTOMAC
RIVER

293

Wythe St.

↑To ⑯

Pendleton St.

⑮

⑨ Oronoco St.

⑩ Princess St.

Quay St.

Queen St.

⑪ Cameron St.

⑫ King St. ⑧ ⑦ ⑥ ⑤
①

⑰ ② ④
⑱ ⑭ Prince St.

⑲

⑬ Duke St.

③ Wolfe St.

Wilkes St.

Gibbon St.

Franklin St.

Henry St. Rt. 1 S
Patrick St. Rt. 1 N
Alfred St.
Columbus St.
Washington St.
St. Asaph St.
Pitt St.
Royal St.
Fairfax St.
Lee St.
Union St.

Potomac River

N

KEY

① Ramsay House Visitors Center
② Stabler-Leadbeater Apothecary Shop
③ Old Presbyterian Meeting House
④ The Athenaeum
⑤ Torpedo Factory Art Center
  & Alexandria Archaeology
⑥ Carlyle House
⑦ Market Square/ City Hall
⑧ Gadsby's Tavern Museum
⑨ Boyhood Home of Robert E. Lee
⑩ Lee-Fendall House

⑪ Lloyd House
⑫ Christ Church
⑬ The Lyceum
⑭ Friendship Veterans
  Fire Engine Association
⑮ Black History Resource Center
⑯ Alexandria Waterfront Museum
⑰ George Washington
  Masonic National Monument
⑱ Fort Ward Museum
  & Historic Site
⑲ Waterfront Park

Note: Arrows indicate flow of traffic on one-way streets.

SCALE 1"=1,070 FEET

The Carlyle House is Alexandria's "grandest" house, built in 1752 and completed in 1753 by Scottish merchant John Carlyle. It is the city's only example of a Scottish country manor home. It is at 121 North Fairfax Street, two blocks up Cameron Street from the Torpedo Factory Art Center. Before the waterfront was developed, the Potomac River reached almost to the formal gardens at the rear of the house.

Above the park is the Torpedo Factory Art Center, which is home to 83 studios occupied by more than 165 professional artists as well as five cooperative membership art galleries, an art school, and an archaeology laboratory and museum. Artists work in the public view, so you can watch the art being created, may ask questions about the creative processes, and (naturally) buy their work. The art center is in a building which was constructed at the end of World War I for manufacturing torpedo shell cases. At the end of World War II, the building was used by the federal government to store documents and artifacts, and by the Smithsonian Insti-

Boating Season Activities in Alexandria

There are several special annual events that occur during the Memorial Day to Labor Day period in Alexandria. Busy waters and marinas will be more crowded when these celebrations take place. I have listed the usual time for each event, but you can get details by calling the Alexandria Convention and Visitor's Bureau.

- *Alexandria Red Cross Waterfront Festival*, second weekend in June. A celebration of Alexandria's historic importance as a seaport and the vitality of the Potomac shoreline today. Historic ships, boat rides, fireworks, children's events, ship tours, arts and crafts shows, entertainment, food booth, and water safety demonstrations. Admission.

- *Annual Civil War Living History Weekend*, date varies in June/July. On Saturday and Sunday, authentically equipped Civil War military units demonstrate camp life with drills, music, and a review of the troops at the Fort Ward Museum and Historic Site. Four miles from Old Town Alexandria Torchlight tours of the camp on Saturday night. Admission.

- *Annual Virginia Scottish Games*, fourth weekend in July. This two-day annual Celtic festival is one of the largest in the U.S. It features Highland dancing, bagpiping, national professional heptathlon, animal events, and national fiddling competitions, all at the Episcopal High School grounds. Admission.

tution for an urban archaeology laboratory that focused on 18th- and 19th-century items revealed in excavations in Alexandria. The laboratory/museum is still here but it is now Alexandria Archaeology and is open to the public Tuesdays through Saturdays from 9:00 a.m. to 5:00 p.m.; laboratory hours are Fridays and Saturdays from 11:00 a.m. to 5:00 p.m. Alexandria Archaeology is the nation's first municipally supported urban archaeology

program. The Torpedo Factory Art Center renovation has been hailed as an imaginative example of adaptive reuse architecture, but I think that, at least from the outside, it still looks like a torpedo factory.

Just inland on Royal Street, three blocks up Cameron Street from the Torpedo Factory Art Center, is Gadsby's Tavern Museum, which is known for its Georgian architecture. The tavern was a center of political, business, and social life in early Alexandria. (Birthright celebrations honoring George Washington were held in the second floor ballroom.)

Dockages. The Alexandria City Marina is next, probably the best place to tie up to land. It is easily picked out by the large wooden gazebos on its two piers. It is operated by the city and, unlike most marinas, is designed primarily for transients; there are no provisions for long-term stays. Even staying for an overnight or two requires special permission. The marina can accommodate about a dozen boats of the 30-foot class and 15 to 17 small powerboats; there is additional space alongside the pier ends. The dockmaster is on duty from 9:00 a.m. to 9:00 p.m. on weekdays and 10:00 a.m. to 10:00 p.m. on weekends. Transients are expected to arrive during those hours.

A little farther up is the Alexandria Waterfront Museum, actually the first of four locks built as a part of the Alexandria Canal. The tidal lock's excavation and preservation is portrayed in a 10-minute video; additional photographs, maps, and drawings explain how the canal worked.

WASHINGTON, D.C.

Charts: 12285, 12289

Slightly more than 2 miles above the bridge, on the Virginia side just south of Washington National Airport, is Washington Sailing Marina, where you can get facilities and supplies and make arrangements for transportation into Washington. To approach the marina, take your departure from the green "1" can adjacent to the main Potomac Channel and head directly for the pair of red "2" and green "3" daymarks that indicate the entrance channel. From there, follow the markers around the point into the marina basin.

Washington, D.C.

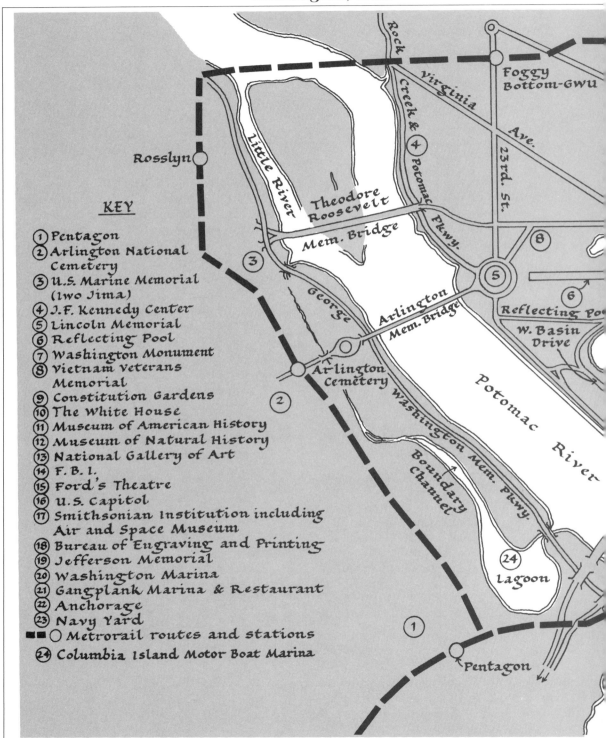

KEY

1. Pentagon
2. Arlington National Cemetery
3. U.S. Marine Memorial (Iwo Jima)
4. J.F. Kennedy Center
5. Lincoln Memorial
6. Reflecting Pool
7. Washington Monument
8. Vietnam Veterans Memorial
9. Constitution Gardens
10. The White House
11. Museum of American History
12. Museum of Natural History
13. National Gallery of Art
14. F.B.I.
15. Ford's Theatre
16. U.S. Capitol
17. Smithsonian Institution including Air and Space Museum
18. Bureau of Engraving and Printing
19. Jefferson Memorial
20. Washington Marina
21. Gangplank Marina & Restaurant
22. Anchorage
23. Navy Yard
▪▪◯ Metrorail routes and stations
24. Columbia Island Motor Boat Marina

SCALE 1"=1,900 FEET

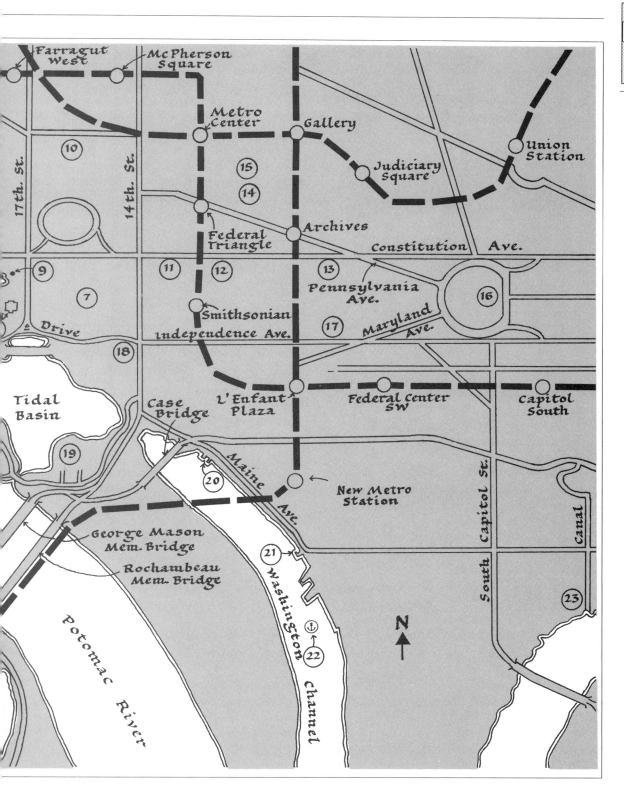

Farragut
West

McPherson
Square

Metro
Center

Gallery

Union
Station

17th. St.

10

14th. St.

15

14

Judiciary
Square

Federal
Triangle

Archives

Constitution   Ave.

9

11

12

13

16

7

Pennsylvania
Ave.

Smithsonian

17

Maryland   Ave.

Drive

Independence Ave.

18

Tidal
Basin

Case
Bridge

L'Enfant
Plaza

Federal Center
SW

Capitol
South

19

20

New Metro
Station

Maine Ave.

South Capitol St.

Canal

George Mason
Mem. Bridge

21

23

Rochambeau
Mem. Bridge

Washington channel

Potomac River

22

N

About 4 miles above the bridge, the Potomac divides into three "channels," the Anacostia River to the east, Washington Channel in the middle, and the Virginia Channel to the northwest. Haines Point divides the Potomac into the Virginia Channel, which is actually the main Potomac River, and the right fork or Washington Channel. A few hundred yards further, Greenleaf Point, on which is Fort McNair, divides the right fork into the Washington Channel and the Anacostia River.

ANACOSTIA RIVER

Charts: 12285, **12289**

Small powerboats can follow the Anacostia River almost to Bladensburg, but the route is uninteresting, except perhaps to history buffs interested in following the route taken by the British Marines who set fire to the White House during the War of 1812.

Dockages/Facilities. The James Creek Marina and Buzzard Point Marina, immediately to the east of Fort McNair, are on Greenleaf Point right in the mouth of the Anacostia River. Both marinas welcome transients.

Things to Do. A little above the South Capitol Street Bridge (a swing bridge with a closed vertical clearance of 40 feet) are the Port of Bladensburg & Safford Marine and the Anacostia Marina, both of which offer facilities and a place to tie up to visit the nearby Navy Memorial Museum on the Washington Navy Yard.

The Washington Navy Yard was established in 1799 and has been in continuous operation ever since. It is the oldest naval facility in the country. For many years, it was the Naval Gun Factory, the primary facility for design and production of large naval guns and ordnance. The United States Navy Memorial Museum, housed in one of the old factory buildings, is dedicated to the history of the U.S. Navy in war and peace, from the Revolutionary War to the space age. More than 4,000 items,

including the first working submarine built in the U.S. and the *Triest*, the deep sea oceanographic submersible, are on display both within the building and outdoors in the waterfront park. Admission is free, a refreshing change in this day and age. Museum hours are 10:00 a.m. to 5:00 p.m., seven days a week.

The next two bridges are fixed and the vertical clearance of 28 feet limits passage. Those boats requiring no more than 8 feet vertical clearance can continue upriver almost to Bladensburg, Maryland. The only reason I can imagine for making the trip is to be able to say that you have done it. I settle for the Navy yard or the marinas nearby.

WASHINGTON CHANNEL

Charts: 12285, **12289**

Washington Channel can be considered headquarters for most of the Washington yachting fleet. During the past 15 years, the area has been revamped as a part of the Southwest Washington Redevelopment Program. Initially, long-range plans called for a wide pedestrian mall along the waterfront with several hundred slips for yachts, a commercial dock, excursion steamer docks, and several other attractions designed to upgrade the quality of the waterfront. While far from complete, the redevelopment project has made significant progress toward these goals.

Dockages/Facilities. The main marine facilities, all to starboard as you enter Washington Channel, include the Gangplank Marina, followed by the Capitol Yacht Club and the Washington Marina. All accept transient yachts for a short stay. The yacht club expects you to have some standing with a recognized yacht club and, even then, discourages prolonged stays.

Things to Do/Where to Eat. To the west is the East Potomac Park with its public golf course and visitor center.

Hogates Restaurant and the Flagship Restaurant are easily accessible on the waterfront side of Maine Avenue. Hall's Seafood Restaurant is located on Buzzards Point at the foot of 1st Street.

For theatergoers, there is the Arena Stage, at the intersection of Maine Avenue and 6th Street. Depending on the play and the time of the year, reservations (well in advance) are recommended but not always necessary. The ticket office is close enough that you can easily stroll over to inquire about available seats.

At the north end of Washington Channel on the banks of the Tidal Basin is Jefferson Memorial. This monument is difficult to reach from here by foot because of the road pattern and traffic, but worth the trouble.

Ranging farther afield, a walk of about three-quarters mile takes you to the mall. Here you can visit the Smithsonian Institution to your front and left; the Washington Monument, White House, and Lincoln Memorial to your left; and the U.S. Capitol to your right. Often overlooked by tourists, the Botanical Gardens are to the right, just before the Capitol building. Directly behind the Capitol are the impressive buildings of the U.S. Supreme Court and the Library of Congress.

If you are not up to walking, the new Waterfront Metro Station (on the Green Line) recently opened at the junction of 4th and M Streets, just a couple of blocks from Washington Channel. You can go to L'Enfant Plaza and walk from there or change to the Blue Line and ride that to the Smithsonian stop. The maps are easy to understand and the system is designed to be user-friendly.

Once you have seen the main attractions of Washington, consider a visit to the Navy Museum in the Washington Navy Yard, 2 miles east of Arena Stage on M Street. If this is too far to walk, you might consider taking your boat around Greenleaf Point to one of the Navy docks or one of the marinas there. Check with the Visitor Center (202/433-3731) at the Navy Yard before you try to use any Navy facilities.

Washington has far too many points of interest to list here. In Washington Channel you are close to the heart of the city and within easy reach of most of its "must see" places—without traffic, parking, and related hassles.

VIRGINIA CHANNEL

Charts: 12285, **12289**

Approaches. For almost all sailboats the first bridge over the Virginia Channel must be considered the head of navigation because of the 18-foot vertical clearance of the fixed bridges. Powerboats may continue upstream some distance above the Key Bridge (which crosses the river by the Lincoln Memorial), to the vicinity of the Fletcher's Boathouse and the Kennedy Center—possibly a little farther.

Anchorages/Provisions. While the river does narrow down and you should follow the chart carefully (there are rocks here), the water is deep—7 to 36 feet deep almost from shore to shore. You can anchor here, but there are no facilities for cruising boats nor is there is any practical place to tie up and land, except for the Columbia Island Motor Boat Marina, which is in a shallow basin adjacent to the Pentagon. Fletcher's Boathouse, on the Washington side, is a possible site, but you have to ask permission there at the time.

REGION 6

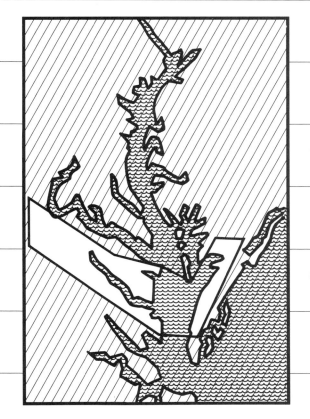

Potomac River to Wolf Trap Light

Potomac River to Wolf Trap Light

POTOMAC
RIVER
TO
WOLF
TRAP
LIGHT

302

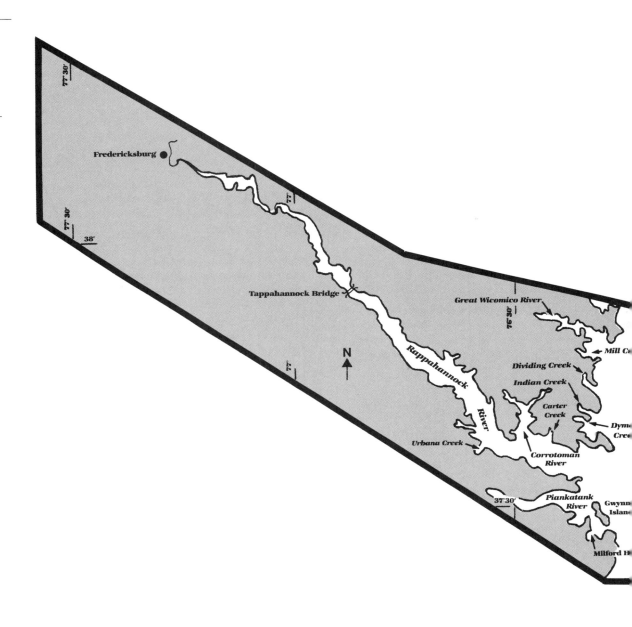

POTOMAC
RIVER
TO
WOLF
TRAP
LIGHT

303

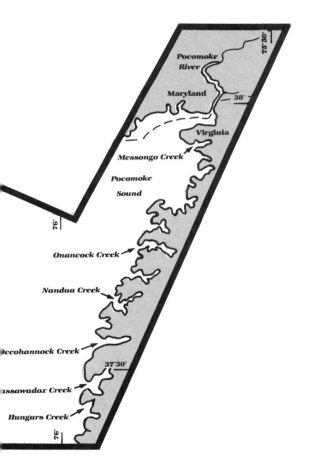

From the Potomac River on south, the Chesapeake Bay widens and the low lying land on the Eastern Shore makes the Bay look even wider than it is. For some distance below Tangier Island, it is more than 20 miles across and you can easily be out of sight of land, an unusual feeling for those used to the Upper Bay. The water is almost indistinguishable from the ocean, being only slightly less salty and full of comparable marine life. Although the average depth here is still only about 40 feet, the waves tend to be bigger and farther apart than in the more northern regions. While you are still in what the Coast Guard classifies as "semi-protected waters," you can almost convince yourself that you are sailing "blue water."

You are still in the Chesapeake Bay, however, and never very far from a sheltered harbor. If you are reasonably prudent and alert, you won't be caught out if the weather turns nasty.

Contrary to the character of the Bay farther north, the best harbors from the Potomac River on south are on the Western Shore. With a few notable exceptions, those on the Eastern Shore are small, shallow, and relatively difficult to negotiate. The rivers, creeks, and coves on Virginia's Western Shore are comparable to those on Maryland's Eastern Shore; they constitute the best cruising grounds in the Southern Bay.

Eastern

Shore

Although Tangier Island is actually located south of the Potomac River, I included it in Region 4, making it part of the Crisfield-Smith Island-Tangier Island triad.

Just about in the middle of the Bay, west southwest of Tangier Island, you find markings on the chart showing a series of shipwrecks within a circle labeled "Prohibited Area." When you cruise in this area, you see what appears to be a perfectly normal ship, apparently headed in an easterly direction straight toward Tangier Island. This, and the other wrecks, are all targets for a Navy bombing range, so stay away from them.

Southwest of Tangier Island and due south of the center of the "Prohibited Area," is another marking on the chart warning of the wreck of the *San Marcos*. (See Region 4, "Tangier Island," for more on the *San Marcos*.)

POCOMOKE SOUND

Charts: 12225, 12228, **12230**

Of the two approaches to Pocomoke Sound, the easiest is from the south past the southern tip of Watts Island. The other is from the Little Annemessex River, near Crisfield, through the Broad Creek dredged cut, which shortens the run through Pocomoke Sound by about half. However, the controlling depth for this shorter route keeps getting shallower, as it does in all dredged channels on the Chesapeake. If your draft is more than 5 feet, check on the latest controlling depth, especially at the southern end, before trying it. If you have a draft even approaching 5 feet, try this approach on a rising tide to take advantage of the 2-foot average range of tide. Do not attempt this if a strong northerly wind has been blowing for any appreciable period of time.

POCOMOKE RIVER

Charts: 12225, 12228, **12230**

The entrance to the Pocomoke River is via a 3½-mile–long, dredged cut, across The Muds 16 miles up Pocomoke Sound from the southern tip of Watts Island. As a result, most cruisers don't visit this river. Their loss, I say, because the Pocomoke offers excellent scenery and easy cruising in deep water, once you get past the entrance.

Approaches. Once into Pocomoke Sound, navigation is straightforward for most of the way to the cut through "The Muds," as the shoal in the mouth of the Pocomoke is known. Be especially careful of the large number of fish stakes, nets, and the thousands of crab pot floats. Be sure to honor the green and the red buoys just west of North End Point so that you avoid the shoal in the middle of the sound there. Incidentally, the white/orange buoys spaced throughout the sound mark the Maryland-Virginia border, they are *not* navigational markers.

From the last green marker in Pocomoke Sound, flashing red 4 second "12," make a small dog-leg to the left and head directly for the lighted green "1" at the entrance to the cut. Proceed slowly and carefully through the cut, sounding all the way. Be especially careful of shoaling in the section of the cut that closely parallels the shore. Once you reach the part of the cut through Fair Island, the controlling depth is fairly reliable at 6 feet minimum. As you clear the last green marker at the end of this cut, you are in the deep (11 feet or more) water of the Pocomoke River.

From here on, there are no navigational markers—none are needed as there is deep water from shore to shore and there are no noticeable protruding shoals. For about 8 miles, the shore is mostly marsh with occasional pockets of heavier vegetation.

Provisions. In Shelltown, to port a mile above the exit from the cut, the small country store has some piles and a bulkhead where a boat can tie up to visit.

About 4 miles up, you will see a pair of huge cypress trees right at the edge of the water. When you see them, look for a beautiful 18th century plantation house, known as "Thrumcapped" (not open to the public).

Eight miles upriver is the town of Rehobeth, which has a post office and a small country store.

Just above Rehobeth, the character of the river changes. Here the river passes between high banks lined with tall trees and the water itself turns darker, stained near black by the huge cypress trees lining both sides of the slow-moving, freshwater stream. This is the real cruising ground of the Pocomoke. Dense cypress woods, mixed with maple, pine, and dogwood, give the impression of virgin territory. The few breaks in the woods, which give glimpses of farms, and the few small boats tied at the water's edge do little to dispel this feeling.

Pocomoke City, about 14 miles upstream from the river's mouth, can provide all kinds of supplies, but you may have some difficulty in finding a good place to land.

Dockages/Anchorages. Pocomoke City Municipal Park offers 100 feet of service dock, but in boating season space is in demand and rare so it might be wiser to anchor and land by dinghy there or at the City Boat Landing, a little farther upstream.

A fixed bridge 1 mile above the railroad bridge at Pocomoke City limits further navigation to those boats with a vertical clearance of less than 35 feet, effectively making this the head of navigation for most cruising sailboats. Powerboats can continue for another 14 miles to the town of Snow Hill before shoaling and snags make further exploration unwise, although possible. If you continue 10 miles above Pocomoke City, you come to Shad Landing State Park, which has a 6-foot deep basin at the end of a dredged channel. Here you can anchor to enjoy this lovely park and its facilities.

MESSONGO CREEK

No facilities

Charts: 12210, 12225, **12228,** 12230

On the southeast side of Pocomoke Sound, between the long shoal extending to the southwest from Long Point and Guilford Flats, Messongo Creek looks attractive at a casual glance but is too shallow for any save very shallow-draft vessels, such as runabouts.

Anchorages. Boats drawing less than 4 feet can find a marginal anchorage just inside Drum Point, but it just doesn't seem worth it. There is nothing else to recommend this creek.

GUILFORD CREEK

No facilities

Charts: 12210, 12225, **12228,** 12230

Approaches. Less than 3 miles south of the mouth of Messongo Creek, the approach to Guilford Creek lies between two long shoals. Find the quick-flashing, 18-foot–high light at the western tip of Guilford Flats for proper orientation to start your approach into the harbor. From this light, assume a course of 105 degrees (magnetic) which is aimed slightly south of the tips of Flood and Ebb Points (you probably cannot distinguish between them from a distance). As soon as Lower Bernard Island comes abeam, swing in a wide arc to a course of 50 degrees (magnetic) to head directly for the red "2" marker northwest of Ebb Point. Leave red "2" and the red "4" daymark just beyond it close to starboard. From red "4", you need to take a dogleg to the north of a course directly toward the red "6" light east of Sandy Point. A course of 117 degrees from red "4" helps you avoid Bernard Flats to port and the shoal northeast of Sandy Point to starboard. The Muddy Creek green "1" northeast of red "6" can serve as an aiming point. When red "6" is approximately 45 degrees off your starboard bow; swing to leave it close to starboard.

Anchorages. Once you round Sandy Point, Guilford Creek offers a reasonably protected anchorage in 5 to 6 feet of water in the main part of the creek. Boats drawing 5 feet or less can find a nice anchorage tucked just inside Sandy Point off an isolated beach. If you are looking for seclusion, this spot is hard to beat.

Stay out of Young Creek to the south in anything but a dinghy. In spite of the encouraging red "2" daymark at its entrance, the maximum depth inside is 2 feet.

Muddy Creek to the east offers a challenge to the gunkholer. If you draw 4 feet or less you can get in, but feel your way carefully. The markers on Muddy Creek are deceptive. You cannot follow a straight course between them as the channel wanders back and forth. If you do make it in, try the nice little anchorage northwest of Poulson Point.

The upper reaches of Guilford Creek, where it necks down to a tight squeeze at Graven Point, are also accessible to craft with 4-foot drafts. Again, it is unmarked and you have to feel your way in. Do not proceed beyond the first point to starboard past Graven Point, there isn't any water.

With the exception of Sandy Point, the shores are muddy and marshy. The creek could be used as a jump-off point for a trip to or from the Pocomoke, but has little attraction of its own.

THE THOROFARE

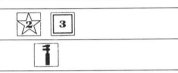

Charts: 12210, 12225, **12228**

"The Thorofare" seems to be a popular name on the Bay. Usually, it refers to a passage from one body of water to another through a section of land. This one goes to a deadend and the town of Hopkins, although it does provide a common entrance to both Hunting and Bagwell Creeks. There are a couple of reasonable anchorages, but no special attractions.

Approaches. The initial approach is the same as for Guilford Creek. First find the beacon at the end of Guilford Flats. From this beacon, hold a course of about 120 degrees, toward Simpson Point, until Lower Bernard Island comes abeam. Then swing to starboard to head south southeast until you can pick up the red and green markers east of Halfmoon Point, at the entrance to The Thorofare. Hold close to the green "3" daymark and swing a little to port after passing it in order to avoid the shoal off Halfmoon Point.

Anchorages. Once inside The Thorofare, you can anchor near the middle in 7 to 8 feet of water. Boats drawing 4 feet or less can find a nice spot tucked in the curve of Half Moon Island about 300 yards south to about 800 yards south southwest of the tip of Half Moon Point—take your choice but watch out for shoaling extending southeast from the point to an imaginary line drawn south southwest from green "3." The land in this area is so low that there is little or no protection from wind, but you are fully protected in all directions from waves.

Facilities. Boats with drafts of 5 feet or less can continue to follow the markers into Hunting Creek as far as the little town of Hopkins, where there is a marine railway and a concrete launching ramp. No supplies are available and there is little or no room to anchor, so come this way only if you have sustained damage requiring immediate repair.

Additional Anchorage. Bagwell Creek offers well-protected anchorage in near pristine surroundings for boats with drafts of less than 4 feet. Its entrance is easy, just swing to port past the green "7" daymark southwest of Weir Point and hold to the middle of the creek. You can proceed for about one-half mile, to where the creek bends sharply to the north, before the creek shoals.

DEEP CREEK

No facilities

Charts: 12210, 12225, **12228**

Approaches. It is 8 miles up a winding but well-marked channel to the town of Deep Creek. As you approach the green "11" marker just south of Scott Island, the channel narrows drastically to a dredged channel used by watermen from Deep Creek. This channel is for shallow-draft powerboats only, according to the chart. However, the local watermen claim that there is more than 10 feet of water at high tide. Whatever the real depth, there is little to attract cruising boats up this creek. Although the village of Deep Creek is probably one of the busiest fishing villages on Virginia's Eastern Shore, there is no anchorage here.

Do not attempt entering Island Bay. While you can get in if your draft is less than 4 feet, the numerous unmarked shoals make it slow going. Pass this one by.

CHESCONESSEX CREEK

Charts: 12210, 12225, **12228**

Approaches. About 2 miles north of the better known Onancock Creek on Virginia's Eastern Shore is the channel into Chesconessex Creek. It is wide and well-marked—a 5-foot shoal lies between "3" and "4"— until you reach the red "6" daymark, where the creek

Chesconessex and Onancock Creeks

SCALE **1"=1.45** NAUT. MILES   **Good anchoring**

 Mooring area   **Launching site**

makes a right-angle turn to the south. Do not head directly toward the next marker; the shoal between markers bows to the west. Keep red "8" on your port bow until you are about two-thirds of the way to it. Then turn to head directly toward it until it is a little more than 50 feet away before swinging to port and heading for the next marker. There is supposed to be a stake opposite red "8" to mark the shoal on the opposite side of the channel, but don't depend on it. The channel carries 6 to 7 feet of water all the way to the last set of markers.

Dockages/Provisions.

As you near the red "10" daymark, you will see some of the crab buildings ahead of you. On the eastern side of the creek, just past Tom's Railway Service directly across from red "10," is the North Chesconessex County Wharf where you can tie up to walk into the village of Chesconessex. From the channel, head directly toward the center of the wharf, then pivot to lay alongside. Be careful when approaching the wharf because there is little water to either side of it, although there is more than 10 feet alongside.

The marine railway has a gas pump (no diesel), but the water depth is debatable. Ask before trying to approach.

At the red "12" daymark, the channel turns abruptly to the west where it ends at the State Launching Ramp and a small service dock. There is a gas pump on the wharf, but if you draw over 4 feet you won't be able to lay alongside. Since the channel runs very close to the wharf, you might be able to get close enough to have the hose passed to you, but don't try this on a falling tide. You can obtain supplies at small country store here.

If you are the adventurous type, proceed a few hundred yards past the last channel dogleg—carefully, the creek shoals quickly. Other than this region and a small area to the east of the red "6" daymark near Tobacco Island, there is no good place to anchor out on this creek. The anchorage near Tobacco Island is exposed to the Bay on the west side.

ONANCOCK CREEK

Charts: 12225, **12228**

Approaches.   This is probably the most easily accessible creek on Virginia's Eastern Shore. The channel is well marked and maintained with controlling depths of 10 to 11 feet all the way to the town of Onancock at its headwaters, a distance of about $3\frac{1}{2}$ miles. In reasonable visibility, the channel entrance is found by orienting yourself relative to the southern tip of Tangier Island and Watts Island. At night the 4-second flashing green "1" beacon is easily seen from several miles away. If you do enter at night, be sure to have a good spotlight so you can pick up the daymarks.

Anchorages.   If you prefer to anchor out in seclusion, there is an excellent anchorage off a sandy beach to the north of the channel, just inside Ware Point. The area is well protected from wave action although the low-lying land does little to stop wind. The marshes here are attractive, but they do mean mosquitoes at night, so be prepared.

There is a secure anchorage in the mouth of Parkers Creek, about 2 miles in from the green "1" marker at the channel entrance. Parkers Creek has over 6 feet all the way to the last marker (this isn't very far), but it is probably best to anchor just inside the tip of East Point.

As you proceed up the creek, the channel narrows somewhat but still has plenty of room. The marshland at the entrance quickly gives way to farmland. The homes dotting the shore are widely spaced and many of them date back to the colonial era.

The Town Wharf is located in North Branch, at the headwaters. It is easily identified by a large sign which proclaims, "Onancock, the Cobia Capital of the World" (cobia is a food and sport fish). Dockage is free, but you may have trouble finding space on weekends. The waterfront is busy and noisy well into the evening. A more comfortable anchorage is in the North Branch basin or a little downstream near the mouth of Titlow Creek, also known as the South Branch.

Founded in 1682, the Onancock covers only a

square mile, in spite of having had 300 years to develop. It is still composed of a considerable number of homes built in the late 1700s through the 1800s. Scotts Hill, built in 1779, looks like the fortress that it was, complete with trap doors and hiding places.

Things to Do.   One of the better known buildings is Kerr Place, built in 1799. It is owned by the Eastern Shore of Virginia Historical Society, which uses it as a museum, complete with period furniture. It is open to visitors weekdays and Saturday between 10:00 a.m. and 4:00 p.m. for a small admission fee.

Provisions.   The Hopkins & Brother Store Museum on Market Street contains a general store circa 1842 and a steamboat wharf. It offers cruises to Tangier Island. Recently, it has added a small selection of groceries, a gift shop, and a small restaurant (open April through December) that serves three meals a day. Gas and diesel fuel are available. Since there are only a few transient slips near the museum, reservations are recommended.

Hopkins & Brother Store Museum with workboats at the docks. Gas and diesel fuel are available here.

The town has several shops, at least two drugstores (which serve meals), and a post office. There is a supermarket about 1 mile down the road and an ice house 2 miles out of town. You should be able to find all the supplies you may need here, although you may have to walk a ways to find it all.

Actually, it is worth the visit simply to walk around the town. As in most places on the Eastern Shore, the people here are friendly and helpful.

PUNGOTEAGUE CREEK

Charts: 12210, 12225, **12226**

About 4 miles farther south from Onancock, this creek rivals Onancock Creek as an attractive place to visit. The channel is deep and well marked as far as the town of Harborton, about 4 miles from the entrance. There are no good anchorages until you reach this part of the creek. Stay out of Underhill Creek—there's no water. Pungoteague Creek, itself, appears broad but wide shoals on both sides prevent you from pulling far from the center of the creek to anchor.

A quick-flashing marker lies about a mile into the Bay from the two points of land that indicate the (unnavigable) entrance to Butcher's Creek. The actual entrance to Pungoteague Creek is between the marshy Bluff Point and Finneys Island, about 2 miles northeast of the quick-flashing marker and nearby green "1" daymark, both of which are to be left to port on the way in. Just inside the quick flasher is a tilted concrete base, the remains of the old marker. The rest of the way into the creek just honor the markers; the channel is easy.

HARBORTON

Charts: 12210, 12225, **12226**

Anchorages.   Probably the best place to anchor for the night is near the red "13" light, just short of Harborton. You have room there to swing and on a hot night you can get a cooling breeze. Pull out of the channel to avoid the workboats, which will probably go out early in the morning.

Provisions.   Harborton has a public wharf where you can tie up to visit the tiny town. At the end of the dock there is at least 6 feet of water and gas (no diesel) is available here. Be careful as you move toward the end of the wharf where the gas dock is located, since the water depth is a little uncertain. An easier stop for gas is at the Eastern Shore Yacht & Country Club across the creek from Harborton. The post office is in town; the grocery store, about a mile down the road.

Past Harborton, the creek is unmarked. Taylor Creek shoals rapidly so stay out of it. You can proceed, with caution, nearly 2 more miles up the main (north) fork of the creek in 5 to 6 feet of water. Here you can find a number of secluded anchorages. Houses are few here, although there may be a little pulpwood traffic. Past Boggs Wharf, now only a ruin, the water shoals abruptly. Larger boats better stop, although you can still explore by dinghy for a mile or more up both of the remaining forks.

NANDUA CREEK

Charts: 12210, 12225, **12226**

Just 2 miles south of the entrance to Pungoteague Creek is the winding channel into Nandua Creek. The channel is well marked, but the shoals frequently shift so proceed cautiously. The controlling depth in the channel was 5 feet a few years ago; it could be less now. Approach the first marker at the entrance to the channel, green "3," on a southeast course to avoid the unmarked shoal on the south side of the entrance. (The first marker, a green "1" beacon, is over a mile offshore in 12 feet of water.) The channel is rather narrow until you pass Milby's Point and the channel hooks to the south. From here on it is wider and more forgiving.

NANDUA CREEK

ANCHORAGES

No facilities

Charts: 12210, 12225, **12226**

Anchorages. Once you are inside the shelter of Milby's Point there are several places to anchor, all the way to the headwaters of the creek. On the north side of the creek are several large homes or estates. On the south side are more modest homes and the village of Nandua. There are no marine facilities and the public wharf has long since decayed into nothing. The anchorages are snug and well protected and there is little traffic on the water. If you are looking for seclusion, you will find it here; if you need resupply of any kind, you are out of luck.

OCCOHANNOCK CREEK

Charts: 12210, 12225, **12226**

This creek is a pleasant, quiet place to visit, with some snug anchorages. The channel is easy to find from the Bay and reasonably well marked. There is a problem between daymarks green "5" and red "6," southwest of Killmon Cove, where it is shoaling in. Even so, if you can manage to stay in the channel, the controlling depth is close to 7 feet until you reach red "16," which is just east of Poms Point, well inside the creek. In that region, it has shoaled to about 5 feet.

Other than that, the channel is wide and reasonably deep as far as Fisher Point, about 2½ miles past the creek entrance at Old Neck. Beyond there, the creek is unmarked and the water depth is iffy. Those adventurous souls in shoal-draft boats might be able to pick their way as far as the fixed bridge at Belle Haven.

OCCOHANNOCK CREEK

ANCHORAGES

Charts: 12210, 12225, **12226**

Provisions/Facilities. At the place marked Morley's Wharf on the chart, there is the Wardtown Public Launching Ramp and a small service dock. Morley's Wharf no longer exists, save as a ruin.

Across the creek is Davis Wharf where you can get gas and visit the small store/post office. The depth at the fuel dock is supposed to be 5 feet.

Anchorages. That is the extent of marine facilities on this creek. It offers quiet, secure anchorages and a good place to visit.

NASSAWADOX CREEK

Charts: 12210, 12225, **12226**

This creek is reserved for boats drawing less than 3 feet and skippers with good nerves. The chart indicates that it is a tricky creek to negotiate—and it is. The depth at the entrance to the channel keeps changing. For several years, it has been holding between 3 and 4 feet, but don't depend on it. We recommend checking with one of the locals before trying the entrance. The channel itself is normally marked with stakes by the local boat owners, in addition to the standard daymarks. However, this plethora of marks can be confusing.

NASSAWADOX CREEK
ANCHORAGES

Charts: 12210, 12225, 12226

If you can get into this creek, you should be able to go anywhere once inside, giving proper consideration to the numerous shoals. You certainly won't be crowded by

other boats. Don't try Church Creek; the entrance is closed by a shoal.

Facilities. Hull and engine repairs are available at Zimmerman Marine to port beyond the radio tower. There is another marina to starboard, but it is private—members only.

The rest of the creek is a significant challenge to the true gunkholer.

NASSAWADOX
CREEK

HUNGARS
AND
MATTAWOMAN
CREEKS

311

HUNGARS AND
MATTAWOMAN CREEKS

Charts: 12210, 12225, **12226**

While these creeks share a common entrance, Hungars Creek is the only navigable one. Mattawoman Creek has only one foot of water.

HUNGARS CREEK

No facilities

Charts: 12210, 12225, **12226**

Approaches. The channel into Hungars Creek is marked for about 2 miles, which is about as far as you can expect to go. There is 6 to 7 feet of water until a little past the points of land that mark the entrance to the creek proper. Past that, it shoals to about 4 feet for a little over one-half mile. Beyond that, you would make better progress if you were to step overboard and walk.

Obviously there are no supplies or marine facilities on either creek. Hungars Creek offers some shelter in an emergency but, unless you are an incorrigible gunkholer, you should find more rewarding creeks elsewhere.

Western

Shore

LITTLE
WICOMICO
RIVER

312

As you pass Smith Point, just below the mouth of the Potomac River, note the wind and current conditions. A significant current can develop in this area, passing over or near shoals, sometimes with an opposing wind. Some rather impressive, although localized, seas have been encountered just outside Smith Point Light under these conditions. By moving your course one-half mile farther out you can improve the comfort of your passage.

LITTLE WICOMICO RIVER

Charts: 12225, **12233**

One of four Wicomico Rivers on the Chesapeake Bay, the Little Wicomico lies almost hidden beyond the tip of Smith Point at the entrance to the Potomac River. Unfortunately, the entrance shoals are constantly changing, so don't completely trust any charts or entrance instructions, including these, unless you first check with Smith Point Sea Rescue on VHF channel 16 for entrance instructions.

Even then, feel your way in. The bottom here is firm sand, so be careful. The current at the entrance is often strong. I recommend entering on an incoming tide.

LITTLE WICOMICO

ANCHORAGE

Charts: 12225, **12223**

Approaches. Make your approach to the jetties from the southeast. Assume a due west, or slightly south of west, course to keep Smith Point Light dead aft (to the east) until the red "2" marker for the river entrance comes nearly abeam. Then set a course for that marker. Don't pass too close to red "2." Once you can see the red and green markers at the end of the jetties, head to leave the green marker about 200 yards to port before swinging to port to head directly between the jetties. Past the jetties, favor the south (port) side where you should find at least 6 feet of water. As you enter between the red and green markers, note that the channel doglegs to the north as you pass green "3." The small island ahead of you must be left to port. Once past the daymark "6," you are in and can expect to find 6 to 10 feet of water in most of the branches.

Facilities.   There are three marine railways on the Little Wicomico, but the only marine facilities useful to transient cruisers are in the second branch of the river to the south. Look to port after passing red "4" for the daymarks leading to the two marinas. The channel lies quite close to shore. Don't hold too close to green "5" and "7." As you clear the point into this little branch, you can see the Smith Point Marina, which has ice, gas, diesel fuel, and some groceries. Jett's Marina is a little farther in.

Anchorages.   There are several anchorages in the other branches of the river, with 8 to 10 feet of water, where you can drop the hook in relative seclusion. Keep an eye out for bald eagles, which are known to nest here.

Just past green "7" is one of the Chesapeake's few remaining cable ferries. They are interesting to watch in operation, and this one you can ride for free.

GREAT WICOMICO

Charts: 12225, **12235**

The Great Wicomico River offers numerous anchorages in relative seclusion as well as several points of resupply or refueling. The approach is easy: Leave Great Wicomico Light, a steel spider, to starboard and you enter Ingram Bay at the mouth of the river.

From here, you have several choices. You can head

southwest to enter Mill Creek, which shares a common entrance with the Great Wicomico; north into Cockrell Creek for resupply, or northwest up the Great Wicomico itself, which has many attractive anchorages.

COCKRELL CREEK

Charts: 12225, **12235**

Cockrell Creek, sometimes referred to by the name of its only town, Reedville, is the home port for much of the menhaden fishing fleet. The fish processing plant is across the creek in what is actually Fleeton. If the plant is in operation, proceed well north of it to avoid its malodorousness. There are plenty of anchorages.

The area is unique in that it is the center for the entire menhaden fishing and processing industry. Here is where the fleet brings its catch to be turned into fish oil, meal, fertilizer, and scrap, which is used in animal feed, paint, and cosmetics. When the plant is in operation, the stacks emit great billows of "smoke"— actually steam from the process of drying the meal after the oil has been pressed out.

Provisions.   Jennings Boat Yard in the cove below Tims Point, opposite the large stack marked on the chart, offers gas and diesel fuel, as well as ice (block and cube), limited hardware, and a few slips for transients.

Anchorages.   The best anchorages are in the main, north fork of Cockrell Creek. This is usually far enough away from the processing plant to be practically unaffected by it, and the surroundings are quiet and pleasant, although heavily residential. You can continue up this branch nearly to the end before it starts to shoal. Anchor wherever it appeals to you. The entire fork is well protected and the holding is generally good. Beware of the unmarked shoal protruding into the creek just past the first cove to starboard. Favor the west half of the creek in this region. For the rest of the way, keep to the middle. Buzzard's Point Marina, near the end of the west fork of the creek, has gas and diesel fuel, and offers ice, and a few transient slips.

Things to Do. Visiting Reedville, a town included in the Virginia Historic register, is like taking a trip back in time. The only street in town is lined with homes from the turn of the century, the oldest dating to 1875. Part way down the street is a monument to Elijah W. Reed, the town's founder. The Reedville Fisherman's Museum, on Main Street just inland of the Reedville Marine Railway, is open weekdays from 3-5 p.m., and weekends 1-5 p.m. There's no admission fee, although donations are gratefully accepted.

Additional Provisions. You can either anchor in the east branch of the creek and take a dinghy in to the Reedville Marine Railway, or tie to the old wharf at the southern tip of the peninsula near the old ice house, where there also is a good machine shop. The ice house used to have one of the best block ice bargains on the Bay. As of 1989, however, it only carries cubes. Ten-pound block ice is available at the gas station about one-third mile up the road, a little beyond the church.

CRANES CREEK

Charts: 12225, **12235**

A course of 307 degrees from red "6" in the middle of Ingram Bay takes you to the first red "2" daymark at the entrance to this creek. The entrance is tight and just a little tricky. If you draw more than 5 feet, you may not be able to get over the bar just west of the tip of Bussel Point.

CRANES CREEK

ANCHORAGE

No facilities

Charts: 12225, **12235**

Approaches/Anchorages. Approach on a line with the two red daymarks and proceed slowly, holding fairly close to both of them. Hold close to red "4," then swing sharply to port, holding close to the end of the pier just past the marker, and head directly toward the sandspit on the end of Bussel Point. Squeeze past the end of the sandspit and you quickly find yourself in 8 to 11 feet of water in a well-protected basin. You can anchor anywhere in quiet rural surroundings here.

Overhead power cables prevent cruising sailboats from proceeding up the forks to either side of Bailey Prong. These cables are supposed to have a vertical clearance of 40 feet, but it may be a little less.

SANDY POINT

Charts: 12225, **12235**

While it is part of the main Great Wicomico River, Sandy Point gets special mention because it is one of the most popular anchorages on the river.

SANDY POINT ANCHORAGE

No facilities

Charts: 12225, **12235**

Anchorages. In the bight north of Sandy Point is a well-protected, deep-water (15 feet) anchorage off a sandy beach. The deep water holds quite close to the beach and the area is better sheltered than a glance at a chart indicates. There is enough room for many boats to anchor without crowding each other.

Things to Do. The point proper is excellent for sunbathing, beachcombing, building sandcastles, and (if the nettles aren't in) swimming. In years past, cruisers used to go ashore here to have beach cookouts. Recently, some "No Trespassing" signs have cropped up on the point, a trend in many parts of the Bay. You will have to figure out and observe the limits yourself.

HORN HARBOR

Charts: 12225, **12235**

There are other little creeks branching off the Great Wicomico before you reach Horn Harbor, but none is accessible to cruising boats; sand bars across their mouths block entrance.

HORN HARBOR

ANCHORAGE

Charts: 12225, **12235**

Anchorages. Horn Harbor, about 3 miles above Sandy Point, is something special. It is one of the snuggest hurricane holes on the Bay. The entrance is a little tricky but, once in, you find 7 to 8 feet of water.

Provisions. Just to the west of the entrance is the Horn Harbor Restaurant at the Great Wicomico Marina. Supplies in this area are limited to the gas and ice available here.

Approaches. The Horn Harbor entrance is unmarked and the numerous fish stakes around it add

to the confusion. Ignore the stakes and approach the beach about 100 feet east of the entrance, then turn to port to parallel the beach until you can turn directly into the entrance. There used to be some private floats marking the channel, but there is no guarantee that they are still there. Favor the starboard (east) side as you negotiate the entrance. Once in, dogleg to starboard to avoid the little shoal on the west side of Horn Harbor just after you enter. The surrounding fields and woods rise more than 80 feet above the water to provide near-total protection, which also means that you don't want to be in here on a hot, muggy summer night.

BARRETT CREEK

Charts: 12225, **12235**

Across from and a little upstream of Horn Harbor, Barrett Creek offers a lovely rural anchorage that fascinated us.

The mouth of the creek is crowded with confusing oyster stakes. They don't mark shoals, so it is best to ignore them.

BARRETT CREEK

ANCHORAGE

No facilities

Charts: 12225, **12235**

Approaches. Shoals protrude from each side of the entrance. The best approach is to continue up the Great Wicomico to just beyond Ferry Point, then turn and head right for the middle of the entrance to Barrett Creek. Once you pass between the two points of land at the entrance, swing to port and favor the east side of the creek the rest of the way.

Anchorages. Anchor in the region just short of where the creek forks. Here you have good holding in mud with 7 feet of water.

TIPERS
CREEK

UPPER
GREAT
NICOMICO

316

In the southern fork of the creek, a small peninsula juts into the water. Several times we watched horses come down in both the morning and evening to play here in the water and with each other, amusing us to no end.

Things to Do. Directly across from this peninsula, there is a small marsh pond that is nearly landlocked. When we took our dinghy in to explore, we saw raccoons, deer, and opossums as they came down to the water later in the evening.

There are few houses and no facilities here. You are likely to be all by yourself, something which is getting harder and harder to achieve on the Bay.

TIPERS CREEK

Charts: 12225, **12235**

Tipers Creek, just past Barrett Creek, is another tight little anchorage that few manage to find their way into. A bar here limits access to boats with drafts of less than 5 feet. If you can clear that bar, the entrance if easy.

TIPERS CREEK

ANCHORAGE

No facilities

Charts: 12225, **12235**

Approaches/Anchorages. Stay in the middle and squeeze over the bar off the tip of the narrow finger of land, which nearly closes the mouth of the creek, and you will find yourself in 10 feet of water in a secluded little cove. You can proceed about halfway up the creek before the depth drops to less than 6 feet, but the best anchorage is just inside the spit.

UPPER GREAT WICOMICO

Charts: 12225, **12235**

At Glebe Point, there is a swing bridge (vertical clearance 9 feet) over the river but it presents little obstacle to exploring the headwaters of the river. Until 1984, most cruising sailboats had to consider this the head of navigation because of an overhead power cable on the other side of the bridge which had an authorized clearance of 40 feet. Then a storm came through with violent winds, which snapped one of the power poles. Two poles were replaced with 65-foot ones, providing an authorized clearance of at least 54 feet at mid-channel—adequate clearance for all but the largest sailboats. Boats can continue to explore the river for about another 3 miles.

HEADWATERS OF THE

GREAT WICOMICO

Charts: 12225, **12235**

Anchorages. There are plenty of attractive and secluded anchorages. Except for Balls Creek, stay on the main part of the Great Wicomico since the remaining offshoots are too shoal. You can anchor just about anywhere in good security.

Balls Creek is also accessible for most of its length, flowing between high wooded banks. It carries a depth of 7 to 8 feet for about 1 mile before starting to shoal. The creek has no markers; none is needed provided you stay clear of the small shoal on the north side of the creek entrance. The high, tree-lined banks make this a well-protected harbor in blustery weather or storm. By the same token, it can be hot on a summer's night. There are only a few houses on this creek and they are

Great Wicomico River and Mill Creek

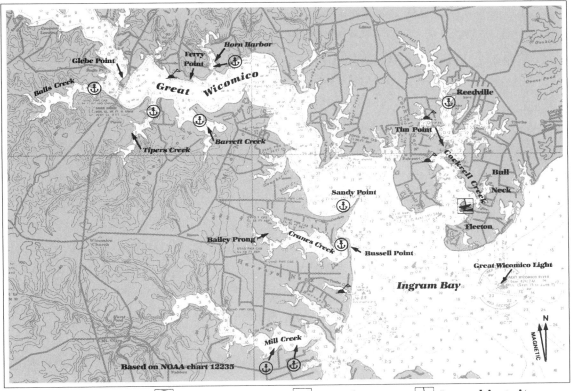

SCALE **1″=1.22** NAUT. MILES | ⚓ **Good anchoring** | **Mooring area** | **Launching site**

---

inobtrusive. There is a development, Tipers Landing, planned for a 192-acre site on this creek.

MILL CREEK

Charts: 12225, **12235**

Mill Creek, one of the prettiest waterways in the region, shares a common approach with the Great Wicomico. Once you pass the Great Wicomico River light, head directly toward the red "2" daymark, to the southwest in the mouth of Mill Creek. Be sure to honor the next two markers, giving green "3" a wide berth and holding fairly close to red "4." As you pass red "4," swing sharply to starboard and you enter Mill Creek proper. Favor the east side when you enter as a shoal makes out from the western point at the entrance.

MILL CREEK ANCHORAGE

⊗4 | 3

No facilities

Charts: 12225, **12235**

Approaches. The creek is unmarked from here on, but it has few protruding shoals to snag you. Just be wary of getting too close to any of the points of land. You can proceed nearly to the end of the creek, passing though scenic wooded surroundings that are dotted with homes.

Anchorages. Anchor anywhere that strikes your fancy; the holding is good in soft mud.

There are no facilities of any kind on this creek and

you will encounter few other boats. If you are looking for a quiet, secluded anchorage, this is it.

DIVIDING CREEK

Charts: 12225, **12235**

Although exposed to the southeast for most of its length, Dividing Creek offers some secure anchorages in its tributaries. There are no facilities here, so most of the people you encounter will be locals or cruisers looking for an out-of-the-way anchorage.

DIVIDING CREEK

ANCHORAGE

No facilities

Approaches. The approach is easy. Simply pick up the first marker, a lighted green "3" (there is no "1" marker) and follow the markers to the northwest into the mouth of the creek. Beware of the unmarked shoals off Kent Point and the point north of Prentice Creek.

Anchorages. There is an excellent anchorage just inside Jarvis Point, although you need to feel your way past the shoal on the way in. Take your course from the green "7A" daymark north of Jarvis Point and head directly toward the red "2" daymark in the entrance to Jarvis Creek. When you are about 100 yards from red "2," turn to the south and feel your way along the shoal to port until you are 100 yards past the end of the Jarvis Point hook. You can anchor just inside this hook or proceed carefully around the next point to starboard. In either case you anchor in 7 feet of water, well-protected in all directions.

To enter Prentice Creek, depart from a little upstream of the red "8" daymark west of Hughlett Point and head for the center of the opening into Prentice Creek, leaving green "1" close to port. There is good anchorage in 7 to 8 feet of water around the second bend. Some gas and ice may be available in Ditchley, but this is not a sure thing. This area is a little more populated than we anticipated; if you likewise prefer seclusion, try farther up Dividing Creek.

Lawrence Creek, about 1 mile above Prentice Creek, is easy to enter. Simply cruise in and drop the hook anywhere past the first bend. You shouldn't have any significant boat traffic.

The last anchorage is in the north fork of Dividing Creek where it bends to the north. The mouth of Natty Point Cove offers the prettiest anchorage in the area. It is quiet and secluded.

FLEETS BAY

Charts: 12225, **12235**

This bay serves as an entryway to four cruising creeks, Indian, Dymer, Tabbs, and Antipoison.

INDIAN CREEK

Charts: 12225, **12235**

Like Dividing Creek, Indian Creek is easily entered. It is also exposed to the southeast for more than two-thirds of its length and anchorages are to be found only in tributaries and in the last third of the main creek. Indian Creek has some excellent marine facilities and is much more built up than Dividing Creek. Even so, Indian Creek is pretty cruising ground.

Approaches. The approach and entrance are straightforward. Follow the markers, holding within about 100 yards of a line between the red entrance markers. The channel is wide and the only problem is an unmarked shoal to port off the southern side of the entrance.

Anchorages. The first anchorage is in Henrys Creek, to starboard just before you reach red "6." Don't try to enter Barnes Creek just inside Bluff Point. There is a 1-foot bar at the mouth of that creek. Simply stay in the middle of the entrance to Henrys Creek, favoring the starboard side as soon as you pass between the points of land at the entrance. Usually a stake marks the shoal to port and more mark the one to starboard a little farther in. Here you can anchor anywhere in 7 to 11 feet of water. The overhead power cable in the west fork of the creek has a clearance of 30 feet, so sailboats beware.

About one-half mile past Henrys Creek, Balls Creek opens to starboard. The entrance is easy if you stay in the middle as you enter; this avoids the shoals on either side. Balls Creek offers snug anchorage in 8 to 11 feet of water, depending on how far up it you go.

Longs Creek and Arthur Cove, to port and starboard respectively, each offer snug anchorage for the few boats that manage to squeeze in the unmarked entrances.

Pitmans Cove is one of the more attractive anchorages on Indian Creek. Stay in the middle on entering and anchor anywhere except in the inviting-looking cove to port. It's the only part that is a little shy of water. The bottom is mud and the entire creek is well protected from all directions.

Pass up Waverly Cove in favor of either of the two forks at the headwaters of Indian Creek. Both forks offer snug, well-protected anchorages in pleasant surroundings.

Provisions. The Chesapeake Boat Basin, located on the point of land labeled Kilmarnock Wharf on the chart deserves some special mention. Kilmarnock Wharf was once a steamboat landing in the long-gone days when steamers were a major source of transportation in the Bay. The marina is nicely laid out and has some transient slips, ice, gas, and diesel fuel. The marine store's inventory rivals that of marine wholesale stores. There is also a gift shop. The town of Kilmarnock lies about 2 miles down Wharf Road from the marina. Transportation to town can usually be arranged at the marina.

DYMER CREEK

Charts: 12225, **12235**

Like both Dividing and Indian Creeks, Dymer is exposed to the southeast for most of its length. Honor the markers on the way in and you enter easily. The best anchorages are in the tributaries or coves sprouting off from the main creek. Virtually all are readily accessible and—with the exceptions of Lees Cove, Chases Cove, and the unnamed cove just before it—all have 6 or more feet of water.

Facilities. There is a marine railway at the entrance to Georges Cove and the Ocean Boat Shop, with 165 feet of dockage, is farther into the cove. No fuel or ice is available on the water but transportation may be arranged into Kilmarnock for supplies if you ask.

Anchorages. The first cove to starboard on the way in, Rones Bay, makes a nice anchorage. Favor the starboard side when you enter, then just stay well offshore. Watch out for the shoal extending out from the northeast corner of the cove.

The third cove to starboard, Hunts Cove, provides the best anchorage on this creek. Stay in the east half of the entrance on the way in to avoid the shoal on the other side. Look for a stake, which you should leave to port. Once you are well into the creek, stay in the middle until you select your anchorage.

If you are looking for more seclusion, move on up toward the headwaters of Dymer Creek proper, past Chases Cove. Once up this far, you have a choice of relatively private spots in which to drop the hook.

TABBS CREEK

No facilities

Charts: 12225, **12235**

This creek is just south of Dymer Creek and shares a common approach. The entrance looks forbidding on the chart, however, we have been told that it has been dredged and that boats with drafts of not more than 5 feet should be able to enter through the privately marked channel. Proceed slowly; there is no telling when or how much this channel may have shoaled in. Once inside, you have 9 to 12 feet of water and are fully protected from all directions.

ANTIPOISON CREEK

Legend has it that this creek is where Indians provided Captain John Smith with a poultice that counteracted venom from a stingray's dart, hence the name Antipoison.

Approaches. As you approach the mouth of Antipoison Creek, there is an enticing little cove inside North Point to port. Don't try it—there isn't any water inside.

Antipoison Creek is well marked and the approach easy. Honor the red "2" daymark west of North Point and swing wide of the red "4" flasher before you turn to head directly into the creek mouth. As you enter, favor the north side to avoid the small shoal to port. Once inside, you will find 8 to 10 feet of water almost to the head of the creek.

Anchorages. The entire creek is well protected from all directions. You can anchor anywhere, however the best anchorages are in the first two coves to starboard after entering the creek. The first offers room for several boats to swing in 8 feet of water.

To get into the second cove, proceed far enough past the entrance so that you enter in the middle when you swing to starboard. This ensures that you avoid the shoal on the east side of the entrance. The shoal is normally marked by a stick with a cloth tied to it, but don't depend on it. Inside, there are several other sticks—oyster bed stakes, not shoal markers. This anchorage offers pleasant, rural surroundings with little boat traffic. You won't find fuel or marina facilities here but you

can find some supplies on the north shore at the Little Bay Ice & Seafood Store, under an Amoco sign.

RAPPAHANNOCK RIVER

Charts: 12225, 12235, 12237

The northernmost of three major rivers that penetrate nearly 100 miles into Virginia's tidewater region, the Rappahannock River bears a strong resemblance to the Potomac. Both have a long point on the northern side of their mouths, both have their best cruising grounds within less than 30 miles from their mouths, and both anchor their navigable headwaters in a sizable city (Fredericksburg for the Rappahannock).

Although the river is navigable for 95 miles of its length, extensive marshes begin just below the bridge at Tappahannock, 39 miles upriver. At that point, the river begins to narrow, the marshes become more extensive, and there are no more marine facilities upstream.

When approaching the mouth of the Rappahannock, give wide berth to both Windmill Point on the north side and Stingray Point on the south. When approaching from the north, you can cut inside Windmill Point Light by almost a mile and still be in 6 to 8 feet of water. The shoals come up rather suddenly. If you are not a very good judge of distance, hold close to the light. In addition, numerous fish traps and crab pots in the shallows of Rappahannock Spit drastically decrease the appeal of cutting inside the light.

Stingray Point Light, on the south side of the river's mouth, gives you no choice in approach. If you don't honor this mark, you may have to get out and walk.

WINDMILL POINT

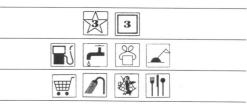

Charts: 12225, 12235

North Shore of the Rappahannock River:
Dividing Creek to Corrotoman River

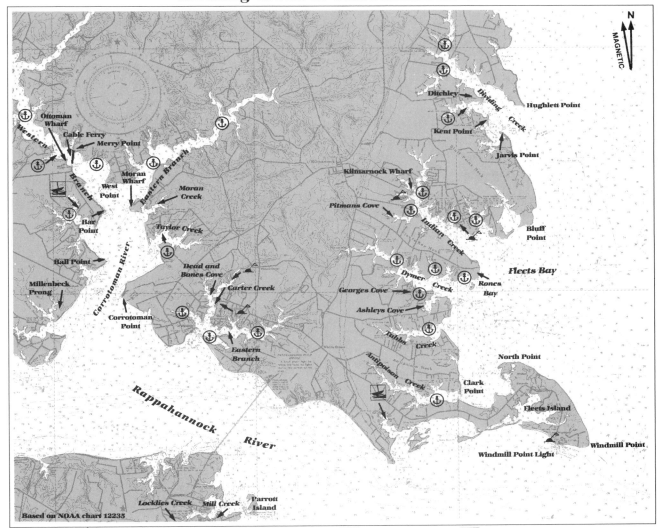

N
MAGNETIC

Ditchley
Dividing Creek
Hughlett Point

Kent Point
Jarvis Point

Ottoman Wharf
Western
Cable Ferry
Merry Point
West Branch
Moran Wharf
Eastern Branch
West Point

Kilmarnock Wharf

Bluff Point

Moran Creek

Pitmans Cove
Indian Creek

Taylor Creek

Bar Point

Ball Point

Dead and Bones Cove
Carter Creek

Dymer Creek
Rones Bay
Fleets Bay

Georges Cove

Millenbeck Prong

Corrotoman River

Ashleys Cove

Corrotoman Point

Tubbs Creek

North Point

Eastern Branch

Antipoison Creek
Clark Point

Rappahannock

River

Fleets Island

Windmill Point

Windmill Point Light

Based on NOAA chart 12235

Locklies Creek   Mill Creek   Parrott Island

SCALE 1"=1.90 NAUT. MILES   **Good anchoring**   **Mooring area**   **Launching site**

Based on NOAA chart 12235

Dockages/Facilities. On the south side of Fleets Island, just inside the tip of Windmill Point, is Windmill Point Marine Resorts. If you like shoreside, resort-type facilities, this is a must-stop location. Simply honor the privately maintained markers to make your way into the dredged basin. The channel tends to shift, and if you draw 6 feet or more entering can be a challenge. Forget any ideas of anchoring out; it's not that kind of harbor.

The resort is nicely situated on a sloping beach overlooking the mouth of the Rappahannock and the Bay. It has tennis courts, golf, a pool, pedal boats, bicycles, and a nature trail. All this is in addition to the "standard" marina facilities and a motel. Many townhouses have been erected nearby, indicating that at least some people who have come here decided to stay. The original resort developers of some 25 or more years ago, Dr. and Mrs. Wallace Atwood, are still (actually back) in control and looking after their enterprise with "TLC."

Don't try to enter any of the other inviting-looking inlets between Windmill Point and Mosquito Point; not a one has any water.

BROAD CREEK

All facilities

Charts: 12225, **12235**

Dockages. Just inside Stingray Point, on the south side of the mouth of the Rappahannock, is Broad Creek, a small harbor loaded to capacity with boat yards and marinas. On last count I noted an even dozen of them.

Approaches/Facilities. Depths are reported to be 6 feet at mean low water, both in the dredged entrance channel and the harbor basin. Most of the marinas cater to transients as well as residents. There are no restaurants here, but transportation to nearby Deltaville is easy to arrange. This is a good spot for repairs or other marine services, but if you are looking for seclusion, try elsewhere.

MILL CREEK

No facilities

Charts: 12225, **12235**

Approaches. The first navigable creek to appear on the south side of the Rappahannock River past Broad Creek, Mill Creek looks interesting at first glance. However, the entrance gets somewhat tricky after the initial set of markers. If you do attempt the entrance, don't try it in anything with a draft of much over 3 feet; it is shoal inside.

The only boats that use this creek are the local fishing boats. There are no supplies for cruisers in here; this is not a cruiser's anchorage.

The more adventurous may want to try the passage inside Parrott Island to approach Locklies Creek. You have to feel your way through and I rather doubt anyone would do it a second time.

LOCKLIES CREEK

Charts: 12225, **12235**

Approaches. Because of the shoals off Parrott Island, this creek is best approached by holding well out into the Rappahannock until you can line up the flashing 4-second 14-foot 4M"9" marker near the south end of the Rappahannock River bridge and the flashing red "2" marker west of Parrott Island. A course that keeps you about 50 yards east of a line between these two markers brings you into the channel entrance.

Anchorages/Provisions. Follow the markers at least to the first cove to starboard, which will serve as an anchorage for boats with less than a 5-foot draft. There are two small marinas in this area, but only the one by Locklies has gas and diesel fuel.

Past this point, the creek shoals and the chart doesn't give you much to go on. If you draw less than 3 feet, try it just to look. For spending the night, pass this creek by in favor of Carter Creek or the Corrotoman River.

CARTER CREEK

Charts: 12225, **12235**

Approaches. Just beyond the Rappahannock River bridge, on the north side of the river, the entrance to Carter Creek appears. No entrance instructions are necessary—just follow the markers. Past the entrance, the creek fans out into a spray of coves or branches of the creek, one of the prettiest in the southern Bay. Yopps Cove and the Eastern Branch are to starboard; the main creek continues ahead until it forks into Church Prong and Dead and Bones Cove, and Carter Cove is to port. Take your pick!

Dockages/Provisions. Carter Creek is a favorite with cruisers. In fact, its major drawback is that it draws too many boats! There are nine marinas in the main branch of the creek, including the luxurious Tides Lodge & Marina and the Tides Inn, plus the friendly and informal Rappahannock River Yacht Club. The latter has a tendency to attract big yachts. By the way, the Tides Lodge requires that men wear a jacket to the dining room after 6:00 p.m. and that women dress accordingly. There are several other less posh restaurants right in the area. A friend of ours says that there is a "neat maritime antique store in nearby Irvington."

Anchorages. The creek offers complete security—whether you tie up or anchor out—all the facilities and amenities you could ask for, and hospitable people. If you prefer relative privacy, put into Yopps Cove to starboard just inside the entrance, Carter Cove to port, or head well up the Eastern Branch. A tour around the

creek and its various branches clearly illustrates why it so attracts cruisers.

CORROTOMAN RIVER

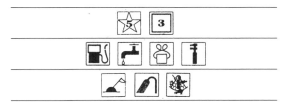

Charts: 12225, **12235**

Approaches. About 3 miles past the Rappahannock River bridge, the Corrotoman River offers peaceful cruising grounds where you easily could spend several days exploring or simply enjoying its relatively unspoiled, thickly wooded shoreline. Poke around all parts of the Corrotoman to take in the scenery. The few protruding shoals are well marked. If you pay attention to where you are going then trouble will be hard to find. Nearly the entire length of the Corrotoman has plenty of water (7 feet or more) for most boats. Plan to spend at least one day exploring it.

Anchorages. The first creek to port, just before you enter the Corrotoman River proper, is Whitehouse Creek. (This creek could be considered to be branching off either the Corrotoman or the Rappahannock, considering its location.) The Corrotoman has better anchorages, but this one recently became far easier to enter than it used to be thanks to some locals who installed private pilings, with tops painted to indicate the channel. The easiest way to enter is to depart from the lighted red "2" marker off Corrotoman Point on a course of 240 degrees. Use a depth sounder to guide your way into the creek's mouth along the edge of the northern shoal until you can come to a due south course into the main part of the creek. Here is a well-protected anchorage in 6 feet of water.

If your draft is 4 feet or less, you can also squeeze past the bar into Millenbeck Prong, which is to starboard as you are about to enter Whitehouse Creek. As the area is still subject to shoaling, this is an exercise for the more adventurous.

As you clear the red "2" light, Town Creek, the harbor at Millenbeck, is apparent to port. This looks to be a pretty harbor but it is rather shoal and full of oyster stakes and crab floats. There probably won't be any room at the docks for your craft among the workboats. You might find some supplies in town, but it isn't worth the effort. If you need supplies, you are in the wrong river.

A course of 063 degrees from red "2" takes you to Taylor Creek, one of the good anchorages on the Corrotoman. The entrance appears to be formidable, with 2 feet indicated on the chart adjacent to the green "1" daymark at the creek entrance. However, there are rows of sticks, which you can use to guide you to the green "1" daymark close to the east shore. Be careful of the pile to port (probably capped by an osprey nest), hold close to green "1," swinging to port just as you clear it, and you should have 6 feet all the way in. Inside you have a beautiful anchorage in 7 to 8 feet of water. Don't proceed past the point to the southwest where the creek forks since it shoals quickly.

Dockages/Facilities. The next creek, to port, is Myer Creek, which lays claim to the only marina on the Corrotoman River, Yankee Point Sailboat Marina, just inside the north fork of the creek. The marina has some limited marine supplies and a dockside sewage pumpout facility for holding tanks. From here, you should be able to arrange for transportation to a nearby store for other supplies.

Additional Anchorages. There is an excellent anchorage farther up this branch, about one bend past the marina. Sailboats cannot go past the marina because of the overhead power line (35-foot clearance) just beyond it. No matter; one of the area's best anchorages is in the left fork of this creek in 7 to 8 feet of water. With a few homes tucked back in the wooded banks, this anchorage is serene and at least gives the impression of seclusion.

Moran Creek, the next creek to starboard, is an inveterate gunkholer's delight. Don't even attempt entry if your draft is 4 feet or more. The entrance is unmarked and shoals are on either side. The simplest approach is to take a course of 35 degrees from the red "4" daymark northeast of Ball Point and hold it until you are about 200 yards from the bank by Moran Wharf. Then swing to starboard and feel your way in around the sandbar to port, favoring the starboard side of the creek entrance.

Just past the bar is a nice anchorage in 5 to 6 feet of water. You can explore nearly to the headwaters, but take it slow and feel your way.

Past Bar Point, 2 miles upstream from the river entrance, the Corrotoman forks into the Eastern Branch and the Western Branch, each of which is navigable for another 2 to 3 miles. Anchorages abound. Both branches are well protected from wind and wave. Pull to the side, out of the way of passing traffic, and drop your hook.

In the Eastern Branch, only Hills and Bells Creeks offer a reasonable water depth past their entrances. The most favored anchorage in this branch is in the mouth of Bells Creek, off a nice sandy beach. Stay out of the other small tributaries as they shoal quickly.

The two significantly protruding shoals in the Western Branch, off West Point and the point opposite it, are well marked. These are the last navigational markers on this branch, but prudent cruisers need no more. Unlike the Eastern Branch, most of the little tributaries in the Western Branch are navigable, at least for a short distance past their entrances. The large bight to starboard just past West Point is an excellent hot weather anchorage. Farther upstream are well-protected coves and tributaries if you feel the need for their additional shelter. Don't plan on proceeding more than one-half mile past Little Branch as the river quickly shoals.

You may still be able to get into John Creek, but I strongly advise against trying it due to the growth of the bar at its mouth—unless you are fond of dredging new channels. The same is true of Davis Creek about a mile farther upstream. Lowrey Creek and both branches of Senior Creek offer tight refuges should you need one, but they are a little snug for hot weather. Anchoring in one of the many coves on the main part of this branch is normally preferable.

Things to Do. One of the few remaining cable ferries on the Chesapeake still runs (since 1869) between Ottoman Wharf and Merry Point. If you approach while the ferry is in transit, leave plenty of room both ahead and astern of the ferry to avoid fouling the cable. One of the few free rides left in this day and age, there is no charge to ferry across the river. If you ever tour the area by car, try this interesting trip. Merry Point Mansion, built in 1767, is on its namesake point on the north side of the river. It isn't open to the public but is worth a look.

URBANNA CREEK

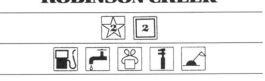

Chart: 12237

Like many rivers and creeks on the Bay, Urbana has been through many name changes. Its earliest recorded name was Nimcock Creek, but the source of that name is unknown. By 1680 the creek was known as Wormeley's Creek, after Ralph Wormeley who built his estate, Rosegill, nearby. In 1705, the town of Queen Anne's City was established. The town's name was modified to Urb Anna (Anne's City). It wasn't long before the creek assumed the town's name, both contracted into a single word, and so it remains today. Rosegill still exists and we have been told that it is worth the one-mile walk from the town to visit, although we have yet to do so.

Approaches. Entering Urbanna Creek is simplicity itself, although the creek entrance may be a little difficult to see from the main part of the Rappahannock. The easiest way to find it is to run a course of about 290 degrees from the red "6" bell buoy off Towles Point until you can see the first marker, the red "2" light on the end of the jetty on the starboard side of the entrance to the creek. From there, simply follow the markers on into the creek, favoring the starboard side after passing Bailey Point at the entrance.

Dockages/Facilities/Provisions. You will soon see the facilities offered by the four marinas there. The first one is really a restaurant (Windows) with 35 slips to accommodate transients. The other three are more conventional marinas, two of which (Urbanna Marine and Urbanna Bridge Marina) have dockside sewage pumpout facilities. You can find nearly any kind of shoreside facility here.

Anchorages. For the best anchorage, go almost to the bridge, opposite Urbanna Boatyard. While the creek is navigable for some distance beyond the fixed bridge, the vertical clearance of 21 feet sets the bridge as the head of navigation for all sailboats.

Things to Do. During the Oyster Festival (normally the first weekend in November), don't expect to find any room anywhere in this creek. If you want to join this three-day party, make your reservation at one of the marinas early in the summer. The rest of the year, this is a quiet small town, which prides itself on maintaining its character as a tidewater settlement. History buffs must tour the town. You can land just to the right of the grain elevators and walk in, or land at one of the marinas. The drugstore has great ice cream and the Urbanna Inn offers excellent meals. The library used to be a tobacco warehouse, circa 1777. There is a supermarket about a mile inland, as is the Rosegill Mansion (mentioned earlier). Urbanna's people are warm and friendly and willing to share tales of the town's history with you. Be sure to ask about Fort Nonsense, a favorite tale of the spoofing of the British raiders during the War of 1812.

However, for the seclusion of a quiet cove, try elsewhere.

ROBINSON CREEK

Chart: 12237

Dockages. One mile upstream from Urbanna Creek, the dredged 9-foot channel of Robinson Creek offers ready access to its two marinas. Unfortunately, the Joseph Conboy Shipyard is long since out of business. For boats with drafts of less than 5 feet there is some anchorage room, but there are more interesting anchorages in the area.

LAGRANGE CREEK

Chart: 12237

Approaches. Just above Robinson Creek is Lagrange Creek. A red daymark off Long Point gives promise of ready entrance to this 2-mile long creek. Unfortunately, the water shoals quickly a short distance past the daymark, limiting access to shallow-draft (less than 3 feet) boats.

Provisions/Facilities. Just over a mile above the red daymark is Remlik Marine, offering gas, limited hardware, and inboard/outboard boat sales and repair.

This is a powerboat creek, so much so that cruising sailboats cannot even enter it.

GREENVALE CREEK

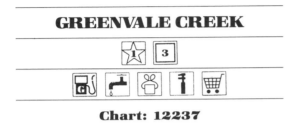

Chart: 12237

Facilities. About 2 miles above Lagrange Creek and on the east side of the Rappahannock, Greenvale Creek offers the facilities of two marinas where gas and ice are available. There is a well-marked, dredged 6-foot channel, which you have to negotiate to gain access to the creek.

Anchorages. Once inside, the creek opens out a little, allowing room to anchor between the two marinas.

PARROTTS CREEK

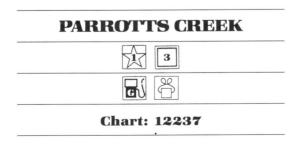

Chart: 12237

Three miles farther upstream, just below Punchbowl Point is the narrow, marked entrance to Parrotts Creek on the west side of the Rappahannock. Although facilities are available, this is a daytripper's country. Gas and ice are available at the Waterview Packing Co., but the water is too thin for comfort unless you are in a vessel that you can step out of and push. Cruisers should forget this creek.

TOTUSKEY CREEK

No facilities

Chart: 12237

Approaches. The creek is on the east side of the Rappahannock, about 4 miles below the Tappahannock bridge. There is a long, narrow, well-marked channel, nominally 6 feet deep, stretching from the red nun "2" buoy about three-fourths mile off Waverly Point for a good 3 miles upstream.

Anchorages. You can find some nice, secluded anchorages just out of the channel, where local watermen comprise most of the traffic. If you are a true gunkholer, try this one.

PISCATAWAY CREEK

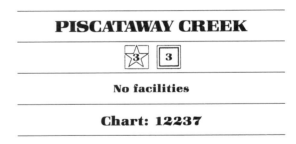

No facilities

Chart: 12237

Approaches. On the west side of the Rappahannock, about 2 miles below the Tappahannock bridge, Piscataway Creek offers an interesting anchorage to those with drafts of less than 6 feet. The entrance is unmarked but easy. Beware of a 5-foot spot just past the point at the entrance; from there to about 2 miles from the entrance you have 6 to 10 feet of water.

Anchorages. You can anchor just about anywhere after the first bend, fully protected from wind and wave. Not many cruising boats penetrate this far, but those that do are likely to want to return. There are no marine facilities of any kind here, so plan accordingly.

TAPPAHANNOCK AND UPSTREAM

Chart: 12237

The town of Tappahannock is located on the west side of the Rappahannock River, just downstream from the bridge (fixed, 50-foot vertical clearance). Gas is available at the Haven Marina, a short distance up Hoskins Creek. The creek was dredged to 10 feet a few years ago, but check locally or with the Coast Guard to determine when the approach was last dredged—it frequently shoals in.

Dockages/Provisions. Boats with draft of less than 4 feet can gas up at the Tappahannock Marina just above the bridge. Other supplies are available in town. There is no secure place to anchor so, unless you can take a slip at Haven or Tappahannock Marina, you probably should not try to spend the night here.

While the river is navigable for another 50 miles above the Tappahannock bridge (all the way to Fredericksburg), this is normally about as far as cruising boats ever go. There are no marine facilities or even really good anchorages above this point—just the simple adventure of exploring the headwaters of this famous river. Should you try it, make sure that you have adequate fuel and other supplies for the 100-plus–mile round trip. Don't count of refueling at Fredericksburg or anywhere along the way; you will have to haul jerrycans. There are no marine facilities above the Tappahannock Bridge.

PIANKATANK RIVER

Charts: 12225, **12235**

For those running north or south on the Chesapeake Bay, a favorite course is to follow the rhumb line between Smith Point and Wolf Trap lights. This course neatly avoids most of the fish traps and crab pots by keeping you in 30 to 50 feet of water yet well out of the shipping lanes. By deviating about 5 miles from this course, you easily can enter the Piankatank River. It is one of the prettier tributaries on the Bay, with a wide selection of well-protected anchorages and plenty of marine facilities.

The entrance is broad and well marked, but don't try to cut inside any of the markers once you are into your approach. Some markers will let you get away with it, but many won't.

A course of 255 degrees from the flashing green "1" buoy should take you a good three-fourths mile south of Stingray Point Light if you are approaching from the north. There is an extensive shoal extending to the east of Stingray Point.

If you are approaching from the south, head for the flashing green "3" marker, about 1½ miles northeast of Cherry Point, and come to the same course until you can pick up red "6." From here, you can swing either to the northwest to enter Jackson Creek or sharply to the south to head upstream into the rest of the Piankatank. Be sure to honor the red "8" marker southeast of the tip of Stove Point—the bar between this point and the marker has caught more than one unwary captain! Watch out for fish traps during your initial approach.

The river is navigable for some 15 miles, from its entrance all the way to Freeport, but most larger cruising sailboats are stopped at about the 10-mile point by the 43-foot vertical clearance of the fixed bridge between Wilton Point and Dixie.

JACKSON CREEK

All facilities

Charts: 12225, **12235**

Approaches. Right at the apex of the angle formed by the southern shore of Stingray Point and northern end of Stove Point Neck is Jackson Creek, the first of several excellent harbors off the Piankatank

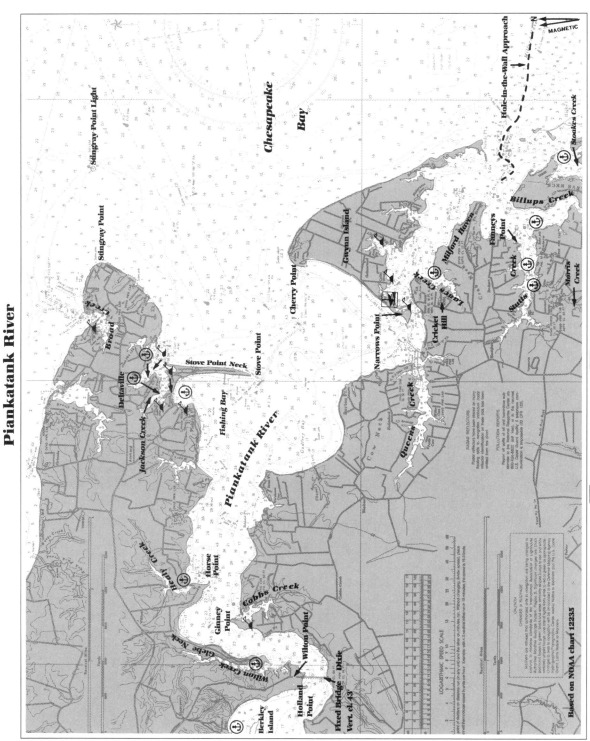

Piankatank River

Chesapeake Bay

Stingray Point Light

Stingray Point

Broad Creek

Deltaville

Jackson Creek

Stove Point Neck

Stove Point

Fishing Bay

Godfreys Bay

Cherry Point

Gwynn Island

Narrows Point

Cricket Hill

Lanes Creek

Milford Haven

Finneys Point

Stutts Creek

Morris Creek

Billups Creek

Stoakes Creek

Hole-In-the-Wall Approach

N MAGNETIC

Piankatank River

Queens Creek

Cow Neck

Berkley Island

Holland Point

Wilton Point

Fixed Bridge and Dixie Vert. cl. 43'

Wilton Creek

Cobbs Creek

Ginney Point

Horse Point

Glebe Neck

Healy Creek

RADAR REFLECTORS

POLLUTION REPORTS

CAUTION

LOGARITHMIC SPEED SCALE

Nautical Miles

Based on NOAA chart 12235

SCALE 1"=1.31 NAUT. MILES   Good anchoring   Mooring area   Launching site

River and one of three areas rife with marine services. Looking at the chart, you might wonder if you will have trouble negotiating the entrance. Indeed, the long shoal to port has snagged many a skipper who failed to notice the second pair of red and green daymarks ("3" and "4") close to shore almost due north of the first pair. The next two pairs ("5" through "8"), after you take a sharp turn to port beyond green "4," are also a little difficult to pick out against the shoreline. However, with some forethought and attention to where you are and where you are headed, the entrance can be made without incident. There is a minimum of 9 feet all the way in. Simply follow the markers and stay near the middle of the channel, as the edges rise sharply.

Facilities/Provisions.

Once past the entrance, the creek splits into two forks. The right fork contains the Club on Jackson Creek, offering a full set of marina services including gas, diesel, ice, some marine supplies, and a laundromat. In the left fork is the Fishing Bay Yacht Club. It tends to be crowded and you must be a member of a yacht club with reciprocal privileges in order to use the facilities.

Anchorages.

Both arms of the creek have good anchorages that are fairly well protected in most directions. Pick a spot out of the way of traffic and make sure you have adequate room to swing. The area is rather built-up so you may have difficulty finding a place to land other than at the marinas.

Additional Provisions.

Deltaville, a nice, quiet little town, is less than a mile stroll up the road from wherever you manage to land. In town are grocery stores, a hardware store, a bank, and a post office. There is also a reasonably priced, informal restaurant, Taylor's Restaurant, in the middle of the three-block-long town. Taylor's will provide transportation to the restaurant if you call them from a marina.

This little harbor is a welcome refuge from bad weather as you can get into it quickly from the Bay. On the other hand, if you are looking for seclusion, keep heading on up the Piankatank.

MILFORD HAVEN

All facilities

Charts: 12225, 12235

Approaches. I have a little difficulty categorizing Milford Haven, other than as the body of water that makes Gwynn Island an island. The main entrance is from the Piankatank, past Narrows Point on the western tip of Gwynn Island, and through the swing bridge which connects the island to the mainland. This is the straightforward, "easy" approach.

Facilities. There is a cluster of marine facilities, on both sides of the bridge on Gwynn Island. These marinas range from the full-service Narrows Marina, complete with motel, restaurant, pool, and laundromat, to the Gwynn Island Landing State Launching Ramp, which is just that.

Alternative Approach. There is another entrance, locally called the Hole-in-the-Wall, which is for gamblers. If you are heading north looking for a harbor or leaving the Piankatank heading south, the Hole-in-the-Wall offers a time-saving shortcut and a challenge to boatmen. If you draw less than 4 feet, give it a try but go slowly and watch the markers carefully. Entering on a rising tide is recommended. Do not try this passage if you draw more than 4 feet. As you pass the red "6" light on the way in from the Bay, feel your way carefully, especially between red "8" and red "14." Note that after you pass red "14" on the way in, the marker numbers in Milford Haven are referenced from the Narrows Point entrance, decreasing from "12" on down. So, when entering from the Hole-in-the-Wall, keep red markers to the right until you pass red "14," then keep red to the left as you head toward the Narrows Point entrance.

Once into Milford Haven, all you have to do is pay attention to the markers and keep an eye on the water itself. It is frequently clear enough to warn you of any shoals with a glance at the shelving edges. There is no excuse for going aground.

Anchorages. Anchorages abound so you can veto tying up at any of the marinas near the bridge. Skip Edwards Creek unless you are heading for either Powell's Boatyard or the Edwards Railway here; other anchorages are less public.

One anchorage is just inside the mouth of Lanes Creek where the depth just starts to decrease from 7 feet. Barn Creek looks like another nice snug anchorage, but we haven't investigated it.

Stoakes Creek, just to the south of the Bay entrance to Milford Haven, calls to true-blue gunkholers as it is totally unmarked and the shoals on either side require that you feel your way in. Again, if you have a draft of 4 feet or more, don't try it. No one should anchor here, regardless of draft, on hot, windless summer nights as the marshes are thick with mosquitoes and no-see-ums. The same holds true for Billups Creek, although the entrance is easier and there is 6 feet or more of water well into the creek.

Stutts Creek has the best anchorage, just about anywhere upstream of the mouth of Billups Creek. This creek is navigable (depth at least 6 feet) for a good mile past Fanneys Point and you should explore it at least once. It is a pretty creek.

The more adventurous might attempt to squeeze into Morris Creek to the south. Owners of larger boats should plan to ask locally or sound the entrance from a dinghy as the entrance might have shoaled in. If you can get inside, I recommend a snug little anchorage in 6 feet of water just past the entrance. Sailboats should not go beyond the first bend because the water starts to get shallow and the overhead power cable has a 30-foot clearance.

History. Gwynn Island deserves some attention. Its 1500 acres makes it one of the larger islands in the Chesapeake. Unlike most of the other islands, it has had a remarkably slow rate of erosion, thanks to its relatively sheltered location on the west side of the Bay.

The island was originally settled by a Colonel Hugh Gwynn in 1634. The legend holds that the colonel and two of his servants were admiring the island when they saw a sudden squall upset a small dugout canoe containing a young Indian girl. Upon rescuing the girl, they discovered her to be the daughter of the chief of the Piankatank tribe that inhabited the area. In gratitude, the colonel was given the island from which they made the rescue. He just as promptly managed to obtain an official grant to Gwynn Island from its English "proprietor."

Gwynn Island played a part in the Revolutionary War. After burning Norfolk, Lord Dunsmore, the Royal Governor of Virginia, assembled a fleet of more than 180 ships loaded with loyal Tories and some British troops, moved up the Bay, and took over Gwynn Island. Looting the island and devouring all the livestock, they then used the island as a base of operations, raiding other settlements—notably the Eastern Shore islands such as Tilghman, James, and Sharps. Dunsmore's group was finally driven off by the local militia, which mounted cannon at Cricket Hill on the mainland. It is debatable whether it was the cannon or the outbreak of fever, which killed more than 500 of the Tories, that really drove Dunsmore and company off the island. Today, a Coast Guard station occupies the site of the cannon batteries.

Until 1884, when a ferry started operating between Gwynn Island and the mainland, access was by individual boat only. The ferry has since been replaced with a modern swing bridge.

Much of Gwynn Island retains the flavor of an authentic turn-of-the-century fishing and seafaring community, despite the summer influx of tourists. The island has given the U.S. Navy and the maritime fleet many a ship captain.

QUEENS CREEK

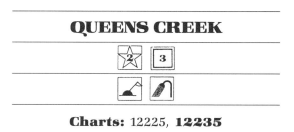

Charts: 12225, **12235**

Approaches/Anchorages. Just west of Narrows Point on Gwynn Island is a narrow, marked channel leading into Queens Creek. A few years ago, the controlling depth in this channel was 5 feet. Since then, chances are good that it has filled in so that it is something less than that. If you carry more than a 3-foot draft, check the controlling depth with one of the local watermen before trying it. The creek opens up inside, providing a fair amount of anchoring room in a snug little harbor with 6 to 7 feet of water.

On the other hand, the shore is relatively built-up and the Queen's Creek Marina offers little for the transient. Go for the better anchorages farther upstream.

FISHING BAY

Charts: 12225, **12235**

Anchorages/Moorings. With a little imagination, the chart representation of Stove Point Neck looks like the head of a pterodactyl. Beneath the dinosaur's neck and west of the thin peninsula forming its beak lies Fishing Bay, one of the most popular anchorages on the Piankatank. Unfortunately, save for the set of marinas located here, all the property is private. The marinas have put in a number of moorings recently, but there is still plenty of room in which to anchor. On a hot, windless, summer night, this may well be the best place in the area to spend the night. It is well protected but still sufficiently open to the south and southwest to permit even the slightest breeze of southwesterly air (usually bug-free) to move over and through your boat.

Facilities. The marinas on the western side of Fishing Bay are sometimes a little difficult to pick out as you enter. You can find just about any marine facility you need, from ice to complete engine and hull repair. Fishing Bay Marina also has a pool (necessary if the nettles are in).

This is a nice but busy anchorage. For a snugger, more secluded harbor, investigate the remaining creeks and harbors upstream on the Piankatank.

HEALY CREEK

No facilities

Charts: 12225, **12235**

Approaches. Healy Creek, on the north shore of the Piankatank, is easier to enter than the chart might lead you to believe. Beware of the unmarked shoal on the east side of the approach to the creek entrance. Stay near the middle of the Piankatank until you can line up the first set of daymarks at the Healy Creek channel entrance. Do not confuse these with the red "14" Piankatank River daymark southeast of Horse Point. Once the entrance markers are lined up, head directly for them and be sure to keep them on the correct side of you. At the last marker, head directly for the opening, which should be clearly visible at this stage.

Anchorages. There is an exceptional anchorage just past the sandy hook at the entrance. You can anchor anywhere from just inside the entrance to the fork in the creek in about 7 feet of water. Here you will find a few slips, which belong to the Horse Point Estate and Marina, and a couple of other boats already at anchor. The marina has no facilities for transients.

The whole creek is quiet and relatively secluded. It provides plenty of protection from wind and wave in a blow but is still open enough to permit a cooling breeze in hot weather.

COBBS CREEK

Charts: 12225, **12235**

Approaches/Anchorages. On the south shore of the Piankatank, just east of Ginney Point, is Cobbs Creek, offering an excellent, sheltered anchorage in 8 feet of water. The approach is straightforward, but be careful of the shoal north of the final red daymark. After you clear the sandy hook to port at the creek mouth you can drop your hook. Aside from a few watermen, you probably won't find much boat traffic.

Provisions/Dockages. Ginney Point Marina is located here but all you are likely to obtain is ice or, possibly, a slip for the night. Most cruisers just anchor.

WILTON CREEK

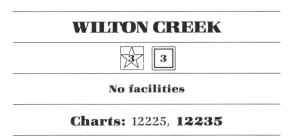

No facilities

Charts: 12225, **12235**

This is our favorite anchorage on the Piankatank—partly due to the attractiveness of the creek itself and partly due to some special memories we have of the place. It was here that our daughters (both still preschool at the time) learned to row the dinghy by themselves. They insisted that they knew how, so we tied 100 feet of line to the painter of the dinghy and "cast them adrift." Within 15 minutes, they each learned to row well enough to get the dinghy more or less to where they wanted to go.

About that time, a local resident rowed over and offered to let us land on his dock if we wanted to stretch our legs. Then he asked if we needed any ice or if he could drive us into town for supplies! We didn't need anything, but is it any wonder that we have a warm feeling for the place?

Approaches/Anchorages. Although unmarked, the entrance is easy. Swing wide around the southern tip of Glebe Neck and head directly into the mouth of the creek. Once in, there is 8 feet of water, gradually decreasing in depth to about 5 feet a mile upstream. There are 10- to 20-foot cliffs on either bank for a good portion of the creek's length. Anywhere in here is snug anchorage. The icing on the cake is the creek's

Two young Shellenbergers fish from their dinghy. Wilton Creek is where they learned to row by themselves.

north-south orientation, which allows a cooling breeze from the typical southerly in hot weather.

If you are looking for a snug, secluded anchorage in beautiful surroundings, stop in here.

WILTON POINT BRIDGE

AND UPSTREAM

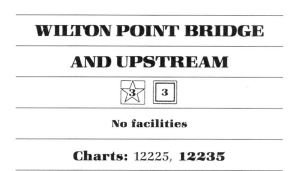

No facilities

Charts: 12225, **12235**

Approaches. The 43-foot vertical clearance of the fixed bridge between Wilton Point and Dixie makes this the head of navigation for most cruising sailboats. Some excellent cruising grounds await those who can get past the bridge. The overhead power lines just past the bridge have a vertical clearance of 68 feet, and so present no problem.

After passing through the bridge, swing wide around the tip of Wilton Point and head directly toward the east end of Berkley Island. This takes you past the unmarked shoal off Holland Point. The best anchorage is in 9 feet of water, north of Berkley Island. The island is uninhabited but has two docks, which facilitate landing should you wish to explore; one is on the north side, the other on the west side of the island.

Anchorages. The west side of the island is relatively high, tapering down toward the east until it ends in a long shoal extending to the southeast of the island. Holding is good and the whole area is relatively wild. Since few cruising boats penetrate this far, this area offers seclusion.

The deep water continues for several miles upstream, all the way to Freeport. There are several potential anchorages from which to pick; most are comparatively exposed. By far the best is the one by Berkeley Island. You have to contend with several unmarked shoals, but if you simply avoid all points of land, you should have no trouble.

You cannot get supplies in this part of the Piankatank.

REGION 7

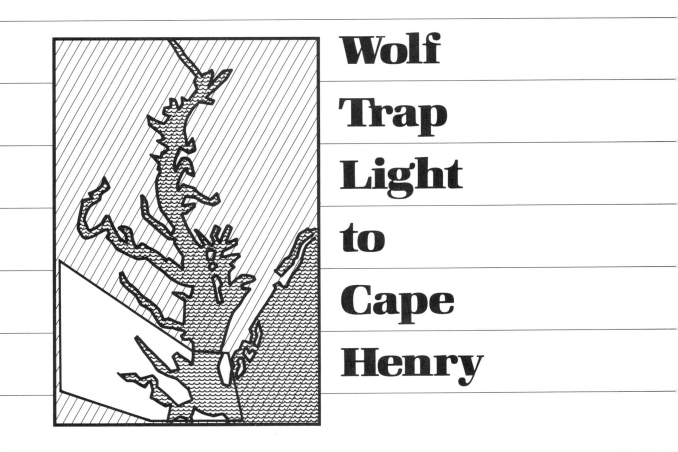

Wolf Trap Light to Cape Henry

WOLF
TRAP
LIGHT
TO
CAPE
HENRY

336

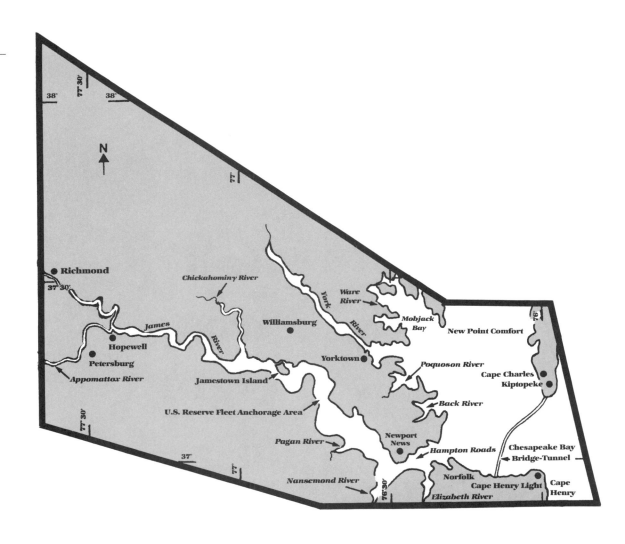

From Wolf Trap Light on south, you are in the bottom of the Bay. Here the wave action is similar to that near the Atlantic Coast in this latitude until the edge of the continental shelf. However, you are still in semi-protected waters and won't experience anything like the wave heights encountered in the open ocean. This is still the Chesapeake Bay, until you proceed past the protection of Cape Henry and Cape Charles into the Atlantic Ocean proper.

Wolf Trap Light is placed to warn shipping traffic of the Wolf Trap Shoal. This shoal extends eastward from the western shore, approximately in the middle of a 10-mile stretch from the "Hole in the Wall" entrance to Milford Haven (south of Gwynn Island) to the mouth of Mobjack Bay, which is devoid of hospitable harbors (with the possible exception of Horn Harbor about 3 miles north of New Point Comfort). Wolf Trap Shoal takes its name from the British frigate, *HMS Wolf*, which ran aground thereby trapping itself on this shoal during the American Revolution. The frigate was captured by American revolutionaries, reputedly local watermen!

The shores in the four cardinal directions in this part of the Bay each have a distinct and different character. To the south is the cosmopolitan atmosphere of Norfolk with the conspicuous presence of the enormous ships docked or anchored by the Navy base. This is Hampton Roads, made famous by the classic battle between the first Union and Confederate ironclad ships, the *Monitor* and the *Merrimack* (renamed the *Virginia*). Here, also, is the entrance to the channels of the Intracoastal Waterway leading all the way to Florida.

To the southwest and west are the cruising grounds of the York and James Rivers, as well as the numerous tributaries fanning off Mobjack Bay.

To the north is the entire balance of the Chesapeake Bay with its fantastic collection of creeks, rivers, and harbors luring the cruiser.

To the east is the bottom of the Delmarva peninsula where there are only a few harbors to be found and explored by the cruiser, unusual for anywhere on the Chesapeake.

WOLF
TRAP
LIGHT
TO
CAPE
HENRY

337

The 17.6-mile Chesapeake Bay Bridge-Tunnel connects the Eastern Shore with the Virginia mainland.

CHEERYSTONE
INLET,
KINGS
CREEK
AND
CAPE
CHARLES
HARBOR

338

Eastern
Shore

South of Wolf Trap Light, there are few harbors on the Eastern shore of the Chesapeake. The real cruising grounds are on the western shore. There are only three sets of harbors worth mentioning here; the cluster of three harbors around Cherrystone Inlet, Kiptopeke Harbor of Refuge, and Cape Charles Channel. There are a few other creeks shown on the chart, but none of them are even close to navigable.

CHERRYSTONE INLET, KINGS CREEK, AND CAPE CHARLES HARBOR

Charts: 12221, 12222, **12224**

These three harbors, the last natural ones on the Eastern Shore, have been lumped together here because they share the same approach. The entrance is relatively long, but well marked. Interestingly enough, you can safely ignore the first few markers in the entrance channel (all of those associated with Bar Channel), and directly approach the red "4" lighted spar near the beginning of Cherrystone Inlet Channel. From red "4" on, remain in the marked channel. At night there are ranges for each of these channels which bring you safely to the mouth of Cape Charles Harbor. Range A for Bar Channel, which runs from the Bay to the quick-flashing red "2" channel marker at the start of Cape Charles Harbor Channel, consists of a quick-flashing 19-foot-high front range light and an equal interval 6-second 33-foot-high rear range light. Range B, from the quick-flashing red "2" channel marker to the entrance to Cape Charles Harbor Basin, is a quick-flashing red 16-foot-high front range light and an equal interval rear range light.

CAPE CHARLES
HARBOR

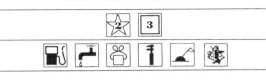

Charts: 12221, 12222, **12224**

As you proceed through Cherrystone Inlet Channel, the harbor basin appears off your starboard bow. Immediately to starboard as you enter the basin is the Cape Charles Refuel Dock where ice, gas, and diesel fuel are available. Here is where you can arrange for a slip in the landlocked municipal basin behind the Coast Guard Station. It is possible to tie up here with no charge, long enough to go into town and return. Most of the bulkheads along the harbor basin are taken up by commercial clamming boats so you are not likely to find space to tie up. You can anchor past the ferry slips provided that there is not a strong west wind.

Provisions. Cape Charles has several stores along its main street where you can obtain supplies. There are also a couple of good restaurants and two hotels. Outside of the main street, the town is residential with several stately old homes which are worth the stroll to see.

Dockages. Unless you rent a slip at the Municipal Marina, we recommend proceeding on to either Kings Creek or Cherrystone Inlet to spend the night. The harbor is open to the west and there is only a little room to anchor.

KINGS CREEK

Charts: 12221, 12222, **12224**

The entrance to Cape Charles Harbor, looking south. VA MARINE RESOURCES COMMISSION

Kings Creek is still relatively unspoiled. The shore is lined with a marsh, backed by pine trees with a few houses scattered among them. The only drawback is that it is unreachable by boats with drafts of 5 feet or more. If you draw less than 5 feet you can find your way at least as far as Kings Creek Marina on the south shore, just inside the entrance. There is an overhead power cable (vertical clearance 33 feet) but no cruising sailboat has any business going that far in; the water depth quickly drops to well under 4 feet, with 1 foot not uncommon.

Approaches/Provisions. Simply follow the markers into the creek, proceeding cautiously and checking the depth as you go. You will see the marina to starboard. Head into it just before reaching daymark "10." However, if you had trouble getting into the Kings Creek channel, you won't make it to the marina nor will you get much farther upstream. Head back out and try Cherrystone Inlet.

CHERRYSTONE

INLET

★4	3

No facilities

Charts: 12221, 12222, **12224**

Approaches. To get into Cherrystone Inlet, just continue up the channel, past Kings Creek, and head for Wescott Point. Keep close to the spit making up Wescott Point to avoid the shoal to starboard. This shoal is frequently marked with bush stakes. If you see them, leave them to starboard.

Anchorages. This creek has a number of nice anchorages but no marine facilities or services of any kind.

You can anchor anywhere inside Wescott Point off a nice sandy beach in good security. There is a large campsite on the opposite shore below Mill Point, so you might want to continue upstream beyond Mill Point. There is at least 7 feet of water in Cherrystone Inlet for a distance of about 2 miles above Wescott Point. Proceed

cautiously, as the band of deep water is not all that wide.

A shoal extends out from the western shore of the inlet about 2 miles into Cherrystone Inlet. The chart shows a house on the shoal, and as you are coming up the inlet, the house appears to be sitting right in the middle of the waterway. Under no circumstances proceed beyond the house; it marks the end of deep water—if 4–5 feet can be called deep.

To starboard, just after you pass Kings Creek on the way in, is Cherrystone Aqua Farms. Dr. Michael Pierson started raising clams there in 1984 and now markets several million each year. The facility is not open to the general public, but it is possible that the occasional visitor, especially one by water, might manage to arrange a tour if he or she asks nicely.

To port, the first house on Savage Neck keeps several peacocks. You may not be able to see them from the water without glasses, but you will probably hear them on occasion. They were kept in "the old days" as intruder alarms.

Savage Neck is quite low and there is little vegetation toward the end of the point. The result is that you can easily look across the Bay from your secure anchorage to see ships passing up or down the Bay. You couldn't ask for a better location to observe a beautiful sunset. Following sundown, it gets rather dark. The lack of shoreside lights tells you that you are in the country.

KIPTOPEKE BEACH

Charts: 12221, 12222, **12224**

First, I should point out that this is not really the name of this harbor. Kiptopeke is simply the name of the nearest town, which I am using as a geographical reference. Kiptopeke Beach is indicated on the chart, but there is nothing there anymore. Kiptopeke used to be the terminal used by the Cape Charles ferry until it was replaced by the Chesapeake Bay Bridge-Tunnel. The ferry slip is protected by a breakwater constructed by the process of sinking nine WWII surplus ferrocement ships, between the slip and the Bay.

KIPTOPEKE HARBOR

OF REFUGE

Charts: 12221, 12222, **12224**

Anchorages. There is an excellent barrier to wave action from the west, a little less from the north and south unless you anchor on the lee side of the old ferry slip itself. There is at least 6 feet of water on both sides of the ferry slip, provided you stay a prudent distance from the shore.

Approaches. One advantage of this spot is ease of approach. The two lines of concrete ships have plenty of water on all sides of them and can be made out from a considerable distance. As you approach, the apparently solid breakwater soon resolves itself into the shapes of individual hulls, with noticeable gaps between them. There is a white light on either end of the breakwater. The old ferry passage is right in the middle, where the northern line of four ships and the southern line of five ships overlap. It doesn't look like there is a great amount of room between the lines, but this is an illusion. After all, the ferries used to pass through here.

Kiptopeke Beach is now a Virginia State Park complete with a boat launching ramp and a fishing pier, but no slips. Boaters are asked to keep clear of the swimming beach to the north of the boat ramp. You will have to land by dinghy. You are not permitted to tie up at the dock, but there is still room to anchor behind the concrete ships without too much disturbance from the boat ramp. Normally, this is a pleasant and popular anchorage. However, in a strong south to southeast wind, it can be a rough ride. Fresh water and showers are available.

It is interesting to see the concrete ships, if only once. This is a different kind of Bay anchorage with comparative isolation.

Concrete, World War II ships, sunken to form a breakwater to protect the old ferry dock, make a good harbor of refuge off a sand beach. The marina construction began in 1988. PETER McCLINTOCK/VA MARINE RESOURCES COMMISSION

CAPE CHARLES CHANNEL

Charts: 12221, 12222, **12224**

This channel is little more than a shallow passage from Wise Point on the Bay side at the southern tip of Cape Charles to Magothy Bay on the eastern side of the cape. Magothy Bay leads north to "The Thorofare" (another one!) which eventually connects to Sand Shoal Inlet on the Atlantic Ocean side of the Delmarva peninsula.

The 40-foot vertical clearance of the fixed bridge stops nearly all cruising sailboats. Shallow-draft powerboats with an adventurous crew might attempt channel passage to explore Magothy Bay, after checking with one of the locals regarding the current depth.

Western

Shore

The Western Shore of the Bay south of Wolf Trap Light to the mouth of the Bay is where this region's cruising traffic is concentrated. Excellent, attractive harbors ranging from very popular to some which are rarely visited by cruisers pepper the area. I have chosen to treat the region from Hampton Roads to Cape Henry on the Atlantic side as part of the Western Shore cruising grounds although technically this region is the southern shore of the Bay. A glance at the chart shows that it is for the most part contiguous to the Western Bay shore and the dearth of anchorages in this region of the Eastern Shore increase the probability that you will approach Hampton Roads from the Western Shore. (Conversely, if you are entering the Bay at its mouth, you are more likely to proceed from the Roads up the Western Shore than to try the sparse offerings of the Eastern Shore here.)

HORN HARBOR

Charts: 12221, **12238**

Unless you count the extremely narrow, shallow, and twisting entrance to Winter Harbor (which nearly all sizable cruising boats should avoid) a couple of miles to its north, Horn Harbor is the first acceptable harbor in a long stretch of the western shore of the Chesapeake as you are heading south from the vicinity of the Piankatank. (This is not the same Horn Harbor as the snug little hurricane hole near the headwaters of the Great Wicomico River. Many different creeks and harbors on the Bay share the same name.) This Horn Harbor is about 3 miles north of New Point Comfort on the north side of the entrance to Mobjack Bay.

HORN HARBOR

ANCHORAGE

⭐2 3️⃣

Charts: 12221, **12238**

Approaches. The well-marked entrance was dredged in January of 1990, making it readily accessible to boats with drafts up to 6 feet. Deep draft boats also can squeeze through the entrance channel as long as no northerly blow is expected (or in progress). The safest first-time approach to the channel entrance is a 288-degree departure from the Mo (A) "HH" buoy in the Bay to the red "2" light mounted on a peculiar-looking casement structure. The channel has shoaled somewhat from the north and you should give the next marker, red "2A," a moderately wide berth. Then swing to pass close by the green "3." Take it slow through this area until you pass green "3" since the shoal tends to shift with the winter storms. This is the only tricky spot. From here on in, simply follow the markers. You may find that the markers do not agree with those shown on the chart. When there seems to be a conflict, honor the markers that are actually there and your entrance should be accomplished with no problem.

Anchorages. After clearing red "12," about one-half mile past Mill Point, the channel bends to the right, fairly well indicated by sticks. You will need to avoid the inevitable crab pots in the channel. Once you pass the red "14" daymark, you can anchor nearly anywhere in the creek or continue on past the next two bends to visit Horn Harbor Marina. Here you will find gas, diesel fuel, ice, and some limited hardware (mostly for powerboats). Shortly beyond the marina the water quickly thins. Near the marina is a good place to anchor in a blow.

MOBJACK BAY

Charts: 12221, 12241, **12238**

Mobjack Bay covers a considerable area. You can spend literally days exploring it. The mouth of this bay is 3½ miles wide from New Point Comfort on the north to the edge of Guinea Marshes on the south. From New Point Comfort, the bay extends a good 7 miles to Ware Neck Point, where it divides into the North River and Ware River. Two-thirds of the way from the mouth of this bay to Ware Point, the East River splits off to the north and the Severn River to the southwest. I will address four other anchorage areas, but these four rivers are the principal tributaries of Mobjack Bay.

As you approach the mouth of the bay, beware of the extensive fish traps. This is definitely a working waterman's territory. At times, the traps are so thick that you may think that there is no way through them. There is; you just have to take the time to find and follow the fairways, indicated by the black and white nuns (being replaced with yellow ones now). Needless to say, making your way through this fish trap maze in the dark can be a nightmare. If you are not completely familiar with the area, do not approach at night.

One of the most prominent manmade landmarks in the area is the old New Point Comfort Lighthouse off the southern tip of New Point Comfort. It's indicated on the chart by the notation "ABAND LT HO." This 63-foot–high sandstone structure, built in 1804, was replaced by a lighted buoy (or pair of buoys depending on your perspective) in the early 1950s. However, the lighthouse remains a prominent structure, even as a ruin.

For ease of narrative, I cover the creeks and rivers in a counterclockwise direction around Mobjack Bay, starting with Davis Creek, just over a mile upstream from the New Point Comfort Lighthouse.

DAVIS CREEK

Charts: 12221, **12238**

Approaches. From a glance at the chart, Davis Creek appears to be a difficult, narrow entrance. Actually, even with a bit of sea running, it isn't hard.

The first leg is almost due north. It is the longest and, with a channel width of about 50 feet (less than the 80 feet indicated on the chart), the most difficult because of the distance between the first two markers. After that, the markers are much closer together and following the channel is easy. Be very cautious between red "4" and red "6" where you must negotiate your way between the outlying shoals before entering the creek proper. You should be able to see the shoals by the change in color of the water (varying degrees of brown). To starboard, you can probably watch the assorted sea birds *walk* on the mud flats nearly up to the channel. The controlling depth was 3 feet in 1986 and, unless it has been dredged in the interim, that limits the use of this creek strictly to shoal-draft vessels.

Once you pass between the two arms of land at the entrance, you will be able to stay in deep water even though the shoals to either side appear to be uncomfortably close.

Dockages. Near the final mark in the creek, a long dock extends nearly to the edge of the channel. This is the public landing where you can tie up—if you can find room. A little farther up is "The Crabbers and Fishermans Wharf," a red building with white trim. I assume that the gas pumps here service the local water-

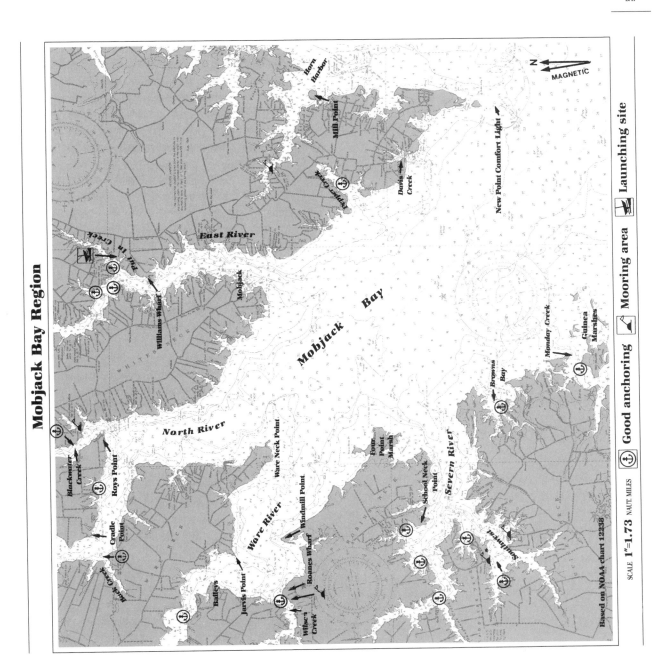

Mobjack Bay Region

Horn Harbor

Mill Point

New Point Comfort Light

Davis Creek

Pepper Creek

East River

Mobjack

Put In Creek

Williams Wharf

WHITES

Mobjack Bay

Monday Creek

Guinea Marshes

North River

Browns Bay

Blackwater Creek

Roys Point

Ware Neck Point

Windmill Point

Four Point Marsh

Severn River

School Neck Point

Cradle Point

Back O' Creek

Bailleys

Jarvis Point

Roanes Wharf

Wilson Creek

Sandbanks

SCALE 1"=1.73 NAUT. MILES

Based on NOAA chart 12238

⚓ Good anchoring   ⚓ Mooring area   ⚓ Launching site

men as this creek does not even pretend to cater to cruising boats.

If you plan to explore Davis Creek, do it early in the day. Then if you can't find a place to tie up for the night, you have time to look elsewhere before nightfall. This is an interesting place to visit, but better and more attractive anchorages beckon cruisers farther into Mobjack Bay.

PEPPER CREEK

No facilities

Charts: 12221, **12238**

Approaches. The entrance to Pepper Creek lies about 3 miles above New Point Comfort. The green "1" daymark at the outer end of the approach to this creek is a bit difficult to see until you are fairly close to it. The easiest way to start your approach is from the 15-foot–high flashing 4-second red "6" light in Mobjack Bay, southwest of Dutchman Point. From this light, a course of 345 degrees takes you directly to Pepper Creek green "1." Leave this daymark a good 50 yards to port and head directly for the red "2" daymark which looks like it is squarely in the middle of the creek entrance. Leaving red "2" close to starboard, swing to starboard and remain in the middle of the creek. Watch out for the 2-foot spot to port about 100 yards past the red "2" daymark.

Anchorages. Once inside, you can anchor nearly anywhere in the main part of the creek. Six feet of water is carried for half of its length before it starts to shoal to nothing. (Stay out of the first cove to starboard; it only has 1 foot of water.) Here you are protected from all but the southwest. Even from that direction, the outlying shoals and the twist in the entrance channel moderate any waves. This is a pleasant anchorage, but be prepared for mosquitoes; the entire shoreline is marshy.

EAST RIVER

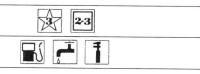

Charts: 12221, 12225, **12238**

The East River is perhaps the closest and most easily reached of the four main rivers off Mobjack Bay. It offers a number of nice anchorages in pleasant surroundings. But it doesn't offer much in the way of marine facilities.

Provisions/Facilities. Just inside the mouth of the river, on the west side, is the town of Mobjack, where the large tanks and sizable fuel dock of the Tidewater Oil Company are clearly visible. These are strictly commercial docks. If you are in need of fuel, there is a narrow, well-marked channel, just below Sharp Point, that leads to Mobjack Marina. Mobjack Marina is for members only, but you probably can get fuel and water there if you ask nicely. There is 7 feet of water at the bulkhead by the fuel dock.

Stay out of the inviting looking little coves along the way upriver. With the exception of Tabbs Creek, which has 5 feet of water well past its mouth, they are all shoal. Tabbs Creek has an overhead power cable (vertical clearance 40 feet) but water depths in that portion are so shoal that you are in trouble if you do pass under it. About 2 miles up the East River, just past Weston Creek on the east bank, is one of the last tide mills on the Chesapeake. Of course, it is no longer in operation, but it remains in a relatively good state of preservation. Consider stopping to visit. There is no dock, so you have to land by dinghy.

If you are in need of hull or engine repairs, try Zimmermans Marine, to port opposite Williams Wharf. No other facilities are available here.

Anchorages. The first good anchorage area is past Williams Wharf in Put In Creek. As you enter Put in Creek, stay in the middle to avoid the shoals to either side. They are not extensive, but it is still better to avoid them. The creek carries at least 6 feet of water for a good mile past its entrance. You can anchor anywhere in here that pleases your fancy, well protected from all directions.

Continuing past Put In Creek, the main branch of the East River from here to well past Woodas Point offers a number of choice anchorages. Perhaps the most attractive is in the mouth of Woodas Creek or tucked just below Woodas Point. The rest of the river beyond Woodas Point carries a minimum of 4 feet of water for another mile, at least in the middle, but the best anchorages are near the junction of Put In Creek with the East River.

NORTH RIVER

Charts: 12221, 12225, 12235, **12238**

With a width of about a mile, the first 3 miles of the North River past Ware Neck Point at its mouth are too broad for comfort and there are no anchorages until you reach Blackwater Creek. Davis Creek to port (not to be confused with the Davis Creek near the mouth of Mobjack Bay) may look like a possible stop until you notice the lack of water depth; pass it by.

Approaches/Anchorages. Blackwater Creek splits off to the north from the North River. In fact, the main river takes nearly a right-angle turn to the west here so, if you don't turn sharply to port, you could enter Blackwater Creek accidentally. (In reality, you would have to try hard to do this.) Leave the red "2" light close to starboard, then favor the port side of the creek until Roys Point comes abeam. Thereafter, stay near the middle and you will find 7 to 10 feet all the way upstream to just short of the point where the creek forks for the last time. You can anchor nearly anywhere in here. Perhaps the best anchorage is right in the mouth of Hampton Creek. Don't enter the creek itself as it shoals quickly. Oakland Creek on the way in provides a really snug anchorage for boats with drafts of less than 4 feet, if it hasn't shoaled in some more. Proceed carefully.

Dockages/Provisions. The only marine facilities on the North River are in Greenmansion Cove, just over one-half mile beyond the red "2" at the mouth of Blackwater Creek. Here Mobjack Bay Marina and The Yacht Yard (same place) offers gas, diesel, ice, limited hardware, and some transient slips. Just across from the marina is a large home called Greenmansion. Now a private home, at one time it was a summer resort. Whether the building got its name from the cove or vice versa, I don't know.

Additional Anchorages. Proceeding on up the main North River, the next really good anchorages occur after the river again bends to the north. Belleville Creek is a possible anchorage for powerboats with drafts of less than 3 feet, but the 30-foot–clearance overhead power cable at its mouth prevents sailboats from even trying it. In fact, powerboats with high radio antennas had better be careful, too.

At the northerly bend in the river, Back Creek offers an anchorage just inside its mouth for boats drawing less than 4 feet. Hold close to the green "7" daymark at the river's mouth and head for the middle of the creek mouth. Don't proceed past the second bend as the water gets shallow fast. Stay a good hundred yards or more to the east of the overhead power line there.

None of the other little creeks off the North River have much in the way of water in them; stay out. You can anchor wherever you choose in the main river from Cradle Point to just past the unnamed point to starboard beyond Toddsbury Creek. Most cruisers choose to anchor in the vicinity of the cove between Auburn Wharf and Roys Point, but there is no particular reason not to proceed farther upstream for a bit more seclusion.

WARE RIVER

No facilities

The third of the main rivers off Mobjack Bay, the Ware, offers no marine facilities for transient cruisers, in spite of the presence of a tiny marina in Wilson Creek. It does offer some nice scenery and very pleasant cruising.

Approaches. The approach to the Ware River is straightforward. Just swing well wide of the shoal off Four Point Marsh, especially the region northwest of Ware River Point where there is a 1-foot spot well offshore. From here on in, simply honor the markers. There are a number of substantial shoals but all are well marked. The biggest one to watch out for is the one extending to the southwest of Jarvis Point. The Jarvis Point red "6" lighted spar is well south of where you might expect to find it after clearing green "5" north of Windmill Point. There is no question of cheating and passing to the north of red "6"; you simply won't make it.

Anchorages. The first, and probably best, anchorage on the Ware is just inside Wilson Creek. There is a slight trick to entering this creek safely. Do not attempt this entrance for the first time in poor visibility. The easiest approach is to take your departure from Jarvis Point red "6" on a course of about 305 degrees. Follow this course to within a couple of hundred yards from the end of the long dock ahead. Then swing to port and parallel the shore until you can see the private aid with white arrows pointing to the channel. When you pass the red triangular private marker beyond what's left of Roanes Wharf, you will be in a snug, secure, little anchorage. Simply anchor in the middle of the creek in 6 to 8 feet of water. The shore is full of docks tenanted by both the typical Bay workboats and a number of pleasure boats. Vessels with less than a 5-foot draft can continue on around the first bend in the creek. Deeper draft boats shouldn't proceed much beyond the first little cove to port. Wilson Creek is a favorite spot for the lower Bay cruising clubs and it is not unusual to find more than 30 boats anchored there on a summer weekend.

Should you elect to remain in the main river, continue around Jarvis Point and the next bend if you are looking for a more secluded area. You can anchor nearly anywhere past Baileys Point, but watch the depth as you move to the side of the river, the shoals are extensive. One other note of caution: The shoreline is marshy in much of this area; expect to be visited by mosquitoes and no-see-ums at dusk.

SEVERN RIVER

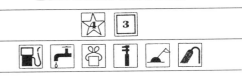

Charts: 12221, 12241, **12238**

Somehow, seeing the name "Severn River" in conjunction with Mobjack Bay always gives me a little jolt. Granted, there are many different rivers and creeks on the Bay which share names, but I still can't help the gut feeling that the Severn River of Annapolis and Naval Academy fame should be the only Severn on the Bay.

Approaches. That is not meant to slight *this* Severn River, which is very accessible and probably offers the best set of anchorages in the Mobjack Bay region. The entrance is easily found and negotiated. Simply pick up the 4-second flashing green "1" light located about midway between the marshy points on either side of the river's mouth.

Anchorages. Leave this marker to port and stay in the middle of the river until you select your anchorage. There are a few protruding shoals but with the exercise of a little prudence and attention to your chart and position, they present no problem.

Caucus Bay, to starboard beyond green "1" at the mouth of the Severn River, allows entrance to boats with less than a 4-foot draft. While negotiating this entrance, be sure to favor its western side to avoid the wide shoal to starboard. While interesting to poke into, Caucus Bay doesn't offer a good overnight anchorage as the eastern through southern part of this bay is wholly exposed to the long sweep of Mobjack Bay. In addition, the entire shoreline is a muddy marsh. It's not a recommended anchorage.

Whittaker Creek, also to starboard, offers a possible anchorage to boats with less than a 4-foot draft. Favor the western side of the approach from well out in the Severn River in order to avoid the 2-foot shoal extending a good distance into the river on the east side of the creek approach. Don't pass beyond the overhead power cable (30-foot clearance) here unless you draw well under 3 feet; it shoals quickly. The shoreline is another muddy marsh and there are better anchorages. Pass this one by, too.

SOUTHWEST BRANCH

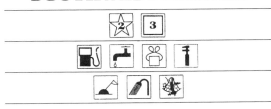

Charts: 12221, 12241, **12238**

Approaches. The Southwest Branch, to port, offers the first set of excellent anchorages on the Severn. The entrance is well marked and straightforward, provided you remember that you come to the Severn River green "3" light just before reaching the green "1" daymark at the entrance to the Southwest Branch. Leave them both to port and you'll have no problem. Swing sharply around the green "1" daymark and leave the red "2" daymark to starboard. All shoals from here on are well marked.

Anchorages. The small cove to starboard just past red "2" is an excellent anchorage if you don't try to go too far in. In fact, you can anchor anywhere in this branch, as far up as one-half mile into either Willets or Heywood Creeks, the two forks of the Southwest Branch. The whole branch is well protected but still open enough to permit a welcome cooling breeze in hot weather. You can get a good fetch to the northeast, so watch the weather or be very selective in your anchorage.

Dockages/Provisions. There are two marinas in the Southwest Branch, the only ones on the Severn River. However, the water depth is uncertain at both marinas for boats with drafts over 4 feet; ask first. The first is Holiday Marina, on the south side, just beyond the entrance to Rowes Creek. Here you will find both gas and diesel fuel, ice, some hardware, and a few slips for transient cruisers. The other is Glass Marine (really a builder of work boats) on the north side, right at the entrance to Willets Creek. Gas and diesel are available here, as well as some slips for transients.

NORTHWEST BRANCH

No facilities

Charts: 12221, 12241, **12238**

The Northwest Branch offers a series of anchorages that are somewhat prettier than those of the Southwest Branch. It has a slightly higher shoreline, fewer marshes, and presents a generally more attractive set of surroundings. Lack of marine facilities and a source of supplies here means less traffic and more seclusion than the other branch.

Anchorages. There is an excellent anchorage in the bight to the north, just past School Neck Point. This bight is actually the mouth of Free School Creek, which is only navigable to boats drawing less than 4 feet. The preferred anchorage is in the bight in 7 feet of water.

Just to the west of Free School Creek is Bryant Bay, another excellent anchorage, except for the considerable fetch to the southeast. Don't proceed too far into the two forks to the west and you will find good holding in 5 to 7 feet of water. Be wary of the shoal extending to the east of the marshy point between these two forks.

Past Bryant Bay, simply pick an appealing spot. Most of the rest of the branch is reasonably well protected. If you are one of the more adventurous, consider feeling the way into Vaughans Creek. Don't try it with a draft of more than 5 feet.

BROWNS BAY

Charts: 12221, 12241, **12238**

Approaches. Just south of the entrance to the Severn River, Browns Bay lies squarely in the middle of an extensive salt marsh. The entrance is well marked and easy to follow all the way into the little bay. Beyond the last marker, red "4," swing to starboard past the marshy point and you will find a nice little anchorage in 5 to 7 feet of water, unprotected only from due east. Even to the east, the entrance shoals tend to break up and greatly reduce any waves from that direction, if not the wind. There is a white pole in the water just past red "4," treat it as a red marker and leave it to starboard.

Provisions. A public dock is clearly visible as you enter. While cruisers are welcome, it is used almost totally by workboats (oyster, crab, and fish) to offload their catch. There is nothing there for the visitor unless you are interested in buying fresh fish, or perhaps some crabs as they come in. There is no marina, but there is a fuel dock operated by Shackleford-Thomas Seafood, a wholesale fish house next to the public pier. The fuel dock has diesel fuel and gasoline.

If you choose to head for the public pier, take your departure from the white pole past the red "4" marker and head directly toward the end of the dock. There is 5 feet of water all the way to the pier and for most of the length of the pier. Be more careful approaching the fuel dock. Ask about the water depth first; there is less than you might expect.

Anchorages. In either case, don't plan to spend the night—or even any great amount of time—at the pier; anchoring out is definitely preferable. There will be some workboat traffic going in and out, but you can expect to be the only boat anchored there.

Pick your weather if you plan to stay overnight here, it's not a place to be locked into for several days during an extended blow, especially one from the northeast. However, if you enjoy observing the marsh wildlife in their natural habitat, you will be hard pressed to find a better location. Don't try to enter Johns West Creek, to the south of Browns Bay, in anything other than a dinghy. But if you are interested in seeing pristine marshland, by all means take out a dinghy and have a look at it. As a point of interest, there is a lone "TREE" marked on the chart about halfway up the creek. Don't look for it; either it has fallen or it is not very large and is screened.

There are no supplies, restaurants, or much of anything else on or within walking distance of Browns Bay, just marsh and countryside. To us, that is its main attraction! Remember that marsh means lots of mosquitoes in the evening; come prepared or you will be the main attraction.

MONDAY CREEK

No facilities

Charts: 12221, 12241, **12238**

Everything said about the environment of Browns Bay holds true here except that the channel is unmarked and you won't even see any workboat traffic. If you are looking for a secluded anchorage to observe marsh wildlife, this is it. The odds are that you will be the only boat for at least a mile in any direction.

Approaches. The approach to this creek is a gunkholer's delight! While there is plenty of water in the channel on the way in (7 feet minimum), the trick is to find and stay in the channel. There is no good reference in Mobjack Bay from which to take a reliable departure. The easiest way to enter is to start from a couple of hundred yards to the east of the red "2" daymark at the entrance to Browns Bay and travel due south until the water depth decreases to between 6 and 7 feet. This should be the edge of the shoal on the west side of the approach. Continue sounding your way along, keeping in 6 to 7 feet of water, until you find your way to a hard-to-see stake marking the narrow part of the channel entrance. Leave the stake to starboard. From here, feel your way slowly into the creek, keeping in a water depth of 7 feet. The sides come up sharply in places, but, if the water has any visibility at all, you can see the change in water color where it shoals.

Anchorages. Anchor just past the point on the north side of Big Island in 7 feet. This is one of the few anchorages where you can look out into the main Chesapeake Bay from a harbor protected from waves, if not wind, in all directions.

YORK RIVER

Charts: 12221, 12241, 12243, **12238**

Together with the James River, the York River forms one of the borders of the famous Gloucester Peninsula, which embodies a significant portion of this nation's history. On this peninsula can be found the historic towns of Yorktown, Williamsburg, and Jamestown, not

to mention Newport News at its tip. The latter two are covered in the section on the James River, but a cruise up the York River makes a visit to Yorktown and Williamsburg relatively easy. In Yorktown there is an information center where you can arrange for tours of Yorktown, as well as more extensive excursions to Jamestown or Williamsburg.

While there is deep water at Yorktown, the docks do not lend themselves to tying up nor are there any marine facilities. Because of the water depth off the town

York River to Poquoson Flats

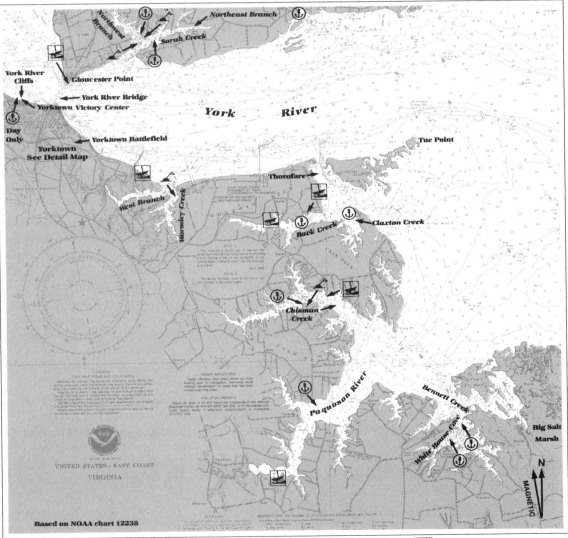

SCALE **1"=1.57** NAUT. MILES ⚓ **Good anchoring** ⚓ **Mooring area** ⚓ **Launching site**

Virginia's Tri-Town Vacationland

While most of the sites and attractions of the Chesapeake Bay are designed for easy access from the water, some of the major points of interest, clustered on the Gloucester Peninsula are not.

WILLIAMSBURG. The colonial town of Williamsburg is located very nearly in the geographical center of the Gloucester Peninsula, bounded on the northeast by the York River and on the southwest by the James River. It was established in 1632 as a small settlement with a stockaded outpost to help defend Jamestown against Indian attacks. At the time, the settlement was known as Middle Plantation. Unlike virtually all of the other settlements of that and the following century, Middle Plantation was not located with immediate access to a navigable body of water. The stockade was over six miles inland from the banks of the James River and about the same distance from the shores of the York River.

In 1693, a charter granted by the king and queen of England established the College of William and Mary, named after them, at Middle Plantation. This became and is the second oldest college in the United States and is still using the oldest academic building in the country, the Wren building, which was designed by Sir Christopher Wren in 1695.

In the fall of 1698, a fire destroyed the State House at Jamestown, although the colonists did manage to save all of the vital records. That fire, combined with the unhealthy and swampy conditions of the original Jamestown site, provided the incentive to relocate the capitol of the colony to Middle Plantation. The town was laid out by Governor Nicholson in early 1699 and construction started almost immediately.

Nicholson planned well. He divided the town into half-acre residential lots and included plans for government buildings, especially the Capitol and a courthouse, as well as the Governor's residence (promptly dubbed the Governor's Palace). All of the buildings, residences and government buildings alike, were constructed in the style of the English homes and gardens popular during the reign of William and Mary, 1687 to 1709. The elegant Governor's Palace and formal gardens provided the centerpiece for what was to become perhaps the most beautiful colonial town established in this country. This style and elegance has been maintained ever since, in spite of a few disastrous fires.

With the move of the colonial capitol from Jamestown to Middle Plantation in 1699, the town was renamed Williamsburg in honor of King William III. It quickly grew to a fair-sized town with a population of around 1800 people. Twice each year this population would nearly double during the "Publik Times" when the General Court and the legislature were in session. Williamsburg prospered! In addition to being the political center, it also soon became both the social and cultural center of the entire colony, especially during the "Publik Times" when balls, plays, and horse races were held.

Prior to the Revolutionary War, Williamsburg served as host to George Washington, Thomas Jefferson, James Madison, James Monroe, John Marshall, and Patrick Henry. Here in 1775 at the Williamsburg Capitol, Patrick Henry delivered his "Give me Liberty" speech against the Stamp Act. The Capitol also unanimously passed the "Bill of Rights" drafted by George Mason.

In 1780, while the Revolutionary War was still in progress, the capitol of the Virginia Colony was moved from Williamsburg to Richmond, considered a far safer location in those trying times. With that move of the capitol, Williamsburg reverted to a quiet country town, although it was still the county seat and the college town of William and Mary.

Today, the Capitol City of Colonial Virginia is the largest restored 18th-century town in America. The public buildings and several exhibit homes are open to the public (admission fee) and there are displays and exhibits of colonial crafts, occupations, and gardens, as well as plentiful shopping, dining, and lodging for visitors. Maps are available at the Visitor's Center, which is open from 8:45 a.m. to 5:20 p.m. every day.

(For more information, contact The Williamsburg Area Convention and Visitor's Bureau, P.O. Drawer GB, Williamsburg, VA 23187, 804/253-0192.)

Amid Williamsburg's rolling hills is Busch Gardens, The Old Country, one of the most action-packed and diverse theme parks in the world. A visit to the 360-acre European-theme park is reminiscent of old-world Europe, complete with quaint villages, exciting rides, exquisite cuisine and an array of entertainment and shops. The Old Country is open from April through October and consistently ranks as one of the state's most popular tourist attractions.

Busch Gardens Old Country offers visitors "hands-on" entertainment such as close encounters with the Anheuser-Busch Clydesdales and "refreshing" amusement park rides.

The old-world Europe theme is a reminder of the roots of settlers who came to nearby Colonial Williamsburg and other historic sites in the area. Extensive research and exploration trips to European countries are the basis of numerous details found in the park's architecture, rides, shows, restaurants, strolling characters, shops, and games. Entertainment offerings include the Talers of Threadneedle Faire who offer the rowdy merriment of a Renaissance fair, and more than 20 new strolling characters ranging from the Three Musketeers to a beefeater.

In addition to entertainment, the park's architecture helps transport visitors to another place in time. Castle walls, turrets, and brightly colored flags highlight the English hamlet of Hastings. Sidewalk cafes, blooming flower boxes, chromatic shutters and awnings dot the French village of Aquitaine. The "Wilkommenhaus" German town hall features a glockenspiel in Rhinefeld where cobblestone streets and handcrafted stained glass windows complete a picture-perfect scene.

Differing from many amusement parks, Busch Gardens' effort to transfer theming to its food offerings has resulted in a wide array of unique and delicious items.

Rides also stick closely to the park's European theme. The "Big Bad Wolf" suspended roller coaster sends riders on a free-flight course through a rustic Alpine village and quaint German town filled with cottages and a rural church as well as over rugged terrain and the Rhine River. The ride is based on research of two German towns, Dinkelsbuhl and Rottenburg. One of the park's newest adventures, "Roman Rapids," is another elaborately themed ride. The white-water–raft ride takes guests through ancient Roman ruins including broken columns, statues and a "decaying" aqueduct where spouting water douses unsuspecting guests.

(For the latest information on admission fees and hours, call 804/253-3350.)

YORKTOWN. Next, follow the Colonial Parkway to Yorktown where American and French troops forced Cornwallis' British troops to surrender in 1781. Points of interest include the Yorktown Victory Center and surrounding battlefields. There is also Waterman's Museum, which serves as a unique tribute to the life of Chesapeake Bay watermen and On the Hill, a cultural arts center which focuses on the visual arts and contains the work of a 30-member cooperative, as well as displays by regional guest artists. For more on Yorktown, see the main text.

JAMESTOWN. The third corner of the historic triangle is occupied by Jamestown, the first permanent English Colony in America. At Jamestown Settlement, guests can board full-

Jamestown Settlement and Yorktown
Victory Center feature living
history recreations of colonial and
revolutionary war eras.

sized replicas of the *Susan Constant, Godspeed*,
and *Discovery*, the small ships that brought the
colonists to the New World in 1607. Jamestown
is also covered at length in the main portion of
the text.

(50 to 80 feet), anchoring is not very convenient either.
A better course of action is to anchor or take a slip at
one of the marinas in Sarah Creek across the river from
Yorktown. From there you can take a 2-mile walk to
Yorktown or arrange for transportation at one of the
marinas.

As is the case with many of the rivers with broad
mouths fronting on the Bay, one has a choice in approach of the York River entrance. If you are approaching from the south, it is essential to stay more than 2
miles offshore from Big Salt Marsh in order to avoid the
outer reaches of Poquoson Flats. Save for the black and
white fishtrap area markers, these shoals are unmarked. The safest approach from the south is to either
follow the fishtrap marker fairway until you can parallel

the York River entrance channel or to pick up and follow this shipping channel well offshore. The alternative
is to keep a close watch on your depth sounder and be
constantly aware of your exact location until you enter
the York River proper. Once you are clear of Poquoson
Flats, the rest of the approach is easy.

From the north, there are two approach routes: the
easy one and the short one. A long shoal extends well to
the east of Guinea Marshes on the north side of the
York River entrance. This shoal hooks to the south for
another 2 miles past Swash Channel Light, which, itself, is a good mile offshore. The safe passage is to continue south until you can pick up the last pair of lighted
red and green buoys marking the end of the York River
channel, then swing to starboard to enter the York
River. The shorter route is to use Swash Channel, a natural channel through the middle of the shoal. This approach really isn't hard and can save you a couple of
miles. Simply take a departure from the red "2" light
southeast of New Point Comfort on a course of 248 degrees. This course, which includes a dog-leg to the
north to avoid the north end of the shoal south of the
channel, takes you to the green "3" Swash Channel
light *which you must leave to starboard*. Hold about
100 yards east of Swash Channel Light and swing to
port to a course which leaves the red "2" daymark south
southwest of the green "3" light *to port*. (A good look at
the chart shows the reason for this anomaly.) Once past
red "2," you can easily run to green "1" and enter the
rest of the York River.

PERRIN RIVER

Charts: 12238, **12241**

The first harbor you reach on your way upstream from
the Bay is the Perrin River on the north shore of the
York. A cursory glance at the chart may give those with
deeper draft vessels some pause. In actuality, those with
drafts up to 6 feet will have no problem negotiating the
entrance channel and finding a good place to anchor.

Approaches. As you make your approach, keep the red "2" nun well to starboard to avoid the extensive shoal off Sandy Point. Come close to the red "4" light on a spar before swinging to port and following the rest of the markers into the river. Favor the west side of the channel, especially as you pass the "No Wake" sign to starboard.

Dockages / Facilities / Provisions. Stay out of the inviting-looking cove to port as you enter the river; that cove has less than 2 feet of water in its deepest part. Ahead to starboard are the docks of Cook's Landing Marina where you will find plenty of marine facilities, including transient slips, fuel, ice, some marine supplies, a swimming pool, and a dockside sewage pumpout facility.

Anchorages. The best place to anchor is just past the place where the Perrin makes a sharp turn to the west, right after the green "11" daymark. Here, you have good holding in 6 feet of water, with plenty of room to swing. Boats with less than a 6-foot draft can proceed upstream several hundred yards past where the river bends back to the north. Proceed slowly and watch your depth. Like most parts of the Bay, this area is subject to silting in.

While a satisfactory harbor, the Perrin River is not the area's best, at least not when compared to Sarah Creek farther up the York.

WORMLEY CREEK

Charts: 12238, **12241**

Approaches. Generally overlooked by cruising boats, Wormley Creek is on the south shore of the York, about 2 miles downstream from Yorktown. There is a large generating plant with several huge smokestacks which dominate the area. While these stacks serve as an excellent guide to the creek's entrance from a long way off, they aren't nearly as noticeable once you are in. The

entrance to Wormley Creek is just past the piers belonging to the power plant. The rest of the approach is easy: Simply line up the entrance markers and follow them on in. There is at least 5½ feet in the channel at mean low water.

Dockages/Facilities. The one marina on the creek, Wormley Creek Marina, is to port just inside the entrance. There is a 6-foot depth at the marina and, although transients are rare, they are always made welcome. The marina offers slips for transients, gas, diesel, and a dockside sewage pumpout facility. Ice doesn't seem to be available. Incidentally, this marina is also the only place in the creek where you can stay for the night. There isn't much room here to anchor.

Just past the marina, the dredged channel turns to the west, into the West Branch of the creek. Stay out of the main branch; it's too shoal. The channel continues for about one-half mile until it terminates at the docks of the Coast Guard Training Center. Follow the channel at least once, if only to satisfy curiosity.

For a secluded anchorage, try elsewhere.

SARAH CREEK

All facilities

Charts: 12238, **12241**

This creek is the most popular harbor on the York River and with good reason: The entrance is easy; there is plenty of water depth; the surroundings are pleasant; and you have the choice of anchoring out or visiting the excellent marine facilities here. Creek depths range from 7 to 14 feet throughout most of the creek, facilitating exploration.

Approaches. Make your approach by leaving the first Sarah Creek marker, the red "2" light, to starboard. From there, simply honor the rest of the markers. Hold close to the sand spit to port as you first enter the creek, there is a shoal to starboard which is unmarked.

Facilities/Dockages. Immediately past

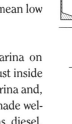

this sand spit is the York River Yacht Haven, in the small bight to port. Here you can find just about all the marine facilities you could need, including a ship's store, a pool, bike and car rental, and a dockside sewage pump-out facility. There is also a laundromat, some groceries, a courtesy car, and four nearby restaurants. In addition, they do offer slips for transients. They even have a sail loft, which replaced their restaurant.

Two more marinas, Jordan Marine Service and Gloucester Point Marina, are located well up the Northwest Branch of the creek. The former caters primarily to workboats and doesn't offer much for the transient cruiser, but Gloucester Point has gas, diesel, ice, some marine supplies, and transient slips.

Anchorages. You can anchor just about anywhere in Sarah Creek. It is all well protected and the surroundings are pleasant. Try to stay to the side so you don't block the passage of other boats. The most popular anchorage is in 9 feet of water, just inside the Northeast Branch of the creek. Stay out of the little tributaries to the north and south of this anchorage area if you have more than a 4-foot draft.

Sarah Creek is probably the ideal place to leave your boat if you plan to visit historic Yorktown, the scene of the surrender of the British General Cornwallis at the close of the Revolutionary War. Alternatively, you may want to rent a car or arrange for some other transportation to visit Williamsburg or Busch Gardens just a few miles farther away. Whether you take a transient slip or anchor out, you can leave your boat here with the full expectation that you will return to find it safe and secure. Any of the marinas will be happy to help you to plan these excursions and assist in arranging transportation. For the hardier souls, it is only about a 2-mile walk into Yorktown from any of the marinas on Sarah Creek.

YORKTOWN

No facilities

Charts: 12238, 12243, 12241

This is the Yorktown of Revolutionary War history. But there is more to the story than the victory of the Continental army.

History. The town was established in 1691 on the bluffs above the river. A mere 6 years later, it became the county seat and developed as a thriving business center for the area. It also became a major port for the tobacco trade. By the mid-18th century, the center of tobacco production moved farther south, as soil in the Yorktown area became exhausted. Yorktown began to decline and, by the time of the Revolution, was no longer a major port.

Prior to and during the Revolution, the majority of the residents and town leaders supported the patriot cause. In fact, they held their own "tea party" in December 1774. Although the town provided many troops to the cause, it saw little of the war until the British troops under General Cornwallis occupied the town in August of 1781, driving out the small colonial garrison.

General Lecompte de Rochambeau saw a chance and persuaded General Washington to delay his attack on New York to make a concerted effort to stop Cornwallis at Yorktown. The plans were laid: French Admiral Le Compte de Grasse would engage the British fleet and take control of the Chesapeake Bay and the York River to prevent the resupply or withdrawal of Cornwallis by sea. General Le Marquis de Lafayette, with a combined French and American force, would prevent Cornwallis from withdrawing by land until Washington and his army could join Lafayette to launch a combined attack. As we know, the plan worked: By late September, General Cornwallis was effectively surrounded and outnumbered.

On October 3, 1781, the fighting began. By 17 October, the British had lost several key positions. Cornwallis finally realized that his position was hopeless and raised a flag of truce. Two days later, on October 19, Cornwallis accepted the surrender terms and, for all practical purposes, the war was over. Some desultory fighting continued until the Treaty of Paris, signed on September 3, 1783, formalized the peace between Great Britain, France, and what was to become the United States of America.

The surrender of Cornwallis gave Yorktown an immortal place in history, but the siege devastated the already diminished town. It never recovered its pre-Revolution size and activity. Today, it is a small, peaceful town which looks with pride on its historic bat-

Yorktown

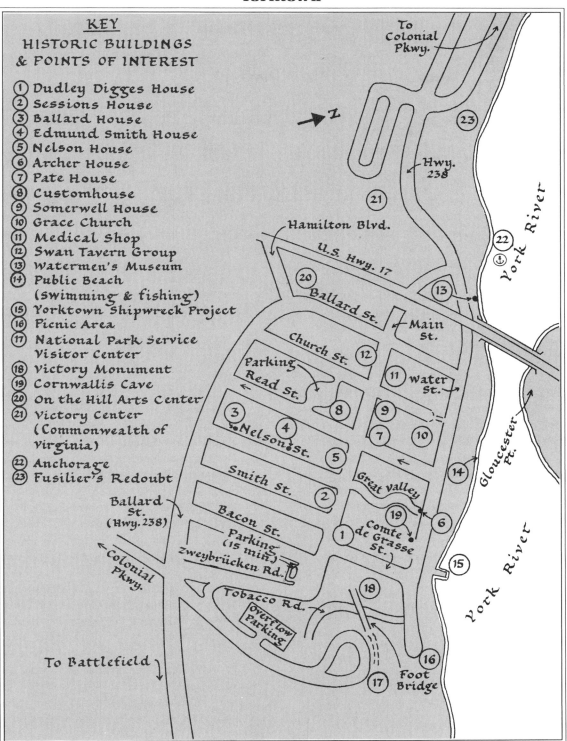

KEY

HISTORIC BUILDINGS & POINTS OF INTEREST

1. Dudley Digges House
2. Sessions House
3. Ballard House
4. Edmund Smith House
5. Nelson House
6. Archer House
7. Pate House
8. Customhouse
9. Somerwell House
10. Grace Church
11. Medical Shop
12. Swan Tavern Group
13. Watermen's Museum
14. Public Beach (swimming & fishing)
15. Yorktown Shipwreck Project
16. Picnic Area
17. National Park Service Visitor Center
18. Victory Monument
19. Cornwallis Cave
20. On the Hill Arts Center
21. Victory Center (Commonwealth of Virginia)
22. Anchorage
23. Fusilier's Redoubt

N

To Colonial Pkwy.

Hwy. 238

York River

Hamilton Blvd.

U.S. Hwy. 17

Ballard St.

Main St.

Church St.

Parking

Read St.

water St.

Nelson St.

Great valley

Smith St.

Ballard St. (Hwy. 238)

Bacon St.

Colonial Pkwy.

Parking (15 min.)

zweybrücken Rd.

Comte de Grasse St.

Gloucester Pt.

York River

Tobacco Rd.

Overflow Parking

To Battlefield

Foot Bridge

SCALE 1″=680 FEET

Waterman's Museum Pier with the York River bridge to the northeast.
This beach is a good spot for landing in a dinghy to tour Yorktown.

tlefield. (The Yorktown Victory Center tells the tale of those historic days.)

Anchorages. By all means, visit Yorktown! There are, however, a few complicating factors regarding access by boat. The town is no longer a port and there are no docking facilities. The water off the town is deep, around 80 feet, and the bottom rises abruptly near shore making anchoring difficult. If you plan to spend the night, put into Sarah Creek, directly across the York River and either walk the 2 miles to Yorktown or arrange transportation at one of the marinas.

To visit Yorktown just for the day, in fair weather, there is another choice. There is an area just above the York River Bridge where you can pull near shore by the York River Cliffs to anchor in 7 to 10 feet of water. You have to land by dinghy; there is no place for larger boats to tie up. The York River Bridge presents no obstacle to navigation. It is composed of two swing bridges which, when closed, have a vertical clearance of 60 feet. The only problem is that the area is open for the entire sweep of the river in both directions and is not a good place to be in a blow. There is some serendipity in anchoring here. First, you can land just a little downstream at the Waterman's Museum dock and visit the museum. Then, turn right on the road by the museum and walk a little way up the hill to visit the Yorktown

Victory Center or turn left and walk through the town itself up to the Yorktown Battlefield Park and its fabulous Visitor Center.

Things to Do. The Waterman's Museum is dedicated to telling the story of Virginia's working watermen—crabbers, oyster tongers and dredgers, net fishermen, menhaden fishermen, and boatbuilders—from the Indians up to today's watermen. Inside the building, there are assorted models and displays about fishing, crabbing, clamming, and oystering. Outside, there are displays of workboats and the oystering tools used. The dock by (or on) which you landed is a replica of an old tobacco wharf. Here you can also try your hand at tonging for oysters.

The Waterman's Museum is open Monday and Thursday through Saturday from 10:00 a.m. until 4:00 p.m. and on Sunday from 1:00 to 4:00 p.m., from Memorial Day to Labor Day.

Your next stop should be the Yorktown Victory Center (admission charged), a short walk west along the road to the top of York River Cliffs. Here, you walk down an indoor multimedia re-creation of an 18th century lane where voices and figures recount major events leading up to and including the American Revolution, culminating with "The Road to Yorktown" shown in the museum theater. This film depicts the crucial sea battle between the French and British fleets and the siege of Yorktown that led to the British surrender. Outside, there is an 18th century military encampment where you can speak with both soldiers and camp-followers who relate stories of life in the period. A proper tour of the victory center takes at least 2 hours. By the time you leave, you will have a far better understanding of the events leading up to and including the siege of Yorktown—brought home even more when you tour the redoubts on the actual battlefield. The Yorktown Victory Center is open daily 9:00 a.m. to 5:00 p.m. year-round, except Christmas and New Years's Day. (For more information, contact Yorktown Victory Center, P.O. Box 1976, Yorktown, VA 23690, (804)887-1776.)

As you retrace your steps back along the road, continue east on Water Street for just under a mile to where the road turns up a hill to the east of the town, on Compte de Grasse Street. A little beyond the top of the hill, you come to the Victory Monument. It's big—you can't miss it! By the monument is a footbridge that takes you directly to the National Park Service Visitor Center (no charge) on the actual battlefield. Here you can see the original field tents used by Washington, walk through a re-creation of about one-quarter of an 18th century ship-of-the-line right in the building, see a 12-minute film, "The Siege of Yorktown," and go to the observation deck for an elevated view of the battlefield. There is a driving tour laid out, complete with a tape cassette and recorder that you can rent at the Visitor Center Bookstore. Unfortunately, the whole battlefield is far too large to tour on foot. However, adjacent to the Visitor Center is the British Inner Defense Line and Hornwork, an untouched British redoubt, part of the Second Allied Siege Line, and a French artillery emplacement. Two more redoubts are near the cliffs overlooking the York River. Free maps are available at the Visitor Center.

As you walk back to your boat, walk along Main Street to take a look at the stately homes, many of which date back to the 18th century.

Finally, should you be cruising in the area in October, every October 19th is celebrated as Yorktown Day, the day of the British surrender. There is a parade, wreath-laying ceremonies, military drills, colonial music, and a traditional Brunswick stew luncheon.

Don't miss a visit to Yorktown.

UPPER YORK RIVER

No facilities

Charts: 12241, **12243**

The York River is navigable as far as West Point, where it divides into the Mataponi River to the northwest and the Pamunkey River to the west. However, the more than 20 miles between the York River Bridge and West Point are relatively uninteresting. There are no suitable safe harbors and the shoreline is low and marshy. West Point has a paper and pulp plant which does little to enhance the surroundings with its "fragrance." There are no marine facilities, except launching ramps. In short, don't bother going upstream beyond Yorktown, save to be able to say that you've "been there." The Restricted Area in the York River restricts anchoring, but only ships would even consider anchoring here—it is too exposed for small craft. The Naval Weapons Station on Stony Point is a supply depot, so you could see some sizable Navy ships tied up there.

BACK CREEK

Charts: 12221, **12238**, 12241

Not to be confused with the Back *River* about 8 miles to the south, this particular Back *Creek*, one of close to a dozen on the Bay with this name, is located just south of the mouth of the York River.

BACK CREEK

ANCHORAGE

Charts: 12221, **12238**, 12241

Approaches. Unlike any other Back Creek, this one has a "back door," called "The Thorofare," which allows a direct access, for some boats, from the York River. Unfortunately, The Thorofare has silted in recently and the controlling depth is debatable. Don't even think about it if you draw more than 3 feet. If you still want to try it, ask a local waterman or sound it by dinghy first. Better yet, wait for low tide and then land and wade the channel in the critical region between markers "10" and "14." There certainly can be no surer way to determine the true condition of the channel.

Back Creek itself presents easy access from the Bay through a well-marked channel, but give the shoal east of Tue Point a wide berth during your approach. Start your entrance from the flashing 5-second red "2" light. Actually, you can cut a couple of hundred yards inside red "2," but watch out for the 4-foot shoal directly north of it. From there, just follow the markers. If you continue more or less straight past green "7" you could find yourself in the entrance to The Thorofare with shoals closing in on all sides! Swing to the left as you pass the green "7" daymark off Green Point to head into the main part of Back Creek.

Provisions/Dockages. The numbers on the markers up to this point are referenced to the Thorofare, continuing in ascending order into the York River. As you proceed into Back Creek past green "7," the next marker is the Back Creek green "1" daymark. Ahead to port are the docks of Mills Marina, which offers gas, diesel, ice, and some limited groceries. The marina also can provide some transient slips, but prior reservation is strongly recommended if you prefer to tie up at a marina.

Anchorages. Just to port, midway between green "7" and Back Creek green "1," is the unmarked entrance channel to Claxton Creek. Sound your way in carefully, staying near the middle, and you will find a nice anchorage in 5 to 6 feet of water. Although the shore is low and marshy, "bugs" aren't much of a problem as long as some wind is blowing. On the plus side, you will probably be all alone in a serene, secluded anchorage, well protected from waves in all directions.

A little farther on, to starboard, is the Back Creek Park, a 26-acre area donated to the county by the Amoco Company. There are a couple of floating docks, launching ramps, a playground and picnic area, and six tennis courts.

Back Creek is a pleasant creek—which may be why it is rapidly filling up with homes and docks. You can anchor nearly anywhere in here provided you pull out of the main channel so as not to block traffic. The creek has at least 7 feet of water up to about 200 yards past green "3," a little short of where the creek forks. There is 5 feet of water in most of the north fork of the creek, but it is umarked so sound your way in. Be sure to take into account the state of the tide, which can range up to 3 feet in this area.

POQUOSON RIVER

Charts: 12221, **12238**

There is only one approach to the Poquoson River. Poquoson Flats on the south and the shoal off Tue Point, by the mouth of the York River, to the north dictate that a course parallel to (if not within) the channel, marked by the pairs of buoys starting in the middle of the approach to the York River, be followed.

As you approach York Point on the north side of the entrance to the Poquoson, you need to make a choice. The Poquoson River itself has little to attract the cruiser, quickly becoming shoal before there is much in the way of protection. However, there are two creeks off it that are worth looking into. The first of these, Bennett Creek, has its entrance just to the southwest of the green "11" light between York Point and Cow Island. The other, Chisman Creek, curves to the north after you round the red "14" marker just south of York Point.

POQUOSON RIVER

ANCHORAGES

☆2 2-3

⛽ 🚰 🍽 ⚓

🛶 🛒 🚿 🍴

Charts: 12221, **12238**

Approaches. Bennett Creek offers some protected anchorages, four marinas, and an interesting

Poquoson, on the river of the same name, is home port for many watermen. VA DIVISION OF TOURISM

challenge to the gunkholer with the nerve to explore it. After rounding the Poquoson green "11" light, hold close to the Bennett Creek green "1" daymark and head directly for the red "2" marker ahead. Ignore the first cove to starboard, Lyons Creek; it is too shoal to be useful.

Dockages/Anchorages.

The next cove to starboard is White House Cove where there are some protected anchorages as well as four marinas, at least two of which offer slips to transients. The channel is well marked. Just honor the markers. Don't proceed past the last marker into either fork of this cove as the forks shoal quickly.

If you continue past White House Cove, you find some secluded anchorages in 8 feet of water, provided you don't go too far and enter any of the five coves splitting off at the end of Bennett Creek. The shore is low and marshy, which means mosquitoes in the evening hours.

For the adventurous, there is a narrow, unmarked channel leading between Cow Island and Marsh Island directly opposite Lyons Creek. This channel holds 6 to 7 feet of water through the marshes, all the way to Lloyd Bay. In truth, there is little to attract most cruisers—no good anchorages, no attractive scenery, just marshland. However, for those who like the challenge of finding a passage that no one save another gunkholer would appreciate, this one is a real novelty.

Additional Anchorage/Facilities.

In Chisman Creek on the north shore of the Poquoson,

there are three marinas, none of which advertise slips for transients but which do have most of the other marine facilities that you may need. The best anchorage is in the main creek, just past the mouth of Goose Creek and the two marinas on the south shore. Stay out of Goose Creek and the inviting-looking coves near the entrance, first to starboard then to port; there isn't much water in them.

While interesting to visit at least once, there is little on the Poquoson or its tributaries to cause a cruiser to seek them out more than once.

BACK RIVER

Charts: 12221, **12222**, 12238

This is Back *River*, located about midway between the mouths of the York and James Rivers, not the Back *Creek* right at the mouth of the York. There are well over a dozen Back Creeks, Rivers, etc. on the Bay, possibly as many as two dozen. I don't think that anyone has ever taken the trouble to make an exact count.

In any event, *this* Back River can provide a harbor of refuge in a blow but is not likely to be sought as an anchorage by choice. It is now home to several marinas, at least two of which offer slips for transients and most of which offer the usual marine facilities sought by cruisers, with the exception of a restaurant. There are dredged channels to the marinas, most of which are located on the south shore, just inside the river entrance.

Back River

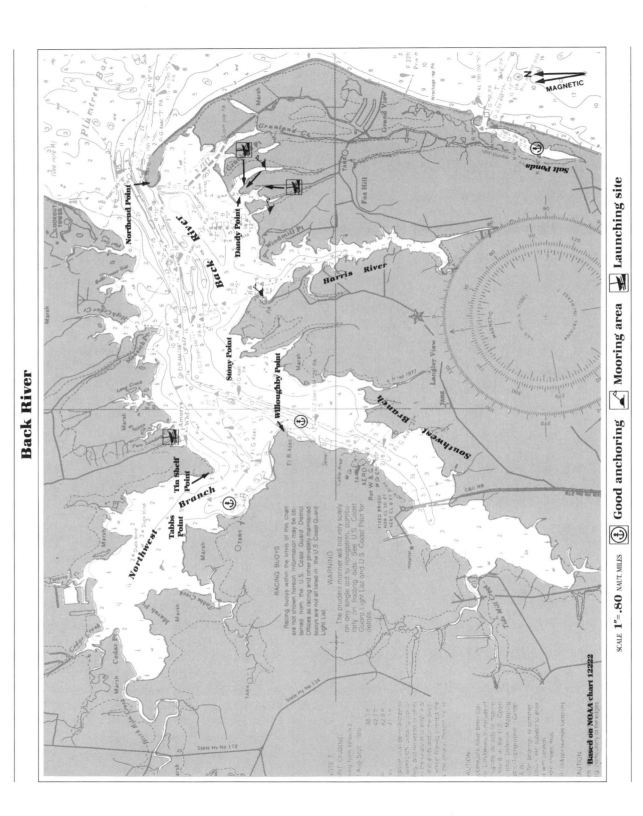

SCALE 1" = .80 NAUT. MILES   ⚓ **Good anchoring**   ◭ **Mooring area**   🚤 **Launching site**

BACK RIVER ANCHORAGES

Charts: 12221, **12222,** 12238

Approaches. Follow the markers on the way in, holding close to Northend Point as you enter the river. Immediately after passing Northend Point, swing hard to port to enter the channels to the marinas. Head directly for the green "1" daymark ahead. If you proceed too far past Northend Point before making your turn, you may "survey" an unmarked shoal.

Anchorages. If you are looking for an anchorage, proceed up the river and on into either the Northwest or Southwest Branches. In the Northwest Branch, anchor just west of the tip of Tin Shelf Point, near the western shore. Don't continue beyond Tabbs Point if you draw more than 4 feet. In the Southwest Branch, favor the western shore and anchor wherever you find a presentable spot. Beware of the underwater cable area near the white-orange can "A" by the tanks on the shore.

You soon will discover that Langley Air Force Base is located nearby. The noise of the planes may force you to look for a more peaceful harbor.

SALT PONDS

Charts: 12221, **12222**

The Salt Ponds are located about midway between the entrance to Back River and Old Point Comfort. The easiest way to find the entrance is to run up or down Horseshoe Channel, the rows of markers denoting a fairway through the designated fish trap areas on Horseshoe Shoal, until you can pick up the pairs of privately maintained entrance daymarks leading to the stone jetties of the entrance to Salt Ponds. The channel has a bad habit of shoaling in right at the ends of the stone jetties, especially on the north side. It was supposed to have been dredged in 1987, but enter cautiously any-

way. There normally is a sort of yardstick on the south side of the entrance which is helpful in indicating the water depth in the channel at different stages of the tide. We hope that it has been kept up to date.

SALT PONDS ANCHORAGE

Charts: 12221, **12222**

Approaches/Anchorages. Inside the entrance are markers that lead to a canal on the west side where there is a residential community, and the Salt Ponds Marina. Still under development, the marina is in full operation, with 300 slips, floating docks, a pool, and sewage pumpout. Don't try to anchor or tie up in the canal. Continue past the last marker, checking the depth as you go until you can anchor. There is room for five boats, although the area is becoming more crowded. Land by dinghy on the east side to walk over and explore the Bay side.

HAMPTON ROADS

Charts: 12206, 12207, 12221, **12222,**

12253, 12254, 12256

Every schoolchild has heard of Hampton Roads, the scene of the battle between Civil War ironclads, the *Monitor* and the *Virginia* (*Merrimac* to unreconstructed Yankees). This battle was fought in sight of Fort Monroe, located on Old Point Comfort. The fort has been in continuous existence and use since 1823 and is currently the home of the Casemate Museum and headquarters of the U.S. Army Training and Doctrine Command.

Many think of Hampton Roads as a bay or wide river mouth where the Union blockade formed a picket line

Hampton Roads Region

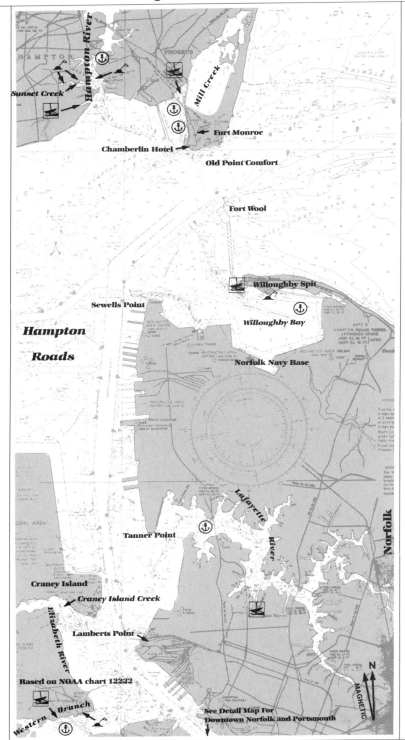

SCALE **1"=1.41** NAUT. MILES ⚓ **Good anchoring**   ◣ **Mooring area**   ⛵ **Launching site**

of warships. In reality, Hampton Roads is not a river, creek, or bay; it's a region, and a relatively small region at that. It comprises only the last half dozen miles or so between the mouth of the James River and the Chesapeake Bay, but in that distance it encompasses Fort Monroe, the Hampton River, Willoughby Bay, the entrance to the Elizabeth River, the huge Norfolk Naval Base, and the Nansemond River.

There is a certain amount of argument over whether Hampton Roads should be considered as an entity or as

Hampton Roads and the Hampton Roads Bridge-Tunnel are in the background of this aerial view of the U.S. Naval Station, Norfolk, Virginia. U.S. NAVY PHOTO

a part of the James River. Certainly there is justification for both viewpoints. From a chart, it is easy to conclude that the major river in the area, the James, continues its sweep down to the Bay, including the Hampton Roads region within its lower reaches and mouth. Traditionally, Hampton Roads has been considered the junction of several rivers, including the James, and looked upon more as "Hampton Roads Harbor" than anything else. In that light, I have chosen to go with tradition and treat Hampton Roads as a major entity of its own. For that purpose, we shall define the start of the James River as the region between the tip of the point at Newport News on the north side and the western bank of the mouth of the Nansemond River. The rest of the area down to the Bay is defined as Hampton Roads.

Almost in the middle of Hampton Roads, the Elizabeth River splits off to the south to lead into the docks of Norfolk and Portsmouth and the entrance to the Intracoastal Waterway. A short distance to the east, beyond the long Bay Bridge-Tunnel, lies the Atlantic Ocean. To the north is the entire expanse of the Chesapeake Bay. To the west is the entire length of the James River.

MILL CREEK

Charts: 12222, 12256, 12245, 12221

Of the more than a dozen Mill Creeks on the Bay, this one is probably the easiest to locate and enter but also the least attractive as an anchorage. The primary redeeming factor, which makes this creek well worth a visit, is the fascinating star fort of Fort Monroe located on Old Point Comfort, just east of the anchorage on Mill Creek.

Approaches. The massive, seven-story, red brick structure of the Chamberlin Hotel on the tip of Old Point Comfort is an unmistakable landmark, visible for miles, which makes locating and entering Mill Creek simplicity itself. Head for the hotel until you can see the

Old Point Comfort Lighthouse, just outside the Fort Monroe moat.

The main sallyport entrance over the moat to Fort Monroe.

large concrete abutments of the northern terminus of the Hampton Roads (Hampton to Norfolk) Tunnel to the west of the Chamberlin. The approach to Mill Creek lies directly between these two landmarks. Be sure to honor the green "3" daymark, to port as you enter. It marks the end of a shoal extending from the tunnel abutments. Once past green "3," you can leave the marked channel and pick your spot in which to anchor.

In fact, you never truly enter Mill Creek! The navigable portion is really the approach, bounded on the east by Old Point Comfort and on the west by the causeway approaching the tunnel terminus. You can look under the low causeway toward the western part of Hampton Roads, although the causeway provides fair protection from wind and wave. A fixed bridge with a vertical clearance of only 6 feet effectively prevents all but dinghies and runabouts from entering the true mouth of Mill Creek. Even those are pretty much stopped by the shoal waters beyond the next bridge, a couple hundred yards farther on.

Anchorages/Provisions.
There are only two choices for anchoring here. The maximum protection is near the fixed bridge by the fishing boat docks ahead, but be sure that you don't block access to the docks by the fishing trawlers, for obvious reasons. Just past the fixed bridge is Sam's Seafood Restaurant. By all means, take your dinghy under the bridge, tie up to

Sam's piers, and have a meal there if you can. Ice and groceries are also available at Sam's.

The other anchorage area is just off the Fort Monroe Marina, right inside the tip of Old Point Comfort. You can't tie up at the marina—its use is restricted to Fort Monroe military personnel—but you can anchor off and land at the dinghy dock to visit Fort Monroe for the day or to visit the sumptuous Chamberlin Hotel for dinner in their magnificent dining rooms. For that matter, just take a stroll through the huge lobby and visit their gift shop and small museum with relics of the "old days" of the Chamberlin and its predecessor from the days of steamboats. That, by itself, is worth the trip!

History/Things to Do.
Fort Monroe, the largest stone fort ever built in the United States, was named in honor of President James Monroe. Its construction was started in 1819 and it has been continuously occupied since 1823. Today, the installation is a National Historic Landmark and serves as the headquarters for the U.S. Army Training and Doctrine Command. Both the star fort and the rest of the Army post that surrounds it, is an active military installation and most of the buildings are either residences or offices. Be sure to respect their privacy and work areas.

To get to the fort from the marina, walk to the far end of the Chamberlin Hotel and turn left on Ingalls Road. A short distance ahead is a pedestrian bridge over the moat which surrounds the entire fort, leading to a small sallyport through the ramparts. As you pass through the sallyport, turn right and you will be at the entrance to the Casemate Museum, housed directly within the walls of the fortification. This should definitely be your first stop at Fort Monroe. Allow about 1½ hours to complete a walking tour of all the sights indicated in a pamphlet guide available at the Casemate Museum.

Casemates are rooms within the walls of a fortification. Many of those at Fort Monroe were used as living quarters from the time the fort was built until the end of the Civil War. Bachelors were given one room and families two. On occasion, some of the casemates were made into cells. One such cell was used to imprison Confederate President Jefferson Davis after the Civil War. His cell, sample living quarters, gun emplacements, and many other exhibits about Fort Monroe and the Coast Artillery Corps are included in the well-done museum. Admission is free and it is open daily 10:30 a.m. to 5:00 p.m.; closed Thanksgiving, Christmas, and New Year's Day.

Upon exiting the Casemate Museum, the building directly across the street served as the quarters of the then Lieutenant Robert E. Lee when he was stationed at Fort Monroe (1831–1834). The house is a private military residence and is not open to the public.

Turn right on exiting the museum and head up the steps to the Jefferson Davis Memorial Park at the top of the ramparts for a view out over the lower Chesapeake and Hampton Roads. Fort Wool, started in 1819 (but not completed until 1834) as a sister fort to Fort Monroe to protect Hampton Roads and the James River, is easily visible, a mile away, across the entrance to Hampton Roads. A stroll counterclockwise along the ramparts takes you past the rear of the imposing General Officer's quarters to the Old Point Comfort Lighthouse, all located just outside the moat.

The Old Point Comfort Lighthouse has been in continuous operation since 1802. The classic lighthouse and adjacent lighthouse keeper's cottage are worth investigation, only from the outside; visitors are not permitted in either structure. The lighthouse is still in operation and the old lighthouse keeper's cottage is now being used as military housing.

After you descend the ramparts, you have a choice of exiting the fort through the east sallyport and returning past the Chamberlin Hotel along the seaside walkway or taking a shortcut through the parade ground within

Fort Monroe's Casemate Museum contains exhibits of seacoast articles, the cell in which Confederate President Jefferson Davis was imprisoned after the War Between the States, and exhibits depicting the fort's history.

the fort to return the way you came in. If you choose the latter, be sure to take a look at the "Lincoln Gun," the first 15-inch Rodman gun ever made. It was cast in 1860, inspected by President Lincoln in 1862 (when it was named for him), and used to bombard Confederate batteries near Norfolk during the Civil War.

As you exit the fort through the main sallyport, the YMCA across the street offers refreshments and snacks for the hungry and thirsty—a good stopping place before you return to your boat.

For more information, contact: The Casemate Museum, P.O. Box 341, Fort Monroe, VA 23651, (804)727-3391.

HAMPTON RIVER

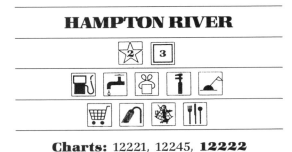

Charts: 12221, 12245, **12222**

Approaches. The entrance channel to the Hampton River is located on the north side of the entrance to Hampton Roads, just to the west of the massive concrete structure where the Hampton Roads (Hampton to Norfolk) Tunnel dives under the surface by Old Point Comfort. Even if you have any trouble locat-

Hampton River: An Ignoble End for the Infamous Blackbeard

Whether Captain Edmund Teach, better known as Blackbeard, was truly the fiercest and most cold-blooded pirate in history or simply the best showman, he still represented the epitome of the classic pirate image, one which equally inspired fear in his victims, his foes, and his own crew! His long, black beard, which began immediately below his eyes, was festooned with ribbons, twisted into tails and tied behind his ears. Various stories tell of him going into battle with

burning slow matches (or fuses) in his beard or under his hat, producing sulphurous smoke around his head. He carried a huge sword and three brace of pistols on slings over his shoulders. A huge, powerful man, he was the very image of a nightmare incarnate!

Operating mostly in the Carolinas, Blackbeard blockaded the port of Charleston through most of 1717 and 1718. Some said that he even blockaded the mouth of the Chesapeake. However, since by now nearly every act of piracy in the vicinity was being attributed to Blackbeard, the latter is doubtful. Carolina's Royal Governor Charles Eden tolerated and accommodated him there, probably lining his own pockets in the process. Eden officiated at Blackbeard's marriage to a 16-year-old lady of Bath Town and even offered Blackbeard and crew amnesty if he would mend his ways. Blackbeard gave it a try, but obviously didn't like it and returned to pirating.

It was Governor Spotswood of Virginia who finally caused the demise of this notorious pirate, appointing British Navy Lieutenant Robert Maynard, commanding two sloops-of-war, the HMS *Jane* and the HMS *Ranger,* to seek out and destroy this menace. This he did, tracking the pirate to his lair in the Carolina Outer Banks and engaging the larger and better armed *Adventure* of Blackbeard. Maynard actually won by a ruse, sending nearly all of his crew below and tricking Teach into boarding the *Jane,* thinking all were dead. Then Maynard's men swarmed out and the final battle began.

The battle of Ocracoke Inlet lasted for only a few minutes but casualties were high on both sides. Blackbeard, himself, fell dead only after suffering at least twenty-five wounds.

On January 3, 1719, Maynard arrived in Hampton Roads aboard the captured pirate ship *Adventure* with the severed head of Edward Teach hanging under its bowsprit, a grisly trophy to be presented to the Colony of Virginia!

Legend has it that Blackbeard's head was raised upon a pole at the mouth of the Hampton River, where it remained for years. It goes on to say that the skull was later fashioned into a huge drinking cup that is reputedly still in existence. Blackbeard probably would have approved!

ing that, you can't miss the massive Chamberlin Hotel described above for Mill Creek. The channel is well marked and leads to a snug harbor with a variety of marine services.

Dockages/Provisions.

You may not be able to find a good place to anchor here, with the exception of near the Settlers Landing Bridge upstream. The channel is too narrow in most places. However, you should have little trouble finding a slip for the night at one of the many marinas. Hampton Roads Marina, in Sunset Creek to port just past the river entrance, advertises transient slips, as does the Bluewater Yacht Yard. Hampton Roads Marina also offers a courtesy car. Joy's Marina, to starboard, doesn't seem to have any transient facilities. For those with a membership in a recognized yacht club, the Hampton Yacht Club, to port just beyond Sunset Creek, is most hospitable and will help visitors find a slip. Jones Marina, just past the Hampton Yacht Club, also offers transient slips.

Stop at the Hampton Visitor's Center, to port just before the bridge at the head of navigation. They have a dock, and will provide you with more information on the area than you can use. They also may be able to point out some possible areas to anchor. Be sure to visit the new Air & Space Science Museum in downtown Hampton. Next to the museum is one of the few remaining wooden horse Merry-Go-Rounds, a relic from the old Buckroe Beach Amusement Park.

The large white bridge a little beyond the Visitor's Center marks the head of navigation for sailboats. Even if a sailboat can clear the bridge, the shoal water on the other side stops everything except shoal-draft vessels and waders.

WILLOUGHBY BAY

Charts: 12206, **12222**, 12221,

12245, 12254, 12256

Approaches.

This is a well-protected, sizable harbor, which, although lacking in attractiveness, offers plenty of anchoring room and is an easily entered harbor of refuge. It is on the south side, immediately inside the entrance to Hampton Roads after you clear Fort Wool. Be sure to honor the first pair of markers as you enter this bay's channel because of the pincer-like shoals at its mouth. Once you pass the second green daymark, you need not worry too much about the rest of the markers provided you err to the west, not the east, should you drift out of the channel. There can be a fair tidal current that tends to push you out of the channel, so keep tabs on your position and the markers fore and aft.

Dockages/Facilities.

As you clear the last set of entrance channel markers, there are three marinas to port, followed by the municipal boat ramp with 150 feet of dockage. However, the depth at the municipal dock is not certain, so feel your way. Sailboats should avoid the area around the municipal boat ramp because the water is very shallow with several shoals. The marinas are clustered inside the curl at the tip of Willoughby Spit. Willoughby Bay Marina and Willoughby Harbor Marina offer transient slips and the latter even has a laundromat. Rebel Marine Service has a towing service with a salvage crew and divers on call, a fairly unique service on the Bay. They also have an unadvertised paperback book library in which you can exchange your paperbacks for others at no cost. This is something we would like to see more of on the Bay! Rebel Marine is the home of a rather unique vessel; the auxiliary sail-powered 51-foot "Tugantine," the *Norfolk Rebel*. If it is in port, go take a look.

Anchorages.

If you choose to anchor, Willoughby Bay is somewhat open to the northwest, but the entrance shoals minimize the wave action and you can tuck into the northeast corner of the bay and find reasonably good shelter even from that direction.

As stated earlier, this is not a pretty anchorage. Interstate Route 64 emerges from the Hampton Roads Tunnel and runs along a causeway for the entire length of Willoughby Spit. As a result, expect constant road noise. Save for the marinas, the area borders on being barren. All of the southern and eastern shoreline of this bay is a restricted area belonging to the Norfolk Navy Base. Landing or even anchoring close to these shores is prohibited. (Have you ever been chased away by a helicopter?) Many charts will show a seaplane landing lane right down the middle of Willoughby Bay. Don't worry about that—it has been discontinued.

As a harbor of refuge, a short-term stop for a lunch break, or a visit to a marina or restaurant, Willoughby Bay is just fine. If you are coming out of the James or heading north from the Intracoastal Waterway, it serves as a good jump-off place in the area for a cruise up the Chesapeake or out into the Atlantic. But as an attractive, secluded, quiet anchorage in its own right, forget it!

Fort Wool

In the mouth of the James River, about a mile south of the tip of Old Point Comfort and the bastions of Fort Monroe, is a totally man-made island with a somewhat checkered history. The island came into being from decades of ship ballast being dumped on a shoal, long before there were any conscious efforts to stabilize the resulting pile of stones into an island that could be used for anything.

Although Fort Monroe, constructed on Old Point Comfort, was intended to defend the mouth of the James River, the artillery of the day wasn't quite up to the task due to lack of accurate range to cover the whole entrance. In an effort to better protect the mouth of the river, construction of an island on the site of the ballast pile (or rip rap), to be followed by the construction of a fort, began in 1819. At that time and for several decades, it was called Fort Calhoun, in honor of John C. Calhoun, President Monroe's Secretary of War at the time.

The task of stabilizing the island turned out to be more difficult than anticipated. The dumping of rock and other material for the construction of a foundation for the fort went very slowly, with the blocks sinking into the deep mud. It wasn't until 1823 that the foundation was raised to a mere six feet above mean high water. Even then, it took until 1826 before the cornerstone of the fort was laid. Everything was done with hand labor, but it was done well. The construction of the fort was solid and it was built to stand in spite of the possibility of cannonballs being bounced off it. Man-made assault it could withstand; Nature's was another story.

Even after construction of the fort was completed, the island was not yet stable. The weight of rock and masonry caused the island to continue to sink into the mud. During his tour of duty at Fort Monroe, a young lieutenant of Engineers, one Robert E. Lee, was assigned the onerous task of stabilizing the island. This he accomplished by the process of adding rock and more rock, finally succeeding in stabilizing the island in the last three months of his 1831–1834 tour there.

At times, the fort was used as a summer resort by government dignitaries, notably Presidents Andrew Jackson (in 1831 and 1833), and John Tyler (in 1842). With the commencement of the War Between the States, the fort was selected by the commandant of Fort Monroe, General Wool, as a good place to send prisoners of war and other federal convicts for punishment. (The fort was later renamed for him.) However, the Army soon determined that imprisonment on this early version of Alcatraz was a form of "cruel and unusual punishment" and the practice was discontinued in 1862.

President Lincoln visited Fort Wool in May 1862 to observe an artillery bombardment of Confederate batteries on Norfolk's Sewall Point. This was also the occasion of the testing of the experimental Sawyer rifled cannon, now displayed on Fort Monroe as "The Lincoln Gun." The last active bombardment by guns on Fort Wool ended with the landing of Union forces on a Norfolk beach and the surrender of Norfolk on May 10, 1862.

Fort Wool remained in active Federal service—without any further significant activities—until abandoned by the Army as surplus in 1967. Today, the island is uninhabited, save by pigeons and sea gulls (and, perhaps, a few ghosts), but it is worth a visit to walk around the remains of the fort and muse about the conditions endured by the soldiers assigned to such a barren place in days long gone by. In spite of its closer proximity to Willoughby Spit, off the shores of Norfolk, the 15-acre, kidney-shaped island is now a park owned and operated by the city of Hampton, visited daily by tour boats based in that city.

ELIZABETH
RIVER
(NORFOLK
AND
PORTSMOUTH)

372

ELIZABETH RIVER (NORFOLK AND PORTSMOUTH)

Charts: 12206, 12207, 12221,

12222, 12245, 12253, 12254

There is probably some argument as to where, exactly, the Elizabeth River begins. For purposes of continuity and description, we locate the entrance to the Elizabeth River as just to the west of Sewells Point, down the large, clearly marked, north/south-oriented channel. In all probability, you will never notice Sewells Point. You will be too busy gawking at the huge Navy ships, aircraft carriers, and the like, berthed at the piers all along the eastern side of the channel from Sewells to Tanner Point. (There is a seasonally available guided tour of the

The Elizabeth River channel is busy; you will be dodging shipping traffic and huge Navy ships, carriers, and the like. The Norfolk Navy Base piers extend from Sewell Point to Tanner Point on the eastern side of the channel. U.S. NAVY PHOTOS

Norfolk Navy Base. Call (804)627-9291 for the latest information on times and starting point.) You may also find yourself dodging other shipping traffic if you pick an inopportune moment to enter this channel. As a matter of fact, you don't have to remain in the shipping channel. It is smarter to parallel its path just to the west of the line of red markers, where the water depth averages 15 feet. Don't even think of stopping in this region. The first place you can get out of the traffic pattern is at the Lafayette River.

For approximately the first 15 miles, the Elizabeth River is bounded on the east by the City of Norfolk, founded in 1680 by an Act of the Virginia Assembly that set aside 50 acres on the banks of the Elizabeth River to establish a town. From then on, the town grew and kept growing, as the City of Norfolk is still trying to do today. (Ask any citizen of Virginia Beach about that last item!)

However, this growth wasn't without its rough spots. At the beginning of the American Revolution, on January 1, 1776, a British fleet under Lord Dunsmore bombarded the town. What was left after the bombardment was burned to the ground by the patriots to prevent British occupation, an extreme but effective measure. The sole survivor from that time is the St. Paul's Episcopal Church, still an active parish, which holds one of Lord Dunsmore's cannonballs embedded in one of its walls to this day.

Norfolk quickly recovered from this disaster and, by the end of the 18th century, was booming with ship-building and maritime activities. But it had two more severe blows to absorb. In 1855 a yellow fever epidemic devastated the population and brought shipping activities to a halt. Less than 10 years later, the city was occupied by Union troops as the *Monitor* and the *Merrimac* clashed in Hampton Roads during the Civil War.

Today, as in the beginning, Norfolk is heavily reliant on the shipping industry (it is one of the two largest ports in the States) and a growing U.S. Naval presence. (Norfolk has the largest Navy base in the world.) Downtown Norfolk, once a dingy area of wharves and "low class establishments," has been revitalized and now sparkles with life and activities. (See the section on downtown Norfolk for more detail.)

Across the Elizabeth River from downtown Norfolk is the City of Portsmouth. Sometimes thought of as a "suburb of Norfolk," Portsmouth has a separate identity and is undergoing its own renovation. Founded in 1752 and surrounded by water on three sides, this city has always been associated with ships and the sea.

The Norfolk Naval Shipyard, the oldest naval shipyard in the United States and the largest ship repair yard in the world, is located in Portsmouth—not Norfolk—and it is Portsmouth's largest employer. The first cruiser, the first battleship, and the first aircraft carrier of the U.S. Navy were all built here. The first drydock, built here in 1831, is still in use, along with more modern ones. The first ironclad, the *Merrimac* (renamed the *Virginia*) was fitted out in the Portsmouth shipyards prior to her successful engagement with the blockading wooden vessels of the U.S. Navy and the fateful, if inconclusive, battle with the *Monitor*.

Commercial shipping commands its share of attention. Container ships regularly visit the docks between Pinner and Love Points.

The city itself has much more to offer than just its shipping, however. It caters to private boats as well as visitors arriving by land, and there is plenty to see and do. Like downtown Norfolk, The Olde Towne has been revitalized and certainly is not to be missed. (See the section on Portsmouth for more details.)

Beyond Norfolk and Portsmouth, you are at the entrance to the Intracoastal Waterway, the main "inside" route to the southern waters all the way to Florida. (The passage through the Intracoastal Waterway is a story all its own and is beyond the scope of this book.)

ELIZABETH
RIVER
(NORFOLK
AND
PORTSMOUTH)

373

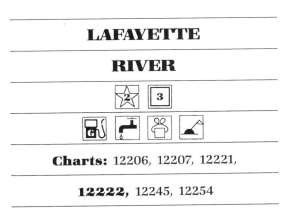

LAFAYETTE

RIVER

Charts: 12206, 12207, 12221, **12222,** 12245, 12254

Approaches. The entrance to the Lafayette River is directly opposite the northern tip of Craney Island, the first solid piece of land to starboard as you are proceeding south on the Elizabeth River. From Craney Island, head due east to pick up the lighted red "2" marker at the entrance to the channel leading into the Lafayette River. This channel is relatively narrow, but well marked. Simply follow the markers.

ELIZABETH
RIVER
(NORFOLK
AND
PORTSMOUTH)

374

Dockages/Provisions. The Norfolk Yacht & Country Club is just outside the first bridge. The club offers reciprocal privileges to member of recognized yacht clubs and service is available on a 24-hour basis. Gas, ice, and water are available at the dock and slips are often available.

The 26-foot vertical clearance of the Route 337 (Hampton Boulevard) fixed bridge makes this the head of navigation for nearly all cruising sailboats, even though there is a minimum of 7 feet of water in the channel for another 1½ miles. There are a couple of small powerboat marinas on the south shore, about a mile past the Route 337 bridge and a little before the next (Route 460; Granby Street) bridge but their facilities are limited.

Anchorages. There is some room to anchor near marker red "14" just short of the bridge. Be careful as you head south out of the channel, it shoals quickly. The permanent moorings in this area serve as a reference. Past the bridge, there is little, if any, room to anchor outside of the channel, except for shallow-draft boats. For sailboats, it is the yacht club or nothing if you can't find anchorage space by red "14."

CRANEY ISLAND CREEK

No ratings

Charts: 12206, 12221,

12222, 12253, 12245

Just south of Craney Island, there is a marked channel leading west to the U.S. Coast Guard Station there. In spite of the fact that the only land battle won by the Americans *during* the War of 1812 was fought on Craney Island, there is nothing to see. (The Battle of New Orleans was fought *after* the conclusion of the war.) The Coast Guard station is all that is there.

WESTERN BRANCH

Charts: 12253, 12222,

12245, **12221,** 12206

Dockages/Facilities. Below Lamberts Point, the marked channel of the Western Branch of the Elizabeth River leads out of Port Norfolk Reach, to the southwest. On the north side of the fixed bridge in the Western Branch, three marinas are clustered, two before and one after the bridge. The vertical clearance of the bridge is 45 feet. If you are in a sailboat whose mast, including any antennas, is taller than that, you have reached the head of navigation.

Anchorages. Even if you are able to get past the first bridge, the next one has a vertical clearance of only 28 feet. The area between these two bridges is the only area in which you may try to anchor on this branch of the Elizabeth River. It is fairly well protected, except from the east. The bottom provides good holding in soft mud and it should be relatively peaceful.

If you are unable to clear the first bridge, forget this one, except for a possible trip to the marinas for resupply or to rent a slip.

SCOTTS CREEK

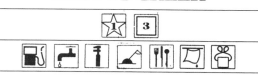

Charts: 12206, **12221,** 12253

Facilities. South of the Western Branch and north of Hospital Point, Scotts Creek opens to the west off the Elizabeth River. Scotts Creek Marina, a full marina with a marina store, provides a shuttle service to Waterside across the river in Norfolk. The City of Portsmouth has approved the dredging of the length of Scotts Creek, and has plans for a marine-related business park on the north shore.

DOWNTOWN NORFOLK

Charts: 12221, 12222, 12253,

12254, 12256

The Main Branch of the Elizabeth River continues for about 2 miles past the junction with the Western Branch. Then, a short distance past Town Point, it forks again into the Southern Branch and the Eastern Branch. The Southern Branch leads to the Intracoastal Waterway. The Eastern Branch holds little of interest to the cruiser save a couple of more marinas.

ELIZABETH
RIVER
(NORFOLK
AND
PORTSMOUTH)

375

This section of the Main Branch of the Elizabeth River, between the junction with the Western Branch and the split to the south, is the region of primary interest to cruisers and many others as well. Here is the location of the attractions of downtown Norfolk on one side and the Olde Towne of Portsmouth on the other.

Just before the fork in the river, on Town Point itself, the city of Norfolk has made a much heralded attempt to revive downtown Norfolk, pumping millions of dollars into the project to clear the old waterfront, build a pretty riverside park, construct a spacious parking garage, and underwrite the brand new $13.5-million pavilion of The Waterside.

Dockages/Provisions. The Waterside, a conceptual replica of Baltimore's Harborplace, is located behind the breakwater of City Marina at Waterside, just past Town Point Park. You can sail right up to the pavilion and dock, although reservations for a slip or dockspace are virtually a necessity during the main boating season. (The City Marina at Waterside monitors VHF-FM channels 16 & 68, or you can phone them on (804)441-2222.) There is always someone eager to

Waterside marketplace. You can cruise right up to the pavilion and dock. Inside the pavilion houses more than 120 shops. DEBORAH WAKEFIELD/NORFOLK CONVENTION & VISITORS BUREAU

ELIZABETH
RIVER
(NORFOLK
AND
PORTSMOUTH)

376

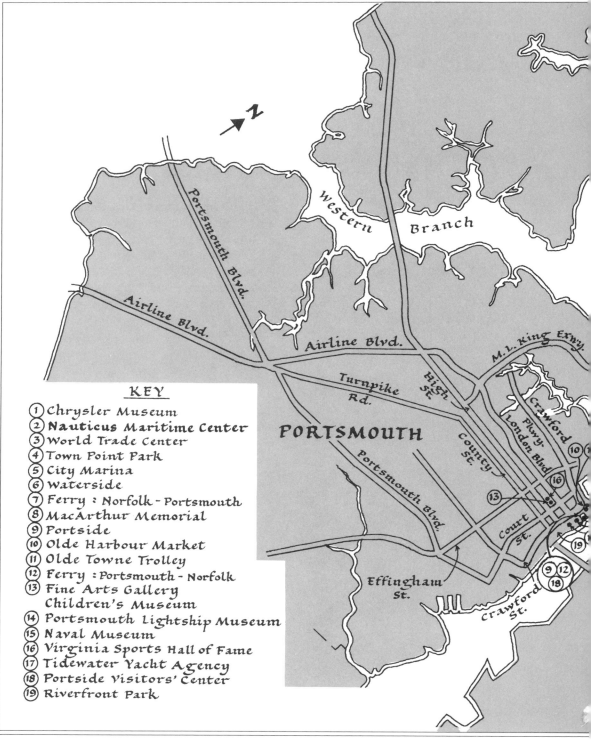

KEY

1. Chrysler Museum
2. Nauticus Maritime Center
3. World Trade Center
4. Town Point Park
5. City Marina
6. Waterside
7. Ferry : Norfolk - Portsmouth
8. MacArthur Memorial
9. Portside
10. Olde Harbour Market
11. Olde Towne Trolley
12. Ferry : Portsmouth - Norfolk
13. Fine Arts Gallery
    Children's Museum
14. Portsmouth Lightship Museum
15. Naval Museum
16. Virginia Sports Hall of Fame
17. Tidewater Yacht Agency
18. Portside Visitors' Center
19. Riverfront Park

PORTSMOUTH

SCALE 1" = .20 MILES

ELIZABETH
RIVER
(NORFOLK
AND
PORTSMOUTH)

377

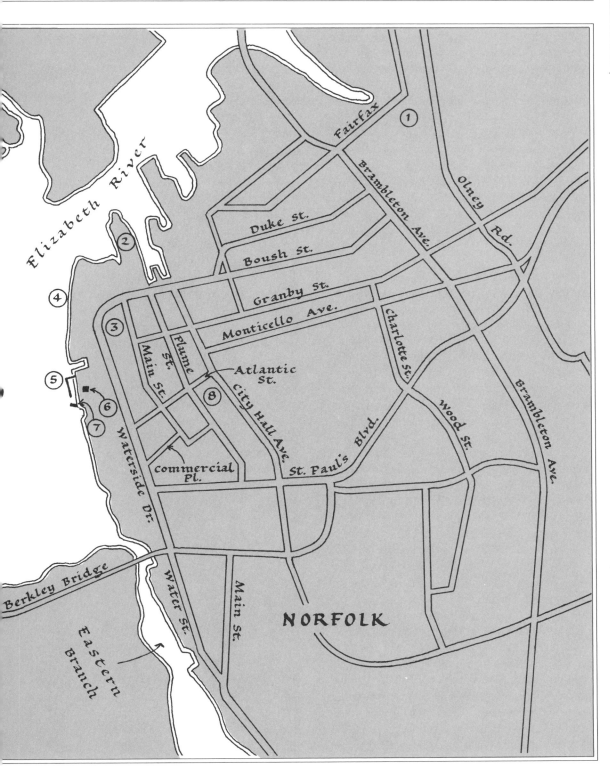

Elizabeth River

Fairfax

Brambleton Ave.

Olney

Rd.

①

②

④

③

Duke St.

Boush St.

Granby St.

Monticello Ave.

Charlotte St.

Plume St.

Main St.

Atlantic St.

⑤

⑥

⑦

⑧

City Hall Ave.

Wood St.

Brambleton Ave.

commercial Pl.

St. Paul's Blvd.

Waterside Dr.

Berkley Bridge

Water St.

Main St.

NORFOLK

Eastern
Branch

take your lines and they won't necessarily be marina personnel!

Within the pavilion are more than 120 shops offering a wide variety of items for sale, including a fantastic assortment of food in numerous stands and restaurants. (There is a fudge-making concession which demonstrates its technique in a singularly entertaining manner. You have to see it, I can't explain properly in words.) The Waterside, billed as a "festival marketplace" is successfully drawing people from outlying areas who, otherwise, might have little reason to go to downtown Norfolk. It seems that Norfolk, like Baltimore, is having a great deal of success in the renovation and revitalization of its waterfront. Open seven days a week, The Waterside has become almost as much a gathering place as a marketplace.

Things to Do. It isn't a coincidence that a variety of festivals, concerts, theater presentations, celebrations, and assorted other entertaining activities are featured, usually free of charge, in the adjacent Town Point Park. This 6.5-acre waterfront park includes a brick promenade that runs the length of the waterfront (including past The Waterside), has an "activities area" and a 5,000-seat ampitheater-on-the-grass. Beyond the amphitheater is the Nauticus Maritime Center, a hands-on maritime museum housed in a building designed to look like a ship.

Behind and to the north of The Waterside pavilion is another World Trade Center, a concept reminiscent of the one in Baltimore, although the building is of a different design. Behind that is the W. T. Brownley Co., which specializes in nautical instruments and charts. They also have a compass adjusting service.

Slightly farther afield, south of the junction of Plume and Bank Streets, is the Douglas MacArthur Memorial, composed of four buildings. The one to visit first is the Theatre, which contains several displays and continuously shows a 22-minute compilation of newsreels featuring General of the Army Douglas MacArthur. There is the Library and Archives housing MacArthur's 4000-volume book collection and more than 2-million assorted documents. The Gift Shop, in addition to the obvious, displays MacArthur's 1950 Chrysler Imperial limousine. The Memorial, where the General is entombed in a large rotunda, is a conversion of the old 19th century Norfolk City Hall. The basic theme is MacArthur's creed: Duty, Honor, Country.

Also in the vicinity is the Chrysler Museum, rated by

The Wall Street Journal as one of the top 20 art museums in the country. Named for Walter P. Chrysler, of automotive fame, the collection encompasses not only Roman, Greek, Oriental and pre-Columbian American art, but paintings and sculpture from major periods of European and American art.

For ranging farther afield, there is a "Discover Tidewater Trolley Tour," which travels around downtown Norfolk and over to the Norfolk General Hospital and Fort Norfolk area. A guide aboard the trolly regales you with tales of the sites and the city along the way. The trolley stops at a substantial number of the sights, allowing you to disembark and explore, then reboard the next trolley that comes along to continue the tour. The fare is $1.50 (as of 1989, subject to change) per person with half-fare for senior citizens and children under 12. It runs 10:00 a.m. to 4:00 p.m., from May to September and noon to 4:00 p.m. in the month of September.

One more item which I should mention: Early each June, Norfolk conducts a three-day long Harborfest, centered on The Waterside, featuring all kinds of activities and entertainment. If you plan to arrive during that time, make your reservations well in advance! (For more information, contact the Norfolk Convention and Visitors Bureau, 236 E. Plume Street, Norfolk, VA 23510, (804)441-5266.)

Speaking of trips, you can leave your boat where it is and take the *Carrie B*, a replica sternwheel riverboat ferry, from the dock in front of The Waterside across the Elizabeth River to visit Portside and the City of Portsmouth. The ferry departs The Waterside every

ELIZABETH
RIVER
(NORFOLK
AND
PORTSMOUTH)

378

The Elizabeth River ferry runs between Norfolk and Portsmouth. The 15-minute ride provides a low-fare easy passage between cities.

half hour at quarter after and quarter before the hour. It returns from Portside, departing every half hour at the hour and half hour. The 15-minute ride costs the staggering fee of $1.00 per person (as of 1992) and senior citizens get a 50-percent discount on the fare. Try it! It provides a new perspective as well as an interesting trip and it's the easy way to get to Portside and vice-versa.

You can cruise the Elizabeth River on the *American Rover*, a 135-foot, three-masted topsail schooner modeled after Chesapeake Bay cargo schooners of the past century. She is the largest such passenger-carrying schooner under U.S. flag. The *American Rover* departs from The Waterside Marina; for information or reservations, call (804)627-SAIL. The *American Rover* offers daily 2- and 3-hour tours of Hampton Roads nautical landmarks, allowing you to see the sights and let her captain worry about the shipping and naval traffic. In 1992, the futuristic-looking *Spirit of Norfolk* began offering lunch, dinner, and moonlight cruises.

PORTSMOUTH

All facilities

Charts: 12206, 12221,

12222, 12253, 12245

ELIZABETH
RIVER
(NORFOLK
AND
PORTSMOUTH)

379

Just across the Elizabeth River from The Waterside is Portside, Portsmouth's complement. You can lay alongside the quay opposite the Portside-Waterside Ferry landing at no charge for at least a few hours. However, you may find the climb up to the top of the quay a bit on the arduous side.

Anchorages. There is a possible anchorage off either side of Hospital Point, but you have to stay well out, not far from the channel because of shoaling. It is exposed to wakes from passing traffic and you still have the problem of landing. Finding a place to take a dinghy

Portside, the Portsmouth complement to Norfolk's Waterside, and the ferry docks. You can lay alongside the quay (not shown) opposite this landing for two hours at no charge.

ELIZABETH
RIVER
(NORFOLK
AND
PORTSMOUTH)

380

in and leave it is not insurmountable, but you really don't need another nuisance here.

Dockages/Facilities.   A far better idea is to put into the Tidewater Yacht Agency a couple hundred yards to the north of Portside, behind a large wooden breakwater. Here are all the marine facilities you have dreamed of, including a dockside sewage pumpout facility and a laundromat. Take a slip here and you can wander Portsmouth and Norfolk to your heart's content, assured that your boat is in good hands.

Be sure to make your first stop the large Visitor's Center, just above the ferry landing, to collect all manner of information and brochures on the area. There are rest rooms here, as well as the ticket counter for a trolley tour, a counterpart to the one in Norfolk.

Things to Do.   Open from spring through early fall, Portside offers a dozen open-air shops with everything from plants to seafood (the Olde Harbour Market), a variety of entertainment on its floating stage (free), and roving entertainers (The Portside Players). Nearby is the starting point for a 45-minute trolley tour of Olde Towne, with its collection of historical houses and five museums (Children's Museum, Fine Arts Gallery, Virginia Sports Hall of Fame, Naval Shipyard Museum, and the Lightship Museum). In all, more than 50 points of interest are highlighted. Actually, all are within easy walking distance from Portside, but the narrated tour by trolley guide makes a good introduction to the whole area with little effort on your part. The fare is only $1.50 per person, half price for senior citizens and children under 12.

To the north is Hospital Point with the large Portsmouth Naval Hospital. Nearly everything else to see is to the south and west of the Visitor's Center.

On the quay, just a little south of the ferry landing area, is the Portsmouth Lightship Museum. The museum is an actual 1915 Coast Guard Lightship, *Lightship Charles,* which you can board and examine, together with exhibits and artifacts which describe the era of lightships.

Next, just a little farther down Water Street, past Riverside Park (the only open space left in Portsmouth), is the Naval Museum, where "Naval history comes alive" with displays of weapons, ship models, flags, and pictures. Some of the guns there were actually used by the British during the Revolution in the shelling of Norfolk from Portsmouth.

From there, turn down High Street to visit the Children's Museum and Fine Arts Gallery; both are in the old 1846 Portsmouth Courthouse. The exhibits in the Children's Museum are right out in the open and touching or working with them is encouraged. Next door is the Virginia Sports Hall of Fame with exhibits from major sports figures from the entire state.

There is so much more that I won't even attempt to address it all. Get a copy of the "Olde Towne Lantern Tour" pamphlet from the Visitor's Center for a guide on where else to go and what to see in the area. This provides more details and anecdotes on the sights you saw briefly during the trolley tour, but now you can take your time. You will find a warm welcome everywhere you go.

For more information, contact the Department of Economic Development, 801 Crawford Street, Portsmouth, VA 23704, (804)393-8804.

A 45-minute trolley tour of Old Towne (Portsmouth) includes a guide whose talk serves as an introduction to the historic district and area museums.

EASTERN BRANCH

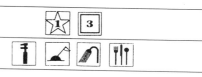

Charts: 12206, **12207,** 12221, 12253

There is little to say about the Eastern Branch of the Elizabeth River. While it is navigable for a few more miles, it has no particular points of interest and is not an especially attractive route to take. Pass it by.

SOUTHERN
BRANCH (ICW)

All facilities

Charts: 12221, 12207, **12206**

Approaches. The Southern Branch of the Elizabeth River leads to both branches of the Intracoastal Waterway: the Albemarle Canal (route #1) and the Great Dismal Swamp Canal (route #2). The Albemarle Canal is shorter, wider and deeper, but there is a long stretch down the Currituck Sound and then across Albemarle Sound at the southern end of it, which seems to be rather uncomfortable as a general rule. The Dismal Swamp route is longer, but more interesting. It runs straight as an arrow, except for one bend, for 22 miles with a controlling depth of 6 feet and terminates at the village of South Mills in North Carolina.

Facilities. If you expect to need any marine facilities along the way, take the first route. If you want a more interesting trip and can hold out for any marine facilities until you reach Elizabeth City, North Carolina, take the second one.

Unless you plan to take the ICW, at least as far as Lake Drummond, this branch of the Elizabeth River holds little interest.

NANSEMOND RIVER

Chart: 12248

Although readily accessible from Hampton Roads, the Nansemond River is permanently spoiled for cruisers. Aside from the marshy shores, which can be a plus, the area is heavily commercial and oil and gravel barges frequently ply the channel.

Dockages/Provisions. Anchorages are effectively nil because of shoals outside the marked channel. Bennett Creek Marina, on the south shore just before the drawbridge at Town Point, offers some facilities for powerboats. Brady Marina is one-half mile up the shallow Western Branch, which is over 10 miles up the Nansemond River from its mouth. Eight feet of water is carried in the channel of the Nansemond all the way to Suffolk, although I don't recommend the trip unless you just want to take a look.

JAMES RIVER

Charts: 12221, 12248, 12251, 12254

The James River has its origins west of Virginia's Blue Ridge Mountains. From there, it meanders through the Piedmont, passing names notable in the history of this country: from the Blue Ridge, through Lynchburg, over the Piedmont Plateau, past Richmond, joining with the Appomattox River (which passes nearby Petersburg), swelling in size to flow by the stately plantations of Shirley, Westover, Berkley, Brandon and others, on past the Jamestown Colonial National Historical Park, by Newport News, to Norfolk and the famous Hampton Roads, where it empties into the Chesapeake Bay. Admittedly, urban and industrial development has made its impact on the river's scenery. For instance, over 10 years ago, there was a large industrial spill (some say deliberate dumping) of the toxic kepone chemical which polluted a large portion of the James River, causing a prohibition of harvesting of all marine life from most of the James River for several years. The chemical sank to the bottom and remains there slowly being buried in silt but retaining its toxicity for years to come. I am not sure of the current status of the restrictions, but believe that most of them have now been lifted. While this event— and those like it—of the recent past give one pause, the names associated with this river and the history these names bring to mind continue to stir our imaginations, and the basic beauty of the river itself, in most of its reaches, still remains to draw the cruiser.

The James River bridge, at Newport News, is a minor obstacle to some ships due to its 65-foot vertical clearance when the lift bridge is closed. There normally is an operator on duty, and the clearance is 145 feet with the lift raised. The James is navigable for about 90

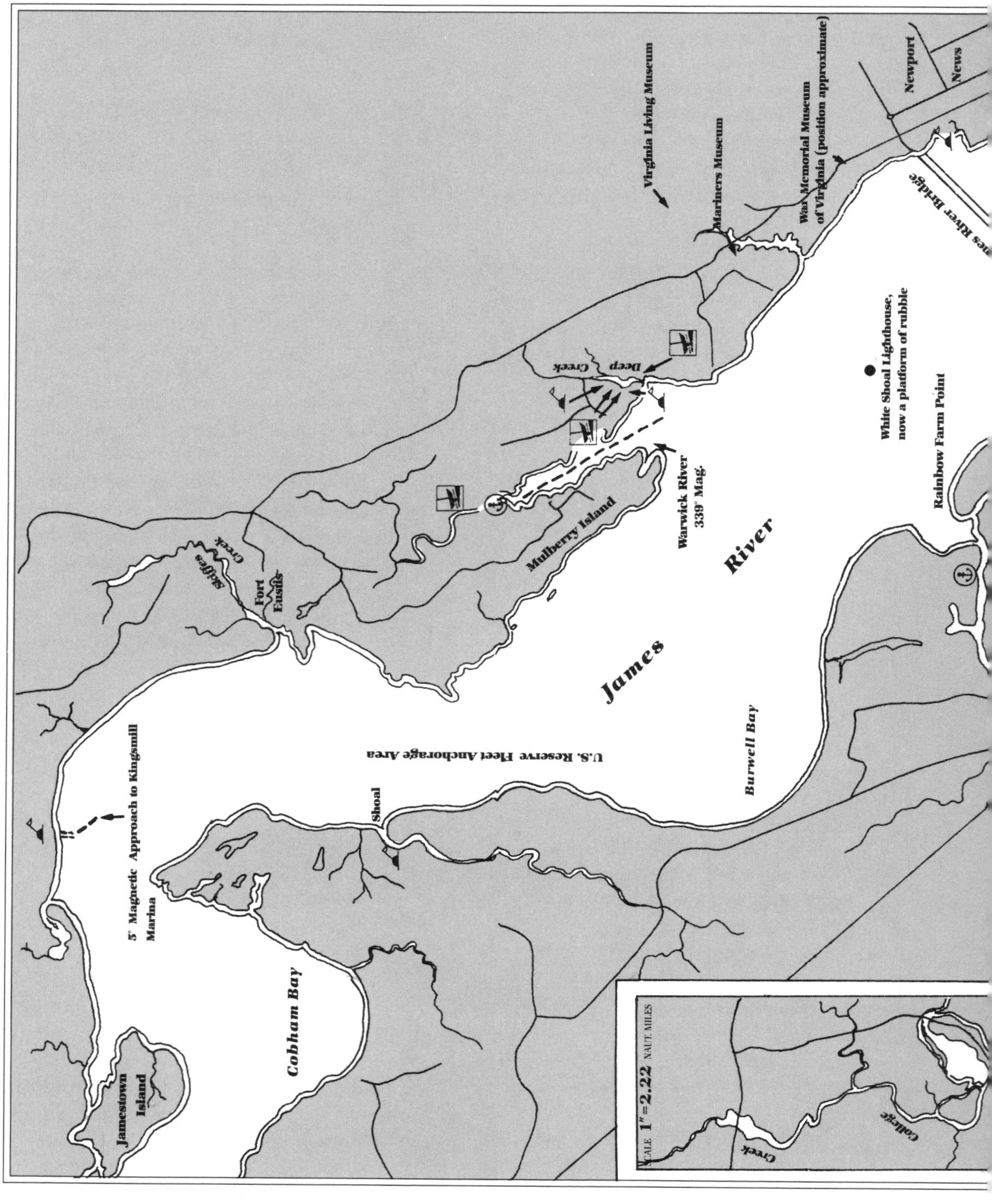

Lower James River

Virginia Living Museum

Mariners Museum

War Memorial Museum of Virginia (position approximate)

Newport

News

James River Bridge

Deep Creek

White Shoal Lighthouse, now a platform of rubble

Rainbow Farm Point

Warwick River 339° Mag.

Mulberry Island

River

James

Burwell Bay

U.S. Reserve Fleet Anchorage Area

Skiffes Creek

Fort Eustis

Shoal

5' Magnetic Approach to Kingsmill Marina

Cobham Bay

Jamestown Island

SCALE 1" = 2.22 NAUT. MILES

College

Creek

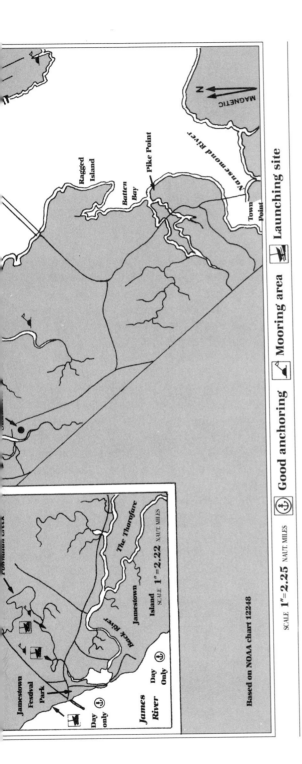

The James River bridge has a closed vertical clearance of 65 feet. VA PENINSULA TOURISM BUREAU

miles, all the way to Richmond, although few choose to cruise that far. Like many Bay rivers, the best cruising grounds are near its mouth.

But the James is a unique Bay river in that, above its junction with the Chickahominy, it has twists and turns and islands splitting the channel, making it more reminiscent of tales of the Mississippi River than of Chesapeake Bay cruising. Beyond this junction, you are into river cruising of a type closer to wilderness trekking on the water than you will find on any other river with direct, navigable access to the Bay. Few cruisers proceed upstream of the junction with the Chickahominy, feeling that the trip is not worth the trouble. But, if you are looking for something well out of the ordinary character of Bay cruising, try making the trek to Richmond. If you do, allow plenty of time to poke into the bights where the river has changed its course, creating islands such as Turkey, Jones Neck, and Hatcher Islands. Bear in mind that, in the upper reaches, you must navigate a relatively narrow channel where there is occasional shipping traffic.

NEWPORT NEWS

Charts: 12221, 12248, **12254**

While not exactly the best cruising country, the city of Newport News offers some attractions—beyond the usual amenities of fuel and supplies—which are well worth visiting. The difficulty lies in finding a secure place in reasonable proximity to the points of interest in which to leave your boat. One choice, for a day stop in fair weather, is to anchor in the James River near the shore and land by dinghy. For an overnight stay, there is little choice other than to take a slip in one of the marinas.

Dockages/Provisions.
Although Newport News Creek, at the southern tip of the point, looks like a potential anchorage on the chart, this is not an attractive harbor for cruising boats. It is crowded with commercial boats and is distinctly unappealing to cruisers. It is also well beyond walking distance from the prime points of interest. There are three marinas located here. Crockett's Marina and Davis Boat Works offer dockage, which would be a smart choice if you stay here. Anchoring in the harbor doesn't seem to be a good idea.

The Municipal Marina-Peterson Yacht Basin is located roughly midway between Newport News Creek and the Hampton River, but it is restricted to smaller boats because of a fixed bridge with a 12-foot clearance.

A better choice for those wishing to visit Newport News and its many attractions would be to put in to the Leeward Marina, located behind a breakwater, just south of the James River bridge (Route 17). Simply head for the base of the bridge and daymarks will guide you to the opening in the breakwater. This marina was opened by the city of Newport News in mid-1988 and is operated by its Parks and Recreation Department. Ice is available at the marina and grocery stores; restaurants and two large shopping malls are within walking distance.

Things to Do.
The Mariners Museum (admission fee) is probably the prime attraction for cruisers in this area. Located on a 550-acre park and wildlife sanctuary about 2 miles north of the James River bridge, the museum itself offers an extensive collection of figureheads, navigation instruments, whaling equipment,

The Newport News Shipbuilding & Dry Dock Company is the largest privately owned shipyard in the nation. Shown here is the *Dorothy*, the company's first vessel. The 90-foot tugboat worked the New York Harbor until 1912. NNS&DD CO.

lighthouse and lifesaving devices, numerous ship models, marine paintings, and temporary special exhibits. The museum opened a Chesapeake Bay wing in the fall of 1989. The museum is open seven days a week, year-round, except Christmas Day. The hours are Monday through Saturday, 9:00 a.m. to 5:00 p.m.; Sunday, noon to 5:00 p.m. For more information, contact The Mariners Museum, Newport News, VA 23606, (804) 595-0368.

Just north of the bridge is the War Memorial Museum of Virginia, which is dedicated to U.S. military history from 1775 to the present. The collection contains more than 30,000 artifacts, including uniforms, weapons, artwork, aircraft, vehicles, and other materials that relate to every U.S. military involvement from the Revolution to Vietnam. Special programs are also available. (For more information, call (804)247-8523.)

A little harder to get to, but still worth a visit, is the Virginia Living Museum, located at 524 J. Clyde Morris Boulevard. Formerly the Peninsula Nature and Science Center, it has been transformed into a combination natural history museum, zoological park, aquarium, and planetarium. It is open seven days a week. Summer (mid-June to Labor Day) hours are: Monday through Saturday 9:00 a.m. to 6:00 p.m.; Sunday 10:00 a.m. to 6:00 p.m. Winter (Labor Day to mid-June) hours are: Monday through Saturday 9:00 a.m. to 5:00 p.m.; Sunday 1:00 to 5:00 p.m. It is also open every Thursday evening from 7:00 to 9:00 p.m. (For more information, contact Virginia Living Museum, 524 J. Clyde Morris Boulevard, Newport News, VA 23601, (804)595-1900.)

BATTEN BAY AND
CHUCKATUCK CREEK

No facilities

Charts: 12248, 12254

Here's a bit of a gunkholers challenge! Both Ragged Island Creek and Chuckatuck Creek split off from Batten Bay, but only Chuckatuck Creek offers any possibility of entry—and don't try it at all with a draft of 4 feet or more.

Approaches. To approach the first marker of the channel through Batten Bay, you should be on a course of about 270 degrees toward the southern tip of Ragged Island. As soon as you are able to see the red "2" daymark, southernmost of the cluster of red and green markers, head directly toward it. Leaving red "2" close to starboard, swing to leave the next marker, lighted Green "3," close to port. Leave the rest of the green markers close to port until you reach green "7." At this marker, swing hard to port to line up with the opening to the creek just north of Pike Point. You should be able to see the lighted red "8" marker ahead, which you should leave close to starboard.

Anchorages. Once past the red "10" daymark beyond Pike Point, you can anchor near the southern shore in the mouth of the second cove to port.

The drawbridge has 21 feet of vertical clearance when closed. It may require prior notice to have the bridge open and it probably isn't worth the effort; there are no good anchorages past the bridge and the creek shoals to less than 4 feet in about a mile.

Try it for the experience, but it is unlikely that you will want to do it again.

PAGAN RIVER

Chart: 12248

Approaches. A little over 2 miles beyond the James River lift bridge, you should be able to see the channel markers for the Pagan River to port. The first set of markers are southwest of the abandoned White Shoal Lighthouse (actually, nothing is left of the lighthouse but rubble on a platform) on the downstream side of White Shoal in the middle of the James River. The channel has a controlling depth of 6 feet, is well marked, and is easy to follow. Don't stray far from the markers as the channel has a nominal width of only 80 feet. For those with drafts of less than 4 feet, it may be tempting to make some short cuts. This is a bad idea due to the numerous fish and oyster stakes outside the channel, many of which are barely at or below the surface.

Facilities. As you pass Rainbow Farm Point, Jones Creek opens to port. This creek leads to the limited marina facilities at Rescue, about one-half mile up the creek. As you pass Battery Park (featuring the Battery Park Fish & Oyster Co.), just remain in the middle and honor any of the private marks you encounter. Consider the fixed bridge at Rescue to be the head of navigation. The vertical clearance of 10 feet may allow some powerboats to pass, but the one-half– to 1-foot shoal on the other side quickly discourages those trying to continue upstream.

Anchorages. There used to be a reasonable spot to anchor in the Pagan River, where the channel opens out past the first bend beyond Battery Park. That is now taken up by the Gatling Pointe Yacht Club, a private facility associated with a new housing development. There is a possible anchorage in a small bight in the first creek to port beyond the Gatling Pointe Yacht Club. Don't go too far in as it shoals rapidly! The shores in this region are low and marshy, promising mosquitoes, and you won't find anyplace to land except in mud. If you plan to go ashore, continue on. There really is no good place to anchor on the Pagan River until you reach Smithfield.

The narrow Bob Shoal Channel on the Pagan River begins about 1½ miles past the mouth of Jones Creek. It runs for just over one-half mile and is reputed to have a controlling depth of only 4 feet. If you draw more than that, you are on your own!

Things to Do. The town of Smithfield (of Smithfield Ham fame) lies about 2 miles up river from Battery Park. Here, you can tie up at the dock of the Smithfield Station, a combination marina, restaurant, hotel, and river cruise station. The 35-slip marina can accommodate boats up to 70 feet LOA. Rates vary according to your length of stay. From here, it is a short walk to tour Smithfield's historic district, do a little shopping (remember those hams?), or just relax and enjoy your stay in a quiet country town. Smithfield was settled in 1752, primarily by British merchants and ship captains. Ten of the houses in town pre-date the Revolutionary War. After the War Between the States, it was a center for the flourishing peanut industry, resulting in the construction of a number of elaborate Victorian houses with their turrets, towers, and stained glass windows. Smithfield is the main reason for any cruising boat to enter the Pagan River. (Special note: The Pagan River in this area can have a tidal current flow as high as 4 knots. Be prepared for it when anchoring or maneuvering in this river.)

The fixed bridge at Smithfield has a vertical clearance of 15 feet. If you can pass that obstacle and the 16-foot vertical clearance bridge one-half mile beyond it, the river is navigable for about another 2 miles for those boats with less than a 4-foot draft. This part of the river wanders through some very sparsely settled territory—a real drawing card for gunkholers.

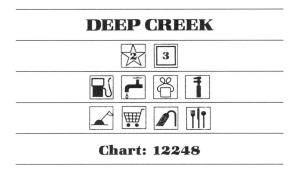

DEEP CREEK

Chart: 12248

Deep Creek is on the east shore of the James, about 2 miles due north of the upstream end of White Shoal.

Approaches. The inviting basin in Deep Creek is accessible through a mile-long, well-marked channel. The approach is a little deceptive as the channel initially appears to be leading into the mouth of the Warwick River directly to the north. It soon bends to the right, leading to the entrance to Deep Creek, just visible between a grassy knoll on the starboard side and a white building (city jail) on a small bluff to port. Unfortunately, the controlling depth in the channel is uncertain. If you have a 4-foot draft or more, check locally before attempting the channel. (The James River Marina advertises that they monitor VHF-FM Channel 16.)

Facilities/Dockages. As you pass between these two "landmarks," the basin inside opens out. The city dock is beside the spit, but it is usually cluttered with commercial boats. Easily visible are the three marinas and the Warwick Yacht & Country Club. Most of the marine facilities you need are there, including a dockside sewage pumpout facility at the Menchville Marine Supply Corp. Transient slips are not advertised, but are probably available for the asking. Herman's Harbor House Restaurant is also right on the water.

Anchorages. For anchoring, try the bight to starboard beyond the city dock, just short of a bunch of workboat tie stakes. Do not go beyond the range mark unless you are in the channel leading to the Warwick Yacht Club. The rest of the area is shoal.

It may not be secluded, but it is a secure harbor if you can get into it.

WARWICK RIVER

No facilities

Chart: 12248

Approaches. It is possible to get into the Warwick River if you have less than a 4-foot draft, but the channel is not well marked and there are extensive shoals. Start your approach in the same channel that leads into Deep Creek. Instead of turning to starboard at the channel dogleg, swing about 20 degrees to port and head directly for the red "2" daymark ahead. Leave this daymark and all following red markers close to starboard. Be very careful just before and after red "8" as there are shoals just under the surface in that vicinity. Feel your way past this marker slowly.

Anchorages. As you pass the two marshy points, swing to starboard to leave the green "11" daymark to port. You can anchor in 6 to 8 feet of water in this region, toward the middle of the river. It is possible to proceed for nearly another mile if you feel your way carefully past the next bend in the river. Fort Eustis covers the entire Mulberry Island peninsula, to port as you enter the river. There are no marine facilities anywhere on this river and nothing in particular to attract the cruiser, with the possible exception of the U.S. Army Transportation Museum at Fort Eustis. However, the museum is not readily accessible from the shores of the Warwick River. For that, Skiffes Creek is a far better choice.

Cruising into the Warwick River offers an interesting challenge to the gunkholer, but repeat visits are unlikely.

U.S. RESERVE FLEET

No rating

Chart: 12248

As you proceed up the James River, you see what appears to be an enormous fleet of ships anchored along the western side of the river. This is the "mothballed" reserve fleet. Be advised that the Maritime Administration, which has jurisdiction over this fleet, has designated the anchorage as a restricted area with the following admonition: "No vessels or other watercraft, except those owned or controlled by the U.S. Government, shall cruise or anchor between Reserve Fleet units, within 500 feet of the end vessels in each unit, or within 500 feet of the extreme units of the fleet, unless specific permission to do so has first been granted in each case by the enforcing agency."

Keep your distance, but get a good look as you go by. It's an impressive sight.

SKIFFES CREEK

No facilities

Chart: 12248

Things to Do. Past the northern end of the Reserve Fleet, just before the James makes a 90-degree left turn, a deep (11 feet), well-marked channel leads into Skiffes Creek. While all facilities in this region are the property of Fort Eustis, you may be allowed to tie up temporarily while you visit the U.S. Army Transportation Museum located in Building 300, Washington Boulevard, on the post, about a mile away.

The museum is the only one of its kind, having a complete display of military transportation depicting more than 200 years of U.S. Army history. The displays include aircraft, helicopters, trains, marine vessels, and one-of-a-kind experimental vehicles, such as the Avrocar Flying Saucer. Admission is free.

While entrance to this creek is not specifically restricted, we recommend skipping this one, save for a deliberate visit to the museum.

KINGSMILL

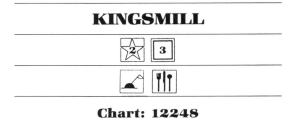

Chart: 12248

This is neither a creek, river, or cove. Nor is it an anchorage. It's a marina, and a private one at that! OK; so why am I singling out this marina in a book on harbors and gunkholes? There are two main reasons.

Dockages/Where to Eat. First of all, it's the only refuge for a considerable distance on this part of the James, with the possible exception of Skiffes Creek, which is described above. Kingsmill is really a resort, as well as a residential community, both developed by Anheuser-Busch. The marina is privately owned, but they do reserve a few transient slips (perhaps as many as 10), which can accommodate boats as large as 50 feet. The Kingsmill Restaurant is within walking distance. (I'm told that men are supposed to wear jackets and reservations are a must.) A van is available to take you to the Kingsmill shops or even to Busch Gardens a few miles away. Reservations for slips at the marina are recommended. The resort offers vacation packages; the toll-free number is (800)832-5665.

Things to Do. Second, it gives me the opportunity to mention the starting (or ending) point for a unique cruise, either in your own hull or aboard one of the cruiser boats out of Richmond. Operated by Harbor Cruises of Newport News, these boats regularly cruise between Richmond and Kingsmill, providing a guided tour of the upper reaches of the James and a long series of great plantations. The tour could never be achieved by land in like manner. If you don't want to tackle the rest of the James in your own hull, this cruise is a good alternative. The trip takes about six hours. At the terminus, buses return you to your starting point.

Approaches. To get to Kingsmill, follow the shipping channel from the vicinity of Skiffes Creek to the point where it bends to head west. Take your departure from buoy red "38" on a course of 310 degrees or from red "40" on a course of 352 degrees. The jetties at the entrance quickly become apparent. The final approach to Kingsmill can be a little nerve-racking if you haven't been there before because of the wide shoals on either side of the entrance jetties. Don't worry about it, simply head straight between the jetties and you will find yourself in the sheltered waters of the marina.

For a jumping-off place to somewhere else or to stay at the marina overnight for those who prefer it, this is a great spot. For those who like to anchor out in seclusion, forget it; this is not an anchorage.

JAMESTOWN

No facilities

Charts: 12248, 12251

Not far from the western tip of Jamestown Island, there is a monument to commemorate the establishment of the first English colony in the New World. The inscription at the base reads: "Jamestown, the first permanent colony of the English people. The birthplace of Virginia and of the United States. May 13, 1607." The island is administered by the National Park Service and is classed as a National Monument.

Here, too, is a statue of the indomitable Captain John Smith and a monument to Pocahontas, the Indian princess who pleaded with her father, Powhatan, for Smith's life.

These landmarks are relatively recent, all constructed in the 20th century. There is but one landmark that dates back to the original Jamestown: the Jamestown Church Tower, constructed in 1639. A walking tour leads to the remains of the other structures that have been unearthed in a continuing excavation program.

There is no place to tie up a boat to land on Jamestown Island. The Thorofare, a wide passage of water that leads to the north of Jamestown Island and connects into the Back River, making it truly an island, is too shoal to even consider entering in anything you won't be able to step out of and push. Stay out of it! Your

The Jamestown Church Tower dates back to the 1640s. It is the one landmark on Jamestown Island from the original settlement. (The church behind it is a reconstruction built on the original foundation.) NATIONAL PARK SERVICE

only choice if you are in a sailboat is to anchor out in the James and land by dinghy. The best place is about 500 yards downstream of the "monument" indicated on the chart where there is a section of 9 to 15 feet of water. Other than that, the river is either too deep or too shallow to anchor comfortably.

Things to Do. In 1957, on the bank of the James River just north of James Island, the State of Virginia constructed a replica of the first stockade built by the colonists, as well as a number of buildings which were used during the Jamestown Exposition that year. All of these remain and are open to visitors. It is now designated Jamestown Settlement, a living history museum that depicts life in America's first permanent English settlement. Moored at the dock below the buildings are three ships, replicas of the *Susan Con-*

stant, the *Godspeed,* and the *Discovery,* which brought the 105 colonists who settled Jamestown in 1607. All three faithful reproductions were built in Norfolk and launched in 1984; and they are worth a visit. If you do visit the settlement, plan to spend 1½ to 2 hours simply wandering around the indoor and outdoor exhibits. Take your time and get the flavor of the place.

Visiting Jamestown Settlement or the ships by boat—"Aye, there's the rub!" as William Shakespeare put it. The problem is that unless you are in a shoal-draft boat (2-foot maximum draft) your only choice is to anchor out in the James River and land by dinghy or to put in to another harbor and visit by car. Under no circumstances tie up to the ferry dock as it is in use and you could find yourself in real trouble.

Landing at Jamestown Settlement by dinghy may present a slight problem of a different sort. The settle-

The *Susan Constant*, *Godspeed*, and *Discovery*
replicas at the Jamestown Settlement. Visitors can
board and tour the *Susan Constant*, the largest
of the three. JAMESTOWN-YORKTOWN FOUNDATION

Approaches. This creek is located on the
southwestern shore of the James River, almost directly
opposite the Jamestown Church Tower on the western
tip of Jamestown Island. The easiest approach is to
head on a course of 230 degrees from the red "55"
marker in the James River. This will take you to the
first of a set of three pairs of red/green markers that
will guide you into the creek. You need to negotiate
the entrance carefully as the creek is full of assorted
snags, obstructions, and submerged pilings outside the
channel. The channel has 6-7 feet over a muddy bottom and there is deeper water once you are past the
2-foot bar at the creek mouth. Favor the port side and
feel your way in slowly as the shoals have a tendency
to shift.

Anchorages. Once you get in, there is plenty
of water in the creek for a distance of more than 2
miles. Eagle's Point Marina is to port, just past the first
bend in the creek. There is a definite down-home feel
to this marina that makes it well worth stopping by,
if only to chat with the owner for a bit. You can lay
alongside the fuel dock for fuel and supplies—perhaps
even overnight. However, we recommend anchoring
somewhat beyond the marina in 12-15 feet of water,
where you will be well protected from weather by the
high banks to either side.

Understandably, there is little traffic on this creek,
so it will be quiet. The shores are marshy, which means
mosquitoes after dark. Be prepared for them.

From the marina, it is just a short walk into Scotland (a little over one-half mile). You can take the ferry
from Scotland directly to the landing just above Jamestown Settlement, secure in the knowledge that your
boat is safe.

ment is not set up to receive visitors by water and there
is an admission fee ($5 per adult, less for children, as of
1989).

Shoal-draft boats with a vertical clearance of less
than 12 feet can pass under the bridge between Jamestown Island and the exposition area on the mainland
into Powhatan Creek. There are two marinas about a
mile upstream from the bridge. The problem is getting
by the shoal area just inside the bridge, between daymarks red "10" and green "11." Don't try it in any vessel
that you can't get out of and push.

In any event, be sure to visit Jamestown Island and
Jamestown Settlement. If you can't make it by water,
come by car from wherever you do make port.

GRAYS CREEK

CHICKAHOMINY RIVER

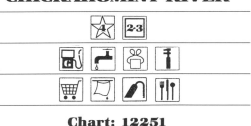

Chart: 12251

Chart: 12251

Chickahominy River

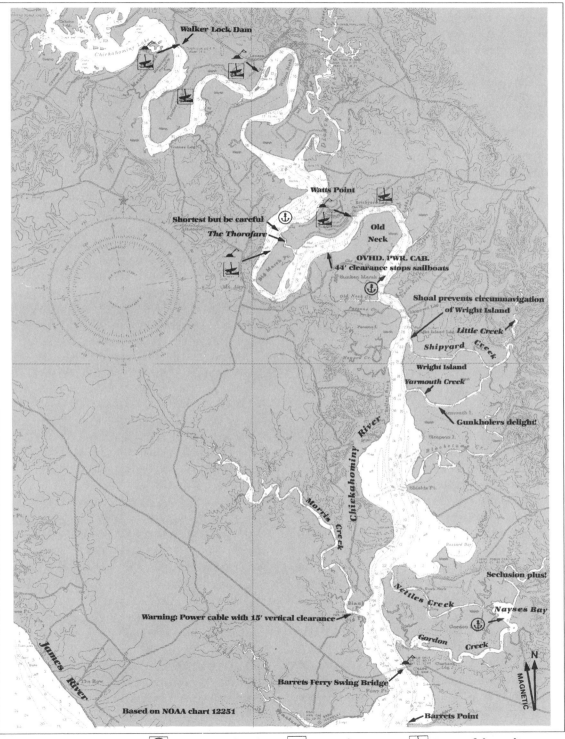

Walker Lock Dam

Watts Point

Shortest but be careful

The Thorofare

Old
Neck

OVHD. PWR. CAB.
44' clearance stops sailboats

Shoal prevents circumnavigation
of Wright Island

Little Creek

Shipyard Creek

Wright Island

Yarmouth Creek

Gunkholers delight!

Morris Creek

Chickahominy River

Seclusion plus!

Nayses Bay

Nettles Creek

Warning: Power cable with 15' vertical clearance

Gordon Creek

N

MAGNETIC

Barrets Ferry Swing Bridge

Based on NOAA chart 12251

Barrets Point

James River

SCALE **1″=1.28** NAUT. MILES   ⚓ **Good anchoring**   **Mooring area**   **Launching site**

About 4 miles above Jamestown lies the entrance to the Chickahominy River, the first James River tributary worth exploring to any extent in its own right. From Barrets Point at the entrance to the Walker Dam Lock 18 miles upstream, the river winds its way through the countryside. Aside from the main river, there are a number of narrow but navigable creeks to poke into and examine. The river is used only by pleasure craft and a scattering of local fishermen. Unlike the James, there is no commercial traffic with which to contend.

Approaches. The approach to the Chickahominy is easy, at least from downstream on the James. The channel through the flats at its entrance is well marked and the few shoals beyond the Barrets Ferry swing bridge have strategically located daymarks. The sole exception is Buzzard Bay: It is unmarked, but stay out unless you intend to walk!

Dockages/Facilities/Provisions.
Just beyond the bridge, the Riverside Resort is to starboard. There is no fuel available, but you can get ice, some groceries and beverages. They also have a laundromat. There are no more marinas until you reach Old Neck. From there to the Walkers Dam Lock, six marinas are scattered along the river. They are evident as you pass by. None carry diesel fuel, however.

Anchorages. There are numerous places to anchor along the Chickahominy. Simply pick a spot off to one side of the river, taking advantage of the twists and bends to minimize the fetch from any direction, and drop the hook. The gunkholers among us may prefer to pull into one of the creeks along the way to find snug anchorages, but it isn't really necessary.

The first of the navigable creeks to appear is Gordon Creek, less than one-half mile to starboard past the swing bridge. If you can squeeze past the shoal encroaching from the north just beyond the first bend, you will find a minimum depth of 5 feet all the way to Nayses Bay, about 2 miles upstream. If you are looking for a secluded anchorage, this one will be hard to beat! The creek carries 5 feet for about another one-half mile beyond Nayses Bay, but sailboats had better watch out for the overhead cable at the first bend, its vertical clearance is only 40 feet. The cable makes this river bend the head of navigation in Gordon Creek for most cruising sailboats.

Next to appear, to port, is Morris Creek with its 10-foot deep entrance appearing between the marshy banks of Pig and Blank Points. Although the creek carries a minimum depth of 8 feet for a distance of more than 2 miles past its entrance, exploration of this creek is limited to smaller powerboats without tall radio antennas because of an overhead power cable, with a vertical clearance of only 15 feet, about 100 yards inside the entrance.

Nettles Creek, to starboard, is extremely narrow but has at least 5 feet of water to just beyond its first bend, where there is a 4-foot spot. Intriguing it may be, but don't proceed beyond the second bend or you may run afoul of the snag reported there.

Yarmouth Creek is the next navigable creek. If you can get past the 4-foot bar at its entrance, you can almost circumnavigate Wright Island by swinging to port at the junction with Shipyard Creek. Unfortunately, there is a 2-foot bar just inside the mouth of Shipyard Creek which prevents direct access to the Chickahominy for most boats. That's why I say, "almost circumnavigate." Yarmouth Creek has 5 to 10 feet of water as far as its junction with Little Creek, just under one-half mile beyond Shipyard Creek. Don't try to proceed beyond this junction as the creek shoals rapidly.

Beyond Shipyard Creek, the Chickahominy narrows somewhat and begins a series of twists and turns, which make for an interesting trip. Sailboats should beware of the overhead power cable across the river about midway between Old Neck and Big Marsh Points, less than one-half mile past the Chickahominy Marina to starboard. It has a vertical clearance of only 44 feet. Most cruising sailboats have to consider this cable the head of navigation on the Chickahominy.

There are no more navigable creeks off the river beyond this point, with one possible exception. The adventurous might attempt the shortcut through Big Marsh Point via The Thorofare to cut more than 1½ miles off the trip upstream. It is supposed to have a controlling depth of 5 feet but that probably should not be believed.

Just short of Watts Point, beware of a shoal in the middle of the river, indicated by green daymarks at either end of it. Be sure to honor them.

The rest of the way to Walker Dam Lock, you are really into river cruising. With a little prudence, you'll have no problems as there is plenty of water nearly from shore to shore, save for a few fairly evident shoals. It may be possible to proceed past Walker Dam Lock and on into Chickahominy Lake, but we have no information on it and so can't recommend the passage.

UPPER CHIPPOKES CREEK

No facilities

Chart: 12251

Approaches. About 5 miles up the James from the mouth of the Chickahominy is the hard-to-find entrance to Upper Chippokes Creek. The entrance channel, marked by private poles or stakes, is close to the southern side of the creek mouth. The channel is narrow and winding with a controlling depth of 5 feet. If you do manage to make your way in, you can find an anchorage beyond the long, marshy point, which looks like a finger pointing north. The creek is navigable for at least 3 miles and offers some good gunkholing but little else.

Provisions. Just below the mouth of the creek, on the south shore of the James River, is Claremont Beach Campgrounds. There are no docking facilities, but they do have ice, showers, and a restaurant. You can also get gasoline, but you will have to carry it in jerry cans.

POWELL CREEK

No facilities

Chart: 12251

Approaches. Fourteen miles above Upper Chippokes Creek is an extremely narrow, but deep, little creek which is rarely visited by cruising boats. There are two poles marking the entrance to Powell Creek's 9-foot–deep channel through the marshy delta. If you make your approach at or near low tide, you should easily be able to see the channel—it's where the water is and the grass or mud isn't!

Once inside, you can follow this winding creek for

James River Plantations

Between the intersection of the Chickahominy and James Rivers and just above the Appomattox River are a series of historical and prominent Virginia plantations that are well worth seeing even if you don't or can't tour them. In most cases, shoals on the river prevent a close approach to shore and the buildings are generally placed some distance from the riverbank. A good pair of binoculars and a telephoto lens for your camera are a must.

Although Powell Creek and the Appomattox River are interspersed between the plantation locations on the James River, the plantations have been listed sequentially for ease of presentation.

TETTINGTON. Just past the entrance to the Chickahominy River, by Sandy Point on the north side of the James River, is the old Lightfoot home, Tettington. The chief point of interest on this estate is the beautiful lawn and garden which center about the boxwood shrubbery. This is a private residence and is not open to the public, but be sure to take a good look as you go past.

BRANDON. On the south side of the James, at the next bend on the river upstream from Tettington, are two famous homes—Lower Brandon and Upper Brandon. Lower Brandon is the original residence of the Brandon Plantation which was granted to a John Martin, a compatriot of the Captain John Smith of note and, later, a member of "His Majesty's first council in Virginia." The present house at Lower Brandon was built in the mid-1700s and the house at Upper Brandon in the 1820s. Neither estate is open to the public.

SHERWOOD FOREST. Sherwood Forest Plantation is located on the south side of the James River, at the top of the bend in the river opposite the Brandon Plantation.

The manor house on Sherwood Forest Plantation—a working plantation for over 250 years and the home of two U.S. presidents, William Henry Harrison and John Tyler—is not typ-

Middle James River

Berkeley
Plantation

Herring Creek

Evelynton

Queens Creek

Sherwood Forest Plantation

Jordan Point

Westover
Plantation

Bucklers
Point

Windmill Point

Bachelor Point

Flowerdew Hundred
Plantation

Upper Brandon Plantation

Fort Powhatan

Lower Brandon Plantation

Tettington
Plantation

Wards Creek

James

Approach marked
private stakes

Chippokes Creek

Upper

Based on NOAA chart 12251

SCALE **1″= 2.33** NAUT. MILES   **Good anchoring**   **Mooring area**   **Launching site**

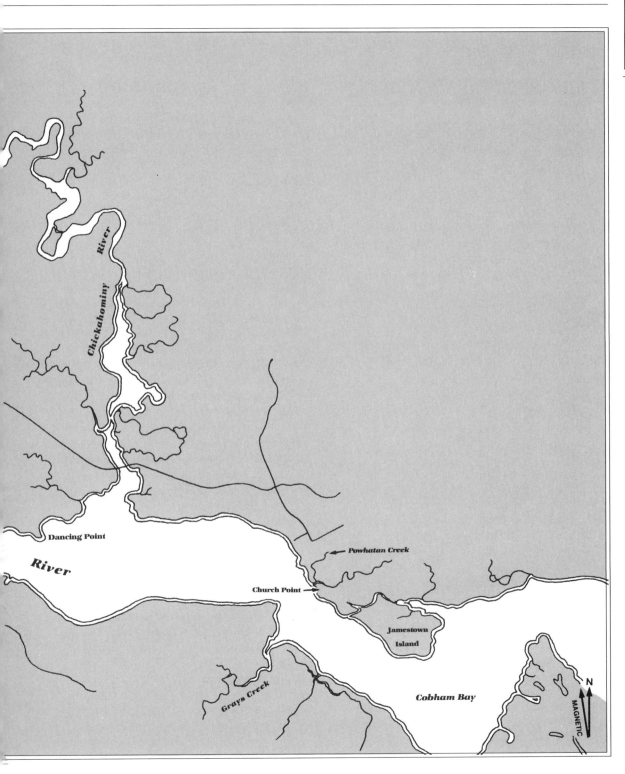

Chickahominy *River*

River

Dancing Point

Powhatan Creek

Church Point

Jamestown
Island

Grays Creek

Cobham Bay

N

MAGNETIC

Sherwood Forest Plantation.
VA STATE TRAVEL SERVICE

ical of the other plantation houses in the area. The white frame building is 300 feet long. The original building was constructed in 1730. Extensions were added to the ends of the house in stages, the final stage by President John Tyler after his term of office. Tyler also gave the estate its unique name, ostensibly to reflect his own belief that he was a kind of "political outlaw" of some sort. It is said that he bolted the name of the estate to the door so securely that it has remained exactly as he placed it ever since.

The estate is a National Historic Landmark and the grounds are open to the public daily. Tours of the mansion can be arranged by appointment; call (804)829-5377.

FLOWERDEW HUNDRED. Located on the south side of the James River, at the top of the bend in the river opposite Charles City, is the site of one of the earliest English settlements in Virginia. Today, the culture and history of the region is studied and interpreted here. Escorted tours include a "Walk Through Time" in the museum; an 18-century–style reconstructed windmill; the pontoon bridge used by Grant's army during the Civil War; and archaeological excavations. More than 65 sites have been excavated and literally thousands of items, some dating as far back as 9,000 B.C., have been found.

There is a museum shop and bookstore where reproductions and cornmeal ground at the windmill are for sale. Hours are Tuesday through Sunday, 10:00 a.m. to 5:00 p.m., April to November. Admission is $2.50 for adults and $1.50 for children. It is operated by the Flowerdew Hundred Foundation, a nonprofit organization, which you can contact at 1617 Flowerdew

Hundred Road, Hopewell, VA 23860, (804)541-8897.

EVELYNTON. Between Charles City and the Benjamin Harrison bridge, on the north side of the James river, are a series of three plantations: Evelynton, Westover, and Berkley; each of which has its own story to tell. The first of these as you proceed upstream is Evelynton, originally a part of William Byrd's colonial Westover Plantation and named after his daughter, Evelyn.

In 1862, Confederates under Generals J. E. B. Stuart and Stonewall Jackson, on the ridge overlooking Herring Creek, held off Union forces until they ran out of ammunition and had to retire. The Union troops then almost completely destroyed the plantation, burning the house and slave quarters and destroying the largest trees. In 1864, Evelynton was purchased by the Ruffin family, in whose hands it has remained to the present day. The house was restored in the 1930s by John Ruffin, grandson of Edmund Ruffin, who bought the estate. The present house, a Georgian manor, is built atop the original foundation and constructed of 250-year-old brick.

The house, grounds, and gardens are open to the public from 9:00 a.m. to 5:00 p.m. daily. There is also a gift shop and a nursery.

WESTOVER. Just the other side of Herring Creek from Evelynton is the stately mansion and plantation of Westover, built by William Byrd II in 1730. The house is probably one of the finest examples of Georgian architecture in the country, complemented by a long sweep of lawn down to the James River and an abundance of 100- to 150-year-old tulip trees.

The grounds, outbuildings, and garden are open year-round for an admission fee of $2.00 for adults and $.50 for children. The main house is open only for the five days of the Annual Historic Garden Week.

BERKELEY. On the north shore of the James River, just downstream of the Benjamin Harrison bridge, is the beautiful Berkeley Plantation. Built by Benjamin Harrison IV in 1726, the Georgian mansion, which is said to be the oldest 3-story brick house in Virginia, sits on a

Berkely Plantation.
VA CHAMBER OF COMMERCE

Unique to this country, there is a complete set of 18th century brick buildings which form a classic Queen Anne forecourt. These include a two-story kitchen, a laundry house, and two barns, one of which has an icehouse beneath it. There is also a stable, a smokehouse, and a dovecote. The manor house proper features unique architectural facets and artistry, and is filled with original family portraits, furniture, crested silver, and many other items. Its famous three-story–high, carved walnut staircase, the only one of its kind in America, rises to the top floor with no visible means of support!

small hilltop overlooking the river. Ten acres of formal terraced boxwood gardens and lawn extend from the mansion for a quarter of a mile down to the James River.

There are some interesting "firsts" which took place at Berkeley. What Virginia claims to be the first official Thanksgiving was conducted on 4 December 1619 by newly arrived settlers from England who came ashore at Berkeley. Sometime later, in 1621, Berkeley Plantation distilled the first bourbon whiskey in America. Benjamin Harrison, a signer of the Declaration of Independence, was born here as was William Henry Harrison, ninth President of the United States. In 1862, during the Civil War, Union forces under General McClellan were camped here and the haunting notes of the famous "Taps" were composed here by General Bill Butterfield, who was part of that command. The plantation is open daily from 8:00 a.m. to 5:00 p.m. For more information, contact Berkeley Plantation on Route 5, Charles City, VA 23030, (804)829-6018.

The Coach House, on the estate, is open daily for refreshments and traditional colonial dining. Reservations are highly recommended. (804)829-6003.

SHIRLEY. After the Benjamin Harrison bridge, Shirley Plantation lies on the east side of the James River, just around the next point, about 1½ miles past the mouth of the Appomattox River. This is the oldest plantation in Virginia, founded a mere six years after the arrival of the first permanent English settlers at Jamestown in 1607.

Shirley Plantation.
MRS. HELLE K. CARTER

The plantation is designated as a National Historic Landmark and it is no exaggeration to state that a visit to Shirley is a bit like stepping into American history. Shirley has been the home of the Carter family since 1723; it was home to Ann Hill Carter, mother of Robert E. Lee, and is owned and operated by the ninth generation of the family. Shirley is open to the public year-round, except Christmas Day, between 9:00 a.m. and 5:00 p.m. The admission fee helps to preserve and improve the plantation. For more information, contact Shirley, Charles City, VA 23030, (804)829-5121.

almost 2 miles before the water depth decreases to less than 8 feet. This happens shortly after you reach the marsh to starboard at a sharp bend in the creek. Call a halt as soon as the water depth starts to decrease as it shoals relatively abruptly a little farther along.

This is not a cruising area for the fainthearted. The narrow, winding stream between the comparatively high banks can be somewhat claustrophobic for those in larger boats, in spite of the deep water. On the other hand, isn't this exactly what a gunkholer finds most intriguing?

APPOMATTOX RIVER

☆2   2

⚓

Chart: 12251

Approaches. From Powell Creek on upstream, pay careful attention to the chart and don't stray too far out of the marked channel, even to avoid passing commercial traffic. The James shoals quickly outside of the marked channel.

About 3 miles above the Benjamin Harrison bridge over the James River at Jordan Point, the Appomattox River branches off to the west. The fixed Route 10 bridge at Hopewell, right at the mouth of the Appomattox, has a vertical clearance of only 40 feet, which denies most cruising sailboats access to the river. A mile beyond that bridge is a swing railroad bridge with a vertical clearance of 12 feet, closed. (Presumably it opens on demand, but I am not sure.) If you can clear the bridge, there is a well-marked channel most of the way to Petersburg. The controlling depth is 6 feet to the Lone Star Company Basin, about two-thirds of the way past Gatling Island, just under 8 miles from the James River. The controlling depth then drops to 2 feet for the next half mile to the Appomattox Small Boat Harbor just past the tip of Gatling Island. You can't quite make it all the way to Petersburg. If you want to tour the Petersburg area, you have to rent a car or find some means of motor transportation. Touring on foot is not feasible.

Things to Do. The city of Hopewell is located on the south side of the junction of the James and Appomattox Rivers. It is possible to land on City Point, but

Lower Appomattox River

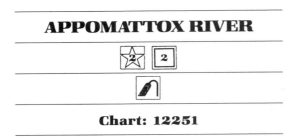

SCALE **1″=.84** NAUT. MILES   ⚓ **Good anchoring**   **Mooring area**   **Launching site**

only from the James River side where there are piers to lay alongside. The Appomattox River side is barred by a 1-foot shoal which extends nearly one-half mile into the Appomattox from the James River to the Route 10 bridge. Here, the City Point HIstoric District offers a walking tour of about two dozen homes, many of which were used by the Union Army during the War Between the States. General Grant was headquartered on the grounds of Appomattox Manor, now the City Point Unit of the Petersburg National Battlefield Park. The manor house and grounds, together with Grant's cabin, are open to the public daily from 8:00 a.m. to 4:30 p.m. Admission is free.

For those who can make it past the Route 10 bridge, one of the few plantation houses left on the Appomattox, Weston Manor, is accessible. Built before the American Revolution, Weston Manor is an excellent example of late Georgian plantation architecture. It still retains much of its original furnishings. You can tie up to some of the piers below the manor, but you must ask permission first. The manor, itself, is located on 21st Avenue and Weston Lane.

For information on Hopewell, contact the Hopewell Visitors Center, 201-D Randolph Square, Hopewell, VA 23860, (804)541-2206.

One mile past the railroad bridge, a cluster of islands center in the river, starting at Point of Rocks at the tip of Cobbs Island. The left fork leads on up the Appomattox. The right fork leads to Port Walthall Channel, which is navigable for another 2 miles, opening the potential for exploring and gunkholing. There are high banks to starboard on the mainland and Cobbs Island; to port is low and swampy. The channel forks again at Cat Island. Only the right (west) fork is navigable, leading to Swift Creek and the head of navigation for the Port Walthall Channel.

The main channel of the Appomattox splits again at Long Island. The right fork is the "Old Channel," no longer navigable, although it is possible for shoal-draft boats with strong-nerved skippers to make it all the way past Back Creek Island to the tip of Gatling Island. However, you can't make it back into the main channel without retracing your course. This one is reserved for gunkholers.

Anchorages/Facilities. In spite of the historical perspective of the area and the undeniable appeal of gunkholing around the cluster of islands, the Appomattox River is not of great appeal to cruisers. Al-

though it is quite feasible to simply anchor to one side of the river, there are no good harbors and there are no marine facilities catering to cruising boats, with the possible exception of Appomattox Small Boat Harbor near Prince George. This marina caters mostly to small boats (runabout class), although it does have a 50-ton marine railway and the only shower facility in the area accessible to cruisers.

UPPER JAMES RIVER TO RICHMOND

Chart: 12251

Once you proceed beyond the junction of the Appomattox River with the James, the river changes again. Now you are truly into river cruising of a different sort than anywhere else in the Chesapeake Bay area. The river takes three big loops, each of which is cut off by the main commercial channel to form islands. Here are harbors and cruising grounds for you to explore at your leisure with no concern for the commercial traffic that threatens in the main channel. This is the prime reason for venturing so far up the James River.

TURKEY ISLAND

No facilities

Chart: 12251

Approaches. One-and-one-half miles above the Appomattox River, the James makes a big loop around Turkey Island. The commercial traffic follows Turkey Island Cutoff to the south of the island, leaving a stretch of nearly 6 miles for you to explore in peace. There is farmland on the southern third of the island, reached by a cable ferry in the middle of the cutoff. The rest of the island is covered by the uninhabited Presque

Upper James River

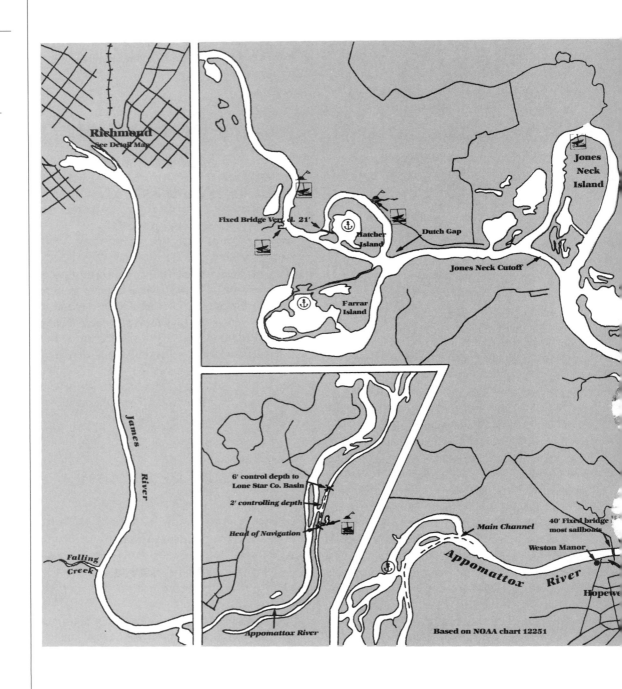

Richmond
See Detail Map

Jones
Neck
Island

Fixed Bridge Vert. cl. 21'

Hatcher
Island

Dutch Gap

Jones Neck Cutoff

Farrar
Island

James

River

6' control depth to
Lone Star Co. Basin

2' controlling depth

Head of Navigation

Main Channel

40' Fixed bridge
most sailboats

Weston Manor

Falling
Creek

Appomattox River

Hopewe

Appomattox River

Based on NOAA chart 12251

SCALE 1"=1.28 NAUT. MILES   Good anchoring   Mooring area   Launching site

Pickett Wharf

Neck

Turkey Island
Bend

Curles Swamp

Curles

Turkey Island

key Island
utoff

Cable Ferry

● Shirley Plantation

Shirley Hole

Harrison Point

Eppes Island

Lift Bridge

oint

← Piers to lay alongside

Jordan Point

N

MAGNETIC

Isle Refuge, which is a swamp, and the marsh in Turkey Island Bend.

Favor the mainland side of the river on your way around the island, especially in the northwest corner near Pickett Wharf. Favor the island side along the southwestern half of the island, by the steep bank, to avoid the shoal on the mainland side by Curles Swamp. Circumnavigation of the island is easy and worth the trip.

Anchorages. Should you choose to spend the night, simply pick your spot. But remember that this is a swamp and marsh area; you should expect mosquitoes and other insects and come prepared.

JONES NECK ISLAND

No facilities

Chart: 12251

Approaches. Two miles above Turkey Island, the James makes its next big loop, around Jones Neck. Jones Neck Cutoff makes Jones Neck into a true island. The eastern half of the island is a marsh and the western half farmland. How the farmers managed to get vehicles onto the island is not apparent, but somehow they did it. There is what appears to be a channel into a basin in the middle of the island on the eastern side, but the depth is uncertain. Don't try it in anything but a dinghy and be prepared to get out and push.

Anchorages. Circumnavigation of the island is easy, as is finding a nice spot to anchor for the night. There is a public launching ramp directly north of the island, so you can expect some local rowboat and runabout traffic. At dusk, the traffic disappears and you are alone in a quiet, peaceful anchorage.

Just west of Jones Neck, at Varina Farm, there is a basin off the north side of the James. It looks intriguing, but there is no information on it and it may well be private. Leave it alone.

FARRAR ISLAND

No facilities

Chart: 12251

Approaches. Directly opposite the point labeled "Dutch Gap" on the chart, about 2 miles upriver from the west end of Jones Neck Island, is the 400-yard–long false mouth of the waterway leading to an interesting basin in the middle of Farrar Island.

The deceptively wide mouth quickly necks down to the true entrance, marked by the quick-flashing green marker on the east side of the entrance. Be sure to leave this marker to port as you head southwest into the "creek." There is a quick-flashing green "151" James River marker almost onshore at the west side of the entrance. Hold a course between these two markers, then remain about in the middle until the creek starts to curve to the west, about three-quarters mile from the entrance. At that point, hold close to the west shore, guiding carefully between the zero-foot shoal and the main part of the island until you can enter the narrow channel leading into the basin.

Anchorages. When the channel opens out into the basin, remain in the northern quarter of the main basin to anchor.

There were some buildings on the point protruding into the basin from the west side, but the access bridge to them is in ruins and they must be abandoned by now. There are several underwater wrecks scattered through the basin and a shoal in nearly the geometric center of the basin, all to be avoided. The rest of the basin is a gunkholer's delight.

If you are looking for a private, secure, secluded anchorage, try this one. However, you will be surrounded by swamp and marsh, so be prepared for mosquitoes.

HATCHER ISLAND

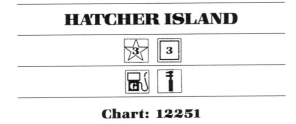

Chart: 12251

Just past the entrance to Farrar Island, the James makes its last big loop before the long, barren stretch to Richmond. At Dutch Gap, the river makes a 1½-mile loop to the north around Hatcher Island.

Facilities. Here is the only marina to offer gas and some repairs on this part of the James, Richmond Yacht Basin. Little else in the way of marine facilities is available to transient cruisers.

Favor the mainland side of the river as you circum-navigate the island, except on the western side where you should favor the island side.

Anchorages. There is one unique feature to Hatcher Island; it has a large navigable basin right in the middle of it, which offers an excellent anchorage in 7 to 23 feet of water. Stay in the center as you enter from Dutch Gap Cutoff and anchor anywhere in the eastern half of the basin. There is a marsh to the east, but you can anchor far enough out that insects should be only a minor problem.

JAMES RIVER ABOVE

HATCHER ISLAND

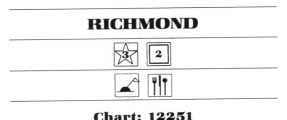

Chart: 12251

Facilities/Approaches. Above Hatcher Island, you are well advised to remain in the main channel of the James for the entire 18 miles to Richmond. Except for King's Landing about a mile past Hatcher Island, and Falling Creek Marina at the entrance to Fall-

ing Creek, which offers only engine repairs, there are no facilities upriver. It is not an unpleasant trip, but it can be a bit tedious. The only reason to make it is to visit Richmond by water. Sailboats cannot make the trip to Richmond at all without dropping their masts due to the 21 foot vertical clearance of the fixed bridge over the James River a few hundred yards upstream of Hatcher Island.

The channel ends at Richmond, just past the railroad marshaling yard, a few hundred yards before the first bridge over the James. If you pass the docks at Shiplock Park where the James River Cruise Boats dock, stop! You run out of water very quickly because you have reached the head of navigation of the James River.

RICHMOND

Chart: 12251

History. The city of Richmond's location is very much due to a quirk of nature. Seven miles of falls, 125 miles above the mouth of the James River, form the upper limit of navigation on the river and block access to the more than 200 miles of the James River which extend into the interior of the country. Early settlers recognized the commercial opportunities presented by the falls blocking navigation on the river and soon formed a settlement there. Richmond's history is one of steady growth, greatly enhanced by its selection as the state capital. The establishment of the big tobacco companies and heavy industry didn't exactly hurt either.

During the War Between the States, Richmond was the capital of the Confederate States of America and was the South's largest industrial center at the time. The city has a substantial national military park along its eastern perimeter, most of it the result of seven major attempts to capture the city by Union forces. The Confederates successfully repelled all of those attacks. Richmond fell only after the capture of Petersburg, following a 10-month siege, broke the Confederacy's defenses.

The defeat of the Confederate States, while immediately traumatic, was only a temporary setback to Rich-

Richmond

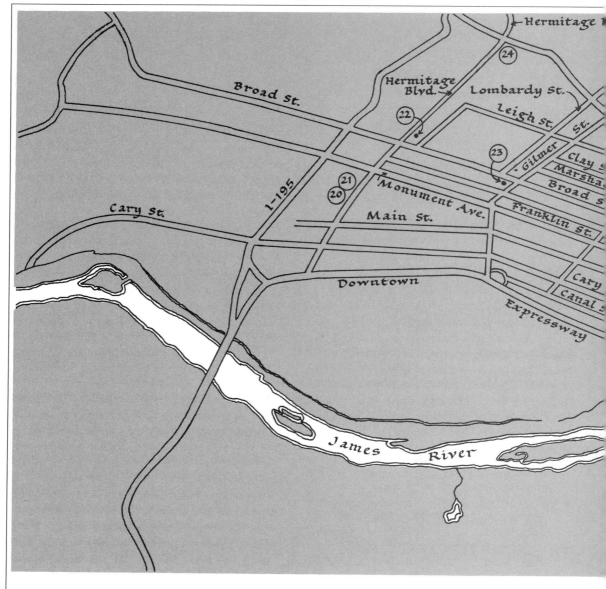

KEY

1. Annabel Lee Riverboat
2. Shiplock Park
3. Kanawha Locks
4. Edgar Allen Poe Museum
5. Farmer's Market
6. Kanawha Locks
7. Shockoe Slip
8. Governor's Mansion
9. State Capitol
10. Bell Tower
11. St. Paul's Church
12. Old City Hall

SCALE 1"=2.85 MILES

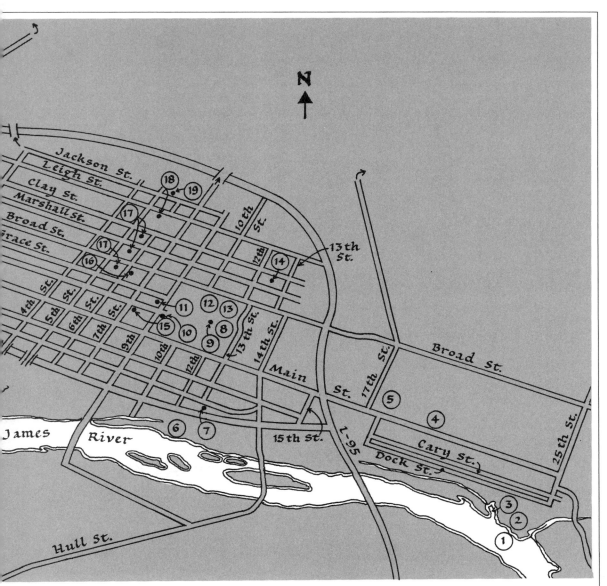

N

Jackson St.
Leigh St.
Clay St.
Marshall St.
Broad St.
Grace St.

10th St.
12th
13th St.
13th St.
14th St.
Main St.
17th St.
Broad St.
25th St.
Cary St.
Dock St.
15th St.
I-95
Hull St.
James River

4th St. 5th St. 6th St. 7th St. 9th St. 10th 12th 13th St. 14th St.

⑬ State Library
⑭ Museum of the Confederacy
⑮ Lee House
⑯ Carpenter Center
⑰ 6th St. Marketplace
⑱ Coliseum
⑲ Richmond Children's Museum
⑳ Virginia Museum of Fine Arts
㉑ Virginia Historical Society
   (Battle Abbey)
㉒ Science Museum of Virginia
㉓ American Hist. Foundation Museum
㉔ Metro Richmond Visitors' Center

mond's growth. Today, Richmond is a busy, bustling city, the cultural leader of the state, with a suburban region extending most of the 23 miles south to Petersburg, forming a sort of megapolis much like the one between Baltimore and Washington, D.C. in Maryland.

Things to Do.

The waterfront area, known as Shockoe Slip, was once a bawdy, low-class district, avoided by the "better class" of citizens. Today, it has been renovated and is an attractive area of shops and restaurants with a terminal for James River Cruise Boats and a city dock where private craft can tie up (on a space available basis) to visit the city. Some of the points of interest are within easy walking distance, but many require some form of motor transportation. Both bus tours and self-guided car tours are available. I mention only a few of those points within walking distance from the city dock.

Perhaps the best place to start is at Chimborazo Park, to the east of the city dock, where the Richmond National Battlefield Park Visitor's Center is located. Dedicated to the battlegrounds that were the setting of the 1861–1865 defense of Richmond, the center offers exhibits, an audiovisual program and maps for a 97-mile tour through the battlefield sites. Needless to say, you aren't going to walk all of that one.

As you leave the visitor's center, head back west along Broad Street to stop at St. John's Church. Built in 1741, this church was the site of the 1775 Revolutionary Convention during which Patrick Henry gave his famous "Give me liberty or give me death!" speech. On summer Sunday afternoons, there is a re-enactment of his speech.

Head down 24th Street and turn right on Main Street for about five blocks to find the Edgar Allen Poe Museum, which is housed in "The Old Stone House," believed to be Richmond's oldest surviving stone building, built in 1737. The museum contains Poe memorabilia and artifacts from the days when he lived, wrote, and romanced there. It is open daily.

A jaunt up 19th Street and left on Broad Street soon takes you to a cluster of sights. To the right on 12th Street is the Museum of the Confederacy, containing the world's largest collection of Confederate memorabilia. Jefferson Davis's home during the war, "The White House of the Confederacy," is right next door.

Two blocks west is the Valentine Museum, presenting the life and history of Richmond, as it was and is.

Three blocks south you come to Capitol Square, site of the beautiful Virginia State Capitol building. Designed by Thomas Jefferson in 1785, this was the first building in America constructed in the form of a classic Greek temple. This is the home of the oldest known legislative body in the Western Hemisphere, the Virginia Legislature. It also houses Houdon's statue of George Washington.

Continue south from Capitol Square on 12th Street to return to the waterfront and the site of the Kanawha Canal Locks, two remaining locks from the first canal system built in America. At one time the canal extended from the bottom of the falls at Richmond, past Lynchburg, to Buchanan on the far side of the Blue Ridge Mountains. The canal was started at the impetus of George Washington in 1784 and finally completed in 1851. It served this country well until the railroads superseded it, as they did virtually all of the canals in this country. A narrated audiovisual presentation describes the history and significance of the old Kanawha Canal. I recommend visiting it.

There are many other points of interest in Richmond. I have barely scratched the surface. Most lie a bit farther afield and are beyond the scope of this book. For all practical purposes, the falls at Richmond mark the end of cruising the James River by any vessel that you can't pick up and carry.

LITTLE CREEK

Charts: 12205, 12207, 12221, **12222**

Just 2 miles west of the southern end of the Chesapeake Bay Bridge-Tunnel is the entrance to Little Creek, the last good, easily entered, harbor before leaving the Bay and entering the Atlantic Ocean.

LITTLE CREEK

ANCHORAGE

⭐2 | 3

⛽ 🚰 ☕ ⚓ ⛏

🛒 🚿 ⚓ 🍴

Charts: 12205, 12207, 12221, **12222**

Approaches. The approach is wide open and the broad entrance channel is readily located by the 70-foot–high, lighted green "1" beacon on the end of the east jetty. Depth is no problem; it's 20 feet all the way into the basin.

As you enter the channel into the creek, you can't help but become well aware of the Coast Guard Station and the Navy Amphibious Base (part of the Atlantic Fleet); they take up most of the harbor area and assorted good-sized vessels are frequently moored there. You are free to take a swing around the harbor and look at these boats, but tying up at any of the docks belonging to these facilities is not permitted.

Dockages/Facilities. All of the marina facilities in Little Creek are in the first (western) branch to starboard, just past red "8" as you enter. Favor the south side of this branch as there is some shoaling on the northern side, especially past the green "3" daymark. There are seven marinas on this branch. Among them, you should be able to find any type of marine facility for which you may be looking, except a laundromat (and likely one of them is not too far away). You should have no problem finding an overnight slip. A large shopping center, less than a mile from any of the marinas, includes a supermarket and a large department store, as well as assorted other shops. Any of the marinas can help you find transportation, if you aren't up to the walk.

This is not a harbor where you can expect to anchor out at all, let alone in any seclusion. It's a busy and crowded place, but it is the closest reasonable jumping-off place for a trip offshore. If you prefer to anchor out, head back inside Hampton Roads to Willoughby Bay, a distance of about 9 miles from Little Creek. Boats that

can clear an overhead limit of 35 feet might consider Lynnhaven Inlet, 4 miles to the east.

LYNNHAVEN INLET

Charts: 12205, 12207, 12221, **12222**

The entrance to Lynnhaven Inlet is just 2 miles east of the Chesapeake Bay Bridge-Tunnel or 4 miles west of Cape Henry Light, depending on your perspective. It leads to an interesting series of inland waterways and bays providing a "back door" to Virginia Beach. Unfortunately, the use of this entire area is limited to power-boats or small sailboats that can pass under the fixed bridges (vertical clearance 35 feet) at its entrance.

LYNNHAVEN INLET

⭐3 | 3

⛽ 🚰 ☕ ⚓

⛏ 🚿 ⚓ 🍴

Charts: 12205, 12207, 12221, **12222**

Approaches. Because of the fairly exposed position of the entrance channel to the ocean, the entrance channel shifts constantly. Buoys are moved regularly to correspond to the channel shifts but, for obvious reasons, we don't recommend trying the passage under rough conditions with an onshore wind. There is also a strong tidal current, especially under the bridges. Considerable caution is advisable during any time other than slack water. Controlling depth in the channel is not normally a problem; it's at least 6 feet.

You could proceed for about a mile south southeast into the Lynnhaven River or follow markers from the Lynnhaven River into the Western Branch, but there are no good anchorages or marine facilities. The other route is far preferable.

Dockages/Facilities. Once past the bridges, turn to port and follow the markers to the east

Lynnhaven Inlet (foreground) with Chesapeake Bay Bridge-Tunnel in the background.

into Long Creek (actually a canal for the first mile). This is where most of the marinas, with plentiful facilities, are, and it is the start of the passage to Virginia Beach. Lynnhaven Municipal Marina also has a dockside sewage pumpout facility.

Anchorages. The first anchorage is in Broad Bay, reached simply by following the markers to the east until the waterway opens into the bay. You can anchor here or proceed through The Narrows into Linkhorn Bay. Linkhorn Bay offers a number of little coves, especially along its western shore, which seem to offer more attractive anchorages than Broad Bay. If you choose to anchor in either Broad Bay or Linkhorn Bay, be careful of submerged piles as you approach shore.

Additional Dockages. If you want to visit Virginia Beach, head up the east fork of Linkhorn Bay and take a slip at the White Heron Motel & Yacht Club or anchor nearby and land by dinghy. The Barco Marine Railway, in the same vicinity, has 10 service slips and it may be possible to rent one overnight.

CAPE HENRY

Charts: 12205, 12207, 12221, **12222**

There are two lighthouses on Cape Henry within a few hundred yards of each other. The "old" lighthouse was built in 1791 and, while no longer in service, is still in such good condition that visitors are allowed to climb to its top for an excellent view of Virginia Beach and the entrance to the Chesapeake. The oldest Federal lighthouse in the country, it was authorized by the first Congress of the newly formed United States. It served well for almost 90 years, until 1881.

The nearby "new" lighthouse is new only in comparison. It was built in 1879 and now houses one of the world's most powerful lights, visible 20 miles at sea.

Near the base of the "old" lighthouse stands a stone cross, marking the site of the first landing, in 1607, of the colonists who went on to found Jamestown. Adjacent to the cross is a commemorative placard which reads, in part:

The new and old Cape Henry lighthouses.
The new tower houses a powerful light, visible
20 miles at sea. Visitors can climb to the top of
the old tower for a view of Virginia Beach.

"On April 26, 1607 three small ships approached the Chesapeake Bay from the southeast and made their landfall at Cape Henry, the southernmost promontory of that body of water. The Virginia Company expedition had set sail from England in December, 1606. Released from their four month confinement, the colonists, led by the Reverend Robert Hunt, gave thanks to God for their safe voyage. Before them lay the vast American wilderness known as Virginia."

Here, where it all began, it seems fitting to end this guide to the "Land of Pleasant Living," the Chesapeake Bay.

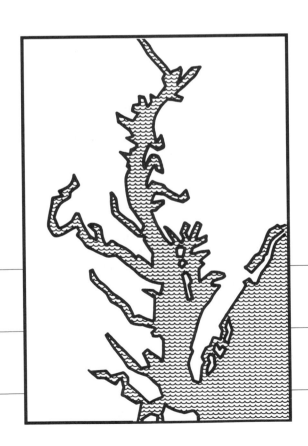

Appendices

Radiotelephone
Usage

More and more boats on the Chesapeake Bay, as well as elsewhere, are installing and using VHF-FM Marine Radiotelephone sets. This is an excellent safety measure, provided you know the proper radiotelephone procedure and channel usage. Laxity here results in chaos. For that reason, I have included this primer on correct usage.

Channels

As a result of an FCC action in September of 1985, we now have one less VHF-FM "chatter" channel available for our use. The FCC has limited the use of Channel 70 to automated calling only. Recreational use is now prohibited.

A new transmitting technology called Digital Selective Calling (DSC) soon will allow the equivalent of "direct dialing" on Channel 70; when the channel receives a coded signal, the radio will automatically switch to another channel for the message. This is also due to become part of the Future Global Maritime Distress and Safety System (FGMDSS), which is now under development. The cost of DSC equipment will likely limit its use to commercial ships.

Although the uninformed continue to use Channel 70 for chatter, its reclassification is official. Use of this channel can result in a "nastygram" and fine from the FCC. Stay off it!

Recreational boaters may use Channels 9, 68, 69, 71, 72, and 78 as working channels. Channel 72 is for ship-to-ship use only and Channel 9 is shared with commercial vessels.

NOTE: All Marine Radiotelephone Operators (Ch 24–28) and Bridge Operators (Ch 13) are to be called directly on their assigned working channels. All others must first be contacted on Channel 16 before switching to a working channel.

The following is a compilation of VHF-FM radiotelephone channels that are pertinent to pleasure craft. With few exceptions, all other channels are restricted to commercial or government purposes and are not for recreational boaters' use. If you want more complete information, BOAT/US offers a free FCC publication regarding the use of VHF-FM radios to its members. They also offer the "Marine Radiotelephone User's Handbook" (Item 912502 at $4.00 ppd).

Channel 16: For distress and calling. In anything short of a Mayday situation, shift to a working channel as soon as possible.

Channel 6: Reserved for ship-to-ship safety purposes, not to be used for general conversation. Often employed in Search and Rescue Operations.

Channel 9: An alternate calling channel to Channel 16. May use as a working channel, but shift to another working channel as soon as contact is made.

Channel 13: Bridge-to-bridge frequency for commercial craft. Also used for contact with drawbridge operators and C&D Canal Control.

Channel 22: Primary Coast Guard working channel. Contact Coast Guard on Channel 16 first; they don't monitor Channel 22.

Channel 81: Secondary Coast Guard working channel.

Channels 25 and 26: Baltimore, MD, Marine Operator.

Channels 25 through 27: Norfolk, VA, Marine Operator.

Channel 26: Point Lookout, MD, Marine Operator.

Channel 27: Prince Frederick, MD, Marine Operator. Lewes, DE, Marine Operator.

Channel 28: Wilmington, DE, Marine Operator. Cambridge, MD, Marine Operator. Washington, DC, Marine Operator.

Channels 68, 69, 71, 72, and 78: Noncommercial ship-to-ship, general communications (chatter channels).

Channel 70: As of 1986, reserved for Digital Selective Calling. Do not use!

WE-1, WE-2, and WE-3: NOAA Weather Broadcast.

Radiotelephone
Calling and Response
Procedures

NORMAL

To call other boats: Make sure set is turned on. Set to Channel 16. Call with following procedure:

"(Name of other boat), (Name of other boat), THIS IS (Name of your boat), (Your call letters)."

RESPONSE: ⟨(Name of calling boat), THIS IS (Name of responding boat), (Call letters of responding boat).⟩

When the other boat answers, call and say:

"THIS IS (Name of your boat), (Your call letters),

SWITCH AND ANSWER ON CHANNEL (68, 71, 72 ⟨pick one⟩), PLEASE ACKNOWLEDGE."

RESPONSE: ⟨(Name of responding boat) SWITCHING CHANNEL (selected channel).⟩

An alternative response:

RESPONSE: ⟨THIS IS (Name of responding boat). NEGATIVE CHANNEL (Selected channel). SWITCH CHANNEL (pick another channel), OVER.⟩

Wait for at least five seconds or until the other boat answers, then switch to the channel you picked. Listen to see if someone is already on that channel. If so, *wait until they are done*, then call:

"(Name of other boat), THIS IS (Name of your boat), (Your call letters), OVER."

Wait for the other boat to come back. If it does, go ahead and talk. If it doesn't, call again and wait. If it still doesn't acknowledge, return to Channel 16 and start over.

Remember, when you are transmitting you cannot hear and when the other boat is transmitting it cannot hear. The word *over* indicates that you are done speaking and are ready to listen. Don't forget to release the microphone button to stop transmitting.

Others are probably waiting to use the channel over which you are conversing. As a matter of courtesy, limit your conversation to the essentials and clear the channel as soon as possible. A good rule of thumb: If you don't have anything to say, don't say it over the air!

When your call is finished, each party should transmit, in turn: "THIS IS (Your boat name), (Your call letters), OUT." Then switch back to Channel 16 to monitor.

EMERGENCY

If you have a real emergency that you cannot handle yourself, call following this procedure:

Switch to Channel 16 and *stay on Channel 16 until told to switch to some other channel by the Coast Guard or Marine Police!*

Call: "MAYDAY, MAYDAY, MAYDAY. THIS IS (Name of your boat), (Your call letters), MAYDAY, MAYDAY, MAYDAY, WE ARE (describe what the problem is in 10 words or less), OUR LOCATION IS (read the Loran display or give the nearest object such as a buoy or marker and nearest point of land), MAYDAY, MAYDAY, MAYDAY."

Release the microphone button and listen for someone to acknowledge your call. If no one returns the call, wait 30 seconds and repeat the process. Keep repeating the process until someone does answer, then tell them what the problem is. *Stay on Channel 16 until the Coast Guard or Marine Police tells you to switch to another channel or the emergency is solved.*

If you should hear a Mayday distress call, *stay off the air unless you are in a position to render immediate assistance.*

Any message headed by one of the emergency signals (MAYDAY, PAN-PAN, or SECURITY) must be given precedence over routine communications. This means listen. Don't transmit. Be prepared to help if you can.

The following outlines the proper use of the three emergency signals:

MAYDAY: This distress signal, pronounced "MAY DAY," indicates that a vessel is in grave and immediate danger and requests immediate assistance. MAYDAY has priority over all other communications.

PAN-PAN: This urgency signal, pronounced "PAHN-PAHN," indicates that the safety of a vessel or person is in jeopardy. For example, "man overboard" messages are sent with this signal. PAN-PAN has priority over all other communication with the exception of MAYDAY traffic.

SECURITY: This safety signal, pronounced "SAY-CURITAY," is used for messages concerning safety of navigation or preceding important meteorological warnings. For example, it may be used to warn of the approach of a severe thunderstorm with high winds. SECURITY has priority over routine traffic but not over MAYDAY or PAN-PAN.

PHONETIC ALPHABET

All radiotelephone users should learn and use the International Phonetic Alphabet for use when you give your call sign or when it is necessary to spell out any words, such as the name of your boat, especially when requesting assistance or reporting a hazard or accident. At the very least, you should know the phonetic letters for your boat name and call sign.

The International Phonetic Alphabet is:

Alpha	November
Bravo	Oscar
Charlie	Papa
Delta	Quebec
Echo	Romeo
Foxtrot	Sierra
Golf	Tango
Hotel	Uniform
India	Victor
Juliett	Whiskey
Kilo	X-ray
Lima	Yankee
Mike	Zulu

HANDHELD VHF-FM RADIOS

A good friend of ours, Jim Parker, went to considerable effort to distill the following report on VHF-FM Handheld radios. Originally produced by the staff of BOAT/US and published in their quarterly BOAT/US Boating Equipment Reports in early 1987, the condensed form presented here appears with the permission of both parties:

It seems that no one, including the manufacturers, knew what the range of 3-watt Handheld VHF-FM Marine Radiotelephones should be, so the staff of BOAT/US set out to find out. One FCC engineer punched in variables in his calculator and came up with a range of 794 miles for a 3-watt handheld under ideal conditions (flat earth, no atmosphere)! Obviously, we can't achieve that sort of range, so there has to be another, overriding factor.

In fact, antenna height is the most important variable in the real world; VHF will work at about 20 percent better than line of sight. A useful formula is the square root of twice the transmitting height plus the same for receiver antenna height (heights in feet and range answer in miles).

The BOAT/US staff took out two boats, each with the handhelds under test and each with a 25-watt primary transceiver with masthead antenna. Tests were made with the handheld unit on one boat communicating with the other systems on the other boat or the Coast Guard ashore. The test results are summarized as follows:

Test Condition	Measured	Predicted
Handheld (6′) to handheld (8′)	3.25 mi.	7.5 mi.
Handheld (6′) to masthead (48′)	6.75 mi.	13.5 mi.
Handheld (12.5′) to masthead (48′)	10.75 mi.	14.5 mi.
Handheld (6′) to C.G. (90′)	10.5 mi.	17.25 mi.
Handheld (12.5′) to C.G. (90′)	14.5 mi.	18.25 mi.

So we see that the handheld unit actually gets about one-half to three-quarters the expected range. In each case, when they added about one-half mile to the range, the reception got rather chancy and quit altogether with yet another half mile.

The staying power of the handheld's batteries was also tested. They imposed a continuous cycle of 15 minutes standby, 15 minutes receive, and 5 minutes of transmit, then measured the transmit power. Both of the units tested started with greater than the 3 watts specified (4.5 and 5 watts). After the first test period, the power dropped to about 4 watts and held up at that level until after the three-hour point, at which time the power dropped precipitously. That is the characteristic of Ni-Cad batteries.

The BOAT/US staff came up with the following conclusions: (1) The handheld makes a good primary unit for those who wouldn't have one—small boats, day sailers, fishermen, etc. (2) Handhelds make a good secondary radio for larger boats under several conditions—emergency backup for the primary radio, dinghy to mother ship, or when the user doesn't want to leave the cockpit. (3) The staff suggested to the manufacturers that a device similar to a cordless telephone for operating the primary radio from anywhere on the boat would be very useful.

The report also included information about licensing rules for these devices. If you use the handheld as a secondary unit on your boat, you do not need an additional license. If the handheld is your primary unit, you need a regular ship's license. If you use the handheld on another craft (dinghy or charter), you need a "portable" license. If you use the handheld from shore to call your dinghy, the FCC will not like you. If you use the handheld on your own boat to talk from the foredeck to the cockpit, the FCC will not like you. An operator's license is no longer required for VHF-FM radiotelephones.

A Partial Listing of Charter Services on the Chesapeake

KEY

S	SAILBOAT CHARTERS
P	POWERBOAT CHARTERS
F	FISHING CHARTERBOAT SERVICE
H/B	FISHING HEADBOAT SERVICE
H	HOUSEBOAT CHARTERS
C	CREWED CRUISES
	(Medium to Large Cruise Boats)

There are many, many charter services available in the Chesapeake. I know I did not *find* them all, let alone list them here. What I have gathered is designed to provide a reasonable starting point. The services are broken into the regions covered in the text, in the same order in which the body of water on which the service is located is covered. While the name and particular office of the actual charter service may differ from what I've listed here, the location should be correct. In most cases, the name listed is that of the marina where the service is located, but not necessarily the name of the service itself. (Services can relocate or change hands; marinas can change hands but they tend to stay put.) Regardless of these differences, the name and number I have given will be a viable point of contact for a charter service.

TYPE   NAME, ADDRESS & PHONE NUMBER

REGION 1
Head of Bay to Pooles Island

S   HAVRE DE GRACE MARINA
Water St.
Havre de Grace, MD 21078
(410)939-2161

S&P   SKIPJACK COVE MARINA
P.O. Box 208
Georgetown, MD 21930
(410)275-2122

S   SAILING ASSOCIATES, INC.
P.O. Box 6
Georgetown, MD 21930
(410)275-8171

S   LA VIDA YACHTS, INC.
22174 Great Oak Landing Road
Chestertown, MD 21620 (Fairlee Creek)
(410)778-0329

REGION 2
Pooles Island to Bay Bridges

S TOLCHESTER MARINA
P.O. Box 503, RR 2
Chestertown, MD 21620
(410)778-1400

S SWAN CREEK MARINA
Yard A
Gratitude Point
Rock Hall, MD 21661
(410)639-7813

S GRATITUDE BOAT SALES, INC.
Lawton Ave.
Rock Hall, MD 21661
(410)639-7111

S THE HAVEN CHARTERS
Gratitude Road
Rock Hall, MD 21661
(410)639-7140

S GREAT RIVER YACHT CHARTERS
5649 Walnut Street
Rock Hall, MD 21661
(410)639-2166 or (800)677-2166

S THE SAILING EMPORIUM
Green Lane
Rock Hall, MD 21661
(410)778-1342

F ROCK HALL SEAFOOD
Rock Hall, MD 21661
(410)639-2261

S&P WILD DUCK CHARTERS
Piney Narrows Yacht Haven
210 Piney Narrows Road
Chester, MD 21619
(410)643-7200

S MARYLAND MARINA CHARTERS
3501 Red Rose Farm Road
Baltimore, MD 21220
(410)335-3898

S&P NANTICO MARINE CENTER
402 Key Highway
Baltimore, MD 21230
(410)962-1171

S,P,C CHESAPEAKE CHARTERS
418 E. 31st Street
Baltimore, MD 21230
(410)235-7224

C THE BALTIMORE PATRIOT
Pratt & Light Streets
Baltimore, MD 21230
(410)685-4288

C CLIPPER CITY, INC. (Tall Ship)
1003 Old Philadelphia Road
Baltimore, MD 21230
(410)539-6277

C SCHOONER NIGHTHAWK CRUISES
1715 Thames Street
Baltimore, MD 21230
(410)327-7245

S CHESAPEAKE CRUISES
White Rocks Yachting Center
1402 Colony Road
Pasadena, MD 21122
(410)437-2123

S GIBSON ISLAND YACHT BASIN
487 New York Ave.
Pasadena, MD 21122
(410)255-3488

REGION 3
Bay Bridges to Little Choptank River

S LIPPINCOTT CHARTERS
Rt. 1, Box 545
Grasonville, MD 21638
(410)827-9300

S&P C & C CHARTERS
Mears Point Marina
Box 535AA
Grasonville, MD 21638
(410)827-7888

S&P EASTERN SHORE YACHT CHARTERS
Box 589
Oxford, MD 21654
(410)226-5000

S MEARS YACHT HAVEN
502 E. Strand
P.O. Box 130
Oxford, MD 21654
(410)226-5450

S&P AMERICAN POWERBOAT SCHOOLS
125 Riverview Ave.
Annapolis, MD 21403
(410)721-7517

A

PARTIAL

LISTING

OF

CHARTER

SERVICES

ON

THE

CHESAPEAKE

417

REGION 3
Bay Bridges to Little
Choptank River—*Continued*

S&P ANNAPOLIS BAY CHARTERS
Box 4604
Annapolis, MD 21403
(410)269-1776

S&P ANNAPOLIS CITY MARINA
410 Severn Ave., Eastport
Annapolis, MD 21403
(410)268-0660

S AYS CHARTERS & SAILING SCHOOL
7416 Edgewood Road
Annapolis, MD 21403
(410)267-8181

S BIGHT SERVICES, INC.
Annapolis Landing Marina
992 Klakring Road
Annapolis, MD 21403
(410)268-2414

S CHESAPEAKE & POTOMAC YACHT
SERVICE
301 Burnside Street
Annapolis, MD 21403
(410)263-7224

S&P PIER 4 MARINA
301 Fourth Street
Annapolis, MD 21403
(410)268-2987

S LILLY BROS. YACHT YARD
726 Second Street, Eastport
Annapolis, MD 21403
(410)263-8881

S NORTH-EAST-WIND CHARTER, LTD.
306 Second Street
Annapolis, MD 21403
(410)267-6333

S HORN POINT HARBOR MARINA
121 Eastern Ave.
Annapolis, MD 21403
(410)263-0550

S&P ATLANTIC SAILING YACHTS
7078 Bembe Beach Road
Annapolis, MD 21403
(410)268-4680

S CHESAPEAKE SAILING SCHOOL
Port Annapolis Marina
7074 Bembe Beach Road
Annapolis, MD 21403
(410)269-1594

P CHESAPEAKE BAY TRAWLERS
690 Fairview Ave.
Annapolis, MD 21403
(410)263-2838

C CHESAPEAKE MARINE TOURS, INC.
Box 3350
Annapolis, MD 21403
(410)268-7600

S MOONSHADOW YACHT CHARTERS
Box 6529
Annapolis, MD 21403
(410)266-9060

S&P PARADISE BAY YACHT CHARTERS
215 Severn Ave.
Annapolis, MD 21403
(410)268-9330

S&P HIGHSPIRE YACHT SERVICES
P.O. Box 4249
Annapolis, MD 21403
(410)263-2838

S&P CRUISING YACHT CHARTERS
Liberty Marina
410 Westbury Drive
Riva, MD 21140
(410)956-5530

H OAK GROVE MARINA
Rt. 2
Edgewater, MD 21037
(410)266-6696

FREE STATE YACHT CHARTERS
Liberty Yacht Club
64 Old South River Road
Edgewater, MD 21037
(410)266-9060

F BAY VIEW MARINA
1061 Turkey Point Road
Edgewater, MD 21037
(410)269-6887

F BLUE WATER MARINA
1024 Carrs Wharf Road
Edgewater, MD 21037
(410)798-1232

S&P WEST RIVER YACHT HARBOUR
Box 125
Galesville, MD 20765
(410)867-0650

S HARTGE CHESAPEAKE CHARTERS
Church Lane
Galesville, MD 20765
(410)867-7240

TYPE	NAME, ADDRESS, & PHONE NUMBER		TYPE	NAME, ADDRESS, & PHONE NUMBER

F   **DEALE MARINA**
485 Deale Road
Deale, MD 20751
(410)261-5220

F   **HAPPY HARBOUR MARINA**
Deale, MD 20751
(410)867-0949

F   **HERRINGTON HARBOUR**
Rose Haven on the Bay
Rt. 261
Friendship, MD 20758
(410)741-5100

F   **SEASIDE CRAB HOUSE**
Chesapeake Beach, MD 20732
(410)257-7269

F&H/B   **ROD 'N' REEL DOCK**
P.O. Box 99
Chesapeake Beach, MD 20732
(410)257-2191

REGION 4
Little Choptank to Potomac River

F   **QUEEN ANNE MARINA**
410 Congressional Drive
Stevensville, MD 21666
(410)643-5065

F   **KNAPP'S NARROWS MARINA**
Bay Hundred Restaurant
P.O. Box 279
Tilghman, MD 21671
(410)886-2622

F   **CAP'N BUCKS SEAFOOD**
Tilghman, MD 21671
(410)886-2244

F   **HARRISON'S CHESAPEAKE HOUSE**
Tilghman, MD 21671
(410)886-2123

S   **DICKERSON BOATBUILDERS, INC.**
RR 2, Box 92
Trappe, MD 21673
(410)822-8556

S   **MADISON BAY MARINA**
P.O. Box 41
Madison, MD 21648
(410)228-4111

S   **SHEPHERDS'S MARINA**
P.O. Box 559
Solomons, MD 20688
(410)326-3939

S&P   **SPRING COVE MARINA**
Box 160
Solomons, MD 20688
(410)326-2161

F   **BUNKY'S CHARTER BOAT MARINA**
Main Street
Solomons, MD 20688
(410)326-3703

F   **RIPPON BROS.**
Hoopersville, MD 21642
(410)397-3200

F   **TOWN CREEK MARINA**
Rt. 2, Box 62
California, MD 20619
(410)862-3553

F   **CLARKE'S LANDING**
Rt. 1, Box 891
Hollywood, MD 20636
(410)373-9819

F   **SCOTT'S COVE MARINA**
Chance, MD 21816
(410)784-2363

F&H/B   **CRISFIELD FISHING CENTRE, INC.**
Jersey Island
Crisfield, MD 21817
(410)968-3162

REGION 5
Potomac River

H/B   **POINT LOOKOUT STATE PARK**
Scotland, MD 20687
(410)872-5688

F   **SWANN'S PIER**
Piney Point, MD 20674
(410)994-0774

F   **YECOMICO MARINA**
P.O. Box 38
Kinsale, VA 22488
(804)472-2971

F   **KRENTZ MARINE RAILWAY**
Harryhogan Point, VA 22435
(804)529-6800

S   **FT. WASHINGTON MARINA**
13600 King Charles Terrace
Ft. Washington, MD 20744
(410)292-7700

A
PARTIAL
LISTING
OF
CHARTER
SERVICES
ON
THE
CHESAPEAKE

419

TYPE	NAME, ADDRESS, & PHONE NUMBER
C	ELENA—QUEEN OF HEARTS (PADDLEWHEELER) 600 Water Street Washington, DC 20024 (202)488-1249
C	POTOMAC RIVERBOAT CO. (PADDLEWHEELER) 205 The Strand Alexandria, VA 22314 (703)684-0580

REGION 6
Potomac River to Wolf Trap Light

TYPE	NAME, ADDRESS, & PHONE NUMBER
F	SMITH POINT MARINA Rt. 1, Box 312 Little Wicomico River Reedville, VA 22539 (804)453-4077
C	BUZZARD'S POINT MARINA Reedville, VA 22539 (804)453-3545
S	RAPPAHANNOCK YACHTS, INC. Irvington, VA 22480 (804)438-5353
S&P	IRVINGTON MARINA Irvington, VA 22480 (804)438-5113
F	LOCKLIES MARINA Topping, VA 23169 (804)758-2871
S	DOZIER'S DOCKYARD, INC. Rt. 33 & Broad Creek Deltaville, VA 23043 (804)776-6711
F	BURRELL'S MARINA P.O. Box 203 Urbanna, VA 23175 (804)758-5016
S	URBANNA MARINE CORP. P.O. Box 520 Urbanna, VA 23175 (804)758-2342

REGION 7
Wolf Trap Light to Cape Henry

TYPE	NAME, ADDRESS, & PHONE NUMBER
F	GARTZ MARINA 127 East River Road Poquoson, VA 23662 (804)868-6821
H/B	CHESAPEAKE CHARTER SERVICE Jones Marina 519 Bridge Road Hampton, VA 23669 (804)723-0998
F	LITTLE BOAT HARBOUR SUPPLY 201 Jefferson Ave. Newport News, VA 23601 (804)245-7796
F&H/B	SHORE DRIVE MARINA 8180 Shore Drive Norfolk, VA 23518 (804)463-8800
F	COBB'S MARINA 4514 Dunning Road Norfolk, VA 23518 (804)588-5401
F	BUBBA'S MARINA & BOAT RAMP 3323 Shore Drive Virginia Beach, VA 23451 (804)481-9867
F	LYNNHAVEN MUNICIPAL MARINA 3211 Lynnhaven Drive Virginia Beach, VA 23451 (804)481-7137
F	D&M SPORT FISHING CENTER 3311 Shore Drive Virginia Beach, VA 23451 (804)481-7211

Chesapeake

Bay

Dockside

Sewage

Pumpout

Facilities

CHESAPEAKE
BAY
DOCKSIDE
SEWAGE
PUMPOUT
FACILITIES

421

(Note: Listings are subject to change; please call ahead.)

FACILITY	LOCATION	PHONE #

REGION 1
Head Of Bay to Pooles Island

FACILITY	LOCATION	PHONE #
Locust Point Marina	Locust Point, Elk R.	(410)392-4994
Schaefer's Marina	C&D Canal	(410)885-2204
Bohemia Bay Yacht Harbour	Bohemia R.	(410)885-2601
Long Point Marina	Bohemia R.	(410)275-8181
Two Rivers Yacht Basin	Bohemia R.	(410)885-2257
Duffy Creek Marina	Georgetown, Sassafras R.	(410)275-2141
Georgetown Yacht Basin	Georgetown, Sassafras R.	(410)648-5112
Granary Marina	Georgetown, Sassafras R.	(410)648-5112
Skipjack Cove Yachting Resort	Georgetown, Sassafras R.	(410)275-2122
Sassafras Boat Co.	Georgetown, Sassafras R.	(410)648-5355
Gregg Neck Boat Yard	Georgetown, Sassafras R.	(410)648-5360
Green Point Marina	Worton Cr.	(410)778-1615
The Wharf, Handy's Point	Worton Cr.	(410)778-4363
Worton Creek Marina	Worton Cr.	(410)778-3282
Mears Great Oak Landing	Fairlee Cr.	(410)788-5007
Riverside Ponderosa Pines	Northeast R.	(410)642-3431
Anchor Boats & Marina	Northeast R.	(410)287-6000
Pat's Marina	Northeast R.	(410)287-5298
Tidewater Marina	Havre de Grace, Susquehanna R.	(410)939-0950
Havre de Grace Marina	Havre de Grace, Susquehanna R.	(410)939-2161
City Park Marina	Susquehanna R.	(410)939-9448
Bush River Boat Works	Bush R.	(410)272-1882

FACILITY	LOCATION	PHONE #

REGION 2
Pooles Island to Bay Bridges

Facility	Location	Phone
Tolchester Marina	Main Bay	(410)778-1400
Gratitude Marina	Swan Cr.	(410)639-7011
Haven Harbour	Swan Cr.	(410)778-6697
Pelorus Marine, Inc	Rock Hall Harbor	(410)639-2224
Sailing Emporium	Rock Hall Harbor	(410)778-1342
Castle Harbour Club	Kent I., Chester R.	(410)643-5599
Anglers Restaurant & Marina	Kent Narrows	(410)827-6717
Lippincott Marine	Kent Narrows	(410)827-9300
Mears Point Marina	Kent Narrows	(410)827-8888
Piney Narrows Yacht Haven	Kent Narrows	(410)643-6600
Scott Marine Sales & Service	Kent Narrows	(410)827-8150
Long Cove Marina	Langford Cr., Chester R.	(410)778-6777
Kiblers Marina	Chestertown, Chester R.	(410)778-3616
Gunpowder Cove Marina	Gunpowder R/Taylors Cr.	(410)679-5454
Porters Seneca Marina	Seneca Cr., Middle R.	(410)335-6563
Norman Creek Marina	Norman Cr., Middle R.	(410)686-9343
Essex Marina Boat Yard	Hopkins Cr., Middle R.	(410)687-6149
Riverwatch Restaurant & Marina	Hopkins Cr., Middle R.	(410)687-1422
Chesapeake Yachting Center	Frogmortar Cr., Middle R.	(410)335-5390
Key Yacht Club	Back R.	(410)477-2578
Millers Island Yacht Club	Back R.	(410)477-9676
West Shore Yacht Center	Muddy Gut, Back R.	(410)686-6998
Anchor Bay East Marine	Bear Cr., Patapsco R.	(410)284-1044
Middle Branch Moorings	Middle Br., Patapsco R.	(410)539-2628
Lighthouse Point Marina	NW Harbor, Baltimore	(410)522-1881
Riverside Marine	NW Harbor, Baltimore	(410)686-1500
Inner Harbor Marina of Baltimore	Inner Harbor	(410)837-5339
Magothy Marina	Magothy R.	(410)647-2356
Pleasure Cove Yacht Club	Sandy Point	(410)757-8000
Sandy Point Marina	Sandy Point State Park	(410)974-0772

REGION 3
Bay Bridges to Little Choptank River

Facility	Location	Phone
Pier One Marina	Kent I., by Bay Bridges	(410)643-3162
St. Michaels Hbr Marina	St. Michaels, Miles R.	(410)745-9001
Knapps Narrows Marina	Knapps Narrows	(410)866-2720
Gateway Marina	Choptank R.	(410)476-3304
Bachelor Point Harbor	Tred Avon R. (mouth)	(410)226-5592
Town Cr. Rest. & Marina	Town Cr., Tred Avon R.	(410)226-5131
Crockett Bros. Boatyard	Town Cr., Tred Avon R.	(410)226-5115
Easton Point Marina	Dixon Cr., Tred Avon R.	(410)822-1201
Dickerson Marine Services	La Trappe Cr., Choptank R.	(410)822-8556
Cambridge Municipal Yacht Basin	Cambridge, Choptank R.	(410)228-4031
Yacht Maintenance Co.	Cambridge Cr., Choptank R.	(410)228-8878
Gateway Marina & Ship's Store	Rt 50 Bridge, Choptank R.	(410)476-3304
Annapolis Landing Marina	Back Cr., Severn R.	(410)263-0090
Bert Jabin's Yacht Yard	Back Cr., Severn R.	(410)268-9067
Port Annapolis Marina	Back Cr., Severn R.	(410)269-1990
Annapolis Harbor Boat Yard	Spa Cr., Severn R.	(410)267-9050
Bay View Marina	Selby Bay, South R.	(410)798-6060
Liberty Yacht Club	Rt 2 Bridge, South R.	(410)266-5633
Parrish Cr. Marine & Boatyard	Parrish Cr., West River	(410)261-9662
Herrington Harbour South	Herring Bay	(410)741-5100

FACILITY	LOCATION	PHONE #

CHESAPEAKE
BAY
DOCKSIDE
SEWAGE
PUMPOUT
FACILITIES

423

REGION 4
Little Choptank to Potomac River

FACILITY	LOCATION	PHONE #
Wicomico Yacht Club	Wicomico Cr., Wicomico R.	(410)749-9856
White Haven Marina	Wicomico R.	(410)873-2662
Port of Salisbury Marina	Salisbury, Wicomico R.	(410)548-3176
Somers Cove Marina	Crisfield, L. Annamessex R.	(410)968-0925
Halls Marina	Breezy Point, Main Bay	(410)257-2561
Flag Harbor Yacht Haven	Flag Harbor, Main Bay	(410)586-0070
Calvert Marina	Solomons, Patuxent R.	(410)326-4251
Spring Cove Marina	Solomons, Patuxent R.	(410)326-2161
Zahniser's Sailing Ctr	Solomons, Patuxent R.	(410)326-2166
Boatel California	Town Cr., Patuxent R.	(410)737-1401
Weeks Marina	Cuckhold Cr., Patuxent R.	(301)373-5124
Broomes Island Marina	Island Cr., Patuxent R.	(410)586-0304
Cape St. Marys Marina	Cat Cr., Patuxent R.	(410)373-2001

REGION 5
Potomac River

FACILITY	LOCATION	PHONE #
Point Lookout State Park	Point Lookout	(410)872-5688
Point Lookout Marina	Smith Cr.	(410)872-5887
Dennis Point Marina	Carthagena Cr., St Marys R.	(410)994-2288
Tall Timbers Marina	Herring Cr	(410)994-1508
Lewisetta Marina	Coan R.	(804)529-7299
Coan Marina	Coan R.	(804)529-2032
Sandy Point Marina	Shannon Branch, Yecomico R.	(804)472-3237
White Point Marina	Shannon Branch, Yecomico R.	(804)472-2977
Yecomico Marina	West Yecomico R.	(804)472-2971
Kinsale Harbor Marina	West Yecomico R.	(804)472-2514
Olverson's Lodge Cr. Marina	South Yecomico R.	(804)529-6341
Cather Marine Inc.	St. Patrick Cr.	(410)769-3335
Kopel's Marina	St. Patrick Cr.	(410)769-3121
Combs Creek Marina	Combs Cr., Breton Bay	(410)475-2017
Harbor View Marina	Combs Cr., Breton Bay	(410)475-3030
Capt. John's Crabhouse	Neale Sound	(410)259-2315
Cobb Island Marina	Neale Sound	(410)259-2032
Saunders Marina	Neale Sound	(410)934-9266
Shymansky's Rst & Marina	Neale Sound	(410)259-2221
Ragged Point Marina	Ragged Pt. near Lower Machedoc Cr.	(410)472-3955
Port Tobacco Marina	Port Tobacco R.	(410)870-3133
Outdoor World Hbr View	Mattox Cr.	(804)224-8164
Stanford's Marine Rlwy	Monroe Cr.	(804)224-7644
Fairview Beach Yacht Club	S. of Potomac Cr.	(703)775-5971
Waugh Point Marina	Potomac Cr.	(703)775-7121
Willow Landing Marina	Aquia Creek	(703)659-2653
E-Z Cruz	Neabsco Cr.	(703)670-8115
Tyme 'N' Tyde, Inc	Occoquan Bay	(703)491-5116
Capt. John S. Beach Marina	Occoquan R.	(703)339-9650
Hoffmasters Marina	Occoquan R.	(703)494-7161
Ft. Washington Marina	Piscataway Cr.	(410)292-7700
Tantallon Yacht Club	Swan Cr.	(410)292-3349
Belle Haven Marina	Hunting Cr., Alexandria	(703)768-0018
Alexandria City Marina	Alexandria	(703)838-4265
Washington Sailing Marina	Alexandria	(703)546-9027
James Creek Marina	Anacostia R.	(202)554-8844
Port of Bladensburg	Anacostia R.	(410)779-4133

FACILITY	LOCATION	PHONE #

REGION 5
Potomac River—*Continued*

Gangplank Marina	Washington Channel	(202)554-5000
Columbia I. Marina	Columbia I. (Pentagon)	(202)347-0173

REGION 6
Potomac River to Wolf Trap Light

Ocean Pines Marina	Isle of Wight Bay	(410)641-7447
Shad Landing Area Marina	Shad Landing, Pocomoke R.	(410)632-2566
Onancock Wharf	Onancock Cr.	(804)787-7911
Leroy's Marina	Little Wicomico R.	(804)453-6806
Smith Point Marina	Little Wicomico R.	(804)453-4077
Ingram Bay Marina	Ingram Bay, Great Wicomico R.	(804)580-7292
Tiffany Yachts/Marine	Headwaters, Great Wicomico R.	(804)453-3464
Windmill Pt. Marine Resorts	Windmill Pt. Rappahannock	(804)435-1166
Chesapeake Cove Marina	Broad Cr., Rappahannock R.	(804)776-6855
Deltaville Dockside Inn	Broad Cr., Rappahannock R.	(804)776-9224
Greens Marina & Boatyard	Broad Cr., Rappahannock R.	(804)776-9645
J & M Marina	Broad Cr., Rappahannock R.	(804)776-9860
Norview Marina	Broad Cr., Rappahannock R.	(804)776-6463
Waldens Marina	Broad Cr., Rappahannock R.	(804)776-9440
W & E Marine	Broad Cr., Rappahannock R.	(804)776-9592
Tides Inn	Carter Cr., Rappahannock R.	(804)438-5000
Irvington Marina	Carter Cr., Rappahannock R.	(804)438-5113
Regent Point Marina	Locklies Cr. Rappahannock	(804)758-4457
Yankee Point Marina	Corrottoman R., Rappahannock R.	(804)462-7018
Urbanna Yacht Sales, Inc	Urbanna Cr., Rappahannock	(804)758-2342
Urbanna Bridge Marina	Urbanna Cr., Rappahannock	(804)758-5124
Locklies Marina	Robinson Cr. Rappahannock	(804)758-2871
Regent Point Marina	Robinson Cr. Rappahannock	(804)758-4457
Greenvale Creek Marina	Greenvale Cr. Rappahannock	(804)462-7350
Whelan's Marina & Campground	Tarply Point, Rappahannock	(804)394-9500
Deltaville Marina	Jackson Cr. Piankatank R	(804)776-9633
The Narrows Marina	Milford Haven, Piankatank	(804)725-2151
Club on Fishing Bay	Fishing Bay, Piankatank	(804)776-6911

REGION 7
Wolf Trap Light to Cape Henry

Northampton Marine	Cape Charles Inlet	(804)331-4400
Horn Harbor Marina	Horn Harbor	(804)725-3223
Mobjack Bay Marina	Blackwater Cr., North R.	(804)725-7245
Shelter Harbor Marina	Severn R.	(804)642-2800
Holiday Marina	SW Branch, Severn R.	(804)642-2528
Cook's Landing	Perrin R., York R.	(804)642-6177
Jordan Marine Service	Sarah Cr., York R.	(804)642-4360
York River Yacht Haven	Sarah Cr., York R.	(804)642-2156
Wormley Creek Marina	Wormley Cr., York R.	(804)898-5060
Chisman Creek Marina	Chisman Cr., Poquoson R.	(804)898-3000
Poquoson Marina	Bennett Cr., Poquoson R.	(804)868-6171
Marina Cove Boat Basin	Harris R., Back R.	(804)851-0511
Customs House	SW Branch, Back R.	(804)723-8959
Rebel Marine Sevice	Willoughby Bay	(804)588-6022
Willoughby Harbor Marina	Willoughby Bay	(804)583-4150

REGION 7
Wolf Trap Light to Cape Henry—*Continued*

Facility	Location	Phone #
Bluewater Yacht Sales	Hampton R.	(804)723-0795
Hampton Roads Marina	Hampton R.	(804)723-6774
Lee's Yachting Center	W. Branch, Elizabeth R.	(804)484-2652
VA Boat & Yacht Club	W. Branch, Elizabeth R.	(804)484-0308
Western Branch Diesel	W. Branch, Elizabeth R.	(804)484-6230
Tidewater Yacht Agency	Portsmouth, Elizabeth R.	(804)393-2525
City Marina, Waterside	Norfolk, Elizabeth R.	(804)441-2222
Brady's Marina	Nasemond R.	(804)539-8221
Menchville Marine Supply	Deep Cr., James R.	(804)877-0207
Pagan River Marina	Pagan R., James R.	(804)357-7405
Rescue Yacht Basin	James Cr., James R	(804)357-4621
Kingsmill Marina	Kingsmill, James R.	(804)253-3919
Jamestown Yacht Basin	Jamestown, James R.	(804)229-8309
Eagle's Point Marina	Grays Cr., James R.	(804)294-3050
Jordan Point Yacht Haven	Jordan Point, James R.	(804)458-3398
Kingsland Reach Marina	Hatcher I., James R	(804)796-1213
Little Cr. Dry Storage Marina	Little Cr.	(804)583-3600
Cobb's Marina	Little Cr.	(804)588-5401
Taylors Landing Marina	Little Cr.	(804)587-3480
Marina at Marina Shores	Lynnhaven Inlet	(804)496-7000
Lynnhaven Yacht Marina	Lynnhaven Inlet	(804)481-6909

CHESAPEAKE
BAY
DOCKSIDE
SEWAGE
PUMPOUT
FACILITIES

425

In addition to these locations, there is now a waterborne pump-out station that offers its service to Chesapeake boaters at no charge. The 48-foot *H.J. Elser* can be located by calling radio channel 16. During the boating season the *Elser* frequents the Annapolis, St. Michaels, Oxford, Fairlee Creek, and Solomons Islands areas from Thursday through Sunday. The operation is funded by Maryland's boat excise tax.

Bibliography

Blackistone, Mick, *Sun Up to Sundown: Watermen of the Chesapeake;* Washington, DC: Acropolis Books, Ltd., 1988.

Blair, Carvel and Ansel, W. D., *Chesapeake Bay Notes and Sketches;* Centreville, MD: Tidewater Publishers, 1970.

Boating Almanac, Volume 4, Chesapeake Bay, Delaware, Maryland, D.C., Virginia; Severna Park, MD: Boating Almanac Co., Inc., 1985 and 1986.

Chapman, Charles F., *Piloting, Seamanship, and Small Boat Handling;* New York: Motor Boating and Sailing Book Division, 1974.

de Gast, Robert, *The Oystermen of the Chesapeake;* Camden, ME: International Marine Publishing Company, 1970.

"Hampton Roads: Where Rivers End," *National Geographic;* Washington, DC: National Geographic Society, July 1985.

Hays, Anne and Hazelton, Harriet, *Chesapeake Kaleidoscope;* Centreville, MD: Tidewater Publishers, 1975.

Hedeen, Robert A., *The Oyster;* Centreville, MD: Tidewater Publishers, 1975.

Holly, David C., *Steamboat on the Chesapeake:* Emma Giles *and the* Tolchester Line; Centreville, MD: Tidewater Publishers, 1987.

Horton, Tom, *Bay Country;* Baltimore: Johns Hopkins University Press, 1987.

Johnson, Paula J., *Working the Water;* Charlottesville, VA: The University Press of Virginia, 1988.

Klingil, Gilbert, *The Bay;* Baltimore: Johns Hopkins University Press, 1984.

Lippson, Alice Jane and Robert L., *Life in the Chesapeake Bay;* Baltimore: Johns Hopkins University Press, 1984.

Peffer, Randell, *Watermen;* Baltimore: Johns Hopkins University Press, 1985.

Rothrock, Joseph T., M.D., and Jane C., *Chesapeake Odysseys: An 1883 Cruise Revisited;* Centreville, MD: Tidewater Publishers, 1984.

Schubel, J. R., *The Living Chesapeake;* Baltimore and London: Johns Hopkins University Press, 1981.

Shomette, Donald G., *Pirates on the Chesapeake;* Centreville, MD: Tidewater Publishers, 1985.

Shomette, Donald G., *Shipwrecks on the Chesapeake;* Centreville, MD: Tidewater Publishers, 1982.

Townsend, Sallie and Ericson, Virginia, *Boating Weather;* New York: David McKay Company, Inc., 1978.

Warner, William M., *Beautiful Swimmers;* New York: Penguin Books, 1976.

Wennersten, John R., *The Oyster Wars of the Chesapeake Bay;* Centreville, MD: Tidewater Publishers, 1981.

Whitehead, John H., III, *The Watermen of the Chesapeake Bay;* Centreville, MD: Tidewater Publishers, 1979.

There are so many rivers and creeks off Chesapeake Bay, it seems they ran out of names. The echoes of identical—or nearly identical—names bounce north, south, east, and west. Among others, there are six Back Creeks and two Back Rivers listed here, there are three Church Creeks, a couple of Hunting Creeks, eight Mill Creeks, a Smith Cove, two Smith Creeks, and two Smith Points. It can get confusing. Where duplication exists, the following index pinpoints a location by adding a nearby, larger body of water or identifying landmark. The Back Creek listings, for example, are further identified by the addition of *Back Creek, Honga River,* or *Back Creek, Solomons Island.*